A Guide for Women in Religion

A Guide for Women in Religion

Making Your Way from A to Z

Edited by Mary E. Hunt

Writers:
Rebecca Alpert
Karen Baker-Fletcher
Valerie E. Dixon
Mary E. Hunt
Janet R. Jakobsen
Rosamond Cary Rodman
Katharina Von Kellenbach

palgrave
macmillan

First published 2004 by
PALGRAVE MACMILLAN™
175 Fifth Avenue, New York, N.Y. 10010 and
Houndmills, Basingstoke, Hampshire, England RG21 6XS.
Companies and representatives throughout the world.

PALGRAVE MACMILLAN is the global academic imprint of the Palgrave
Macmillan division of St. Martin's Press, LLC and of Palgrave Macmillan Ltd.
Macmillan® is a registered trademark in the United States, United Kingdom and
other countries. Palgrave is a registered trademark in the European Union and other
countries.

Library of Congress Cataloging-in-Publication Data
ISBN 1–4039-6647–8 hardback
ISBN 1–4039-6648–6 paperback

A guide for women in religion : making your way from A to Z /
    edited by Mary E. Hunt ; writers, Rebecca Alpert ... [et al.]
        p. cm.
    Includes index
    ISBN 1–4039-6647–8 (hc)—1–4039-6648–6 (pbk.)
        1. Religion-Study and teaching-Vocational guidance. 2. Women scholars-
Vocational guidance. 3. Women and religion. I. Alpert, Rebecca T. (Rebecca
Trachtenberg,), 1950- II. Hunt Mary E., 1951-
BL41.G94 2004
200'.82 —dc22

                                                                2004050525

A catalogue record for this book is available from the British Library.

Design by Autobookcomp.

First edition: November 2004
10 9 8 7 6 5 4 3 2 1

Printed in the United States of America.

With gratitude to the pioneer women in religion, and

with high hopes

for the women who will follow.

Contents

Acknowledgements

Scores of women too numerous to name shared their experiences as religious studies professionals for this book. Each submission was read and incorporated into this final product. Gratitude abounds for their generosity and candor.

The writing committee is largely responsible for the form and content of this book. Special thanks go to readers who improved the early draft of this book by their astute critiques and helpful additions: Laurie Wright Garry, Julie Kilmer, Rachel Magdalene, Heather McKay, Jacqueline Pastis, Judith Plaskow, Rosetta Ross, Susanne Scholz, Gwendolyn Zohara Simmons, Ilene Stanford, and Kerry Wynn. Jane Webster contributed important material on the Society of Biblical Literature–related topics. Rita Nakashima Brock added the voice of experience on many pages. Shannon Planck brought an American Academy of Religion perspective to bear.

Appreciation flows to Judith Plaskow, Rita Nakashima Brock, and their Committee on the Status of Women in the Profession of the American Academy of Religion. They started this process more than a decade ago and produced the *Guide to the Perplexing: A Survival Manual for Women in Religious Studies,* the forerunner to this volume. Equal gratitude goes to the current Committee members: Rebecca Alpert, Mary C. Churchill, Janet Jakobsen, Sarah Heaner Lancaster, Karen Pechilis, and Gwendolyn Zohara Simmons, who saw the importance of keeping it going. Special thanks are due to the Committee Chair, Rebecca Alpert, and to Shannon Planck, the AAR Staff Liaison, who shepherded the early part of the process with style.

Publishing colleagues helped to direct this book to its eventual home at Palgrave. Elizabeth Castelli, Pamela Johnson, Frank Oveis, and Gayatri Patnaik provided invaluable expertise. Palgrave editor Amanda Johnson offered smart ideas and effective technical assistance. To all of them a grand thank you for demonstrating that feminist work in religion is worth promoting.

The Women's Alliance for Theology, Ethics and Ritual (WATER) provided the infrastructure for editing this book. WATER's Carol

Murdock Scinto and Laura Bernstein edited with their usual eagle eyes. The Women's Studies Program at Temple University hosted the writing committee's meeting. Kudos to these small women's groups that make a big difference.

Introduction

Women are transforming the field of religion in profound and historic ways. There are simply more of us than ever before, though numbers alone do not tell the story. We bring a wide variety of experiences and perspectives to our work. We come from myriad faith traditions or with no personal religious commitment at all. Whether or not we work on women's issues in religion, we are all indebted to the pioneering feminist, womanist, and *mujerista* women who made clear that religion, and, by extension, the study of religion, is gendered activity.

We need and welcome newcomers and students as colleagues who share the challenges, excitement, and fulfillment of working in a field where women are creating new approaches. This guide is intended to elucidate some of the complexities and to smooth the path for those who follow us.

This guide is a collegial project. The writing group looked at how the interstructuring of sexism, racism, Christian hegemony, economic injustice, postcolonialism, and discrimination based on sexual choices has made work in religion difficult for many women, especially for women from marginalized racial, ethnic, sexual, and religious groups. We agreed that we need to grapple critically with the structural inequalities built into the fabric of the United States and an increasingly globalized world that privilege some at the expense of others. We also need to consider carefully the patriarchal religious traditions that bar women from having access to information and to informal networks where decisions are made. Understandably, many women enter the field lacking self-confidence, searching in vain for the support that their male colleagues take for granted, needing the collaboration with other women that is usually, but not always, forthcoming.

The American Academy of Religion (AAR) and the Society of Biblical Literature (SBL) are professional societies in the field. Their meetings are opportunities for women to meet one another and develop professional skills. It is inspiring that our senior colleagues, including some who are deceased, were able to work so effectively against long odds that accumulated in the field over the centuries. Women held top leadership positions, including the presidency, of the Academy's prede-cessor organization, the National Association of Biblical Instructors. For example, the first woman president of the AAR served in 1974. Six of the last ten presidents have been women, and a woman has served as the chief executive for more than a decade.

Some AAR and SBL members started the Women's Caucus of the American Academy of Religion in 1971; it became part of the official program in 1972. In 1986, the Caucus began a series of successful preconference workshops that continue to the present. These are opportunities for women to network, discuss common concerns, and share skills. Many of the themes of the Caucus gatherings are reflected in this guide.

For example, caucus members and other activist women introduced the idea of childcare at the Annual Meeting. The Committee on the Status of Women in the Profession (SWP) made the case and the AAR Board of Directors agreed. SWP developed policies and procedures against sexual harassment, and established the expectation—long since an Academy policy—that job interviews be conducted on a safe and level playing field.

Religious feminist pioneers founded the *Journal of Feminist Studies in Religion,* created institutes that focus on women's issues in religion, and developed women's studies programs in their institutions, all the while fulfilling their responsibilities as scholars and teachers. Scholars, most of them women, pushed the theoretical edges of their respective disciplines to ensure that women would not be ignored or left aside in the study of religion, historical as well as contemporary. Behind the scenes, they networked and connected in order to survive and thrive as professionals in a field in which men predominated.

One useful tool these creative women produced was a camouflage-covered book, *Guide to the Perplexing: A Survival Manual for Women in Religious Studies* (Atlanta: Scholars Press, 1992). It was conceived so that successive generations of women would not have to start from scratch to assure their own well-being. "The Guide," as it was fondly known, was the work of the Academy's Committee on the Status of Women in the Profession, under the leadership of Susan Brooks Thistlethwaite, the Committee's first chairperson. Rita Nakashima Brock and Judith Plaskow wrote the majority of the volume with additional material provided by Committee members including Susan Thistlethwaite, Kelly Brown Douglas, Paula Fredriksen, Adele McCollum, and James Poling, in consultation with other colleagues. Many of the themes in the first guide were also agenda items in preconference Women's Caucus workshops.

Several scholarly generations found our way in the field thanks to this practical and insightful book. A decade later, the field has changed appreciably, in no small measure because those who went before us took the time to share their wisdom. Moreover, this now sizable percentage of women in the academy has grown older and wiser still! Thus, the Committee on the Status of Women in the Profession decided it was time to publish an updated guide to bring new collective wisdom to public expression in a second version that, we hope, will have a similar impact.

Women are making substantive changes in the field. For example, it is possible to study feminist/womanist/*mujerista* and Asian feminist work in religion on the undergraduate level in many institutions. There are a number of doctoral programs where feminist work, gender studies, and queer theory are part of the mix. Women are now presidents of theological schools and universities, as well as deans and chairs of departments. Of course, many women are also working in the traditional fields of study and contributing from other perspectives as well.

The program units of the American Academy of Religion and the Society of Biblical Literature that feature women's work are at the cutting edge of scholarship in religion. Women outnumber men in some seminaries. While this is significant progress, it does not mean that women, especially women of color, have an easy time. Indeed, with the growth in our numbers and in the diversity of our social locations and ideologies, some of the camaraderie of an earlier time has dissipated. Nonetheless, new coalitions are being forged across differences by colleagues who seek to empower those whose voices have been underrepresented in the field.

Unfortunately, some things have not changed at all. For instance, men are still the majority of those teaching on religion faculties. The task of balancing work and family continues to fall disproportionately on women. After some early gains as faculties sought to include at least some women in their ranks, it can be especially hard for women to find jobs in a market that is far more competitive than it was years ago. Women are sometimes pitted against each other on ideological grounds, allowing some institutions to hire women without introducing women's issues into their curriculum or institutional commitments. For example, explicit feminist work is as often punished as rewarded. It is a complex situation, made more so for women who come into religion from other fields and for women who come from countries other than the United States and seek to enter the U.S. job market.

The current AAR Committee on the Status of Women in the Profession, ably chaired by Rebecca Alpert, continues to see the need for a "survival guide," because women are still far from receiving equal opportunity, fair treatment, and equal pay. This time the focus is on women thriving as well as surviving.

I accepted with enthusiasm the Committee's invitation to edit a new volume, with the proviso that the process and the product would reflect our diversity and our commitment to advocate for women in the field. Thanks to the American Academy of Religion's generous support, I was able to design and implement a process that would bring multiple voices to the task. The writing of this guide began as a project of the Committee on the Status of Women in the Profession. However, its publication is indebted to but independent of SWP and of the American Academy of Religion.

I issued a call through the AAR and SBL to the various women's groups, including womanist, Asian women, and *mujerista* colleagues, the Feminist Liberation Theologians' Network, and the Women's Caucus. I invited women to share their insights and experiences. Scores of women (too numerous to name) sent valuable, heartfelt information. Responses came from many women, ranging from students to faculty and staff; from U.S.-based women and women living elsewhere in the world; from women representing a range of racial/ethnic groups and sexual orientations; from professors and librarians; from artists and authors. I hope that this guide effectively reflects their insights.

The wonderful writing committee I convened was comprised of Rebecca Alpert, Karen Baker-Fletcher, Valerie E. Dixon, Janet R. Jakobsen, Rosamond Cary Rodman, and Katharina Von Kellenbach. Together we sifted through the replies, conceived of the overall framework, refined the title, and drafted many of the alphabetical entries. I wrote the rest based on the input we received, with occasional help from persons with special expertise.

Our rich conversation was reminiscent of the early AAR/SBL Women's Caucus sessions, proving that *la plus ça change, la plus c'est la même chose.* Issues of scholarship and spirituality abound. Finding one's voice, handling a commuter partnership, paying off student loans, juggling a career and family life, negotiating a contract, building a case for tenure—all of these remain current areas of concern. But there are new issues not found in the earlier volume—choosing an administrative career, teaching on-line, retiring and moving to emerita status, among others—that simply were not concerns of most women in religion ten years ago, when the average age of women in the field was younger.

Another significant change is that ten years later the increased numbers and participation of lesbian, racial and ethnic minority, Muslim, Hindu, and other diverse women in the academy bring to the fore more questions of multiple layers of discrimination against women. These include racism, sexism, heterosexism, ageism, ableism, colonialism, and more. We now listen to diverse voices in the field and take seriously the complexity of our struggles.

The writing committee had consensus around the fact that each of us is trying to make a life and a living, but we noted the wide range of ways we are doing it. That is why we decided that moving seriatim as in the earlier guide through the undergraduate and graduate years, to the dissertation, first job, tenure, perhaps a second job, and on to retirement, would simply not do. We could not assume that all of us would get or even seek tenure-track jobs. The academic market is tight and other exciting options abound. We developed this guide in light of the structures of academic life, while recognizing that more and more women will not get, and some do not aspire to, academic jobs.

This is both a fresh possibility and a new tension, calling us to balance the "traditional" route with other innovative options. Our view is that work other than teaching can be equally fulfilling and useful. Indeed, graduate education in religion is great preparation for careers in publishing, libraries and information technology, nonprofit organizations, ministry and religious administration, as well as in politics, social work, and health care–related areas. Far from being second-rate options, we see some of our best and brightest colleagues moving in these directions. Nonetheless, the "default" academic assumptions still rule, especially for women students, who, as newcomers to the field, have a priority claim on our attention and wisdom. Let them be heartened by the growing options available to those trained in religious studies.

Many men will find this new guide helpful, as they did the first one. They confront many of the same challenges. They will get insight into what women face in the field of religion and how men can work in solidarity with them. This guide is also essential reading for hiring and tenure committees, academic administrators, and others concerned with equality. We support efforts by colleagues who come from underrepresented racial and ethnic minority groups to develop their strategies as well.

This guide, like its older sister, is not meant to be a substitute for good legal advice. Difficult issues that require legal expertise arise in our work. For example, issues regarding tenure, publishing contracts, and sexual harassment are legally complex. If you need legal help, consult a lawyer. You might also wish to consult the American Association of University Professors (www.aaup.org), Lambda Legal Defense

and Education Fund (www.lambdalegal.org), Legal Momentum, formerly the NOW Legal Defense and Education Fund (www.nowldef.
org), and the National Women's Law Center (www.nwlc.org).

This guide is not intended to take the place of consultation with
trusted colleagues or to supercede an individual institution's rules and
customs. If you need advice, we recommend that you consult your
colleagues broadly, both those within the field and those within the
institution where you work.

Use this guide as a ready reference for some of the practical issues you
or others you know face while engaged in a career in the study of
religion. You may wish to read straight through to get an overall
picture, to discern some of the trends and customs, pitfalls, and
possibilities in the profession. Or, you may wish to take advantage of
the alphabetical compendium and the crosslistings to focus on a
particular theme. Words/phrases in bold are cross-references to other
entries for your convenience. You will note that we have chosen a
conversational tone in our writing. It reflects women's commitment to
share what we have learned, to honor women's informal networks as
well as our formal, institutional ties, and to invite you, the reader,
to join us.

Consider this guide a compilation of the experiences of many
generous women, shared so that our field may become increasingly
more just for women and thus for everyone, and more collegial for the
doing so. Above all, enjoy your work in religious studies. Thanks to
courageous, innovative women and supportive men, the field of religion is now open wider than ever to your creativity and contribution.

The Guide from A to Z

AAR

This lexicon begins fittingly with the AAR, the American Academy of Religion (www.aarweb.org), the professional association for people in religious studies. It is a key source of information, support, and development. Its sister organization is the Society of Biblical Literature, or **SBL** (www.sbl-site.org). The "alphabet soup" of its many aspects and linkages can be found in this guide under their own entries, such as the Committee on the Status and Role of Women in the Profession (**SWP**).

Most people become acquainted with the AAR through its Annual Meeting (see **AAR, Annual Meeting**) where members present and listen to papers, shop for books, network with other members, and interview for jobs. In fact, the AAR has much more to offer throughout the year as a clearinghouse for information and activities in the field. The *Journal of the American Academy of Religion* (*JAAR*) and the newsletter *Religious Studies News* (*RSN*) are welcome sources of scholarly work and timely articles about goings-on in the field.

If you make the effort to get involved, the AAR can also become a location for friendship networks, support, guidance, and intellectual stimulation. It is a good place to get a sense of the "big picture" in religious studies, a healthy antidote to isolation in your institution. You might consider serving on or even chairing one of the several committees of the Board of Directors. For example, the Committee on the Status of Women in the Profession (the group that created a survival guide for women in 1992 and initiated this book) is charged with monitoring issues of importance to women colleagues. In past years, they have worked on matters such as securing childcare options at the Annual Meeting, sexual harassment policies, job equity, mentoring, and making public the contributions of religious feminists.

There are also committees on Racial and Ethnic Minorities (see **REM**), on Teaching and Learning, and on the Public Understanding of Religion, as well as a Student Advisory Liaison Group (see **SLG**), all of which do important work for the AAR. For further information, consult the Web site, where you will find the governance structure, information about committees and the Annual Meeting, and about the many other activities and publications carried out by the AAR. Find what interests you and volunteer or ask a colleague to nominate you for the task.

AAR, Annual Meeting

The Annual Meeting of the AAR is held in late November in different cities around the continent (for example, Atlanta, Chicago, and Toronto). It has long been held in conjunction with the **SBL Annual Meeting**, though the organizations plan to hold separate meetings beginning in 2008. Upward of seven thousand members gather for a long weekend of seminars and lectures, book buying and job hunting, meetings, and social events. It is important to attend the Annual Meeting for the opportunity to catch up on scholarship in your field and to meet the people from around the world who are doing similar work.

The gathering can be intimidating. Plan ahead by highlighting in the program what you want to attend. Make dates with your friends and colleagues before you arrive on site. A refreshing encounter with someone you have not seen in a while can be as productive as attending a program session.

It is important to pace yourself as you go through the meeting. Make strategic choices about which sessions to attend. Consult with colleagues about what they are doing so you can find out which sessions might be interesting, even if they are not in your field. Keep a careful schedule of your commitments and your "free" spots so you can quickly suggest a meeting time when you run into someone on site with whom you want to chat.

The Annual Meeting includes cultural sessions, films, local tours, concerts, and the like. These events provide a great way to "rest" while still being stimulated intellectually. They are also good places to meet people with similar interests and appreciate just how rich and diverse our field can be.

Spend some time in the book display. It is helpful to catch up on the latest publications and to find books for next year's syllabi. It is a great place to run into people, or to track down a publisher with whom you would like to work. Many books are sold at discounted prices. Publishers' catalogs announce forthcoming works and advertise their current lists. This can be helpful as you decide what review or desk copies you wish to request. The program book for the Annual Meeting includes a guide to the book displays so you can plan where you want to go in the cavernous room to get the books you want.

Don't be shy about introducing yourself to someone whose work you admire, whose name you've noticed on his or her badge (without staring rudely). Usually, colleagues are grateful for the contact. After a paper has been delivered, it is quite common to present your business card to the author and ask for an electronic copy. Or, if you miss a paper and would like to read it, simply contact the presenter and ask her/him to share it with you. This is what it means to work collegially. Anyone who has presented a paper at the Annual Meeting will be listed in the membership directory, available on the AAR Web site to all current members.

Make sure you have fun at the meeting! Find people to chat with and share meals. Connect with graduate school friends or old colleagues. Take walks, use the hotel health facilities, go to a movie or museum, and maybe treat yourself to room service. Remember to breathe! Do whatever you need to do to keep from running yourself ragged, especially if you are in the job market. Go easy on alcohol at receptions and remember that professional expectations do not end when you have delivered your paper. If you itemize deductions for income tax purposes you can often deduct a portion of your meeting expenses. Ask an accountant for details and save your receipts.

The Annual Meeting can be hard on introverts. So many people, so little silence. Anyone who has been involved in a large institutional structure knows that the best way to survive is to get involved with a small group within that structure. The Annual Meeting provides many opportunities for you to do just that. You might, for example, get involved with the Women's Caucus. This group holds a premeeting every year the day before the convention begins, and addresses issues of importance especially to those new to the profession. Womanist Scholars, the Feminist Liberation Theologians' Network, and others meet that day, too, so it pays to go early. Besides, by the time the actual meeting starts you will know how to navigate the scene.

The **Women's Caucus** sponsors a reception during the Annual Meeting, as well as mentoring programs that are good chances to meet other women. There is a student group and an elected student director who serves on the AAR Board of Directors (see **SLG**). The students provide a session introducing the AAR to new members at each Annual Meeting. They have a lounge in which to relax and meet people. Many international colleagues attend the AAR/SBL. There are often special events for them as well.

Another important way to make connections is to attend the business meeting of the section(s) or group(s) in your field of study. Through these meetings, you can become acquainted with scholars in your area of interest, be involved in crafting the topics for the Call for Papers for the following year, and make yourself available to serve on the committee that decides which papers will be accepted for presentation. Like most things, what you put into it will mirror what you get out of the AAR, so consider it a worthwhile investment, especially if professional service is important for your tenure and promotion.

AAR, regional

The AAR is broken down into geographic regions. If you are an AAR member, you automatically are part of a region. Each year the regions sponsor conferences, usually in the spring. You can attend, give a paper, or become involved in the governance and organization of your region. It is usually less expensive and more convenient to go to a regional meeting. It is a good way to accomplish what may be more daunting on the macro level, namely, to meet people in the field and display your work on a smaller scale before you tackle the Annual Meeting (see **AAR, Annual Meeting**).

Ableism (see also Disability)

Ableism is the systemic discrimination against and exclusion of people who have physical, mental, and/or emotional disabilities. It is a way to devalue and disregard people with disabilities. It is a set of normative assumptions about how bodies work (many work differently) that is codified in law, architecture, education, and virtually every other sphere of life based on often arbitrary values with regard to physical well-being. It is a form of oppression that, when combined with sexism and racism, for example, assures that women and people of color who are disabled will suffer disproportionately. Many institutions have offices and/or officers who handle these matters.

Academic freedom

Academic freedom is a time-honored dimension of life in the academy. It typically refers to the respect accorded to each one for her/his work and to the expectation that one can articulate possibly unpopular ideas and beliefs in the classroom. What is not always clear is what it means, how far it goes, to whom and how it applies. In fact, the irony is that many of the people who most need **tenure** for the protection of their rights often do not get it.

Academic freedom is especially tricky when religious matters are involved since the "freedom" to contradict a religious tradition's beliefs may well result in problems on the job in religiously affiliated institutions, though problems with academic freedom are not limited to such institutions. Good advice is to learn the local landscape in this regard early in one's term at an institution, and make choices accordingly, weighing risks and benefits. Still better advice, if sometimes costly, is to keep your banner high even in religious institutions, since they risk the loss of their reputations when they abrogate a basic tenet of academic life. Academic freedom is for all or none of us.

Activism

There is a mistaken notion that the opposite of scholarship is activism, that activism can cloud one's scholarly objectivity. In fact, activism takes many forms, of which scholarship can indeed be an important one. Besides, myths of academic objectivity are widely debunked. Without activism, this guide and all of the accomplishments of women in the field would never have taken place.

Some women in religious studies may become full-time activists, making social change outside the academy rather than through teaching in or changing academic institutions. Options abound to make practical use of our sometimes specialized knowledge. Activism can be considered an integral part of our common project.

A key question is the relationship between activism and scholarship, the balance to be struck, and the logistics of finding time and energy to do both. What are the written and unwritten rules about activism at your institution? What are the possible consequences of your activism on your institution, students, family, yourself? How can one *not* become involved when one has the skills and the expertise to make a difference? How can one learn skills necessary to make a difference? Some institutions have a "town/gown" problem. Other communities depend on scholars to provide leadership for local issues as well as to be resource people on global ones. There are countless ways to be useful.

Women must be especially vigilant not to be lured into so much activity that their scholarship suffers. However, far more common is the tendency to keep one's head down and stick closely to the expected path, especially early in one's career, an approach that can lead quickly to being coopted. This helps no one.

Service learning, sometimes called community-based learning, can be a kind of activism. When professors design courses that require students and/or themselves to work in local settings, they are encouraging community and/or volunteer work that can become a life-long habit. Likewise, using one's position in an academic or other professional setting to leverage ideas and commitments can be a highly responsible use of privilege that the vast majority of the population will never have. These are tough choices, of course, but activism in an unjust climate is crucial to change even if it is at times personally expensive.

Administration

Women are taking on increasing administrative responsibility in the field of religion. Administrative work is often inadequately respected in academia, though at the higher levels, such positions can be better paid and/or more powerful than faculty jobs.

Women who have been involved in administration find that it has many hidden rewards, both personal and professional. Although at the highest levels administration requires time commitments that may not fit into a life that includes raising children or other time-consuming passions, many administrative positions (such as running departments, programs, centers, or organizations) may be more compatible with a lifestyle that allows for leisure or family pursuits. Administrative posts can lead to opportunities to affect the quality of life at an institution. Remember that administrators often control budget, workload and pay adjustments, curricular decisions, hiring, class sizes, and, at higher levels, the overall direction and goals of the institution.

While we have learned from experience that gender does not determine one's ability to govern wisely or justly, the presence of women in administration in general has had an impact on creating more humane governing practices and working conditions. To be a good administrator you need a penchant for multitasking. You need to be able to encourage staff and faculty so that they feel they are working with (and not for or against) you. You need an ability to connect with other administrators (who are both your peers and your bosses), a good sense of budgets and other numbers and systems, a commitment to academic integrity and honesty, and a great sense of humor. You need a real dedication to students or other clients who are served by the organization you are now running. You will also benefit from acute political antennae, an ability to "read" how you are perceived by others, and, especially, good personal boundaries.

If you are interested in and, more important, have discovered you have an aptitude for administrative work, you might try running an interdisciplinary program such as women's studies or American studies, or the practical curriculum at a seminary to get a feel for whether it's a good "fit" for you. If you then find yourself hankering to get back to the classroom or suffering from library withdrawal, this might not be your vocation. However, if you like it—the meetings and strategizing, the memos and long-term planning—you might want to start reading the ***Chronicle of Higher Education,*** an excellent resource and tutorial, and letting your colleagues know of your interest. Your institution might support your attendance at the HERS Summer Institute for Women in Higher Education Administration (http://www.brynmawr.edu/summerinstitute/hers.html), where you will learn all about the issues and find out if administration is your cup of tea. For the high atmospheric ranks of presidencies, the Harvard Graduate School of Education runs an excellent summer training session.

Senior women in the field of religion report a variety of experiences ranging from unexpected fulfillment to unmitigated disasters. However, the key is that administration is an important option for women, and women are important for such leadership posts. Younger colleagues report that on occasion they have been named chair of a department, sometimes before being tenured. While this can look like a plum assignment, it can be way of saddling women with administrative busywork that gets in the way of their own professional development. Beware such offers.

Advisor/advisee relationships

One of the great privileges of academic life is the opportunity to work with students, both undergraduate and graduate, whose area of interest is in some way connected to your own. On the undergraduate level, advising usually includes choice and construction of a major field of study, guidance on graduate school and/or job options, writing recommendations, and, if the program requires one, help in writing a senior thesis.

Being an advisor for graduate students comes with a great responsibility to introduce students to the academic world they wish to enter and/or to acquaint them with other opportunities that correspond with their abilities. Advising tasks include attention to writing and teaching skills. The advisor helps students to develop a CV and/or dossier (see **Curriculum vitae**), encourages them to attend and present papers at academic conferences, to apply for **grants** and **fellowships**. Writing thoughtful, detailed recommendations is an ongoing responsibility even long after a student has graduated. Likewise, introducing your students to your academic colleagues, helping them enter the world of publishing, and counseling them realistically on career options are all part of the job when it is done well.

Graduate students should try to find an advisor who shares their academic interests, of course, but also who has a reputation for nurturing graduate students while simultaneously treating them as adults. Many women want a woman advisor. Given that women are still in relatively short supply in many institutions, it is best to seek someone who can give the time and energy even if that person is not a woman.

The advisor/advisee relationship can be quite intimate. Advisors often are students' first real colleagues in the field, the ones who see them up close and respect what they seek to accomplish. Beware of any sexualizing of the advising relationship that can undermine the purpose of it, which is for the more experienced person to help in the professional development of the colleague being mentored. Such boundaries on both sides are essential to successful advising. An inappropriate relationship with an advisor can compromise a student's relationships with other students, the institutions, or other members of the field, all of which are important to long-term professional success. In addition, some faculty handbooks prohibit intimate relationships by faculty with students under their direct supervision (see **Faculty handbook**).

Affirmative Action

Affirmative Action was intended to mitigate the general exclusion of disadvantaged minority Americans and white American women from a broad range of opportunities, including employment and promotion, and admission to formerly all-white and predominantly male universities and professional schools. Its enemies have interpreted Affirmative Action as reverse discrimination, or, even more insidiously, as a covert means of promoting unqualified persons for college admission or jobs. Federal laws bind institutions in this regard, though informal practices vary. For a good list of controlling statutes including Title VII of the Civil Rights Act of 1964 prohibiting employment discrimination, the Equal Pay Act of 1963 prohibiting discrimination on the basis of gender in the area of compensation, etc., see www.eeoc. gov (U.S. Equal Employment Opportunity Commission).

Concerted attacks on Affirmative Action across the United States, especially in the courts, mean some gains made by minorities and white women are being eroded. Women, particularly those of color, must be vigilant against increasing resistance to diversifying college and university faculties and student bodies. People on hiring committees must be reminded of the benefit of diversity to faculties and student bodies. Women already on the inside must struggle to get onto hiring and admission committees to advocate for the hiring and entry of qualified minorities and white women. The successes that the enemies of Affirmative Action have made in diminishing and/or dismantling these programs call for increased efforts to keep programs in place that assure diversity of faculty and student bodies.

Aging

One obvious consequence of having women thrive in the field of religious studies in large numbers is that many women will age there. Hence, some of the new challenges to consider are **retirement** and **emerita** status. There are also simply the inevitable realities of growing older, with a diminishment of energy that, happily, is paired with an increase in wisdom. Moreover, some colleagues will enter the field of religion as a second and third career. Age discrimination in hiring is a real problem even for a newly minted Ph.D. at forty.

As baby boomers turn into middle-aged professionals, many of the so-called mid-life issues emerge: Am I doing what I want to be doing with my life? Is this all there is? Why are some people seemingly so much better off, happier, more fulfilled than I am? This may mean a midcourse correction in the form of a job change, perhaps even a career change, a makeover that morphs a longtime professor into the head of a nonprofit organization or that catapults a social activist into a university post (see **Mid-career issues**). Increased life expectancy and the fact that many universities and organizations do not have a mandatory retire-ment age mean that many senior colleagues are just hitting their stride at sixty-five. This is especially true for women, many of whom are ten years behind their male counterparts in terms of job progression because of years given to care for children or earlier careers in other fields.

Aging brings economic concerns such as pension funds, 401(k)s, and health insurance that women need to attend to in a culture that renders a high percentage of older women poor. A financial planner can help, and a visit with your institution's benefits officer is a must. Nevertheless, there is no substitute for forth-right conversation with trusted friends who can help clarify options and suggest good choices.

Allies

Finding and developing allies on the job is essential if sometimes difficult work. Women tend to look to one another, often with great success, for help on the job. Nothing is as disappointing as finding out that presumed allies are not, that trusted colleagues are unworthy of trust. While encouraging women to bond, the more realistic approach is to build alliances where one can—with men as well as women in the department, with colleagues in other areas, in cyberspace as well as down the hall, across racial/ethnic lines, and with people of all sexual orientations.

The most important people in any institution are not necessarily the ones with names over their doors, but the secretaries and custodial **staff**, most of whom are women, who make the place run. Cultivating their friendship as equals can go a long way toward creating a less hierarchical environment and making institutional life pleasant.

Appointments, adjunct/part-time

Given the current market, many academic institutions are cutting corners, taking advantage of the abundance of well-prepared people by trimming their full-time faculty rosters and turning to adjunct hires to teach core courses. This makes good economic sense if you are on the budget committee, but is a mixed blessing, at best, if you are on the job hunt. Benefits are minimal and course loads can approximate those of full-timers.

Salaries for adjunct or part-time teaching are generally a fraction of what one would be paid for the same course offering as a segment of a full-time teaching load. One advantage of adjunct teaching is that *in theory* one just teaches and has none of the advising, committee work, and the like that go with a full-time position. Of course, students do not make such distinctions when they want to discuss their vocational plans, request a letter of recommendation, or research a topic about which they consider you the world's expert.

Adjunct teaching may be a foot in the academic door. It may also be a dead end. It is rare for faculties to turn adjunct appointments into full-time positions. Teaching for a year or two while one is finishing one's dissertation can be a good idea, or it may be the fastest route to being "all but dissertation" (commonly called ABD) for a long career. Some people actually prefer to teach part-time, but for most it is not a choice. Women are especially taken advantage of here. If women decide to have children, care for elders, or pursue other worthwhile endeavors, adjunct teaching can be a good stopgap measure to maintain a toehold in academia while still pursing other goals. However, it is all too often a trap.

After several years of it, you should demand full benefits and/or to be hired as a half-time rather than adjunct professor. It will not be financially lucrative long after it has become a good CV item. Whether you teach one or six years as an adjunct is usually of little consequence career-wise. Think about a move to a cognate field or to another form of teaching. Writing or media work, for example, may be areas where your skills will be appreciated, and you will not be blatantly used to provide cheap skilled labor in the classroom.

Appointments, tenure track

Unlike what you get from the dentist, an academic appointment is a fancy way of saying, "Congratulations, you got the job." It means that you are named to a specific task with written responsibilities, a reciprocal relationship of accountability, and remuneration. Be sure to read the fine print. Know your rights and plan to live up to your part of the bargain, indeed, to exceed expectations. An academic appointment usually has a time frame and promotion scale attached to it. Getting a job in the nonprofit world, publishing, or a religious bureaucracy may not have such formalities, but it is equally important to attend to such matters. Be sure to read the **faculty handbook** and familiarize yourself with the expectations and culture of the institution.

Appointments, visiting

A visiting professorship can be a nice change of pace, a chance to see if the grass really is greener elsewhere, and an opportunity to work with different colleagues. It is not usually the prelude to a long-term appointment, so do not go with unrealistic expectations. It can also be a hardship: time away from one's family and usual surroundings, perhaps working in a different language or cultural setting. While many institutions like to have visiting faculty, few know how to welcome and sustain a visitor as part of the community.

Evaluate such offers with care, and negotiate conditions with as much attention as you would for a regular job. Otherwise, it can be a semester or a year wasted. Be sure that expectations are clear and that there are no hidden demands that will compromise what might otherwise be a good time to get some writing done and/or to try out a new course.

Benefits, domestic partner

Many colleges and universities today offer domestic partner benefits. While you probably should avoid asking about the policy at your interview (along with other questions about benefits that are better handled after an offer has been made), you might want to check with the Affirmative Action office at the school to see if it has such a policy. You could also check out the institution's Web site for this information. You can find an up-to-date list of schools that offer these benefits at the Human Rights Campaign Web site www.hrc.org/worknet.

Carefully investigate what is being offered. Some policies include funeral leave, campus privileges (tuition, library, swimming pool, etc.), or inclusion of partners as beneficiaries on life insurance or pension. Some policies allow you to cover your partner on your health care policy, while others provide cash allowances (often subject to taxes) equivalent to some or all of the cost of taking out your own policy. Some policies cover only same-sex partners, while others also cover heterosexual couples. This is an area where moving toward parity is slow but steady. You can help it along by becoming an advocate for equal benefits regardless of sexual orientation or marital status.

Benefits, leaves (family)

Family leave is mandated by federal law for reasons of illness, death, and other life-changing circumstances. Maternity leave is required by law (see the 1978 Federal Pregnancy Disability Amendment to Title 7 of the 1964 Civil Rights Act), so your institution must provide it. What is not as clear is how much time you get, whether partners can also claim it as a family leave matter, or what in other countries (such as Sweden) is seen as shared time taking care of a new addition to the family. If you think it will be an issue, check it out in the negotiating phase just so you know where you stand. Feel free to push the envelope since U.S. institutions are notoriously stingy in granting time off and women are notoriously poor in asking for it. In fact, if you are in a position to make such decisions, urge women to err on the side of **self-care**. It was sad to hear a recently retired, revered colleague give that advice to her friends, admitting that she wished she had taken better care of herself during her working years.

Benefits, leaves (study)

Academic life is considered so demanding and stressful, so lacking in time to keep abreast of developments, that a major concern is when one can leave, bow out for a bit, to refresh. These so-called leaves become coveted parts of the academic benefit package, negotiated furiously to wring the most time away possible. There is a certain irony about the fact that in the flurry to get a job, one is negotiating how to leave! Some nonprofit organizations have imitated that model and make a paid leave part of the package for their research and/or administrative people.

Academic leaves of absence, like sabbaticals, can be paid or unpaid, a semester or a year, on campus or off, usually for a specific project and often with the goal of publication in mind. Know what your institution offers and plan accordingly. If you are required to have a book done or a project completed, be sure you comply or the next leave will be that much harder to justify.

Benefits, medical

Most institutions offer some form of health benefits, though the changing conditions of the U.S. health care system dictate that these can range considerably. Many institutions offer a smorgasbord of choices, all with different costs and benefits associated with them. Take time to study your options in relation to your particular health situation.

If you are considering bearing children, be sure that the pregnancy and fertility benefits are adequate. A dental plan and vision benefits are important. As you approach retirement, an important consideration is what benefits will carry over when you become Medicare eligible. If you are from outside the United States, explore what might apply from your country, and match your choice accordingly.

Don't forget that the best health insurance is preventative care. See if your institution offers benefits in the form of gym or health club access. If not, start a campaign so they will (see **Health, mental** and **Health, physical**).

Benefits, retirement

Every institution has its own **retirement** policy. Of course, everyone is required to pay into Social Security, so, at least for the near future, those benefits will be available. Larger institutions provide a seminar on retirement planning. Virtually all institutions have provisions to reserve a certain percentage of one's salary, usually matched by the employer, for retirement saving. There are popular plans developed to meet the needs of people in the field of education. Find out what is available and save, save, save.

Books

Books are still important tools of the religion trade even though there is some suggestion that people read less and watch television, and surf the Web more. **Publishing** a book, perhaps beginning with the dissertation recycled into a more generally accessible text, is part of the expectation in most religion-related fields. Not everyone writes well; some fabulous teachers never publish a book, and some well-known authors are disasters in the classroom. But books still reign.

Once colleagues get academic jobs, or for that matter jobs in information technology, the nonprofit sector, or the like, they are inundated with announcements and catalogs from publishers advertising their wares. Careful study of selected ones may be useful in helping to develop syllabi for courses. Sometimes it is possible to get a free review copy (yes, you need to write a review) or a desk copy of a book for which you do not normally pay if you adopt the book for classroom use. Publishers want to promote their books for classroom adoption, so this is a win-win for everyone. Just do not request books you will not use, as that puts a crimp in the system for all. As electronic books come into popular usage it is not clear how the whole business of book publishing will develop, but it is clear that writing remains an important component of religious studies work.

Make friends with the manager of the bookstore at your institution. She/he is responsible for ordering books for your classes, and can be helpful in making suggestions on titles you might have missed. Urge your students to write early and often if they plan a career in this field.

In some settings, organizing a book discussion group can be a great alternative to a full course on a topic. It can be a way to test interest in a theme or drum up business for a future course. Such groups are good ways for community people to join those in the academy, as well as to highlight certain materials that would otherwise be ignored.

Children

A career in religious studies does not preclude children in a woman's life. To the contrary, this is a field in which passing on faith and knowledge from generation to generation is an all-important task. It is not easy. Unfortunately, women still usually bear more than their share of child-rearing responsibilities. Having children requires finding ways to balance the needs of young people with the demands of a professional job, accent on the "balance." However, women in academia have some flexibility in hours. With a supportive partner or other means of support, especially good childcare, women can often manage to raise children and build a successful career.

Ways of doing this are as varied as we are. Some women find that planning their children around their career milestones, such as getting pregnant as soon as the ink is dry on the dissertation, is a good way to go. Others already have children when they enter a doctoral program or take a job. Still others find themselves caring for nieces and nephews or grandchildren at times they never expected. Some women adopt children. Many choose to enjoy other people's kids without full-time personal responsibility. It is important to recognize these differences as the fruit of decades of struggle for choice, and to accord each the dignity and support it requires.

Sage advice from the mothers, grandmothers, and aunts boils down to "make time for the children in your life and get all the help you can afford." It is a balancing act. The urgent demand of a child crying at night or at other hours pleading "Play with me" or "Help me with my homework" is serious competition for any dissertation or book, project, class, or conference. Nonetheless, there are still only twenty-four hours in a day, so some accommodation to supply and demand is required. Having a babysitter at home while you are in your study working can provide some respite. Childcare is costly, and in a field where salaries are not usually high, this often creates a strain.

Many women find that spacing children according to other needs, such as not trying to have a baby around the time of general exams, makes sense. However, life does not always work on schedule. So it is perhaps more important to structure a support system—friends, colleagues, partner if you have one, family, neighbors—who can be the "village" the child requires. Despite all of our progress on shared childcare, we note that women still do the lion's share, a problem that needs attention.

Childcare is expensive but some academic institutions and some nonprofits provide it at reduced cost. Check out your options. Also, check on the federal tax credit now available to offset part of such costs. Consult an accountant to be sure. Choose your childcare with safety as a foremost concern. Don't forget about flexibility and reliability so you can tailor your schedule according to the pace of your institution to minimize the inevitable childcare failures.

When kids get into school, they often need their parents in different but no less demanding ways than before. The myth of confining concerns for children to their early years is easily shattered. Consider taking your child with you if you have professional travel obligations. It is generally easy to find babysitters along the way. For example, the AAR Annual Meeting offers childcare by advance reservation. Of course, travel with children is always a challenge. And be sure that their needs are met when you take them along, not just your need to avoid guilt for leaving them at home.

Monitor your benefits package to see if you can get tuition reduction or reciprocity with another institution for your children as they approach college age. Seek low-rate loan programs that your institution might offer to help with education costs.

Christian hegemony

Christianity dominates the field of religious studies. That is hegemony. Many jobs are at Christian seminaries or in the departments of religion at church-related schools. Much of the scholarship on various religions is undertaken by Christians who study "other" religions. The majority of members of the AAR are Christian. This Christian hegemony is a reflection of both the historical development of the field of religious studies and the dominance of white Protestant Christianity in American social and cultural life. Thus, all kinds of Christians—African American and Asian Christians, Catholics, Anabaptists, for example—may find themselves marginalized by Christian hegemony, even as they may simultaneously enjoy certain of the privileges of Christian affiliation.

There are both conceptual and practical implications to this Christian dominance. Because Christians historically formed the field of religious studies, "religion" also contains Christian assumptions. The category of "religion" itself was taken up and shaped by colonialism. Spiritual and cultural practices were recategorized as "religions" on the model of Christianity. For example, the wide variety of South Asian practices were brought together as variations of the single "religion" called Hinduism.

Certain South Asian texts were translated by British colonists and treated as sacred scriptures analogous to the Christian Bible. Thus, the word "religion" as in the American Academy of Religion, or "religious" as in religious studies can indicate the plurality of "religions" studied in the field.

The practical implications range from who is allowed to study which religion, to what types of jobs are available, to the organization of the Annual Meeting, to how the field is structured (including such matters as jobs, panels, anthologies, and departments). While Christians may range widely in their choice of specialization, often those who practice another religion are expected to take up an academic specialization in line with their identity. Those who are not Christian—who practice another religion or who are atheists, or who are conscientious objectors to religious identification—may find their experience of the field alienating. They may need to seek out those spaces and sections at the Annual Meeting, for example, where Christian hegemony is addressed or resisted.

Christian hegemony can mean that even those who are very concerned about diversity may focus on the categories of gender, race, class, or nation, but fail to think through or address issues of religious diversity. Resistance to Christian hegemony requires being able to think through and respond to the crosscutting of issues related to diversity. For women it means conscious efforts to see one another as colleagues across various lines.

The Chronicle of Higher Education (The Chronicle)

The Chronicle of Higher Education (*The Chronicle*) is a weekly newspaper aimed at college and university faculty and administrators. It includes news, employment openings, and other materials related to the field. Subscriptions provide full access to the Web site, www.chronicle.com, and to *Academe Today,* a daily e-mail newsletter. This can be very useful in the job-hunting process and in keeping up with scholarly trends and ideas in and beyond the field of religious studies.

Class, socioeconomic

Class is a changing, challenging, and tricky problem as questions of money, access, education, race, and culture interweave to form layers of privilege and discrimination. For women in religious studies, it is important to realize that academic institutions and many related settings in publishing, library work, and so forth are organized as if white upper-middle-class ways were normative. This involves everything from who can afford to go to graduate school to what fork to use at a faculty dinner, from what your stationery looks like to whether you can pay back your student loans without taking a corporate job.

Women in the field of religion need more frank discussion on such matters. It is often easier to address one's sexuality than one's financial status. In the meantime, structural analysis of class-based oppression in a globalized economy is an integral part of any religious studies program. That means examining our institutions and ourselves to determine how to share resources and recognize and respect substantive differences that result from women's different histories.

Clothing options

Some women colleagues worry about religious *haute couture*. What to wear to interviews, what to wear for professional events, what to wear for teaching, how to dress for office hours, and what to take to the AAR Annual Meeting (toss in a bathing suit, as many hotels have pools) are concerns. Women are creative and one way we show it is by our diversity of dress.

There are guidebooks and academic musings on deciding what to wear. There is also a lot of time lost on the trivial. Does it really matter? Our consensus: Sometimes it does and sometimes it does not. There are horror stories of the results of wearing a too-short skirt for a job interview, or presenting an endowed lecture in pants when a dress/skirt/suit is *de rigeur*. However, who says so? And why do we grant the clothes police such authority? Nonetheless, clothes give a message in a complex social order.

Individual style choices are expressions of oneself to others. Realistically, professional dress, whether skirt or pants, is always dignified and should be comfortable. It may be festive and/or reflect one's heritage. The bottom line is to be comfortable in one's clothes and to dress in a way appropriate to the setting.

Collaborative work

Collaborative work is not regarded as highly as the Lone Ranger approach in our field. The gender of the Lone Ranger may have something to do with it, but we will save that for another day. Just know that when it comes time for a tenure review, your joint publications, your collaborative efforts, will count less than your single-authored work. This flies in the face of all good sense, and passes over the fact that it is often harder, more of a stretch, and therefore more of a growth experience, not to mention often resulting in a better product, to work in collaboration. We recommend it nonetheless, especially when it comes to interdisciplinary teaching and writing. We encourage women to raise this issue with their colleagues and change this outmoded protocol. A caution: When submitting collaborative work for tenure review, be sure to state clearly *your* contribution.

If you are invited to a collaborative process, give it a whirl even if you are a reflector by learning style and prefer poring over a text to discussing an idea in a group. You may find that the stimulation of working collaboratively (and this includes team teaching) is well worth the occasional aggravation.

Coming out

Among the real changes in religious studies is the matter of sexuality. Of course, in many institutions, especially in more conservative ones, it is still a major liability to be an out lesbian, bisexual, queer and/or a transgender person. The price is high. You may not be hired in the first place. If you are a graduate student, you may get clear and distinct signals that you might consider a career in another field that would be friendlier to you.

There is work to be done to correct this injustice, and people need to survive in the meanwhile. None of these choices is easy yet.

Due to lots of hard work, there are now some graduate programs that offer queer theory courses, a number of institutions that realize that some of their best and brightest (faculty, staff, and students) are lesbian/gay/bisexual and transgender persons. There are support networks, conferences, and meetings for **LGBTQ** students and for scholar/activists in religion.

There are new centers at several theological schools that deal with LGBTQ issues in religion and ministry and that archive materials from LGBTQ religious groups. For example, there is the Center for Lesbian and Gay Studies in Religion and Ministry at Pacific School of Religion (www.clgs.org). The Chicago Theological Seminary has the Heyward-Boswell Society (HBS), an outreach and support group for the lesbian, gay, bisexual, and transgender community and their supporters at that school (www.chgosem.edu). CTS houses the Lesbian, Gay, Bisexual and Transgender Religious Archives Network (www.lgbtran.org).

There are prominent professors, directors of organizations, rabbis, and ministers who are out lesbian or bisexual women. In many circles, LGBTQ scholarship is increasingly respected. The landscape has changed enormously in a relatively short time, even if some institutions are still conducting witch-hunts. There is still much work to do to extend the welcome and level the playing field until sexual status no longer matters.

How you position yourself as a student, a job applicant, a young faculty member, an editor, a religious leader is up to you, knowing that some settings are more open than others. No one should be required to commit professional suicide for the sake of being "out." Nonetheless, the onus is on everyone in the field, not just lesbian, bisexual, and queer women, to recognize LGBTQ scholarly and activist work for what it is, namely, work, and to evaluate it on its merits.

Meanwhile, the law guarantees your right to privacy, and your right to separate your professional life from your personal life is important. It is illegal for interviewers to base hiring decisions on your answers to personal questions. Most search committees are advised to avoid questions about your private life and marital status (see **Interviewing**). You may offer such information if you choose, but you can (politely) refuse to answer such questions.

The consequences of staying "in the closet" can be devastating, forcing you to work under stressful conditions. The best advice is to find colleagues who can share their experiences and advise you from their wisdom based on the institutional climate. Obviously, in an ideal world, such matters would never arise, but since they do, we should all work to stop the injustice.

Transgender people will have an especially hard time until our institutions and surrounding culture catch up with the reality of gender diversity. Since so much about gender is rooted in religious language and imagery, people in religious studies have a special professional responsibility to work to overcome the prejudices that abound.

Committee on the Status of Women in the Profession (CSWP)

The SBL Committee on the Status of Women, like its counterpart, the AAR Committee for the Status of Women in the Profession (see **SWP**), addresses issues that women face in religious studies, specifically in the area of biblical scholarship. A standing committee of the SBL council, the CSWP was constituted to assess the status and encourage the participation of women in all professional areas of biblical studies.

In pursuit of this mandate, it continues its efforts in areas of mentoring and networking, opening the Society to greater participation by women, and calling attention to the ways in which the Society through its various activities speaks to and about women. The CSWP encourages networking and mentoring by sponsoring a breakfast for women members. This breakfast is an opportunity to meet new people and to build relationships, to honor excellent mentors with a "Mentoring Award," and to identify, through speakers, panels, demonstrations, or roundtable discussions, new issues that women face in the profession.

The CSWP also offers an orientation session for students, both to enable networking and to introduce people to the complex nature of the Annual Meeting. The CSWP also administers a travel grant that enables women from developing countries, Asia, and Eastern Europe to attend the annual and international meetings. Between meetings, the CSWP keeps members connected through a Web page (www.sbl-site.org/SBLCommittees_CSWP.aspxnd) and a listserve. Your input is welcome.

Committees

Committees are a mixed blessing in our business. On the one hand, much of the work is done this way, especially in large departments or organizations. On the other hand, the burden of meetings, reports, interviews, and the like can double your workload in no time whatsoever.

As a first year faculty member in any institution, you will be invited to join a committee or three. Be prudent and know that what you gain in meeting colleagues and establishing your reputation for being a team player has to be balanced against what you lose in terms of time for your own work, your family and friends, and your sanity in general while adjusting to a new place. Some institutions wisely do not expect new faculty to serve on committees until their second year. If your institution has no such policy, limit what you accept to the base minimum required during your first year.

Women of color are especially vulnerable in such situations, where institutions are anxious to diversify and see them as the means to that end. While women need to say "no" when they have taken on enough responsibility, those holding power in institutions need to cease and desist from overinviting them and expecting them to carry more than their fair share.

Committee work can be fun, a stepping-stone to administrative work, a diversion from the humdrum of teaching core courses. Committees can yield rich results in terms of shaping an organization or a department. However, like so many good things, a little bit goes a long way. Be sure to check whether committee work is taken into account in your institution when it comes time for tenure or promotion before committing too much time.

Commuting

Factor commuting into your decision about employment, your choice of housing, and your allocation of time. In an increasingly mobile society where it seems that fewer and fewer people live near their jobs, commuting is becoming a major issue in quality of life planning. Be realistic. Know that the trade-off for endless hours in your car or on a subway or bus can be positive—the newspaper read, a good novel on tape, some time to yourself for a change. Alternatively, it can be negative—loss of research time, a crowded, unpleasant, stressful part of your daily routine. Some of it is unavoidable, such as plane rides if you and your partner live in different cities or if you take a visiting appointment for a bit. In that case, be sure you book a direct flight, get your frequent flyer points, and travel light.

Some of the hassle of commuting is avoidable now that telecommuting is possible. Academic schedules being what they are, you might be able to keep your on-site workweek to three or four days, create a home office, and join the fray from the comfort of your own modem. Be creative and ecological in all of this, saving yourself and the environment at the same time.

Competition

Our field is as competitive as many, not as cutthroat as some. Recall that at Harvard Law School, students were known to cut assigned articles out of journals so their peers could not read them. Happily, there are few reports of that in religion.

Graduate school is, by history, culture, and structure, competitive. Getting in is competitive, and once in, some faculty thrive on having graduate students compete with one another for their attention. That is the bad news. The good news is that after course work and comprehensive exams, the drive to compete softens up substantially. Dissertations are so diverse that there is little worry about having your work appropriated by someone else.

The issue of women in competition with one another in graduate school and in professional positions can be particularly fraught with hazards. Cultivating cooperative and mutually supportive relationships can be easier said than done in graduate school, since the need to distinguish oneself can make for uneasy liaisons. One of the best ways to see alternatives to the competitive model is just that: to see alternatives to the competitive model. Reading groups and writing groups can be helpful and sanity-producing sites for collegial rather than competitive learning.

A mentor might be able to discuss her own experiences. Professional associations and networks of women are another good source of alternatives to counterproductive competition. At the same time, it is worth keeping in mind that a healthy sense of competition can be enlivening and mobilizing. Just don't overdo it. Keep in mind that virtually all of our progress as women in the field has come about because of cooperative work.

Computers

Computers are now standard equipment in the field. If you are under the age of thirty-five, there is no need to read on. Over thirty-five, you may want to continue.

Many institutions provide broadband access to the Internet and expect faculty and staff to be proficient in its use. If you are not, take a course at a community college, or call your teenage niece and make an appointment with her to tutor you.

Many institutions are offering on-line education, a relatively inexpensive and efficient way to teach and learn. You may be expected to participate, so be sure you and your computer are up to speed. Likewise, a lot of classroom instruction now includes an on-line component—whether papers are submitted that way, class discussion is conducted via e-mail, or research is handled through digital means. This is a huge shift in our pedagogical and communication modes, but it still requires that you read your mail (e-mail), prepare for your (on-line) classes, and be attentive to your students and colleagues. There are increasingly good models for this kind of teaching, so check with your institution's Information Technology department for help. Just be sure to back up data multiple ways, as computer failures are frequent and human error is even more so.

Studies indicate that the gap between women and men when it comes to technological competence is shrinking, but it remains very real across age groups. Nonetheless, if you cannot handle PowerPoint or do not feel comfortable signing on to teach a distance education component of your curriculum, get the help you need. It can be great fun and there is no going back. **On-line courses** are the wave of the future.

Confidence

Many women enter our field with low self-esteem and even less confidence in their abilities. This can plague us as well as our students. It shows up in many ways, including jealousies, nasty competition, and undercutting one another. Many women come by their lack of confidence honestly, because we are still discriminated against due to sexual, racial, national, and class prejudice.

Confidence is hard to instill, easy to undermine. Hopefully, having information, such as that provided by this book, and scheduling regular meetings with friends who are in the best position to assess one's skills, will go a long way toward increasing our individual and collective confidence. Therapy can help, though the problem ought never to be seen as only individual but always as rooted in the often unjust culture in which we find ourselves as women.

There is no substitute for the rewarding hard work, the projects completed, the goals reached to increase our confidence over time. Still, the most effective route to self-confidence for women is to instill it early in our girls, and reinforce it with every step, something institutions and organizations need to assume as their part in this project called equality. Support and **networking** are good ways to reinforce one another's confidence.

Confidentiality

Confidentiality is understood in many professions as maintaining absolute privacy of privileged information. Realistically, in our circles, it is somewhere between the seal of the confessional and what prisoners jokingly call confidence that you will not use what you know against me. Beware of assurances of confidentiality, whether from colleagues or committees, as all too often privileged information finds its way into the public arena. Many women have found their reputations ruined, their trust broken in such situations. There may also be times when the demands of confidentiality serve the needs of the institution and not the greater good, creating a situation of extreme dissonance and ethical dilemma.

At the same time, if you serve on a committee or are in a situation where you are expected to maintain confidentiality, that is, not to spill the beans regardless of what legal fine-tuning may apply, it is considered your professional obligation to act accordingly. Be sure to learn what your institution expects in this regard (for example, whether you are obliged by law to report illegal activities when you learn of them), then make your choices accordingly. You may decide that serving on a review committee is too stressful or that you know the person too well to be objective. Know when to excuse yourself. Be especially careful with electronic correspondence. It is very easy to err on the discretion front when the technology makes it so easy to send things.

Conflict (see also Competition)

Conflict styles vary both culturally and individually. Women are especially vulnerable to differences in style and can be greatly misunderstood. Racial stereotypes can also determine what others expect from women. For some people, arguing means you care; for others, arguing means that the world is about to explode into violence. Some people seek to engage in conflict as a means of engaging in relationships, while others seek to avoid conflict for fear that it will destroy relationships. For some people, any disagreement with their views is experienced as disrespect. For others, vociferous argument can be a sign of respect for another person's views, showing that one takes these views seriously.

Because the United States is dominated by a white, middle-class culture that tends toward conflict avoidance, those who are not white and/or middle-class and who engage directly in conflict may find themselves disciplined in various ways. On the other hand, this dominant culture is much more accepting of anger expressed by white, middle-class men, such that those men become used to expressing their own anger regularly without expecting much response, and can be greatly offended when similar forms of anger are directed at them. This is a recipe for institutional disaster.

As one enters various institutional settings, it is often good to learn to identify one's own style with regard to conflict and that of one's colleagues. As a student, how do I engage in disagreements with my fellow students and with my professors? As a faculty member, how do I engage with other members of my department, the staff, and administrators around conflictual issues? How do I handle conflict in the classroom setting, where I am expected to make room for differing views? It is helpful to acknowledge various styles of conflict directly and to ask the students to identify their own styles, as well as to be aware of gender and racial stereotypes they may impose on expectations of the behavior of others.

Contracts (see also Negotiations)

You did not go to law school, but negotiating a contract is not for lawyers only. Once a job offer has been made, you will be expected to sign a contract that binds you and the institution to mutual agreements. It is a legal matter, so should only be signed after the greatest of scrutiny and, if possible, with someone to help you think through the implications.

Know the salary range at the institution to ascertain whether what you are being offered is in the ballpark. *Academe,* a publication of the American Association of University Professors, publishes annually the salary information for many institutions, as well as for regions of the country. Even if you lack specific information for the institution hiring you, you can get a sense of a fair salary for that part of the country. Salaries can be state secrets, but colleagues will be helpful in orienting you. Insist on having all benefits spelled out in writing, especially when it comes to tenure-track or long-term employment options, leaves and sabbaticals, funding for conferences and equipment, course load, and the like. All of this varies enormously around the country, in small schools and large, for undergraduate and graduate programs, to say nothing of the range in the nonprofit sector or publishing.

The basics are the same: Know that your bargaining power is at its peak when the institution wants you, wants to conclude the search, and wants you to sign immediately. That is the time to call your friendly lawyer for advice and ask the potential employer for your wish list. Most women have not been socialized for asking for what we want or need. This is the point at which your advisor and your friends will be of great assistance. Then get it all in writing to prevent future problems.

Counter offers (see also Negotiations)

The negotiation process may involve offers and counter offers, that is, a package of wages and benefits made by one institution that will be matched or at least responded to in some way by another. This can happen in the hiring process, though in the present climate it is unusual. It is more likely to occur when one is already in a position, for example in the academic world in a tenure-track position but not yet promoted, or for other reasons is not entirely satisfied with the situation. Looking elsewhere is tricky business as it can send a mixed signal to your current employer. However, if you are given an offer, your current employer may decide to match or better it as a way to keep you on board.

The key to this whole process is maintaining integrity, keeping people informed while at the same time looking out for your best interest. A lawyer may be helpful in sorting out contractual details that will affect your decision. In any case, the real winner in these cases is the person who acts honorably.

Curriculum vitae

The curriculum vitae, or CV as it is known, is an important document on paper (or on-line) that conveys who you are to the world. It is expected in our field that you will have one and that you will keep it updated as you progress throughout your career.

Like its cousin, the humble résumé, a CV includes the basic information about you: name, address, phone/fax/e-mail, and professional preparation including education and certification. Then it showcases your academic work by listing your dissertation, published articles, reviews and books, and of course your invited lectures, prizes, fellowships, and other information that conveys your credentials.

There are several keys to a good CV. First, it must be scrupulously honest, not inflating or misrepresenting your accomplishments. Second, it must be simple in design, easy on the eyes, and accessible at a glance. Third, it must be up-to-date, with the most recent accomplishments and publications listed first and the rest in descending order of date. Fourth, it should be proofread carefully, with publications displayed in proper bibliographic form. Some universities have their own required format, so check with your career planning office, your advisor, or the dean.

Computers and word processing make all this so much easier than in years past. But they do not update it for you, nor select the standard white (or other neutral color) paper (bond, or in any case a good quality) that you will print it on. With so much work being done on-line, including job applications, it is a good idea to have a nicely formatted version ready to go at a moment's notice. Resist the temptation to enhance it with graphics, colors, and the like. A CV is a CV is a CV. The major questions about a CV have to do with how much information is too much. Personal information such as date of birth, religious affiliation if any, marital status, citizenship, ethnicity, etc., are entirely discretionary.

It is also a good plan to keep a summary of your CV handy for use when you give a lecture or a talk at another institution. That will save you typing a blurb each time you are asked. Keep that version short—a paragraph or three will do. Get some professional photographs taken while you are at it, as many groups ask for them for publicity purposes. Scanning one or two photos onto your computer will assure they are handy when requested. A **Web page** that includes this personal information is an efficient way to handle all of this.

Computers allow us to tailor documents easily to fit the circumstances. This means you can highlight certain aspects of your CV depending on the need. Bottom line here—keep it simple, complete, honest, and up-to-date.

Disability (see also Ableism, Illness, and Disability)

The middle of the twentieth century saw the beginning of a major shift in the role of people with disabilities within society with the influx of disabled veterans following World War II and the rise of the civil rights movement. The first shift was from medical isolation and marginalization to medical rehabilitation and mainstreaming as a means of normalization. The second shift was to abandon the medical model in favor of a social model that sees the primary issue of disability as a social construct rather than a personal characteristic. This shift is seen in the rise of the disability rights movement and disability studies.

Disability can be defined as any limitation to mobility, communication, learning, or any other life activity based on deviation from the social norm for physical, mental, neurological, and perceptual abilities. Women with physical disabilities often face additional discrimination due to body and gender issues in a sexist society.

The Americans with Disabilities Act of 1990 defines disability as having or being perceived as having a condition that impairs a major life activity. Defining disability as a social construct is not meant to deny the reality of impairment. Rather, it is to highlight the fact that society structures itself according to normative ability rather than the range of ability. The imposition of normative standards that attempt to marginalize or normalize people with disabilities or privilege nondisabled people may be called "ableist" or "normate."

People with disabilities have been entering the academy at all levels in recent years. Civil rights legislation such as Section 504 of the Rehabilitation Act of 1973 and the Americans with Disabilities Act of 1990 have opened the doors of higher education for people with disabilities. Institutions are required to provide accessible programming for people with both visible and invisible disabilities. Religion faculty members will find that they will be called on to make the appropriate accommodations for students with disabilities. This may range from extended time on exams and assignments, to alternative formats for materials, use of assistive listening devices in lecturing, or working with a sign language interpreter in class. Faculty should become aware of their institution's policies and resources for accommodating students with disabilities.

The rights of faculty members with disabilities are also covered by legislation such as the Americans with Disabilities Act, although the rights of an employee differ to some degree from the rights of a student. Faculty with disabilities should become familiar with their rights and the process at their institution for pursuing appropriate accommodation. Current practices in disability accommodation should be seen as a transition stage in enabling people with disabilities. Universal Design is a philosophy that calls for the structuring of facilities, institutions, and instruction in such a way that the range of human ability is addressed rather than accommodation to ableist norms.

The study of religion is a particularly sensitive area for people with disabilities. Care should be taken in identifying ableist attitudes and biases within different faith traditions. Often ableist perspectives arise in the interpretation and translation of sacred texts that are not essential to the faith perspective. Religion often encounters issues of embodiment and normative humanity, such as physical and mental perfection. These ableist views often surface when dealing with issues of faith and healing. Ableist attitudes should be dealt with openly and candidly, where they do appear (see appendix V, "Making Your Presentations Disability Friendly").

Dissertation

Many more women than men in religious studies get through comprehensive exams but never finish the dissertation, a condition coyly referred to as "all but dissertation," or ABD. Much of the explanation is economic and societal in nature, having nothing to do with competence. Writing a dissertation requires uninterrupted time, which is expensive, and it requires overcoming the social conditioning that women have nothing unique and meaningful to say. Happily, as a field we have come some distance on both accounts.

Women are getting more financial aid than ever before (previously it was assumed men would handle the heavy intellectual lifting and the family income, and thus it was unnecessary to waste money to educate a woman). Support groups, women role models, and good colleagues are helping with the conditioning problems. We still are a long way from making the dissertation process user-friendly for most women.

A dissertation is like and unlike anything you have ever written before. In a way it is akin to books you have read throughout your career. It is also the largest project you have taken on to date. Graduate school does not teach you how to develop and sustain an idea over the course of hundreds of pages.

A well-thought-out prospectus can be a good roadmap. Consult it often, since you will undoubtedly hit dead ends in the writing process. It will remind you of the core ideas and how they are structured. There is no formula for dissertations. However, most in religion are five or six chapters, with an introduction, a review of the literature, analytic and constructive chapters followed by a conclusion. Bibliography and the usual scholarly tools are included as well.

A good advisor, a mentor, and a writing group will help you. Only your persistence will get you through it. When push comes to shove, perhaps you only need two things to write your dissertation: a chair and a bucket of glue. Put some glue on the chair. Sit down. WRITE. (An exaggeration, of course, but containing a grain of truth!) Here are some tips:

- Say what YOU want. You have trained too hard to collapse into other people's desires and expectations. This is your unique contribution.
- Allow yourself to share your writing with others—especially your peers, who can give you excellent feedback—before taking your drafts to your advisors.
- Spend lots of time on your thesis statement. The longer and more complicated it is, the harder the writing is. The more crisply stated and brief, the easier the dissertation will be to write.
- Keep writing. Write every day, even if it is only for a brief period.
- Take calculated risks. Your peers and your committee will help you come to terms with the risks that will benefit your project, and the ones that will not.
- Divide the project into blocks. Reward yourself after you have completed each one.
- Write with a wide audience in mind. This will make your rewrite for publication simpler.
- Be patient, and push yourself.
- Understand that this is not the final word on the topic, but simply, and importantly, your best effort.

Emerita

One sure sign of progress for women in religious studies is that we now have some women who are professors emeritae. This means that they have retired officially from active teaching at their institutions. Usually emerita status follows a full professorship. The title is an honorific conferred to signal their accomplishment at the time of retirement.

Depending on institutional policy, it may mean a continuation of certain benefits of the job, for example, an office on campus and, in rare cases, some secretarial help. This needs to be negotiated carefully since such benefits can be very valuable as women live longer lives. Beware, however, of efforts to grant emerita status early as a way of putting feminists "out to pasture" prematurely.

Employment opportunities (see also Appointments)

Religious studies professionals are well prepared for a range of jobs. The easy mistake is to think that when you finish your training you will train others, i.e., that teaching and research at an institution like your alma mater is the expected outcome of a doctorate in the field. This is a limited and limiting notion, the opposite of what professionals in other fields think. For example, most recently graduated medical doctors do not believe they are going to teach in a medical school, nor do new lawyers assume they will teach law. They expect to practice their professions. Graduate students in religion are socialized to think that they will teach, as if that is the only thing for which they are prepared. If they do not get jobs in academia, they are sometimes made to feel that they have failed. Do not fall for that myth.

The market is such that many well-trained colleagues will never teach in academic institutions. This may be a blessing in disguise, given the stories of so many senior women who are dissatisfied, feel underappreciated, stifled, trivialized, and otherwise unhappy in the academic institution they were schooled to think was their only option. In fact, there are countless job options for women who are trained in religious studies and have the skills to consider critically, to analyze carefully, and to think "outside the box."

Libraries and information technology, publishing, the non-profit sector, and certain government departments are just a few of the possibilities. Employment in religious institutions is also an option. Some women with backgrounds in religious studies even find their way into the corporate world; for example, one is in charge of personnel for a huge multinational corporation, while another is in the process of making a bundle in real estate. Career counseling is available at larger institutions and is usually free if you are a student, so take advantage of it.

The key is to think big, think YOU, and think variety. There are more options than you imagine. There is a niche for you. Life is long and you will have various jobs over the course of your career. Do not let the tunnel vision of some academics stifle you. Think, act, and expect big on your terms.

One place to look for employment is the **AAR** resource called *Openings: Employment Opportunities for Scholars of Religion* (www.aarweb.org/openings). Listings are posted monthly with information on how to apply.

Entrepreneurs

One wonderful result of women coming into religious studies in larger numbers is that some of us are able to imagine not simply moving into open slots but actually creating new opportunities for others and ourselves. These so-called entrepreneurs are responsible for the creation of new departments of women's studies and gender studies that simply did not exist before. They have created and endowed lectureships and research programs. They have founded journals like the *Journal of Feminist Studies in Religion* (*JFSR*) (www.hds.harvard.edu/jfsr). They have built organizations like the Center for Women and Ministry in the South; the Women's Alliance for Theology, Ethics and Ritual (WATER) (www.hers.com/water); and the Women's Theological Center, among so many such accomplishments. Consider joining their ranks. The challenge of entrepreneurial action is that such creations take money and time that most of us simply do not have on our own. Therefore, they require intense collaboration, meticulous organization, fund raising ability, and good luck.

The downside is that there are also hucksters out there who will commercialize and commodify your work, sell it to the highest bidder, and profit from your labor. These include companies that tape and sell lectures or lecture notes without proper permission, or people who quote work without attribution or who appropriate ideas without acknowledgement. They are entrepreneurs, too, and their numbers are increasing as business people realize that religion "sells," especially in tough times.

Avoid them, as there are many better ways to get your ideas into the mainstream without reducing them to soup or a bad movie.

Ethnocentrism

Ethnocentrism is one of the many means by which social hierarchy and domination are maintained. Placing a dominant or ethnic group (in the United States, white/Anglo Americans) at the center—of knowledge, of concern, or of activity—marginalizes other groups and reinforces existing hierarchies.

There are any number of ways that ethnocentrism is enacted in the academy. For example, assuming that Euro-American traditions of knowledge are the most important and relegating African American or Asian American traditions to a week or two at the end of the semester is ethnocentric. Even efforts to address race/ethnicity and racism can fall into the trap of ethnocentrism. For example, white parents, in teaching their children to be tolerant, often say that Latino or Native American children are "just like" white children. They rarely say that white children are just like children of color. In this formulation, whiteness remains as the center to which "others" are compared. All important questions and problems ultimately revolve around the concerns of white people. Therefore, for example, white people may assume that the study of race/ethnicity and racism is important for the undoing of white racism. While this may be a laudable goal, it misses the value of, for example, womanist study or Asian feminist work on their own terms. Alternatively, when attending meetings and conferences that address race and ethnicity, white people sometimes attempt to focus discussion on their concerns and antiracist attitudes, rather than accepting the marginalization they might feel when people of color are at the center.

Placing the concerns of nondominant groups at the center is not necessarily ethnocentric. Moving "from margin to center" may be a necessary correction to entrenched racism. In other words, white people should think twice before accusing people of color of ethnocentrism. Such accusations may be just another means of returning white concerns to the center once again.

Ethnocentrism is possible between and among people of color given that there are differences among and within racial groups. In some situations, one of these groups may have an established social dominance and may act in an ethnocentric manner. Ethnocentrism remains a critical problem in the religious academy.

Evaluations, annual, pretenure

In more and more institutions, the tenure process is being carefully monitored on an annual basis. In order to submit the appropriate documentation, you should be sure that your department chair keeps you informed about what is expected of you each year, and how you are expected to document it. If the chair does not notify you about these procedures, make sure to ask her or him what you need to do beginning at the time of your hire. Most schools have well-documented procedures. Often, there is a form that your **curriculum vitae** should follow, and it is best if you begin by formatting it in the prescribed form, then keeping it up-to-date on a regular basis. It is probably more efficient to save materials in a file and update the CV periodically than to add one item at a time.

The most common advice people receive is "save everything." You will need to document your activities. It is not a bad idea to have the **files**, but it also may not be necessary to hand everything in—find out from a trusted friend what the institutional culture requires. If you present a paper at a conference, save the program bulletin. If you receive a note from a colleague or student commending your work, file that as well. You should also be working on a **teaching portfolio;** that means saving your assignments, syllabi, student work, etc. All of this collecting will make it easier to put an annual report together, and those collected evaluations will be a big help when you are ready to put your tenure file together.

Pay careful attention to the letters you receive from the dean each year renewing your contract. They should include clear recommendations for what you need to do to meet requirements for tenure. They may include specific information about what the chair or dean is expecting you to complete or areas in which they wish you to improve. If you do not agree with the evaluation, it is also important to commit your response to writing.

Evaluations, peer

You will sometimes be in the position of having to review your colleagues—for example, when they come up for promotion or tenure (see **Evaluations, annual, pretenure**)—and to be reviewed by them as well. You may also be asked by publishers and journals to do peer reviews of manuscripts. While reviews are meant to be confidential, reviewing the work of your colleagues can be a source of tension, especially in small departments. It is helpful if you remember that the critiques of and by your peers (whether of teaching or scholarship) can be a valuable source of learning and growth. While we may not enjoy being judged or judging, it is part of the learning experience throughout an academic career, and something we need to get used to.

That said, it is important to remember when doing these reviews that even the harshest criticism can be given gently and with a generous spirit. It is often the tone of reviews, rather than their content, that inflicts unnecessary pain and breeds an atmosphere of ill will. You may find yourself in a situation where your best judgment tells you that a colleague's work does not merit tenure or promotion by the standards your university has set. You need to be sure that you have really thought through the situation, have not been unduly swayed by political pressure, and have come to an honest and ethical conclusion. That is all you can ask of yourself. If you do make such a judgment, do your best to treat the person in a supportive and friendly manner, as you will have to live with her or him for at least a year if tenure is not granted.

Evaluations, student

The plain brown envelopes and number 2 pencils with ample erasers come out at the end of each semester so that students can provide their feedback to professors. It is only fair, in that professors grade them as well. Of course, this practice can play into a certain consumer attitude among students, and if negatively evaluated a professor can feel undermined. However, if you are serious about improving your teaching, you will read all evaluations with care, and take them with a grain of salt. Promotion and tenure committees read them, so it is a good idea to take them seriously and invite students to be candid. While there are often one or two who will vent, the vast majority of students, especially in a well-formulated course, will wax poetic about how much they learned, how accessible you were, how much you helped them, and how they appreciated your efforts. What is problematic about the whole procedure is that the results are often so cut and dried, so starkly numerical that it is hard to communicate nuance (for instance, that the student who hated you also failed the course because he never came to class). In addition, there is no way to detect, or account for, student expectations of professional behavior based on gender, sexual orientation, or racial stereotypes, which can affect how they perceive your performance.

One strategy for making student evaluations more useful to your teaching and the success of a course is to conduct your own private evaluation midcourse. Getting student input partway through the term can allow for midcourse corrections or clarify unspoken misunderstandings or dissatisfactions. It can encourage students to participate more actively in the work of a course if they believe you actually care what they think before you turn in grades and the term is over.

Some schools post the results in informal ratings that students share when "shopping" for classes. Other schools guard the results lest your privacy be invaded and that one course you botched follow you for years. Overall, student evaluations are a useful tool for gauging whether you are reaching your audience, whether what you are teaching is being learned, and whether you are fulfilling your part of the bargain as a professor.

Exams, qualifying/comprehensives/generals

Every graduate program has a slightly different route to completion, but exams of some sort are a common feature. They are known as qualifying exams, comprehensives, or generals, depending on the school. These exams are a way to assure that students are well prepared in the field before moving on to write a dissertation.

It is important to work closely with your advisor in shaping the exams, if that option is given, and/or at least in preparing for them. This means getting the requisite book list and taking the courses, especially graduate seminars that will best prepare you. The exams can often be geared to orienting your research for the dissertation, thus speeding along your progress for the program as a whole.

The exams can be an ordeal, or they can be a useful exercise in gaining and demonstrating proficiency. Approach them like a job. Be systematic and thorough in your preparation. Don't let the hype that sometimes develops around them get to you. After all, you have been successful this far, so there is every reason to be confident that with adequate study you will do fine. If the experience becomes a burden, do not hesitate to get the counseling or other support you need to get through it.

Faculty club

If your institution has a faculty club, consider a membership, and/or if it is automatic, consider using it. The club can be a convenient place to lunch with colleagues, conduct meetings, and hear interesting lectures. Some clubs even have overnight accommodations, a great choice for visiting lecturers or colleagues from other institutions. While some of these places look like wood-paneled men's clubs, think about joining and using the club with your women colleagues. The atmosphere will be markedly improved by your presence; some of the pretense and old-school tie feel may diminish. On the other hand, if the faculty club is more than you can bear, repair to your favorite coffee/tea/chocolate shop, simply taking your business elsewhere.

Faculty handbook

Most institutions provide new employees with a book that contains all of the relevant information related to institutional policies, benefits, promotion, and the like. It is important to read it carefully to understand the lay of the land. The handbook is the definitive source for the legally binding information you will need to function effectively in your institution. The faculty handbook is considered in most institutions part of the legally binding contract of your employment, so know its contents well. Unspoken or informal aspects of an institution usually are at least as important as, if not more so than, what is written down. But the law does not respect them in the same way as a written resource.

Family (see also Children)

Families come in an infinite variety of forms. Virtually everyone has one, whether it consists of your parents, your pets, a partner, children, a strong circle of friends, or extended relatives. The point is not to make assumptions about family that privilege the mom, dad, and 2.2 children model to the detriment of the rest. Easier said than done, of course, when pensions, Social Security, and the like are all bound up in that one model. This is the cutting edge for institutions and departments to address in their policies.

Many of us have major responsibility for others whose lives are affected by our choices. Some colleagues support their siblings' children, so they need the same family leave and tuition benefits that would go to their own children. Others care for aging parents who may require as much time, attention, and medical care as is structured to give to children. All of these beings (some of our colleagues consider their pets as their closest kin) are part of the constellation of relationships that brings us love and well-being, as well as anxiety and exhaustion. Thus, paying equal attention to them is part of the twenty-first-century way of being in our field. Set your own priorities and do not be afraid to say "no" when asked to break them.

Fellowships, graduate student

Many institutions offer fellowships for graduate students. Consult your local financial aid office for details on other fellowships offered by various, sometimes quite obscure, groups. A Web search will help, but there is no substitute for knowing someone who is on the committee or has an in with someone who is.

Fellowships are a fact of life for those considering or pursuing graduate studies in religion. At some point, you will apply for fellowship monies to support your studies. For some, understanding the terms of a fellowship begins immediately upon acceptance into graduate school, where the fellowship may be formulated into your acceptance. It may be granted as a multiyear or an annual award. Study the language of your letter of acceptance with care, and be sure you understand the terms of acceptance. Find out whether the fellowship is contingent (on grades, on teaching, on getting outside support to match). A fellowship might cover tuition and fees but offer no stipend to cover living expenses. Alternatively, a stipend might take the form of salary for a teaching or research appointment.

Most students will, at some point, need to garner outside fellowship support, especially during the dissertation writing stage. Generally, applications for such funding are due in the fall semester for the next academic year. Financial aid offices and departments often publish lists and contact information of pertinent fellowships. Many such offices have a fellowship database accessible on-line. Also, ask about selected lists of available fellowships specific to your field, as reading through general fellowship and grant opportunities can be daunting.

The financial aid office or your department might even provide examples of successful proposals, which can be enormously helpful. Read fellowship announcements carefully, noting due dates, intended recipients, length of funding, and specified purpose of the fellowship monies (e.g., final-year dissertation writing, travel, or foreign language acquisition support). Give yourself plenty of lead-time. Applications take longer than you think.

First, you will have to provide several letters of recommendation, and busy faculty members require plenty of notice (a couple of months, with a reminder a month or so prior to the deadline). Be sure they have all the information they need to grant your request with relative ease, and be sure to follow up. Faculty cannot be expected to keep track of your timelines; do not be afraid to remind your recommenders of impending deadlines. Second, you will be called on to provide transcripts, various timelines, proposals, outlines, and synopses of your work. These take time and should be crafted with great care. Vet your work vigorously before sending it out. Schools and departments often lead workshops on fellowship opportunities and grant writing. Ply advanced students with coffee or a meal in exchange for their advice.

Finally, do not be afraid to cast your net widely. Competition is fierce, and your project may appeal to various funders. Capitalize on the interdisciplinary nature of a religious studies project.

When you are awarded your fellowship, note that the Tax Reform Act of 1986 specifies that all grants and fellowships that exceed the cost of tuition, fees, books, and related classroom expenses are subject to U.S. income tax. Often, there are no initial withholdings on stipends, leaving you to take responsibility for reporting stipend amounts and making tax payments when appropriate.

Fellowships, professional

As a professional, you will be eligible for fellowships of various sorts. There is a world of funds available for the enterprising professional who can write good proposals. For example, the National Endowment for the Humanities and the Guggenheim Foundation offer grants for relatively senior scholars with projects. The Women's Studies in Religion Program at Harvard Divinity School offers a one-year residency fellowship, as do many humanities centers at universities and colleges. The **AAR** Web site lists some of these sources, as do university offices of sponsored research.

As you plan **sabbaticals**, which are often for one semester, consider applying for a fellowship that will allow you to extend the time to a year. Some schools encourage faculty to do so and provide grant-writing help to enable them to apply for fellowships. It is in the interest of the institution to help you, as it adds to its faculty's luster when they win prestigious awards. Remember that it may take multiple years and repeated applications to win an award, so keep trying, and begin applying well ahead of when you anticipate a sabbatical. If you are turned down, ask for feedback. You may discover you were close, and it is worth trying again. If you haven't a ghost of a chance, this is also useful to learn, so as to avoid wasting time and energy in repeated applications.

Feminist

Definitions of feminism abound, but the bumper sticker that says, "Feminism is the radical notion that women are full persons" remains a good summary. Feminism arose around the world out of the struggle for women's rights and women's survival. It is a globalized movement and theoretical commitment to securing the well-being of women and dependent children in a world that has long privileged men. Feminism began as a gender-based concern. But due to the influence of womanism (see **Womanist**), *mujerisimo* (see ***Mujerista***), Asian American, and Native American women's work, it now signals a complex analysis of and effort to change racist, sexist, classist, imperialist, colonialist, heterosexist, and other structures of oppression that keep women, especially young, poor women of color, from surviving and thriving.

Early feminist work in religion began in the 1960s when the gendered nature of religion was exposed and the sexist assumptions of many religious traditions were challenged. In the intervening decades, feminist work has reshaped the field, as virtually every religious subspecialty has been subject to feminist analysis and reconstruction.

Festschriften

Festschriften are books written in honor of a colleague, often on the occasion of her/his sixty-fifth or seventieth birthday, or upon retirement. There are other ways to lift up the importance of a colleague's work—for example, with a conference, a special section of a journal, an art project, or the like. However, the most common academic model is a collaborative book that includes an essay about the person and her/his work, or essays on themes related to or sparked by the colleague's endeavors.

It is a privilege to be invited to contribute to a *Festschrift*. The essay or other contribution need not seem like uncritical homage. Rather, it is an opportunity to acknowledge a person's contribution to the field in a polite and professional way, perhaps best by exhibiting one's own work as it has been influenced by hers/his.

Files

Careful filing is the key to success for many professionals. Just ask someone whose work style you admire (you know, the one who always gets her grades in on time, writes her grocery list in triplicate, that sort of thing) and you will probably hear that she keeps her files in good order. This is such a personal and culturally specific matter—oral cultures have no need for such things. However, it is a good basic habit to cultivate, as life just gets more complicated. It may be a good idea to keep some personal files—such as your contract, documentation about sexual harassment, journal notes about a difficult colleague—at home in a safe place. In the event of a legal challenge, you will still have access to them.

Use whatever method works for you—different colors for different topics, various kinds of files depending on the items, perhaps an accordion file or a three-ring binder for a class. File early and often rather than face the mountains of paper that accumulate in a semester. Periodically toss what you have not touched in years, being careful to preserve things that might go into an archive of your work. Now that historians are interested in the progress in our field, archives are increasingly interested in our materials.

The same care needs to go into computer files, keeping back-ups in a separate place in case of emergency, purging and compacting e-mail files on a regular basis. For every one message you delete and need again you will get rid of thousands that clog your system and your life.

A good address book system is worth its weight in gold so you can access immediately those people you need. A good calendar system, whether it is on your computer, in a hand-held electronic organizer, or on a good ol' paper calendar, is crucial to ease in scheduling. Double scheduling yourself or missing appointments happens to everyone on occasion. Done regularly, it is a sure sign that your life is out of control.

If you can live with a higher level of disorder than represented here, feel well accompanied. If you need someone to help you de-clutter once and for all, or need simple ways to streamline the "stuff" of life, give some thought to new systems of organization and file, file, file.

Forerunners

This guide would not be possible if some phenomenal women had not paved the way. They include our personal ancestors as well as our foresisters in the field of religious studies. Rather than name them, and for fear of leaving any out, just use this entry as a reminder to thank them often and to do them proud.

Fund raising

Most graduate programs in religion do not offer courses in fund raising, but it might be a good idea if they did. Learning to raise money is a skill worth having. Many jobs in the nonprofit sector require it. Even getting a fellowship or a post-doctoral grant is a form of fund raising.

The bottom line is ask, ask, ask. Beyond that, there are many specialized workshops in how to write proposals, how to conform your project to the granter's guidelines. There are capital campaigns and direct mail appeals, annual gifts and annuity options. Knowing the basics will help you get and give intelligently.

Globalization

The field of religious studies, like everything else in the world, is increasingly globalized. This means we can be in close communication with colleagues around the planet, but it also means that the United States plays its hegemonic role in our work as in other fields. Women colleagues report that while there are obvious advantages to international networking, cultural differences are often obscured, resulting in a skewed sense of what is important. Our challenge is to utilize those aspects of globalization that link us—the Internet, air travel, and the like—and to resist and reject the dynamics that allow fewer and fewer people to make more and more decisions for the rest of us. One example is the increasing pressure to do theological and religious studies work in English to guarantee a wide audience for publications. It is perhaps our biggest challenge in the decade ahead.

Graduate school

The road to a career in religious studies usually begins in graduate school, so your attention to it is well placed. It starts with choosing your school. Instincts, personal preferences, and research will serve you well in choosing a graduate setting in which to pursue your interests. Your instincts—about whether you can work closely with a faculty person, about the institutional culture, about communication and power dynamics between faculty and students, and even about the geographical setting—are a source of information that deserves respect and attention. Of course, this does not replace thorough research and asking smart questions.

Think carefully about and compare resources (libraries, computer labs, crossregistration with other schools). Get a firm understanding about the financial support (stipends) offered to students, and whether that kind of money is guaranteed throughout your years of study, or whether you must continually compete for it, and exactly when it evaporates. Make a realistic budget. Think about institutional expectations and demands on grad students (teaching, tutoring). Think also about the intellectual tenor of the school and its departments, about available symposia, colloquia, and resources. Compare the programmatic issues: How are the subfields in the department presented and shaped in terms not only of courses offered, but also in terms of course requirements and comprehensive exams? Despite the injustice of it, many academic benefits do depend on the prestige of the institution.

There is no substitute for visiting a place, which gives you both insight you will not get from the institution's brochures and the added benefit of allowing you to meet the people who will be deciding about your acceptance there, should you choose to apply. One common piece of advice is to apply to a large number of schools, though it can be very costly in time and money.

Getting into a good program is a competitive enterprise. This must be weighed against your real interest in the place. Take seriously the requirements of the application, even if you do not like the assignment (writing your life's ambition in a 300-word essay or taking the Graduate Record Examinations). Don't sabotage your future over bureaucratic necessity. Your ability to navigate hoops more or less gracefully will serve you well when you get into the graduate program of your choice. If you are not accepted, you can inquire as to why you were turned down and then try to remedy the matter and apply again. Often, though, it is simply a numbers game, with many solid applicants competing for too few places and even less financial aid.

Once in, the task turns to surviving, nay, thriving! Depending upon your subfield and your personal situation and style, graduate school can take a long time, meaning more than six years. Shorter or longer, it is exhausting. If you enter graduate school with a dissertation topic or research interest in mind, you might take less time than if you enter with only a vague idea of what you really want to write about. In any case, the balancing act between creative risk and disciplined focus will probably serve you best. In fact, thriving in graduate school in general requires an ability to balance: to balance relationships and work, teaching/working and studying, choices between traditional and more risky fields of study. Everyone is different, and there is no right way. Remember, your balancing act is more for the duration of a marathon than a sprint. Be patient with yourself. Being specific with your advisor about your needs and expectations will help, as will forming a writing group. If you can, find and cultivate a mentor relationship. Creating networks of supportive colleagues, both in your cohort and outside, will give you sources of information and advice that will be invaluable. The AAR and SBL offer graduate student orientations at their annual meetings.

Grants

There are a variety of grants available from foundations and other agencies. A good place to start is at the **AAR and SBL Annual Meetings**, which often feature a time for grant-making organizations to meet with grant seekers. Another option is a Web search or a good talk with your institution's grants officer, if such exists, to find out what is available in your field. The Association of Theological Schools, The Lilly Endowment, and other agencies fund religious studies, though be forewarned that competition is keen for the relatively few offerings. Make use of the Internet to keep up on the latest prospects.

Consider a small grant to make something big happen—like a travel grant to attend a conference. Large or small, just be sure you fulfill the terms of the grant, submit all required paperwork in a timely way, and let your imagination be the limit of what you wish to work on, as there may be funding available. For example, the SBL Committee on the Status of Women in the Profession offers a travel grant to women in developing countries, Asia, and Eastern Europe who want to attend the Annual Meeting, especially if they are presenting a paper. See the Web site for details (www.sbl-site.org/SBLCommittees_CSWP_Activities).

Guest lectures

Whether being invited to present a guest lecture or inviting someone to do so, the rules are about the same. The best analogy is to houseguests—as the one invited, you want to be a gracious guest; and as host, you want to provide everything that will make your guest feel comfortable.

That means that when an invitation is offered it must include the topic, time, place, expected audience, honorarium, travel and housing arrangements, and some insight into the local scene. When the invitation is accepted, the speaker needs to provide the lecture topic and/or title, materials for publicity (including CV and photo), Social Security number, mailing address, and anything else (short of shoe size) that may be required.

When the event takes place, the speaker should arrive promptly (early is best), be met and escorted to her room, offered food and drink as appropriate, and allowed a little time to freshen up. She should then be escorted to the lecture locale (nothing worse than wandering aimlessly around a campus). She gives her brilliant presentation, takes questions, and conducts a discussion before bidding a gracious farewell. The host then escorts her back to her quarters or makes sure she gets to her plane, train, or taxi on time. The guest submits her expenses; the host reimburses and sends the honorarium in a timely way along with a cordial note of thanks and copies of any follow-up press.

Okay, that was the textbook case. Most of the time it goes smoothly, but as lecture circuit veterans will tell you, disasters lurk. Advice: get everything in writing, keep correspondence to refer to, make sure you and the host/guest have physical contact (by phone or in person) with each other prior to the event. Nothing is more disappointing than for a speaker not to show up, or to show up late. Likewise, it is embarrassing to have to shake down institutions for honoraria owed months back and held up because the host forgot to submit the expenses. Planes run late, so as the guest plan an earlier one than you actually need. Bring your own hair dryer and travel alarm clock!

Guest lectures can be a wonderful way to diversify curricula and expose students to innovative thinkers in the field. If you are the lecturer, be careful which invitations you accept. How the arrangements are made will often mirror what the experience on site will be. If your host bungles the invitation, chances are good that you will have other glitches as well.

Harassment, racial

Racial harassment is a serious matter. It happens in this field, as in others, with a frequency that is hard to measure since so many instances are covered up or otherwise treated lightly. Policies do not exist in most institutions to deal with racial harassment, though the model provided by sexual harassment (see **Harassment, sexual**) can be helpful. It is an especially difficult circumstance for women of color, who are often subjected to both types of harassment.

Be sure to document instances with as much detail as you can recover. Seek legal advice on the best remedies in your particular case. Know that racial harassment, however subtle or overt, is intolerable and illegal (see **Racism**).

Harassment, sexual

Women have been sexually harassed in the field of religious studies, as in most other fields, since they arrived on the scene. Hair-raising stories of women being propositioned at conferences, during job interviews, and on the job are all too common, the result of unequal power dynamics between women and men in a sexist culture. Lawsuits have been filed, but for the most part these indignities were borne quietly by the women for fear of sullying their reputations, a misplacement of blame.

Sexual harassment has become a serious issue in many workplaces. Be sure to check the policy of the institution where you work to make sure it has a policy against such behaviors. Policies vary widely. Some institutions have rules about dating (faculty and students, for example). Grievance procedures differ, too, so the best advice is to be informed about your local options.

The **AAR** has a policy that applies to the Annual Meeting and to its own office. See appendices I and II for the policy and the grievance procedures as a sample. The SBL also has a sexual harassment policy that serves as a warning or code of ethics but has no governing authority. See appendix III for this model.

If you feel you are being sexually harassed, document events, dates, time, place, witnesses, attire, and exact words spoken. Note as many details as you can remember while the occurrence is all fresh in your mind. Keep those notes at home, not in your office. They will be invaluable if/when you need to seek legal remedy (see **Sexism**).

Health, mental (see also Self-care)

Your good mental health is essential to your career. Clearly, many factors pose a challenge to it—stress, prejudice, economic problems, genetic predisposition, personal history, and physical problems. Do yourself and your colleagues who depend on you a favor by making your mental health a priority to prevent burnout. Consider therapy, a leave of absence, a change in job, anything that will bring you back to mental health and keep you centered. There is no reason to share your mental health history with prospective employers, but be sure to consult the institution's human resources department and get to know and use your options.

Health, physical (see also Illness and disability)

Physical health is a gift and an achievement. Some of us are luckier by genetic and cultural heritage than others, but all of us can prioritize our physical, as our mental, health to rank above our jobs, and encourage the conditions for others to do likewise. Easier said than done when the demands of making a living get in the way of having a good life, but diet, exercise, rest, and relaxation will maximize what nature and nurture have given us. Be sure that your health insurance is current and that you schedule and keep your appointments for yearly check-ups. Do not forget your eye health as the years go by, and of course have extra tests for conditions that may run in your gene pool.

When health adversities strike, decide how you want to manage them. Let colleagues pitch in and help. Designate someone to let the word out, but only as much or as little information as you deem fit.

Heterosexism (see also Coming out)

The normative assumption that a religious studies professional will be a man goes along with the notion that he will be heterosexual. Most of us using this guide are living proof that the first assumption is wrong; some of us disprove the second as lesbian and bisexual women make distinguished contributions to the field. Still, our field is rife with the outmoded assumptions of heterosexual normativity that simply need to be replaced. The price can be high for those who are lesbian/gay/bisexual and transgender in our field. But we are all responsible for resisting heterosexist assumptions. There is a group called the GLBT Activist Scholars in Religion that meets each year at the **AAR and SBL Annual Meetings**. The gatherings are open to all interested colleagues and are a good chance to discuss contemporary concerns.

Hiring (see also Interviewing)

As women have achieved status in the profession of religious studies, more women are responsible for decisions about hiring. Often the best advice in these situations is to try to remember how much tension the process of applying for jobs induced when you were on the other side of the table, and to make sure that you provide an environment for applicants that will reduce stress and bring out the best in them.

Make sure you create job advertisements that clearly reflect the obligations of the position. If you are interviewing at the Annual Meeting, make sure you get a sufficient number of people from your department to participate, or you will run yourself ragged and not make good decisions. When you invite people to campus, be sure you provide them with a combination of opportunities to show what they do well. Get the committee involved with providing transportation, company at meals, and escorts to show the candidate around campus. Informal settings are often the best way to get to know people, and to provide them with useful information about your campus and your city. Remember, the candidate is judging your school and department as much as you are judging her/him, so you do want to leave a positive impression.

If you are interviewing women candidates, do not automatically assume that they would like to teach courses related to women. If you discover that they are also interested in gender issues, be sure you involve the women's studies program on your campus in a social function or invite them to attend the "job talk." The same advice applies to lesbian candidates and candidates of color, although in these cases the candidate may well also want to meet with the **LGBTQ**, black, Native American, Latina, or Asian caucus members to find out about how they will be received on campus. It is important to learn specifics about life for their particular group in your town, and to answer important questions like: Where do black faculty live? Is there a gay community in the area? However, do not schedule such meetings without asking the candidate first. Make sure you understand the **Affirmative Action** guidelines on your campus.

Hiring can be stressful for the people doing it as well as for the candidates, so make sure, if you are chairing the committee, that you are sensitive to their needs, as well as to your own self-care. As a committee member, feel free to speak up if a part of the process seems unjust or discourteous.

Sometimes an unsuccessful candidate will turn to you for feedback. This may involve confidential search committee information that cannot be shared. But sometimes a candidate will sabotage herself. If this is the case, be honest, but kind, about feedback. She may be hurting herself unconsciously and unaware of how she comes across. Feedback can be helpful.

Housing

It is generally advisable that first year and junior faculty members live close to their campus or workplace in order to become acquainted with the institutional culture. Residing nearby allows them to get used to and manage the teaching and service load without the added problem of long commutes. However, financial constraints (exorbitant rental/purchase prices in the surrounding areas), privacy and sexual issues such as running into staff/students frequently (especially for lesbian and/or single women), partner employment, the absence of religious, ethnic, and cultural communities, or research agendas may make long commutes the better choice (see **Commuting**).

Those who opt to commute and choose to consolidate the workweek into several long and intense on-campus days may be faced with suspicion and resentment among colleagues who live closer to campus. Choosing a place of residence at a certain distance from campus or place of employment can be seen as a lack of commitment to the institution, but women faculty have lives and make choices that are multidimensional given the competing demands most women face from family and work.

Illness and disability

There is an old Yiddish proverb that loosely translates, "If you want to make God laugh, make plans." While sometimes-unexpected events can be sources of joy, they often come in the form of tragedy: accidents or illnesses that come upon us or members of our family unexpectedly and change our lives. While planning may not be possible in these cases, and we may not want to think about the possibility of tragedy striking, it is good to be aware of your institution's policies on disability, and to investigate the availability of private disability (and long-term care) insurance as well. It is good to know what your options are, and being prepared in any way you can is a good idea.

That said, it is not possible to prepare for the changes that illness and disability can bring to your life. Of course we all have minor disabilities we need to cope with, from the need for eyeglasses to getting the flu, and the disability rights community will wisely remind us that each of us is only temporarily able-bodied. However, when you or someone you live with is diagnosed with a major illness, your life will change radically. People, of course, respond to these events differently, but most find that they benefit from making others aware of the problem and getting support. You will be the best judge of how your chair or dean will respond to your needs, but they cannot respond unless you are clear about what you are asking for, whether it is an unpaid leave or extra teaching support. While departmental colleagues may also be helpful, you also need to make considered judgments about how much you would like to tell them. Moreover, whether or how much to inform your students is also a judgment call. It is a delicate balance between maintaining your privacy and making sure you get the support you need.

Some people find support groups helpful for thinking through dimensions of a particular illness. Web sites dedicated to particular illnesses such as breast cancer or heart bypass surgery can also be a good source of information about how others have handled a situation you are going through, but beware of becoming overwhelmed. Some people suggest you get a friend or partner to filter information on Web sites, as it cannot only be overwhelming but often scary as well. Mobilizing a network of friends and colleagues is also crucial. From raising funds to providing meals, letting other people support you is a very important way to get through the critical phases of some of these difficult situations.

If you are the caretaker in the situation, it is also important to remember that you will need support. Nurturing and caretaking is expected of women in our roles as partners and mothers (and is often, indeed, a satisfying experience), but it can and usually does become overwhelming. The need for the caretaker to be taken care of, and to take care of herself, is often overlooked, and chairs, deans, colleagues, and bosses may not be as sympathetic about granting time (or cutting slack). Therefore, it is all the more important for the caretaker to find ways to take breaks and get support for herself as well. Mental health holidays, long weekends, and the like will help. So, too, will asking friends to help with shopping and/or provide respite care so you can get away.

Immigration

The situation for faculty and other workers coming from abroad has worsened dramatically since September 11, 2001. Unless asked specifically, one should not volunteer one's immigration status during the job interview. It is not illegal to discriminate against noncitizens, and, indeed, is increasingly encouraged. Some colleges and universities are informally advising department chairs not to extend job offers to international applicants because of the ensuing immigration complications.

If you are not a U.S. citizen, once you receive a job offer and decide to accept, you need to be prepared for a harrowing experience of powerlessness and often humiliation with the Immigration and Naturalization Service (http://uscis.gov/graphics/index.htm), an experience that can only get worse now that the INS has been fused with the Department of Homeland Security.

No visa application should be undertaken without legal counsel by an immigration lawyer. Although large universities have well-established programs for international students and scholars whose staff is familiar with current immigration regulations, you cannot be sure that your university or organization knows the ropes. If anything goes wrong in the process (and something often does), you are the one who will leave the country, not the staff person handling your immigration papers. Lawyers are expensive (and not always successful), but they work exclusively for you.

Since immigration laws are currently being tightened, there is little specific advice one can give other than the following:

1. You should apply for change of status immediately (from a student visa to a temporary worker visa; from a temporary visa to permanent resident alien). There are strict deadlines, which, once missed, will force your institution to undergo another national search.

2. Once you have secured a tenure-track position and have begun the process of applying for permanent residency, you cannot leave your position until your green card is granted. This can take up to three years. If you switch jobs in the middle, you will have to start all over again.

3. Never leave the country while your paperwork is being processed by the INS. Reentry can and has been denied on a whim, and you may get stuck outside the country. You should always leave your immigration paperwork with the responsible staff person at your institution in case of emergencies when you need your employer to intervene on your behalf.

4. Only a tenure-track position will give you a green card. If you have a visiting or temporary appointment, you are only eligible for a temporary worker's permit and you will need to continue searching for a permanent job.

5. Once you have received permanent resident status signified by your green card, you can apply for citizenship after a period of five years. Some people remain on green cards for the duration of their academic careers.

However, resident aliens are often not eligible for certain grants and scholarships and you may have to apply for a reentry permit when you go on sabbatical for more than twelve months. If you leave the country for your sabbatical, your citizenship clock (of five years) begins all over again.

Immigrant status can also become especially problematic for older women, because one is not eligible for certain health and welfare benefits and one pays higher inheritance taxes. All of these issues reflect the tenuous positions of migrants worldwide and the difficult impact of globalization on the freedom of movement of all people. Canadian and Mexican citizens who have an offer of a position that requires a BA or higher have the option of a temporary NAFTA (North American Free Trade Agreement) visa. These are offered only at the border at the discretion of the border immigration officers. These can be hard to get, but be prepared with your CV, job contract, diplomas and degrees, transcript and citizenship papers.

Check with the INS for updates on these matters, and, of course, consult an attorney for legal issues.

Some U.S. workers may wish to emigrate to work in another country. Visas and work permits will vary widely, so the same advice to consult a lawyer and expect certain complications applies.

Inclusive language

Languages reflect cultural changes with regard to gender, race, disability, and other important social matters. Institutions increasingly expect that language used in official documents as well as in teaching and writing will reflect these changes. Therefore, the use of "persons" instead of "men," "night" instead of "darkness," and the like are normative. Far from being an exercise in political correctness, this is simply an evolution of language that serves to include rather than exclude, honor rather than dismiss.

Independent scholars

Some scholars, for various reasons (temperament, scholarly interest, employment choices, or lack thereof) choose to be independent scholars. All this means is that they do not have an academic institutional affiliation, though most of them work for a living somewhere. There are advantages to such a choice: no dull faculty meetings, no boring teaching assignments, the ability to pursue one's own research interests. However, disadvantages accrue as well: often lack of library privileges, no institutional structure for benefits, economic problems, and the need to work outside the field in order to fund one's work inside it. Some of those who are called independent scholars are really religious studies–trained colleagues who work in fields other than academia, so that term can cover a rather dubious assumption about our homogeneity.

Independent scholars are more than welcome as part of the **AAR/SBL**, especially in women's circles where the matter of affiliation is decidedly secondary. The **AAR Annual Meeting** now has a gathering time for independent scholars. Still, we advise sensitivity and awareness all around so that the subtle agenda that we all be employed at recognizably respectable places not rear its ugly head. Some of the best work in the field is still done by people who are not tenured anywhere.

Institutional analysis

In order to survive and thrive in religious studies, it is crucial to analyze the institutions in which we do our work. Academic religious studies takes place in a variety of institutional settings: public institutions and private institutions, large research universities, smaller liberal arts colleges, colleges with religious affiliations, seminaries, community colleges, and independent centers and institutes.

Experiences in the academy will vary greatly depending on the type of institution(s) in which one does one's work and with which one interacts. Requirements for promotion and tenure, teaching loads, expectations about the level of involvement

between faculty and students, expectations about religious identity and practice, all vary with the institution. The rewards or
dangers of particular types of activity will also vary by institution. Spending a great deal of time outside the classroom with
students may be absolutely necessary and highly rewarded at
small liberal arts colleges, but it may not be valued at large
research universities and it may seriously limit the time one
spends on one's own research.

Academic institutions are also part of larger communities, and
the relations between academic institutions and the cities, towns,
and/or neighborhoods in which they reside can often be tense and
conflicted. "Town-gown" equations can range from towns, in
which colleges or in some cases large state universities are the
dominant institutions, to big cities, in which the academic institutions are but one part of the cultural landscape. Because
colleges and universities are class-based institutions, town-gown
conflicts often revolve around economic and cultural issues.

In thinking about the institutions in which we work, we need
to consider how these institutions affect the communities around
us. Efforts at community **activism** or ethnographic research will
be received differently depending on the history of town-gown
relations and the contemporary situation. Is the college, university, seminary, or center open to the community? Does it share
resources or is it closed to the outside community while dominat-
ing or controlling surrounding land, employment, and resources?

Each institution has a culture and hence a politics of its own. In
entering a new institution, whether as a student or worker, it is
important to find out as much as possible about that particular
institution. One can find important information by reading the
institution's Web site, its handbooks and regulations, by asking
questions about institutional history, and by attending to details
ranging from daily interactions to the architecture of a campus.

The structure of higher education as a whole is also going
through major changes. These changes follow broader changes
in public life in the United States today. Broad trends in American
life toward privatization and enclosure within the market of
spaces and functions that have previously been considered public
have also affected colleges and universities. As with other non-

profit institutions, such as hospitals, universities are beginning to move toward profitmaking enterprises and market-based imperatives. In the past thirty years, there has been a massive increase in the administrative infrastructure of universities and a concomitant decrease in the role of democratic faculty governance. The function of institutional presidents has moved increasingly toward an emphasis on fund raising, even at public universities and colleges.

The sections below provide a general outline of how institutions vary by type, but one also needs to learn about and develop skills for reading particular institutions.

Public institutions

When one works for a state university, one is directly faced with the imperatives of the bureaucratic state. Because state legislatures ultimately control funding, the culture of the university may depend on the approach of the legislature. Is this a state that generally supports education, or is it a state that tends to be more suspicious of, or even to downplay, education? What is the role of the state legislature vis-a-vis the education system?

Many state institutions are often research universities. These institutions tend to be larger and have lighter teaching loads and heavier research responsibilities. These institutions are likely to reward publication and to grant money, and are less likely to be concerned about teaching. While the institution will assert its interest in good teaching, when it comes to tenure and promotion, the relative weight placed on various aspects of the job may be skewed by as much as 80 percent on research, 10 percent on teaching, and 10 percent on service. Junior faculty members at these institutions would be wise to put their time and effort into applying for grants and fellowships. Money and prestige are often the terms of reward. Less intimacy is expected between faculty members and undergraduates, although faculty members may be expected to spend large amounts of time with graduate students. Attend to how this labor is divided.

Large institutions may have various types of jobs in addition to tenure-track faculty positions. Research centers, for example, may offer employment opportunities, but these opportunities are often based on "soft money" (grant money that is raised from year to year and may disappear) and, hence, these jobs are less stable. Such institutions are relying increasingly on adjunct faculty labor, rather than on tenure-track jobs (see **Appointments, adjunct**). Jobs often involve intensive teaching loads, for lower pay, with less job security. Organization among adjunct faculty can be crucial to gaining reasonable working conditions in these positions.

Community colleges emphasize teaching. Students at such schools differ from those at flagship research universities. They may be employed full time, be of nontraditional age, and work on a degree part time. They may not have qualified for admission to a university and are preparing themselves for transfer. Some schools practice open admission and provide remedial training for those who need it. The students will be from the local community, whatever its makeup, and commute to campus. All these factors mean that, while the emphasis is on teaching at such institutions, the ability of students to focus on their education will vary considerably. In addition, a faculty member will confront a diverse student population, including some students who may be considerably older than their teacher.

Private institutions

Private colleges and universities offer certain freedoms that are not found in state schools and can present a different set of constraints. While private institutions do not face the need to please state legislatures, they can experience intense pressure from their Boards of Trustees, often made up of a variety of individuals, including alumni/ae of the institution.

As the cost of higher education rises, however, boards are increasingly dominated by wealthy individuals and corporate representatives whose expectations are that the college or university should be run like a corporation. Smaller private institutions may be facing difficulties in fund raising and budget constraints, while larger private institutions, particularly elite research institutions, are increasingly circumscribed by an ethos of profit making. Just as the political culture of state institutions varies depending on the state in which they operate, so the political bent of private institutions also varies. Some have long histories as liberal institutions, while others tend toward the conservative.

Some private institutions are large research universities and some are smaller liberal arts colleges. Private universities, particularly elite research universities, may have even stricter demands for tenure than do state research universities, some requiring two books of junior scholars in the humanities fields. The vast majority of candidates for tenure are approved nationwide. However, the percentages can be much lower at elite research universities, some of which grant tenure only to the rank of full professor, which places someone just six to ten years out from a Ph.D. in competition for a tenured position with colleagues at other institutions who have been in the field much longer. It is often important to inquire about the expectations for receiving tenure along with statistics of how many junior faculty members who are hired in a given institution actually receive tenure. Some elite institutions are notorious for overworking junior faculty, who serve the institution well, only to reject them for tenure because they have not published enough.

Most small colleges are private institutions. Teaching loads tend to be higher and sometimes research responsibilities are lighter, but check with each institution. Presence on campus and participation in a wide range of campus activities are highly valued. Small colleges also often ask faculty members to spend time with students outside of the classroom, not just in office hours, but also in social settings. New faculty members should attend to how their colleagues deal with such expectations and demands. Do these expectations vary by gender and race? Are women expected to be more open and available to students? Are people of color expected to mentor and sustain all the students of color? Speaking openly of these expectations, making them and the division of labor visible, can help departments to develop arrangements that are more equitable.

Religiously affiliated colleges and seminaries

Many institutions of higher education in the United States have religious affiliations. For some institutions, these affiliations are largely dormant. Although they may continue to affect the overall culture of an institution, they are not expressly applied. For other institutions, particularly for seminaries, these connections may be central to the life of the institution. In addition to academic goals, these institutions may have expectations, both stated and unstated, for students and faculty members to participate in the religious life of the community. Both students and faculty may also be rewarded for participating in religious activities in the broader community. It is important to be as clear as possible about these expectations when entering such an institution. For these institutions, questions of how to address religious diversity can be particularly difficult—whether diversity across religious traditions or diversity found within the particular religion or denomination of which the school is a part. In some more conservative establishments, the religious expectations are explicit and enforced. Buyer beware.

Independent centers or institutes

Centers often offer freedoms that are not found in traditional academic institutions, but they can also be less institutionally stable. There is a trend for some large institutions to handle innovative issues and/or issues they want to marginalize (such as those involving women and racial/ethnic minorities) through centers. In some cases, the center moves to the center; in other cases the center is really on the margin.

Setting up one's own center can require an entrepreneurial spirit and fund-raising capabilities (see **Entrepreneurs** and **Fundraising**). It can be done, both within large institutions and independently. It takes real vision and lots of sweat equity but can result in magnificent contributions to our field.

Institutional culture/politics (see also Institutional analysis)

Each institution has its own culture. It includes such intangibles as clothes and lifestyle, willingness to debate, and even whether faculty are addressed by first name by students. It is subtle and nuanced; it also varies according to who you are in the institutional hierarchy. Women and people of color find that out right away. Your best bet is to read everything you can get your eyes on, but then find an ally (see **Allies**). Sit down and ask the hard questions until you feel you have a handle on how the unarticulated power dynamics of the institution work. Your own intuition will kick in, but having somebody to check your perceptions against, and doing it early, will save you a lot of aggravation.

Intellectual property

Laws governing intellectual property are in constant flux as this new area of expertise develops. Be careful on two fronts: First, be sure your own work is copyrighted or otherwise credited to you. Many women report seeing their good ideas in other people's work without permission. Second, be scrupulous in noting your sources and securing your data. There are sad tales of women's careers screeching to a halt when they have, however inadvertently, used their graduate students' work or otherwise appropriated what was not rightfully theirs. When in doubt, a good lawyer is a good investment.

Interdisciplinarity and the disciplines

Religious studies is an interdisciplinary field of study defined by its object of study: religion. The question of object and study are not easily separable. Recent historical and philosophical work has shown how the idea of a transhistorical, cross-cultural phenomenon called "religion" was created in part through the study of religion and how this process was intertwined with European colonialism (see **Religious studies**). Disciplines, on the other hand, are most often organized around method of study. As the concept literally implies, a discipline is knowledge created by controlling and adjudicating the processes by which that knowledge is sought. Historians must meet standards of empirical evidence, sociologists must gather data through recognized quantitative and/or qualitative methods, and philosophers must submit to logic and argument.

Not surprisingly, feminists and other progressive scholars have often criticized these disciplinary practices, since the standards of each discipline were developed by the predominant practitioners—in the United States, white men of privilege—and they reflect the biases of these people. For example, historical standards of evidence have often focused on printed documentation and hence have necessarily produced knowledge primarily about those persons who produced documents. Approaches such as oral history or material cultural studies that might overcome some of these biases have sometimes been resisted by those with the power and authority to protect the discipline.

Disciplines can also be conservative insofar as they create separate, coherent areas of study. Because disciplines are used to police the boundaries of whom and what is studied, scholars who might ally to create new forms of study can be kept apart. After all, it took decades to develop women's studies. Disciplines also contribute to the simplification of complex phenomena and social problems, as only one method of study predominates in a given sphere. Thus, disciplines have been one of the necessary sites for struggles for justice in the academy.

In order to address some of these problems, new fields of study related to progressive social movements—women's studies; racial and ethnic studies; lesbian, gay, bisexual, transgender, and queer studies; and postcolonial studies—have most often developed as interdisciplinary fields. These fields brought together various disciplines to address complex phenomena such as the lives of women and/or people of color. However, interdisciplinarity is not simply the amalgamation of different disciplines. It can also pose questions that cannot be answered, and sometimes not even be asked, within the structure of the traditional disciplines.

Universities and colleges are adaptive institutions, so administrations have sometimes taken up "interdisciplinarity" as a code word for cost-cutting and administrative consolidation. In these cases, rather than opening areas and possibilities for study, interdisciplinarity is used as a justification for closing them down. For example, religion and anthropology departments are sometimes merged, or even religion and film departments, for reasons that remain obscure other than funding cuts. In addition, defining a field in terms of object of study is not necessarily progressive. Taking up the study of religion without questioning how religion is objectively formed means that we may extend European and Christian assumptions and dominance. Just as disciplines separate areas and potential allies, so can fields of study. The separation between and among women's studies, racial and ethnic studies, **LGBTQ** studies, and postcolonial studies has created serious problems for the study of the intersections of the differences named by these fields. It also undercuts possibilities for alliances across these fields, making the resulting transformative demands more easily managed by the university.

Young scholars need to be aware of the policing power of the disciplines, even as they may want to seek out or even develop interdisciplinary programs and methods to pursue the types of projects they value. While pursuing interdisciplinary studies, whether in a traditional department or interdisciplinary program, students may want to protect themselves by also pursuing certification—whether through exams or dissertation chapters—that allows them to apply for positions in a discipline. Remember that tenure is usually granted by a department, which must review a scholar's work, and that positions relate to curriculum, which may be divided by traditional fields. These combine to make it difficult to get interdisciplinary work evaluated adequately for tenure, though this is changing somewhat because of the presence of interdisciplinary programs.

Upon getting a job, one needs to be clear about expectations and review processes within a department or program. Be clear from the start about the type of scholarship you hope to pursue and the materials that you will use. If interdisciplinary methods are new to your colleagues, help to educate them about the growing importance of this work in your field. Share your work with them as you progress. When it is time for review for tenure and promotion, discuss the importance of reviewers who will not object to interdisciplinary scholarship, and suggest senior scholars who can act as reviewers or provide advice on your field as you understand it.

Scholars who work in interdisciplinary ways often must attend a variety of professional meetings: Chicano Studies Association, the Association for Asian American Studies, National Women's Studies Association, etc. Most institutions will fund attendance at one professional association meeting a year, and then only if the faculty member is on the program. To attend other meetings may require you to pay yourself, so, if you need to be active in several learned societies, try to negotiate support for such activity at the time you are offered a position. An institution may be willing to specify an amount for travel to meetings, rather than limit faculty to one meeting, but be sure the amount is adequate for more than one meeting. Taking a proactive stance (in a nonhostile manner) can make a world of difference in terms of keeping open spaces for interdisciplinary undertakings.

International colleagues

The number of international faculty in higher education is rising steadily. Depending on the discipline (especially in the sciences), between one-fifth and one-third of professors are immigrants. Religious studies is no exception, and your department will in all likelihood have an international flavor.

Academe is generally a welcoming place for people from around the world; there is a broad consensus that international, multicultural, and multireligious perspectives enrich the learning environment for students and faculty. For many international scholars, U.S. institutions of higher education provide the economically, religiously, and politically safe environment needed to engage in research that would be impossible in their home countries.

Despite difficulties with the INS (see **Immigration**), **racism,** and **xenophobia,** most immigrants find the United States open and hospitable and develop strong ties to their colleagues and institutions.

International study

In an increasingly globalized world, international study is virtually required for religious studies professionals. It often means equipping oneself with another language (something that notoriously monolingual U.S. residents need to do anyway). It involves travel, intercultural experience, and the reward of friends and colleagues beyond one's shores. It is a great antidote to **xenophobia** and can add a completely new dimension to one's work, regardless of how early or late in one's life it takes place.

Of course, international study is expensive, often a factor for women. It need not last for long periods but must be long enough for solid exposure. Organizations and foundations offer grants for summer research, which can be used for international work. Universities and colleges sometimes have funds for just this purpose. Study can be combined with meetings and conferences abroad, and is best done in concert with international colleagues who handle logistics and form a natural community on-site. The point is to do as much international work as time, money, and interest allow. The world is only getting smaller.

Internet/World Wide Web

Perhaps the single biggest change in scholarship in the past decade is the widespread availability of access to the World Wide Web, or the Internet as we commonly call it. It is virtually impossible to do our work now without the Web: library resources are widely available, e-mail is the preferred mode of communication among us, up-to-the-minute information is on tap, and we are expected to have it readily available. There is a great downside to all this in that it widens the gap between those who have access and those who don't, an issue many people in religious studies have taken seriously in order to remedy it (see **Computers**).

Plan to increase your Web use over time. Consider a personal **Web page** so that people can access your work easily. Place your CV, publicity photo, course descriptions, and the like on it. Just know that it takes time to update it. Students are often more adept at this than faculty, so hire accordingly.

Internships

As you prepare for a career in religious studies, consider internships as a practical, enjoyable, and sometimes life-changing way to get acquainted with the players, organizations, and major themes in the field. Imagine an internship at a nonprofit organization that works on women's spirituality in Santiago, Chile, or a semester interning at a group that works on reproductive health in Washington, D.C.. Consider moving outside of your usual circles in your internship choice. If you are Jewish, think about going to a Muslim agency; if you are Christian, search out a Buddhist option. The sky is the limit. It is often through internships that we find our career direction, and practical ways to move in it. The supervisor makes all the difference in the world, so research and choose as carefully as if you were taking a paid position.

Interviewing

Virtually every job requires an interview. Books have been written on the subject; consultants will prep you on what to wear and how to act. None of it guarantees you a job. Our advice is to treat the interview as the first day on the job. If you do not like it or the "fit" is not right, better to find out sooner rather than later. In the current competitive climate, it can feel as if the interviewers have all the power, especially in academia, with so many candidates and so few jobs. In fact, as the candidate you have plenty of decision-making power as well as control.

Our advice is simple: Be prepared and be yourself. If this sounds simplistic and you prefer to strategize each move, that may work in your case. For the most part, you can expect that the members of the search committee are looking for long-term colleagues with that vague quality called "fit." They want someone they would value as a member of their community and who shows promise of a distinguished career. You may or may not be that person. However, you are yourself and that will have to be enough.

Preparation for the interview includes thorough knowledge of the institution involved, or at least enough to ask intelligent questions. It also involves choosing those parts of your CV you wish to highlight, and a well-thought-out rationale for why you would be the ideal person for the job. You cannot anticipate every question, but some rehearsing with a friend or in front of the mirror does not hurt. You can decide what information is on or off limits and prepare responses accordingly. Remember, your marital status, age, and sexual preference are not necessarily public information.

In academic settings, you may be called to the campus for an interview, proof that you are a strong competitor for the job. You may be asked to present a lecture and/or conduct a class. You will surely have meetings with the faculty, some administrators perhaps, and students. A campus visit gives you a chance to see if this is a place in which you would like to live/work. Be aware that you are being observed throughout, not just at the formal interview. Before you go, be clear on who will pay what expenses.

Interviews can be learning experiences. Mistakes made once need not be repeated, which is why interviewing for a position, even if you do not get it, can be a valuable experience. You might even ask a colleague involved in the process what you might have done differently or what the successful candidate did. Most of the time you will find it just was not a "fit," not a very helpful response but proof that the whole process is quite capricious.

Interviewing at the **AAR/SBL** Annual Meeting is done under controlled conditions. Rules are in place to make the process safe (no interviewing in hotel rooms, for example) and efficient. See the AAR or SBL Web sites for details (www.aarweb.org and www.sbl-site.org).

Isolation, cultural and religious

Many women find that being "the only" anything (racial/ethnic/gender group member, lesbian, professor of Coptic and Ugaritic, etc.) can be a very lonely experience in a large or small institution. It is increasingly common as religious studies programs shrink due to budget concerns. Look to the natural **allies** in women's studies or African American studies or wherever your interest lies. Seek a worship community or other faith-based group in your area if those ties are important to you. Join professional organizations to keep in touch with colleagues in the field.

Keep a strong connection to friends beyond your institution. Consider your phone bill part of your therapy budget. Get out of town on occasion. Use the Internet as a lifeline. In all, take seriously that we are meant for community and you deserve yours as well, even if your job has taken you far afield.

Job sharing

If you are considering a job sharing arrangement, you and the other person should apply together for the job. If you decide later in the process to share one position (referred to as one full-time equivalent or FTE), there are several legal hurdles (**Affirmative Action**, nepotism rules) to navigate. In the negotiation process, make sure your salary is at the upper end of the salary spectrum; insist on separate offices, separate travel funds, and separate (double) pension benefits. Merit reviews and tenure reviews are usually separate. It is wise to put stipulations in your contract regulating the dissolution of the arrangement in case of divorce or separation or the failure of one partner to achieve tenure.

Job sharing arrangements have some obvious advantages: They secure partner employment at the same university or other institution, and help to avoid the academic commuter couple syndrome. They allow people to care for children and/or elderly family members without giving up academic ambitions. In addition, they relieve the pressures of teaching for women who have ambitious scholarship goals but find themselves in environments with heavy teaching loads.

There are also some disadvantages. Most institutions with job sharing arrangements evaluate each member separately. While the teaching load can be divided easily (and evaluated separately), service cannot. Those on half-lines are continually battling against expectations that they should be more present and more active than their half-line salaries warrant. Most institutions get more than one full FTE out of shared arrangements, but only pay for part of it, including the retirement and medical benefits. While job sharing arrangements make for sane and happy family lives, life on one academic salary is rough, and the injustice of being overworked and underpaid can wear on one's conscience and checkbook.

Jobs, changing

Even though the market is tight, there is always a certain amount of job changing that goes on. It used to be that you could reasonably expect to change at least once, that is, from a first job out of graduate school to a second, tenure-track position; or, if you received tenure in the first one, a switch to a place you might prefer. When moving after tenure, it is common to take a leave of absence from your first institution to determine if the new job is good for you. Such leaves must be negotiated with both institutions, so check with colleagues to find out what arrangements are customary in your setting.

In the current climate, all bets are off in terms of job changes. Many people are clinging desperately to the one they have, even if they do not like it, for fear of ending up without any position at all. It is hard to assess how this will play out in time, but two cautions are worth a mention. First, once you accept a job it is considered bad form to hop to another too soon, except under special circumstances. After all, the search committee went to great lengths to fill the opening and does not want to have to do so all over again. Second—and this may seem contradictory—if the job is clearly not a fit once you have been at the institution for a year or more, it is perfectly acceptable to begin to put out feelers. Be cautious, as it is not a given that your institution will match **counter offers**. They may be feeling as negative as you are.

Journals, reading and writing

Journals are the print vehicles that convey solid scholarship in a field. You would be wise to get into the habit of perusing several journals in your subspecialty, as well as the *Journal of the American Academy of Religion* (*JAAR*) (www.aarweb.org/publications/jaar). We are fortunate to have the *Journal of Feminist Studies in Religion* (*JFSR*) (www.hds.harvard.edu/jfsr), which specializes in feminist scholarship. Note that many journals are now considering on-line versions of their offerings, and even more have indices on-line already. It remains to be seen how widespread this will become, but is sure to result in easier, if not cheaper, access to these sources.

Publishing an article in a refereed journal (like *JAAR* or *JFSR*) is helpful to one's academic career. It is not easy, in that the better journals turn down up to a dozen articles for every one they publish. Do not be discouraged. Publishing is a matter of finding a fit between what you have written and a journal or other outlet that wants to publish it. Your rejected submission to one journal may be the lead article in another. Your piece that is too popular for a scholarly journal may be just right for the magazine of your religious community.

A few tips may help you get published. First, submit to only one juried publication at a time, paying close attention to their style sheet and citation method. Most editors and readers are unpaid, so their time is valuable. If they spend time reading and critiquing your piece, and then you decide not to let them publish it, everyone loses. Second, journals are not like the Internet; they are slow moving. When you submit an article, you can expect to wait several months before hearing whether it is accepted or not. If after a decent interval (perhaps four to five months) you have not heard anything, do not hesitate to inquire. It is not fair to you to hold your work any longer than that. Third, always have a list of backup choices and envelopes ready to mail if your article is not accepted at your first choice. The blow of rejection can be cushioned if in the next day's mail you send out another copy to another publication. Finally, be sure that whatever you submit is carefully put together and closely scrutinized by you and at least one other person for typos or other incidentals that may discourage readers from choosing it.

Language requirements

Many degree programs require proven proficiency in one or more languages other than English. These requirements vary considerably across institutions, but the study of many aspects of religion makes the use of a variety of languages necessary. Check on your institution's requirements and consider learning the languages early in your program so you can make use of them in your work. Computer programs aid considerably in the translation process, but they are no substitute for being able to read a text in the original and "feeling" what it means. Likewise, the increasing globalization of the field makes conversation with colleagues in other than hegemonic English a desirable ability.

Leaves of absence (see also Benefits, leaves)

A leave of absence can be granted or taken for a variety of reasons. Health-related issues are common. However, a leave can also be used as a placeholder, a way to save your space in an institution while you are trying out another one. Some faculty take leaves of several years to work in government service or in NGOs related to their field. Each institution has limits on such leaves, so investigate this before you commit. Unpaid leaves can also be taken when one has won a fellowship at a time other than a regularly scheduled sabbatical, or just as a refresher after a windfall.

Depending on the type of leave, you may be able to take benefits with you on leave, especially if a fellowship will pay your award to your institution, which allows you to stay on their payroll. If you win a fellowship, check to see if this is possible. In all cases, it is important for women especially to calculate the full cost of a leave, for example, lost benefits, lost Social Security credits, and the like. While it may seem a good idea in the short run, be sure it also makes long-term sense or risk lower benefits down the road.

Lecture circuit

Various ones of our number find themselves on the lecture circuit after an especially popular book or because they work on issues of wide interest, or just because they happen to be smart, articulate speakers who can offer an audience a lot of food for thought in an accessible way. One can think of this prospect as **guest lectures** writ large, so all the wisdom found under that heading applies here and then some.

Lecturing can be a great way to reach people who are not in the classroom. It can also be a way to take the temperature of the public, to learn what issues and approaches are most helpful. On the downside, the travel and changes involved in any such undertaking (ask anyone who has done a book tour) are strenuous, so be prepared.

When saying yes or no to invitations, the size of the audience is less important than the "fit" between speaker and listeners. A handful of people who really want to hear what you have to say can be far more rewarding than a hall full of restless undergraduates who are there under duress. Be sure to talk with trusted colleagues about lecture fees. They range widely, and women are forever being asked to give their skills away for little or nothing.

LGBTQ

There is no single word to describe the myriad ways people organize their sexual activities and gender identities, so the amalgam of letters "**LGBTQ**" has come to stand for some of the possibilities: lesbian, gay, bisexual, transgender, and queer—or sometimes "Q" stands for questioning.

The terms themselves may be usefully ambiguous as well. Women who identify as lesbians may have sex with other women, or they may organize their lives around other women. They may have sex with people across a range of genders, only with themselves, or not at all. Gay men may organize their lives around resistance to dominant gender norms or they may focus on men in ways that extend misogyny. Bisexual women or men may organize their lives around partners of different genders or one partner in lifelong commitment. Transgender people may inhabit a variety of gender positions that do or do not match their assigned "biological" sex. They may change gender by what they wear, how they carry themselves, how they work out or through hormonal or surgical intervention. Identifying as queer generally means taking up resistance to dominant norms of gender and sexuality, however that resistance is lived out. Heterosexual people may identify as queer, while lesbian, gay, and bisexual or transgender people may not necessarily choose to do so. When taking up institutional authority or projects of social change, keep in mind and make openings for the multitude of ways in which people live their lives. Abundant new religious resources on the topic help to clarify issues and promote justice.

Marketing

The term "marketing" conjures certain images that seem out of place in religious studies. In fact, professional work stemming from this field is not for the faint of heart who are unable to convey their ideas and themselves to others. This is the basis of marketing—persuading people that they want what you are offering.

There is a big difference between marketing and boasting. As women, we are socialized to hide our light under a bushel basket, as it were. Most of us are hesitant to promote ourselves, considering it poor taste, expecting other people will do it for us. There is a balancing point between the crass approach of television evangelists and pathological modesty. A good CV (see **Curriculum vitae**), a good book, and a good reputation are a good start.

Many institutions have administrative departments of public relations, or imbed those functions within the development or alumni/ae office. If asked, they are often willing to help faculty with promotion of books or to offer faculty "experts" to the media. It is to their advantage to promote faculty, so ask for their help.

Media relations

The media are crucial to public discourse, to open, free and vigorous debate. Therefore, our relations with the media go two ways; they call us when they need an explanation or an expert opinion, and we call them when we need publicity for some event our institution is sponsoring that will benefit the public. The **AAR** and **SBL** now offer connections to their members with the media on selected topics through a project called *Religionsource* (see www.aarweb.org/news/Religionsource.asp).

A local religion or education writer may call us for our opinion on a piece of pending legislation or on some current event. A national outlet may want a theological, ethical, or historical explanation of something. A columnist or commentator might want to know how sacred texts inform a current event. It is at this moment that our function as teacher and scholar reaches beyond the classroom, beyond our particular institutions, beyond the academy.

Unhappily, many media people still think that scholars of religion look like their childhood religious leaders, so they are not likely to call women without prompting. This attitude is changing, albeit slowly and with help. Some women scholars of religion have appeared on national television programs, so women's insights are gradually becoming part of the public discourse. Nevertheless, it is still quite unusual to see more than one woman featured with a group of men, especially when it comes to major news events like the death of a pope, clergy sexual abuse, or the funeral of a queen. Then male experts are trotted out in legions as if women knew nothing about the topics.

The key to good media work is clarity. It takes time to learn how to be concise. Most of us are trained to pay attention to nuance and detail, argument and counter argument. Sound bites are just that, ten to fifteen seconds when we must convey very complicated thoughts in glitzy, memorable, and, most of all, short ways.

Media training is important if you plan to do a lot of this. You will learn what to wear (solid colors, little jewelry, avoid white), how to posture (be offensive without offending), when to respond and when to let gratuitous remarks go by, what to do if the microphone goes dead (smile and pray), and above all, how to STAY ON MESSAGE. The latter is especially hard for us, as we have learned so well to elaborate on everything. Good practice for media work is Thanksgiving dinner with your extended family. How they hear things you say, how they respond to you, will give you a good clue about your audience out there in televisionland.

Sometimes we call the media: for example, when our institution brings a world-renowned scholar to our community or sponsors an annual lecture series. Public relations departments of our institutions do this best. If none exists, develop a list of media contacts and issue an advisory to each several weeks beforehand. Then a release goes out just before the event, inviting media representatives to attend (gratis of course). Local newspaper and radio/television stations are obvious outlets. Think also of free weekly papers, of local cable stations, and of course the Internet as ways to get the word out.

The more we as women can develop our skills in media relations, the faster we will change the mistaken impression that all experts on religion are men. A good first step is to see and greet media folks as allies, not as aliens, to welcome their questions, however banal and gum-chewing they may seem, and consider the effort invested in media work to be well expended. It is time that such work is counted as "service" to an institution, a contribution that is not yet recognized in most places.

One caveat: Some institutions have strict protocols and pathways for the creation of a media "presence" or who can speak for them. Be sure you know your institution's rules before you speak on its behalf or in ways that could raise questions.

Mentoring (see also Advisor/advisee relationships)

Finding a good mentor may make or break your academic career. Mentors give feedback on one's intellectual work. They soothe bruised egos after one's scholarship has been rejected by a publisher. Mentors encourage you to "revise and resubmit" a rejected article. They put underhanded, mean comments of senior and junior colleagues into context. Mentors point out the small print in the faculty handbook and give tips for preparing one's tenure file. Mentors cut to the chase of campus politics and help you find **allies,** avoid enemies, and create a network of colleagues beyond the institution. Mentors give inside information about comparative salary structures and benefits packages and help you (re)negotiate your contract. Mentors prevent you from going crazy by pointing out the inconsistencies, contradictions, and double binds of academic life.

White men have always mentored white men, and some women have benefited from male mentors. More often, however, women and people of color have been forced to succeed without the assistance of mentors. As a result, we have not learned to ask for mentoring or to offer mentoring, something that hurts us in the long run. Given that the numbers of junior scholars is many times that of senior scholars, there are not enough such mentors to cover the needs of those entering the field. So finding a good mentor may require some creative searching, and someone may be a good mentor for some aspects of your career but not all aspects.

Mentoring is reciprocal. While the balance of power makes clear who leads and who follows in this dance, the faculty member often derives a good deal, too, from the relationship with the graduate student, both intellectually and emotionally. If you have a good mentor, consider yourself lucky. If you are a good mentor, thanks!

Midcareer issues

There is an expression called the "post-tenure blues." Some women get it and some women do not. It is related to a set of questions about midcareer changes, promotion, or advancement not necessarily related to tenure. Some women, once having attained tenure or having been tenured for a number of years, wonder, "What next?" "Is this all there is?" We may ask ourselves, "How do I keep my career alive?" "How do I teach the same required courses when the repetition becomes boring?"

"Do I want to stay at the same institution?" "What new directions in research and teaching or community activism might I make?"

Of course, the onset of doubts varies from woman to woman. Sometimes it is concurrent with midlife questions, but oftentimes it is not. Age is not necessarily a factor. Many of us reevaluate our careers and regroup. Issues of growth, and whether or not we can continue growing where we are, become a part of the reevaluation and regrouping. Priorities shift and our careers with them. It is all quite normal. The key is to find people and resources that encourage such shifts.

Money management

Money is an unspoken topic in religious studies. It carries so much freight with regard to class background, self worth, discrimination, and mystery that it ought to be in every graduate school curriculum.

There are many books for women on how to manage your money, many financial planners who will be glad (for a fee) to help you make investment choices and plan for retirement. Look into these, as few of us in the humanities are savvy about the finer points of the stock market, the difference between bonds and equities, the advantage of a Roth IRA, or the importance of 529 accounts for children's college education.

Graduate school is a major expense, usually a debt-producing one. It is also an uneven playing field in that it is easier to manage for those who come from families that could save for their education than for those who are, for example, the first in their family to go on to higher education, often without benefit of any such savings. These differences have a long-term impact: for example, who can do an unpaid internship and who cannot afford it, who can study abroad and who cannot. These inequities require structural changes to correct them.

There are simple things we can do that will get us started on the path of sound fiscal management over the life of a career. Begin with your graduate institution's financial aid offices and insist that you get the maximum in grant, work-study, and other outright (as opposed to loan) forms of assistance. Then negotiate student loans at well below market rates through your institution rather than relying on commercial offerings. Once on the job market, a realistic picture of salaries is key to assuring we are being paid commensurate with our brethren. Differentials persist. It is also a good idea to check on salary differences at midcareer. For a variety of reasons, women tend to spend a longer time at the Associate level. Check to make sure you and your female colleagues are not experiencing salary compression while male colleagues have jumped ahead. Sometimes the women's faculty caucus at your institution can be helpful in addressing these issues, and if there is no caucus, it might be helpful to form one.

For some women, the first job is also the first time they have disposable income, so the job of managing money becomes even more important. If you have student loans, how much of your paycheck is really discretionary? What if you want to buy a house instead of renting an apartment? What if the old car just isn't reliable anymore? An accurate budget adhered to strictly, and a moratorium on new debts are an essential combination for financial health. Some people find that by consolidating student loans they are able to decrease monthly payments. Check with an accountant to get your best option.

Another sure bet is to maximize your allowed contributions to your retirement or pension fund. Take advantage of tax laws that favor income saved over income spent. Consult that financial advisor about how to invest any excess income you may have, learning how much risk you can tolerate and when to choose the safest course. All of this is conversation men have on the golf course and in the locker room. We need to start it with one another, always with an eye toward sharing the resources among us so that no one is left out while others have abundance.

Mujerista

Commitment to women's well-being from the perspective of Hispanic/Latina women is called *mujerista,* a term favored by some colleagues in religious studies. It is similar to but distinct from *feminista* in that it is understood not in relation to feminist work (see **Feminist**), which is often perceived as Anglo efforts to achieve women's rights, but rather akin to **womanist** or African American women's efforts to survive in a racist patriarchal culture. *Mujeristas* hear and articulate some of the many voices of Hispanic women on their own terms. They create a framework for social justice based on their experiences. *Mujerista* work involves the whole community, and is done in concert with other women and men who seek the well-being of women, the community, and the earth.

Negotiations (see also Contracts; Leaves of absence)

All job offers result in some form of negotiation until both the institution and the prospective employee are clear about and can agree on conditions for employment. Most women in Western settings have been socialized not to talk about money. We have a lot to learn from our sisters who go to the marketplace and bargain with the vendors, and especially from those who are vendors themselves.

Most professional contracts do not have extensive parameters in the current soft economy. Nevertheless, there is always room to negotiate, especially *before* any contract is signed. Once you do sign, your power all but evaporates. So think carefully about the basics—working conditions, teaching/research/academic load, office, health benefits, retirement plan, disability insurance, sabbatical possibilities, tenure options, professional development, childcare, and the like. It does not hurt to share your contract with an employment lawyer, who might notice a loophole you have missed.

Do not forget to look at the seemingly smaller stuff that can make/break your experience. What about a computer? Will you have secretarial support? Are there teaching, research, or work study assistants available to you? How large will your classes be? How long must you teach that introductory survey course until you get to try your hand at a graduate seminar?

Only after you have ascertained the answers to these and other questions relevant to your kind of employment, and discussed the offer with a trusted friend or colleague, should you consider accepting it. For academic appointments, it is customary to respond to written offers within two weeks. Some institutions will pressure you to do so more quickly, but do not be rushed into a rash decision. Of course, if you are not planning to take the position, it is only courteous to say so quickly so as not to delay the search, allowing the committee to move on to its next candidate. Negotiating an offer is a serious process that institutions understand.

The key is to be honest with everyone along the way. It may turn out that you reject the offer because in the negotiating you realize that dealing with this place reminds you of your first husband during the divorce or an unpleasant relationship you once had. Better to cut your losses, insofar as you can afford to, and find a job in an organization where you feel respected. Remember that you are in your most powerful position *before* you sign, so be sure you will feel comfortable afterward. Barring unforeseen catastrophe, there will be other jobs to consider, other avenues to explore for your considerable talents. Remember, once you are on campus for an interview, it is clear that you have the credentials for the job. What is at stake is the "fit." You can only control half of that, so relax and enjoy the experience.

Networking

Networking is a trendy way of saying keep your eyes and ears open and reach out to your sisters in the field. It is not some magic solution to getting that dream job or a foolproof way to avoid discrimination. It is a result of the fact that we live and work in communities, despite the many pressures to divide us.

In religious studies, networking opportunities begin in the home institution, where links with others in the department or section are important. Do not discount the use of the Internet, where a good discussion group or e-mail list can put you in regular touch with people.

The Womanist Approach to Religion and Society Group at the **AAR Annual Meeting** is a good example of a network. African American women share their work, share the word on the street, and share their wisdom. They meet the day before the AAR Annual Meeting, and even include a community outreach component in their gathering. The **Women's Caucus** in Religious Studies is another good place to go. Its seminar connected with the Annual Meeting is a rich opportunity to meet other women, hear from some of the seasoned members, and profit from their experiences. The Committee on the Status of Women of the AAR (see **SWP**) organizes a lunchtime session for networking. Both AAR and **SBL** have various receptions, breakfasts, and other meetings to encourage networking, for example, for **independent scholars**.

Graduate students, gay/lesbian/bisexual and transgender people, and international colleagues all need and have created their own networks. Ask around and find yours. If it is not readily apparent, gather two or three colleagues and start one.

On-line courses (see also Computers)

Many institutions are offering on-line classes, a natural outgrowth of increased availability of technology. Such classes vary in format and may include on-line video and/or audio lectures, on-line discussion sessions, and the like. They require the same if not more preparation than an off-line course. In order to make them memorable pedagogical experiences, they require a certain flair for writing and communicating that will hold the students' interest and encourage them to delve more deeply into the material even without the face-to-face encounter of the classroom. Since electronic learning is on the upswing in many institutions, one is well advised to learn the mechanics and practice by including on-line dimensions in off-line classes. Many institutions use Blackboard or comparable software to incorporate on-line dimensions into their course offerings.

Postcolonialism

Postcolonial discourse is an emerging area of study investigating oppositional thinking that began at the first breath of European colonial conquest of the world. It is similar to postmodern thought in that it seeks to deconstruct master narratives and challenge binary oppositions. Many institutions understand that the world is growing ever smaller and try to prepare students for this new reality. Therefore, they work to bring in people from other countries and cultures to create a global community. This means that some of our teachers, our students, and our peers will come from countries that have a colonial history.

Not all colonialisms are created equal. The United States, once a colony, is now arguably the most powerful country on the earth, exporting its own hegemonic cultural and economic influence. Postcolonial work requires careful listening and a willingness to see and accept the authenticity of the Others within the definitions formulated by the Other selves. Like racism, sexism, and all forms of oppression, it is a challenge for everyone in the field, not simply for those who suffer its sting. Religions are classic tools of colonialism, so understanding and deconstructing them is essential to getting beyond hegemonic norms.

Poster session

Poster sessions are common in many fields, especially the sciences and medicine, though new to religious studies at the Annual Meeting of the AAR. They are a chance to display current research and engage in conversation with colleagues who may be involved in similar projects. One applies for a poster session just as one does for presenting a paper. The difference is that instead of presenting to an audience, one presents, via a poster board, to individuals who stop to talk during a designated period during the meeting. A sharp, well-written, and well-mounted display on a 4'x 8' board is the medium. Words, pictures, graphics, and other means to convey research and results are made available to interested passersby. Though very different from presenting an academic paper, poster sessions are especially useful for generating interest in new research and connecting with people who have similar interests.

Power, white male

When we think of religious studies in historical terms, the image of a white male bastion of power springs readily to mind. Some would argue that the picture has not changed much: that most religious groups are still headed by men, that predominantly white religious organizations have far more money and political clout than those run by women and/or people of color, that most tenured professors are still white men. True, perhaps, but to leave the story at this point is to ignore the enormous strides many women have made and the valuable solidarity engaged in by many white men who understand their common stake in the increasing diversity in our field.

Nonetheless, power is power. It is the ability to make choices, to deem relevant or irrelevant certain aspects of who we are, to render important or trivial ideas and projects, to fund or defund efforts, to invite or disinvite, in short, to shape the reality in which we do our work. This guide is an investment in consigning this entry to the dust bin, and replacing it with *Power, shared and equal,* which we hope will describe our field in future editions.

Presenting a paper

One of the defining experiences of a career in religious studies is the first attempt to present an academic paper at a conference, notably at the AAR Annual Meeting or a regional meeting. First comes the business of getting a proposal accepted. This is done by submitting a proposal to the blind review process of a program unit of the AAR or SBL (see **AAR, Annual Meeting** and **SBL, Annual Meeting**). Once a proposal is accepted, whether for a panel presentation or for a paper, the hard work begins of writing something that will: (1) fit the time allowed, (2) keep a specialized as well as general audience awake, and (3) showcase your expertise to the max.

Everyone is nervous the first time. Practice helps to calm the jitters. So does wearing something you feel good in. Have a friend time you so that you do not run on endlessly. Then consider a set of hints (written years ago by Mary E. Hunt) that the Women and Religion Section has circulated to its presenters, entitled, "Be Brief, Be Witty, Be Seated."

1. **BE BRIEF:** It takes about twenty minutes to read nine to eleven double-spaced pages. Adjust your time accordingly if your audience is made up of many people who are not native speakers of English or you are not a native speaker of English. Allow a little time for introductory remarks and to repeat for emphasis what you really want to get across. Err on the side of too little material rather than too much. Your audience will thank you. Studies show that the average attention span for spoken words is slightly over ten seconds. A few good ideas with a clear introduction and concise conclusion will stay with your listeners longer than a convoluted argument. Allow time for questions, which offer another opportunity, usually more listener friendly than being read to, for communicating your ideas.

2. **BE WITTY:** Not every religious studies scholar is a Whoopi Goldberg or a Lily Tomlin, but it is important to think of an academic audience as people first and foremost. A touch of humor is always appreciated. It keeps the audience alert. Think of the presentation as needing the clarity of a picture, the precision of an article, the flow of a conversation, and the satisfaction of a good meal. Humor adds levity and makes your remarks memorable. Anecdotes and examples will give you a chance to lighten what might otherwise be a deadly dull performance. Delivering a paper is performance art, so show signs of polish.

3. **BE SEATED:** Honor the time constraints because they assure that everyone will have an equal opportunity to speak. It is boorish not to, a sure sign of inexperience or arrogance. Practiced speakers finish up with a bang on or a little ahead of time. Novices start out strong but end up fumbling because they try to speed-read that last twenty pages of a thirty-page paper in the remaining five minutes. When they realize that their time is rapidly coming to a close, they often exclaim, "Oh, heavens, I am just going to skip the next ten pages and read you the conclusion," or desperate words to that effect, as if the content they are leaving aside has no bearing on the argument. To avoid this faux

pas, keep your presentation to the time allowed. However, if you do not manage that:

a. acknowledge the timekeeper with a nod so as not to distract your audience;

b. summarize your remaining material without reference to the time problem;

c. move smoothly to your conclusion like a practiced speaker and nobody will be any the wiser except you, the next time.

Delivering a paper is learned behavior. It is like preaching a sermon, teaching a class, or giving a lecture anywhere else. You can get it right with practice. Bad things can happen—the microphone can go dead, your PowerPoint presentation can freeze, you might even have an attack of nerves that will cause you enormous stress. Always have a second copy of your manuscript on hand (once a death-of-God theologian lost a page while lecturing, which prompted him to utter "Oh my God," rendering his argument weak). When relying on PowerPoint or other technology, be sure you have back-up materials and overhead transparencies in case the machines fail you.

For the most part, delivering a paper will be a good, even an enjoyable, experience. You can enhance it, Miss Manners would suggest, by offering a warm thank you to your introducer and by thanking your audience at the end. Further, a quick e-mail thank you to the presider and/or the person who chairs the section is a nicety that increases graciousness among us.

Privilege

Whatever your age, gender, race, socioeconomic class, sexual orientation, religion, physical ability status, or ethnicity, it is important to remember that while in some cases these ways of classifying ourselves leave us open to oppression, we also benefit from privilege, both within these classifications and from our status as part of the academic world. We often tend to notice the ways in which we are disadvantaged and ignore the power we have. Therefore, it is also important to recognize that there are situations where, for example, whiteness gives white women the edge over African American, Asian, Latino, and Native American men and women, or Christian hegemony brings Christian women closer to the centers of power than their Muslim, Jewish, Hindu, or Buddhist sisters or brothers. Rather than simply feeling discomfort about that privilege, we can use it well by paying attention to it, and calling attention to it whenever possible to move toward a time when it is shared.

Professional associations

The AAR and the SBL are only two of many professional associations related to our work in religion. Find out the name(s) of one or several that meets your needs, and join. Their newsletters and journals, occasional meetings and on-line discussion groups are great sources of information and **networking**. Activity in one of these groups is also considered part of your service requirement in your home institution (see **Service**).

If you teach in an institution of higher education, you may want to consider joining the American Association of University Professors (AAUP). Their bulletin, *Academe,* addresses many national issues of interest to women in education.

Professional development

Professional development is the umbrella term for all that you do to keep growing and producing in the field of religious studies. It includes teaching effectiveness, especially the development now of computer skills to bring your teaching into line with contemporary modes. Effectiveness of communication is something we can all use help on, whether oral or written.

This is the rubric under which the pretenure and tenure evaluations are carried out, as well as most other evaluations in cognate fields (see **Evaluations, annual, pretenure**). You are expected to publish regularly, whether books, journal articles, and/or reviews. If you know this is your weak suit, start early to get help from colleagues or from private sources (there are writing coaches now) so you will not be caught without a paper trail when you need one.

Presenting papers at professional meetings (see **Presenting a paper**) is considered part of your professional development. Acting as a presider is less important but worth a mention to show your willingness to serve. Speaking on panels, presenting **guest lectures**, getting **grants**, and doing **media relations** can all be part of your professional development. It is important; otherwise, you risk stagnating at the just slightly post-graduate school stage, a natural location one year out, but a problem if five years later you are still there.

Summer seminars and grant acquisitions can be part of your professional development. New research projects, especially collaborative ones that involve people from various departments in your own institutions or work by colleagues from a number of institutions, are considered a big plus. These activities break the monotony of routine teaching and inform your teaching with new and exciting content.

Professional ethics

Professional ethics is a relatively new subspecialty that refers to the many issues we face in the regular course of our work. It includes matters of personal conduct, institutional responsibility, **confidentiality**, as well as the many aspects of our subspecialties, for example, decisions relevant to research protocols or handling of sources. For women, the trickiest aspects can be matters of personal conduct (see **Relationships**), where differences of perception, lapses in judgment, and/or cultural prejudices can result in serious problems.

One suggestion here is to rely on those **allies** within your institution and the networks beyond (see **Networking**) to help alert you to expectations that may be unwritten. This is a reminder to all of us to convene such conversations regularly so as to maintain high professional standards within our field without condemning people unfairly who make honest mistakes because they were uninformed.

Promotion

As long as there is a pecking order, there will be a top rank. In academia, the graduate student assistant is on the bottom, followed by lecturers, who are usually adjuncts. On a tenure-track, one becomes assistant, then associate, and then, perhaps, full professor. Some schools provide endowed chairs or the rank of "university professor" for those they consider the most distinguished full professors. It remains to be proved whether such rankings (which usually carry not only increased salary and benefits but also other privileges as one ascends the scale) are the ideal approach. For now, it is what we all face. Less formal structures for the same dynamic are found in the many other institutions in which we work.

Promotion can be as capricious as **tenure**, as subject to the whims of colleagues and committees, administrations and budgets. In an ideal world, it would be based on the achievement of certain well-specified criteria, the accomplishment of a certain degree of **professional development** commensurate with rank. Sometimes promotion to associate carries with it tenure; sometimes it does not. Sometimes long-term service will be enough to garner a full professorship, often not. There is little rhyme or reason in this system beyond what each institution determines.

Preparing for promotion reviews (see **Evaluations, annual, pretenure**) is essential. Keeping good records (see **Files**) and balancing your work according to the formula prescribed by your institution (see **Service** and **Institutional analysis**) makes the task much easier. Know that promotions are like grades, subject to the prudential judgment of the ones making it, often with little recourse. Similarly, do not be afraid to appeal a blatantly unfair call. While it may not get you the promotion, it will at least force those who made the decision to be forthright about why. Such a process can help you prepare for the next time, and/or reveal such entrenched biases that the only promotion you want is out the door.

Publishing (see also Books; Journals)

Ours is a field that expects members to publish, whether books, journal articles, on-line materials, or in popular outlets. Women have made huge strides in this arena in the last twenty years, producing some of the best-selling and most widely translated materials in the field. Publishing remains a business deal, a way to get the word out while also generating a profit for increasingly fewer companies that are interested in our work. It has been a men's game, so women need to share with one another how it is done and to insist that publishers consider and promote women's work. The book displays at conferences, especially the **AAR and SBL Annual Meetings,** are good places to meet publishing representatives, and begin to develop relationships that will provide a face to go with your written work.

There are things to keep in mind about publishing as a business. First, it changes all the time. Editors change presses, companies are sold or close, so stay abreast of developments. Second, the press is interested in selling books, so, while academic presses will invest in obscure scholarly projects, they support themselves with books that sell. Hence, they are especially interested in "cross-over" books that are intellectually smart but can appeal to a wide, educated audience beyond a scholar's specialization. These are sometimes also called "high-end trade" books.

Third, good writing is important. Graduate work militates against good writing and pushes toward academic-speak because you fill your head with scholarly work, much of it mediocre or worse as writing. Have an objective critic assess your work and give you honest feedback.

If you need writing help, consider taking a course in nonfiction writing or hire an editor to help you. Few presses provide adequate editing help, as editors are required to handle too many projects to do close work with authors. Do not count on the publisher to provide all the editing help you might need. Many successful authors would not think of publishing without a good personal editor, which, in days of old, might have been the professor's wife, who did it for free. As professional writers say,

"There is no good writing, only good editing." Fourth, your odds of finding a publisher are higher with presses that publish material similar to yours. Since you are the expert, you are the person who knows what the best books in your field are. Go to those publishers first. If you are grouped with other books, they know they have an audience and can sell your book. The trick is selling your work to the publisher as different enough from the pack to elicit that audience's attention.

Once you have a good idea for a book, or want to transform your dissertation into something that more than a few loyal friends will read, you need a cover letter, an outline or table of contents, and a sample chapter to send to a publisher. You will want to include some indication of the audience you intend to reach, other books that are published that compete with yours, and why your approach is unique and different. You can send this material to several publishers at once to get a sense of the market. But when one invites you to submit the full manuscript, or if you have one ready and decide to go that route instead of the more abbreviated one, be sure to send the full manuscript to only one publisher at a time. Check with other authors who have recently worked with that publisher about their experience. Some presses are much more heavy-handed about editorial control, which may be fine if this is your first project and you do not yet trust your own editorial skills. However, be careful about the press you choose and how much control you have. The book display at the AAR/SBL Annual Meetings is a good place to meet publishers and talk face-to-face about your projects.

Negotiating a contract, especially for a first book, is standard. Like all contracts, however, read it carefully before you sign. If you do not understand, clarify before you sign. You might have a lawyer look it over. There are no get-rich-quick schemes in academic publishing. Just be sure who has the copyright, whether you are agreeing to right of first refusal for your next book, and whether you have control of the basics, such as cover, price, and whether it will come out initially in paperback or hardcover.

Try to adhere to your agreed-upon deadline, but realize that few deaths will result if you are a little late. Better not to drive yourself mad, though extending the deadline is usually a onetime thing. Then just write it. Be sure to allow time for reading proofs, chasing down lost footnotes, and promotion. Fill out the promotion form carefully to be sure that people and publications you respect get review copies. Then enjoy the fruits of your labor.

All writing can make a contribution. When it comes time for tenure review, however, books are the most important thing, followed by journal articles, and then anthology chapters, and finally book reviews (see **Reviews, book**). Consider setting yourself a yearly goal and then refuse politely other offers to write until/unless the projects fit into your timeline. You will find that if you are a successful writer you will be asked frequently to contribute to anthologies and journals. It is hard to say yes to all such requests and still stay on track with other work. Consider turning all professional papers into articles, and/or collecting some of them for a volume.

Racism

Racism post–civil rights has shifted from its ugly, obvious, overt manifestations to something more sinister and subtle. It is important to recognize and name racism when it is directed against us, or when we ourselves, unwittingly or wittingly, participate in it, but it may be more difficult to detect or define. Racism is both systematic and subtle discrimination against and judgment of an individual based on identity with a particular racial group. It always has both an individual and an institutional manifestation.

How does racism look inside the academy? Racism is experienced in different ways. Sometimes it manifests itself as colleagues', administrations', and students' attempts to overlook race or to focus too much on it, colleagues treating one as if she/he were invisible or as if the only reason she/he is there is because of **Affirmative Action**. Invisibility is a problem on and off campus. People who recognize you on campus may not say hello off campus. Racism happens in committee meetings and faculty meetings. For instance, a person of a minority group making a point may be met with silence while a person of a dominant racial group making the same point is affirmed. This happens for reasons of **sexism** as well. For women of color, dynamics of

racism, sexism, classism, and heterosexism are interlocking manifestations of oppression.

Many students have never before had a teacher who is a
woman of color and do not always respond easily to such a
person in a position of authority. Some of us find that our
colleagues make assumptions about what we are and are not
prepared to teach. White colleagues do not always evaluate
accurately the work of students and professors of color. Professors of color are sometimes labeled "harsh" when we require
very rigorous standards. There are jokes and questions about
Affirmative Action, the assumption being that Affirmative Action
means the school has not hired the best. The problem is complex
and resistant to change.

Because racism can be so subtle these days, it is difficult to
know when one is contributing, however unwittingly, to a racist
atmosphere. Thus, it is helpful if people of all colors are open to
dialogue about ways in which racism manifests itself and ways to
eliminate it. Understanding the ways in which religious studies
and religious traditions have been constructed racially helps to
change them. It is important not to be defensive immediately if
someone suggests that your words, deeds, or attitudes are racist.
In confronting the racism of others, it is also important to
acknowledge at the outset that they may not be aware of it. At the
same time, when one is confronted with the complaint of having
engaged in a racist exchange, it is important to be open to
dialogue. Racial harassment policies are beginning to be defined
and can be a good source of protection and/or redress.

References

It used to be pro forma that if you did a good job your supervisor
would happily provide a letter of reference when you looked
elsewhere. If you did not perform very well, she/he might politely
decline or write something quite tepid. Our increasingly litigious
culture has changed this, especially in jobs beyond academia.
Now it can be hard to get a recommendation because employers
fear legal suits regardless of the quality of your work. Know your
organization's culture in this regard and plan accordingly.

The academic world still treats the letter of recommendation as part of the package, though it is not clear how long it will be before this changes. Admissions decisions are increasingly contested, and some people are understandably loath to get involved. Nonetheless, for now a letter of recommendation is still required for many academic moves, beginning with undergraduate admission, graduate school, and most teaching jobs, as well as grants and fellowship applications. One puzzles to imagine what will take its place.

Be sure that your advisor and/or others who will perform this task for you know you well enough to write intelligently and to distinguish you from the many other students of their acquaintance. It is best to provide your recommenders with an up-to-date CV (see **Curriculum vitae**) as well as the addressed, stamped envelopes to mail off your letters to the proper officials. Decide whether you want to waive your right to see the letters, as most schools will give you that option.

Do not assume that the recommender's fame is a substitute for a good letter. Be certain that your recommenders can write good letters under the deadline constraints. A well-written, nuanced letter from a midrange colleague or scholar can be much more effective than a hastily dashed-off paragraph from a senior scholar too busy to take the necessary care. If you are uncertain about confidential letters in your placement file, you can ask your advisor or someone else on the faculty who you trust to look them over. They cannot tell you the content of the letters, but they can recommend you remove one or more and find other recommenders.

When writing such letters, be honest but strategic. The frank fact is that writing a letter that does not convey much enthusiasm for a student is worse than telling the student to find someone else to write it. Readers on committees spot such letters right away. Likewise, be sure that you do not use some formula that could apply in general terms to many students. Be quite detailed about the individual involved. Otherwise, committees that read your letters often will discount them eventually. Never have a student write the letter and you sign it. Some well-known professors who are asked frequently to write letters have turned to this model, to the chagrin of their students, who accept it in lieu of a better offer. It helps no one and compromises the integrity of letters of reference, as well as the individual using such shortcuts.

We need to preserve the integrity of this system, not inflating our students to get them into graduate school nor writing bogus letters for students we hardly know just because they think our official stationery will look good. Only then can we rely on one another for the kind of candid assessment that other employers seek all the time lest they hire someone who is not right for the job. Professionals reading such letters become adept at spotting vague, hyperbolic praise and appreciate those that come with thoughtful, specific, honest assessments.

Reinventing yourself

Just because a woman begins with one career track does not mean she has to stick with it for life. That is true whether you are moving into religious studies after a career in another field, or whether you have been in religious studies for a number of years and want to change your research/teaching focus. Second career students in the field of religion are common.

Many of us find our minds and hearts moving in a new direction and decide to leave a career in another field to pursue a career in religious studies. Some of us found ourselves placed in a subspecialty in religious studies that we never felt was quite the real fit, but we took it when the job we were looking for or the politics of the moment made it the best choice. Some women simply outgrow an earlier interest in one area and/or their research leads them to a different emphasis. You may outgrow your department and find that there is a different department in your university you prefer. Alternatively, you may outgrow your institution and find that you want an institutional change.

Keep records of the changes you make in your syllabi and research. Develop relationships with the colleagues who work in the area you find yourself shifting toward. Those of us who have made this shift have learned the importance of carrying along others with us as our research and teaching interests change. Presenting papers at professional meetings in your new area is a helpful way to reintroduce yourself. Becoming acquainted with and joining working groups in the field you are moving into facilitate recognition of your work in the area. It helps in the interview process to bring others up-to-date on your work, and even to talk about the process of changing research and teaching emphases. It is a sign of **professional development.**

Relationships

No magic wand here, just a quick word about the fact that all of us have relationships with our work colleagues. The question is how to live them out with integrity while being women in religious studies, given the sexist, racist, heterosexist, and colonialist assumptions that reign. For example, how does a single, heterosexual woman date someone in her immediate circle without having her personal life influence her first-year performance review? Or, how does a woman of color on a small campus develop her social life without having that fishbowl feeling? Or, how can a lesbian woman have a commitment ceremony without fearing the loss of her job at a conservative school?

There are no easy answers, and many women have spent their professional lives trying to make it easier for others. Some basics help. First, your right to privacy is guaranteed by the U.S. Constitution, so do not feel any need to share your personal life in an interview, a faculty meeting, or anywhere else where you do not feel safe, comfortable and/or motivated.

Second, intimate relationships with peers are subject to careful negotiation and discretion. Dating someone in your department may be more complicated than it is worth. However, it is not illegal or immoral, but subject to extreme caution. Third, relationships with students or those you supervise are deeply discouraged if not forbidden. They are simply too front-loaded with power dynamics that are difficult to change. If they occur, be sure they are public so that scandal is not a factor (also, making a relationship public may be a good way to discourage it if it is inappropriate) and that the conditions of power (for example, if you are the professor) change. That is a hard one, but it guards against inappropriate favoritism, and/or recriminations if the relationship ends. Again, it is much better to avoid such boundary-crossing relationships; there are other fish in the sea (see **Professional ethics**). If the relationship is worth pursuing, it is worth delaying until the student is no longer under one's supervision.

Enjoying cordial professional relationships, indeed, developing lifelong friendships with colleagues is one of the perks of this business. Enjoy them carefully.

Religious belief

One need not believe in God, G_d, G*d, Godde, Goddess, or the Divine to work as a religious scholar. One need not be a member of a faith community to do quality work in the field. **Christian hegemony** being what it is, many women have paid a high price for their public agnosticism, atheism, and/or belief in Goddesses. There is a subtle pecking order here, too, with Christianity on top, then Judaism, followed by Hinduism, Buddhism, Islam, and on to the many other traditions, with pagan and Wiccan folk toward the bottom. This is a regrettable and changing phenomenon, one rendered ridiculous by the increasing religious pluralism of an increasingly globalized world. However, it is a real factor in our field and must be recognized in order to be transformed.

A related issue is the place of religious expression in our work. This will vary depending on the setting (see **Institutional analysis**). It is always inappropriate to expect that everyone believes as you do or to engage in public prayer as if that were the case.

Religious studies

Religion is a topic that everyone thinks they know something about. (Beware of mentioning your field of study on airplanes.) This may be a product both of the view that "religion" has to do with "personal experience" and the difficulty that many people have with thinking about "the social." Rather than considering religion in terms of the social relations that produced both religious practices and religion as a category of study, there is an assumption that religion is the most ancient of all human endeavors, that "from time immemorial man [sic] has been religious."

The category of "religion," and the discipline of "religious studies," however, are the product of a specific historical process: to wit, colonialism. The concept of religion as a category was developed at the moment of cultural contact produced by European exploration and colonialism. This category could then be deployed in various ways in service of the colonial project. At different historical moments, indigenous practices were seen as the same as/different from/incommensurate with the emergent European idea of religion.

Thus, in thinking about the field of religious studies today, it is necessary to situate the field in this historical context and to consider the social effects produced by taking up "religion" as an object of study. For example, if the course that serves as an introduction to religion is taught as an introduction to and comparison of canonical scriptures, then the teaching of religion becomes inscribed in the colonial project of establishing and reifying canons of writing. Another example would be the phenomenological approach, in which human experiences and or behaviors are divided into categories such as myth, ritual, the holy, sacred, and profane, cosmology, ethics, and practice. This approach establishes a unified notion of the human that serves as the fundamental basis for comparison. These types of comparisons are often implicated in hierarchies in which some persons or cultures are put down for alleged failure to measure up to the standard of the fully human.

Religious studies is most often taken to be the overarching name for an interdisciplinary field of study that incorporates fieldwork, textual and literary studies, historical inquiries, and ethical and theological writing. Unlike fields such as English or history, there is no single disciplinary method that defines the field of religious studies. In fact, the study of religion is taken up in various institutional settings and transgresses academic boundaries. Depending on institutional setting, scholarship, training, and teaching in religious studies might be formulated as "religion," as "theology or thealogy," as "the history of religions," as "professional training," as "philosophy," as "humanities," as "ethics and values," as "comparative religions"—all to different conceptual, ideological, and social effects. Religion is an interdisciplinary field of study that is also transnational. Like religious studies, transnational studies can produce varying effects. Transnational studies have been taken up as both the cutting edge of progressive efforts to de-center European studies and as the institutionalization of neoliberal globalization that reinscribes the United States and Europe as the centers of world affairs.

Religious studies were not a central part of much university life in the United States until the 1960s, when the Supreme Court made a distinction between "teaching religion" (for example, propagating the Christian faith) and "teaching about religion." This decision allowed state-funded educational institutions to take up the study of religion, but the 1960s was also a time when many intellectuals lived in the expectation of the triumph of secularization. Women's studies in religion began at this time. Changes in geopolitics, however, particularly the Iranian Revolution in 1979 and the rise of the Christian Right in the United States, moved religious studies more to the center of academic life. These shifts were accompanied by the emergence in the academy of multiculturalism. Multiculturalism indexes, if it does not always recognize, the importance of religion as a multivalent subject.

At the beginning of the twenty-first century, religion has become a popular topic of study. The study of religion is taken up in different types of departments—anthropology, area studies, literature, history—in fact, virtually any department in the humanities and social sciences, and perhaps even the physical sciences as the religion/science dialogue deepens. This development of religion as an object of study across the university testifies to the importance of religious studies as a field, but it can also erode the contour of the conversations that constitute the field. This raises a challenge for people who are trained in religious studies to become better conversation partners with their colleagues across the disciplines in order to make work that has been done in the academic study of religion visible. Women have been leaders in this effort and continue to demonstrate through creative scholarship how it can be done more effectively.

REM, Status of Racial and Ethnic Minorities in the Profession Committee

The Status of Racial and Ethnic Minorities in the Profession Committee is part of the **AAR** structure. It recommends policies and practices to assure the full access and academic freedom of persons from racial/ethnic minority groups within the Academy. It develops programs to enhance status in the profession. REM encourages joint intellectual work among the various racial and ethnic program units, sponsors special topics forums, and holds a reception at the Annual Meeting to encourage networking and deepen relationships.

Retirement

It seems remarkable that so many women are now facing retirement in our field. This is not because women do not retire, but because a generation ago there were so few who reached that stage that it was hardly the subject of discussion. Now retirement plans and options, **emerita** status and *Festschriften* are regular parts of our concern, as they should be. Just as women are still often discriminated against in hiring, promotion, and tenure, there are problems with retirement as well.

The major stumbling block is income differential, a result of unequal pay, numerous **leaves** for family and personal reasons that fall disproportionately on women, and lack of proper financial planning (see **Money management**). All of these require correction long before retirement time.

The year before retirement is the time to be sure all such loose ends are tied up, that medical and other benefits are in order, that one uses any that will expire with the contract. It is the time to negotiate any post-employment benefits, such as an office or secretarial help. It is also the time to get one's own materials in order so that the move from an office can also be, if desired, a time to deposit things in an archive. Then enjoy the celebrations and mark the next academic year's beginning with a good vacation. After that is a fine time to begin the next career (one colleague has since become a wonderful painter, for example), take up that long-ignored manuscript again, and otherwise continue to contribute to the field from a position of wisdom.

We have seen cases where progressive women have been eased out of their jobs prematurely. Tactics include legal wrangling or veiled offers to elevate them to nonteaching status for their own good—really ways to get them out the door. Beware such tactics and use your lawyer wisely if they occur.

Reviews, book (see also Publishing)

Book reviews are a common way to analyze and communicate the content and analysis of a recently published volume. Writing them is part of the expectation of our field, a form of publication that "counts" in one's tally for tenure. In some research universities, reviews are counted in the category of **service**.

Several rules of thumb apply here. Only request and review books you are confident you can handle objectively. Choose books you deem important, not simply ones that come your way from publishers. Do not use the occasion to promote your own work. Summarize the contents, provide your opinion of its importance, and sign off. Reserve strong negative judgments for books that may be dangerous or misleading; in other cases offer careful critical comments with appreciation for what you do like. Without attention to such ground rules, reviewing can become an ugly and competitive business. There was a case of a feminist reviewing another feminist's work that led readers to conclude, "She wants her job." It was not pretty.

This is not to suggest that one ought to suspend critical judgment. To the contrary. The job of a reviewer is not to sell books, but to orient readers as to which ones are worth reading. Common courtesy and fair play go a long way toward encouraging all of us to do our best work.

When your book is reviewed, do not take comments too seriously, whether the review is good, bad, or indifferent. It is easy to feel flattered by a spate of good reviews. It is even easier to be deflated and depressed by one line in one review that strikes you as unfair or gratuitous. In any case, reviews are opinions, to which all are entitled, right or wrong as they may be!

Sabbaticals

The historical concept of a sabbatical is agricultural in nature. The land and people need rest periodically. After (usually) six years of work in an institution, you may be eligible for such a wonderful time. It is part of one's employment contract (see **Benefits; Negotiation**) and is intended as an opportunity for rest and refreshment, a chance to write and retool. Sabbatical time clocks vary by institution. Additional leaves and shorter times between sabbaticals can occasionally be negotiated at the time of a job offer.

In practice, the sabbatical (it can be a semester or a year) is typically used to write a book, or engage in some research project related to teaching. Many people like to get away physically as well as emotionally from their institution. Consider a house swap or a stint abroad. Others stay on-site but hidden away from the usual committee, classroom, and advising demands. The biggest temptation, and women are often put upon in this regard, is to do "just a little" work, attend "just one or two" meetings, serve on "just this last" dissertation defense committee. Don't do it! You will regret it. Enjoy your sabbatical; you earned it, and you will not get another one for six more years.

SBL

The Society of Biblical Literature (www.sbl-site.org) is the **AAR**'s sister organization, but its specific focus is, as the name implies, to "advance the public understanding of the Bible and Biblical scholarship." Scholars in the SBL engage biblical studies in a number of areas, including—but not limited to—literary, histori-cal, sociological, ideological, and textual studies. The SBL plays a role in developing technology, research, publishing, and commu-nication for members, and offers a large number of electronic resources. One of its most important functions is to coordinate the **SBL Annual Meeting**.

SBL, Annual Meeting

The SBL Annual Meeting shares time and space with the AAR Annual Meeting (see **AAR, Annual Meeting**), though plans are for the groups to meet separately beginning in 2008. It provides an opportunity for SBL members to share their research through scholarly presentations and seminars, to identify new publications in their field of interest through the book display, and to build networks of colleagues and **allies**. The SBL Annual Meeting format is like that of the AAR—lectures, workshops, panels, plus receptions and other social events. Job interviews are part of the mix.

SBL, International Meeting

To promote the exchange of ideas in an international forum, the SBL has a meeting outside of North America in such places as Europe and Asia. Americans are invited to attend and to give papers; be prepared for presentations in German or French. This is a good opportunity to meet international biblical scholars and to broaden your cultural horizons. The SBL **Committee on the Status of Women in the Profession** travel fund is also available for travel to this meeting if you are from a developing country, Asia, or Eastern Europe.

SBL, regional

The Society of Biblical Literature Annual Meeting can be a little overwhelming for a newcomer. Regional meetings, held in the Pacific, Pacific Northwest, Midwest, and Southeastern regions, are sometimes less threatening and more accessible. They are a good place to make your first presentation and to develop allies outside of your institutions. Some regional meetings occur with the AAR, but not all of them.

Self-care (see also Health, mental; Health, physical)

Self-care is perhaps the best encouragement we can give one another, whether graduate student or professor emerita. This means paying strict attention to physical health, emotional well-being, and spirituality, or, as one colleague put it, "Paying ourselves first."

Diet, exercise, and rest are the cornerstones of physical health. You cannot do much about your genes (yet), but you can make conscious choices about foods and drinks. Exercise is as much about time as energy. Just carving out that hour for a swim and sauna, or that half-hour brisk walk can be the difference between high energy and low, between tranquility and stress. And rest is the opposite of what most of us do most of the time. Therefore, it will take a concerted effort to get your required hours at night and to take sustained time for **vacation**. The point is that there is no formula that works for everyone, just these broad categories that you fill in according to your choices. How about serving herbal tea instead of caffeine at meetings? Why not make a date to walk and discuss a book, or conduct some committee business outside? What about canceling that extra session and sharing the information later by e-mail so everyone can take a nap? Good health is collective as well as individual business.

Academic work is largely self-generated, beyond the demands of the institution. Most of us entered the field because we had personal research interests, and staying alive in our careers depends on this self-generated activity. However, it can take over and consume too much time. Be sure to take time off, regularly. Don't work all summer. Give yourself leisure time. If you find yourself working weekends giving **guest lectures**, finishing reports, grading exams, or leading retreats, find a way to take a day off midweek. Don't fall into the trap of working seven days a week all semester long.

Emotional well-being is equally important. The conditions for it include safe and just working conditions, freedom from discrimination, and supportive colleagues. If any of those are missing, do not be surprised if you are on edge, stressed out, and heading toward burnout. Make a change! If you are responsible for those conditions for others, monitor your situation and change it unless you want to be responsible for the downfall of your colleagues.

Spirituality is a common word in our business, but ironically, one many of us pay more lip service to than actually practice. Choices will vary widely, but cultivating some spiritual practice, whether meditation, prayer, chanting, drumming, yoga, whatever chimes your bells, can be a good antidote to the stresses of professional life. Your practice may be sports—individual or team—or music, whether listening or playing. It may be theater or cooking, handcrafts or gardening. Whatever it is, make time for it, and help others make time for theirs, too, by taking self-care as seriously as you take **professional development.**

Sensitivity, religious (see also Christian hegemony)

One of the implications of increased and welcome religious pluralism in the field is the need for increased sensitivity to various religious beliefs and practices. There is no substitute for knowledge here. However, as one is acquiring it there are many opportunities to break with the convention of the larger culture and acknowledge and/or celebrate other religious expressions. For example, Pagan, Wiccan, and Goddess colleagues are religious; practices, feast days, and customs that are important to them deserve to be recognized. Jews, Hindus, Buddhists, and Muslims do not appreciate being asked how their "Christmas vacations" were. This may mean canceling classes on holidays that do not appear on most calendars and respecting dietary and ritual practices.

Let's look at one example. More sensitivity is needed regarding Muslim colleagues, whose numbers are increasing rapidly in the field. Issues related to Salat (ritual prayers), dietary matters, the fasting month of Ramadan, and Muslim women veiling show how important it is to know something about other religions to be a respectful colleague.

Many Muslims are serious about making their obligatory prayers five times a day. Non-Muslims who are planning meetings, workshops, and conferences should be generally aware of the times of prayer and allow breaks of fifteen to twenty minutes' duration to enable those who make their Salat at the scheduled times to retire for their prayers without having to leave meetings.

Regarding dietary matters, most Muslims refrain from eating pork or anything cooked with or in pork. Therefore, planners for events where food will be served should make sure that neither pork nor pork products are served to Muslim participants and that there are alternatives. As some Muslims refrain from eating non-halal meats (flesh of animals killed during ritual slaughter in which prayers are recited during the slaughter), it is always safe to serve vegetarian meals. Hindus and religious Jews will appreciate this consideration as well. Islam also prohibits alcoholic beverages, and thus there should be nonalcoholic beverage alternatives served with meals or snacks.

During the Islamic month of Ramadan, many Muslims observe the sunup to sundown thirty-day fast, during which they refrain from all food and drink, including water. At sundown, when the fast is broken, provisions should be made for those who are fasting to leave the meeting or conference so they can end their fast for the day. This is usually done by drinking water and eating a few dates. The Maghreb prayer is generally observed when the fast is broken. Therefore, time should be allotted for the light meal and the prayer. The Muslim holiday called the Eid Al Fitr occurs at the end of the month of Ramadan. Muslims celebrate the Eid with prayers at a mosque, feasting, and exchanging gifts. To be aware of this holiday in the life of a Muslim is important. Many will want to take this day off from work. In addition, if possible it is good not to schedule meetings or other events on the Eid. Muslim colleagues appreciate being greeted with "Eid-Mubarak" or "Blessed Eid."

There is a second Eid during the Muslim calendar year, the Eid Al-Adha, which comes immediately after the Hajj. This Eid is an even larger celebration for Muslims, and most Muslims will want to be off on the day of the Eid, and perhaps spend one to three days with their families and other Muslims to commemorate this sacred time.

If Muslim women in the group wear hijab (head coverings) and/or other "Islamic clothing," it is inappropriate to comment on their dress or to ask them why they wear it, even to bring the subject up unless the women raise the issue themselves. This sensitive personal and political matter requires care.

Other faiths have equally unique customs. We need to recognize the importance of understanding and respecting the range of beliefs and practices among us.

Service

Service is an amorphous category used to describe the many ways colleagues contribute to their institutions beyond the classroom and research/writing. This may include your function as the chair or member of a committee, your leadership in your department, your willingness to be the faculty sponsor for a club, your choice to live in a residence hall in a supervisory capacity. It may also include your work outside the institution in **professional associations**. It can even encompass your role as a religious professional, if that is related to your primary responsibilities as a teacher.

The caution here is twofold: First, document all of your service. It will be useful for those pretenure annual reviews (see **Evaluations, annual, pre-tenure; Tenure**). It is easy to spend a lot of time on a committee or a project and then forget about it completely when you are filling out the forms. Second, be sure to balance your service with your scholarship according to your institution's formula (see **Institutional analysis**). Because many women are used to doing three things at once, they tend to get overextended, interested in what is urgent, and run out of time for what is seemingly less pressing, namely, scholarship.

However, the tenure clock waits for no one, and before you know it, you have given generously of yourself with little to show in other areas in which you will be evaluated. There is nothing wrong with such generosity, per se. In fact, some of the very best professors find themselves in this situation, given urgent needs. However, it is not conducive to promotion and tenure, so be clear about your choices. Besides, service is the role to which most women were socialized, and it is about time we got to shape it.

Sexism

Some may suggest that a guide for women in religious studies is itself sexist. Please note, however, that sexism is not about focusing on women or men. Rather, it is a form of discrimination, like **racism**, aimed at women because of their sex/gender. Of course, postmodern deconstructions of sex/gender render it increasingly difficult to say with certainty just which persons are women. It is increasingly easy to see where and how discrimination takes place, and transgender people are very often the objects of discrimination.

The history of religious studies as a field is replete with examples of sexist behavior, including the relatively late entrance of women into the field, the continued prohibition on the full participation of women in many religious traditions (e.g., Catholic ordination), and the persistent recalcitrance on the part of some institutions to grant women full status as faculty. Lack of respect for parenting plays a role, of course. However, this guide is proof that efforts are underway to change all of that.

Staff

Staff members are the backbone of any institution. They include support workers such as administrative assistants. Also included are student personnel workers and those who provide services such as printing, janitorial services, information technology, and the like. Many of them are women, some underpaid and underappreciated but among the finest **allies** one will ever find. If we have made any advances as women in the field, surely it is because many secretaries and administrative assistants have run interference, tipped us off to institutional culture, gone out of their way to give our work priority. Justice and good sense dictate that gains for women in the field begin with staffing. We can support those gains by supporting unions and living-wage efforts as well as by simply being conscientious about working conditions.

If one has become an administrator, supervision of staff comes with the job. This means regular performance evaluations, encouragement of professional staff, and creating a humane work environment. Many administrators find personnel issues among the most difficult and headache-inducing aspects of institutional leadership. It pays to know one's human relations staff and work closely with them.

Student Advisory Liaison Group (SLG)

Students make up nearly one third of the **AAR** membership. There is a Student Director on the Board. The Student Advisory Liaison Group (www.aarweb.org/students) reports to the Student Director to assure input from a wide variety of opinions. Most major graduate institutions have a representative in the SLG. The SLG guides the AAR in designing programmatic responses to the needs of student members. In and through the SLG, the AAR alerts students to current trends in scholarship and teaching, provides them with opportunities to become acquainted with life-minded colleagues, and helps them to navigate the shoals of entrance into the profession.

Superwoman

Now, sisters, the fact is that sometimes we have to reach into our dresser drawers and pull out from under our lacy underwear that Superwoman "S." We have to slap that "S" on our chests, brand its image in our brains, jump into our shoes, and fly. We have to leap tall buildings at a single bound. Even though we may be trying to take one day at a time, several days attack us at once.

Sometimes, we have to get up before daybreak, before that first bird starts to sing her song, before the traffic sounds get heavy, while all the rest of our significant others are still in dreamland, to read the rest of that assignment, write the end of that paper, put the finishing touches on that lecture, make that agenda for the meeting we are chairing today. We often get breakfast for ourselves and the others we live with, take them where they have to go, get ourselves where we have to be, teach the class, chair the meeting, meet with the students one on one, participate in a dissertation defense, attend a community meeting, and then be witty and charming and gracious for dinner with the candidate interviewing for some position or other. Finally, we pick up the family, go home, make sure everybody else is fed and safely tucked in, read a stack of papers and then, and only then, can we take off our shoes, take the "S" off our chests, soak our Superwoman selves in a hot tub, and go to bed.

Now, sisters, this Superwoman stuff gets very old, very fast. Any woman who is in her right Superwoman mind knows that while such days happen, they cannot become an everyday thing. Limiting commitments, doing what you like to do to keep stress at bay, and asking one another for help will help.

If you have to be Superwoman every day, you have lost your Superwoman mind and you are cooperating in your own abuse. You have taken on too many commitments. It is time to rethink and tell some folk a Superwoman's "No thank you" (see **Yes and no**).

SWP, Committee on the Status of Women in the Profession

The Committee on the Status of Women in the Profession (www.aarweb.org/about/board/swp) is a standing committee of the **AAR**. It concerns itself with the range of issues facing women. The Committee recently completed work on the AAR Sexual Harassment policy and its dissemination. It has also been working on issues related to mentoring, using a variety of venues for this project, including lunch sessions at the Annual Meeting, where senior scholars meet with students to provide ideas and advice. The Committee offers a question and answer format ("Academic Abby") on its Web page, and has overseen the revision and republication of this guide, originally published by the Committee in 1992.

SWP has been making targeted efforts to coordinate women's groups, caucuses, and sections of AAR and **SBL** through contacts and sessions at the Annual Meeting. It has advertised and monitored childcare at the Annual Meeting and is involved in assessing its success. SWP has devoted its Special Topics Forums at the Annual Meeting in recent years to increasing the visibility of feminist scholars in religion in discussions of issues of religion and public policy. The Committee also functions as a "watchdog" on gender issues related to initiatives of the AAR. The group is beginning to work on issues of salary equity. Your input is welcome.

Syllabi

Designing your syllabi can be a terrific way to combat the multiple forms of oppression as well as to engage in activism. Your choice of texts and your teaching style make a difference. There are no courses on how to prepare syllabi in religious studies. The art must be developed by looking at models from courses you have taken and/or work your colleagues are willing to share. The **AAR** has a syllabi project (www.aarweb.org/syllabus). The Women's Caucus has gathered and made available syllabi over the years. The Wabash Center has posted a number of useful and creative syllabi for religious studies courses (www.wabashcenter.wabash.edu). Remember, syllabi are like other academic materials. They belong to their authors. If they are published, they can be used like any other source, that is, with proper annotation.

Teaching

Teaching has historically been the most common work of those who train at the doctoral level in religious studies. The all-important first job is usually in teaching, whether in a small institution or large, whether at the high school, undergraduate, or graduate level. Many of the issues are the same: developing courses, deciding on grading, balancing the workload, and "growing" as a teacher. Teaching is a discipline and an art form all its own, beyond the actual content of the subject at hand.

You have had by now hundreds of role models as teachers. Your own style will come in time, but at the outset, it is intimidating to think about imparting information, much less knowledge, to groups of people who may or may not want it. Your best bet is to teach from your strength insofar as your institution will permit. In fact, most first-year instructors (see **Teaching, first year**) teach what needs to be taught regardless of their area of expertise. Nevertheless, negotiate in order to teach at least one course in your main area of expertise. If you do not, you may falsely conclude that you do not care for teaching as much as you thought, when in fact what you do not like is teaching what someone else thinks students need to know.

Course development takes time. You may begin with a general concept, some bibliography and ideas, but by the second or third time through you will find, unless you are just recycling old graduate school notes, that the course will take shape in ways you never imagined at the outset. Rely on colleagues to review your work and make suggestions. Student evaluations will help, too (see **Evaluations, student**).

Grading is a vexed problem that goes along with teaching. There are many good ways to provide useful feedback to students—commentaries on their written work, individual meetings, evaluation of group and/or individual projects. However, when it comes to assigning a letter or numerical grade, comparing them with one another and/or against a norm, the fun stops, and the work begins. Some institutions have dispensed with this ritual entirely, relying instead on Pass/Fail or a similar option. At the other extreme are institutions that expect their professors to correct for the recent grade inflation by grading on a curve. There is no easy solution, especially since students tend to see grades as reward or punishment rather than as evaluative tools.

Women faculty especially are sometimes put upon by students, sometimes even by administrators (for example, when an athlete's eligibility is in question), to "adjust" grading, to put it delicately. Resist this with all your might. Despite the vagaries of grading, your integrity and power are at stake. Consult your chairperson and/or dean for advice on how to handle these delicate matters. But know that you have the final word.

Another serious concern for all teachers is how many and what sorts of courses they can or must offer. Check this carefully in your contract, as workloads vary from institution to institution. See if you are expected to teach in a January session or in the summer; if you can choose in which semester you will carry a heavier load; if you get a reduction for your administrative, committee, and/or research work. Bargain hard. Everyone else does (see **Contracts; Negotiations**).

Still another concern for those who teach is how to keep from getting stale, how to keep learning when the time demands of teaching are so enormous. This is not an easy matter, but attending the Annual Meeting of the AAR and SBL (see **AAR, Annual Meeting,** or **SBL, Annual Meeting**) or other professional meetings is a good start. So, too, is attending a summer seminar in your field, such as the offerings in bioethics or on teaching itself. Consider attending teaching workshops sponsored by your institution or places like the Wabash Center. This is especially important if you are moving into on-line teaching and need some new skills (see **On-line courses**).

Still another means of refreshment built into the system is a leave (see **Benefits, leaves**) and a sabbatical (see **Sabbaticals**), which are part of most academic contracts. In other lines of work, such as usually lower-paid nonprofit positions or in ministry, it is even more important to negotiate such benefits because burnout is a constant worry.

Teaching may be your lifetime work, or it may be something you do for a few years and then decide it is for someone else. Whatever the results, consider it one of the privileged forms of labor.

Teaching, assistantship

Being a teaching assistant (sometimes called a tutor or class assistant) puts you in an interesting position. While some professors approach it as a practicum, an opportunity for you to learn and exercise your pedagogical style, others use you to get their own work done. Your power is provisional and contingent. The expectations vary from course to course; the subject matter may be more or less familiar, making your job that much harder. The grading you do must accord with not only your own sensibility, but even more so with what the professor wants. You may have to run discussion sections only, or you may be expected to lecture several times.

Learn whether the department or the institution or both have stated guidelines about this role. Become familiar with your rights and responsibilities, and the length of duty. Your job will be infinitely easier if you can work cooperatively and communicate clearly with the professor with whom you are working. Before the course begins, schedule an appointment to discuss and clarify the expectations and terms. If you run into trouble, learn to whom you can go to ask for assistance (the chair of the department, the dean, and your advisor). This may be your only "formal" training as a teacher before you are unleashed in front of a class on your own, so take advantage of it.

Teaching, first year

Teaching is a wonderful way to share the fruits of years of study (see **Teaching**). The first year can be difficult as one learns both the ropes of an institution and a lot about oneself as a teacher. Most common mistakes to avoid include putting too much material on the syllabus or taking on too much work on top of the required course load, something to which women are especially prone, given our socialization. People of color are often pressured as well by institutions anxious to show their newfound diversity (see **Tokenism**). Taking on too much is an easy mistake to make because we all want to make a good first impression and show ourselves to be team players. But it will inevitably backfire as the constraints of time and energy make learning the difference between "yes" and "no" (see **Yes and no**) a matter of life or death. Burnout is epidemic among first-year teachers, enthusiasm notwithstanding.

Teaching portfolio

More and more institutions are now requiring a teaching portfolio as part of the essentials for tenure, and many for job applications as well. A portfolio may simply consist of the syllabi and teaching evaluations you have compiled. Portfolios can also include peer reviews and self-reflective narratives about your teaching philosophy, or a narrative analysis of your experience in an individual course, as well as samples of student work you have graded and Web sites or handouts you have created as instructional tools. Include a list of workshops or seminars on teaching in which you have participated. Keep an updated annotated bibliography of books that you have read to help you improve your teaching skills. Add copies of notes sent by grateful students or colleagues. In short, document your growth and development as a teacher. Be sure that you know what your institution requires, and prepare accordingly.

Tenure

Tenure is that much-disputed custom of granting lifelong employment to those members of a faculty or organization who meet the requirements of that institution. The tenure system is intended to protect academic freedom. It is a slippery problem, at the same time guaranteeing creative people a place to work without fear of firing, and keeping the proverbial deadwood in place for years on end. Tenure is the "logical" outcome of a traditional academic career, from secondary and undergraduate levels through the doctorate, to the first job and then tenure.

Relatively few women are fully tenured faculty members. The process involves an exhausting compilation of one's work, letters of reference from outside reviewers, recommendations from one's department, assessment by one's peers, student evaluations, and usually a decision by a Rank and Tenure Committee that is then presented to the institution's highest board or committee, or perhaps to the president, for final action.

Preparing for tenure is very much like preparing for an annual review (see **Evaluations, annual, pretenure**). Be sure to file all relevant papers—records of classes taught, lectures given, service to the institution, outside service, publications, and the like. **Networking** within your institution will help you gauge realistically where you stand. Networking beyond your institution will give you a good list of people who could write to vouch for your work, although institutions prefer that outside reviews come from people in your field who know your work but with whom you are not acquainted. Letters of support can come from anyone.

Despite the most careful preparation, the most deserving candidates sometimes do not get tenure. For example, some elite universities are known for turning down some of the very best scholars (who often go on to get MacArthur "genius" awards and/or tenured positions in other institutions). One question is whether it is better to try for tenure and be turned down, or to accept the handwriting on the wall if it is clear you will not get it. Another question is how quickly you need to look for another job if you will not try for tenure. Still another question is how to appeal negative tenure decisions. All of these issues vary according to institutions. They require your best consultation with trusted colleagues, and a good employment lawyer. Remember that tenure is not the be-all and end-all of your career. Many of our best and brightest will have several careers, perhaps none of them tenured jobs.

Once you have tenure, you may discover that it is not a panacea (see **Midcareer issues**). Nonetheless, it will give you some leverage when you look for another job, as well as peace of mind where you are. Congratulations, and use your tenured position to make change!

Tokenism (see also Racism; Sexism)

Tokenism exists in all the likely places where racism, sexism, and other forms of discrimination lurk. It is the practice, however unconscious, of choosing (read: using) people to create the appearance of diversity when indeed the dynamics of power have not changed one whit. For example, hiring one person of color in an academic department of twenty is tokenism.

Women, especially women of color, know a lot about it. We are becoming increasingly savvy about how to use it to our advantage, for example, insisting that no one woman will join an all-male department, that our subspecialty be integrated into the curriculum rather than the subject of an annual invited lecture. Religious studies remain fraught with tokenism on many levels, a vestige of liberalism that we are in the process of eradicating.

Travel

Work-related travel is slightly more complicated than getting from here to there. It involves cost, choices, convenience, safety, and the unexpected. Whether for a job interview, a professional meeting, a guest lectureship (see **Guest lectures**), research, or just plain vacation, getting there is half the fun for women on the road.

Who pays for the travel is the first point to ascertain. Be clear with the host institution or your own department as to which of them is paying, and to the rules governing travel. Stick to those rules. They may reimburse your initial first-class ticket without dispute, but you can be sure it will be your last. Keep all receipts for reimbursement or do not expect to see your money again. Institutions have accountants, and, post-Enron, they rule. If you are invited to use the institution's travel agency, jump at the chance. It will save you hours on the Internet and will probably mean you will not have to expend your money to be reimbursed. If it is a financial hardship for you to pay for the ticket and wait for what can be an eternity for a department to reimburse you, do not be afraid to say so and get your money up-front, or ask them to make the arrangements and send you the ticket.

Travelers have many choices—plane, train, car, bus, bike, walking. Be sure to factor *all* of the time involved before you decide. For example, flying can take more time than taking the train when you figure in the airport waiting time and ground transportation. Bus or subway will usually be cheaper than a cab and can sometimes be faster. Your time is worth money when it comes to travel. Consider it when you decide on the cheaper ticket with a stop versus the nonstop that costs a bit more. Likewise, think seriously if you really want to drive a long distance or whether your time is better spent working on a plane or train.

If you travel a lot—your first book has really become a best seller and you are in demand for lectures everywhere (see **Lecture circuit**)—consider investing in an airline club. While seemingly elitist, these havens in crowded airports can be a necessary luxury (also tax deductible in some cases) for sanity and productivity on the road. Alternatively, consider the annual fee for a platinum level credit card, such as American Express, which offers free club memberships, on the day of travel, for several airlines and Amtrak.

Safety is a major issue, not simply post–September 11, but especially for women who travel alone. Would that it were otherwise, but always leave your destination phone number with a friend, family member, or with someone in your office. Get in the habit of calling someone when you arrive so at least one person knows where you are. Consider a cell phone as a steady companion, especially if you travel long distances. Choose hotel floors with care, balancing the risk of high floors against the possibility of ground floor problems. Your room number should be confidential. Be sure your room key does not have the number written on it, in case you lose it. Ask for another room if the room clerk inadvertently broadcasts it in the lobby!

There is no preparation for the unexpected, but it will happen. Common sense dictates avoiding the last flight of the night, which is cancelled more often than an earlier one. Know your options for earlier flights. Sometimes business finishes early and you can get home what will seem like a whole day early even if it is just a matter of hours. Tuck away a traveler's check or two for a rainy day on the road when the ATM is out of commission. Maps are printed for a reason. Having one and knowing how to read it will save enormous time. Travel as light as possible; you can usually buy what you need but you cannot ditch extra weight as easily en route. Enjoy your travels.

Undergraduates

So you've decided to major in religion. That is great. A thousand welcomes! Studying religion affords you the opportunity to range broadly, to read comparatively, to engage in interdisciplinary work, or to focus on a specific interest. Further, a major in religion stands you in good stead in learning how to think alongside social scientists and those in the humanities. You may select your minor(s) with that in mind.

Contrary to public opinion, there are many things one can "do" with a major in religion, though in fact it needs no such justification. Going to seminary or graduate school, choosing a religious vocation of some sort, are only a few options. Increasingly, journalists, social workers, doctors, ethicists, politicians, and those in the business and economic sector recognize the validity of attending to religion as an element of human activity and influence.

The usual advice applies: Make sure your advisor is available to help you and to read your work, especially if you write a senior thesis. Do not neglect the crossdisciplinary resources available to help you in your studies, not least of which may be women's studies. Enjoy your major and give it your own stamp. We all stand to benefit.

Unions

Faculties at many state institutions, and increasingly at some private schools, are developing unions. They can be very useful for dealing with workplace issues, so much so that, if your institution does not have one, be sure you know how such issues are handled. Faculty unions help create equity and fight for benefits like making sure the institution pays for contraceptive coverage in the prescription drug program (see **Institutional analysis**).

Increasingly, graduate students are organizing themselves into graduate student unions. While the particularities of the situation that graduate students face differ in some ways from what clerical or autoworkers face, many issues remain the same.

Equity, benefits, workload, and the ability to negotiate the terms of employment have often been denied to graduate students, or been seriously neglected. Some institutions have argued that what graduate students do when they serve as teachers, preceptors, research assistants, teaching assistants, and graders is not work, per se, but pedagogical practice or "good experience." Institutions have argued that unionization threatens the "unique" relationship of student/teacher or mentor/mentee. Such rhetoric can disguise abuses.

The issues are broad and touch on all aspects of graduate student life, from partner benefits to expectations of teaching loads to stipends. Further, the issues of unionization differ from campus to campus. It behooves you to learn about the place, or lack, of the graduate student union in the wider context of institutional practice and culture in the institution that you are planning to attend.

Vacation

Time for rest and renewal is a right, not a privilege, though you would never know it by the average time U.S. workers get off. Indeed, the United States has one of the stingiest vacation deals in the world. Contrast our measly two weeks (if that) with the six weeks or more many Europeans (until recently) expect in their workplace. In academia, the summer can seem like vacation time when in fact it is the only time to prepare courses, do academic writing, and get caught up on correspondence. In cognate fields like the nonprofit sector or publishing, a summer off is unheard of, so this is a serious issue for activism.

For women, the only advice is take vacation time when you can get it, as often as you can, and without guilt. Did you ever meet a woman who felt she had had too much vacation? Try being the first, as you will be a pioneer in an area where we need to help one another do **self-care**. Besides, there are so many great vacation options, including house swaps. One smart group of women in our field rents a house on Martha's Vineyard every year for several fun-filled weeks. One feminist religious nonprofit organization always, but always, closes for the month of August.

Such routinized approaches to vacation assure that we look forward to, take, and enjoy them.

Vocation

A vocation is slightly different from a job or a career. A vocation is a calling. It is a belief, a kind of knowing that you are doing that which virtually no one else but you in the whole of creation could or should be doing right now. Calling work in religion a vocation is no excuse to accept less pay and more work. Beware the spiritualization of such concepts, at the same time that you choose to honor them.

Web page, personal

Many institutions are now putting information about faculty on the school's Web page. Some encourage each faculty member to have a personal Web page that students can use to access information about the teacher and her/his courses. This page can be used for a number of informational aids including posting a syllabus before class actually starts, listing further reading for the class topic, providing access to links to Web pages that are relevant to the class topic, posting instructions for assignments, and/or making personal information about yourself available (such as a CV or a list of classes taught).

If you are given this opportunity, think very seriously about constructing a page. There are advantages and disadvantages. Advantages include the fact that students like to have this information available to them. You can have information in one easily accessible site and this may even reduce some use of paper. Students do not always have to contact you directly to get certain questions answered. Former students can check in to see what you are suggesting now as good reading material. Disadvantages include the fact that there is a time commitment involved in constructing and maintaining a personal Web page. Students who get used to using the Web page expect to have the information up earlier than you may be able to get to it. Anything you post is available to the general public unless you are able to have restricted access with password protection.

Personal Web pages are the wave of the future, along with such instructional aids as Blackboard. They save time when people ask for a bio or photo. Be careful about intellectual property concerns and, as always, consult a legal expert on matters in question.

Womanist

African American women concerned with the well-being of women and the whole community, using their experiences and insights to create theoretical as well as practical strategies for change, call their work "womanist." The term originated in the writings of Alice Walker, who described "womanish" practices as those that aided the survival of black women and their dependent children. In religious studies, womanist work has contributed mightily to the many women's efforts to bring about equality and justice.

Women's Caucus

The Women's Caucus in Religious Studies began more than twenty-five years ago. A group of enterprising women, students as well as faculty, realized that in order to survive the sea of suits that was the AAR/SBL Annual Meetings in those days, they would have to bond. They did so with enormous success, meeting yearly to bring constant critical attention to the needs and contributions of women in the field. They raised the need for childcare at the Annual Meeting and pushed behind the scenes for the election of the first women presidents in each society. The Caucus was the forerunner to the now several academic sections that deal with women-focused content.

The Caucus sponsors a premeeting seminar geared to student and newer members, as well as a **networking** reception. Dues are modest and on a sliding scale. Leadership rotates. Feel free to get involved. The Caucus needs you and you need the Caucus.

Women's studies

Women's studies has emerged as a new field of study, in some instances a new program or department, in the past twenty years. It is still young and changing; indeed, in many instances it has been subject to such intense backlash that it is out of existence already, morphed into gender studies or in some other way forced to back away from an explicit commitment to women's well-being. Women's studies acts as a border field, and lends itself readily to interdisciplinary learning. Women's studies courses treat issues from a perspective that is implicitly or explicitly feminist, multicultural, and respectful of difference.

In religious studies feminist, womanist, *mujerista,* Asian, Native American, and other explicitly women-centered forms of analysis and discourse constitute a rich and powerful example of women's studies. However, in many institutions those gains are eroding. Those who teach and study religion will find many areas of shared interest. Getting involved in women's studies will allow for hybridization, team teaching, and creative approaches to standard material.

A common question from doctoral students is whether they should risk working in women's studies. Or, perhaps, should they do a "straight" dissertation and then concern themselves with women's issues later? This is a hard call, given the virulent pressure on women to conform to patriarchal ways. If we are to have another generation of scholars and activists trained in women's studies in religion, it is imperative that our best and brightest do their work where it matters most.

Xenophobia

The United States of America understands itself as a country of immigrants and is generally open toward newcomers. However, it is also racist toward immigrants of color, people from developing countries, and Muslims (or anybody who looks Muslim, such as Sikhs), especially post–September 11.

This is particularly troubling if your university or institution is located somewhere that white, Christian norms rule unbroken.

You will need the active support of your colleagues on campus to navigate potentially hostile environments of the town and county in which you are located. Make sure to ask about safe neighborhoods, Klan and white supremacist militia activities in the area, whether to list your telephone number, whether to get a post office box. Your social life may depend almost entirely on contacts with your colleagues. You may have to weather a very lonely and isolating period (see **Isolation, cultural and religious**) until you find your people.

Xenophobia may also color your interactions on campus with colleagues, staff, and students. Cultural, religious, and racial stereotypes may influence how people perceive you. Such biases can easily find their way into student teaching evaluations, merit reviews, and fuzzy evaluation categories like "collegiality." Try to become aware of these stereotypes and learn to anticipate and manipulate them in your favor. It is a challenge for which the onus is really on those who occupy the privileged place (see **Privilege**).

Yes and no

The difference between these simple words is something that takes many women a lifetime to learn. We need to help each other say "no" to the myriad invitations we receive that may distract us from our dissertations, books, recreation, or study. We need to be equally helpful in saying "yes" to one another in those instances where a collaborative effort is proposed, a little extra is asked of us, or an opportunity too good to pass up is in the balance. Knowing when to say "yes" and when to say "no" can be the difference between a stressful, unsuccessful career in religious studies and a fruitful, enjoyable one.

Zeitgeist

The Zeitgeist, that is, the spirit or attitude of a particular time, is changing in religious studies. Women, people of color, people from the wide range of religious traditions other than Christianity, are creating a new gestalt in religious studies that corresponds more closely with the religious reality of an increasingly globalized world. You are part of it, and you give it new shape. Thank you.

Appendices

Appendix I

American Academy of Religion Sexual Harassment Policy

At its November 1996 meeting the AAR Board of Directors adopted a policy condemning sexual harassment in academic settings. Building upon the Equal Employment Opportunity Commission's definition of sexual harassment, the statement is designed to elevate members' awareness of the range of behaviors that can be described as sexual harassment, and to articulate the AAR's own commitment to ensuring that its own activities and operations are free from the pernicious effects of such behavior.

The AAR's Status of Women in the Profession Committee drafted the statement, which also draws from statements by a number of other learned societies that have established similar policies. When asked why it was important for the AAR to put forward such a statement, Emilie Townes, a former chair of the AAR's Committee on the Status of Women in the Profession, said "it is important to match the high standards the American Academy of Religion has for scholarship and research with a policy that calls forth the best of each of us professionally and interpersonally. It is important for AAR to make a clear and unambiguous statement against sexual harassment and provide all of the membership of the Academy resources for understanding and combating such dehumanizing behavior."

Sexual Harassment Policy for the American Academy of Religion

Introduction

The American Academy of Religion is committed to fostering and maintaining an environment of rigorous learning, research, and teaching in the field of religion. This environment must be free of sexual harassment. Sexual harassment is a discriminatory practice which is unethical, unprofessional, and threatening to intellectual freedom. It usually involves persons of unequal power, authority, or influence but can occur between persons of the same status.

Sexual harassment is illegal under Title VII of the 1980 Civil Rights Act and Title IX of the 1972 Educational Amendments. Sexual harassment is a gross violation of professional ethics comparable to plagiarism or falsification of research. It should be regarded and treated as such by members of the Academy. The policy of the American Academy of Religion is to condemn sexual harassment. Members of the Academy are encouraged to file complaints about sexual harassment with the appropriate administrative office of the institution where the harasser is employed or where he or she is enrolled, or with appropriate law enforcement authorities.

Background

The Equal Employment Opportunity Commission (EEOC) of the United States Government defines sexual harassment in the workplace or in the academic setting as:

"The use of one's authority or power, either explicitly or implicitly, to coerce another into unwanted sexual relations or to punish another for his or her refusal; or the creation of an intimidating, hostile or offensive working environment through verbal or physical conduct of a sexual nature."

Having friendships with students is common for teachers. It is also possible that teachers will experience attraction to students and experience students' sexual attraction to them. This cuts across gender and sexual orientation. Because of the inherent power differential between teacher and student, it is imperative that members of the Academy maintain the integrity of an environment that is not coercive, intimidating, hostile, or offensive.

The work of the Academy is best carried out in an atmosphere that fosters collegiality and mentoring. Sexual harassment can destroy or undermine this relationship. The impact of this on the life and future of the Academy cannot be belittled or ignored.

When our actions are in violation of the dignity and integrity of another person, these actions are a profound violation of professional and human relationships. These are violations because they are exploitative and abusive.

Descriptions

Sexual harassment includes all behavior that prevents or impairs an individual's full enjoyment of educational or workplace rights, benefits, environments, or opportunities. These behaviors include but are not limited to:

1. sexist remarks, jokes, or behavior
2. unwelcome sexual advances, including unwanted touching
3. request for sexual favors
4. sexual assault, including attempted or completed physical sexual assault
5. the use of professional authority to inappropriately draw attention to the gender, sexuality or sexual orientation of an employee, colleague, or student
6. insults, including lewd remarks or conduct
7. visual displays of degrading sexual images or pornography
8. pressure to accept unwelcome social invitations

Sexual harassment occurs from these behaviors and other verbal or physical conduct of a sexual nature when any or all of the following conditions apply:

1. Submission to or rejection of such conduct by an individual is used, implicitly or explicitly, as a basis for employment decisions or academic decisions affecting such individuals; or
2. Such conduct has the purpose or effect of unreasonably interfering with an individual's work or academic performance or creating an intimidating, hostile, or offensive working or academic environment.

Such an atmosphere cannot and does not foster intellectual rigor or valuable, trusting human relationships. Both are necessary ingredients for good scholarship and professional excellence.

The impact on the victim of sexual harassment can be profound. Studies on the effect of sexual harassment reveal disturbing consequences, such as loss of self-confidence, decline in academic performance, and inhibited forms of professional interaction. Sexual harassment has no place in the American Academy of Religion at any organizational level—formal or informal. It is behavior that we must seek to identify and eradicate.

Resources

Baridan, Andrea P., Working Together: The New Rules and Realities for Managing Men and Women At Work. New York: McGraw-Hill, 1994.

Bouchad, Elizabeth, Everything You Need to Know About Sexual Harassment. New York: Rosen Publishing Group, 1990.

Grauerholz, Elizabeth, ed., Sexual Coercion: A Sourcebook on Its Nature, Causes, and Prevention. Lexington, MA: Lexington Books, 1991.

Paludi, Michele A., Ivory Power: Sexual Harassment on Campus. Albany: State University of New York, 1990.

Sexual Harassment on the Job: A Guide for Employers. Washington, DC: U.S. Commission on Civil Rights, 1982.

Available at http://www.aarweb.org/about/board/ resolutions/sh.asp.

By permission of the American Academy of Religion (www.aarweb.org).

Appendix II

American Academy of Religion Sexual Harassment Grievance Procedure

At its November 1996 meeting, the AAR Board of Directors adopted a policy condemning sexual harassment in academic settings. At its April 1998 meeting, the Board approved a Sexual Harassment Grievance Procedure.

The AAR's Status of Women in the Profession Committee formulated the procedure. In announcing the procedure for the membership, Emilie Townes, chair of the Committee, said, "The Sexual Harassment Policy of the American Academy of Religion is designed to foster and maintain an environment of rigorous scholarship and professional excellence. Such an environment cannot be achieved when sexual harassment is present. The Policy is a clear and unambiguous statement against sexual harassment and it also provides resources for understanding and combating unprofessional and dehumanizing conduct. The Sexual Harassment Grievance Procedure provides an equitable mechanism to implement the sexual harassment policy of AAR. The Procedure seeks to provide confidentiality and a fair procedure for all parties involved. It, along with the Sexual Harassment Policy, provides the membership of AAR with a clear statement concerning sexual harassment, resources that are educational in helping combat it, and a procedure for the Academy to address any cases that may arise from official activities of AAR. Together, the Policy and Grievance Procedure, help AAR create and maintain the highest standards of professional conduct and academic freedom in our mutual pursuit of excellence in scholarship."

Introduction

The Grievance Committee has primary responsibility for interpretation of the AAR Sexual Harassment Policy, for the evaluation of complaints brought under it, and for recommendations to the Board of Directors pertinent to such complaints. The Grievance Committee will review those cases arising out of formally constituted activities of the AAR and for which it is the most appropriate forum, if it considers the matter important to the profession, and if it deems the AAR's resources to be adequate to yield a fair judgment. The Grievance Committee will not accept complaints it deems capricious or principally vindictive, and, except in unusual circumstances, it will not pursue a case while the dispute is pending in another forum. Review of a complaint by the Grievance Committee should not be regarded as substitute for legal action.

Composition of the Grievance Committee

The Grievance Committee should have direct lines of accountability to the AAR Board of Directors and the membership. It should be representative of the diversity of the members of AAR and avoid unnecessary bureaucratization.

1. President
2. President Elect
3. Vice President
4. SWP Chair
5. Secretary or Student Director in cases that involve a student

The Executive Director serves as the investigating officer.

No person who has been accused in the complaint will participate in the investigation or resolution of the complaint.

1. If any member of the Grievance Committee is named in the complaint, he or she is replaced by an appointment from the President. If the President is named in the complaint, the President Elect appoints a replacement for the President.
2. If someone comes forward with a complaint against the Executive Director, that complaint should be directed to the AAR President who will replace the Executive Director in her/his role as investigator and/or member of the Grievance Committee.

Complaint Procedure

1. The complainant should present the complaint as promptly as possible with the Executive Director after the alleged harassment occurs. Failure to present a complaint promptly may preclude recourse to legal procedures beyond the jurisdiction of the AAR should the complainant decide to pursue such action at a later date.

   • The initial discussion between the complainant and the Executive Director should be kept confidential, with no written record.

   • The Executive Director has the authority to make a good faith effort to resolve the complaint through informal processes at this stage. There may be cases that can be resolved through efforts of mediation and for which the alleged offender apologizes for her/his actions.

   • If the complainant, after the initial discussion with the Executive Director, decides to proceed, the complainant should submit a written statement to the Executive Director.

   • The Executive Director then informs the alleged offender of the allegation and of the identity of the complainant in writing. A copy of this is sent to the complainant. Efforts should be made to protect the complainant from retaliatory action by the person(s) named in the complaint.

2. The Executive Director alerts the Grievance Committee that a complaint has been filed and promptly calls a meeting of the Committee. Each member of the Committee shall receive a copy of the written statement of the complaint.

3. The Grievance Committee may vote to either accept the complaint for full review or decline to consider the complaint. The Grievance Committee will base its decision on its judgment of its capacity to handle the matter in light of its resources and competence; the seriousness of the complaint; the degree to which the complaint alleges specific violations of the AAR Sexual Harassment Policy; the likelihood that the AAR will be able to make a positive contribution to resolving the problem; the availability of a more suitable forum, such as a university grievance procedure or the AAUP. If the Committee decides to decline consideration of the complaint, it will submit an explanation in writing to the complainant and the alleged offender.

4. The Executive Director will gather all facts pertinent to the allegations of the complaint.

   - The investigation will be conducted promptly and objectively.
   - The investigation will include statements by the complainant(s), person(s) accused, and others as necessary.

5. The Grievance Committee has the following options:

   - If the Committee concludes that on the basis of the investigation insufficient evidence of harassment exists to warrant any action, may close the investigation and so notify the complainant and alleged offender in writing.
   - If the Committee concludes on the basis of the investigation that sexual harassment has occurred the following disciplinary actions may be taken:

   i. Letter of reprimand to the offender.

   ii. Training and education regarding sexual harassment and appropriate and inappropriate behaviors with documentation to the Committee that this training has been completed. Failure to comply may result in the rescinding of membership.

   iii. Rescinding of membership in the AAR for a duration deemed appropriate by the committee.

   iv. Repeat offenders are subject only to disciplinary action iii.

6. Every effort will be made to maintain confidentiality throughout the process, but total confidentiality cannot be guaranteed. The Grievance Committee will protect the privacy of both the complainant and persons accused in every way possible during the process of the complaint and thereafter.

7. The AAR prohibits any form of retaliation against any member or employee of AAR filing a complaint against a member. Any retaliatory action of any kind taken against a complainant under this procedure is prohibited and will be the basis for a separate complaint subject to disciplinary action by the Grievance Committee.

8. If, after investigating a complaint the Grievance Committee determines that a complainant knowingly made a false complaint or knowingly provided false information regarding a complaint, the Committee may decide that disciplinary actions, as above, are warranted.

9. The decision of the Grievance Committee is final.

Available at http://www.aarweb.org/about/board/ resolutions/shg.asp.

By permission of the American Academy of Religion (www.aarweb.org).

Appendix III

Society of Biblical Literature (SBL) Ethics Statement

The members of the SBL constitute a community of scholars dedicated to promoting the critical investigation of biblical literature, together with other related literature, by the exchange of scholarly research both in published form and in public forum. While freedom of inquiry is at the heart of this enterprise, such freedom carries with it the responsibility of professional conduct. As a learned society, the SBL assumes professional conduct of its members as they exchange scholarly research in SBL publications or at SBL annual, regional, or committee meetings wherever they are held. Professional conduct includes, but is not limited to, conduct which is based on respect for others and which does not in any way exploit power and/or status differences such as those that exist between faculty and students or between senior and junior scholars. Professional conduct is conduct free of sexual or any other form of harassment and discrimination.

Discrimination means a distinction, whether intentional or not, relating to personal characteristics of an individual or group, which has the effect of imposing burdens, obligations, or disadvantages on such individual or group not imposed on others; or which withholds or limits access to opportunities, benefits and advantages available to other members of the SBL.

Harassment means vexatious comment or conduct in relation to a person or group of persons which has the effect or purpose of creating a hostile or intimidating environment when such treatment abuses the power that one person holds over another or misuses authority; or such treatment has the effect or purpose of offending or demeaning a person or group of persons on the basis of race, ancestry, place of origin, color, ethnic group, citizenship, sex, sexual orientation, disability, creed, age, or marital/family status. Sexual harassment includes any unwanted sexual attention or behavior by a person who knows or ought reasonably to know that such conduct is unwanted; or any implied or expressed promise of reward for complying with a sexually orientated request; or any implied or expressed threat of reprisal, in any form either of actual reprisal or the denial of opportunity for the refusal to comply with a sexually orientated request; or any inappropriate verbal or physical conduct that has a focus on sexuality or sexual identity in what reasonably may be perceived as a hostile or intimidating environment. The SBL is committed to the creation and maintenance of a discrimination- and harassment-free environment in all of its sanctioned activities. The professional conduct of all members who participate in such activities is essential to the achievement of this standard.

By permission of the Society of Biblical Literature, "SBL Statement of Ethics," Available at http://www.sbl-site.org/EIS/ EIS_EISA+TheAnnualMeeting.aspx.

Appendix IV

Making Your Presentations Disability Friendly

Accessible Facilities

- Clear aisles of any obstacles to individuals with mobility impairments.

- Remove chairs at the end of rows for those using wheelchairs, scooters, or guide dogs so they are not forced to sit in the front, back, or in an aisle.

- Seating should be made available in the front row for those who use assistive listening devices, who use sign language interpreters, or who lip-read.

- If it is possible to regulate the lighting, lights should be adjusted to meet the individual needs of those with visual impairments. (Note: This could mean dimming lights as well as raising them depending on the nature of the impairment.)

- Speakers and interpreters should be well lit for attendees who read lips or use sign language.

Accessible Materials

- Provide copies of all handouts in 16–18 point font.

- Provide copies of handouts in electronic format (e.g. .txt, .rtf, or .doc).

- Provide hard copies of overheads and PowerPoint presentations.

- Read and describe overheads and PowerPoint for those with visual or learning disabilities.

- Allow time for location and review when referring to visual materials.

Accessible Presentations

- Speak clearly and distinctly with a rate of speed and volume usually considered appropriate for public speaking.
- Use a microphone when provided. Microphones should be held at a distance from the mouth such that it will pick up your voice while not muffling the sound.
- Repeat all questions and comments from the audience into the microphone.
- Presenters should speak one at a time.
- Do not turn away from the audience while you are speaking.
- Speakers should identify who they are for those with visual impairments.
- Do not communicate key information solely in gesture or visual reference.
- Turn off overhead projectors and other equipment when not in use to decrease distracting noises.
- Eye contact and comments should be directed to the person who is deaf and not to the sign language interpreter.
- Comments should be addressed directly to participants with disabilities and not to their companions.
- Allow sessions not being taped through the taping service to be taped by participants with disabilities.
- Allow ample time for questions and answers.

Available at www.aarweb.org/other/accessibility/presentations.asp.
By permission of the American Academy of Religion.

Bibliography

Caplan, Paula J. *Lifting a Ton of Feathers: A Woman's Guide to Surviving in the Academic World*. Toronto: University of Toronto Press, 1993.

Gustafson, Melanie S. *Becoming a Historian: A Survival Guide*. Washington, DC: Committee on Women Historians and the American Historical Association, 2001.

Heiberger, Mary Morris and Julia Miller Vick. *The Academic Job Search Handbook* (3rd edition). Philadelphia: University of Pennsylvania, 2001.

Hornig, Lilli, ed. *Equal Rites, Unequal Outcomes: Women in American Research Universities*. New York: Kluwer Academic/Plenum Publishers, 2003.

Lucas, Christopher J. and John W. Murray, Jr. *New Faculty: A Practical Guide for Academic Beginners*. New York: Palgrave, 2002.

Menges, Robert J. and Associates. *Faculty In New Jobs: A Guide to Settling In, Becoming Established, and Building Institutional Support*. San Francisco: Jossey-Bass Publishers, 1999.

Miles, Margaret R. "Institutional Pilgrims: The Task of Women Who Are Both Scholar and Administrator is a Crucial One," *Harvard Divinity Bulletin* 29, no. 2 (2000): 8–9.

Toth, Emily. *Ms. Mentor's Impeccable Advice for Women in Academia*. Philadelphia: University of Pennsylvania Press, 1997.

Williams, Kathy. "Presenting for the First Time at the Annual Meeting: A Graduate Student Shares Her Experience," *Religious Studies News* 17, no. 2 (March 2000): 18.

About the Writers

REBECCA T. ALPERT is Associate Professor of Religion and Women's Studies at Temple University and Chair of the Department of Religion. She was ordained as a rabbi at the Reconstructionist Rabbinical College. She is author of *Like Bread on the Seder Plate: Jewish Lesbians and the Transformation of Tradition* (Columbia University Press, 1997), editor of *Voices of the Religious Left: A Contemporary Sourcebook* (Temple University Press, 2000), and coeditor (with Sue Elwell and Shirley Idelson) of *Lesbian Rabbis: The First Generation* (Rutgers University Press, 2001). She chairs the Committee on the Status of Women in the Profession of the American Academy of Religion.

KAREN BAKER-FLETCHER is Associate Professor of Systematic Theology at Perkins School of Theology at Southern Methodist University. She taught at Claremont School of Theology. She is the author of *Sisters of Dust, Sisters of Spirit: A Creation-Centered Womanist Spirituality* (Augsburg Fortress, 1998) and *My Sister, My Brother: Womanist and Xodus God-Talk* with Garth Kasimu Baker-Fletcher (Augsburg Fortress, 1998).

VALERIE ELVERTON DIXON is Assistant Professor of Christian Ethics at Andover Newton Theological School in Newton Center, Massachusetts. She taught for four years at United Theological Seminary in Dayton, Ohio. Her dissertation was entitled "Reading the Clarence Thomas Hearings: Ideology, Context, Discourse and Meaning."

MARY E. HUNT is the co-founder and co-director of the Women's Alliance for Theology, Ethics and Ritual (WATER), a nonprofit educational center in Silver Spring, Maryland. She has taught at Pacific School of Religion and Iliff School of Theology. Among her publications are *Fierce Tenderness: A Feminist Theology of*

Friendship (Crossroad, 1991), and *Good Sex: Feminist Perspectives from the World's Religions,* coedited with Patricia Beattie Jung and Radhika Balakrishnan (Rutgers University Press, 2001).

JANET R. JAKOBSEN is Director of the Center for Research on Women and an Associate Professor of Women's Studies at Barnard College. She was Associate Professor of Women's Studies and Religious Studies at the University of Arizona. She is the author of *Working Alliances and the Politics of Difference: Diversity and Feminist Ethics* (Indiana University Press, 1998), and coauthor (with Ann Pellegrini) of *Love the Sin: Sexual Regulation and the Limits of Religious Tolerance* (New York University Press, 2002).

ROSAMOND CARY RODMAN is Assistant Professor of Biblical Studies at Macalester College in St. Paul, Minnesota. She received her Ph.D. in 2004 from Columbia University. Her dissertation was entitled "Reclaiming Opacity: Harlem, Heaven's Gate, and John's Gospel," and she has worked as an editorial assistant on several books.

KATHARINA VON KELLENBACH is Associate Professor of Religious Studies and Chair of the Department of Philosophy and Religious Studies at St. Mary's College of Maryland. She is a native of West Germany and received her Ph.D. from Temple University in Philadelphia. She is the author of *Anti-Judaism in Feminist Religious Writings* (Scholars Press, 1994). She is coeditor with Björn Krondorfer and Norbert Reck of *Von Gott Reden im Land der Täter: Theologische Stimmen der dritten Generation nach der Shoah* (Wissenschaftliche Buchgesellschaft, 2001) and coeditor with Susanne Scholz of *Zwischen-Räume: Deutsche Feministische Theologinnen im Ausland* (LIT Verlag, 2000).

Index

Main entries in *bold italics*

158

Index

Our Landed Heritage

The Public Domain, 1776-1936

ROY M. ROBBINS

UNIVERSITY OF NEBRASKA PRESS · Lincoln · 1962

First Bison Book printing March, 1962
Second Bison Book printing December, 1964

Bison Book edition reprinted from the Princeton University
Press edition.

To My Wife

PREFACE

Wiᴛʜ the executive withdrawals of all public lands from private entry in 1935, the opportunity for individual settlement on the public domain officially came to an end. For the future there remained only the consideration of the permanent national domain—national parks, forest reserves, game reserves, grazing and mineral lands. The time is thus ripe for a synthesis on the history of the public lands of the United States.

This volume presents perhaps the first attempt to integrate American land history with the other forces that have shaped our civilization. It is not all political, economic and legal; considerable social history is inextricably bound up with public land settlement, which helps to make the whole story livelier and more interesting. This volume therefore constitutes not only a study in history and in public administration, but also a study in American democracy. Hence it is hoped that the research in this book will help to sustain within certain stipulated limitations that portion of Frederick Jackson Turner's frontier hypothesis as stated in 1903:

"Whenever social conditions tended to crystallize in the East, whenever capital tended to press upon labor or political restraints to impede the freedom of the mass, there was this gate of escape to the free conditions of the frontier. These free lands promoted individualism, economic equality, freedom to rise, democracy. . . . In a word then, free lands meant free opportunities."[1]

The author is deeply indebted to the Social Science Research Council for a grant-in-aid awarded in 1937 for the purpose of making a study of public reaction to the conservation movement in the Rocky Mountain and Pacific Coast regions during the period, 1880 to 1920. Grateful acknowledgment is also made for the considerate assistance of the staffs of the following libraries: the Wisconsin State Historical Society Library, the Western Reserve Historical Society Library, the Library of Congress, the University of Washington Library, the Seattle Public Library, the Bancroft Library of the University of California, and the

[1] See Turner's essay, "Contributions of the West to American Democracy," in his *Frontier in American History* (New York, 1920), 244.

Huntington Library not to mention numerous other libraries where less extensive research was carried on. The author also acknowledges with appreciation the helpful assistance of the staffs of the General Land Office in Washington, D.C., and of the many newspaper offices whose files were so generously opened to him.

Particular thanks are due to Elbert J. Benton, Dean of the Graduate School of Western Reserve University; John D. Hicks, professor of history, University of Wisconsin; Bertha E. Josephson, editorial associate of the *Mississippi Valley Historical Review*; and my father-in-law, Herbert H. Gowen, professor of oriental studies, University of Washington, all of whom carefully read the text and made critical comments and suggestions. A special debt of gratitude is also owed to a number of graduate students—too numerous to mention individually—who, enrolled in the author's seminars during summer sessions at the University of Washington and Montana State University, gave valuable assistance in uncovering much information from old newspaper and periodical files. An exchange of letters with the late Joseph Schafer, superintendent of the State Historical Society of Wisconsin, and Murray Kane of New York City on the "safety-valve hypothesis" also proved very helpful. Finally, tribute must be paid to my wife for her generous and intelligent assistance in the checking and proofreading of this manuscript.

R.M.R.

Indianapolis, Indiana.

CONTENTS

ILLUSTRATIONS

Part I

The Settler Breaks the Way

CHAPTER I

FOUNDING THE SYSTEM

AMONG the grievances listed in the Declaration of Independence was the complaint that the King of Great Britain endeavored to "prevent the population of these States" by "obstructing the laws for naturalization of foreigners; refusing to pass others to encourage their emigrations hither, and raising the conditions of new appropriations of lands."[1]

For over one hundred and fifty years the colonies had enjoyed the privilege of moulding their own land systems, but the Proclamation of 1763, and subsequent Orders in Council leading up to the Quebec Act of 1774, served notice to Americans that frontier policy was no longer a matter for colonial initiative but had become an imperial problem of first order. This interference with the free movement of colonists into the country west of the Appalachians was resented by southern and New England colonies alike,[2] and constituted one of the major causes of the American Revolution.

The policy of the British government was not without its critics even in England. Adam Smith, the chief protagonist of a new school of economics, pointed out in his *The Wealth of Nations,* first published in 1776, that "plenty of good land, and liberty to manage their own affairs their own way, seem to be the two great causes of the prosperity of all new colonies."[3] Looking at the colonies of the different European nations, he observed that British institutions were more conducive to the improvement and cultivation of land than were those of other countries. In British colonies engrossment of uncultivated lands was not very extensive; colonists suffered less from taxation and were allowed a more comprehensive market. The result was a strong demand for labor with correspondingly liberal wages. Hence when the government of George III began to impede the free flow of labor to the

[1] See Clarence W. Alvord, *The Mississippi Valley in British Politics* (Cleveland, 1917), Vol. II, p. 216.

[2] Archibald Henderson, "A Pre-Revolutionary Revolt in the Old Southwest," *Mississippi Valley Historical Review,* Vol. XVII (1930-31), pp. 191-212.

[3] *The Whole Works of Adam Smith* (London, 1882), Vol. III, p. 247.

colonies, or from the colonies into the trans-Appalachian West, it was interfering with one of the vital privileges of empire.

England was just beginning to feel the first impulses of the Industrial Revolution; philosophers everywhere were predicting a new world order. Adam Smith was diligently striving to work out a new philosophy which would synthesize the rising industrialism in England and the political and economic democracy of America. But he spoke too late. The statesmen of the old order, whose minds had been conditioned by mercantilism and the classic literature of Merrie England, were unable to adjust their policies to meet the new situation.

Soon after the Declaration of Independence the problem of disposing of the vacant lands west of the Appalachian Mountains, claimed by seven of the states, became the subject of considerable controversy.[4] If the Revolution was successful and the larger states were allowed to persist in their claims, then the six smaller states with definite boundaries would find themselves hemmed in along the coastline with no future to the west. Was not the sovereignty west of the mountains, the small states asked, being assured more by the artillery of Knox and by the rifles of Morgan than by the parchments issued by some mouldering potentate with little conception of new world geography? Maryland, ringleader of the small states, boldly contended that this unsettled domain to the westward, if wrested by the "common blood and treasure of the thirteen states" should be their common property. The lands should be under congressional control, to be "parcelled out" into "free, convenient, and independent governments, in such manner and at such times" as Congress should determine.[5] It had been imperial policy since 1763, Maryland's leaders recalled, to limit original charter grants. Besides, the seven claimant states could never reconcile differences based on conflicting claims and overlapping boundaries. The State of Maryland thereupon refused to accede to the Articles of Confederation, blocking the establishment of any common government until some concessions should be made by the larger states.

[4] The best works on the land problem during the Revolutionary War period are J. F. Jameson, *The American Revolution Considered as a Social Movement* (Princeton, 1926), and Thomas P. Abernethy, *Western Lands and the American Revolution* (New York, 1937).

[5] Instructions read May 21, 1779, to the Continental Congress. See *Journals of the Continental Congress*, Vol. XIV, pp. 619-22.

Finally, in 1780, to alleviate the dissatisfaction among the smaller states, New York tendered her western lands to Congress without reservation.[6] In the same year Congress passed a resolution "earnestly" recommending that other states having like possessions do the same, and declaring that "the unappropriated lands which should" be ceded or relinquished to the United States by any particular state "should be disposed of for the common benefit of the United States, and be settled and formed into distinct republican states which should become members of the union and have the rights of sovereignty and freedom and independence like the other states—the lands to be granted or settled at such terms and under such regulations as should afterwards be agreed upon by the United States in Congress assembled."[7]

Not until 1784, however, did Virginia magnanimously relinquish her claims to the country northwest of the Ohio, reserving certain areas.[8] Meanwhile, Maryland had agreed to ratify the Articles of Confederation.

These cessions made possible the first legal union of the thirteen states, and conveyed to the government of these united states the title to a body of land known as the *public domain*. Between 1784 and 1802 the remaining five states also ceded their western lands.[9] The public domain thus had its origin in a curious compound of the states-rights feeling which characterized the so-called "critical period" in American history and the growing spirit of nationalism which was to mark the years to come.

The government of the United States thereupon assumed toward the immense bodies of western lands the position of a trustee of society, holding not only the right of eminent domain but also the right of individual ownership. Realizing that this relation should continue no

[6] Clarence E. Carter (comp. and ed.), *The Territorial Papers of the United States* (Washington, 1934), Vol. II, pp. 3-6.

[7] *Journals of the Continental Congress,* Vol. XVII, pp. 806-7.

[8] See *Territorial Papers,* Vol. II, pp. 6-9.

[9] For an analysis of the cession deeds and the various reservations see: Merrill Jensen, "The Articles of Confederation: A Re-interpretation," *Pacific Historical Review,* Vol. VI (June 1937), pp. 120-42; and "The Cession of the Old Northwest," *Mississippi Valley Historical Review,* Vol. XXIII (1936), pp. 27-49; and "The Creation of the National Domain, 1781-1784," *ibid.,* Vol. XXVI (1939), pp. 323-43; Abernethy, *Western Lands and the American Revolution,* Chaps. XIX and XX; Payson J. Treat, *The National Land System* (New York, 1910), pp. 7-14; H. B. Adams, "Maryland's Influence upon Land Cessions to the United States," *Johns Hopkins University Studies,* Third Series, No. 1 (1885); Thomas Donaldson, *The Public Domain; Its History* (Washington, 1884), pp. 65-86.

The Land Claims of the Thirteen States.
From Nathaniel W. Stephenson, *A History of the American People.*
By permission of Charles Scribner's Sons.

longer than was absolutely necessary, it became the anxious desire of the Confederation government to transfer the title into private hands.

By 1784, financiers, ex-soldiers—in whom General George Washington was vitally interested—and many other persons were already calling upon Congress to adopt some sort of policy for the alienation of western lands. This was the one national problem upon which most of the states agreed that Congress could act. Several workable plans were presented by individual citizens, but the congressional committee overlooked these for the most part, and proceeded to formulate a policy based upon land systems already in operation among the various states.

Colonial experience attested to the fact that the nature of society was to a very great extent determined by land policy. New England had been settled compactly under a well-regulated township system. A group of individuals desiring to break away from the more established community was required to incorporate, whereupon it received from the colonial legislature a rectangular tract of land definitely bounded and surveyed. This "was an admirable method for assimilating the wilderness to a definite civilization, but too deliberate, restrained, and social for eighteenth century pioneers of the Kentucky breed."[10]

In the proprietary colonies land had been disposed of for revenue purposes, the proprietor exacting an annual quitrent from the grantee.[11] This aristocratic system provoked the wrath of the colonists, especially in Pennsylvania, and was one of the main forces leading to the establishment of a democratic government in that state. With the Revolution, most of the new state constitutions abolished quitrents and other aristocratic incidents. The type of survey constituted another distinguishing feature of land policy in the proprietary colonies. In most of the middle and southern colonies land was located indiscriminately. This practice tended to scatter the population over a wide area; it favored squatters at the expense of permanent settlers; and it encouraged irregular surveys, as well as carelessness in the recording of titles.[12] Both the New England and the southern systems had merits. The former "afforded a security of title which facilitated an orderly settlement of new lands," while the latter "encouraged initiative and resourcefulness."[13] One made for the evolution of a community type of life, while the other tended to develop the plantation type of civilization.[14]

Congress devoted a year of study to the western land problem. Thomas Jefferson was chairman of the committee and the first draft of an ordinance, dated 1784, is in his own handwriting. But Jefferson's appointment as ambassador to France removed this important southern

[10] Samuel E. Morison, *Oxford History of the United States* (New York, 1927), Vol. I, p. 191. By permission of Oxford University Press.

[11] Clarence P. Gould, "The Land System in Maryland, 1720-1765," *Johns Hopkins University Studies*, Vol. III (1919), pp. 9ff.; Beverley Bond, *The Quit-Rent System in the American Colonies* (New York, 1919).

[12] Oliver P. Chitwood, *A History of Colonial America* (New York and London, 1931), Chap. XXI.

[13] Treat, *National Land System*, p. 25. By permission of Professor Payson J. Treat.

[14] Lewis C. Gray, *History of Agriculture in the Southern United States to 1860* (Washington, 1933), Vol. II, p. 639.

and democratic influence from the drafting committee, and the Ordinance of May 20, 1785, reflects a predominant New England influence.

In line with the earlier abolition of feudal incidents, the ordinance adopted allodial tenure, that is, land was to pass in fee simple from the government to the first purchaser. After clearing the Indian title and surveying the land the government was to sell it at auction to the highest bidder. Townships were to be surveyed six miles square and alternate ones subdivided into lots one mile square, each lot consisting of 640 acres to be known as a *section*. No land was to be sold until the first seven ranges of townships were marked off. A minimum price was fixed at $1 per acre to be paid in specie, loan-office certificates, or certificates of the liquidated debt, including interest. The purchaser was to pay surveying expenses of $36 per township. Congress reserved sections 8, 11, 26, and 29 in each township, and one-third of all precious metals later discovered therein. In addition the sixteenth section of each township was set aside for the purpose of providing common schools.[15]

Despite its many defects, the Ordinance of 1785 "proved to be one of the wisest and most influential of all the acts of the Revolutionary period."[16] It inaugurated a system of land surveys which, perfected by practice and experience, has been adopted by nearly every civilized country in the world. No act of the Confederation government evinced a more genuine national spirit. This ordinance together with the better known Ordinance of 1787 "guaranteed the American colonist against exploitation" by the national government or by any of the original thirteen states, and thus formed the basis for the American colonial system.[17]

The new federal constitution of 1787 did not interfere with the democratic principles of empire established in these two ordinances. A liberal western colonization policy was among the first subjects discussed in

[15] *Journals of the American Congress*, Vol. IV, Ordinance of May 20; 1785, p. 5207; J. C. Fitzpatrick (ed.), *Journal of the Continental Congress*, Vol. XXVIII, pp. 375ff.; *The Territorial Papers*, Vol. II, pp. 12-18.

[16] Treat, *National Land System*, p. 40.

[17] E. C. Kirkland, *A History of American Economic Life* (New York, 1927), p. 142. Also consult, Elbert J. Benton, "Establishing the American Colonization System in the Old Northwest," Illinois State Historical Society, *Transactions* (1918), pp. 47-64; and Homer C. Hockett, *Western Influences on Political Parties to 1825* (The Ohio State University Bulletin No. 2, Vol. XXII [1917], The Ohio State University Studies—Contributions in History and Political Science, No. 4), p. 42.

the Constitutional Convention,[18] and to the southern delegates must go the credit for preserving the policy of free and unhampered development of the West. The Constitution when finally completed gave Congress power "to make all needful rules and regulations respecting the territory of the United States." The new federal government, under this general provision, accepted with but little discussion the legislation of the Confederation Congress. Probably none of the Fathers of the Constitution then imagined that this liberal settlement policy would lead to rapid settlement of the West and that this newer region would ultimately hold the balance of power in national affairs.

Well might this national land system be considered democratic in comparison with the aristocratic systems of the Old World, but as compared with the land systems of the original thirteen states, it was strongly conservative. Lands in western New York were selling at 20 cents to $1 an acre, with credit advanced to the purchaser.[19] Massachusetts had reduced her Maine lands to 50 cents an acre to check possible migration to the West. Pennsylvania's rates were low at its state office; and Virginia's rich lands in Kentucky were selling at give-away prices. So also were the Tennessee lands owned by the Carolinas and Georgia. Consequently for some years the eastern states were able to outbid the national government for settlers.[20]

Regardless of the comparatively democratic character of the Ordinance of 1785, the American settler found little within its provisions that was attractive. The policy appealed more to speculators and men of money than to hardy yeomen who were usually unable to compete with the former at the auction. The pioneer generally hated the speculator who offered him smaller parcels of land at advanced prices. He therefore had to risk the uncertainties of squatter settlement on government land or else to seek his future on the state lands of the East.

The fact is that much of the history of the national land system centers around the struggle between these two forces of squatterism and speculation, between the poor man and the man of wealth. Ever since early colonial days the danger of frontier revolt had menaced established society. The opening of vacant lands to the westward always stimulated a frontier spirit—a peculiar democratic levelling influence,

---

[18] See debates of June 25 in Max Farrand, *Records of the Federal Convention of 1787*, Vol. I.
[19] A. M. Sakolski, *The Great American Land Bubble* (New York and London, 1932), p. 111.
[20] Henry Tatter, "State and Federal Land Policy During the Confederation Period," *Agricultural History*, Vol. IX (1935), pp. 178-82.

likely to be arrogant, daring, dangerous, and even uncontrollable. The frontiersmen wanted free access to the soil, but the forces of established order, on the other hand, contended that free land would destroy the economic and political values upon which government was founded.

All the colonial governments in America had very early adopted iron-clad policies to control these peculiar levelling influences from the backwoods. So long as the movements of population were on a small scale, and for the most part onto vacant lands within the eastern states, the dominant forces of established order could control this frontier spirit. But once settlement spread beyond the reach of the colonial governments, and the western population of squatters and trespassers stood ready to defy the law of the land, danger became imminent. By 1785 the state governments of North Carolina, Virginia, and Pennsylvania with their far-flung frontiers, had found it advisable to compromise with these revolutionary forces by granting the right of preemption.[21] Briefly, the government pardoned the squatter for his illegal settlement and in addition confirmed his title on condition that he buy at a much-reduced price. Preemption was at best an expedient by which established law and order were made to conform to the lawless and uncontrollable spirit of the American frontier.[22] But it was the means by which thousands of acres of land were to be settled by a sturdy and enterprising population. The next half century was to see constant friction between the squatter and the speculator, each seeking indulgences from the national government on the pretext that he was doing more than the other in developing the nation's resources.

The land policy established under the Ordinance of 1785 benefited the speculator at the expense of the settler. In truth, the ink was scarcely dry on the statute book when the Congress of the Confederation, in dire need of money, departed from the provisions of the ordinance and sold extensive tracts of public land in Ohio to eastern speculators at prices far below the minimum price established in the ordinance.[23] Under the direction of the Reverend Manasseh Cutler, a group of Revolutionary veterans of New England organized the Ohio Company

[21] Amelia C. Ford, "Colonial Precedents of Our National Land System as It Existed in 1800," *University of Wisconsin Bulletin No. 352* (Madison, 1910), pp. 23-43.

[22] Consult the author's article, "Preemption: A Frontier Triumph," *Mississippi Valley Historical Review*, Vol. XVIII (December 1931), p. 332.

[23] For resolution of 1787, changing conditions of each sale of land under Ordinance of 1785, consult *Territorial Papers*, Vol. II, p. 78.

of Associates and signed a contract on October 27, 1787, for a million and a half acres of land on the Ohio and the Muskingum rivers, to be known as the Ohio Purchase. The price if paid in depreciated Continental certificates was to be 8 to 9 cents per acre.[24] At about the same time certain members of Congress organized the Scioto Company and dealt out to themselves at similar prices, five million acres along the Ohio River east of the Scioto. A third contract was made in 1788 with Judge John Cleves Symmes, a member of Congress from New Jersey, for the tract between the Great Miami and the Little Miami rivers, at the same bargain rates.

These three grants, together with Connecticut's Western Reserve in northeastern Ohio, the Virginia Military Reserve in southern Ohio, and Clark's Reserve in southern Indiana, marked the beginning of a period in which the national government attempted to settle the western country through the agency of land speculators. It was an unfortunate experience. The most that can be said in favor of this policy is that it led to the establishment of Marietta, Cincinnati, Manchester, Chillicothe, Gallipolis, Cleveland, and other towns, and hence the conquest of the Ohio Wilderness was begun. From the standpoint of land policy, settlement by large land companies was a failure. The Scioto Company collapsed soon after the arrival of a coterie of poor French immigrants who had been induced by rather questionable tactics to settle at Gallipolis. The Ohio Company met only its first payment. Symmes made his first payments then proceeded to sell the land which did not legally belong to him.[25]

When the federal government began to function in 1789 the land question immediately assumed extraordinary importance. Representatives from the frontier regions agitated for a general preemption law and some went so far as to demand free land.[26] A representative from western Pennsylvania voiced the typical western argument for a democratic policy when he inquired, "What will these men think who have placed themselves on a vacant spot, anxiously waiting its disposition by the government," when they "find their preemption right engrossed

---

[24] *ibid.*, Vol. II, p. 80.

[25] For a detailed account consult Beverley W. Bond, Jr., *The Civilization of the Old Northwest* (New York, 1934), Chap. X; Sakolski, *The Great American Land Bubble*, Chap. V; also *Territorial Papers*, Vol. II, consult index for the numerous documents concerning the operations of these companies.

[26] *Annals of Congress*, 1 Cong. 1 Sess., pp. 411-12, 624; *ibid.*, 1 Cong. 3 Sess., p. 1841.

by the purchaser of a million acres? . . . They will do one of two things: either move into Spanish territory, or . . . move on United States territory, and take possession without leave. . . . They will not pay you money. Will you then raise a force to drive them off? . . . They are willing to pay an equitable price for those lands; and, if they may be indulged with a preemption to the purchase, no men will be better friends to the government. . . . The emigrants who reach the western country will not stop till they find a place where they can securely seat themselves."[27]

That settlers would seek the lands of Spain in Florida and Louisiana was a real threat, for at this time the Spanish policy was very lenient.[28] The Spanish "hold out temptations," complained Governor St. Clair of the Northwest Territory, "that will succeed with many who have little other governing Principle beside the Desire for Wealth—a thousand acres of land, free of Purchase and Taxes—ten Dollars per hundred for Tobacco, and six Dollars for Pork or Beef delivered at New Orleans are offered to all who will remove into Florida, and produce those Articles."[29] St. Clair even went so far as to recommend "laying open a part of the Western Territory for those who want land and cannot pay for it immediately." These lands "might be set at a moderate rate and an Office opened, where any person might locate them in small Quantities, and where, upon the payment of the purchase Money, which should run upon Interest, they should receive Patents." As for the sale of large tracts of land to speculators, he commented further: "It seems certain that the Sale of the Country in large Districts, if it ever was an eligible manner of disposing of it, is now over. . . . The Expectation that the Domestic Debt might be paid off . . . by selling that Country in large Portions, was never very well founded," and is now "very much lessened." Building up the population in the Northwest, with adequate military protection, he felt, would do much to check British influence and guarantee control of this region to the United States.[30]

Congress listened attentively to the arguments for a more liberal land policy until the condition of the treasury was pointed out, when prospects for a revolutionary change in policy at once disappeared. Congress

[27] ibid., 1 Cong. 1 Sess., p. 411.
[28] Louis Pelzer, "Economic Factors in the Acquisition of Louisiana," Mississippi Valley Historical Association Proceedings, Vol. VI (1912), pp. 109-29.
[29] Memorial of St. Clair to President Washington, (August 1789), in Territorial Papers, Vol. II, p. 210.
[30] ibid., Vol. II, pp. 210-12.

did, however, put an end to the practice of selling extensive tracts of land to proprietors.

While no liberal policy was forthcoming, President Washington's administration did much to put the western domain in order. In 1790 the President warned the American public by proclamation against the questionable speculative activities of the Yazoo Land Company of the Southwest. In 1789-90 Governor St. Clair established many counties in the Northwest Territory. The year 1790 also saw the creation of the Territory Southwest of the Ohio. A treaty was signed at New York City with the powerful Creek Indian Confederation of the Southwest, and in the course of the next four years the federal government moved against the Indians of the Northwest. The Treaty of Greenville, concluded in 1795, relieved the Northwest of the Indian menace for the next few years and opened up to settlement much of the present state of Ohio. The treaty with Spain in 1795, which assured free navigation of the Mississippi River and settled the Florida boundary, encouraged migration into the new Southwest. This forceful, paternalistic and protective policy on the part of the federal government did more than anything else to lessen the dissatisfaction in the western country. The admission of Vermont, Kentucky, and Tennessee into the union attested to the faith of the administration in the western country.[31]

It was not for lack of interest on the part of President Washington that no important land legislation was passed until the end of his administration. With eastern lands cheap and plentiful, with Indians menacing settlers throughout the West, with Easterners disinclined to run the hazards of western pioneering, and eastern land interests jealous and reluctant to open up western lands, there was little need for a change in land policy.

Alexander Hamilton's report on federal land policy, which was included in his important analysis of the country's resources and economic prospects, published in 1790-91, did not attract much immediate attention. Men of Hamilton's way of thinking placed considerable emphasis upon the financial benefits to the government which might be derived from the proceeds of the sales of public lands.[32] And these men

[31] For a careful treatment of the summary points of this paragraph consult A. P. Whitaker, *The Spanish-American Frontier* (New York, 1927), Chaps. IX-XIV.

[32] Hamilton's report of 1790 on the Public Lands, *American State Papers, Public Lands* (Washington, 1832) Vol. I, p. 81; also, Donaldson, *The Public Domain*, p. 98.

exercised power out of all proportion to their numbers in the early days when the federal government was trying to establish its credit. Hamilton feared that all was lost if the agricultural classes remained dominant in the new government. Instead of a landed aristocracy or an agrarian democracy in which he had little faith, he wished to see a powerful industrial order such as was coming to the fore in England. He built his financial program around the banking and business interests of the North Atlantic States.[33] Their support would be of little avail unless there were some assurance that the supply of industrial labor would increase, and that wages would remain relatively low. Cheap land would lure labor from the East and cause wages to rise. Concentration of labor on farm lands would, he feared, produce an agricultural surplus.

On the other hand, Hamilton had no desire to bring more money into the treasury than was necessary to establish credit, because a surplus would remove one very plausible reason for enacting a protective tariff. He did not oppose immigration, but he insisted that the flow of incoming labor should be regulated so that the economic order could easily absorb it. In short, then, it would seem that Hamilton desired not only to use the public domain as an important source of revenue for the United States treasury, but also to dispose of it in such a way as to guarantee a stable economic and social order.[34] It is not surprising, therefore, to find Hamilton in 1790 proposing that public lands be sold at 30 cents an acre and in lots not larger than 100 acres each.[35] He apparently felt that low-priced land set off in tracts too small to be conducive to speculation would bring more money into the treasury than large tracts sold to speculators who could not meet the terms of their contracts. This does not mean that he was opposed to offering the land in large tracts, that is to say, townships of even uncertain size. In truth

---

[33] James Truslow Adams (ed.) *Hamiltonian Principles: Extracts from the Writings of Alexander Hamilton* (Boston, 1928), p. 40; "Report on Manufactures," pp. 142, 155-61.

[34] This viewpoint is not so much in accord with Hibbard, *History of the Public Land Policies*, p. 1, or Treat, *The National Land System*, p. 115, as it is with Morison, *Oxford History of the United States*, Vol. I, p. 190. It will be observed that forty years before the time of Edward G. Wakefield (see below Chap. VIII) Alexander Hamilton was anticipating his plan for systematic colonization—though it must be admitted that the factors determining these respective views varied somewhat. In England there was a redundancy of labor; in America labor was scarce. Wakefield was well acquainted with the American land system, and undoubtedly understood Hamilton's general economic philosophy.

[35] *American State Papers, Public Lands*, Vol. I, p. 8.

he hoped the day would soon appear when men of money would buy large tracts at prices far above the 30 cent minimum.

It was the condition of the United States treasury which finally led to the passage of new land legislation. Two committees of the House, the Committee on Ways and Means and a Land Committee, were working toward the same end—the reduction of the public debt. The bill when first reported embodied little change from the provisions of the Ordinance of 1785. The Land Committee realized the great difficulty of formulating a new policy, for upon presentation of the bill the chairman invited thorough discussion of the whole public land question. A storm of debate broke loose. Before the House was through with the matter practically every principle of the land system had been discussed.

This bill was not a liberal measure. It provided for selling land in lots three miles square, which at $2 an acre would cost $3,840. Scarcely had the House begun its consideration when various members demanded sale of land in smaller tracts and on more lenient terms. Representative Robert Rutherford, who had lived on the frontier of Virginia for many years, hoped that Congress would destroy that hydra—speculation— which had done the country great harm. Let the government, said he, dispose of this land to original settlers; a hundred and fifty thousand families were waiting to become occupants. Moreover, he added, the "monsters" in Europe were ready to join the "monsters" here, to swallow up this country. John Nicholas of Virginia observed that if the bill were to be changed and provision made for sale in small lots there would be no encouragement for men of property to come forward, for the best lands would be bought by farmers and none left. William Findley of Pennsylvania was opposed to any policy which would engross land into the hands of the few. "Land," he declared, "is the most valuable of all property and ought to be brought within the reach of the people."[36]

At this juncture Albert Gallatin, representing the frontier region of western Pennsylvania, arose and presented an amendment providing that part of the land be surveyed and sold in small tracts. He claimed that the public debt could thus be extinguished in ten years, and he was in favor of the plan that would bring in the most money. A certain proportion of farmers, he observed, men of small property, who were

[36] *Annals of Congress*, 6 Cong. 1 Sess., pp. 329, 337, 339.

able to pay for land and remove to the West, would purchase; at least, he wished to give them the opportunity. The farmer, according to Gallatin, would not buy land to sell, and he reminded his hearers that poor persons must purchase on long credit and pay out of profits from the land. So far as he was able to comprehend, there were only two sets of interests opposed to the opening up of the public domain: those of the self-centered speculators, and those of the vested interests of Easterners who feared too great an emigration from the Atlantic States. Gallatin claimed that before the Revolution the policy of favoring the actual settler prevailed from one end of the country to the other, and that to this principle a great deal of happiness and prosperity was due. "If the cause of the happiness of this country was examined into," he conjectured, "it would be found to arise as much from the great plenty of land in proportion to the inhabitants . . . as from the wisdom of their political institutions."[37]

William Cooper of New York, one of the leading speculators in lands of his state, claimed that in the history of land sales in Pennsylvania and New York, where land was sold in small lots, there were not twenty instances of farmers buying it. Gallatin retorted that the gentleman was totally mistaken. With respect to Pennsylvania, he would maintain that not more than one thousand men had purchased large tracts, the other seventy thousand were possessors of small tracts. Supporting Gallatin in his stand were Edward Livingston and James Madison, later to become prominent in the Jefferson administration.[38]

Gallatin's amendment was adopted, and before the House was through the bill had acquired a markedly democratic character. Unfortunately, the Senate refused to accept Gallatin's changes and as finally signed the measure was far more favorable to speculators than to actual settlers.[39]

This Act of 1796 retained the basic institutions of rectangular survey and auction. The minimum price, however, was raised to $2 per acre as compared with $1 under the Ordinance of 1785. Approximately half the lands were to be disposed of in tracts containing 5,760 acres, the rest in tracts of 640 acres. This was quite different from the 160-acre tracts pro-

---

[37] This was the same opinion as that of Adam Smith, see *supra*, pp. 3-4. *ibid.*, pp. 339, 354, 408-9, 411.

[38] *ibid.*, pp. 342, 859, 862, 868.

[39] *Statutes at Large*, Act of May 18, 1796, p. 464; Treat, *National Land System*, p. 85; *Territorial Papers*, Vol. II, pp. 552-7.

posed by Gallatin. An unattractive one-year credit provided little inducement to settlers to take up land. The best feature of the act was the provision establishing local land offices at Pittsburgh and Cincinnati. Indeed, it is little wonder that dissatisfaction with the national land system began to grow immediately after 1796.

Since only the exterior lines of the townships in the first seven ranges of Ohio had been run under the Ordinance of 1785, it was necessary to divide the townships before any 640-acre tracts could be sold. There were delays in the appointment of a surveyor-general and his staff; Congress was slow to appropriate the necessary money; every tract had to be fully described as to nature of soil, rivers, etc., a process which took more time than had been expected. By 1800, only fifty thousand acres of land had been sold under this act, and by that time politicians were beginning to realize that a more attractive and effective system was essential.

Conditions in the western country were indeed in a muddle. Squatters were appearing in choice localities. Numerous petitions were pouring into the Treasury Department and into Congress asking for a more liberal land policy. One of these, dated 1798, from a group of squatters on the Scioto River asked that a tract of land thirty miles square be set off, one-half to be surveyed into tracts containing 160 acres and the other half, 640 acres, and begged leave "to suggest whether it would not tend to the more speedy settlement of the lands and bringing the Value Thereof sooner into the publick Treasury was the price lowered or the present mode of sale altered." The newly-appointed Surveyor-General of the United States, Rufus Putnam, anxiously called the attention of the Secretary of the Treasury to the fact that the population along the Scioto was growing daily and that these people meant "to hold the Lands by Settling or without purchasing provided their members should increase so far as to give them a prospect of Succeeding in a measure of that kind."[40] Governor St. Clair expressed the belief that these inhabitants on the Scioto, and others on the Great Miami—altogether about two thousand in number—would buy their lands, but that few would be prepared to pay for more than 160 acres at $2 an acre. Again he reminded the government that "in Pennsylvania, under its proprietary Government, the people were indulged in taking up lands in quantities not exceeding three hundred acres, on credit, at a

[40] ibid., Vol. II, pp. 639-40, 654; Vol. III, pp. 26-66.

moderate price." And he concluded with the terse warning that "very considerable difficulty may attend" any attempt to remove these settlers.[41]

Events in the nation at large were now moving toward a climax. Already the democratic forces under the leadership of Thomas Jefferson were exerting noticeable influence on national legislation. Such tendencies in the national political firmament naturally found reflections in the newer agricultural regions of the country. In 1799 Congress advanced the Old Northwest to its second stage of territorial government under the provisions of the Ordinance of 1787. The territory elected William Henry Harrison to the position of delegate to Congress. Harrison at once established his reputation by conspicuously launching a plan to reform the land system.[42] As chairman of the land committee of the House of Representatives, he successfully defended the bill against the opposition of many capable minds. He demonstrated the dangerous consequences of the old system which resulted in preventing sales to actual settlers and encouraged the engrossment of extensive tracts of land by nonresident proprietors. Aiding Harrison in the framing of the bill was the discriminating genius of Albert Gallatin, who had crusaded in 1796 for a liberal land measure and who was soon to become Secretary of the Treasury under Jefferson.[43] In spite of the fact that the bill became an act before Jefferson was elected President, the measure was a product of those democratic forces that were bringing into being a new era.

This act of May 10, 1800, is one of the most important measures in the history of the public domain.[44] It provided for a liberal credit system, a reduction in the minimum amount of land to be offered for sale, and establishment of administrative machinery. Local land offices were to be opened in Cincinnati, Chillicothe, Hamilton, and Steubenville, each with a register and receiver paid from fees. The minimum amount of land that could be purchased was reduced to 320 acres; the minimum price was kept at $2 per acre. While a discount of 8 per cent was allowed for cash payment, more important was the fact that liberal

[41] ibid., Vol. III, pp. 7-8. Report of the Governor of the Northwest Territory on subject of Western Lands, January 1799.
[42] Annals of Congress, 6 Cong. 1 Sess., p. 209.
[43] James Hall, Notes on the Western States (Philadelphia, 1838), p. 170.
[44] Statutes at Large, Vol. II, p. 73; Territorial Papers, Vol. III, pp. 88-97.

credit was tendered to the settler. One-fourth part of the purchase price was due in forty days, a second fourth in two years, a third in three years, and the remaining fourth in four years. W. C. Claiborne of Tennessee attempted to have the principle of preemption included in the act, but eastern interests voted this down.[45]

[45] *Annals of Congress,* 6 Cong. 1 Sess., p. 652. At this time half of Tennessee was public domain, though due to discrepancies in the cession deed these lands later reverted to North Carolina.

CHAPTER II

THE SETTLER BUYS ON CREDIT

THE advent of Jeffersonian Democracy, contrary to expectations, did not bring revolutionary changes in national land policy. In the same year that Jefferson aided in drawing up that liberal document, the Declaration of Independence, he averred that "the people who will migrate to the westward . . . will be a people little able to pay taxes. . . . By selling the lands to them, you will disgust them, and cause an avulsion of them from the common union. They will settle the lands in spite of everybody,—I am at the same time clear that . . . [the lands] should be appropriated in small quantities."[1] In the later years of the Revolutionary period Jefferson more than any other person had been responsible for the democratic changes in the Virginian land system. Throughout the Federalist period of the 1790's, while many of the nation's great men and his own colleagues were engaged in land speculation, he consistently maintained his opposition to aristocratic tendencies in political economy. It would seem, then, that personally Jefferson was probably in favor of drastic changes in the national land system. But the responsibilities of the presidency appear to have moderated any revolutionary tendencies in that direction. To do away with the revenue system in the disposal of public lands would have brought strong repercussions regarding the rest of his program. Besides, little was to be gained by encouraging more rapid expansion of the frontier which was already seething with discontent and constantly threatened by danger of Indian wars if not foreign war. In retrospect it appears that Jefferson's contribution to the problem transcended mere details to set for federal land policy a new and more democratic course.

As Hamilton brought strength to his party by teaching infant industries the art of politics, so Jefferson built up his following by teaching the principles of a modest agrarian imperialism. Jefferson was confident that more land and not less land would save the American people from

[1] Jefferson to [Edmund Pendleton], August 13, 1776, Paul L. Ford (ed.), *The Works of Thomas Jefferson* (New York, 1904), Vol. II, pp. 239-40.

what seemed to him the pitfalls of Hamilton's industrialism. He saw
clearly that possession of the great valley of the Mississippi meant more
to the agricultural interests of the country than any other gift of man-
kind. This Virginia philosopher, exponent of economy and strict construction, may have experienced trouble with his conscience, but it is
certain that "We, the people of the United States" experienced unbounded and pleasurable astonishment when it was announced in 1803
that the United States had purchased Louisiana. The addition of 756,-
961,280 acres of land to the public domain at a cost of 3.6 cents per
acre[2] was one of the greatest bargains ever struck off by the hand of
man. It secured to the United States the greatest and richest valley of
land in the world, which when filled with a hardy and free population
would guarantee the perpetuity of American democracy throughout
the years to come.

As one examines the undercurrents of the westward movement it is
evident that Jefferson was the instrument for carrying out a step which
economic forces had already conditioned.[3] At any rate, the treaty of
1803 gave official encouragement to the process by which Americans,
insatiable in their quest for more land, carried American authority to
the shores of the Pacific Ocean. Economic control of the Mississippi
Valley came first, then a step over into West Florida, a misstep in the
direction of Canada, and finally, a definite move against East Florida.
By these short steps the principle of paramount interest and the doctrine of a modest agrarian imperialism added many broad acres to the
public domain in the period, 1803 to 1820.[4] The purchase of Florida
from Spain in 1819—37,931,520 acres at a cost of 17.1 cents per acre—
climaxed the first period of westward extension.

In less conspicuous fashion the same process operated against the
American Indians. While Jefferson professed the most benevolent principles toward the aborigines,[5] nevertheless he coveted their lands for
the expansion of the white man's arcadia. The Treaty of Greenville of

[2] Donaldson, *The Public Domain,* p. 21.
[3] Louis Pelzer, "Economic Factors in the Acquisition of Louisiana," Mississippi Valley Historical Association *Proceedings,* Vol. VI (1912), p. 129; Theodore Roosevelt, *Winning of the
West* (New York, 1889-96), Vol. IV, p. 276.
[4] I. J. Cox, "American Intervention in West Florida," *American Historical Review,* Vol. XVII
(1912), pp. 290ff.; Julius W. Pratt, *Expansionists of 1812* (New York, 1905), pp. 19-38; Louis
M. Hacker, "Western Land Hunger and the War of 1812; A Conjecture," *Mississippi Valley
Historical Review,* Vol. X, pp. 365-96.
[5] See his view in 1792 in *Territorial Papers,* Vol. IV, pp. 130-1.

1795 brought to an end a period in which the Indians for the most part had taken the offensive; the inauguration of Jefferson opened one in which the Americans assumed the offensive.[6] Between 1795 and 1809, the Indians of the Northwest were rounded up by government officials and plied with oratory and whiskey until they had signed away their rights to forty-eight million acres of land. This procedure was primarily responsible for the Tecumseh revolt of 1811 which merged into the War of 1812. In 1814 the Indians of the Northwest found themselves deserted by their British allies. By 1820 the armies of General Harrison and General Jackson had removed the Indian menace east of the Mississippi River. Indian title to much of the Southwest was extinguished by 1818, to the southern half of Indiana by the so-called New Purchase of 1817, and to all of Illinois by 1819. Considerable inroads had also been made into lands held by Indians in other parts of the public domain.

Coincident with the purchase of Louisiana and the admission of Ohio into the union as the first public-land state there developed another period of speculation. This time the speculation involved lands of the public domain, and while it resulted in some significant settlement, it was nevertheless frought with much evil. "To such an extent," declared a frontier newspaper, "had the hateful spirit of inordinate speculation in lands proceeded, that it had corrupted the fountains of legislation and the courts of justice, as well as the body politic. The rapacious spirit of accumulating large bodies of land, pervaded the whole country and nation, engendering a mass of corruption in every state of the Union; and . . . menaced the existence of the Union itself."[7]

This outburst of speculative enterprise was due for the most part to two factors: the existence of claims to land based on foreign title, and the credit system established by the Act of 1800. Various claims were advanced to tracts either by right of occupancy under the laws of the United States, or by virtue of grants made by England, France or Spain before the territory passed to the United States. The Spanish authorities in the Louisiana territory before 1803 acceded to overtures and collusions for the purpose of personal aggrandizement. Lynx-eyed speculators eagerly sought claims of this character and soon an active commerce sprang up between the artful land-jobbers and the docile,

---

[6] Morison and Commager, *Growth of the American Republic* (New York, 1937), Vol. I, p. 308.

[7] *The Frankfort* (Kentucky) *Palladium*, January 25, 1806.

Indian Cessions in the Northwest, 1789-1816.

From Asa Martin, *History of the United States.* By permission of Ginn and Co.

unlettered settlers, with the result that titles, complete and incomplete, multiplied in endless variety.

These conflicting claims had to be adjusted. Congress therefore appointed boards of commissioners in the several territories, to look into the validity of such claims and either to pass judgment upon them, or to report to Congress the facts upon which they were founded together with their opinions. In this mode, claims derived from legitimate authority were confirmed, as well as other claims which it seemed expedient to place upon a fixed basis, although in many cases legal titles had not been clearly perfected.

Administrative difficulties and the arrogant pretensions of the Spanish government relative to the purchase of Louisiana prolonged litigation for many years. Without doubt the adjustment of foreign titles was one of the most complicated administrative problems which the government of the United States has ever encountered.[8] But this adjudication was a necessary preliminary to systematic land administration. In most cases the government felt that it was making a concession in allowing a confirmation of title on the payment of the minimum price per acre. Between 1804 and 1830, there were sixteen acts passed by Congress, granting preemption in a limited form to special groups in the various territories and states.[9]

The credit system provided for under the Act of 1800 worked badly and necessitated almost as much congressional relief as was required to quiet foreign titles.[10] Attracted by the fertility of the soil, the prospect of its increase in value and the easy terms of sale, individuals made extensive purchases of public lands for speculation. Exhausting their resources to pay the first installments, they expected an advance in the value of their lands to enable them to take care of the remainder. In 1803 a large number of petitions presented to Congress prayed for essential changes in the land system, such as sale of land in smaller tracts, abolition of all charges of interest upon these sales, selling for cash instead of credit, reduction of prices, and granting of small tracts to actual settlers. Gallatin, Secretary of the Treasury, therefore advised the aboli-

---

[8] Vols. I, II, and III of *American State Papers, Public Lands* are devoted almost entirely to this subject. For an excellent brief discussion see Treat, *National Land System*, Chap. IX.

[9] Robbins, "Preemption—A Frontier Triumph," p. 338.

[10] The best treatment of this subject is to be found in C. F. Emerick, *The Credit System and the Public Domain* (Vanderbilt Southern Historical Society Publication No. 3).

tion of the credit system, proposing in its place reduction of the minimum price from $2 to $1.25, and sale in small tracts of 160 acres. In the Act of 1804 Congress reduced the minimum cash price to $1.64 per acre, and the minimum amount to a quarter section, but refused to alter the credit system.[11] As for those settlers who could not meet their payments, the government chose to grant them relief rather than allow them to forfeit their lands. After 1806, in fact, relief acts came to be passed almost as regularly as annual appropriation bills.

Meanwhile the timeworn problem of intrusions on public lands continued to press upon Congress. Petition after petition begging for relief through preemption came from western squatters who knew that they would lose their holdings at the auction. The public lands committee of the House of Representatives reported in 1801 a typical petition of certain persons who "with much labor and difficulty" had "settled upon, cultivated, and improved certain lands, the property of the United States between the waters of the Scioto and Muskingum rivers," and had thereby "not only enhanced the value of the lands" upon which they had "respectively settled, but of the lands in the vicinity of the same, to the great benefit of the United States."

The signers prayed for "a preemption right to those lands at $2 per acre, and such credit as Congress" thought "proper to extend to them, clear of interest." To these petitioners the congressional committee offered sympathy but, feeling that there were many other settlers in the same predicament, it decided that "granting the indulgence prayed for would operate as an encouragement to intrusions on public lands, and would be an injustifiable sacrifice of the public interest. . . . The prayer . . . [therefore] ought not to be granted."[12] In 1806 the public lands committee declared that "when it is considered that these individuals settled without authority, or any reasonable ground of expectation from the government, it is evident that any hardships to which they may be exposed are chargeable only to their own indiscretion."[13]

To cope with the lawlessness of these backwoodsmen Congress adopted stringent legislation. As early as 1802, John Randolph introduced a bill to prevent intrusions on the public domain.[14] Not until

11 Act of March 26, 1804 for disposal of land in Indiana Territory; *Statutes at Large*, Vol. II, pp. 279-81.
12 *American State Papers, Public Lands*, Vol. I, p. iii.
13 *ibid.*, p. 264.
14 *Annals of Congress*, 7 Cong. 1 Sess., p. 421.

1807, however, did Congress seriously take up this matter. The Intrusion Act, passed in that year, admitted in its very terms the inability of the government to administer the law. It provided that unlawful settlers could become tenants at will until they were able to pay for their land or until someone else bought it. But if the intruder on public land did not register his tenancy he was subject to a six months' imprisonment and a fine of one hundred dollars. The frontier army was to imprison settlers who did not conform to these regulations. But inasmuch as the frontier army was made up mainly of frontiersmen, including many squatters, it is not clear just how Congress expected the law to be enforced. This act was a typical example of eastern ignorance of western conditions. It was partially repealed seven years later, although much of it remained on the statute books for decades.[15]

In spite of the multifarious and complex problems which the government faced, the westward march of settlement continued. In fact, it threatened to depopulate Connecticut, and the legislature sought means of alleviating the "Ohio fever." One observer said: "Young people in their plays at social gatherings marched to rude melodies which taught them to dream that toward the setting sun lay an earthly paradise with gates open to welcome them. From hill and valley the processions hurried away."[16] Washington Irving described in his *Legend of Sleepy Hollow* Ichabod Crane's desire to marry the fair Katrinka Van Tassel and with her dowry to purchase the supplies, oxen and covered wagon necessary for the trek west. This is a contemporary delineation of the Connecticut Yankee's urge "to go West"—to the Holland Purchase in western New York, by way of the "Pittsburgh Pike" to the public lands of Ohio, or by the Buffalo gateway to the fertile plains of the Western Reserve.[17]

In the Southwest, however, the competition of state lands was sharp, and few settlers were attracted onto the public domain. Kentucky was selling 400-acre tracts on a liberal installment plan at 25 cents an acre,

[15] *Statutes at Large*, Vol. II, Act of May 3, 1807, p. 445. For attempts at enforcement: See *Niles' Register*, Vol. XV (1819) p. 301, Vol. XXXVIII (1830), p. 99; *Official Opinions of the Attorney General of the United States* (Washington, 1852), Vol. I, pp. 471, 475; *American State Papers, Public Lands*, Vol. II, pp. 242-51.

[16] Sakolski, *Great American Land Bubble*, pp. 122-3.

[17] *ibid.*

and Georgia was disposing of her lands under a lottery system at a nominal price of 6 or 8 cents an acre.[18]

On the whole, the government of the United States was more lenient than its laws would lead one to believe. Its generosity reached out in many directions. While with one hand it tried to prevent speculation and illegal settlement, with the other it was ready to help the settlers out of their difficulties. In addition to the legislative relief already noted with respect to foreign titles and land indebtedness, a great amount of land was doled out by the government, in the period 1800 to 1820, as compensation for military and naval services, in grants for asylums for the deaf and dumb, in donations to religious organizations, for the benefit of sufferers in the New Madrid earthquake, for the encouragement of the growth of vine and olives, etc.[19] But even this benevolence dwindled into insignificance when compared with the broad grants made for public advancement, for schools and for internal improvements.

When Ohio, the first public-land state, was admitted into the union in 1803, the federal government adopted the policy of retaining title to all land within the state boundaries, excepting one section in each township which was set aside for a state fund for common schools. In addition, 3 per cent of the net proceeds of the sales of public lands were earmarked for building roads.[20] Such allowances were made on condition that the state, county, or township should not levy taxes on the land sold by the United States for five years after the sale.[21] This Ohio precedent guided policy for every public-land state later admitted to the union. Had the states of the Old Northwest handled their school grants wisely, they would have aided considerably the support of local schools, but too frequently careless and sometimes corrupt legislatures hastily sold the lands and improperly invested the proceeds.[22]

[18] R. S. Cotterill, "The National Land System in the South, 1803-1812," *Mississippi Valley Historical Review*, Vol. XVI (1929-30), pp. 504-5.

[19] For military bounty grants see Treat, *National Land System*, Chap. X; and for special grants, Chap. XII.

[20] Donaldson, *The Public Domain*, pp. 225, 238; Ohio Enabling Act of April 30, 1802, *Statutes at Large*, Vol. II, pp. 173-5.

[21] In later years, out of this provision was to rise the issue of states' rights vs. the federal government's right of eminent domain. Lands exempt from taxes for five years were to prove quite an attraction to foreigners.

[22] Treat, *National Land System*, p. 285; G. W. Knight, "History and Management of Land Grants for Education in the Northwest Territory," *Papers* of the American Historical Association, Vol. I (1885).

The last important event in the history of public land administration during this period occurred on the eve of the outbreak of the war with Great Britain. In 1812, a General Land Office was established in Washington as a bureau of the Treasury Department,[23] and a commissioner took over the duties formerly performed by the Secretary of the Treasury. This arrangement lasted until 1849 when the Land Office was transferred to the newly created Department of the Interior.

With the outbreak of the War of 1812, westward migration slumped and land sales ceased. But soon after the return of peace in 1814 the movement revived and shortly expanded to incredible proportions. Like a mountain torrent it poured thousands of settlers onto the fertile lands of the Mississippi Valley. This Great Migration, as it was called, was a movement of peoples comparable to the barbarian invasions of Europe in the fourth century, but unlike those invasions it consisted for the most part of a native population moving out of the eastern states.

A number of events prepared the way for this exodus. The Louisiana Purchase, the Burr Conspiracy, the Yazoo Company speculations, the Lewis and Clark and the Pike expeditions, the expanding interests of the fur trade and the campaigns of the War of 1812—all advertised the West. Continued discussion of a system of internal improvements linking the East and the West, the beginning of construction of the National Road, the fight in New York state over the possibilities of an Erie canal, the opening up of steam navigation on the Ohio and Mississippi rivers—these factors also pointed the way to a great western boom. In the East conditions were never more propitious. The rise of the factory system in New England, the falling off of commerce, and the disbanding of the armies in 1815 had contributed to produce for the first time in the history of the American economic order a considerable oversupply of labor. Since the best of the eastern state lands were now taken up, there was nothing apparently to alleviate the situation but a movement onto the public domain of the transappalachian West where land could be purchased on credit.

Towns grew and villages sprang up over night. Mt. Pleasant, a little Ohio hamlet of seven families before the war, grew in 1815 to a town of five hundred souls boasting seven stores, three taverns, a meeting-house, a schoolhouse, a market house, and within a radius of six miles,

---

[23] *Statutes at Large*, Act of April 25, 1812, Chap. 68.

nine merchant mills, two grist mills, twelve saw mills, a paper mill, and a factory for woolen cloth.[24] When cotton rose to 30 cents a pound in 1816, and to the unprecedented price of 34 cents two years later, people poured into the virgin wilderness of the Southwest like the swirling eddies of rushing waters. Lands still stained by the blood of Indian wars sold at prices as high as $50 or even $100 an acre.[25] The Reverend John Peck, a traveller of the period, declared that the pioneers poured into Missouri faster than it was possible to provide corn for breadstuff. "It seemed as though Kentucky and Tennessee were breaking up and moving to the 'Far West'," he declared. "Caravan after caravan passed over the prairies of Illinois, crossing the 'great river' at St. Louis all bound for Boone's Lick."[26]

Six frontier states were admitted into the union between 1816 and 1821, of which all but Maine were public-land states. Over a million acres of public land were sold in 1814, and by 1818 the figure had climbed to the three-and-a-half-million mark. The population of Ohio increased from 230,000 in 1810 to 400,000 in 1816, and to 581,295 in 1820. That of Indiana rose from 24,000 in 1810 to 70,000 in 1816, and to 147,178 in 1820. Illinois had acquired a population of 55,162 by 1820. Alabama in 1818 counted 45,000 whites and 21,000 slaves, while Missouri in 1820 had 56,000 whites and 10,200 slaves. In 1820 Indiana could boast a 600 per cent increase of population in ten years. Illinois showed 350 per cent; Missouri, 215 per cent; Mississippi, 89 per cent; Tennessee, 68 per cent; Ohio, 50 per cent, and Kentucky, 39 per cent. As Professor Turner aptly put it, "A single section had arisen and was growing at such a rate that a description of it in any single year would be falsified before it could be published."[27]

In Missouri the zeal to purchase land amounted to a fever. Another traveller, Timothy Flint, recorded that "land speculators constituted a particular party. It required prodigious efforts to become adroit. The speculator[s] had a peculiar kind of slang dialect . . . and when they walked about it was with an air of solemn thoughtfulness upon their

[24] McMaster, *History of the People of the United States*, Vol. IV, Chap. 33.

[25] Thomas P. Abernethy, *The Formative Period in Alabama; idem*, "Andrew Jackson and the Rise of Southwestern Demorcracy," *American Historical Review*, Vol. XXXIII (1927), pp. 64-77.

[26] Walter B. Stevens, "The Travail of Missouri for Statehood," *Missouri Historical Review*, Vol. XV (1920), pp. 1-36.

[27] Frederick J. Turner, *Rise of the New West* (New York, 1906), p. 70. By permission of Harper and Brothers Co.

countenance[s] as though wisdom would die with them. The surveyors of course were very important instruments in this business, and a great and fortunate land speculator and landholder was looked up to with as much veneration by the people, as any partner in the house of Hope in London or Gray in America."[28]

Bounty land warrants originally granted by the government for military service brought severe strictures upon the government. The West felt much dissatisfaction at throwing open land for the location of these warrants. Doubtless feeling would have been less strong if the soldiers themselves had taken possession of the land so generously bestowed, but military scrip was transferable and considerable amounts of it had been bought up by speculators. It was claimed, for instance, that the right to 320 acres in central Indiana was purchased for $17.50 and sold for $5,000.[29]

This "monster," speculation, fixed its eager grasp upon some of the best lands in the West and held them for a rise in prices. Everywhere, especially in Alabama, lands were selling at advances out of all proportion to their actual value.[30] Throughout the length and breadth of the frontier the cry went up against the speculator. The situation was due to the "disgrace of our legislation, which grants every facility to the rich without consulting the poor," declared a contemporary authority on the subject.[31]

While the speculator waxed fat on milk and honey in the new West, the actual settler did not fare so well. Many settlers had invested in lands on credit hoping to pay out of the increase in the value of their holdings or out of its produce. Some were able to do so but many were not. The continual introduction of new lands into the market diminished the value of those that were already purchased. The importation of merchandise from the eastern seaports drained the West of its money, and the products of the newer regions however abundant could command only low prices because of the lack of means of transportation. All the capital that could be procured was sufficient for the improvement of but a small portion of the land already purchased. In

[28] Timothy Flint, *Recollections of the Last Ten Years* (Boston, 1826; Reprint, Knopf, 1932), p. 192.
[29] David Thomas, *Travels Through the Western Country in the Summer of 1816* (Auburn, New York, 1819), p. 159.
[30] Henry B. Fearon, *Sketches of America* (3rd Ed., London, 1819), p. 215.
[31] Samuel R. Brown, *The Western Gazetteer* (Auburn, N.Y., 1817), p. 111.

truth, much of the public domain which the government had sold to actual settlers remained in a state of primeval wilderness.

The relief problem inherited from the period before the War of 1812 became even more pressing during the period of inflation following the year 1815. The only cure for land indebtedness seemed to be the granting of more relief to the debtors, and so Congress passed relief act after relief act. Attempts to bring about forfeiture of the settlers' interests because of non-payment generally brought forth public outcry. Forfeited land offered at auction often went at prices lower than those in the settler's contract. In some regions the force of public opinion was such that no one would bid against the original claimant, and in most of such cases he was permitted to re-enter his land.[32]

An estimate submitted in 1816 to the House of Representatives showed that land sold at the auctions, most of it to men of money, brought only ten and a half cents more than the minimum price per acre.[33] The government had already disposed of 212,000 acres of land to actual settlers at bargain prices under special preemption legislation. The question arose whether it would not be better to allow all settlers a general preemption and thus provide for actual settlement than to sell to speculators who merely held lands for higher prices. This would solve the land-indebtedness problem to some extent. But rather than make such a radical change the national government persisted in following the policy of 1800.

The Second United States Bank established in 1816 did not succeed, as its founders hoped it would, in checking bank inflation, which was prevalent especially in the West where state banks were established in wholesale lots for the precise purpose of manufacturing credit to be used in buying land and constructing internal improvements.[34] An attempt in 1817 to require payment for public lands in specie served only to increase the numbers of persons buying on credit.

Regardless of the failure of Congress to stem the tide of inflation, economic laws were taking their course. In the laws of speculation like those of gravitation, all that goes up must eventually come down. In the latter part of 1816 a sudden reduction in prices in the Atlantic states and

---

[32] *ibid.*, p. 288.

[33] *American State Papers, Public Lands*, Vol. III, p. 170.

[34] For a discussion of this wildcat banking consult Harry J. Carman, *Social and Economic History of the United States* (Boston, 1930), Vol. I, pp. 530*ff.*; Turner, *Rise of the New West*, pp. 300*ff.*; J. B. McMaster, *History of the People of the United States*, Vol. IV, pp. 280*ff.*

the failure of many banks in the western country pointed to catastrophe ahead. As long as land prices remained high and emigrants continued to arrive bringing money to buy, as long as there was an abundant and unnatural circulation of money, both good and spurious, speculation and rising values continued. But the moment the pressure began to prevent people from selling their lands, the tide began to ebb.

No sooner was the bubble pricked and panic burst upon the country than public opinion turned against the moneyed interests and consequently against the national government. The western country joined wholeheartedly in criticizing the Bank of the United States. And a general hatred of banks appeared which was to result finally in political action.[35] The hard times following the Panic of 1819 did much to produce the wave of democratic sentiment which swept eastward out of the Mississippi Valley under the leadership of Andrew Jackson. A Kentucky newspaper declared that land speculation was the sole cause of the depression in the West, "the most portentous evil that ever existed in America; it *threatens the dissolution of the union.*"[36]

The truth is that both the speculator and the actual settler were responsible for this unhealthy condition in the national land system. The liberal credit features of the Act of 1800, while leading to much settlement in the West, nevertheless played an important part in bringing on the Panic of 1819.[37] A report of the Secretary of the Treasury in 1819 revealed the startling truth that since 1789 the government had sold land to the value of forty-four million dollars, but had received as yet but half of this sum.[38] Between 1815 and 1819 the amount of money owed the government increased from three million to seventeen million dollars.[39] In view of the prostrate conditions existing throughout the country and the hatred that was arising against the creditor interests, the government was compelled at last to take steps to put its house in order. Thorough revision of the land laws was essential to a more orderly and systematic settlement of the public domain, but such alteration would necessarily involve the abrogation of credit—the very life blood of the West.

[35] For the attack upon banks, see: Ernest L. Bogart "Taxation of the Second United States Bank by Ohio," *American Historical Review*, Vol. XVII (1912), pp. 312ff.
[36] Quoted from the *Kentucky Reporter* in *Niles' Register*, September 4, 1819, pp. 10-11.
[37] Samuel Reznick, "The Depression of 1819-20: A Social History," *American Historical Review*, Vol. XXXIX (1933), p. 37.
[38] *Niles' Register*, May 8, 1819.
[39] *American State Papers, Finance*, Vol. III, p. 718.

Western newspapers suddenly grasped the significance of any change in the land system. Every possible atom of praise for the existing system was sought out by western interests and broadcast to the countryside. The editor of the *National Intelligencer,* speaking of the land system of the United States, eloquently declared that "so wise, beautiful, and perfect a system was never before adopted by any government or nation on earth. In regard to rights of man, and dignity, and happiness of man, it triumphs over the legislation of Europe and laughs at the barbaric pomp of Asia. . . . No other country or age has produced a land system so sublime in principle, so perfect in practice, so magnificent in prospect. . . . The titles to land . . . are derived from the public authority, whose arm is extended to maintain the rightful possession. . . . The banner of freedom which waves over the whole proclaims the character and protective power of the United States. . . . Greece in its wisdom, Rome in its grandeur, Europe in its glory, never realized a system so deserving the admiration and applause of human-kind."[40] State legislatures were quick to support public opinion. The legislatures of Indiana and Louisiana drew up memorials praying that no change be made in the land laws, and describing the injurious effects such change would have on the western country.[41] Many eastern business interests, particularly the rising manufacturers and the enterprising builders of canals, turnpikes, and railways, roundly denounced any alteration of the existing system.[42]

The Senate of the United States took the initiative in the matter. Ninian Edwards of Illinois who led the opposition preferred confirming the sale of public lands to actual settlers. "Can it be a dictate of wisdom," he asked, "to predicate a general system upon a particular and extraordinary case which is gone by, and in all probability will never again occur? Can it be wise to select that moment for abolishing all credit upon the sale of public lands when money is scarcer than it has ever heretofore been, and thereby retard settlement of those lands at the very time when the state of things which produced the supposed evils of the credit system is rapidly disappearing?"[43] But the efforts of Ed-

[40] Signed ["Hampden"], quoted in the *Scioto Gazette and Fredonian Chronicle,* July 30, 1819.
[41] Presented to the Senate in February 1820. *Annals of Congress,* 16 Cong. 1 Sess., pp. 260 and 478, respectively.
[42] Carman, *Social and Economic History of the United States,* Vol. I, p. 527.
[43] *Annals of Congress,* 16 Cong. 1 Sess., p. 483.

wards and other frontier leaders were of no avail; the reform bill became a law on April 24, 1820.

The Act of 1820[44] lowered the minimum price of land to $1.25, required full payment in cash, and reduced the minimum amount that could be purchased to eighty acres.

Thus closed an era in the settlement of the public domain. Jeffersonian Democracy had opened the fight for the disposal of western lands to actual settlers, rather than to speculators and proprietors. The credit system may not have brought much money into the national treasury, but the settlement of the West was of incalculable value to the country. The abolition of the credit system was for the moment a blow to the settlers, but some consolation could be found in the provisions of the Act of 1820 which reduced the minimum price to $1.25 an acre and the minimum amount of land which the government would sell to eighty acres.

The cash-payment requirement, however, benefited the speculator at the expense of the settler. It deprived the latter of the advantage which the installment plan had heretofore given him in bidding against speculators at the auction. Competition with men of money for choice tracts of land would henceforth be difficult unless wildcat banks should come to the rescue. American settlers however had already learned the art of turning well-intentioned laws to their own purposes. Profiting by past experience, they immediately initiated a crusade to democratize the land system—to give all men an equal opportunity to acquire land. What the settlers lost through the operation of the credit system they would regain in the next twenty years through the success of the preemption movement.

[44] *Statutes at Large*, Vol. III, p. 566. The Act of 1804 provided sale for cash at $1.64 per acre, and reduced the minimum amount to 160 acres.

CHAPTER III

SECTIONALISM

IN 1820 President Monroe, just reelected by an electoral vote lacking but one of unanimity, waxed eloquent over "the prosperous and happy condition of our country." Said he, "It is impossible to behold so gratifying, so glorious a spectacle, without being penetrated with the most profound and grateful acknowledgements to the Supreme Author of all Good for such manifold and inestimable advantages."[1] In the realm of national politics it was an "Era of Good Feeling." The old Republican Party of Jefferson had at last triumphed to the extent of not only ousting the Federalist Party but also of becoming the only national party in the country. Yet Monroe's statement appears extravagant when one considers the manifold sufferings in the nation at large, particularly in the newer parts of the country. Nor did his exaggeration take into consideration the undercurrents of politics which were seething with discontent, for factionalism was sticking up its ugly head, and sectionalism had never been more pronounced.

When the question of the admission of Missouri into the Union arose in 1818, eastern interests were as much afraid of building up a powerful West as they were of increasing the slavery power of the South. The *Missouri Intelligencer* published at Boone's Lick called attention to the fact that "the eighty-seven members of the House of Representatives who voted" for "the restriction . . . to be imposed upon us . . . were those exclusively of the eastern states. They view with a jealous eye the march of power westward, and are well aware the preponderance will soon be against them; therefore they have combined against us; but let them pause before they proceed further, or the grave they are preparing for us, may be their own sepulchre. As well might they arrest the course of the ocean that washes their barren shores, as to check our future growth. Emigration will continue with a giant stride until the wilderness shall be a wilderness no more; but in its stead will arise flourishing towns, cultivated farms. . . . Let those who are raised by the voice of the people to watch over and protect their rights and liberties, beware

---

[1] J. D. Richardson (ed.), *Messages and Papers of the Presidents* (Washington), Vol. II (1899), p. 55.

how they abuse so sacred a trust, lest they find in every injured freeman the spirit of a Hampden [to] rise and hurl them from their posts."[2]

While it has been stated that the slavery issue struck in national politics like a "firebell in the night," nevertheless, close observation reveals that between 1820 and 1845 the slavery issue was kept out of national politics and other sectional issues such as those pertaining to the public lands, internal improvements, and the protective tariff challenged public attention. Again, as in the 1790's, the pendulum swung toward a national economy which professed to establish a more balanced economic-social order. The American people once more faced the question whether they desired to continue a régime in which the agricultural interests would remain dominant, or whether they preferred a Hamiltonian program which would encourage, and ultimately make predominant in national policy, a group of manufacturing interests. So far the agricultural expansion of the country had been at the expense of the East. The Great Migration had drained the Atlantic States of a valuable labor population, and there had been little foreign emigration to fill up the ranks. The depression period following the Panic of 1819, coupled with the more drastic effects of the European depression of 1825, thus provided American statesmen with a reconstruction problem of considerable dimensions.

John C. Calhoun in 1820 addressed to John Quincy Adams a discriminating comment on American conditions. "There has been within these two years," he observed, "an immense revolution of fortunes . . . and a general mass of disaffection to the government, not concentrated in any particular direction, but ready to seize upon any event and looking out anywhere for a leader."[3] Ultimately that leader was to be a military man, Andrew Jackson, but for the time being the prominent statesman, Henry Clay, attempted to fill that place.

Perhaps Clay did not desire to go as far as Hamilton in granting extensive bounties to manufacturing interests. But he did want to grant some new direction to American industry which would help to bring about a balance in the economic system. By building up manufacturing centers in the country he sought to create a home market which would

[2] Issue of May 17, 1819, quoted by Frank H. Hodder, "Sidelights on the Missouri Compromise," American Historical Association *Report*, 1909, p. 153.

[3] Charles F. Adams (ed.), *Memoirs of John Quincy Adams* (Philadelphia, 1875), Vol. V, p. 128.

absorb the agricultural surplus of the South and West. To build up these centers it would be necessary to protect manufacturing interests from foreign competition by means of a protective tariff. Moreover, to bring about the exchange of products between the manufacturing East and the agricultural South and West, a system of extensive internal improvements was essential.[4] This scheme became known as the American System, and the name carried an appeal to men's emotions even when the principles back of it failed to appeal to their reason.

The passage of the protective tariff of 1824 and the eloquence of John Quincy Adams attested to the rising strength of Hamiltonian forces. Adams looked upon the public domain as a great national resource from which funds should flow for the well-being, happiness, and education of all people.[5] This idea of distributing the proceeds from the sales of public lands among the states for purposes of education found support, as one would expect, in many state legislatures, especially in eastern states which expected to get the greater share.[6]

But Adams believed even more strongly that the land of the West should be disposed of without injuring the real estate and manufacturing interests of the East. "The bee that robs the hive of his neighbor," he observed, "becomes idle and improvident—and is never known to profit even by the flowers in his own garden, and the outrage usually results in the death of the robber and the robbed."[7] Professor Wellington declared that "John Quincy Adams used all his influence to perpetuate the revenue attitude toward the public domain. . . . [He] looked upon the American public domain from the general point of view of the European administrator, seeing how instrumental it might be in the national administration of social and economic interests. His attitude was not unlike the physiocratic point of view of Edward Gibbon Wakefield, a contemporary English economist. . . . If the United States had been controlled by men of property, and more respectful of European practice, the plan of John Quincy Adams might have been adopted."[8]

[4] *Annals of Congress,* 18 Cong. 1 Sess., pp. 1022-40, 1970, 1978.

[5] Message to Congress, December 1825; for extract see Commager, *Documents of American History.*

[6] For example, see *Niles' Weekly Register,* Vol. XXI, pp. 248, 253, 277, 281, 282, 299.

[7] Quoted in Kirkland, *History of American Economic Life,* p. 146. By permission of F. S. Crofts and Co.

[8] Raynor G. Wellington, *The Political and Sectional Influence of the Public Lands, 1828-1842* (Boston, 1914), p. 3. By permission of Professor Wellington.

However, the attempt in the 1820's to convert the American people to a Hamiltonian philosophy was even more short-lived than it had been in the 1790's. It merely served to bring about a closer political alliance between the South and the West. When the East mustered sufficient strength to push through the protective tariff of 1824, John Randolph of Virginia exclaimed in the solemn chambers of the Senate: "If, *ad artem,* you draw the last shilling from our pockets, what are the checks of the Constitution to us? A fig for the Constitution! When the scorpion's sting is probing us to the quick, shall we stop to chop logic?"[9] The defeat of Jackson for the Presidency in 1824, in spite of the fact that he carried the popular vote of the country, did much to gird the West for political action. The South and West alliance, together with aid from the Middle Atlantic States, made possible a powerful coalition against Adams and Clay. In the years of the Adams administration this coalition became effectively organized into the new Democratic Party which was to be triumphant in 1828. In the rise of this Jacksonian Democracy one cannot minimize the part played by the agricultural interests of the West which met with counterproposals each measure on the program of the Adams-Clay group.

The Land Act of 1820 brought the whole population of the frontier to the brink of ruin. Had the federal government proved a rigid creditor it could have turned the Mississippi Valley into a scene of desolation.[10] Faced with the possibility of having to relinquish their holdings, settlers from far and wide frantically petitioned Congress for relief from their obligations under the new law. The problem was complex as well as embarrassing. If Congress refused relief these frontiersmen would become squatters or else seek lands in Mexico. On the other hand, if some indulgence were granted the return of prosperity might enable them to pay their debts. In such circumstances it seemed expedient for Congress to compromise the issue rather than antagonize a region where population and political strength were increasing from day to day.

Accordingly, in 1821 the first relief act was passed, extending the time of payment and authorizing purchasers to secure a portion of their

[9] *Annals of Congress,* 18 Cong. 1 Sess., p. 2,361.
[10] James Hall, *Notes on the Western States* (Philadelphia, 1838), pp. 174-5.

lands by relinquishing the remainder to the government.[11] As might
have been expected, a temporary measure was not sufficient to satisfy
frontier needs. In 1822 Congress extended the relief act of 1821. This
policy of extending credit, once begun, was continued in one form or
another until by 1832 eleven relief acts had been passed.[12] Hence the indebtedness incurred under the Act of 1800 was eventually reduced
without injury to the citizenry of the West and with but little loss to
the government. Such a solution, however, also had unfortunate aspects.
Perceiving the willingness to compromise displayed by eastern leaders
with regard to extending credit, frontier forces were encouraged to
gather their growing strength behind other measures which in fact endangered the whole land policy.

In the long struggle over land policy there were many congressmen
from the New West who presented forcefully and effectively the problems of that rapidly growing section. But perhaps the most outstanding
of these was that "veritable champion of the West," Thomas Hart Benton, Senator from Missouri. Whatever peculiar traits the West may or
may not have had, it certainly cannot be doubted that Benton thoroughly understood and quite as thoroughly represented its economic
and social interests. He began his legal career in St. Louis as a representative of Spanish land claimants, and was elected to the United States
Senate chiefly because of his views on land policy.[13] This Missouri Senator well understood the people who would "settle the lands in spite of
everybody." He exaggerated little when he declared that the thirteen
British colonies had been settled upon gratuitous donations or nominal
sales."[14] But perceiving the immediate futility of working for "gratuitous donations," he gave his attention to "nominal sales."

While the Senate, in 1824, was discussing Clay's tariff bill, Benton
introduced his own bill providing for graduation in the price of land.
"By the present rule," he declared, "the good and bad land are held at
the same price. The best can be got for $1.25 per acre—the worst cannot
be had for less. . . . It is unjust to the people, because it prevents them

---

[11] *Statutes at Large*, Act of March 21, 1821, Vol. IV, Chap. 12. Ninian Edwards of Illinois
led the fight for this indulgence in the Senate.

[12] For an analysis of these relief measures see: Treat, *National Land System*, p. 161.

[13] Jonas Viles, "Missouri in 1820," *Mississippi Valley Historical Review*, Vol. XV (1928), p.
50.

[14] Amelia C. Ford, "Colonial Precedents of Our National Land System as It Existed in 1800,"
University of Wisconsin Bulletin No. 352 (Madison, 1910), p. 95.

from getting the inferior land at a fair price; unjust to the states, because it checks their population and deprives them of their right of taxation; unjust to the nation, because it prevents the public treasury from receiving the money which such land is worth and for which it would sell."[15] His bill set 50 cents an acre as a second minimum price for poorer lands, and the refuse lands that would not sell for even 50 cents an acre were to be given away to poor people who would cultivate them. This bill received little attention.

In the same year the House Committee on Public Lands, in answer to petitions from Illinois and elsewhere which prayed for a grant of preemption, expressed flatly its opposition to such indulgence: "It cannot be perceived by what principle persons having no color of title should, after lands on which they have settled were known to belong to the United States at the time of making their settlement, claim the right of preemption." If the government sanctioned this indulgence there would be a mad rush for valuable lands with the result that there would be no regard for surveys or boundaries. Lawlessness would abound everywhere, and the years of labor which the government spent in building up a respected land system would be lost. The report concluded: "A system of indulgence to those who trespass by making unauthorized settlements upon the lands of the United States after those lands are known to belong to the government, would in the opinion of the committee, be productive of much perplexity to the government as well as perjury to those concerned in the purchase and settlement of the national domain."[16]

Petitions continued to pour in upon Congress from the public-land states asking for graduation and preemption.[17] In the debates on the graduation principle in 1826 Benton clearly maintained his stand "that it is better economy to sell the lands, or the best of them, in eight years, for twenty millions, than to sell them in the progress of ages and centuries for three hundred millions. One would enable us to get rid of the debt; the other would not. The lands were ceded to the federal government to pay the debt. . . . In eight years they will extinguish a debt of eighty millions if the present ruinous system is abandoned, and a new and judicious one adopted."[18] Enormous quantities of land had failed to sell after being placed on the market. Yet large numbers of men desir-

15 *Annals of Congress*, 18 Cong. 1 Sess., p. 583.
16 *ibid.*, p. 2,481.   17 *American State Papers, Public Lands*, Vol. IV, p. 529.
18 In the Senate, May 16, 1826, *Congressional Debates*, 19 Cong. 1 Sess., p. 724.

ing farms had been unable to buy land. He pointed out that if the lands could be occupied by those men, their production would result in greatly increased revenues. Population was the crying need of the West. Congress should graduate the price of the lands in relation to their value, which would be determined by the number of years they remained on the market unsold.[19]

But this prophet who could foresee the time when the valley of the Columbia would be the granary of China and Japan was too far in advance of those who lived in the psychological wilderness of Congressional halls. A resolution introduced by Senator David Barton of Missouri providing for donation of small tracts of the public lands that had remained unsold for a given time, to such persons as would actually live on and cultivate the same for some reasonable term of years, received but little attention.[20] In the same Congress Senator T. W. Tazewell of Virginia proposed that all public land be ceded to the states in which it lay.[21] The following year a bill was introduced in the Senate giving to persons who had relinquished their lands under the various relief acts the right of preemption at one-quarter the original contract price. This bill passed the Senate, but after a heated debate was tabled in the House.[22]

Finally in 1828 a committee reported to the House that it was "just and proper that he who renders a benefit to the public, who by his enterprise and industry has created for himself and his family a home in the wilderness, should be entitled to his reward. He has afforded facilities to the sale of the public lands, and brought into competition lands which otherwise would have commanded no price and for which there would have been no bidders, unless for his improvements."[23] Benton again brought forward his graduation bill, but this time with a provision that all lands which did not sell for a certain minimum price should be ceded to the states in which they lay.[24] Regarding the proposal of cession the committee reported that "each state would have a system of sales differing from that of the other states. . . .

[19] Turner, *Rise of the New West*, p. 142.
[20] 19 Cong. 2 Sess., *Congressional Debates*, p. 6.
[21] 19 Cong. 1 Sess., *Senate Document* No. 99.
[22] 19 Cong. 2 Sess., *Congressional Debates*, pp. 308, 334, 1,485.
[23] *American State Papers, Public Lands*, Vol. V, p. 401.
[24] 20 Cong. 1 Sess., *Congressional Debates*, p. 609.

Serious collusions would necessarily occur; speculation, fraud, and corruption would be attempted in state legislatures."[25]

Thus in the short period of four years from 1824 to 1828 the South and the West brought before Congress, in answer to Adams's proposal to distribute the proceeds from the sales of the public lands among the states for purposes of education and internal improvements, such radical propositions as graduation, donation, and preemption. The conservative interests of the North Atlantic States were much alarmed at this trend of events.

In 1827, Richard Rush, Adams's Secretary of the Treasury, warned the country in very plain words of an imminent crisis in which certain agrarian tendencies threatened the very economic concepts upon which the nation was founded. "The maxim" he held to be "sound . . . that the ratio of capital to population should, if possible, be kept on the increase. . . . The manner in which the remote lands of the United States are selling and settling, whilst it may tend to increase more quickly the aggregate population of the country, . . . does not increase capital in the same proportion. It is a proposition too plain to require elucidation, that the creation of capital is retarded, rather than accelerated, by the diffusion of a thin population over a great surface of soil. Anything that may serve to hold back this tendency to diffusion from running too far and too long into an extreme can scarcely prove otherwise than salutary."[26]

Adams himself recorded in his diary that on December 31, 1828, Clay spoke to him "with great concern . . . [over] the prospects of the country—the threats of disunion from the South, and the graspings after all public lands, which are disclosing themselves in the Western States."[27] Eastern newspapers expressed considerable anxiety over the agrarian tendencies of Congress and of the nation at large. The editor of the New York *National Advocate* complained bitterly that the House public-lands committee appointed by the "Jacksonian" Speaker was completely dominated by southern and western men—a situation which he regarded "as a material sacrifice of the just rights of the nation for

---

[25] *American State Papers, Public Lands*, Vol. V, p. 445.
[26] Report of the Secretary of the Treasury on the State of Finances, 1827, *American State Papers, Finance*, Vol. V, p. 638.
[27] Adams, *Memoirs of John Quincy Adams*, Vol. VIII, pp. 87-8.

the purpose of pandering to the *land appetite* of the west."[28] He characterized the propositions introduced in Congress as "so wild and extravagant as to induce a belief that they intended by them nothing more than to show their constituents that they were deserving their support at the next Congressional election."

"What in the name of common sense," this editor asked "is the hurry to get rid of the public lands, that the government is thus crowded from year to year to reduce the price of them, overstock the market, invite speculators, and in the end take back the poorer portions, and forgive the indebtedness of those who have gone beyond their means and their discretion.... It is certainly time for Congress to adopt a little Yankee management on this subject. It may not be improper or unwise, perhaps, to help the western people to their farms gratis, as concerning the past, but we protest against trusting out the public lands only to give in the debt a few years hence, or permitting speculators to make large purchases only to trouble the government with taking them back again." In conclusion he advised the government to "make fair bargains, gives credit only where payment can reasonably be expected, and then hold the parties to strict accountability."[29]

While agrarianism was concentrated mainly in the frontier West, nevertheless it had counterparts in the East. In New York City at Military Hall the preachings of Thomas Skidmore on Equal Rights led such newspapers as *The Courier and Enquirer, The Evening Journal,* and *The Commercial Advertiser* to discuss this subject.[30] Skidmore's scheme, which provided that the whole property of the state be taken from those who possessed it and redistributed on an equal basis, must have brought shudders to Wall Street and to the landed aristocrats of the Hudson River Valley. In 1828 the first labor newspaper, *The Mechanics' Free Press,* suggested to Congress the propriety of placing all public lands without delay within the reach of the people at large by the right of a title of occupancy only, supporting this memorial with such arguments as the following: "The present state of affairs must lead to the wealth of the few"; "all men have a natural right to the soil, else they will be deprived of life, liberty, and the pursuit of

[28] Editorial printed in full in *Canal of Intelligence* (Norwich, Conn.), January 2, 1828.
[29] *ibid.*
[30] As commented upon in *The Free Enquirer* (New Harmony, Indiana), Vol. II (1829-30), pp. 356-7.

happiness."[31] In 1835, George Henry Evans, editor of *The Man*, a New York labor newspaper, proclaimed to the workingmen's associations the vital relationship between a labor surplus in the East and the public domain of the West.[32] Instead of defending resort to strikes, he therefore advocated a crusade against land monopoly. The origins of the so-called Loco-Focoism, the agrarianism of the East, are clearly to be found in the equal rights and labor movements.

But it was too late to stem the tide. The alliance of the South and West, together with the agricultural forces from the Middle Atlantic States, had already made possible a new Democratic Party.[33] In 1828 this new party supporting the presidency of Andrew Jackson was victorious, and again the East was compelled to recognize frontier values.

Out of the forests and the plains of the Mississippi Valley was born this new democracy of the common man. By 1830 one-third of the American people were "men of the western waters," as they liked to style themselves. Jackson was their natural leader. He had "smashed" the Indians; he had inflicted a stinging defeat on the British at New Orleans; he had met all the problems of the most rapidly growing part of America. It is true that few people knew what to expect after his election as President. When one considers that in the campaign of 1828, four-fifths of the preachers, practically all the manufacturers, and seven-eighths of the bankers opposed Jackson, one begins to understand fully what the Democrats meant when they cried: "Down with the aristocracy!"

As Professor Turner has so ably demonstrated, the victory of Jackson "meant that an agricultural society, strongest in the regions of rural isolation rather than in the areas of greater density of population and of greater wealth, had triumphed for the moment over the conservative, industrial, commercial, and manufacturing society of the New England type. It meant that a new, aggressive, expansive democracy, emphasizing human rights and individualism, as against the old established order which emphasized vested rights and corporate action, had come

[31] *Mechanics' Free Press*, October 25, 1828, in John R. Commons et al. (ed.), *A Documentary History of American Industrial Society* (Cleveland, 1910), Vol. V, pp. 43-5.

[32] *The Man*, May 21, 1835, as quoted in *ibid.*, Vol. V, pp. 46-7.

[33] For the party transition see Homer C. Hockett, *Western Influences on Political Parties to 1825* (The Ohio State University Bulletin No. 2, Vol. XXVII [1917]. The Ohio University Studies—Contributions in History and Political Science, No. 4), Chap. IV.

into control."[34] For the first time in world history, a frontier society came into control of national polity.

The West of the Mississippi Valley was by 1830 a distinct section of nine states, possessing one-third of the nation's population, and controlling 30 per cent of the votes in the electoral college. It had a population greater than that of the original thirteen states when they declared their independence from the most powerful empire on the globe. No reasonable person, thirty years before, would have been likely to foresee the importance the West was to assume in national life by 1830. Probabilities were altogether against it. History and experience could furnish no precedents. All that extremist admirers had dreamed and prophesied had been more than realized.

In this new era there could be little doubt that the subject of land, so vital to the newer sections of the country, would play an all important part. A contemporary authority declared that "the greatest cause of prosperity in the West is the wide extent of good lands open to the reception of emigrants, and the flourishing state of agriculture." In that country the subject of public lands is "a matter of vital interest, and is every day growing in influence, and expanding in magnitude. . . . When the population of a country is thus rapidly increasing, where that increase tends inevitably to a transfer of power from one section of the Union to another, and where the anticipated change is so near at hand, . . . the subject becomes deeply interesting." It is one "calculated to awaken sectional feelings, and upon which, therefore a great deal of opinion may prevail."[35] The West hoped and had reason to expect that the Jackson administration would do something for those who were settling the frontier. The subject of land, so vital to the nation and to the newer agricultural sections of the country was bound to play an important rôle.

In December 1829 Samuel A. Foot, Senator from Connecticut, who had consistently opposed western influences, suggested that an inquiry should be made into the advisability of placing no more public lands upon the market at least for a time.[36] He was anxious to know, more-

[34] Frederick J. Turner, *The United States, 1830-1850* (New York, 1935), p. 30. By permission of Henry Holt and Co.
[35] "The Public Domain of the United States," article based on Report of Select Committee of House of Representatives, 20 Cong. 2 Sess., in *American Quarterly Review*, Vol. VI (1829), pp. 263-83.
[36] 21 Cong. 1 Sess., *Congressional Debates*, p. 3.

over, if the office of surveyor-general—the most important administrative office in the General Land Office—should not be dispensed with.

This challenge was accepted by Benton of Missouri, who exclaimed: "The manufacturers want poor people to do the work for small wages; these poor people wish to go to the West and get land; to have flocks and herds—to have their own fields, orchards, gardens, and meadows—their own cribs, barns, and dairies, and to start their children on a theater where they can contend with equal chances for the honors and dignities of the country."[37]

Robert Y. Hayne of South Carolina saw clearly that both the West and the South were fundamentally opposed to the economic policy desired by the North Atlantic States, though for different reasons. The West desired a lower price on public lands, which would mean that eastern manufacturers would have to pay higher wages. The South wanted a lower tariff, which was opposed by the northeastern manufacturers because it would mean increased foreign competition and hence a cut in their profits. Hayne proposed that the South work with the West on a basis of their common enmity toward the Northeast. He gave a clear statement of the case as it pertained to the land question: "On the one side, it is contended that the public land ought to be reserved as a permanent fund for revenue and future distribution among the states; while on the other it is insisted that the whole of these lands of right belong to, and ought to belong to, the states in which they lie."[38]

The debates might have been resolved into a serious discussion over the principles of distribution and cession had not Daniel Webster moved to the defense of New England. This onetime protagonist of free trade, but now eloquent defender of infant industries and friend of the wealthy manufacturer, Abbott Lawrence, was moved to the defense of certain Hamiltonian interests.[39] For five days he discoursed on matters

[37] Wellington, *Political and Sectional Influence of the Public Lands*, p. 28.

[38] 21 Cong. 1 Sess., *Congressional Debates*, p. 23.

[39] John Quincy Adams wrote in his diary that Lawrence "has been for many years devoted to Webster, and the main pillar of his support, both pecuniary and political." In May 1828, Lawrence had written Webster regarding the tariff bill that "This bill if adopted as amended will keep the South and West in debt to New England the next hundred years." Lawrence believed that a reduction in either the tariff or the price of the public lands would drain his state of its population and wealth. (Quoted in Wellington, *Political and Sectional Influence of Public Lands*, p. 27.)

Thus the manufacturing industries had little interest in the welfare of either agriculture or the West. They, "eager to secure an abundance of cheap labor as to find shelter behind a tariff

which touched the emotions of the nation. He was successful in turning the debate into a discussion of the nature of the Union and the
question whether a state could nullify an act of Congress, as Calhoun
had maintained in 1828. But Benton remained quite unconvinced that
the interests of the West were compatible with those of New England.

While the Hayne-Webster debate sidetracked the real issues in the
Senate, conservative interests in the lower house were making a concerted attempt to push through a distribution bill before the census of
1830 should change the complexion of that chamber. Representative
John Test of Indiana, in defense of the new states, asked why Congress
should "cram this measure down their throats before they shall have
acquired the strength which the new census bill will give them? . . . If
we must have a scramble for this property, give us a chance with you—
do not take the advantage of our present representative weakness, when
you know we have a large portion of original physical strength just
ready to organize and bring into action." James Blair of South Carolina
claimed that too many gentlemen were worried about the accumulation
of a surplus in the treasury and were already providing for its distribution. All this reminded him, he said, of the story about the hunter who
sold the skin before he had killed the bear. He felt that "the friends of
stockholding interest" were combining "with the advocates of high
protecting duties and the friends of internal improvements, in order
to squander away the public funds for selfish and sinister purposes."[40]
Representative Dixon H. Lewis of Alabama protested that the lands
were pledged for the sole purpose of redeeming the public debt. He
had yet to learn that it was constitutional for the federal government
to enter either the field of internal improvements or education. As for
the value of the public lands, he contended that it "has been imparted
to them by the industry, enterprise, and sufferings of that hardy population who preceded the comforts and conveniences of a more advanced
condition . . . who levelled the forests, who opened the roads, who
established the towns, who gave, in fact, a determinate value to all the
lands in the country, by converting a wilderness into a country possessing all the comforts of cultivated life." He was opposed to distribution

barrier, viewed with grave concern the westward rush to the land in the public domain."
(Quoted in Charles A. Beard and Mary A. Beard, *The Rise of American Civilization* [New
York, 1927], Vol. I, pp. 562-3). By permission of the Macmillan Co.
    [40] 21 Cong. 1 Sess., *Congressional Debates*, pp. 495, 497.

because it would mean continuing the protective tariff. "The Southern states," he continued, "had hoped for some alleviation of their burdens after the payment of the national debt. They had thought that after the necessities of the revenue had ceased, these duties would be taken off. But, sir, the race of politicians who believe that a national debt.is a blessing is not yet extinct. They exist full force in this House."

Representative Spencer Pettis of Missouri exclaimed: "Has it come to this, sir? We have had American systems, antislavery systems, the Lord knows what; and now we are to have an anti-emigration system to cripple the West, and to prevent the poor of the East from going to the West. . . . Do you fear the increased and increasing power of the West?"[41]

But neither in the Senate nor in the House was a decision reached on either of the principles of distribution or cession. Benton's graduation bill passed the Senate in May 1830, but was tabled in the House. All of the eastern senators north of the Potomac voted against it, but the South and the West pushed it through.[42]

While Webster and Hayne were proclaiming their love for the West, the frontier forces seized the opportunity to put through Congress a much-cherished piece of legislation. Since the passage of the Act of 1820 the situation of settlers had been serious. The various relief acts of the 1820's enabled many farmers to get rid of lands they could not pay for under their contracts, but this type of legislation did not aid new settlers in the purchase of their lands.[43]

The situation in Illinois, which probably had more arable land than any other state in the Union, is a case in point. Ninian Edwards, then governor, was waging a campaign for a more liberal land policy comparable to the fight Benton was making in the Senate. As late as 1829, six-sevenths of the land of this state was still owned by the federal government, which paid no taxes to the state government notwithstanding the fact that every public improvement made by the state government commensurately enhanced the value of the federal lands. The

---

[41] *ibid.,* pp. 506, 530.

[42] Wellington, *Political and Sectional Influence of the Public Lands,* pp. 33-4.

[43] The government land sales do not provide an adequate measure of the extent of settlement made in the decade of the 1820's. On the contrary, many settlers bought lands from speculators who were glad to unload for prices below the government minimum, or else preferred simply to squat on the land hoping that the government might ultimately grant them a preemption to their holdings.

whole quantity of land sold in Illinois up to July 1, 1828, was little over a million acres, which if divided into 160-acre tracts would make around 7,000 such farms. The actual number of votes cast in Illinois in the August election of that year was nearly 17,000. If allowance is made for, say one person in eighteen not voting, then the number of persons entitled to suffrage was at least 18,000. If the land sold had been equally distributed, the number of farms should nearly correspond with the number of voters. The ratio would then be eighteen voters per every seven farms. And when one considers that many farmers owned more than 160 acres, that many men of property in the state owned extensive tracts, and that a great many tracts were held by nonresidents, then the disparity becomes all the more apparent. In other words, fewer than one-third of the voters were freeholders.[44] Perhaps one should allow for a small proportion of trades people, professional, etc. If these figures are to be relied upon, somewhere near two-thirds of the population of Illinois were persons who were squatting upon lands belonging to the United States government.

The Illinois governor argued that settlers should be able to possess their lands, "that the government should not *hold up* its land, that it ought not to sell *for a profit,* that the land" was held "to the use of such as choose to settle it," that the people had the right to a "*reasonable* price," and that a price was "*not* reasonable which the people residing on, or near the land, and anxious to purchase, *will not* or *cannot* give."[45]

From a frontier point of view these settlers on government lands were not squatters. The word "squatter," it was insisted, originally applied to persons who settled upon the unimproved lands of individuals in the older states, with the express intention of acquiring titles by occupancy, or of profiting by defects in the legal titles of the rightful owners. But in Illinois there was no intent to defraud any one. In many regions surveys were lagging far behind the edge of settlement, not because of the difficulty of surveying prairie land but because of congressional slowness in appropriating the necessary money. One can well appreciate the feelings of the frontiersmen when certain New England congressmen, early in 1830, proposed restrictions on surveys and settlement in the West.

[44] Figures taken from article, "The Public Domain of the United States," *American Quarterly Review,* Vol. VI (1829), pp. 263-83.
[45] *ibid.*

The Preemption Act of 1830 was forced through Congress primarily by the alliance of the South and West.[46] Under its terms any settler who had migrated to the public domain and had cultivated a tract of land in 1829 was authorized to enter any number of acres up to a maximum of 160 by paying the minimum price of $1.25 per acre.[47] Although the act was temporarily in character it nevertheless constituted a general pardon to all inhabitants who had settled illegally. It also served in some respects as a further indulgence to those settlers for whose assistance the relief legislation of the 1820's had been designed. But the act had still more far-reaching significance. Once the government had granted this concession—preemption—it was exceedingly difficult to refuse it on later occasions. In practice, therefore, the act encouraged illegal settlement, for settlers immediately took up the best lands they could find and petitioned Congress for preemption. Why not pardon us, they queried, as well as the unlawful settlers of 1830? So in 1832 Congress renewed the Act of 1830, and again in 1834. In fact, as Edward Everett complained in 1835, the preemption bill was coming up as regularly as the annual appropriation bill.[48]

Another widely celebrated victory for the West was the removal of the Indians beyond the Mississippi. The insatiable desire for Indian lands constituted an embarrassing problem for the national government, a problem that became more alarming as settlement in the late 'twenties again began to spread out into the West. Some observers were beginning to wonder if the total annihilation of the red race was not only a matter of time.[49] In 1814 British peace commissioners had proposed the setting aside of an Indian state in the West, but this had been vetoed by the Americans who were convinced that England was more interested in Canada's fur-trading interests than in the fate of the red man.

[46] The yea's and nay's were not recorded in the House, but in the Senate the vote on January 13 was as follows: Yea's: Missouri, Kentucky, Illinois, Indiana, Ohio, Pennsylvania, Vermont, Massachusetts, North Carolina, South Carolina, Georgia, Alabama, Louisiana, Mississippi, Tennessee; Nay's: Delaware, New Jersey, Connecticut, Maine; Divided: New Hampshire, New York, Rhode Island, Maryland. Vote: 29 to 12. 21 Cong. 1 Sess., Senate Journal, p. 83.

[47] Statutes at Large, Vol. IV, Act of May 29, 1830, p. 420.

[48] ibid., Vol. IV, Act of July 14, 1832, p. 603; Act of June 19, 1834, p. 678.

[49] "The Public Domain of the United States," American Quarterly Review, Vol. VI (1829), p. 282.

Major Stephen S. Long's expedition in 1819 into the region beyond Missouri and the pronouncement that the High Plains country was a great desert quite unfit for white men led several high officials of the government to consider it a suitable location for the Indian tribes of the eastern states. John C. Calhoun, then Secretary of War, continued to agitate this plan until finally in 1825 President Monroe recommended it to Congress. The idea was accepted and negotiations began at once with the Plains Indians to prepare the way for the incoming of the eastern tribes.[50]

But governmental machinery moved too slowly to suit the impatient spirits of the frontier states. The spreading of population into western Georgia and into the Southwest, as well as into Illinois, brought demands that the army remove the Indians at once. The situation in Georgia aroused a controversy of national importance, and did much to ruin Adams' chances for re-election in 1828. This southern state contended that in 1802 when it ceded its claims to western lands the federal government agreed to remove the Indians from its boundaries. After that agreement was made, the federal government had cleared the title of some of the Indian lands, but millions of acres of the best lands still remained in the hands of aborigines. By 1825 the insatiable whites, supported by local public opinion, were breaking in upon these lands from all sides. In the course of the next three years, the governor of Georgia berated the national government for its slowness, and actually defied that authority by ordering the survey of Indian lands. The Cherokees brought suit in the courts. Their case finally went to the United States Supreme Court where Chief Justice John Marshall upheld the Indians in their claims.[51]

At the opening of Jackson's administration the issue was thus squarely drawn between the federal government and the State of Georgia—an issue which might easily have resulted in civil war. In Alabama it was estimated that fifteen to twenty thousand persons were quietly settled on Indian lands, and that while several spirited letters passed between the Secretary of War and Governor Gayle the army had not dared to remove these white settlers. It was declared that "all difficulty would

[50] Grant Foreman, *Advancing the Frontier* (Norman, Oklahoma, 1933); Frederic L. Paxson, *History of the American Frontier,* Chap. XXXI, "The Permanent Indian Frontier, 1825-1841."
[51] 5 *Peters* 1; also consult Annie Heloise Abel, "History of Events Resulting in Indian Consolidation West of the Mississippi River," American Historical Association, *Report,* 1906, Vol. I.

Indian Cessions in the South, 1830-1834.

From Asa Martin, *History of the United States.* By permission of Ginn and Co.

probably have been avoided had the national government not succumbed to the will of Georgia in a similar case."[52]

The situation in Illinois was just as alarming. Governor Ninian Edwards was entirely out of patience with federal policy. The lead mines of the Fever River region of northwestern Illinois brought an influx of white settlers beginning in 1825. The challenge was met by the Indians, and the Winnebago War of 1827 was the result.[53] Forts in that region were strengthened, for Governor Edwards was convinced that this was not the end but only the beginning of trouble. He wrote to General Clark on May 25, 1828: "I have only time to ask you whether any, and what, definitive arrangements have been made for removing the Indians. . . . The general government has been applied to long enough. . . . If it declines acting with effect, those Indians will be removed, and that very promptly."[54]

Such definitive action on the part of frontier states convinced Andrew Jackson that the removal of the Indians should be carried out with all available speed. He struck so suddenly that the Indians had little chance to resist. The problem was so efficiently handled that by 1835 Jackson could proudly declare that the removal process was nearing completion.[55] Difficulty was encountered, however, on two fronts. The disturbance in northwestern Illinois, as has already been related, led to the Black Hawk War.[56] While it is outside the scope of this book to treat the war itself, it may be noted that in the wake of the United States army flocked settlers ready to take up the most fertile lands. The area between Lake Michigan and the Mississippi and eastern Iowa was cleared of Indian title by treaty, and almost immediately Congress created Iowa and Wisconsin Territories.

The Seminoles of Florida and the Cherokees of western Georgia and eastern Alabama also caused serious trouble, the former by refusing to migrate westward and the latter by procrastinating after having agreed to move. Not until the government threatened force did the Cherokees move. The Seminoles resisted and later embarrassed the Van Buren

[52] "View of Public Affairs," *American Quarterly Register*, Vol. II, p. 190.
[53] Annual Report of Quartermaster General, 20 Cong. 1 Sess., *S. Doc.*, Vol. I, p. 79.
[54] E. B. Washburne (ed.), *The Edwards Papers*, in Chicago Historical Society *Collections*, Vol. III (1884), p. 338.
[55] See Jackson's annual message of 1835 in Richardson, *Messages and Papers*, Vol. III, pp. 171ff.
[56] Ruth A. Gallaher, "The Military Indian Frontier, 1830-35," *Iowa Journal of History and Politics*, Vol. XV (1917); Frank E. Stevens, *The Black Hawk War* (Chicago, 1903).

administration with a costly war. The remnants of the tribe had to be tracked down in the Florida swamps and moved forcibly to the West.[57] By 1840, however, the ugly and bloody business of Indian removal was for the most part finished, and millions of acres of rich Indian lands east of the Mississippi had been opened for white settlement. The Indian's only consolation was the promise that the white man would never again disturb him in his habitat. An act of Congress in 1832 created the Bureau of Indian Affairs and another in 1834 set off the region of the High Plains as Indian Country. The government's interest for the red man appeared to be sincere but scarcely was the permanent Indian frontier established than white settlers were cutting across it on their way to Oregon.

As soon as the title to these rich Indian lands was cleared there immediately arose a strong demand for surveying these areas and opening them to settlement. From 1830 to 1834 the Commissioner of the General Land Office complained of lack of sufficient appropriations to carry on the surveys. The establishment of more local land offices also became necessary. The Land Commissioner pointed out that if surveys kept abreast of the line of settlement and there were a sufficient number of land offices, there would be no need for preemption. Intruders and trespassers could then be left "to the local tribunals of justice for such relief as they may be entitled to on any principle of legal right or equitable jurisdiction."[58]

By 1831, with the increase in sales due to augmented immigration from Europe, pressure on the land office was greater than had been expected. At the beginning of the new administration in 1829, the business of the office was four years in arrears. One would think, the Land Commissioner pointed out, that a business which concerned three millions of people in the Mississippi Valley certainly deserved more attention from Congress.[59] The pressure became even greater when by Act of April 5, 1832, Congress provided for the survey of lands in as small tracts as forty acres—otherwise known as quarter-quarter sections.[60]

[57] Grant Foreman, *Five Civilized Tribes* (Norman, Oklahoma, 1934).
[58] *Report of the Commissioner of General Land Office,* 1830, 21 Cong. 2 Sess., *S. Doc.* No. 1, Vol. I, p. 60.
[59] *ibid.,* 1831, 22 Cong. 1 Sess., *H. Ex. Doc.* No. 3, Vol. I, pp. 60, 64.
[60] *ibid.,* 1832, 22 Cong. 2 Sess., *H. Ex. Doc.* No. 3, Vol. I, p. 53.

Finally after 1832 Congress responded by making special appropriations. This action so much encouraged the Land Commissioner that he took steps toward certain important administrative reforms. He called attention to the propriety and necessity of keeping the land-office documents in fireproof bags. Also he asked for an appropriation to be applied toward collecting and compiling the statutes of the state legislatures and the adjudicated decisions, which were vitally important in the conduct of business in the General Land Office.[61] The Act of March 2, 1833, provided for the appointment of a secretary to sign patents in the name of the President. In fact by 1834 much progress in the solution of administrative problems was evident: surveys were progressing nicely, additional land offices had been created, and many additional clerks had been hired to handle the details of business. In fact, an administrative setup had been established which would be able to handle the unprecedented land purchases of 1835-36.

The question of the public lands policy of the Jackson administration came to a head in 1832. On March 22, a combination of western and southern interests referred certain measures on tariffs and public lands to the Committee on Manufactures of which Henry Clay was chairman. Clay discerned the motive which prompted the action and wrote to F. T. Brook as follows:

"You will have seen the disposition made on Thursday last of my resolution respecting the tariff. On that occasion some developments were made of a scheme which I have long since suspected—that certain portions of the South were disposed to purchase support [for] . . . the anti-tariff doctrines by a total sacrifice of the public lands to states within which they are situated! A more stupendous, and a more flagitious project was never conceived! It will fail in its object; but it ought to be denounced. A majority of the Senate referred a resolution concerning public lands to the Committee of Manufactures! Can you conceive a more incongruous association of subjects? The first object has been suggested. The second was to affect me personally by placing me in a situation in which I must report unfavorably to the western and southwestern states which are desirous of possessing themselves of the public lands. I think I shall disappoint the design, by presenting such news of that great interest as will be sustained by the nation."[62]

[61] ibid., 1833, 23 Cong. 1 Sess., S. Doc. No. 9, Vol. I, pp. 52, 54.
[62] Works of Henry Clay (New York, 1896), Vol. I, p. 483.

The report of the Committee on Manufactures thereupon presented some strong arguments against reducing the price of public lands and contended that the briskness of the land sales was evidence that the prices were not too high.[63] A reduction, said the committee, would be a pernicious tendency toward the accumulation of large quantities of land by speculators, as had happened with military bounty lands. This would operate unjustly and injuriously to the government and to former purchasers. Since the proceeds from the sales of public lands would no longer be wanted for ordinary revenues, which were to be abundantly supplied from imports, the committee proposed to distribute the proceeds among the states according to their federal representation in Congress after 10 per cent had been deducted for the new states. The states could apply the funds to education, internal improvements, colonization of free Negroes, or redemption of debts.[64] A number of the older western states immediately began counting their chickens not yet hatched. "The amount received annually" under Mr. Clay's plan, calculated the editor of the *Steubenville Herald,* together "with the income from the public lands now owned by Ohio, would pay the entire interest of the canal debt for the said five years. And if the net income of the canals should be equal only to the support of the state government, the people of Ohio might be relieved altogether from state tax."[65]

Benton was convinced that the protective tariff and distribution interests were working hand in hand against strengthening of the power of the federal government over that of the states.[66] The Committee on Public Lands immediately challenged the right of the Committee on Manufactures to deal with the subject of public lands. The Land Committee after study of the subject presented a report refuting every point of the Manufactures Committee report, challenging the principle of distribution, and favoring the idea of cession.[67] It urged that the price of public lands be reduced for the two-fold purpose of diminishing the amount of revenue derived from the sales thereof and of placing

[63] Report on Committee on Manufactures on subject of public lands, April 16, 1832, in *American State Papers, Public Lands,* Vol. VI, p. 478; 21 Cong. 1 Sess., *Congressional Debates,* p. 35.

[64] Abstract from *National Intelligencer* in *New England Magazine* (Boston), Vol. II (1832), pp. 515-17.

[65] Quoted in *The Cincinnati Mirror,* Vol. I, p. 130.

[66] 22 Cong. 1 Sess., *Congressional Debates,* p. 1,162.

[67] *American State Papers, Public Lands,* Vol. VI, p. 445.

within reach of every man, however poor, the opportunity to acquire a home for his family. Much attention was devoted to the effects upon the western states of annually withdrawing so much money from the West and expending it in other portions of the country. Congress, the report concluded, "should retain the unrestricted control of the public domain. . . . National legislation over the same should be guarded by a policy which shall regard it rather as a means to build up flourishing communities, than as a source of revenue to the general government or of wealth to the individual states."[68]

Jackson, fresh from the victory over Clay in the election of 1832, stepped into the controversy at this point. The times were threatening. Sectional lines had been drawn upon every national issue. South Carolina had just nullified the tariff law of 1832, thus threatening the integrity of national authority. The President himself in his attack on the National Bank had contributed to the feeling of West against East, and of class against class. Sectionalism was driving the nation to the brink of civil war.

While the land question was not as serious as the tariff and bank issues, nevertheless Congress spent just as much, perhaps more, time on it than on the other issues. It was not surprising then that a considerable part of Jackson's message to Congress was devoted to this problem. "The wealth and strength of a country," declared the President, "are in its population, and the best part of that population are the cultivators of the soil. Independent farmers are everywhere the basis of society, and the true friends of liberty." The public lands should "be sold to settlers in limited parcels, at a price barely sufficient to reimburse to the United States the expense of the present system, and the cost arising under our Indian compacts. . . . It is desirable, however, that, in convenient time, . . . the right of the soil, and the future disposition of it, be surrendered to the States, respectively, in which it lies."[69] The population of the West, he went on, besides contributing its equal share in taxation under the tariff system, had also paid into the Treasury a large portion of forty million dollars, of which sum only a very small part was spent in the western country.

As for distribution, he reminded the old states that it was labor alone that gave real value to the lands, and that he could not favor a system of

[68] Abstract in *New England Magazine*, Vol. III (1832), pp. 67-8.
[69] 22 Cong. 2 Sess., *H. Ex. Doc.* No. 2, Vol. I, pp. 10-11.

distributing proceeds among states which had not originally any claim to them, and which had enjoyed the original emolument arising from the sale of their own lands. Nor would the new states be likely to remain contented with the present policy after the payment of the public debt. In order "to avert the consequences which may be apprehended from this cause, to stop forever all partial and interested legislation on this subject, and to afford every American citizen of enterprise the opportunity of receiving an independent free-hold," it seemed to Jackson "best to abandon the idea of raising future revenue out of public funds."[70]

Nevertheless, the conservative forces, aware of the rupture in the South and West alliance, passed Clay's distribution bill. The measure passed the Senate in December, and was finally approved in the House by a vote of 95 to 39. Calhoun denounced the bill in no uncertain terms. To denationalize public funds, he declared, was not only dangerous but unconstitutional. Might not distribution be applied to taxes and tariff duties as well as to proceeds from public lands? He suggested the calling of a convention of the states to decide the matter, though he felt that the prejudices of the time were too strong to permit wise action on the subject. Clay in reply opposed postponement and the calling of a convention of the states.[71]

The distribution bill passed too late in the session, however, to escape Jackson's pocket veto. In his message the following December the President gave his reasons for the veto. He declared that distribution would come to mean federal aid for internal improvements, which he considered unconstitutional; that it meant creating a surplus with the danger that the tariff might be used for this purpose. He reiterated his stand of the previous December that the timely interest of the new states "consists in the rapid settling and improvement of the waste lands within their limits. As a means of hastening these grants, they have long been looking to a reduction in the price of lands upon the final payment of the national debt. The effect of the proposed system would be to prevent that reduction."[72] Clay very angrily termed Jackson's action unconstitutional as well as disrespectful to the Senate of the United States.[73]

[70] ibid.   [71] 22 Cong. 2 Sess., *Congressional Debates*, pp. 234-5, 1,980.
[72] 23 Cong. 1 Sess., *S. Doc.* No. 3, Vol. I, p. 11.
[73] 23 Cong. 1 Sess., *Congressional Debates*, pp. 14-15.

CHAPTER IV

SPECULATION AND PANIC

WHILE Clay and the National Republicans were still smarting under the distribution bill veto, Jackson asked for the removal of the government deposits from the National Bank. These deposits were redistributed among so-called "pet-banks," that is, state banks selected by the government as depositories. Hence many small banks in the wilderness with capital of only two or three hundred dollars were suddenly placed in possession of three times that amount of workable funds. The removal of the deposits from the National Bank thus not only weakened the credit structure of the country, but proved to be a highly inflationary measure, dangerous and ominous. Wildcat banking soon reached proportions unparalleled in the history of the Republic. Speculation every day became more extravagant and more universal.

The first effects of this state of things, like the proverbial first stages on the road to ruin, were delightful. Property doubled in value, industry was stimulated by the increased price of its products, capital was abundant and profitably employed, labor commanded unprecedented wages —indeed, the magic lamp of Aladdin could not have produced more admirable results. In 1833, sales accounted for 3,856,228 acres; but in 1835 over twelve million acres went for sixteen million dollars; in 1836, twenty million acres sold for the all-time high of fifty-four million dollars. The unprecedented interest in internal improvements following the successful venture of the Erie Canal, the competition among eastern cities to tap the supply centers of the West, mounting commodity prices, easy credit, all gave an impetus to western development such as had never before been witnessed.

In this new era of prosperity, land and real estate more than any other commodities became the objects of rampant speculation.[1] Within six years after 1830 the value of real estate throughout the country rose 150

---

[1] Professor Arthur H. Cole, in a study on land sales in the period 1825 to 1845, has shown the close cyclical relationship existing between general commodity prices and receipts of sales from the General Land Office. See Arthur H. Cole, "Cyclical and Sectional Variations in the Sale of Public Lands," *Review of Economic Statistics*, Vol. IX, p. 45.

per cent.[2] From a Wisconsin newspaper came the estimate that in the newer sections of the country, real estate investment for the ten years between 1825 and 1835, paid a 20 to 30 per cent return per annum.[3] In 1836 Manhattan Island was surveyed, divided into lots, sold and resold.[4] The speculators in Maine nearly beggared the state. Men left their warehouses, counting-rooms and stores and rushed off to buy townships, village lots, or mill privileges. "So crowded were the mushroom cities," remarked one commentator, "that barns, sheds, and the privilege to lean against the gate posts were in requisition for lodging places."[5]

What was phenomenal in the East was a mere introduction to what was taking place in the West. Twenty-eight million acres of rich lands dumped onto the market by the government in 1834-35 sharply contrasted with the average of two or three millions offered annually in former years. The whole frontier region was regarded as a lottery office, to which individuals from all over the world might resort to accumulate wealth, under the favors of the capricious and blind goddess, Chance. Good lands in the East were high in price. An item in a New England newspaper to the effect that "twenty farms have been sold in the town of Worthington within a few months, nearly all the owners of which are bound for the West," indicates the extent of the exodus.[6] The danger of depopulation in parts of the East was ameliorated somewhat by the increase in foreign immigration. Political troubles in Germany were driving hundreds of Germans to seek land in the American West.[7] But in spite of foreign immigration, labor was scarce; agriculture everywhere, and indeed all substantial enterprise, was being neglected. Log houses swarmed with eager buyers and settlers when there was scarcely food enough in the country to maintain its permanent population.[8]

In the Southwest the abundance of bank credits which the operations of wildcat banking produced, together with the stupendous rise in the

[2] Reginald McGrane, *The Panic of 1837* (Chicago, 1924), p. 44.

[3] Navarino (Michigan Terr.) *Green-Bay Intelligencer,* July 1, 1835.

[4] George Combe, *Notes on the United States of America* (Philadelphia, 1841), Vol. I, p. 41.

[5] "Speculations" in *Hunt's Merchants' Magazine,* Vol. XXIX (1853), pp. 54-5.

[6] *Green-Bay Intelligencer,* May 10, 1835, quoting *Northampton* (Massachusetts) *Gazette.*

[7] *Cincinnati Mirror and Chronicle,* Vol. IV (1835), pp. 259, 267; Columbia *Missouri Intelligencer,* October 4, 1834.

[8] James H. Lanman, "The Progress of the Northwest," *Hunt's Merchants' Magazine,* Vol. III (1840), p. 40.

price of cotton, rendered planting profitable beyond all former experience. Young planters from the Atlantic States, migrating to the banks of the Mississippi with slaves from their paternal estates, were supported in their enterprise by this state banking system feeding on money from the East and from London. Almost thirty million dollars was invested by eastern capitalists for improvements in the state of Mississippi alone. These new planters entered lands at astoundingly high prices, and immediately became stockholders in the property banks—that is to say, they mortgaged their Negroes and lands to the banks for money to carry on their planting, the banks receiving the cotton and controlling the bills. Sums were loaned on interest as high as 10 per cent.[9]

The large sales of lands, from 1834 to 1837, were all under the whip and spur of this type of inflation. The southern part of the state of Mississippi came into the market first, followed shortly afterward by the sale of that fine tract of land in the northern part of the state known as the Chickasaw Cession. These sales were attended by gambling traders from all parts of the United States, and bona fide settlers had little chance to secure land. Consequently much of the rich loam fell into the hands of a few wealthy proprietors. In the southwestern states during the three years before 1838, over thirty-eight million dollars was invested mostly in the production of cotton. Over twelve million acres of the most prolific land came into culture. The great increase in production brought falling cotton prices, and ultimately led to the ruin of both the planters and the numerous land banks.[10]

The admission of Michigan and Arkansas into the Union in 1836 by overwhelming congressional majorities evidenced the feeling of cordiality and kindly interest in the unexampled growth and prosperity of the West.[11] In the northwestern states the sales of land, stimulated primarily by the Erie Canal, were just as stupendous as those in the Southwest. Choice locations along state canals in Ohio sold at a premium,[12] but Michigan seemed to be the converging point of the new migration. This state, which had escaped the ravages of the land mania after the Panic of 1819, was now in the path of a speculative hurricane. Of the twenty-five million dollars paid into the federal treasury in 1836, five

9 "Commercial Chronicle and Review," *ibid.*, Vol. XIII (1845), p. 470.
10 *De Bow's Commercial Review*, Vol. IV (1847), pp. 86-7.
11 *New Yorker*, July 23, 1836.
12 William O'Bryan, *Travels in the United States of America* (London, 1836), p. 125.

million were paid for lands in Michigan. This new state, declares one authority, recklessly "created a brood of banks, exempted by act of incorporation from redeeming their notes in specie wherever they should be organized—an unprecedented piece of quackery. The state authorized a loan of five million dollars and her bonds were sold by her governor, acting as commissioner, in so unguarded and heedless a manner, that a large portion of their amount was never realized."[13] Although the population of Michigan in 1831 was but 31,639, there were twenty banks within her bounds, and by 1837 there were forty.[14] Enormous purchases of land were frequently blocked in together, and settlers noticeably shunned these areas. Steamboat companies practiced such gross deceptions upon immigrants and travellers that the reputation of the state suffered for years to come.

Speculators in the Wabash Valley of Indiana were pointing out the unusual advantages of the canal route from Lake Erie to the Ohio.[15] In Illinois speculation was rampant. Even in the Territory of Wisconsin, whose population numbered scarcely five thousand souls, the price that land brought at the sales was beyond all reasonable expectation. At Manitowoc prices rose from $10 to $250 per acre within a week.[16] At the Green-Bay land office eight million acres of land out of the thirteen million sold in 1835, lands rich in timber and minerals, were said to have gone to speculators.[17] In Milwaukee, "speculators went to bed at night hugging themselves with delight over the prospect that the succeeding morning would double their wealth."[18] And from Missouri came the report that "many people after three weeks' absence," had "returned from the far West, having purchased everything up to the Rocky Mountains," and were "now so rich" that they talked of "casting every man into the poor house" who was not "worth more than $10,000."[19]

Coincident with this speculation in potential farming lands developed the rage for townsites. There was no part of the public domain

[13] J. R. Williams, "Internal Commerce of the West," *Hunt's Merchants' Magazine,* Vol. XIX (1848), pp. 19-23.

[14] "Debts and Finances of the States of the Union—Michigan," *ibid.,* Vol. XXII (1850), pp. 133-4.

[15] A. D. Jones, *Illinois and the West* (Boston, 1838), pp. 183-91.

[16] *Green-Bay Intelligencer,* March 2, 1836.

[17] Joseph Schafer, *Four Wisconsin Counties, Prairie and Forest* (Madison, Wisconsin, 1927), p. 69.

[18] John G. Gregory, *History of Milwaukee, Wisconsin* (4 vols., Chicago, 1931), Vol. I, p. 72. By permission of S. J. Clarke Publishing Co.

[19] *New Yorker* (September 3, 1836), quoting the *Coatsville Advertiser.*

that did not succumb to the fever for setting up towns on paper. Near New Orleans, the townsite of Bath which nine months previous had cost but $35,000 now brought $600,000. The townsite of Uncle Sam, sixty miles from New Orleans sold under the hammer for $500,000! And Harlen, Louisiana, which had cost $40,000, went for $200,000![20] If these sales were sensational, then perhaps no words can describe the mad scramble for choice locations which took place in the Northwest. There was no fork, or falls, or bend in any river; no nook or bay on Lake Erie or Lake Michigan; no point along any imagined canal or railroad, in fact, not even a dismal swamp or a dense forest, but could be classed as a choice location for a flourishing metropolis—at least on paper! The wildest sort of speculative mania centered around the townsites of Toledo and Chicago.[21] In 1833 Chicago was a mere frontier post; by 1836 it was the fastest growing "metropolis" of all Christendom. Speculators were running steamboat excursions to this town and on to Milwaukee. It seemed as though almost all of northeastern Illinois was laid out in towns—on paper. One site which was actually destined to become a great city, could boast but one humble dwelling, yet the lots on that site were commanding $1,000 to $2,500 each.[22] A Chicago gentleman, observing the increasing activity for town plotting and building, seriously advised with some of his friends on the subject of reserving one or two sections of land in every township for farming purposes![23]

Cairo, Illinois, furnishes perhaps one of the best examples of the madness which accompanied these townsite speculations. The junction of the Ohio and Mississippi rivers, apparently one of the most strategic sites in America, was overnight laid out as a great city. Streets were graded, house and store lots were laid out for miles up the banks of both rivers. Elegant colored maps were exhibited in eastern cities, most minutely particular in design. "There was to be a bank here, a customhouse there, a church in another place, and fine brick and stone dwellings in every direction. A hundred steamers were lying at the wharves, painted like life, and merchandise was piled about in perfect looseness and profusion. Drays were industriously engaged in removing the

[20] Quoted in Green-Bay *Wisconsin Democrat*, March 31, 1837.
[21] A. M. Sakolski, *The Great American Land Bubble* (New York and London, 1932), pp. 246-8.
[22] S. A. Mitchell, *Illinois in 1837* (Philadelphia, 1837), p. 135.
[23] Mineral Point (Wisconsin Terr.) *Miners' Free Press*, September 1, 1837.

merchandise back into the populated streets. Men, women, and children were thronging the squares and sidewalks!" Indeed, from the pictured description, one would suppose, according to this graphic description by a contemporary authority, "that both Cincinnati and New Orleans were to be removed and combined to make Cairo." But after all the speculations of 1836 the city of Cairo remained to be built. Extensive operations were started, it is true, but the first spring flood carried everything downstream, leaving only a dilapidated wharf boat, a long wooden portico with a shanty behind it, called the United States Hatch, a flock of geese, a lean pig, and a jackass.[24]

As the wave of speculation in western lands reached its peak, glaring abuses and even scandalous frauds were brought to light. Speculators dominated the legislatures of Michigan and Wisconsin.[25] Even some officials of the local land offices were involved in questionable activities.[26] In 1834, discovery of great frauds in Alabama and Mississippi led the Senate to pass five resolutions providing for investigation.[27] The fraudulent practices of speculators at auctions were also investigated.[28] It is little wonder that in such circumstances the more substantial element of the pioneer community spoke of the General Land Office as a "den of thieves and robbers, a curse to the nation, and the destroyer of morals."[29]

Abuses were discovered in the operation of the Preemption Act of 1830 and its consequent renewals. The Renewal Act of 1832, it will be recalled, provided that in the case of two settlers on the same quarter section of land, one settler was to be given a preemption-float which would allow him to enter a like quantity from any surveyed but unsold land. This provision offered almost unlimited opportunity to select choice lands.[30] One claimant making use of this provision attempted to gain title to about half the town of Milwaukee.[31] Land Commissioner E. A. Brown, in 1836, reported that he knew of "armies of slaves or hire-

---

24 "Speculations," *Hunt's Merchants' Magazine*, Vol. XXIX (1853), pp. 54-5.

25 McGrane, *Panic of 1837*, p. 58; 24 Cong. 2 Sess., *Congressional Debates*, p. 768; "Debts and Finances of the States of the Union—Michigan," *Hunt's Merchants' Magazine*, Vol. XXII (1850), p. 34.

26 Carl Russell Fish, *The Civil Service and the Patronage* (Cambridge, 1920), pp. 136-8.

27 22 Cong. 2 Sess., *Congressional Debates*, p. 1,743.   28 *ibid.*, 23 Cong. 1 Sess., p. 754.

29 McGrane, *Panic of 1837*, p. 45.   30 24 Cong. 2 Sess., *Congressional Debates*, p. 764.

31 *Land Commissioners' Letters*, Preemption Bureau (in General Land Office, Washington, D.C.), Vol. XVIII (1844), p. 39.

lings" employed by speculators to reap by fraudulent means numerous advantages from the Act of 1830.[32] As for preemption-floats, he said that there were not thirty honest ones in the whole district of Louisiana.[33] The free Negroes, Spaniards, and Indians who inhabited these regions were nearly all in the employ of the speculators. Affidavits printed in large quantities were distributed to these persons who, with the paid cooperation of an ignorant or corrupt justice of the peace, secured preemption-floats.[34]

The provision in the Act of 1830 and in subsequent renewal acts which required proof of cultivation was also considerably abused. The hearings disclosed that such pretenses as the cutting and burning of a small patch of cane, the placing of rails around a spot scarcely as large as a small garden, the planting of a few culinary vegetables, and even the scattering of an undefined quantity of grass-seed had passed as cultivation.[35]

With all the abuse of the land laws during the speculative craze which preceded the Panic of 1837, a major part of the difficulty apparently centered around the auction, an institution which favored the speculator to the injury of the actual settler. Referring to the rich cotton lands in Alabama and Mississippi, Clement C. Clay of Alabama observed that "in sales which embraced three million acres of such cotton lands, the price realized was only $1.27, out of which was to be taken all the expenses of the sale."[36] It was originally intended that competition at the auction should be free and untrammelled in order to guarantee the highest price, but unfortunately collusion among speculators defrauded the government out of much of its expected profit. In fact, the average price for all lands sold in 1836, the year of the most stupendous sales in public-land history, was only $1.25, the minimum price established by law. The legislature of Alabama had petitioned Congress in 1832 praying for the abandonment of the auction, on the ground that it was "not . . . beneficial to the government, and in prac-

---

[32] *American State Papers, Public Lands,* Vol. VIII, p. 612, Doc. 1507.

[33] 24 Cong. 2 Sess., *Congressional Debates,* p. 766.

[34] 24 Cong. 2 Sess., *S. Doc.* No. 168; 24 Cong. 2 Sess., *H. Ex. Doc.* No. 151.

[35] 24 Cong. 2 Sess., *Congressional Debates,* p. 765; also, Harriet Martineau, *Society in America* (London, 1837), Vol. II, pp. 91-2.

[36] 23 Cong. 1 Sess., *Congressional Debates,* p. 4,469.

tice," it was found "to operate injuriously and oppressively upon the purchasers."[37]

A contemporary description gives some idea of the operation of a land sale: "The hour approaches: the poor squatter runs about the town; he has been laboring all the year that he may buy the land on which his house is situated; perhaps for want of a dollar or two, it will be taken from him by greedy speculators. Anxiety and trouble are depicted upon his honest and wild countenance. A jobber accosts him, pities him, and offers to withdraw his pretensions for the sum of three dollars; the poor simpleton gives them to him, not doubting the jobber. . . . This is what is called hush money. . . . And now, the sale being over, the speculators, their titles in their pockets have returned home . . . the planter gone to seek his Negroes and his family; the poor squatter is returned to his home . . . not having been able to realize his hope and being obliged to go still once more in search of a spot on which to settle; it may also be that he is hired as manager to the planter who has bought his house and lands."[38]

Representative Balie Peyton of Tennessee gave an eloquent and pathetic picture: "That poor man who had blazed the trees and planted the potatoes had chosen that spot as the home of his children. He had toiled in hope. He had given it value, and he loved the spot. It was his all. When the public sales were proclaimed, if that poor man attended it, he might bid to the last cent he had in the world, and mortgage the bed he slept on to enable him to do it. He might have his wife and children around him to see him bid; and when he had bid his very last cent, one of these speculators would stand by his side and bid two dollars more, and thus he would see his little home, on which he had toiled for years, where he hoped to rear his children and to find a peaceful grave, pass into the hands of a rich, moneyed company. . . . Such a policy would but teach the republic to alienate her children."[39]

And Edmund Flagg, a traveller who witnessed a land sale at Edwardsville, Illinois, declared that "during that public land-sale, indeed, I beheld so much of the selfishness, the petty meanness, the detestable heartlessness, of man's nature, that I turned away disgusted, sick at heart for a race of which I was a member."[40]

[37] *American State Papers, Public Lands,* Vol. VI, p. 384.
[38] Achille Murat, *A Moral and Political Sketch of North America* (London, 1833), p.62.
[39] 23 Cong. 1 Sess., *Congressional Debates,* p. 4,480.
[40] Edmund Flagg, *The Far West* (New York, 1838), Vol. I, p. 76.

Finding that the government had little interest in preserving their rights, western settlers took the responsibility into their own hands. Numerous claims clubs or settlers' associations sprang up all along the frontier.[41] Convinced that the "man who obeyed the law was at a disadvantage in comparison with either the speculator or the preemptioner," settlers of certain districts banded together to protect their claims at the auction. Over one hundred of these extralegal organizations existed in the Territory of Iowa alone.[42] These clubs had constitutions which, in fact, resemble the mining law of a later day. They had secretaries who kept records of all the claims of the settlers. Notices and resolutions were always published in the local newspapers which sympathized with their actions.[43] Any speculator who bid against a claimant, if not beaten up or harried out of town, was at least outlawed. The settlers pledged their honor "not to borrow of him, nor lend to him, nor sell to him, nor to associate with him in any manner whatsoever." In Mitchell County, Iowa, the settlers were so well organized that at the auction they demanded an extra quarter section of land apiece, and after a hard struggle with the speculators they got their demands.[44]

The claims clubs also dealt with disputes among their own numbers. Frequently settlers would find when the surveys were made that they were on school lands. Knowing that it would be impossible to remain on these lands a settler might try to run some other settler off his claim.[45] Such an unruly settler was treated no better than a speculator. He was regarded with contempt as no better than a thief or robber.[46] If the claim jumper persisted in using force in trespassing on another's claim, a vigilance committee was appointed to arrest him and a genuine frontier trial was held in his honor.[47]

The spirit manifest in the organization of these claims clubs penetrated even into the sphere of the territorial governments. In 1838, the

---

[41] See Benjamin F. Shambaugh, "Frontier Land Clubs or Claims Associations," American Historical Association *Report*, 1910, Vol. I, pp. 67-85.

[42] Frederic L. Paxson, *History of the American Frontier* (Boston, 1924), p. 388; Hibbard, *Public Land Policies of the United States*, Chap. XI; Shambaugh, "Frontier Land Clubs or Claims Associations," *loc. cit.*, p. 72.

[43] Burlington *Wisconsin Territorial Gazette*, September 7, 1837; *Racine Argus*, March 9, 1838; Chicago *Wisconsin Territorial Democrat*, January 20, 1841; *La Crosse Independent Republican*, December 20, 1854.

[44] *New York Daily Tribune*, May 18, 1857.   [45] *Chicago Democrat*, May 5, 1841.

[46] *La Crosse Independent Republican*, December 20, 1854.

[47] George M. Stephenson, *The Political History of the Public Lands from 1840 to 1860* (Boston, 1917), p. 21.

territorial legislature of Wisconsin passed a law protecting settlers in their claims against other settlers.[48] In 1835 an editorial in the *Chicago Democrat* stated the settlers' point of view. "Public opinion is stronger than law, and we trust that a stranger who comes among us, and especially our own citizens, will not attempt to commit so gross an act of injustice as to interfere with the purchase of the quarter sections on which the settler has made improvements."[49] The claims club constitutes a good example of the frontier's ability to rule itself without dependence on any absentee governing power.

It would be a mistake to presume that the Jackson administration was ignorant of the dangerous tendencies inherent in the speculative mania. In fact, the entire spirit of such speculation was completely out of keeping with Jackson's determination to reserve the public lands for actual settlers. Indeed, public-spirited men everywhere were discussing means of putting an end to speculation. The congressional advocates of graduation, distribution, and cession each redoubled their efforts to get their own cherished principles adopted, seeing in them a cure for the speculation mania. Senator Foot's proposal to restrict the sales of public lands, which had seemed absurd to many people in 1829, was again brought forward, but western forces fought stubbornly against it. Another panacea suggested was the raising of prices on lands. Certain senators proposed to allow the states to tax the federal lands within their borders. There was considerable support for the recommendation to eliminate the auction.

Among all the plans suggested in Congress, the proposal of Senator Robert J. Walker of Mississippi to limit the sale of lands to actual settlers came nearest to adoption. When Walker, who was Chairman of the Committee on Public Lands, introduced his bill he declared, "In vain shall we have struck down the feudal system with its accompanying relation of lord and vassal, if we create and continue here this worse than feudal vassalage, the system of American landlords, engrossing millions of acres, and regulating the terms of sale and settlement."[50] He pointed out that in the single year, 1836, an extent of territory as large as the combined states of New England had passed into the hands of speculators. One speculating company, he claimed, was at that very

---

[48] *Racine Argus,* March 9, 1838.   [49] *Chicago Democrat,* June 3, 1835.
[50] 24 Cong. 2 Sess., *Congressional Debates,* p. 420.

moment advertising for sale a million acres of land. Another company having a capitalization of six million dollars was progressing with its entries. Our territories, he exclaimed, will soon become dominated by speculators who will dictate to the national government. And the East, too, he pointed out, was losing its wealth. "There is thus opened a golden stream from the East to the West," Walker exclaimed, "which, whilst it drains the East of millions of capital, ... condemns to a period of long sterility a vast portion of the beautiful valley of the West, containing soil inexhaustively fertile, but remaining in the hands of speculators barren and unproductive." He warned the manufacturing interests that a union with those who desired to maintain a surplus in the treasury would be an embrace with death. The coalition of the surplus and tariff interests would no longer continue to exist, or else, he averred, it would destroy the people's will.[51]

The essential provisions of the Walker bill were as follows: sales were to be made only to actual settlers and cultivators, and were limited to two sections of land; authority of parents to purchase for their children was recognized; a general preemption was granted to all cultivators; and the States were to be allowed to tax public lands within their borders. The bill underwent very extensive debate. Especially heated were the discussions of the preemption provisions, the principle being challenged on the ground that in the recent sales it was a tool of speculation. Calhoun moved to include in the bill his plan to cede the public lands to the states, but his amendment lost by an overwhelming vote. The Walker bill finally passed the Senate by a vote of 27 to 23 on February 8, 1837. It was introduced in the House on March 1, but after several heated arguments it was tabled by a vote of 107 to 91.[52]

Meanwhile the surplus in the Treasury was increasing at an alarming rate. The national debt had been extinguished at the beginning of 1835, and it was expected that the surplus would amount to about nine million dollars annually for the next three years.[53] Clay had been proposing for years the distribution of the proceeds of the sales of public lands, but Jackson had vetoed his bill in 1833. On June 23, 1836, Congress passed Calhoun's bill which provided for distribution of the surplus among the states according to their federal representation in both

[51] *ibid.*, pp. 419-28.   [52] *ibid.*, pp. 428, 736, 770-3, 777.
[53] Turner, *United States, 1830-1850*, p. 435; E. G. Bourne, *History of the Surplus Revenue of 1837* (New York, 1885).

houses of Congress, the said distribution to be a mere loan to the states and to be placed in certain depositories. Jackson signed the bill reluctantly, explaining that since the representatives of the people had favored it he would not stand in the way.[54]

Of far greater consequence to the immediate situation was the executive order known as the Specie Circular—probably drafted by Senator Benton—which was promulgated on July 11, 1836. This order required that after August 15 the local land officials should accept only gold and silver in payment for public land, with an exception in favor of actual settlers buying not more than 320 acres.[55] Jackson in his annual message gave his reasons for the order. The time had come to put an end to the wildcat bank inflation in the West on which speculation was feeding. The order was an expedient to save the new states from nonresident proprietorship, "one of the greatest obstacles to the advancement of a new country and the prosperity of an old one." He concluded by recommending the policy of selling public lands to actual settlers only, for immediate settlement and cultivation.[56]

Almost immediately the country sensed the serious import of the Specie Circular. The very psychology which nourished the speculative bubble had been brought into question by the chief executive of the United States. Public confidence was seriously shaken. Public opinion was keenly divided on the subject. The creditor sections of the country were bitter in their denunciations of the President's interference with the natural operation of economic forces.

This point of view is embodied in the comment of Horace Greeley (later to become the outstanding antagonist of western speculation) who at this time was satisfied with existing conditions and was preaching the doctrine of let well enough alone. He averred that the Specie Circular "may produce a scarcity of money; it may embarrass the Banks, Atlantic and Western; it may even check the impetuous current of speculation generally; but we fear its evils will not fall mainly on those whom it is intended to reach—that it will bear at least equally on the regular business of the country." He questioned the policy of restricting sales to actual settlers because, he said, the restriction would

54 *National Intelligencer,* July 12, 1836.

55 Richardson, *Messages and Papers,* Vol. III, pp. 104-5; Commager, *Documents of American History,* Vol. I, Doc. 153.

56 *ibid.,* Vol. I, Doc. 154; Richardson, *Messages and Papers,* Vol. III, p. 249.

"amount to nil after the land speculators" got used to it. In general, he observed that "speculation, in its broadest sense," was "not an evil in itself, but the contrary," and relieved "public distress far oftener" than it created it. Had not agriculture been stimulated to an increased production by the prospect and the realization of an increased reward; had not commerce expanded; had labor ever commanded a better remuneration; had not enterprise and industry been encouraged? And still as late as May 6, 1837, after the panic had broken, Greeley insisted that land speculation was not the origin of the financial troubles, but that undoubtedly credit was the source of most of the evil.[57]

Whatever the merits of speculation, the fact remains that the penalty had to be paid. Those commodities which had been the objects of the wildest speculation were the first to be affected. The Specie Circular sent land sales into a precipitous decline. The eastern section of the country could not come to the rescue. Everywhere commodity values began to sag along with land values. Decline ran pell mell into panic. By June 1837 there were at least twenty thousand mechanics and thirty thousand seamstresses in New York City unemployed. Greeley was convinced that their only salvation was to go West and take up land for a living.[58] A winter of fearful, unexampled severity was in prospect. "Do not wait to share and increase its horrors," Greeley admonished, "Fly—scatter through the country—go to the Great West—anything rather than remain here. . . . Away then, hardy adventurers, to Ohio, Michigan, Illinois, and Wisconsin. . . . The West is the true destination."[59] It was too late, however; few workers had money enough to get beyond the corporation limits of New York City. Besides the West was no longer a haven of happiness and prosperity. In the wake of speculation had come desolation, chaos, and ruin. The Panic of 1837 was taking its toll.

[57] *New Yorker*, September 10, December 10, 1836; February 18, April 1, May 6, 1837.
[58] Roy M. Robbins, "Horace Greeley: Land Reform and Unemployment, 1837-1862," *Agricultural History*, Vol. VII (1933), pp. 18-41.
[59] *New Yorker*, June 3, 1837.·

CHAPTER V

PREEMPTION: A FRONTIER TRIUMPH

IN 1837, as in 1819, the American public tasted the bitter dregs of depression. Bankruptcy, unemployment and suffering were the order of the day. In the West wildcat banks crashed, internal improvement projects folded up, land speculation automatically ceased, and nine western states with their resources squandered contemplated repudiation. The era of infatuation, inflation, and folly had come to an abrupt end.

It is difficult to tell whether the state, the speculator, or the actual settler suffered most. At any rate, the individual in residence on the soil now had the advantage. Legislatures of many western states immediately put through laws providing for higher taxes on lands. This move hastened the process of liquidation, compelling many absentee landlords to sacrifice holdings, in some cases at prices below the government minimum. Bona fide settlers who had been unable to participate in the speculative years, at last found it advantageous, provided they had the money, to take up land. Laborers were no longer diverted from the field as they had been during the boom era. The lax spirit which had pervaded the West was now discountenanced, and the energies of the people quietly sank down into channels of substantial industry. With harder times, more accurate information on lands became current in contrast to the inaccurate glowing accounts of 1835-36. Everywhere conditions seemed more favorable to settlers than to speculative interests.

It had been contended that the Panic of 1837 stimulated migration to the West. With nine-tenths of the factories of the East closed, one might have expected that the armies of unemployed would heed Horace Greeley's advice to go West and take up land.[1] Many eastern newspaper editors expected, as Greeley did, that laborers would scatter to the West, and western editors naturally welcomed their coming.[2] But recent research bears out the belief that migration for the most part ceased with

[1] Roy M. Robbins, "Horace Greeley: Land Reform and Unemployment," *Agricultural History*, Vol. VII (1933), pp. 18-41.
[2] See, for example, *Boston Mercantile Journal*, April 14, 1837, and *Chicago Weekly American*, May 13, 1837.

the advent of the panic.[3] Few people heeded Greeley's advice, for few had money for transportation and few knew very much about farming. Fewer still had the money to buy land after reaching the West.[4] Extensive settlement was not again resumed until the middle 1840's. At that time settlers took up lower-priced lands offered by speculators before buying at government sales, and even then there was no wholesale migration of redundant population. It is true that cheap land acted as a safety-valve for the discontented but only during good times. In general, cheap land can be considered as an aid in balancing the economic order only if viewed over a long-time perspective.

It was, in fact, the failure of the "back to the land" panacea which led Greeley and others to consider other means of ameliorating the lot of the eastern poor and discontented. The movement to establish economic and social opportunities for the masses which began in Jackson's administration became almost a crusade following the Panic of 1837. Liberal thought that had been deemed radical, agrarian, socialistic, or communistic now found more favorable consideration. Workingmen's associations became more popular in the larger cities of the Atlantic coast. Much might be said of their impracticable and visionary character, but one thing is certain, that two terrible panics within one generation had convinced many that the economic order of the country was more unbalanced than in the earlier period of the Republic. The remedies that were offered were quite levelling in character, but it must be recognized that even so the socialistic and communistic movements in America stood in striking contrast to the extreme revolutionary character of the same movements in Europe. Most Americans were in fact homeowners, and the institution of cheap land really acted as a deterrent against the genuinely radical tendencies of the day. At any rate, one may soundly conclude that eastern conditions served to bring the agrarianism of the West into more favorable light.

Economic and social reform was in the air. Many felt that a system which permitted perpetual artificial fluctuations in values was utterly subversive to the best interests of the country and that steps should immediately be taken to steady the currency system and thus diminish the irresponsible control by private corporations. It was contended that

[3] Murray Kane, "Some Considerations of the Safety Valve Doctrine," *Mississippi Valley Historical Review*, Vol. XXIII (1936), pp. 169-88.

[4] Robbins, "Horace Greeley," *loc. cit.*, p. 25.

the speculative spirit was merely slumbering and that a reunion of Bank and State would waken it to renewed activity.[5] Although it is beyond the scope of this study to deal with currency and banking reform, it is pertinent to consider the relation of the public lands problem to these other economic and social reforms. It was a conceded point that the reckless land speculations of 1835 and 1836 had been the cause as well as the center of the great convulsion of 1837. While banking and currency reform were essential to immediate reconstruction, nevertheless, further action was necessary to relieve the situation in the West. With widespread condemnation of the speculator, and with agrarian sentiment running rampant, the times were never more propitious for the securing of the public lands to actual settlers.

The Panic of 1837, instead of dampening the ardent spirits of the various protagonists on the land question, served to intensify sectional desires to bring about an immediate change. Benton again introduced his graduation bill, but it failed to make much headway against the determined opposition of Henry Clay who argued that it would bring on another decline in land values just as liquidation was supposed to have reached the bottom.[6] Calhoun found a more favorable reception for his cession plan which, modified slightly from previous bills, now provided that the federal government should receive approximately 12.5 per cent of the proceeds, the federal land laws should remain unchanged, no state should be allowed to cheapen its land without consent of Congress, and that books should be kept by the state authorities for federal inspection.[7] But even this bill was tabled in the Senate.

With the failure of the cherished plans of Calhoun and Benton the way was now cleared for consideration of preemption. On January 25, 1838, Senator Robert Walker of Mississippi again presented the bill which had been tabled in the House in 1837.[8] This bill, considerably modified, received unexpected support in the Senate where much of the debate was confined to technicalities and details.[9] Petitions had been pouring in upon Congress from state legislatures and from private citizens asking for relief in the form of indulgences for those who in

[5] "True Principles of Commercial Banking," *United States Magazine and Democratic Review*, Vol. II (1838), p. 126.

[6] *Congressional Globe*, 25 Cong. 2 Sess., p. 564. [7] *ibid.*, *Appendix*, 25 Cong. 3 Sess., p. 96.

[8] *supra*, p. 69. [9] *Cong. Globe*, 25 Cong. 2 Sess., p. 136.

spite of the collapse of speculation still feared the auction.[10] As one memorial declared: "If the lands are brought into the market this summer, a large portion of the settlers . . . who have spent two years of trial and hardship together with large sums of money in improving their lands would be wholly unable to purchase them even at the minimum price. . . . [The national debt has] been discharged, and the great effort for the last few years has been to diminish rather than increase the sources of the public revenue."[11] Credit and extensions had been granted upon customhouse bonds, and the banks throughout the country had been permitted to suspend specie payments without impunity, hence it was reasonable that some consideration should be given the actual settler. And the backers of the preemption measure received added prestige when President Van Buren who was interested in the eastern laborer as well as in the western settler took a decided stand in its favor.[12]

Henry Clay almost alone poured forth bitter invective on Walker's bill. He denounced the squatters on the public domain as "lawless rabble" and claimed that they might as well seize upon the forts, the arsenals, and the public treasure as to rush out and seize on the public lands.[13] "The whole preemption system," he declared, "is a violation of all law, and an encouragement to persons to go on the public lands and take the choicest portion of them."[14] The congressional debate was "nothing more than a struggle between those who would violate the law and those who would maintain its supremacy."[15] He saw preemption as a reward for the violation of the law. The editor of the *New York Courier and Enquirer* observed that "the bold and manly, and patriotic stand which Mr. Clay has taken in this debate will probably injure him politically in the Western and Southern States. Will it give him friends in any quarter of the country? It may not, but it ought to rally around him those men who honestly wish to preserve the national domain from the plunder of a lawless band of squatters."[16]

The same newspaper spoke of the preemption law as one "granting bounties to squatters engaged in cheating the government out of the

[10] 25 Cong. 2 Sess., *H. Ex. Doc.* No. 208; 25 Cong. 2 Sess., *S. Ex. Doc.* No. 317; *Racine Argus*, February 14, 1838.
[11] *ibid.*
[12] James D. Richardson (ed.), *Messages and Papers of the Presidents* (Washington, 1879-1903), Vol. III, p. 388.
[13] *National Intelligencer*, February 5, 1838.   [14] *Cong. Globe*, 25 Cong. 2 Sess., p. 142.
[15] *Niles' Weekly Register*, February 3, 1838.   [16] *ibid.*, January 27, 1838.

best tracts of public lands." As for Van Buren and Benton, the editor continued with the assertion that they were "vying with each other for Western popularity" which was "to be purchased if they or either of them" could "accomplish their views with the public lands." They apparently believed "this property" was "ample to satisfy the most craving among the mercenary," and it was "therefore to be squandered away in a profligate manner upon the unprincipled speculator or worthless squatter, and woe betide him who attempts to arrest their career." From Horace Greeley, came the observation that the bill seemed "calculated to set our western people hunting after sudden fortunes in making a claim upon some choice tract of land—so as to buy for a hundred dollars what may be worth five or ten thousand—instead of striving to improve their circumstances by regular and patient industry. It looks like a premium on thriftlessness and gambling adventure."[17]

So important had the problem become that the House of Representatives took up a bill similar to the Walker preemption bill and passed it on June 14.[18] The Senate dropped the Walker bill and concurred in the House bill. It was a sweeping Democratic victory, and carried along some of the western Whigs.[19]

By the Act of June 22, 1838, every settler of the public lands who was the head of a family or over twenty-one years of age, and who was in personal residence thereon at the time of the passage of the act and four months next preceding, was entitled to all the benefits of the privileges granted in the preemption act of 1830.[20] In other words, the Act of 1830 was practically revived and was to continue in operation for two years. However, the preemption-floats allowed in the previous acts were now outlawed, and wherever two persons were found settled on the same quarter section, the land was to be divided between them. Furthermore, an ironclad oath was to be taken by every claimant that he had entered upon the land "in his own right, and exclusively for his own use and benefit," and that he had not "directly or indirectly made any agreement or contract in any way or manner with any person whatever by which the title which he might acquire from the government should inure to the use or benefit of anyone except himself,

---

[17] *The Jeffersonian*, June 23, 1838.
[18] *Cong. Globe*, 25 Cong. 2 Sess., p. 452. See *Appendix* for vote in the House.
[19] The vote in the House was 107 to 53, and in the Senate 42 to 2.
[20] *Statutes at Large*, Vol. V, p. 382.

or to convey or transfer the said land or title to any other person whatever at any subsequent time." This oath was a security against speculation.

No sooner had this act providing for retrospective preemption been passed than western interests began working for the enactment of a measure incorporating the preemption principle permanently into the land system. This new bill, introduced in the House in 1839, was the natural culmination of the series of acts of temporary and remedial character which began in 1830. Never were the times more favorable to the passage of such an agrarian measure. Notwithstanding the anxiety of western members for its passage, however, the measure was not acted upon, due to the absorbing character of the currency problem.[21]

In 1840 a renewal of the Act of 1838 was easily secured by which the operation of preemption was continued down to June 22, 1842.[22] Undoubtedly, the preemption issue had become the most important land issue of the day, and one which rightly demanded a stand from both major parties in the ensuing presidential campaign. President Van Buren, and in fact the whole Democratic party, was now working openly in favor of the principle. Prominent partisan periodicals were printing full discussions of the *pro* and *con* of the subject.[23] Governor David Campbell of Virginia, speaking on the land problem in general, declared: "I know of no matter in regard to which this Commonwealth has, and ought to feel a deeper interest." From Connecticut came the desire to accept the challenge from the West.[24] Again it appeared that the East was lining up the advocates of Clay's distribution plan to block the preemption crusade from the West.

As the campaign of 1840 approached it was obvious that the West was destined to play a leading rôle. Calhoun in 1838, pointing to the belief that after the census of 1840 the West would command five-twelfths of the votes in the electoral college, predicted that the presidential candidate who catered to the West would secure the election of 1840.[25]

[21] *United States Magazine and Democratic Review*, Vol. IV (1839), p. 180.
[22] *Statutes at Large*, Vol. V, p. 382.
[23] For example, see: *United States Magazine and Democratic Review*, Vol. IV, pp. 137-43.
[24] Message to Virginia Legislature, January 7, 1839, quoted in *The Jeffersonian*, January 26, 1839.
[25] *Cong. Globe*, 25 Cong. 3 Sess., *Appendix*, p. 95.

From all over the country there burst forth unbounded praise of the Valley of the Mississippi. The following excerpt is typical: "That the glorious West of ours is destined ere long to become the seat of population and wealth, with their natural accompaniments of literature, art, and science, before which the pride of our past and present superiority must soon be forced to bow, we know full well; and hailing the approach of that day, we would speed the course of time that is to bring it around."[26] And from a periodical devoted primarily to economics and business rather than to politics came the farsighted observation: "Should the country arrive at that period when these [western] products are exported abroad, the eastern cities must be the depots of shipment for the produce of the west to foreign markets, as they now are and long will be the distributors into the interior of all important foreign goods. The arteries of western commerce will circulate the lifeblood to the heart of our commercial metropolis. Every pulsation of that heart is felt to the remotest borders of the west."[27] Undoubtedly, political and economic observations of this type focussed public attention on potential resources of the West.

But the West of 1840 desired more than empty words. It was already convinced of its greatness, and it was far more concerned about its present situation. With the states of Ohio, Indiana, Illinois, Michigan, Arkansas, and Louisiana practically bankrupt, the West was interested in remedial legislation. Indiana was the only Whig state among the bankrupts. Hence while the Democrats were lining up in favor of preemption, the Whigs proposed the assumption of state debts, hoping to gain the support of the bankrupt Democratic states.[28] This proposal brought forth considerable protest from the East. When the Whigs nominated Harrison of Ohio, the East in return for its support of a western candidate, received an agreement to hush up all the talk on assumption. Clay, who many thought would secure the Whig nomination, was seemingly appeased by the agreement to support his distribution plan. The decision to have no platform relieved many Whigs of embarrassment.

The Whigs were immediately set upon by the western Democrats who had heard with their own ears the Whig overtures regarding

26 "The Poetry of the West," *United States Magazine and Democratic Review*, Vol. IX, p. 9.
27 James H. Lanman, "The Progress of the Northwest," *Hunt's Merchants' Magazine*, Vol. III, p. 22.
28 Raynor G. Wellington, *The Political and Sectional Influence of the Public Lands, 1828-1842* (Boston, 1914), p. 76.

assumption, but the Whigs now denied that anything had been said on the subject.[29] When Benton, in December 1839, introduced into the Senate certain resolutions declaring against assumption, his real if unannounced motive was to bring the Whig position on that subject out into the open.[30] The nervous Whigs tried unsuccessfully to table the resolutions. Calhoun asserted that they had dropped the idea for fear that it would mean a higher tariff which would be unpopular among the southern Whigs.[31] But Benton's resolutions, instead of smoking out the Whigs on assumption, brought them more clearly in line with distribution. On February 10, 1840, Senator Crittenden of Kentucky brought forward resolutions on distribution. Benton's action had thus "aroused the South against the passage of assumption, had endeavored to reveal the Whigs in their true light to be settlers of the West, and had weakened their appeal to the moneyed class for support in the ensuing presidential campaign."[32]

While Benton was embarrassing the Whigs, Calhoun introduced his cession bill, a move which drew fire from the Whigs who charged Calhoun with making overtures to the West.[33] Before the session was over, the Democrats had pushed through a preemption act which renewed the Act of 1838. The forces were now aligned for the presidential campaign.

The Democrats nominated Van Buren and came out openly in favor of preemption and distribution. The Whigs, having no platform, talked of the prowess of their candidate Harrison, the hero of the West, the author of the Land Act of 1800, the victor at the Battle of Tippecanoe and at the Thames. Of course he favored the West! They appealed to the West, but they made no definite promises. Their enthusiasm for log cabins and hard cider was after all a sort of protective coloring. While Harrison reminded a Dayton, Ohio, audience in September 1840 that he had been a Democrat in 1800 and "had devised a bill which had for its object to snatch from the grasp of speculation all this glorious country which now teems with harvests under the hands of honest, industrious, and virtuous husbandmen," yet in the East Whig organizations resolved in favor of distribution.[34] The Whigs won the election, making extensive gains in the older West but failing to carry the newer states which had given unqualified support to

[29] ibid., p. 78.
[30] Cong. Globe, 26 Cong. 1 Sess., p. 82.
[31] Wellington, loc. cit., p. 79.
[32] ibid., p. 83.
[33] ibid., p. 85.
[34] The Log Cabin, September 26, 1840; October 3, 1840.

preemption—Illinois, Missouri, Arkansas, and the Territory of Iowa.[35]

An analysis made a few years later explains the Whig victory: "No one fact of circumstance had so powerful a control over the minds of the great masses in the Mississippi Valley in winning their affections to General Harrison as that he had been a pioneer himself, a settler, in the western sense of that term, had lived in his log cabin, and had favored all the laws which had tended to the protection and security of the squatter. Here was the consideration which threw confusion into the ranks of the Democratic party. This was the lever by which the Whig party raised themselves from a hopeless minority into an unexpected and triumphant majority. The supposed sympathy of General Harrison, and the reputed aversion of Van Buren for the poor man, for the humble citizen, is the true secret of the great and tremendous political revolution of 1840."[36]

The convening of the lame duck Congress in December 1840 commanded the attention of the country. No one section of the country had control of the national legislature, but in view of the courting of the West by both parties during the campaign it was expected that this section by playing its cards carefully, might now gain a complete victory over the conservative East. The ensuing congressional struggle was one of the most bitter and one of the most violent in the history of the land question—the culmination of over twenty years of sectionalism. Evidence of the importance of the land issue is found in the statement made by John C. Calhoun on January 12, 1841: "I regard the question of public lands, next to that of the currency, the most dangerous and difficult of all which demand the attention of the country and government at this important juncture of our affairs." At the same time Senator Ambrose H. Sevier from the frontier state of Arkansas was insistent that the West considered it the most important question of the day.[37]

When Congress met in December, Clay, interpreting the Whig presidential victory to mean the approval of his cherished distribution plan, soon introduced into the Senate a resolution calling for information on public land receipts since the year 1828.[38] But Benton rose to the occasion to demand a showdown on the friendship which the Whigs

[35] George M. Stephenson, *The Political History of the Public Lands, 1840-1862* (Boston, 1917), p. 43.

[36] Speech of Jacob Thompson in House of Representatives, July 9, 1846; *Cong. Globe,* 29 Cong. 1 Sess., *Appendix,* p. 777.

[37] *ibid.,* 26 Cong. 2 Sess., *Appendix,* pp. 52, 64.

[38] Wellington, *The Political and Sectional Influence of the Public Lands,* p. 87.

had pledged to the West in the course of the campaign. The introduction on December 14, of his so-called log cabin bill providing for permanent, prospective preemption took the Whigs quite unawares.[39] Jackson, still in touch with politics, declared that Benton's move was an excellent one because it placed "Clay in a position that he must vote for the bill, or expose his hypocrisy. . . . The battle" was now on "between the log cabins and the palaces." Jackson had "no doubt when the vote" was taken on Colonel Benton's bill, that Clay would "forsake the Cabin Boys and betake himself to the palaces."[40]

On January 4, 1841, the log cabin bill was reported from the Public Lands Committee by Senator Clement C. Clay of Alabama. Clay asserted that the settlers of the West were living in an era of good feeling, that during the campaign they had been the constant theme of praise. He showed that there would be no sacrifice of pecuniary interest worthy of consideration if permanent, prospective, preemption were adopted. He very ably presented evidence to the effect that the average return from the sale of land varied only from $1.26 per acre in 1828 to $1.31 in 1834. In 1836, the year of the largest sales in land history, the price averaged scarcely more than $1.25 per acre. If the expense of the auctions were taken into consideration, the average return per acre was probably considerably less than the established minimum. "Was not the question distinctly presented," asked the Senator, "whether the government was to sell the public domain in small quantities to men of small capital, who would immediately occupy, improve, and render it productive, or whether it was better policy to sell [land] at auction to bands of speculators and capitalists in large quantities, to lie idle and unprofitable till they could extort the desired profit from those whose necessities compel them to have it?"[41]

On the same day, January 4, Benton explained further his log cabin bill, and expressed the desire that graduation might be linked with preemption, since both ideas were being considered by the President and Secretary of the Treasury as revenue measures. He saw no reason why the bill should not meet the approval of all sides of the Senate, particularly the anti-Democratic side which was calling out for new taxes to defray the current expenses of the government and to retire the new national debt.[42]

[39] *Cong. Globe*, 26 Cong. 2 Sess., pp. 420-1.
[40] Jackson to Blair, January 5, 1841, quoted in Wellington, *loc. cit.*, p. 87.
[41] *Cong. Globe*, 26 Cong. 2 Sess., *Appendix*, pp. 18, 19, 83.   [42] *ibid.*, p. 21.

When Senator W. P. Mangum of North Carolina moved an amendment limiting the preemption to citizens of the United States, a tense situation appeared. Clay of Alabama contended that the privileges of the temporary preemption laws had all been open to aliens, but Clay of Kentucky visualized an exodus of the peoples of Europe to America, who might in a short time take up the remainder of the public domain and establish alien governments. The amendment to exclude aliens was rejected by vote of 30 to 12, the Whigs almost to a man voting in favor of alien exclusion.

Senator John J. Crittenden of Kentucky then proposed limiting preemption to persons possessing less than $500 in wealth. The aim of this proposal was to keep the wealth of the East intact and to put a damper on emigration. But this Whig proposal was voted down 26 to 14,[43] although by doing so, Clay contended, they gave their opinion "in favor of admitting the barons and millionaires and nabobs upon an equality with poor men."[44] On January 6, Senator S. S. Prentiss of Vermont, who had opposed all preemption measures heretofore, moved to substitute for the whole measure another extension of the Act of 1840. And on the same day Senator Jabez Huntington of Connecticut made a biting denunciation of the whole preemption system.[45]

It is clear that almost from the outset the struggle settled down to a strict party contest. The Whig position indicated that their praise of the West in the campaign of 1840 was largely camouflage. Jackson's prophecy was realized. Failing to block the log cabin bill by these flanking operations, the Whigs now shifted their tactics. On January 11, Crittenden moved to amend the measure to provide for distribution of the proceeds from the sales of public lands. Crittenden declared he could accept the log cabin bill, provided the Democrats would vote for distribution.[46] This was the first indication of the strategy that the Whigs ultimately adopted: to attach distribution as a rider to the log cabin bill. But at the moment Whig strategy only served to confuse the whole situation, for in order to counteract the distribution amendment Calhoun on January 12 moved an amendment to provide for the cession of the public lands to the states in which the lands were located. Thus instead of having a clear-cut discussion of preemption, the struggle over the log cabin bill resolved itself into a sectional combat with each section putting forward its own cherished solution of the problem.

[43] ibid., pp. 27, 29.   [44] Quoted in *Cleveland Daily Herald*, January 13, 1841.
[45] *Cong. Globe*, 26 Cong. 2 Sess., *Appendix*, p. 38.   [46] ibid., pp. 23, 24.

Debates waxed hot throughout the rest of the month with Benton of Missouri standing up against fire from all sections. Within a single day, January 18, the Senate voted down all the amendments to the log cabin bill, and it appeared that the bill would now have clear sailing. But not so, the Senate still wrangled over the amendments that it had killed—which Benton dubbed unparliamentary tactics—and finally Webster was brought into the arena to hold back preemption in favor of distribution.[47]

The Whig offensive was applauded by Horace Greeley, editor of the official Whig newspaper, *The Log Cabin,* who declared that every member who had opposed distribution was a Van Buren man. Regarding the lame duck Democrats of the eastern states, he charged: "They know that their votes do gross wrong to their several States—they have been told by their legislatures and the popular votes of their constituents that the Bentonian policy with regard to the Public Lands is as execrable to their judgement, as [it is] ruinous to their prosperity—and yet they heap the full measure of their iniquities by voting on every point directly in defiance of their constitutents."

On the subject of preemption and graduation Greeley voiced the Whig opposition perhaps as adequately as did Clay, Crittenden, or Webster. "The direct object and effect of the Locofoco propositions now pending before the Senate is the spoliation of the Old States. . . . [The] thriftless, industry-hating adventurer who shall first pounce upon a section at the junction of two rivers, or at a head of navigation, or in the midst of valuable timber—worth probably fifty to five hundred dollars an acre before his foot touched it—shall be entitled to purchase it whenever he gets ready at a dollar and a quarter an acre. What justice, what policy, can there be in this? . . . The triumph of the preemption and graduation schemes must be the death warrant of the rights of the Old States and the Union. . . . We feel and know," he continued, "that the triumph of preemption and graduation will rob the Old States of an incalculable property, at the same time that it will debauch and demoralize the New, plunging the whole country into another whirlpool of delirious speculation like that from which it has just emerged. . . . The West will be overrun by squatters, its choice locations secured for next to nothing and its best timber destroyed, leaving the residue

[47] Webster's speech and Benton's defense attracted much attention, see: *The Log Cabin,* January 23, 1841; *The Boston Quarterly,* Vol. IV (1841), pp. 230-56.

comparatively worthless. At length, when the price has run down to twenty-five cents, rich speculators will monopolize the land by counties, and the next generation will become their tenants and vassals. Such are the deplorable results toward which Locofocoism* is now driving the country."[48]

When the month of January passed, and it looked as though the log cabin bill would come to a vote, the Whigs again produced a series of amendments undoubtedly intended to obstruct its passage. In turn, cession and distribution were again voted upon and defeated. On February 2 the bill itself was forced to a vote and passed by 31 to 19, fourteen Whigs and five Democrats from the Atlantic Coast states voting against it.[49] Almost every division taken on the land question in the course of the month had been on a strictly party basis. Upon the passage of the bill the official Whig newspaper commentator, Horace Greeley, declared: "We acknowledge that preemption to a great extent will be the law of new sections whatever may be the law of Congress, and that there is a seeming cogency in [preemption] . . . better legalized and regulated than fruitlessly forbidden. . . . But there is consolation yet. The bill of iniquities cannot probably get through the House at the present session. . . . Then the next Congress will pass a distribution bill; and it will be easier for a caravan of camels to go through the eye of a needle than for such a bill as Benton's to pass that body."[50]

The *Republican Journal* of Belfast, Maine, asserted that the land problem had become the leading issue of the day, that it was now "a struggle between Aristocracy and Democracy. . . . The Democracy have contended for the rights of the poor man . . . to settle upon and improve a portion of the public domain." This log cabin bill was "emphatically a bill for the good of the many," and was "founded on sound democratic principles; but Clay, Webster, and other federalists," had "battled with all their might against the bill and its very principles."

The editor further contended that the lands yielded a revenue of some millions annually which went to aid in the support of the government, thus lightening the burdens of the people. If the federal distribution measure should take effect, the revenue of the government would be diminished, the proceeds being distributed to the individual states to be disposed of as they saw fit. This deficiency in the national

---

[48] "H.G." in *The Log Cabin*, January 23, 1841.
[49] *Cong. Globe*, 26 Cong. 2 Sess., *Appendix*, pp. 99, 104, 230.
[50] "H.G." in *The Log Cabin*, February 6, 1841.

revenue would have to be supplied by imposing duties upon goods imported, or by direct taxation upon the people. The latter course would not be submitted to and a protective tariff was the only alternative. The editor believed that "the working man, bad as his condition may be, can yet be worse off. He sees now the West ready to receive him, and give him shelter from northern oppression; he can buy a good farm under the preemption bill at a reasonable price. He has no guarantee that under the distribution scheme, the avarice of the old states will not raise the price so high as to prohibit him from buying. Moreover, the whole northern legislature is so much in the hands of capitalists, it will be the intent of the laws to keep the people at home, by lessening the prospects of emigrants; the more laborers there are, the lower is the price of labor, and the more means are wielded by rich employers to crush any *insubordination* among the employed.

"The distribution scheme," he concluded, "like that of a national bank, is unconstitutional. . . . The lands were originally ceded to the government by the old States,—they cannot demand them back without some violation of compact."[51]

To return to Congress, the Whigs had not been successful in preventing the passage of the log cabin bill, but they had so delayed its passage that it was doubtful whether it could be pushed through the lower chamber. In the House, the Whigs had been able to prevent any such measure from being considered. A resolution introduced on December 24 by John Reynolds of Illinois had proposed instructions for a preemption bill, but William Johnson of Maryland had immediately amended the measure to include provision for distribution. Not until March 3 was the motion made in the House to suspend the rules in order to take up the Senate log cabin bill. Edward Everett of Vermont moved a call of the House, but the members, anxious to go home, refused to allow the bill to be considered.[52] Thus faded the hopes of the Van Buren Democrats to gain a clear-cut victory on preemption.

The Whig victory at the election of 1840 produced in the new Senate a Whig majority of seven, and in the lower house a Whig majority of forty-four. With such a composition Clay of Kentucky was anxious for a special session, and Harrison, influenced by a party caucus, agreed.

[51] Belfast (Maine) *Republican Journal*, February 4, 1841.
[52] *Cong. Globe*, 26 Cong. 2 Sess., p. 58.

But before Congress convened the death of Harrison jeopardized Clay's plans. Tyler, who succeeded to the presidency, was a strict constructionist, an antiprotectionist, and was opposed to a national bank. In his message to Congress he declared in favor of distribution "provided such distribution does not force upon Congress the necessity of imposing upon commerce heavier burthens than those contemplated by the act of 1833."[53] From the southern Whig press came unqualified approval. In fact, Tyler was skeptical of Clay's plans and even seemed inclined to support preemption.[54]

Clay decided, nevertheless, to gain sufficient votes among the western Democrats to compensate for the loss of some of the southern Whigs who feared a rise in the tariff. To accomplish this he proposed to combine distribution and preemption in one bill. It will be recalled that Senator Crittenden, Clay's colleague, had promised the West in January that Clay's Whig following would agree to preemption if the frontier would support distribution.[55] Hence, without the backing of the frontier interests, a combined distribution-preemption bill was introduced in the House on June 24.[56] For the next few days the House debated distribution and some members, disgusted with this turn of events, demanded that the purpose of the special session be redefined.[57] Political grievances appeared to be the order of the day, and Clay seemed determined to ride roughshod over both the Chief Executive and the Democratic minority.[58] The Democrats, at first taken by surprise, rallied strongly against the bill, for they knew that in practice distribution would nullify preemption.[59]

Finally on July 6 the debate in the House reached its climax. Over one hundred amendments were introduced to delay its passage. After ten hours of debate, the House was only warming up to its highest pitch. While the forensic battle raged within, a terrific thunderstorm raged without seemingly keeping time and tune with the unruly chamber. The last stages of the struggle were aptly described by an eye-witness:

[53] Richardson, *Messages and Papers*, Vol. IV, p. 47; Stephenson, *The Political History of the Public Lands*, p. 53.

[54] Wellington, *Political and Sectional History of the Public Lands*, p. 96.   [55] *supra*, p. 82.

[56] On June 22, W. C. Johnson of the Committee on Public Lands reported the distribution bill, see *Cong. Globe*, 27 Cong. 1 Sess., p. 89. On June 24 the bill was reported to include permanent, prospective preemption in practically the same form as Benton's Log-Cabin bill of the previous session.

[57] *ibid.*, pp. 133, 135.   [58] Stephenson, *loc. cit.*, p. 54.

[59] Wellington, *loc. cit.*, p. 98.

"The noise was now so great, and so many members were addressing the chair at once, that it seemed as if 'chaos were come again.' . . . The chair exerted itself to the utmost to restore order, but in vain. The uproar continued, while the rain fell, and the thunder rolled in terrific peals, and the blue lightning glaring at intervals through the hall, appeared to be mocking the storm that raged within. . . . The House having been in session for ten hours, a proposition was made that adjournment take place. . . . This was rejected by the majority. So amidst a terrific storm of thunder and lightning and rain, which at intervals rendered voices inaudible, the bill was forced ahead."[60]

After the storm had cleared away it was found that the distribution-preemption bill had passed by the close vote of 116 to 108.[61] In commenting on the passage in the House, Horace Greeley declared: "The Whig phalanx was compelled at last to resort to a bayonet charge, and they did the work gallantly." As to the compromise character of the bill, he believed "The people of the New States have an immediate, present, tangible interest in getting the public lands for little or nothing. The interest of the Old States in resisting them is equally strong, but unhappily less direct and immediate. One-half our people know and care nothing about it. But the passage of the land bill will remedy this, making the interest of the Old States equally palpable with that of the new. As a measure of precaution and security, therefore, this bill is invaluable."[62]

In the Senate the bill met with even greater opposition. It had been introduced on June 10.[63] On June 14, Robert J. Walker of Mississippi moved a strategic amendment providing that distribution should be discontinued if the tariff should be raised above the 20 per cent level.[64] The Senate, awaiting action by the House, did not seriously consider the bill until August 11. On that day Senator Richard M. Young of Illinois proposed that graduation be included in the bill, but the Whigs rejected this amendment by vote of 27 to 18. Young then offered another amendment to authorize the States to tax the land from the date of purchase from the government but this was also defeated, by vote of 22 to 18.[65]

After their failure to add any amendments to the bill, the Democrats resorted to logrolling. Mississippi was demanding that the Senate pass the bankruptcy bill. Clay agreed to act on that bill provided the advo-

---

[60] *Cong. Globe*, 27 Cong. 1 Sess., pp. 155-6.
[62] *The Log Cabin*, July 10, 1841.
[64] *ibid.*, p. 38.

[61] *ibid.*, p. 156.
[63] *Cong. Globe*, 27 Cong. 1 Sess., p. 175.
[65] *ibid.*, p. 322.

cates of the bankruptcy bill would vote for his bill, but this plan was refused. On August 18 an attempt was made to table the bill. Time was flying, and the Whigs found that even their much-desired revenue bill which had passed the House was being held up pending action on the land bill.[66] The Tyler Whigs now insisted that it would be necessary to borrow or tax in order to distribute. Hence, at last, Clay was forced to accept Walker's amendment of an earlier date which provided that if the tariff were raised above the 20 per cent level then distribution should cease. This amendment was later to prove the undoing of distribution. As Professor Wellington put it, "it took the kernel out of the bill." Had Clay not agreed to this amendment, his bill would probably have been vetoed by Tyler.[67]

On August 26 the Democrats made their last stand. Senator Benton moved to recommit the bill with instructions to strike out that part relating to distribution and instead insert graduation. His motion was lost by vote of 22 to 18. The vote on the original bill was then taken, and it was passed 25 to 18, only one Whig voting against it.[68] On August 30 the House and Senate worked over the details, concurring on the main points. The combined distribution-preemption bill was signed by President Tyler on September 4, 1841.[69]

Viewing the whole history of Clay's bill the summary made by Professor Hibbard seems apt: "It was a case of the progressives against the standpatters, and finally the standpatters voted the progressive program through in order to carry their own."[70] Greeley, with his eyes on the distribution part of the bill, declared that in its ultimate consequences this bill was "of greater importance and value than any other measure" which had been before Congress that session.[71] More to the point, the debates and votes indicate that it was not a sectional measure; it was strictly a party triumph, all to the credit of Henry Clay. Yet the great victory was to be short-lived; the anti-tariff amendment forced through by the southern Whigs was to prove its undoing and to give the triumph after all to frontier America.

[66] Wellington, *loc. cit.*, p. 100.   [67] *ibid.*, p. 101.
[68] *Cong. Globe*, 27 Cong. 1 Sess., pp. 388, 405-6. Three Whigs who had voted against the distribution amendment in February were brought over, which, together with the new Whigs elected in 1840, made the sum of 25 votes. Of the 17 votes opposed, all but 1, Clayton of Delaware, were Democratic votes, mostly from the West and South.
[69] *Statutes at Large*, Vol. V, pp. 453-8.
[70] Hibbard, *History of Public Land Policies*, p. 158. By permission of the Macmillan Co.
[71] *The Log Cabin*, September 4, 1841.

The distribution sections of the act provided for an outright donation of 500,000 acres to each new state for the construction of internal improvements and an apportionment of 10 per cent of the proceeds from the sales of public lands, but said apportionment was to be repealed in case the tariff should be raised above the 20 per cent level. In August 1842, both houses passed a tariff measure raising the duties above this level. In fact, the bill specifically repealed the distribution provisions of the Act of 1841.[72] The truth is that with financial stringency there had been little money to distribute. The total sum paid out amounted to only $691,000, a case of "much cry and little wool."[73] Many of the states including New Hampshire, South Carolina, Illinois, and Alabama, in disgust refused outright their shares of the distribution, looking upon the measure as a bribe. The Governor of Maine declared that "the policy of distribution is fully repudiated by both government and people."[74]

Clay and other Whig advocates reluctantly yielded to the repeal of the principle, fearing that they were signing the death warrant of the public domain.[75] During the next two decades the principle was to be introduced again and again in Congress, but for practical purposes it received its last rites in 1842. Only the preemption portion of the act remained to carry on the memory of the bitter fight of 1841. Thus by an abrupt turn of events, the frontier interests at last triumphed.

The preemption provisions of the Act of 1841 repudiated the retrospective policy of preemption and recognized that settlement prior to purchase was no longer per se a trespass. The act provided that an individual, henceforth, could legally venture forth upon public surveyed land and stake a claim to the exclusion of all others.[76] The maximum amount that a settler could purchase was 160 acres, to be paid for at the government minimum price of $1.25 per acre. Exception was made in the case of the government's alternate sections of land grants to railroads, canals, etc., which could be preempted at $2.50 per acre. Any person was eligible for preemption who could comply with the following conditions: The individual must be the head of a family (any age), a widow, or a single man over the age of twenty-one; the person must

[72] *Statutes at Large*, Vol. V, p. 567.
[73] Donaldson, *The Public Domain*, p. 753; Hibbard, *History of Public Land Policies*, p. 188.
[74] Message to the Legislature, *Niles' Weekly Register*, Vol. LXV, p. 340, cited in Hibbard, *loc. cit.*, p. 188.
[75] *Niles' Weekly Register*, Vol. LXVI, p. 299.
[76] *Statutes at Large*, Vol. V, Act of September 4, 1841, pp. 453-8.

be a citizen of the United States, or have filed a declaration of intention to become a citizen.[77] Also the settler must not be the proprietor of 320 acres or more of land in any state or territory; and he must not quit or abandon his residence on his land to reside on the public land in the same state or territory. Lands included in any reservation, school lands, certain Indian lands, lands already granted to railroads, canals, or other public improvements, land included in the limits of any incorporated town, land already selected for townsites, certain lands set aside for trade or agricultural purposes, and mineral and saline lands were not open to preemption.

Frontier interests "accepted the law as a concession wrung from a reluctant Congress whose sympathy for the West was far from cordial."[78] They never forgave Henry Clay for stealing Benton's thunder. For the last twenty years Clay had consistently sided with the Atlantic Coast in its condemnation of the frontier. Knowing him to be the author of the hated principle of distribution, they believed him insincere in his attempt to reconcile such diametrically opposed principles as distribution and preemption. They called him "the worst enemy of the squatter." An Arkansas newspaper in 1844 said that he had done all in his power "to oppress the poor and hardy settlers upon the public lands, striving to place them in the merciless hands of speculators, and proposing to send a military force against them and force them out of their hard-earned homes at the point of the bayonet."[79]

In reciprocal manner, the East had no love to spare for the belated preemption victory. Horace Greeley—later one of the outstanding advocates of homesteading—professing a true interest in the West, declared: "We detest the whole business [preemption], believing that nothing has wrought so fearful a woe to the industry, morals, and prosperity of the West."[80] When the *Milwaukee Sentinel and Herald* answered this challenge, Greeley retorted: "The Milwaukee editor well knows that we have done more to commend the natural advantages of Wisconsin and direct the attention of our eastern people than any editor east of Buffalo. But while ever advising our friends to emigrate west-

---

[77] *ibid.*, p. 455; *Opinions of Attorney-General*, Vol. IV, p. 147.
[78] Stephenson, *loc. cit.*, p. 97. By permission of Chapman and Grimes Co., Inc.
[79] Little Rock, *Arkansas Banner*, April 24, 1844.
[80] *New York Weekly Tribune*, June 15, 1843; also consult issue of May 4, 1843, and the *Daily Tribune*, April 29, 1843.

ward privately as well as publicly, we have uniformly counselled them not to wander beyond the bounds of civilization—to stop off this side of the jumping-off-place, select land that is surveyed and pay for it." And later he added: "We said then, what we repeat, that the preemption system, with its facility of trespassing on the public lands, is a curse to the West and to the whole country."[81]

The historian may well conclude that the Preemption Act of 1841 marked the end of the old conservative land policy established in 1785. This new policy in general recognized four important principles: first, it was evident that Congress at last regarded the settlement of the public domain as more desirable than the revenue that might be obtained from it; second, that Congress intended that the domain should not fall into the hands of those who already had enough land; third, that the domain should be settled in small farms so as to extend the blessing of cheap land to the largest number; and fourth, that settlers should be protected from all intrusion and allowed a reasonable time to earn or gather together a sum sufficient to buy the land. It was at last intended that the actual settler be placed on an equal basis with the speculator in competition for land.

While the Preemption Act of 1841 served as a remedial measure in the reconstruction period following the great Panic of 1837, nevertheless, its enduring effects gave evidence that it was something more than a temporary panacea. Some contemporary observers went so far as to predict that it would serve as a deterrent against speculation. Indeed, it was the most important agrarian measure ever passed by Congress.[82] It was a victory of pioneer America over the more established eastern order of society.[83] It was the capstone in the democratization of the public land system. The fundamental truth of Jefferson's prophecy made in 1776 in reference to frontiersmen, namely, that "they will settle the lands in spite of everybody," had at last been realized.

[81] *New York Weekly Tribune*, June 15, 1843.
[82] Shosuke Sato, "The History of the Land Question in the United States," *Johns Hopkins University Studies* (Baltimore, 1886), Vol. IV, p. 159.
[83] Roy M. Robbins, "Preemption: A Frontier Triumph," *Mississippi Valley Historical Review*, Vol. XVIII (1931), pp. 331-49.

CHAPTER VI

LAND FOR THE LANDLESS

BY the 1840's the West was beginning to sense its power and to look askance upon the scanty pittance that was being doled out so grudgingly by Congress. The most rapidly growing part of the country was being frightfully neglected, while Congress—so the West charged—granted millions of dollars for splendid ships upon the Atlantic Coast, and for commerce.[1] In fact, the amount of outlay on the Delaware breakwater alone exceeded "all appropriations of every sort" for "intercommunication for commercial purposes" in the "whole immense region included between the lakes and the Gulf of Mexico and stretching from the Appalachian range to the Rocky Mountains." Eastern manufacturers and merchants, so the Westerners claimed, exerted an influence out of all proportion to their relative wealth and numbers; they acted in "masses, and their appearance" was "in that way, much more imposing, and their real power greatly strengthened." The western agricultural section, they maintained, was being treated "as a foreign territory"; and Congress seemed "hardly to have been aware that this far country had any interests to foster."[2]

Notwithstanding western feelings, this favoritism toward the East was already disappearing. With millions of dollars from England and the East invested in western lands and improvements, banking interests were becoming deeply concerned about the welfare of the West. The exploiters of the West, many of whom had suffered much in the Panic, were now ready to aid the West, doubtless hoping thereby to increase the returns from their own investments. Even that spokesman of New England, Daniel Webster, who had personally invested money in western lands, began to express a sympathy for that section. In the 1840's considerable wealth from Boston was being invested in Lake Superior mineral lands. Other eastern interests were sinking capital into the forest lands of Michigan, Wisconsin and the Southwest. The returns from investments in canals and railroads would to a very large extent be

[1] Josiah Bond, "Wisconsin and Its Resources," *Hunt's Merchants' Magazine,* Vol. X (1844), p. 552.
[2] William Kirkland of New York, "The United States' Census of 1850 With Reference to the Political Relations of the Eastern and Western States," *ibid.,* Vol. XIV (1846), p. 116.

determined by the prosperity of the regions which these improvements served. The East began to realize that as long as the representative principle continued in operation, the Mississippi River Valley would hold the dominant place in the Republic.

When the Preemption Act of 1841 failed to satisfy the West, the East became fearful lest this triumph be turned into another victory march for the West. This fear is evident in the concerted effort among the Whigs to reenact their cherished distribution plan which, after being skilfully pushed through Congress by Henry Clay in 1841, had been automatically repealed in 1842 when the tariff was raised above the 20 per cent level.

Horace Greeley, editor of the *New York Tribune,* headed the Whig press campaign in the East to make the land question an important issue in the election of 1844. His editorial on July 9, 1842, succinctly stated the eastern view that distribution was "a measure of strict justice to the states, of relief to the impoverished and bankrupt, and of encouragement to education and internal improvement." It was essential that distribution should be secured at once, "since the very next Congress" would "feel the influx of an enormously increased proportion of Representatives of the squatter interest, clamorous for the spoliation of the Old States altogether, by measures of graduation, loose preemption, or direct cession of these lands."

The East believed the "adoption of either of these measures would be at once a robbery of the Old States and a demoralization of the New, by alluring their citizens from the pursuits of industry to swarming in search of choice tracts of land on which to pounce at a nominal price. But beyond all this, . . . there can be no efficient and steady protection to home industry without the land distribution; for, one year of prosperous industry will lead to heavy purchases of public lands; then comes an excessive revenue, next a reduction of the tariff in the midst of good prices, next excessive importations followed by derangement, bankruptcy and distress. Friends of American industry!" the editorial concluded, "stand by the land distribution! it is the sheet anchor of our safety!"

A month later Greeley, in answer to an editorial in the *Portland* (Maine) *Argus,* took a stand against Calhoun's cession proposition and Benton's graduation scheme, though he admitted that these plans had a good chance of passage as soon as "Iowa, Wisconsin and Florida take their place in the Union."[3] *The Whig Almanac,* the next year affirmed its belief that this "noblest patrimony ever yet inherited by any people" should be "husbanded and preserved with care, in such manner that future generations shall not reproach us with having squandered what was justly theirs, and left them penniless."[4]

Van Buren voiced the Democratic viewpoint that the income from the public domain would be more faithfully and equitably applied to the common benefit of the country if retained in the national treasury.[5] The South naturally approved Van Buren's view, for as long as revenue was coming into the treasury from the public lands there was less likelihood of a higher tariff. Thus the issue was joined between the Whig and Democratic parties.

On December 11, 1843, Robert J. Walker of Mississippi introduced into the Senate a bill to graduate the price of public lands in favor of settlers and cultivators, thus inaugurating a new western drive for graduation.[6] The *New York Tribune* and a few other eastern newspapers threw themselves into the thick of the battle hoping to make land policy the leading issue. To a subscriber who complained that the Whig program of distribution and protection would lead to monopolies which would "work great mischief to a community," leading perhaps to the necessity of regulating "the prices of labor in manufacturing industries . . . by law," Greeley replied: "We must watch and foil the demagogues who are incessantly trying to squander the public lands by reducing their price. Let any graduation bill be passed which reduces the price of these lands ultimately to twenty-five cents an acre, or nothing, and whole counties . . . will be monopolized by heavy capitalists and speculators, and covered with a dependent tenantry, or held for exorbitant prices. The public lands are the great regulator of the relations of Labor and Capital, the safety valve of our industrial and social engine; and woe to this people should [they by] any cheating pretense of favoring 'poor settlers' be alienated, or suffered to be absorbed by the few."[7]

But land policy did not become a leading issue in the campaign of 1844. The Democrats found a more popular issue in expansion, though it must not be forgotten that the Whig campaign for protection and

---

[3] *ibid.,* August 3, 1842.   [4] *Whig Almanac,* 1843, p. 17.
[5] *Congressional Globe,* 28 Cong. 1 Sess., *Appendix,* pp. 628-9.
[6] *Cong. Globe,* 28 Cong. 1 Sess., pp. 13, 22, 373.
[7] *New York Weekly Tribune,* February 3, 1844.

distribution fell short of ultimate victory by only a few votes in the electoral college. Polk's appointment of Robert J. Walker of Mississippi as Secretary of the Treasury heralded a new day for the South and West. Second only to Benton in his championship of graduation, and an apostle of free trade, Walker was to add great impetus to the western movement for cheaper land.

The Polk administration, from Land Commissioner to President, was one in its demand for graduation.[8] In his annual message to Congress in December 1845, Polk asked that "lands some time since surveyed and still remaining unsold because they are inferior quality, that is, swampy, or sterile, or difficult to bring into cultivation . . . be reduced in order to let the poor buy them."

Greeley pointed out that so long as the government persisted in bringing into the market some ten or twenty million of acres of land annually, while the demands for settlement required but one to three million, a heavy and increasing surplus of unsold lands was inevitable. Because lands remained unsold did not therefore necessarily prove they were of bad quality. Any hardy settler, he declared, should be able to save the price of an eighty-acre homestead out of the proceeds of a year's faithful industry.[9] A little later Greeley paid his respects to graduation. He believed that "if ever there was a scheme full of mischief and injustice, this is one. It ought to be entitled 'A bill to discourage and prevent all payment for the public lands, and enable speculators to get them ultimately for a song.'"[10] But in spite of this view, Greeley himself was soon to take a stand in favor of homesteading.

The speech of Jacob Thompson in the House of Representatives, July 9, 1846, clearly portrays the Whig position on the land question. The entire responsibility for the poor showing of the Whig party, he insisted, must rest on the shoulders of Henry Clay whose "course on the public lands" had "always lost him the vote of the new states, and it must and will be the fate of all those who" followed "in his footsteps." Pointing to the eastern interests, he wondered whether they would "never learn that distribution of the proceeds of the sales of the public lands among the States is an exploded, an 'obsolete idea,' condemned by the people, unauthorized by the Constitution, and founded in injustice and a false economy?" Speaking of Mr. Clay he observed that

[8] 29 Cong. 1 Sess., *S. Doc.* No. 16, p. 12.
[9] *New York Weekly Tribune*, December 13, 1845.   [10] *ibid.*, January 3, 1846.

"there were many points in his character which challenged the admiration of our people. His boldness and frankness in taking his positions, his glowing eloquence, and his manly bearing, were traits which would have won the esteem of the daring pioneer. But his opposition to preemption; his unjust and impolitic aspersions . . . [upon] honest squatters; and his advocacy of distribution which led him into opposition to graduation . . . gave to the cup, which otherwise might have been sweet and palatable to the taste, such gall and bitterness as to induce the people of those states to turn away with odium and disgust."[11]

Here was the key to the Whig difficulties. Their program had no appeal to the most rapidly growing part of America. In fact, the more rapid the growth of the West the faster the strength of the Whigs in that area decreased.

The ever-increasing political power of the Mississippi Valley was evident in the fight over the graduation bill in 1846. The bill passed the Senate by a strict party vote, but was tabled in the House on August 5 by vote of 104 to 79.[12] After the passage of the bill in the Senate, Horace Greeley saw "but one hope left. That rests on the principle of the *freedom of the lands* in small tracts (not over 160 acres) to actual settlers only, each paying the sum adequate to the cost of survey, etc. for the right of occupancy only, subject to the right of eminent domain [by] the whole people, of course, inalienable except by the free consent of the holder, and not alienable then except to one who possesses no other land."[13] This rather surprising statement by the long prominent Whig spokesman offered to the Whigs a new approach to the land problem. The question was: would the Whigs accept it?

It is important to understand, however, that Greeley's sudden demand for homesteads was not entirely due to his intense hatred of graduation. In fact the Mexican War which had used up the treasury receipts from public lands had put a temporary damper on the demand for graduation. Greeley's stand was rather an outgrowth of his ever-increasing humanitarian interest, his sympathy with the poor and unemployed, his interest in socialism and, after 1844, his cooperation with the National Land Reformers. To understand the nature of this over-

---

[11] *Cong. Globe*, 29 Cong. 1 Sess., *Appendix*, p. 777.
[12] *Cong. Globe*, 29 Cong. 1 Sess., p. 1,196.   [13] *New York Weekly Tribune*, July 18, 1846.

whelming force of humanitarianism, it is necessary to go back a few years to 1837.

The attempts to secure "equal opportunities for all" during the Jackson administration had brought forth few real advantages for the common man of America.[14] The "right to vote" was after all an empty victory in view of the economic and social disruption emanating from the Panic of 1837. As the first effects of panic began to paralyze the economic structure around New York City, a few eastern editors began to preach emigration, not as a cure for the distresses of the time, but as a means of alleviating their most malignant consequences. Horace Greeley, then editor and joint owner of a none too successful literary sheet, *The New Yorker,* observing that there were already twenty thousand mechanics and thirty thousand seamstresses out of work in New York City alone, began to advise "every laborer, of whatever trade, to take up the march for the new country."[15] In early June, pointing out that a winter of fearful and unexampled severity was in prospect, he cried: "Do not wait here to share and increase its horrors. Fly—scatter through the country—go to the Great West—anything rather than remain here."[16] The horrible conditions produced by the Panic of 1837, in addition to the wretched environment of his youth, gave to Greeley a social viewpoint. Here was the beginning of the "back to the land" gospel, and the conception of that famous epigram, "Go West, young man, go forth into the country"—or as it is often quoted, "Go West, young man, and grow up with the country." For its effects upon American thought and action, the social crusade thus inaugurated is comparable to the Wakefield experiment in England.

The failure of the country to return to better times after the panic led many people to join the crusade for reform. Many of the intellectuals of the country studied conditions in England, fearing that similar conditions might arise in the United States. In 1840 the Reverend William Ellery Channing, in a series of sermons on "The Elevation of the Laboring Classes" which were published in Greeley's paper, noted that the improvement in steam navigation had placed Europe and America side by side. Channing hailed this development, but asked what was "to be the effect of bringing the laboring classes of Europe twice as near as they are now . . . anything, everything should be done to save us from

---

[14] This section of the chapter is abstracted from the author's article: "Horace Greeley: Land Reform and Unemployment, 1837-1862," *Agricultural History,* Vol. VII (1933), pp. 18-41.

[15] *New Yorker,* April 22, 1837.   [16] *ibid.,* June 3, 1837.

the social evils which deform the old world. . . . One thing is plain," he concluded, "that our present civilization contains strong tendencies to the intellectual and moral depression of a large portion of the community."[17]

The presidential campaign of 1840 was fought out in favor of the West and the common man, but politics offered no solution to the depression problem. Meanwhile Greeley, groping for a cure for the nation's ills, became acquainted with Albert Brisbane, an earnest advocate of Fourieristic socialism, who had just returned from France. Brisbane in an editorial in Greeley's *Tribune* declared: "Social evils are less intense in this country than in Europe, it is true—and why? Because we have a vast extent of soil and a thin population, and because there are outlets and new fields of action offered to the increasing population, and to those who cannot find employment, or who have been mired in their fortunes. But we are verging gradually toward the frightful misery which exists in older civilized countries; nay we are already a part of it."[18]

Greeley came under the scathing attack of some of his Whig friends for allowing Brisbane to preach his socialistic doctrines of Association in his newspaper. Ridicule of Brisbane became so strong that Greeley finally came to his defense with the challenge: "Do not stand there quarreling with those who have devised or adopted a scheme which you consider absurd or impracticable, but take hold and devise something better. For, be assured, friend! that this generation will not, must not pass without the discovery and adoption of some method whereby the *right to labor* and to receive and enjoy the honest reward of such labor, shall be secured to the poorest and least fortunate of our people."[19] For four years Greeley preached Association in his *Tribune,* but in 1847 he suddenly dropped it.

While the "intellectuals" were initiating and encouraging Fourierism, a new movement—agrarianism—had sprung up from the ranks of the laboring classes. The Land Reform movement originated with a few intelligent workingmen of New York City. Prominent among these men were George Henry Evans and John Cummerford. Evans was a labor leader whose hopes for a new industrial order had been blasted by the Panic of 1837. Realizing the difficulties of gaining the

[17] *The Log Cabin,* July 18, 1840.   [18] *New York Weekly Tribune,* April 23, 1842.
[19] *ibid.,* July 20, 1843.

desired ends by organizing labor, these men in 1844 hit upon the idea of free land as a means of attracting the redundant population westward and consequently bringing about higher wages and better working conditions for laboring men in the eastern industrial areas. With the eastern laboring interests launching a crusade for free land, the time seemed ripe for an agrarian alliance between the East and West.

In 1841, the Westerners secured the passage of the Preemption Act, an agrarian measure which democratized the land system, legalized trespassing on the public domain, and allowed persons who had settled a quarter-section of land the preference of buying that land at the established minimum price to the exclusion of all other persons. To the West, free land was the logical next step after this preemption victory. The success of an East-West political union would depend largely upon the strength of labor forces in the East, which was the stronghold of conservatism, a region dominated by manufacturers, employers, and property holders fearful of all leveling influences and determined to maintain the established order.

Evans centered his Land Reform crusade around the *ager publicum*— the vast public domain. His party was always to remain weak as to numbers, but because of the intelligence of its members and the publicity of their ideas it began to attract considerable attention. Evans went further than Fourierism in his crusade to assure "equal opportunity for all men." His program aimed to insure the individual's right to the natural resources of the country against creditors by the enactment of a law exempting homesteads from attachment for debts. More than that, the homestead was to be made inalienable. He would prohibit disposal of the public lands in large blocks to moneyed and speculative interests by granting to every poor man a farm of 160 acres of public land. In fact, the Land Reformers' program embraced: free homesteads, homestead exemption, and land limitation.[20] In spite of persecution, these intellectuals steadfastly adhered to their conviction that Land Reform was destined to affect a social revolution which would place the country beyond the possibility of disunion, which would check speculation in land, and at the same time open up an avenue whereby the industrial classes in town and country would be enabled by the strength of their own right arms to avoid being crushed by capital, or becoming bondsmen to cunning speculators.

[20] Selig Perlman, *A History of Trade Unionism in the United States* (New York, 1922), p. 38.

That Horace Greeley, supporter of Whig principles and the exemplar of Clay conservatism, should connect himself with this radical, agrarian movement for Land Reform seems almost incredible. Perhaps his deep humanitarian feeling is the explanation. Throughout 1844 and 1845 Greeley carefully watched the activities of Evans and his crusade to establish "the Right to Labor and the Right to the Soil." The reports of the workingmen's associations and their conversion to Land Reform were printed in the columns of the *Tribune*. When the *Courier and Express* charged that he was a "Fourierist, an Agrarian, and an Infidel," Greeley replied, "We admit and insist on the *legal* right of the owner of wild lands to keep them uninhabited forever, but we do not consider it *morally* right that he should do so when land becomes scarce and subsistence for the landless scanty and precarious . . . yes . . . something will be done, in spite of any stupid clamor that can be raised about 'Infidelity' and 'Agrarianism,' to secure future generations against the faithful evils of monopoly of land by the few."[21]

On October 1, 1845, the World's Convention of Reformers met in New York City, adopting as their motto, "Let's All be Unhappy Together." Robert Owen was elected president of the gathering. John A. Collins diagnosed the nation's ills: "All agree that society is sick—very sick—but few can agree as to the nature of the complaint, whether it is dyspepsia or dropsy—headache or heartache. . . . But all agree in one thing—that it is high time to send for the doctor." L. W. Rychman insisted that the lands were owned by society—that "the only true title to land" was "the obligation to cultivate." George Henry Evans voiced the plea of his organization of National Reformers for free land. And finally, Alvan E. Bovay "contended for the right of every individual to a free use of the soil for the purposes of subsistence."[22]

Greeley was more than lukewarm in his sympathy for the principles of these reformers. He studied the columns of Evans's paper, *Young America;* he attended their weekly meetings; and when they decided to enter politics by nominating individuals for the state elections, he reprinted their ideas in the *Tribune*. Placards reading "Vote Yourself a Farm" were distributed everywhere by these men who aspired to form a true American party which would advocate the cessation of public

---

[21] *New York Weekly Tribune*, August 4, 1845. For a discussion of Horace Greeley and the National Reform Association, see B. H. Hibbard, *A History of the Public Land Policies*, pp. 358-65.

[22] *ibid.*, October 11, 1845.

land sales and the grant to every landless man of a quarter-section from the public domain.[23] If this measure could be enacted, they argued, wealth would consist of the accumulated products of human labor, not of the "hoggish monopoly of the products of God's labor," and strife between capital and labor would cease.

On October 14, 1845, the Industrial Congress of Workingmen assembled and the Young Americans were admitted into the Industrial Brotherhood.[24] The principles of the Land Reformers were thus incorporated into the platform of the Industrial Brotherhood, and organized labor became a sponsor of the Land Reform movement.[25] The eastern Land Reformers, by enlisting the strength of the workingmen's associations of New England and the Middle States, attracted much attention, but they still lacked a real spokesman for their cause. Evans's *Workingman's Advocate,* like other reform papers, could not reach all classes. At this time, Greeley had not accepted the cause of the Land Reformers. In fact, after an attack by the New York *Courier and Express,* Greeley openly denied support of the Land Reformers and dared the *Express* to state just why it opposed the idea of free land.[26]

The winter of 1845-46 brought intense suffering to the less fortunate in New York City, and Greeley once more championed their cause. He estimated the number of jobless at thirty thousand heads of families, and called attention to the daily increases from immigration.[27] This problem of destitution was peculiarly acute in New York City alone, a fact which made it difficult for the rest of the country to understand Greeley's plea. Still under the influence of Fourierism, he proposed the erection of a charitable institution on an estate two miles square, with workshops, cotton and woolen factories, and surrounded by farms. He asked for private aid and demanded a public levy, but these bounties were to serve only as temporary expedients. He advised the unemployed to go to the farming districts, but the unemployed lacking money to buy land, and knowing almost nothing about farming did not act on his suggestion.

Under such conditions Greeley decided to risk a new adventure which he hoped would prove more successful than his participation in

---

[23] See John R. Commons, *A Documentary History of American Industrial Society,* Vol. VII, pp. 305-7; and *New York Weekly Tribune,* October 18, 1845.
[24] Evans's followers were called Land Reformers, National Reformers, Young Americans, etc.
[25] *New York Weekly Tribune,* October 25, 1845.   [26] *ibid.,* December 6, 1845.
[27] *ibid.,* January 3, 1846.

the Fourieristic movement. On January 23, 1846, he stated the problem and made his resolution:

"Every day's reflection inclines us more and more to the opinion that the plan of holding and settling the public lands of our Union proposed by the little band who have taken the name of 'National Reformers' is the best that can be devised. . . . This system, with such modifications and safeguards as wisdom and experience may suggest, would rapidly cover the yet unappropriated public domain with an independent, substantial yeomanry, enjoying a degree of equality in opportunities and advantages such as the world has not seen. . . . Secure all, so far as possible, a chance to earn a living; then if they *will* run away from the soil and shiver and starve in cities, why there is no help for them but such as charity will afford. But shame on the laws which send an able, willing man to the almshouse or to any form of beggary when the soil on which he would gladly work and produce is barred against poverty and accorded by this government of freedmen to those alone who have money to pay for it, and therefore are to some extent able to do without it."[28]

This new proposal brought a storm of objurgation and vituperation from the opposition press. The *Express* declared that the *Tribune* certainly deserved "the cap and bells."[29] The *Goshen Democrat* prophesied that, "If the plan should be adopted, we should soon have the whole contents of European poorhouses emptied down upon our fertile West." To this Greeley replied in a two-column editorial: "If 'the whole contents of European poorhouses' are to be 'emptied down' on us *anywhere* we certainly prefer that they should be planted on our public lands rather than in our almshouses."[30] Similar attacks appeared in the Buffalo *Commercial Advertiser;* the Boston *Daily Mail* believed it "much better in the long run . . . that a man should purchase his land, and pay for it, than take it as a *pauper entail.*"[31]

The fire of the opposition newspapers continued throughout 1846. In July Greeley, boldly addressing the New York Constitutional Convention, asked that august body to declare itself in favor of Land Reform. "To save the public lands from . . . monopoly—to make them practically free to actual settlers, otherwise landless . . . is the duty of

[28] *ibid.,* January 26, 1846; *New York Daily Tribune,* January 23, 1846.
[29] From the New York *Courier and Express,* quoted in the *New York Weekly Tribune,* January 31, 1846.
[30] *ibid.,* February 14, 1846.   [31] *ibid.*

Congress, but," he pointed out, "there are still duties devolving upon *you*. . . . The Convention can forbid future aggregations of great landed estates . . . by breaking up of those which now exist in our State." "*Our* plan," he continued, "would save our city a good part of the heavy expense of pauperism. . . . Who ever heard of a farmer starving *on his* land?" The Philadelphia *Public Ledger* and the New York *Globe* answered Greeley in threatening tones; the latter, although admitting the frightful nature of poverty in New York City, stated that it could have no sympathy with the idea of land for the landless.[32] The *Express* asserted that it had knocked Fourierism out of the *Tribune* and that very shortly it would knock Land Reform out of it.[33]

In spite of the severe indictment which Greeley received at the hands of the opposition press, no editor was to be successful in forcing Land Reform out of the *Tribune*. Greeley's agrarian crusade boded ill for the conservative interests of the East; it created dissension within the Whig Party, which appealed to the laboring classes, but did little for them.[34] Thurlow Weed was delighted to get the support of the *Tribune*, but deplored Greeley's adventure on the land question. In 1847, the New York *Courier and Express* attempted to read Greeley out of the party.[35] It looked as though Land Reform would very shortly become a national political issue. Such might have been the case had not this issue been engulfed in the slavery controversy and in the politics of the Mexican War.

Early in 1847 Greeley called attention to Britain's unemployment problem and the famine in Ireland. He elaborated Lord John Russell's proposal to devote one million pounds sterling to the improvement of nearly five million acres of waste land in Ireland. He lauded Roebuck, a leading Liberal of the House, who had exclaimed, "Sire, I say that it is the duty of England . . . to *insist that the land* shall maintain the people of Ireland." And with biting sarcasm he asked: "Where are the *Courier and Enquirers* and *Expresses* of Great Britain?"[36]

In the light of Greeley's interest in the Land Reform movement it is not difficult to understand his unbounded sympathy for the Irish. The opposition to his Irish program was considerable in New York and elsewhere, but he put his humanitarian crusade on a world-wide basis

[32] Philadelphia *Public Ledger*, July 11, 1846; New York *Globe*, July 11, 1846.
[33] Quoted from the *Courier and Express* in the *New York Weekly Tribune*, July 11, 1846.
[34] *New York Weekly Tribune*, December 2, 1846.
[35] New York *Courier and Express*, August 14, 1847.   [36] *ibid.*, March 6, 1847.

when he stated his belief "that the right of the human race to live is older, stronger, more sacred, than the right of any individual to retain uncultivated or to exact his own price for liberty to cultivate a whole county or province of God's earth."[37] The Irish should be welcomed, for they would "bring and create wealth to an indefinite extent. The untilled lands of the great West," that required "but moderate attention to be abundantly productive," could "receive, occupy and reward a nation of industrious laborers. . . . Judging of the future by the past, the completion of this century" would "exhibit a mighty empire resting upon the Great Lakes and the Northern Mississippi."[38]

After this spirited fight, Greeley took a trip into the Northwest, his first west of the Alleghenies since 1831. He displayed considerable interest in the development of the copper mines in the Superior region.[39] In Illinois he deplored the amount of vacant land held for speculation. His sincere belief in the imminent greatness of the West led him to predict that by 1900 Chicago would surpass New York City in population.[40] He proposed a Pacific railroad.[41] He praised Wisconsin for its adoption of the homestead-exemption principle.[42]

With considerable pride Greeley surveyed the growth of Land Reform: "None who have not taken a decided interest in the subject can realize the rapidity with which the idea of a reform in the laws governing the acquisition and disposition of land is spreading and finding favor in this country. Hardly two years have passed since it first attracted any share of public regard, yet at this moment we think not less than fifty periodicals earnestly advocate it."[43]

[37] ibid., April 24, 1847.
[38] ibid.
[39] ibid., July 17, 1847.
[40] ibid., July 31, 1847.
[41] ibid., June 26, September 8, 1847.
[42] ibid., September 11, 1847.
[43] Among these journals Greeley named the Cincinnati Herald of Truth; New York Young America; Cleveland Spirit of Freedom; Salem (Ohio) Homestead Journal; the Albany Freeholder; and Rochester National Reformer. See New York Weekly Tribune, October 9, 1847. Greeley forgot to mention any of the German newspapers, such as the Volk's Tribune.

CHAPTER VII

FREE LAND AND FREE SOIL

THE introduction of the homestead measure into Congress coincided closely with the rise of the Land Reform movement. On January 4, 1844, Robert Smith of Illinois introduced into the House a resolution providing for a grant of eighty acres of land to any settler who was "the head of a family, and living with the same, and not the owner of land, and who, through misfortune or otherwise," was "unable to purchase said land." The selection was to be made, however, "from any lands belonging to the government which" had been "on the market and subject to entry not less than ten years."[1] On March 9, 1846, McConnell of Alabama presented a homestead measure.[2] Three days later, Andrew Johnson of Tennessee asked leave to introduce his bill, but was refused.[3] Mr. Richard P. Herrick of New York who attempted at the same time to introduce a memorial embracing the principles of the Land Reformers, was also refused. In commenting on these events, the New York *Tribune* declared that "Messrs. McConnell of Alabama and Johnson of Tennessee evidently" supposed they were "acting in accordance with the purpose of the National Reformers. . . . But they could not [have been] more utterly mistaken. . . . To offer each [poor man] a quarter section of public land as a free gift with liberty to sell the fee simple to anyone, would be simply aiding the speculator to obtain . . . second hand for a few dollars what now costs him hundreds."[4]

In the following month, Representative Orlando Ficklin of Illinois introduced a homestead bill providing that the land was to be inalienable for debt for the space of ten years.[5] Hearing of this action, Greeley observed that Ficklin had the National Reformer's platform, but had not gone far enough; in ten years' time, Greeley averred, the eighty acre tracts would become the "football of speculation."[6] Here the matter rested until after the Mexican War.

[1] 28 Cong. 1 Sess., *House Journal*, p. 165; *Congressional Globe*, 28 Cong. 1 Sess., p. 106.
[2] *ibid.*, 29 Cong. 1 Sess., p. 473.   [3] *ibid.*, p. 492.
[4] Issue of March 21, 1846.
[5] 29 Cong. 1 Sess., *H. Jour.*, p. 599; *Cong. Globe*, 29 Cong. 1 Sess., p. 526.
[6] *ibid.*, April 18, 1846.

Attention now began to center around the campaign and election of 1848. In 1847, the second session of the Industrial Congress agreed to support the Liberty Party if it selected a candidate favoring Land Reform.[7] Horace Greeley later that year expressed hope that the Whig Party would adopt measures for the improvement of social relations, especially for Land Reform.[8] But he continued his flirtations with the Liberty Party headed by Gerrit Smith, which was already displaying Land Reform on its banners. At the same time he urged the Free-Soilers to "secure to each and all . . . a really Free Soil!—especially free from the hated speculators."[9]

At the beginning of 1848 Greeley again denounced Congress for its failure to take up Land Reform. "Wages in many sections are falling while rents and food grow dearer, and employment becomes more and more scanty and precarious."[10] He hailed with delight the convention of National Reformers at Cleveland on May 17, declaring that these were "among the first mutterings of a gathering tempest."[11] The Industrial Congress in its third annual meeting at Philadelphia nominated Gerrit Smith of New York for President and William S. Wait of Illinois for Vice-President, endorsing "Land Reform" as their main plank.[12] The Land Reform movement was rapidly spreading westward to the region where it would naturally find ready support.

The slavery and the expansionist issues, however, kept Land Reform in the background. Greeley caused much disruption in the Whig ranks by his refusal to support General Taylor, the Whig nominee; at the same time he bitterly attacked General Cass, the Democratic candidate, for his extensive speculation in western lands. Cass had just repudiated free soil;[13] Taylor was an expansionist, and the Mexican War had resulted in the addition of territory which Greeley hoped would remain open to free institutions.

Probably Greeley would have supported in 1848 any party which openly favored Land Reform. When the Free-Soil Party met in convention at Buffalo in July, the Land Reformers hoped that it would adopt the principle of free land as well as free soil. But, while it nominated Martin Van Buren for president, it hedged on the issue of free land.[14]

[7] *New York Weekly Tribune*, June 12, 1847.   [8] *ibid.*, October 2, 1847.
[9] *ibid.*, November 20, 1847.   [10] *ibid.*, April 1, 1848.
[11] *ibid.*, June 3, 1848.   [12] *ibid.*, July 1, 1848.
[13] *ibid.*, August 5, 1848.
[14] George M. Stephenson, *The Political History of the Public Lands, from 1840 to 1862* (Boston, 1917), p. 136.

Greeley did not at first feel that the Free-Soil platform was ambiguous. He wrote to Schuyler Colfax: "If I could make Van Buren president tomorrow, I would. . . . I do like the principles he now embodies—Free Soil and Land Reform. . . . The Free-Soil party is the only live party around us."[15] But the Free-Soilers "missed a great opportunity of drawing in a large western vote by not featuring the homestead issue."[16]

In the East, the free-soil principle had the open support not only of Greeley's *Tribune,* but also of the New York *Globe* and the Philadelphia *Daily Sun.* With only Gerrit Smith's party embracing Land Reform, the campaign was not too far gone to win Greeley back to the Whig fold. The Whigs sorely needed his support. Thurlow Weed therefore placed Greeley's name on the New York ticket as a candidate for Congress to fill an unexpired term, and the *Tribune* returned to the support of Taylor and the Whigs.

Economic forces were now rapidly moulding a situation that would bring to fruition the Land Reform movement. The influx of immigrants from Ireland and Germany afforded a supply of labor which could not be drained off by the West. An ocean transport system was being developed which would aid in the maintenance of the labor reserve in the East. The growth of the factory system called for wide markets. Farms carved from the forests and prairies would supply this need. The development of canals and railroads was creating an East and West economic alliance. Never before were prospects brighter for the realization of Clay's American System which Greeley was advocating almost daily in the columns of the *Tribune.* But if the Whigs were to sponsor this new economic order, they must discard their old scruples on western agrarianism and admit the principle of free land. This gradual shifting of the economic center of gravity was soon to cause many manufacturers and employers to align themselves with the Land Reformers.

Greeley, the foremost proponent of Land Reform, was not slow in sensing these economic tendencies. In the 1840's he had emphasized the advantages of free land to the working classes; in the 1850's his philosophy of the soil broadened, and included a direct appeal to the manufacturers and employers of the East. This new turn in the crusade for

---

[15] Quoted in Constance M. Rourke, *Trumpets of Jubilee* (New York, 1927), p. 298.
[16] Stephenson, *loc. cit.,* p. 138.

free land was clearly evident in the columns of the *Daily Tribune,* which circulated mainly in the population centers of the East.[17]

"Every smoke that rises in [the] Great West marks a new customer to the counting rooms and warehouses of New York," wrote Greeley.[18] Fewer paupers and fewer tenants would mean more produce, more markets, and consequently more wealth.[19] "Every thousand hardy, efficient workers who float West on free lands would leave places open for as many others; and these taking a step upward, would leave room for advancement of as many more and so on. Even to those workers who will never migrate, free land at the West would be a great and lasting benefit." Moreover, he avowed, "It [free land] will enable us to appeal forcibly to the settler of the new states for protection to the exposed industry of their Atlantic brethren by whom they have been dealt with generously."[20]

Greeley's appeal also became broader in its humanitarian aspects. The soil, he declared, was God's gift to man. Frequent references were made to the laws promulgated by Moses.[21] At one time he quoted *Leviticus* xxv:23, "The land shall not be sold forever; for the land *is* mine; for ye are strangers and sojourners with me."[22] From this quotation he deduced the principle that to sell land as "mere merchandise, like molasses or mackerel" was a sin.[23] Later he asserted that "every bird, every beast has a home, which he inhabits and enjoys without apprehension of ejection or deprivation, at least by his own species. Man alone erects houses for others to inhabit and enjoy. And is the time not at hand when every free citizen shall have his own home if he will?"[24]

The first two editions of his book, *Hints Toward Reforms,* appearing in 1851 and 1853, respectively, included important essays on "The Right

[17] In 1845 it was estimated that there were two thousand newspapers published in the United States, and that six hundred of these supported Land Reform in 1850. See Selig Perlman, *A History of Trade Unionism in the United States* (New York, 1922), p. 38. In one year, 1852-53, the circulation of the *New York Daily Tribune* increased from 17,640 to 26,880; the *Semi-Weekly Tribune,* from 3,120 to 11,400; and the *Weekly Tribune,* which circulated mostly in the Mid-West, from 51,000 to 103,680. By 1854 Greeley's *Tribune* wielded more influence in America than any other newspaper. See Willard G. Bleyer, *Main Currents in the History of American Journalism* (New York, 1927), p. 228. Bayard Taylor wrote that it came next to the Bible throughout the West. See James Ford Rhodes, *Lectures on the Civil War* (New York, 1913), p. 30. The *Tribune* grew in circulation and influence until in 1860 the *Weekly Tribune* reached the almost incredible figure of 217,000.

[18] *New York Daily Tribune,* March 9, 1849.   [19] *ibid.*
[20] *ibid.,* May 6, 1852.   [21] *ibid.,* December 28, 1849.
[22] *ibid.,* March 9, 1849.   [23] *ibid.*
[24] *ibid.,* May 6, 1852.

to Labor," and "Land Reform," and "Coming to the City." His deep agrarian sympathy is evident in his statement that "The defeasance or confiscation of man's natural right to use any portion of the earth's surface not actually in use by another is an important fact, to be kept in view in every consideration of the duty of the affluent and comfortable to the poor and unfortunate. . . . What nature indicates and justice requires is *equal opportunities* to all. . . . National reform is the broad and sure basis whereon all other reforms may be safely erected. . . . It would hardly be possible to exaggerate the ultimate benefits of the proposed reform, and the day of its triumph should be hailed by the poor and lowly as the birthday of their independence, as the Fourth of July is celebrated as that of the nation."[25]

Slowly, the northern Whig leaders were attracted to the ideals of the Land Reformers. The Democratic Party, on the other hand, was confused on the land question. Thomas Hart Benton of Missouri had inaugurated the fight for free land in the early 1820's, and by 1852 the West was almost completely won over to homesteading.[26] Conspicuous in the organization of the movement in the Northwest was the National Reform Association of Chicago.[27] The Germans of this region also were becoming an important influence in favor of homesteading. In fact, Representative Sutherland of New York, discussing Johnson's bill in 1852 dubbed it—absurdly enough—the "offspring of the German school of socialism [Marx] and 'higher law' transcendentalism."[28]

By 1850, such progressive Democratic leaders as Andrew Johnson of Tennessee, Stephen A. Douglas of Illinois, and Sam Houston of Texas, had taken up the cause and were embarrassing the conservative slavery interests of the Old South, who already realized that free land meant free soil.[29] More dissension was added to the ranks of the party in 1852 when a leading representative of northern democracy, Galusha A. Grow, from David Wilmot's district in Pennsylvania, considering himself the true inheritor of Benton's views, entered the crusade for Land Reform in the interests of the laboring classes.[30]

[25] Horace Greeley, *Hints Toward Reforms* (New York, 1853), pp. 315, 317, 318.
[26] *Cong. Globe,* 31 Cong. 1 Sess., p. 263.
[27] Arthur C. Cole, *The Era of the Civil War, 1848-1870* (Springfield, Ill., 1919), p. 91.
[28] *Cong. Globe,* 32 Cong. 1 Sess., *Appendix,* p. 731.
[29] Cited in Cole, *Irrepressible Conflict,* p. 137.
[30] Andrew Johnson was the leading advocate of the principle in Congress. His first bill was introduced in 1846. See *supra,* p. 105. For Douglas' bill, see *Cong. Globe,* 31 Cong. 1 Sess., p. 87. For Houston's bill, see *ibid.,* p. 262.

As for the politics of the years 1849 to 1854, one finds the columns of the *Tribune* alive with editorials, letters, and comments relating to the progress of Land Reform. Greeley was highly pleased when such Whig leaders as Seward and Webster took up the issue. However, in 1852, in thanking Webster for his continual support of Free Land, Greeley frankly told him that if he had pushed Land Reform as hard as he had ridden the "Union" hobby, he would have been "nearer to the Presidency than he is now."[31]

The *Tribune* carefully reported the details of the Sixth Industrial Congress. Seward and Greeley had been seriously considered by these Industrialists as possible candidates for the Presidency of the United States, but they were passed over at the last moment in favor of Isaac Walker of Wisconsin.[32] Greeley's decision to support Walker was due to the fact that Tammany, in May 1851, had begun to bid for the support of the Land Reformers. A huge mass meeting was held in Tammany Hall "of all those in favor of land and other industrial reform, to be made elements in the Presidential contest of 1852." Their platform included the principles of the Land Reformers, and urged that the Democratic Party adopt the homestead principle. Senator Walker of Wisconsin was nominated as their candidate for President.[33]

There was considerable doubt in Greeley's mind whether Land Reform could be made an issue in the campaign and election of 1852. The old parties were "exceedingly shy of the new questions which come up to divide the country. . . . For the moment at least, compact and thorough-going parties" existed "only with reference to a few questions of long standing."[34] He apparently agreed with the stand taken by the Albany *State Register* that "the Whig Party needs purification."[35] He was more than lukewarm in support of Webster for President, but he

---

[31] See his speech of March 30, 1852, in the *Cong. Globe*, 32 Cong. 1 Sess., *Appendix*, pp. 426-7. Grow's speeches contain many expressions that are the replica of those of the Land Reformers. Inasmuch as he was a close observer of the columns of the *Tribune*, having taken that newspaper since its first issue, one may conclude that Greeley, as well as Benton, had considerable influence upon Grow. See James T. Du Bois and Gertrude S. Mathews, *Galusha A. Grow, Father of the Homestead Law* (New York, 1917), p. 288. Professor Commons declared that Grow's speeches were "merely an oratorical transcript" from the *Working Man's Advocate*; see John R. Commons, "Horace Greeley and the Working Class Origins of the Republican Party," *Political Science Quarterly*, Vol. XXIV (September 1909), p. 484.

[32] *New York Weekly Tribune*, March 20, 1852.

[33] *ibid.*, June 14, 1851.

[34] Perlman, *History of Trade-Unionism*, p. 38.

[35] *ibid.*, June 14, 1851.

felt that his connection with the Fugitive Slave Law did not make him a desirable candidate.[36]

General Winfield Scott, in accepting the Whig nomination, stated that he favored settlement of the public domain by actual occupants *only*.[37] But this was really a "hedge" on the issue. The Democrats did no better, and Greeley bitterly took both parties to task for dodging Land Reform.[38] The remnants of the Free-Soil Party of 1848 organized themselves into the Free Democrats, with John P. Hale of New Hampshire as their candidate. Though they adopted free-labor and free-homesteads as planks in their platform, it was obvious from the beginning that they were more interested in repudiating the Compromise of 1850 than in furthering the cause of homesteading. Greeley thus remained with the Whigs, though his support was not enthusiastic.

The overwhelming Democratic victory meant a setback for the homestead cause. However, the Democratic Party was daily becoming more and more embarrassed by the Land Reform movement. With the election of Pierce, Greeley's hopes seemed shattered. Several times he declared that he was through with politics. He became more and more dissatisfied with the Whig Party and talked earnestly in favor of a "Northern" party. Because he was in this frame of mind, the rise of the Kansas-Nebraska question easily started his thoughts along a new course.

In 1848, as has been stated, the prospect that the Free-Soilers would adopt free land as one of their planks brought the land issue more prominently before the country. Altogether it was a big year for the Land Reformers. In the United States Senate, John P. Hale, a convert of the movement introduced on July 10 a joint resolution providing that every male citizen owning no other land, might enter one hundred acres and reserve patent after five years' residence thereon. The editor of the *Emancipator* believed the "Land Reform measure" was "destined to prevail." It was "just and democratic . . . a check to the speculation in the public lands, by capitalists heretofore, and at this time, so prejudicial to the honest, laboring masses of the country. The tendency of the measure, if passed" would be "adverse to the prevalence of slavery, and its extension into the territories of the Union—as the lands" would be "taken up and settled by a laboring and nonslaveholding population."[39]

[36] Quoted in *ibid.*, June 12, 1852.   [37] *ibid.*, March 20, 1852.
[38] Stephenson, *Political History of the Public Lands, 1840-1862*, p. 146.
[39] *New York Weekly Tribune*, June 12, 1852.

At the same time the opinion of the South was reflected by the editor of *De Bow's Commercial Review,* who "urged against the too free a use of the public lands," proposing that such lands be retained for national emergencies.[40]

Here the matter rested in Congress until after the election of 1848. With the Whig victory, Horace Greeley became a member of the short session of Congress convening in December. On the second day of the session he swung into action by giving notice that he would introduce a homestead bill. This he did on December 13, but the bill was not again referred to until February 27 when the committee asked to be released from further consideration of the subject.[41] A western member of the House wanted to know why a New Yorker should busy himself with the disposition of the public domain. Greeley replied that "he represented more landless men than any other member" on the floor of Congress.[42] The bill was tabled, only twenty members seeming to favor it, and thus ended Greeley's personal attempt to convert Congress to Land Reform.[43] Neither party, for the time being, wanted to sponsor a measure so close to the dangerous slavery issue. With the conservatives of both parties in control, there was little immediate hope for Land Reform.

The homestead measure gained its first prominent attention in the Senate on December 27, 1849, when Stephen A. Douglas of Illinois introduced a bill providing for free land.[44] Early in 1850 another well known Democrat, Sam Houston of Texas, presented a resolution requiring that the Committee on Public Lands be "instructed to inquire into the expediency of granting to each family (not land holders or owners of property worth the sum of $1500), citizens of the United States, or emigrants who are now here or may arrive previous to March next, 160 acres of land."[45] Houston argued that actual settlement was more valuable than the small amount of revenue which the government might derive from the sale of the lands. And many poor people living in the cities and dependent on charity would be benefited by this measure. But his bill went to the Committee on Public Lands which

[40] Vol. VI (July 1848), p. 98. See also "Freedom of the Public Lands," *Emancipator,* Vol. XIII (July 19, 1848), p. 2; and in the same issue, "Hale and Land Reform," p. 1.

[41] *Cong. Globe,* 30 Cong. 2 Sess., pp. 13, 605.

[42] Greeley, *Recollections of a Busy Life* (New York, 1869), p. 217.

[43] *The Whig Almanac* (New York, 1850), pp. 37-8.

[44] *Cong. Globe,* 31 Cong. 1 Sess., p. 87.   [45] *ibid.,* p. 262

refused to report it out. Not to be outdone by these western Democrats, William H. Seward, Whig magnate of New York State, and close friend of Greeley, introduced his own bill providing for free land.[46] This was followed, on January 22, 1850, by a resolution of Daniel Webster, Whig leader from Massachusetts, conforming quite closely to the demands of the Land Reformers and eliciting favorable comment from Greeley's *Tribune.*[47]

On January 28, Isaac P. Walker of Wisconsin introduced an interesting bill providing for the cession of the public lands to the states in which they were located on condition that the states convey such lands to actual occupants only in limited quantities for cost of survey and transfer.[48] Walker's bill gained considerable attention, though when it came up for vote, only Dodge and Walker of Wisconsin, and Seward of New York voted for it. In the course of debate some fear was expressed, particularly by Senator William C. Dawson of Georgia that free land would lead to an increase in the tariff; however, Houston of Texas, who was opposed to a higher tariff, stated that he had no such fear. Speaking of the provisions of Walker's bill, the *Whig Almanac* commented: "they embody the first principle of *Land Reform,* which is destined to exert a powerful influence on the future action and welfare of our people."[49]

In the House of Representatives, Andrew Johnson, having failed heretofore to obtain favorable action from the Committee on Public Lands, adopted the strategy of making a report from the Committee on Public Expenditures embracing his cherished homestead bill. The House, however, refused to take it up, ruling that the bill had nothing to do with public expenditures.[50] On February 25 he reintroduced his bill and insisted that it be referred to the Committee on Public Lands, where its fate was sealed.[51] Again on June 4, Johnson introduced his bill, this time succeeding in getting it referred to the Committee on Agriculture which reported favorably on it. Considerable debate ensued.[52] Johnson declared that five years before when the homestead idea was first introduced in Congress it was regarded as "wild and visionary"; now, he averred, "there seems to be quite a struggle going on among the most

[46] *ibid.*, p. 263.
[47] *ibid.*, p. 616; 31 Cong. 1 Sess., *Senate Journal,* p. 197.
[48] *Cong. Globe,* 31 Cong. 1 Sess., p. 233.
[49] *Whig Almanac,* 1851, p. 18.
[50] *Cong. Globe,* 31 Cong. 1 Sess., p. 408.
[51] *ibid.*, pp. 423-4.
[52] *ibid.*, pp. 1,122, 1,449.

prominent men of the country as to who should take the lead in this important measure."[53] Albert G. Brown of Mississippi supported Johnson's bill, but he favored a provision which would allow the settler to sell his holding by paying the government the minimum price per acre.[54] This is the first mention of the commutation principle which later becomes so important in homesteading history.

In the second session of the thirty-first Congress, Johnson endeavored to get his bill read, and finally was permitted to present it and state his arguments. He spoke of the great land grab which at that very moment was being executed in Congress. Sixty-five bills in the last few years, he charged, had been presented in Congress—all aimed at dividing the public lands for purposes of canals, railroads, asylums, public schools, etc. Most of these beneficiaries had but one common objective: to realize profits out of those who would settle the lands. Was it not preferable, he asked, to give the land to the homeless, who would make worthy citizens?[55] But however meritorious his bill, it was opposed especially by representatives from Virginia and Pennsylvania, who claimed the free-land measure was not fair to the old states who had equal rights in the public domain.[56]

With the opening of the thirty-second Congress it was obvious that the homestead principle could make no greater headway in the Senate than before. The bill introduced by Isaac Walker of Wisconsin was voted down in January 1852, which action brought forth a tirade in the New York *Tribune*: "Land Reform was slapped in the face Wednesday," it read, "by that illustrious body, the United States Senate, among whom only *seven* members could be found to sustain Mr. Walker's proposition to give a quarter section to each landless improver and occupier. . . . Of course, after voting that the settlers *shouldn't* have land free, the Senate proceeded to vote that the speculators in Bounty Warrants should go at it with a perfect looseness henceforward."[57]

While the Senate persistently refused to take up the homestead bill, the House gave it a free course, listened to the arguments *pro* and *con,* and ultimately passed it by an overwhelming majority. Senator Johnson on December 3, 1851, again gave notice that he would present his bill to "encourage agriculture." It was read on December 10 and referred to the Committee on Agriculture, which later reported favorably. In the

[53] *ibid., Appendix*, p. 950.
[54] *ibid.*, p. 1,459.
[55] *ibid.*, 31 Cong. 2 Sess., pp. 312-13.
[56] *ibid.*, pp. 313-14.
[57] *New York Weekly Tribune*, January 24, 1852.

discussion which began in March 1852, Mr. Skelton of New Jersey favored the bill because "these lands" were the "balance wheel" that regulated "the labor of our country."[58] Galusha Grow of Pennsylvania, like the Land Reformers, insisted that every man had the right to sufficient land on which to rear a habitation, for this was indispensable for the enjoyment of his inalienable rights of life, liberty, and the pursuit of happiness.[59]

Mr. Sutherland of New York was opposed to the homestead principle. He believed that this Homestead Bill would "take labor from the manufacturing states to the land states—from the manufactories of the East to the farms of the West—and thereby increase the cost of labor and the cost of manufacturing." He thought the bill "an attack on the right of property," and "as agrarian, as the first only of measures brought forward to more equalize the distribution of property."[60] But Johnson, the apostle of the poor-white class of the South, in defense of his bill appealed "in behalf of the poor North Carolinian, my own brother." It was contended that the bill would "take away the laboring man from the old states. Look at his condition." Where was the "man, abstractionist, North Carolinian, Virginian, or citizen of any other state, who has a heart that beats with love for his kind, and patriotism for his country, that would say to him, . . . do not go and settle upon the new, rich, and fertile lands of the West, but stay here, linger, wither, and die in your poverty."[61]

Elijah Chastaine of Georgia opposed the principle; he charged that the House was attempting to squander the public domain.[62] Fayette Mc-Mullen of Virginia summed up the debates on the bill. "These gentlemen representing manufacturing interests," he said, "dislike the idea of seeing this bill pass. Why? They fear that the laborers—the manufacturing hands—will leave the manufacturing districts and go to the West, and that, in consequence of the diminution of laborers, the wages of labor will advance among them. This, they fear, will be the effect of immigration of the laborer from the North and the East to the West. Sir, I say let these men go to the West, and emigration invited from abroad to fill their places—the foreigners will take their positions in the manufacturing districts of the North."[63] Besides the fears on the part of the vested interests of the old states, there was some concern

[58] *Cong. Globe, Appendix*, 32 Cong. 1 Sess., p. 381.
[59] *ibid.*, pp. 426-8.
[60] *ibid.*, p. 530.
[61] *ibid.*
[62] *ibid.*, p. 674.
[63] *ibid.*, p. 519.

among Southerners that free land might diminish the receipts in the treasury, and hence lead to demands for a higher tariff. It was asserted that with the passage of the homestead bill, at least one twenty-fifth of the revenue of the government would be taken away.[64]

The homestead bill passed the House on May 12 by a vote of 107 to 56. Obviously it was not a party division, but a sectional one. The cleavage between the old and new states was clearly portrayed, but it is impossible to estimate the effect of the slavery issue—if any—since the South Atlantic States would be opposed to free land on either basis. Greeley observed that more "Southern" members had voted for the bill than against it, but the question arises: should Tennessee, Arkansas, Alabama, Louisiana, and Mississippi be classified at this time as "Southern" or were they still "Western"? It is indeed remarkable that there were so many favorable votes from the North Atlantic States. The South Atlantic States could hardly have failed to sense the rising alliance between the upper Mississippi Valley and the North Atlantic States.

The bill came before the Senate on August 6, was adversely reported by the Committee on Public Lands,[65] and thus did not come up for discussion. Perhaps the remarks of Senator Mason of Virginia to the effect that the bill came from "suspicious quarters" is of significance in interpreting the Senate action.

In the second session of the thirty-second Congress the Senate still persistently refused to take up the House bill. The same was true in the first session of the thirty-third Congress, though Dawson of Georgia, chairman of the Committee on Agriculture, reported favorably on the bill. Unfortunately, each time the bill came up for discussion, the debates inadvertently drifted into the Kansas-Nebraska question; consequently there was less hope than ever that the bill would receive favorable action.

[64] *ibid., Appendix*, pp. 481-2.
[65] Berland of Arkansas said that two members of the Committee, a minority of which he was one, were in favor of the bill. *ibid.*, 32 Cong. 1 Sess., pp. 1,352, 2,100.

Part II

The West Welcomes the Corporation

CHAPTER VIII

LURING THE EUROPEAN

UNTIL the 'forties, the public domain of the United States had been settled primarily by a native population from the Atlantic States. Economic and social conditions in the East together with the attractions of cheap and good lands and more liberal institutions in the Mississippi Valley had impelled the migration westward. However, as the middle of the nineteenth century approached a new set of conditions came into being, which not only affected the settlement of the vacant lands but also influenced the legislation passed by Congress.[1]

Men have always come to America as foreigners, but their sons have called themselves Americans. Many reasons may impel a man to migrate. On one hand, the existing conditions of life have been too difficult to cope with; nature, perhaps, has been harsh, or fellowmen oppressive. On the other hand, distant lands have seemed to beckon to him especially when he had a friend or relative there. Undoubtedly cheap land directly or indirectly attracted many foreigners to American shores. But it must be remembered that the public domain and the American way of distributing the public land among the people did not constitute the only factor which affected foreign migration.

The century from 1750 to 1850 saw improvements in the conditions of life for the people of Europe. Yet in spite of these improvements and the great revolutions that had taken place, there was still much of the old system that was harsh, and there were many new evils accompanying the new order of things. There were still vast areas where men of the lower classes might never hope to own land. Most of those who worked the land in these regions gave much of their time to others, working hard and receiving very little in return. The Industrial Revolution in England, the potato famines in Ireland, the Revolution of 1848 in Germany—all resulted in conditions which were humanly unbear-

[1] For a general account of European emigration to America consult George M. Stephenson, *A History of American Immigration, 1820-1924* (Boston, 1926), and Marcus Hansen, *Atlantic Migration, 1607-1860* (Cambridge, 1940).

able, and hundreds of thousands were thereby forced to leave their homelands for a new world.

England, in this century between 1750 and 1850, underwent the most stupendous industrial revolution the world has ever known. Unfortunately, the great majority of the people reaped few economic advantages from the new system; many were thrown out of work with the consequent evils. In Manchester, in 1826, a city of approximately 120,000 inhabitants, there were about 14,000 dependent upon the poor rates.[2] The English could point with pride to the fact that the looms of England were capable of producing enough goods for 62,700,000 people.[3] But this new efficiency in machinery produced a sharp decline in textile prices. Low prices and overproduction, with subsequent unemployment, brought large reductions in wages.

Concurrent with the industrial revolution came a revolution in agriculture. The Board of Agriculture established in 1773, with Arthur Young as its secretary, fostered improvements in farming methods, such as crop rotation and scientific fertilization of soil, the introduction of farm machinery, and an extension of farm markets. Ultimately this technological advance lessened the demand for farm labor. Conditions in England were alarming; conditions in Ireland became deplorable. It was not uncommon for hundreds to be ejected at one time from a single Irish estate.[4] To make matters worse, the population of Ireland doubled between 1800 and 1840.[5]

The advent of steam transportation between Ireland and England and Scotland lowered the fares and brought many Irish agricultural workers into the English and Scottish cities, increasing the labor supply there and bringing on a further reduction in wages. Furthermore, there was no opportunity for labor to organize, for such organization was held illegal under the Combination Act of 1800. Thus for the excess laboring population of the British Isles, agricultural and industrial, there seemed but one way out—migration; yet, exile was considered the punishment for crime! Moreover, if migration was the answer to the problem, the government of England would have to furnish the means.

[2] Hansard, *Parliamentary Debates*, R. S., Vol. XVI, p. 298.
[3] "Report of the Select Committee on Emigration from the United Kingdom," *Quarterly Review*, Vol. XXXVII (1825-26), p. 573.
[4] *ibid.*, pp. 539-78.　　　[5] George O'Brien, *Economic History of Ireland* (London, 1925).

During the Napoleonic wars the situation in the United Kingdom was held somewhat in check by the great demand for both manufacturing and agricultural products. But after peace came in 1815, prices crashed, farm values depreciated 50 per cent, wages declined, and there was unemployment everywhere. To aggravate the situation, between 1812 and 1817 over 121,000 men were released from the navy alone. Many of the leading men of thought and action became convinced that these ominous conditions were no longer of a transient character but were fundamental and required drastic action. While politicians toiled with the economic problem many people of the United Kingdom became imbued with the idea of emigration. The people of the United States of America were kindred in blood, language, and institutions. In their country across the Atlantic there was a definite need for capital and labor. The new American transportation system was connecting the Atlantic Coast with the greatest valley in the world. A myriad of British travellers were sending back glowing reports of this land of opportunity—opportunity for those interested in an industrial order and in building an empire out of the wilderness. The effect of these reports was undoubtedly considerable.

Immigration to America from the United Kingdom was moderate down to 1845, but after that date it increased with great rapidity. The reasons for this large migration are of great interest to the student of land history. The Reverend T. R. Malthus at an early date had sensed the depth of the population problem. He became convinced that England, Ireland, and Scotland were greatly overpopulated. In pondering upon the subject of population, Malthus came to believe that the food supply of a country tended to increase according to an arithmetical progression, while the population tended to increase according to a geometrical progression. Eventually the growth of population would be checked by the comparative limitations of the slower increase in food supply. The hardships of the masses of the people in an overpopulated country might be mitigated to some degree by foresight. Since it was not probable that human industry would reach its greatest productivity in all parts of the earth at the same time, "the natural and obvious remedy" in the "case of a redundant population in the more cultivated parts of the world," according to Malthus, was migration to those parts that were "uncultivated."[6] This proposal inaugurated a train of thought which became increasingly important during the nineteenth century,

[6] T. R. Malthus, *An Essay on the Principles of Population* (London, 1890), p. 324.

not only to Britain, but to the United States. One American authority writing in 1876 believed that, "But for the theory of Malthus and its influence in shaping the policy of the British and their governments in favor of emigration, we should have lacked a very powerful agency in our national development which European emigration supplied.[7]

Doubtless the hundreds of thousands who migrated to America had no understanding of the play of economic forces. But on the other hand, no great migration of the redundant elements could take place until the official mind of England became aware of the necessity for migration. In this conditioning process the philosophers played their part. Beyond this point, great migration required preparation in the form of capital—money to get the emigrants across the ocean, and money to establish their economic existence in America. A consideration of the more practical aspects of the problem is therefore necessary.

One of Malthus's disciples in the 1820's, Robert John Wilmot Horton, pressed the redundant labor subject before Parliament. In the years from 1823 to 1825, experiments in colonization were carried on in Canada, which were successful within certain limitations. But with the 1830's came a new theory of colonization which was to have widespread effect in the English-speaking countries of the world. Under the inspiration of that fiery Scotchman, Robert Gourlay, Edward Gibbon Wakefield began to preach within the academic walls of Newgate prison a new gospel of systematic colonization. Wakefield had studied Robert Gourlay's three volumes entitled *Statistical Account of Upper Canada,* and Stuart's *Three Years in North America.* Before writing his account, Gourlay had travelled, though not extensively, in the United States. The resultant elaborate theory on colonization was not unlike the land policies of Hamilton, Adams, and Clay. It seems fair to conclude that since Wakefield was acquainted with many English economists who were friends of his father, he was at least indirectly acquainted with American experience. As time passed, Wakefield enlarged and perfected his theory in various publications, among which were *England and America* and *A View of the Art of Colonization.*

Wakefield disagreed with Adam Smith with regard to the influence of free land on the prosperity of colonies. The lack of labor in countries such as the United States was due, Wakefield insisted, to the abundance of free land which attracted men to enterprises of their own. The ideal method, said Wakefield, would be to place a price on the land just high enough to prevent too much from being taken at any one time, and just low enough to cause an acceleration of activity at a reasonable rate. The right price thus would be just "sufficient" to adjust properly the supply of land to the supply of labor.

Like Alexander Hamilton, this great English theorist overlooked the significance of frontier attitudes and behavior patterns on the one hand, and the human weakness for speculation on the other. Self-government and controlled economic action did not synchronize. Nevertheless the theory had a great influence on English minds and called attention to the possibilities of colonization as a solution for the social and economic difficulties which the United Kingdom was experiencing. Because of youthful indiscretions in social life, Wakefield could not obtain a public office, hence Charles Buller represented him in Parliament. After the Canadian Rebellion of 1837, he and Buller went to Canada with Lord Durham, and together they compiled the monumental report on affairs of Canada.[8] The Wakefield theory was written into the report, although some modification in regard to the price of land was necessary because of the low prices prevailing in the United States.[9] When carried into practice Wakefield's scheme was not successful in relieving England either of redundant capital or of surplus labor.

The prime importance of Wakefield's theory of colonization appears not so much in the realm of actual colonization as in its influence upon other movements. While Wakefield, Buller, and Durham worked for free trade, it was the activity of men like Richard Cobden, John Bright, and Sir Robert Peel that secured the repeal of the corn laws in 1846. This latter group of men was in reality at odds with the Wakefield school in that they, remaining true to Adam Smith's philosophy, preached an abundance of cheap land. The tariff on the importation of grain into England had raised grain prices and thereby caused the cultivation of inferior lands. The rent paid was beneficial only to the owners of the land. With the repeal of the corn laws and the improvement of ocean and land transportation, America and the colonies could produce grain at a lower price. They felt that the repeal of these obnoxious

[8] Sir C. P. Lucas (ed.), *Lord Durham's Report on the Affairs of British North America* (Oxford, 1912), Vol. I, pp. 153-5.

[9] *ibid.*, Vol. III, pp. 109-10; 104-6; 125-6.

laws would bring about an extension of the field of production, would release large numbers for emigration, and, by promoting emigration, would greatly expand the market for Great Britain's manufactured goods.

The repeal of the corn laws meant that the small agricultural capitalist in the United Kingdom could no longer compete with foreign grain. Thus he took his small stock of capital and went to America. Henceforth both capital and labor found an attractive field of employment in the United States of America. The migration of capital and labor was facilitated by the improvement in transportation and the cheapening of transport rates which came after 1840. The passage of the Cheap Trains Act in 1844 brought third-class passenger service by rail in England to as low as one penny a mile. A revolution in transportation resulted. In 1845, third-class passengers numbered in round numbers, 13,000,000; in 1850, there were 35,000,000; and in 1860, almost 94,-000,000.[10] The improvement in oceanic transportation after 1838, with an increase in the number of ships, brought not only faster and better service but also lower rates on the seas. In the United States, too, the railroad building era was just at hand. Chicago was connected by rail with the Atlantic Coast in 1853. American shipping on rivers, canals, and oceans was rapidly improving, and all this improvement in transportation and communication made for ease of emigration. It also increased the demand for laborers for further river, canal, railroad and oceanic improvements.

Several other events accelerated the emigration of British capital and labor. The Irish famine brought on by the failure of the potato crop in 1845 was probably the most serious in English economic history.[11] Starvation covered the whole island and tragic repercussions were felt all over the world. The British government made some attempt to help the Irish, but it amounted to little. At the very time that the Irish were dying by the thousands, foodstuffs were being imported by the shipload into England from Ireland. This was due to the fact that some 8,000,000 Irish people were landless; the whole island was owned by about 1200 persons, many of them residents of England.[12] With the repeal of the English corn laws further havoc was wrought upon the Emerald Isle.

10 H. D. Traill and J. S. Mann, *Social England* (London, 1901-04), Vol. VI, pp. 276-83.
11 W. F. Adams, *Ireland and Irish Emigration to the New World* (New Haven, 1932).
12 *Niles' Weekly Register*, Vol. LXXIII (1848), p. 240.

That the flour shipped over the New York canals had increased from
a little less than two million barrels in 1840 to nearly four million in
1847 was a fact that no Irishman could fail to comprehend.[13] Where
England refused to lend a helping hand, America came to the rescue,
first, by direct relief in the form of breadstuffs, later, by the raising of
money to bring the Irish to America. Actual donations from America
up to December 4, 1847, were estimated at more than a million dollars.[14]

Irish farmers who could muster from two to twenty pounds made
ready to start for America.[15] In fact it is said that nearly every family
sent at least one member to America with the expectation that money
would be sent back to take others across the Atlantic.[16] Glowing accounts of success in America were received by the thousands, and more
important still, they were accompanied by remittances. It is claimed
that over a period of three years no less than £1,250,000 were sent annually to pay passage for emigrants to America.[17] The letters might well
have given the impression that if the entire population of Ireland were
to emigrate to America there would be work for all.[18] Thus to the Irish
peasant America was the promised land.

Emigrants from Britain in 1845 totalled 93,501; in 1852, 368,764.[19] In
1846, 45.1 per cent of the emigrants went to the United States; in 1849,
73.3 per cent; in 1851 over 80 per cent.[20] Had the Irish migration continued for twenty years, the Celtic race might have vanished from Ireland. During the year 1849 when the British emigration reached the
then unprecedented number of 279,498 persons—nearly twice the largest number that had emigrated in any previous year—219,450 went to
the United States and 41,367 went to Canada. The migration continued
almost unabated until the Panic of 1857. In 1856, the number of emigrants leaving Great Britain and Ireland was 176,554. In the six months
ending June 30, 96,770 persons left Liverpool alone. In the three months
from March to June 1856, 48,000 sailed in 135 ships for the United
States; 10,505 in 25 ships for Victoria; 6,778 in 25 ships for Canada;

[13] ibid., Vol. LXXIII, p. 258. [14] ibid., p. 299.
[15] "Political and Monetary Prospects," Blackwood's Magazine, Vol. LXXII (1852), p. 9.
[16] "Policy of the Protectionists," ibid., Vol. LXXI, p. 656.
[17] "Gold and Emigration: In their Effects, Political and Social," ibid., Vol. LXXIV (1853),
p. 117.
[18] "Policy of the Protectionists," ibid., Vol. LXXI (1851), p. 656.
[19] "Gold and Emigration," ibid., Vol. LXXIV (1853), p. 118.
[20] Quoting from a review of James W. Johnston, Notes on North America, in ibid., Vol. LXX
(1851), p. 710.

2,032 in 5 ships for New South Wales; 604 in 2 ships for Tasmania; 160 in 4 ships for New Brunswick; 33 in 6 ships for South America, etc.[21] Most of those going to Canada were re-migrating to the United States. Of the 21,982 arriving at Hamilton, Ontario, January to June 1856, 19,432 went on to the United States.[22]

These figures are indeed impressive, but even more significant are the amounts of capital that left Great Britain for the United States.[23] The higher interest rates in America, both in the East and West, had attracted enormous quantities of British capital by 1840.[24] In 1858, a contemporary authority estimated that immigration had given to America three-fourths of the farm implements, three-fourths of the cities and towns built and three-fourths of the railroads constructed. Calling attention to the fact that the immigrants were of the proletarian or working class, this authority estimated that the three million immigrants arriving in this country brought two hundred million dollars in coin to American shores.[25]

The same economic conditions which led to migration from the British Isles existed to a lesser degree on the continent of Europe. Following the Napoleonic wars, Germany underwent a long period of economic distress; the land was devastated and many were out of employment. The rise in the cost of living, crop failures, and the industrial revolution all had their effect. The failure of the potato crop in parts of southwestern Germany in 1846-47, and the failure of vintage in Wurttemburg in 1850-53, added to the prevailing distress.

But more important to American settlement were the political ideas that emanated from the French Revolution. It is not the purpose here to trace the growth of the liberal ideas in Prussia. Suffice it to say that the Revolutions of 1830 and 1848 encouraged the democratic movements.[26] The example of the United States of America tended to promote the movement for a more liberal form of government. But always the answer was repression. The struggle had religious aspects, for many

---

[21] *Hunt's Merchants' Magazine*, Vol. XXXVII (1857), p. 514.
[22] From the *Hamilton Spectator* quoted in *ibid.*, pp. 514-15.
[23] L. H. Jenks, *The Migration of British Capital to 1875* (New York, 1927), *passim*.
[24] 26 Cong. 1 Sess., *S. Doc.* No. 1, p. 22.
[25] Paper presented by S. P. Dinsmore before the American Geographic and Statistical Society of New York, as discussed in *Hunt's Merchants' Magazine*, Vol. XXXVIII (1858), pp. 645-6.
[26] M. L. Hansen, "The Revolution of 1848 and German Migration," *Journal of Economic and Business History*, Vol. II, pp. 630-58.

of the Old Lutheran congregations were subject to discriminations. By 1848 many German liberals were ready to migrate. This great German migration after 1848 was conditioned by the reports of Germans who had gone to America at an earlier period. Their letters were filled with glowing descriptions of the land of freedom. Newspapers contained accounts of immigrants, and books of travel appeared from time to time such as those by Arends, Eggerling, Brauns, Bromme, and Duden.[27]

Although there had been a fairly steady stream of immigrants from Germany all through the nineteenth century an increase in numbers became manifest in the 'thirties and 'forties. In the 'twenties, 5,753 Germans came to this country; between 1830 and 1840 the number mounted to 124,725. The wave of immigration which began in 1846 with 157,500 Germans reached its crest of 215,004 in 1854.[28]

Thus America became an asylum for the oppressed of Europe. The autocratic governments of northern Europe looked with indifference upon the rapid migration of their surplus population and capital to America; England actually encouraged it. But this rapid influx of population and capital changed the whole economic structure of this country. A plentiful labor supply in the East made it possible for the moneyed class to think of the West as a vast home market for manufactured goods. The pressure of immigration hastened the settlement of the remaining vacant lands of America. Moreover, it lent encouragement to those forces who looked beyond American boundaries, ever anxious to add broad acres to the public domain. The demand for wheat, resulting from British conditions in general and from the Crimean War in particular called forth an agricultural revolution in America. Besides expansion onto new soil, for the first time considerable thought was given to more intensive cultivation of all land, a process in which farm machinery was to play an important part. Irrigation and conservation became encouraged. Altogether Americans began to sense the possibilities of their own country. Statisticians were calculating the power of America fifty to a hundred years hence, and the figures were impressive.

As there was unloosed in Jefferson's administration a modest agrarian imperialism which ultimately culminated in an uncontrollable clamor

[27] B. G. Gilbert, "Germans in Texas," *German American Annals*, Vol. X, p. 318; T. S. Baker, "America as the Political Utopia of Young Germany," *ibid.*, Vol. I, p. 65.

[28] A. B. Faust, *The German Element in the United States*, Vol. I, p. 585.

for Canada and Florida, so in the 'forties there appeared a strong demand for the annexation of Texas and the occupation of Oregon. This movement soon reached a crescendo, and under the watchword of "manifest destiny" the cries went up for the conquest of the North American continent and even of the regions beyond.

Expansionist Americans faced England in the Aroostook Valley of Maine, in the Columbia Valley and perhaps in Texas. In northern Maine the United States secured in 1842 a potato-patch one hundred miles in length, from which the Irish could later be fed, and still later, the Italian workers who flocked to New England's factories. As for Texas, Andrew Jackson had sent Anthony Butler to Mexico in the 'thirties to procure not only Texas but California. But Jackson's real-estate agent was not sufficiently adroit to break the "sales resistance" of the suspicious Mexicans, and Jackson was forced to recall the "scamp." Presidents Tyler and Polk, however, understood the principles, if not the terminology of "high-pressure salesmanship," and in 1845, the United States annexed the Lone Star State with its 61,892,480 acres of land.[29]

It soon proved convenient for our manifest destiny that a dispute should arise over this state's boundaries, and soon war existed "by the act of Mexico," in "shedding blood on American soil!" A little over a year later the roll of American drums was heard on the streets of Montezuma's capital, and Nicholas Trist, who had accompanied the American army, was able to secure Mexican signatures to a carefully prepared treaty, by which the Mexicans ceded to the United States for the consideration of $15,000,000 a clear title to Texas, New Mexico, and California. The American field of production was thereby expanded to the extent of 334,443,520 acres.[30] Meanwhile, even England had considered it expedient to divide the Oregon Country at the forty-ninth parallel, thus conceding to the United States the Columbia River Valley. And in 1853, Gadsden's purchase from Mexico of 29,142,400 acres of land, rounded out the American domain to its present boundaries.

Such was the official course of empire. However, the real thriving, throbbing spirit of this rampant, agrarian imperialism is hardly sensed until one turns to the countryside to sample the flavor of public opinion.

[29] Texas, never to form a part of the public domain, was allowed to keep her own lands and to dispose of them in her own way.
[30] Donaldson, *The Public Domain*, p. 12.

In June 1838, the editor of *The Boston Courier,* commented upon a resolution introduced by Caleb Cushing of Massachusetts into the House of Representatives, which provided for the erection of a post on the Columbia River for the defense and occupation of the Oregon Country. "Which shall it be?" he asked, "Can the sense of our true interest, can the honor and pride of the nation hesitate? It is a country ours by right; ours by the necessities of geographical position; and ours it will be in tranquil possession, if we temperately but firmly assert our rights. The world is wide enough for England and for us."[31]

Newspapers and magazines throughout the country brought clearly before the public the advantages and agricultural possibilities of Oregon.[32] Before 1842, the occupation of this region had largely been one of fur traders and missionaries, but beginning with that year hundreds of settlers left Independence, Missouri, headed for the Far Northwest. Frémont's expedition of 1842, Parker's *Travels,* T. J. Farnham's *Travels* of 1843, Irving's *Astoria*—all served to advertise the region. A convention of citizens of the Mississippi Valley assembling at Cincinnati in 1843, urged immediate occupation of the Oregon region by "the arms and laws of the United States of North America." They boldly declared their belief "that it is for the benefit of all civilized nations that . . . [Britain] should be checked in her career of *aggression with impunity, and dominion without right"*; and they concluded by asking: "Had not the Monroe Doctrine definitely stated 'That the American Continents were not thenceforth to be considered subjects for future colonization by any foreign power'?"[33]

The demands for the acquisition of Texas were of the same tenor. Then, having established the significance of Texas, it was not difficult to press the importance of California. "It is not much farther off than Texas," declared the *Family Magazine* in 1840, and continued, "The fact is becoming obvious that Mexico cannot long retain a hold of her unwieldy domain. Great Britain or France will ere long be stretching their hands toward California, if we do not. The plan of a colony on the Gulf, we think, is not a bad one."[34] By 1845, it was being pointed out

---

[31] *The Boston Courier,* June 7, 1838, quoted in the *Jeffersonian,* June 23, 1838.
[32] For instance, consult the article "Oregon Territory," *The Family Magazine* (1840), pp. 493-4; Henry Sherman, "The Oregon Territory," *Hunt's Merchants' Magazine,* Vol. VI (1842), p. 319.
[33] Proceedings reported in the *New York Weekly Tribune,* July 22, 1843.
[34] "California," *Family Magazine,* 1840, p. 559.

that California was even more desirable than Oregon, "especially since the annexation of Texas." Furthermore, it was observed that many persons headed for Oregon had dropped down into northern California and that already the province was "in a state of revolution—even the natives wishing to expel the Mexicans, and having every prospect of success."[35] In fact, the acquisition of California was well under way before the Mexican War even began.[36]

In the Congressional chambers, the expansionist enthusiasm drowned out all opposition. The remark by Mr. Rufus Choate of Massachusetts in the Senate in 1844 to the effect that the annexation of Texas would so seriously disturb the balance of the country that it would not be the same country, that the United States would be merged and lose its identity, was so significant that it was seized upon and widely circulated in the campaign of 1844. But the cries of the Democrats for the "Reannexation of Texas and Reoccupation of Oregon!" and "Fifty-four Forty or Fight!" transcended the opposition. Buchanan after mapping the progress of the nation during its past fifty years asked impressively: "What is a century in the lifetime of a nation?" As for the fear that expansion would endanger the union, there was even deeper conviction "that the spreading of our people, and the extension of the number of unfederated states" did not "weaken, but rather" gave "strength to the American Union. Like the enduring and increasing strength of the concentric arch, the pressure from without" gave "firmness and solidity and harmony to all within. The West, with its increasing greatness and overshadowing weight," was "gradually drawing together the East, and the center, and the South, with a power" that became "more and more irresistible."[37]

Once the boundaries of the United States were extended to the Pacific the nation immediately undertook the task of settling its new possessions. At once there arose the struggle between the free-labor interests of the North and the slavery forces of the South over the settlement of the domain. In 1845 under the caption of "California Next" the editor of the *Cincinnati Herald* commented on the interest in California displayed by the *Nashville Union*. He could not refrain from noting that

[35] "California Next," *Cincinnati Weekly Herald*, April 30, 1845, commenting on a paragraph from the *Nashville Union*.

[36] Frederic L. Paxson, *History of the American Frontier*, p. 361.

[37] William E. Cramer, "The March of Our Republic," *Hunt's Merchants' Magazine*, Vol. XIII (1845), p. 546.

slaveholders were already settling in that region and cotton of the finest quality could be raised there abundantly. The soil was adapted to all staples of slave-labor and slavery would be "planted there." Slaveholders would "strive to make it all their own," and would "enlist on their side the national passion for territorial aggrandizement." The editor of the *Herald* concluded by pointing out that the nonslaveholders of the country had the power in their hands, but "let them not waste their efforts . . . in opposing the extension of our territory. . . . Let them devote all their energies to the limitation and ultimate extinction of slavery."[38] Thus agrarian interest in the expansion of national boundaries was found to be closely linked with the rising slavery issue just as it was in Missouri a generation earlier.

The slavocracy, at first interested in expansion, shortly reversed their position, becoming less and less interested in the West, for the West acquired in the 'forties was not as desirable for slavery as first appeared. But until the slavery issue entirely eclipsed the expansionist issue, the latter was to be regarded as a very important stimulant to the settlement of the West.[39]

In those areas where the land speculation of the 'thirties was the most extensive, the ensuing depression was the greatest. In the three years, 1835 to 1838, over thirty-eight million dollars of capital had been applied to the production of cotton, bringing into cultivation over twelve million acres of most fertile land.[40] Extending the period to embrace the years 1833 to 1848, it appears that in the five southwestern states alone, over twenty-one million acres had been taken up. While a great deal in Louisiana had gone into sugar production, nevertheless, most of the area was planted in cotton. Production of this crop increased during the panic and depression period.[41] The large purchases of lands apparently reached their maximum effect in 1843, when the new states alone produced 1,703,048 bales of cotton, and the total national crop of 2,300,000 bales surpassed all previous records. By 1848, the production of the older plantation-states, that is, the South Atlantic States, was not much larger than in 1833, but that of the Gulf States had tripled.[42]

[38] "California Next," *Cincinnati Weekly Herald*, April 30, 1845.
[39] Discussed more fully in next chapter.
[40] *De Bow's Commercial Review*, Vol. IV (1847), pp. 86-7.
[41] "Commercial Chronicle and Review," *Hunt's Merchants' Magazine*, Vol. XIII (1845), pp. 470-2.
[42] *ibid.*, Vol. XIX (1848), p. 388.

It is clear then, that nearly the whole increase in the production of cotton had taken place in those states where immense sums of borrowed and subscribed capital had been invested in virgin soil of most fertile character, putting in motion the industry of thousands of blacks drawn from the more sterile soil of the old states. As a result, production outran consumption and prices dropped so low that the Atlantic planters could no longer make a profit. Not until the period 1843-45 was the vastly accelerated production overtaken by consumption and the South enabled to look forward to better times.[43]

The concentration of vast tracts of lands in the hands of speculators during 1835 and 1836 had the disastrous effect of excluding great numbers of settlers. As prices on speculative holdings crashed, settlers rushed into the choice locations.[44] In Mississippi, as a result of bankruptcy and repudiation, some of the finest portions of the domain became depopulated.[45] In fact, interest in Mississippi subsided and settlers were "turned aside in the pursuit" of the "rich loam of Louisiana, the new regions of Arkansas, and the varied expanse of the young republic of Texas."[46] Even Alabama attracted more settlement than Mississippi in the 1840's. Not until 1849 could it be said that: "The old régime of Mississippi has passed away. . . . Our lands are now in the hands of earnest cultivators. The banking system is no more."[47]

While the South was searching out opportunities in the West for the extension of its cotton empire, other interests were also establishing their spheres of influence.[48] In the period, 1839-41, New York State yielded its control of the wheat empire to the regions farther West.[49] In 1842 observers pointed out that the six northwestern states and territories, "to which channels of communication" were "now being opened," were already producing twenty-five of the eighty-four million bushels of wheat raised in the United States, and that this region was capable of raising enough to feed fifty millions of people. Should England repeal her corn laws, thus opening her market to American grain, in exchange for which the northwestern farmer would buy manufac-

---

[43] *ibid.*, Vol. XIII (1845), pp. 470-2.   [44] *ibid.*, Vol. XII (1845), p. 174.
[45] D. C. Glen, "Mississippi," *De Bow's Commercial Review*, Vol. VII (1849), p. 39.
[46] *ibid.*, p. 38.   [47] *ibid.*, p. 39.
[48] For a comprehensive account of the spread of agriculture into the upper Mississippi Valley consult P. W. Bidwell and J. I. Falconer, *History of Agriculture in the Northern United States, 1620-1860* (Carnegie Institute, *Contributions to American Economic History*, Wash. 1925).
[49] Josiah Bond, "Wisconsin and Its Resources," *Hunt's Merchants' Magazine*, Vol. XXVIII (1853), p. 481.

tured articles, the western states would be able "to liquidate the load
of debt which they now have," and there would be "a great increase in
business in the Atlantic States."[50] In 1844, it was observed that settlers
were preferring oak-openings to prairie land, and that if this preference
continued, Wisconsin could expect to become a great wheat-producing
region.[51]

With the repeal of the British corn laws in 1846, the way was thus
paved for a great wheat boom in America. In 1853 the English and
French markets could have taken three or four times the amount of
breadstuffs that American farmers were able to furnish.[52] By 1858 it was
openly declared that the grain fields near the Atlantic seaboard had
given out, and that "Genesee wheat, formerly the finest in the world,"
was now "of little account." Speakers at the meeting of the Seneca
County New York Agricultural Society in 1848, pointed out that the
American grower had a margin of thirty-nine cents over the English
grower, and paid considerable attention to the fact that with the increased means of transportation, such as the Erie Railroad, the western
free and fertile lands could in the future greatly increase the American
advantage on the foreign market.[53] With the running of railroads into
the Northwest, America would control the wheat market of the world.
In America itself, by the late 'fifties King Cotton was passing his scepter
to King Corn.

In addition to the repeal of the corn laws and the revolution in transport, a number of scientific factors contributed to the rapid expansion
of the grain frontier into the Northwest and beyond.[54] The introduction
of the improved plow, the McCormick reaper, the horse rakes, the baler,
the drill, the seeder, and finally the harvester, not to mention scientific
fertilizers, brought about before 1860 a virtual revolution in the agricultural industry. What this meant to the prairie country of the West
is attested by an observer of 1860 who with the aid of a spyglass counted
146 reapers at work at one time.[55] Advancing with the corn frontier
was the pork frontier, and the cattle frontier was not far behind. By
1865 Chicago was a great stock market center. With the development

[50] James M. Whiton, "British Corn Laws," *ibid.*, Vol. VI (1842), pp. 329-31.
[51] Josiah Bond, "Wisconsin and Its Resources," *ibid.*, Vol. X (1844), p. 554.
[52] From the *Cincinnati Gazette* quoted in *ibid.*, Vol. XXXI (1854), p. 756.
[53] *ibid.*, Vol. XXII (1850), p. 323.
[54] The best condensed account of these factors is to be found in Arthur C. Cole, *The Irrepressible Conflict, 1850-1865 (A History of American Life,* Vol. VII, New York, 1934), Chap. V.
[55] *ibid.*, p. 107.

of agriculture came a growing interest in agricultural education—agricultural journals and newspapers, fairs, agricultural societies, and finally agricultural colleges. The rise of this great western agricultural industry was without doubt one of the most important factors in bringing about the Homestead Act of 1862.

The appearance of a cheap and democratic press in America and abroad was a powerful influence on the emigration from the East and from Europe. Information about the American West was to be gleaned from literary travel accounts, letters, guide books, and from newspapers and magazines. Horace Greeley might be noted as a prominent example of the eastern forces—newspapers and miscellaneous agencies—which were striving to protect the emigrant, to guide him to the West, and to aid him in establishing civilization on the vacant lands. Very early in his career Greeley assumed the rôle for which he later was to become famous, that of handing out helpful hints to those interested in becoming farmers. By the 1850's his New York *Tribune* was regarded as an authority next to the Bible in most agricultural sections of New York and the Great Lakes country. As early as 1836, he advised would-be emigrants to buy the published guides on the West, declaring: "If there are not more adventurers exploring the far West, there will at least be fewer unfortunate ones."[56] Nearly every published work on the West—exploration, travel account, or economic treatise—received a careful review in the *Tribune's* columns. Very early, too, Greeley encouraged the formation of immigrant associations to protect those coming from foreign countries, and to aid them "in procuring suitable employment, or direct them to that part of the country" where they would "be most certain of employment."[57] Swarms of "land-pirates," he declared, guising themselves as "transportation-agents, runners or forwarders" were succeeding "in robbing the poor immigrant often of his long-hoarded gold." He dedicated himself to expose all these frauds,[58] and even better, he advocated the establishment of one great "Intelligence Office" in New York City similar to those already established in Albany and Boston to supplant the existing philanthropic societies that were too often "partial in character." [59]

56 *New Yorker,* June 18, 1836.
57 *New York Weekly Tribune,* April 6, 1843.
58 Note exposé of "emigrant swindle" in *New York Semi-Weekly Tribune,* March 17, 1857.
59 *ibid.*

To obviate one of the chief objections to migration to the frontier—that of being deprived of society and nearly all the comforts of life—this enterprising editor proposed "that a number of persons should unite and purchase contiguous tracts."[60] At another time Greeley favored the plan of organizing companies to populate the West. Commenting on the efforts of one C. Oakey of Illinois who had organized an immigrant company in England to settle lands in Illinois and the upper Mississippi Valley, Greeley said: "This, at least, is a species of emigration to which even the most fastidious will hardly object."[61] In 1847, he proposed that the government furnish ships to aid the Irish to get to America, and when the idea went begging he came out with a very denunciatory editorial under the label of "murder."[62]

From humanitarian as well as antislavery motives, Greeley lent much support to the Kansas Emigration Society which was organized in 1854.[63] Why not, he conjectured, form an emigrant association that would buy up a county at a cost of say half a million dollars, and by the guarantee of roads, mills, schoolhouses, etc., the country could be settled with "homogeneous and brotherly love."[64] And finally, he heralded the act of the New York Legislature incorporating the American Emigrant Aid and Homestead Company, which was to buy up land in the State of New York for resettlement purposes. "He who seeks land at government price, under the present system," Greeley contended, "must go out of the pale of civilization, out of the sight or hearing of neighbors, to find it."[65] Notwithstanding, the plan of orderly and controlled settlement with which Wakefield and others in the 'fifties were experimenting in the settlement of Australia was hardly a feasible plan for America, although there was some experimentation with group settlement in Kansas. However, no one can doubt Greeley's sincere desire to aid in the building-up of the West, though in truth his interest was national.[66] It was evident that a genuine spirit of cooperation was beginning to manifest itself in place of the older sectionalism of East *versus* West, or established order *versus* frontier.

Considerable information on the American West could be picked up from other agencies more peculiarly western. As early as 1852 Wiscon-

[60] *ibid.*, September 24, 1842.   [61] *ibid.*, January 15, 1842.
[62] *ibid.*, March 20, 1847.   [63] *ibid.*, September 16, 1854.
[64] *ibid.*, April 11, 1857.   [65] *New York Semi-Weekly Tribune*, April 17, 1857.
[66] Earle D. Ross, "Horace Greeley and the West," *Mississippi Valley Historical Review*, Vol. XX (1933), pp. 63-75.

sin passed a law providing for the appointment of a commissioner of immigration who was to reside in New York City.[67] It was the duty of this officer to give out information to immigrants concerning Wisconsin. Wisconsin's example was followed by Iowa in 1860. The Wisconsin commissioner of immigration soon discovered that numerous agencies were bidding for the immigrant trade, especially railroad agents. The New York and Erie, for example, attempted to start the immigrants for the West immediately for fear that they would buy their tickets elsewhere.

When a ship docked it was overrun with agents, runners and peddlers. Gysbert Van Steenwuck, immigration commissioner for Wisconsin, discovered that forwarding agents favored Wisconsin because it was so far west, that it was possible to overcharge for passengers and baggage.[68] Steenwuck made it his business to become acquainted with those persons who were connected with immigration—federal officials, consuls from foreign countries, steamship lines and railroad companies —in order that he might print pamphlets setting forth Wisconsin's advantages, and advertise in the newspapers, particularly those in the German language. In addition, since most German immigrants went to Wisconsin he employed a German assistant, Herman Hartel. Hartel who became the commissioner in 1853, advertised the advantages of Wisconsin in both New York and European papers. His report, which covered a period of eight months, stated that he had received 317 letters from Europe, and that many immigrants, mostly Germans, had visited his office. Hartel was ably assisted by Dr. Hildebrant of Mineral Point, Wisconsin, who was United States consul in Bremen at the time.

The report records the distribution of 30,000 pamphlets, half of which were sent to Europe.[69] Hartel's office in New York was visited by about three thousand people, two thousand of whom were recent arrivals in America. These visitors consisted of Germans, Norwegians, Swedes, Irish, English, Scotch, and Hollanders. During the year he received in the neighborhood of three thousand dollars in five and ten dollar amounts from settlers in Wisconsin for the use of their friends and relatives upon their arrival in New York. Hartel's estimate of the

[67] *Laws of Wisconsin*, 1852, p. 665.

[68] Theodore C. Blegen, "The Competition of the Northwestern States for Immigrants," *Wisconsin Magazine of History*, Vol. III, p. 5.

[69] Kate A. Eveorst, "How Wisconsin Came By Its Large," *Wisconsin Historical Collections*, Vol. XII, p. 320.

number of immigrants arriving in Wisconsin for the year 1853 is as follows: Germans, 16,000 to 18,000; Irish, 4,000 to 5,000; Norwegian, 3,000 to 4,000; others, 2,000 to 3,000. While the total immigration for the United States in the year 1853 actually fell below that of the year preceding, the immigration to Wisconsin increased 15 per cent.

Another state which aided the emigrant considerably was the Mormon state of Deseret. These Mormon people, who first migrated to the Great Salt Lake in 1847, established a fund known as "The Perpetual Emigration Fund." The "Saints" of both America and Europe made liberal donations to this fund which provided that those who were otherwise too poor to help build up the "valleys of the mountains" might be aided in so doing. Converts to this faith were made throughout Europe, and many were induced to migrate and settle in Utah. The Mormons wished to increase the population of their territory as rapidly as possible in order that they might be taken into the Union as a state at an early date. Land was plentiful, of course, even though it had to be irrigated, and it is probable that land as well as religion influenced people to move into the region.

Wherever the immigrants went they retained their contacts with friends and relations left behind. Correspondence was made easier by the reduction in postage rates in Europe and America. The thousands of letters which have been preserved attest the importance of the immigrants themselves as an advertising agency. Professor James F. W. Johnston stated the importance of this sort of advertising in his *Notes on North America*: "A letter from a connection or acquaintance determined the choice of a place to go to, and, without further inquiry, the emigrant starts. Thus for a while emigration to a given point once begun, goes on progressively by a sort of innate force. Those who go before urge those who follow by hasty and inaccurate representations; so that the more numerous the settlers from a particular district, the more numerous also the invitations for others to follow, till the fever of emigration subsides."[70] Of the peoples from foreign countries who had settled in the West there were many who wrote to their friends in Europe of the wonders of the new country. In 1847 a certain Van Raalte wrote from his frontier home in Michigan to his friends and relatives in Holland. His letter was published under the name of *Holland in America, or the Dutch Colony in the State of Michigan*, and it

[70] *Blackwood's Magazine*, Vol. LXX, p. 711.

was circulated throughout the country. Another letter was published in the same country the following year from Henry Peter Scholte of Iowa. These letters together with money sent back to Holland to help friends brought many Dutch to America in the 'fifties.

Scandinavians who had settled in America, or who had travelled there, wrote many interesting letters to their old friends in Europe giving glowing accounts of the advantages to be found in America. One such account, published and widely circulated, stated that land was so plentiful that cattle and pigs were permitted to run at will, and moreover that title to the land could be secured with ease. This made a strong appeal to the peasant who gave his labor for two or three days a week to his landlord in return for the use of a small strip of land. (He could seldom hope to own that land himself.) Many Scandinavians came to America in the following decades because of the influence of such letters.

The activities of the various church organizations in the West cannot be overemphasized. Wherever population went, there also went religion. In the many church periodicals one finds a wealth of material on frontier America. Letters and reports published in religious magazines and newspapers undoubtedly attracted many from the East and from Europe.

Lastly, in the 'fifties, with the organizing genius behind the Illinois Central Railroad came one of the most powerful advertising agencies in all the West.[71] Many of the western railroads secured tracts of land from the public domain for their right of way and in addition for eventual sale to settlers. They were also interested in the rapid settlement of the lands in the hands of the government in order that the country might develop to the point where they could do a profitable business. The part played by the railroad in building up the West, however, will be dealt with more completely in the next chapter. Suffice it here merely to call attention to the railroad as a pioneering agency.

[71] Paul W. Gates, "The Disposal of the Public Domain in Illinois, 1848-1856," *Journal of Economic and Business History*, Vol. III (1930-31), pp. 216-30.

CHAPTER IX

INDUSTRY MOVES WESTWARD

THERE were many other factors which conditioned the great western boom of the 'forties and 'fifties. Of especial importance were those aids which made known the existence of the valuable resources of the West. In the process of exploration in the earlier period of American history the fur trader, the Indian guide, the soldier on the warpath, the land surveyors and various agents, and all those individuals who came in contact with the hinterland had played their rôle either directly or indirectly in attracting settlers onto the best lands. It is true that these frontier characters, later including the missionary, continued far into the nineteenth century to exert an important influence in breaking the way for the white man. But as the wave of settlement flowing over the Appalachians became more and more overwhelming, the individual land locator or director could no longer cope with the situation. Here an enlightened national government stepped in. And through the encouragement of a more scientific advance the government was able to direct and guide to some extent the course of settlement.

The credit for the beginning of a national survey must go to Thomas Jefferson, though it should be noted that Washington had collaborated with Jefferson on western surveys as early as 1770. Jefferson's *Notes on Virginia,* published in 1784, had marked the beginning of a scientific interest in the transappalachian region. The Lewis and Clark expedition into the Louisiana Purchase Territory during Jefferson's administration, should probably be considered as the first national scientific survey. This was followed by Colonel Pike's expedition into the upper Mississippi Valley region and onto the High Plains. In 1819, Major Long explored the High Plains region, condemning it as a desert region "hardly fit for man or beast." In the period between 1818 and 1821 came Schoolcraft's explorations of the lead region of the Mississippi and the Great Lakes.

The reconnaissance type of survey continued into the 'thirties and 'forties, and the numerous publications of these explorers did much to attract settlers westward. Between 1832 and 1837 the Black Hawk War and the Army surveys of the High Plains and upper Mississippi Valley regions necessitated by the removal of the Indians to those regions brought to light much information about the nature of the country. The Reverend Samuel Parker followed the missionaries into Oregon, and in 1836 made observations on the Columbia River Valley from which he wrote his *Travels*. But of the Rocky Mountain and Pacific Coast explorations, those by Farnham and Frémont in the early 'forties, and by Stansbury around Great Salt Lake in 1849, are of most importance. The progress of these surveys was reported in many of the newspapers and magazines of the country.[1]

Meanwhile, scientific geological surveys had begun. In the period of the 1830's it might be said that America became geologically-minded. The first state geological surveys were made in 1820 in Albany and Rensselaer counties of New York. New England was quick to follow with a survey of its resources. But of even greater interest to public land history than what Silliman and Hitchcock were doing for New England in the 1830's, was the appearance of a group of Ohio geologists. So rapidly did scientific geological interest spread into the Northwest that by the end of the 1830's, the new West had as many noted geologists as the Atlantic Coast. Here one found George W. Fetherstenough, John W. Foster, Josiah D. Whitney, William W. Mather, Eugene W. Hildreth, Charles Whittelesey, Charles T. Jackson, Douglas Houghton, David Dale Owen, Bela Hubbard, and others. In 1841, at the annual meeting of the American Geological Association, the State of Ohio had more representatives than any other state; in fact, there was not one representative from either Harvard or Yale.

The Ohio surveys, from 1836 to 1838, brought to light the extent of the bituminous coal deposits. William W. Mather reported that the state possessed sufficient coal "for every contemplated increase in population and manufactures for 2,500 years." And at the end of the second season he had so far increased his already generous estimate as to state that there was "not only sufficient [coal] for domestic use for any reasonable time, but to supply the country around the lakes and throughout the valleys of the Ohio and Mississippi, for as long a time" as it was "proper to calculate."[2] In 1838, an article was published in the *American*

---

[1] George P. Merrill, *The First Hundred Years of American Geology* (New Haven and London, 1924), *passim.*

[2] *ibid.*, p. 172.

Journal of Science on the geology of upper Illinois dealing with its rich mineral formations and pointing out the commercial advantages to be derived by uniting the waters of Lake Michigan with the Illinois River.[3] David Dale Owen, after completing a survey of Tennessee, became state geologist of Indiana in 1837. He soon began to test his conjecture that the coal deposits of Indiana were a part of a vast coal field of Illinois, Kentucky, and Iowa.[4] But most important of all was Owen's survey of the mineral lands of southwestern Wisconsin, Iowa, and Illinois in the late 'thirties. The report of this survey was widely read.

Westerners were very much interested in these geological surveys; in fact, it appears that the geological interest emanated from a public interest. For years every farmer had sought a salt spring or some other mineral wealth. Undoubtedly the value of land was considerably enhanced by the presence of minerals as long as those minerals did not interfere with, or impair to any great extent, the richness of the soil. It was apparent that the geological interest paralleled a scientific interest in agriculture. Whether the agricultural society encouraged the geological organization, or vice versa, it is hard to say; perhaps the two interests supplemented each other.

With the completion of the Erie Canal, the settlement of Michigan and Wisconsin, the geological surveys of the Lake Superior country, and the subsequent removal of the Indian menace, the mineral region of Lake Superior came to demand public attention. Douglas Houghton's surveys, beginning in 1830, continued throughout the decade, and the findings were ultimately published in 1841. In 1842-43 the Chippewa Indian title was cleared, and a year later the federal government issued the first mining permits.[5] That same year, 1844, marked the discovery of iron deposits in this region, and the beginning of the copper and iron industry which was shortly to mean so much to the American industrial order.[6] Meanwhile, David Dale Owen had surveyed the lead region of Iowa, Illinois, and Wisconsin, and his report, published in 1839, revealed not only extensive lead deposits, but also vast deposits of

[3] *ibid.*, p. 181.
[4] *ibid.*, p. 194.
[5] *Hunt's Merchants' Magazine*, Vol. XI (1844), p. 482.
[6] T. A. Rickard, *The Copper Mines of Lake Superior* (New York, 1905), p. 35; *A History of American Mining* (New York, 1932), pp. 12-13, 229-31.

copper, zinc, and coal.[7] In commenting on this report the editor of the *United States Magazine and Democratic Review* said: "Dr. Owen's report will doubtless attract the attention of the scientific writers of Europe, and may be the means of rapidly drawing capital and enterprise from across the Atlantic." He concluded with the recommendation that a geologist be attached to each corps that surveyed the public lands, in order to "take measures for discovering the character and value of our public lands" before they were brought into the market.[8]

In 1841 about 25,000 pounds of copper were shipped east.[9] The completion of a road from Milwaukee to Galena in 1842 increased lead traffic by way of the Great Lakes, and with the completion of the Wisconsin Canal it was expected that this important trade would no longer go to New Orleans, but would be diverted by way of the Erie Canal to New York.[10] The Lake Superior Copper Company, organized by capital from Boston, Washington, St. Louis and Detroit, began operations at Eagle Harbor on Lake Superior in 1844, engaging the services of the geologist, Dr. Houghton.[11] Pointing to the vast mineral resources, an observer of 1844 wrote: "With all these facilities, Wisconsin lacks only capital, without which the greatest natural advantages are useless, to become a dangerous rival to the manufacturing states of the east and even of the world; and capital can only find its way, by easy and hesitating steps, into the wilderness of a new country."[12]

By 1845, fourteen companies formed on a corporation-share basis were already engaged in the vicinity of Copper Harbor; thirty other companies were being organized.[13] By 1850, the Lake Superior country had around 2,000 laborers commanding wages as high as were being paid anywhere in the country. Transportational facilities to the region were being improved, freight rates were coming down, and everywhere the country was "covered with squatters," who had "secured preemption rights to all the promising tracts on the mineral range not otherwise taken up."[14]

[7] Merrill, *The First Hundred Years of American Geology*, pp. 196-8; David Dale Owen, *Report of a Geological Exploration of Part of Iowa, Wisconsin, and Illinois*, 28 Cong. 1 Sess., S. Ex. Doc. No. 407, Vol. VII.

[8] Vol. VIII (1840), pp. 30-42.

[9] "Lead and Copper Trade of the West," *Hunt's Merchants' Magazine*, Vol. VIII (1843), p. 385.

[10] *ibid.*   [11] *ibid.*, Vol. XI (1844), p. 482.

[12] Josiah Bond, "Wisconsin and Its Resources," *ibid.*, Vol. X (1844), p. 555.

[13] From the *Boston Post*, reprinted in the *New York Weekly Tribune*, January 3, 1846.

[14] *Hunt's Merchants' Magazine*, Vol. XXV (1851), p. 255.

With the rise of the mineral industry came a change in the policy of disposing of the mineral lands. The passage of the act of July 11, 1846, inaugurated a general sales policy. Lands supposedly containing minerals were to be put up at sale at the minimum price of $5 per acre; the purchaser might take as much as he chose but not less than 40 acres, the smallest legal subdivision. A person already in possession of a lease might buy his holdings at $2.50 per acre, provided he took the whole tract covered by his permit. This act was just the beginning of the largess of the federal government. Other concessions to encourage the mining industry were to follow in quick succession.

Hardly had the new mineral land policy been formulated when gold was discovered in California. Within a short time the whole mountainous country of California was overrun, no consideration whatsoever being paid to the government's right in the land. There is no need here to go into a description of the mad rush to the new Eldorado, nor to pursue further the effect of the vast squatter population on the public land system. But the economic effect upon the country is of immediate concern. At first it was generally believed that the discoveries of precious metals would not "reach a point to create any disturbance in the relative value of property in the country."[15] There was a feeling everywhere that the government should not interfere with the economic setup in this new mineral region by trying to regulate the land system.[16] It was expected that the increase in currency would cause a rise in prices, because there was more money to represent the same amount of commodities; thus speculation would probably set in.

In less than a year, some 500 vessels had been employed to carry people to California by way of Cape Horn. Within that same year the people of California had drawn up a state constitution and been admitted to the Union.[17] Almost at the very moment of admission gold production began to produce marked economic effects. Boston reported a rise in real estate values, with all sorts of property in demand.[18] Between 1849 and 1854, over three hundred million dollars had been produced by the California mines, and in each single year there was contributed to the currency of the country an amount "equal to the

[15] *Bankers' Magazine*, Vol. IV (1850), pp. 391-4.
[16] "The Gold Region of California," *Hunt's Merchants' Magazine*, Vol. XX (1849), pp. 55-65.
[17] "The Wonders of American Energy," *Star in the West*, Vol. XII, p. 199.
[18] *Bankers' Magazine*, Vol. IV (1850), pp. 927-8.

entire real currency of the whole Union eighteen years ago."[19] An era of inflation was thus inaugurated, which was to have a tremendous effect on the whole country. For every addition of a million dollars in gold three or four million dollars in paper would be issued by existing banks, and it was to be expected that a new crop of banks would appear. This influx of California gold was followed by a "universal inflation of prices, affecting first, stocks, city real estate, and all the more susceptible forms of value, and gradually reaching land itself." Concurrently there was a vast multiplication of new projects. The commentator concluded with the warning that "All this tends to a revulsion. Certainly it must have a limit."[20]

By 1860, less than eleven years after the gold rush, California's population was greater than New Hampshire's. The effect of gold upon the construction of internal improvements and upon land speculation is thus clear. The demand for an Isthmian canal and for transcontinental railroads received tremendous impetus. Agricultural production to feed the new mining empire was an imperious necessity. A new American order was in the making. This economic revolution which resulted from the gold rush to California must be fully appreciated before any estimate can be made of its effect upon land legislation and settlement.

The migration of population and capital to the mineral frontier of America coincided with similar movements to the timber frontier in Michigan, Wisconsin, and other parts of the Northwest, and also to Alabama, Mississippi, and Arkansas in the Southwest.[21] The growth of population in the country, the tremendous increase in manufacturing, the construction of transportational facilities on land and sea, the need for a steady supply of timber for the prairie and plains country—all were important in shifting the lumbering frontier from the North Atlantic States, particularly Maine and New York, to the Great Lake and upper Mississippi Valley regions. The great white pine forests of Michigan and Wisconsin came under the ax in the 'fifties. Even as early as 1842 nearly two millions of shingles had been delivered to Galena, Illinois, by way of the upper Mississippi and its tributaries.[22]

[19] James A. McDonald, "Growth of California," *Friend's Review*, Vol. VII (1854), pp. 747-9
[20] *Hunt's Merchants' Magazine*, Vol. XXV (1851), p. 145.
[21] Frederick Merk, *Economic History of Wisconsin During the Civil War Decade* (Madison Wisconsin, 1916); Edward Kirkland, *A History of American Economic Life* (New York, 1932) pp. 135-8; Isaac Lippincott, *Economic Development of the United States* (New York, 1933) pp. 351-3; Harrison B. Fagan, *American Economic Progress* (Chicago, 1935), pp. 226-9.
[22] *Hunt's Merchants' Magazine*, Vol. VIII (1843), pp. 384-5.

An authority writing in 1853 declared: "The course of the lumber trade may now be considered as permanently changed. The pineries of Wisconsin now control, and will soon hold exclusive possession of the market of the valleys of the Mississippi and its great western affluents."[23] During the four years from 1848 to 1852, the supply of lumber brought into Chicago exceeded the demand, but with the building of the Illinois Central Railroad through the plains of Illinois a great market was immediately opened up. In 1853, there were more than fifty lumber dealers in Chicago.[24] While the Lake States in 1850 produced 6 per cent of the lumber of the country, by 1860 these states produced 13 per cent. But even before 1860, Chicago had surpassed Albany and Bangor as the greatest lumber center of the world.

The lumbering frontier did not push in to the new regions of the Southwest as rapidly as it did into the Northwest. Pensacola in 1850 showed a yearly production of fifteen million feet of sawed timber.[25] In 1852, an acute observer complained: "Here, within the limits of this state [Louisiana], are vast tracts of fine timber land, inviting capital and industry to improve the golden opportunity, and gather fortunes with very little outlay; but no, they defy, procrastinate, and put off, till the 'Eastern lumbermen' will soon come on and 'buy up' and pocket it all."[26] The more progressive lumbering frontier on the Pacific Coast in 1858 was furnishing "China, Australia, and other distant countries" with "great quantities of lumber of their own production." This was "gratifying . . . especially when only a few years since they imported their own supplies of the same article from the Eastern States." Thus by 1860 three industries were already booming along the Pacific Coast: agriculture, mining, and lumbering.

In the period between 1815 and 1860 the improvements in transportation between the Mississippi River Valley and the Atlantic Coast were of incalculable value in promoting emigration from the East and from Europe. During the Great Migration following the War of 1812, it had been possible for the native eastern peoples simply to walk to choice

[23] J. H. Lathrop, "Wisconsin and the Growth of the Northwest," *De Bow's Commercial Review*, Vol. XIV (1853), p. 235.
[24] "Trade and Growth of Chicago," *Hunt's Merchants' Magazine*, Vol. XXVIII (1853), pp. 566-7.
[25] *Pensacola Gazette* quoted in *ibid.*, Vol. XXIII (1850), p. 449.
[26] *De Bow's Commercial Review*, Vol. XIII (1852), pp. 600-1.

lands in the Appalachian frontier or to the country west of the mountains. Along the National Road and the Genesee Pike passed a continuous line of hand carts and covered wagons. No tolls were charged along the National Road; transportation cost almost nothing. Beyond these dirt highways were the waterways of the West, most important of which was the Ohio River. By the 1840's the slopes of the main valleys of the transappalachian country were filled up. The factors of distance and topography made internal improvements necessary. Encouraged by the success of the Erie Canal, the western country in the period between 1830 and 1860 improved waterways for steamboat navigation, and constructed a network of plank roads, canals, and railroads. The East, too, was preoccupied with the same rage for internal improvements. These new improvements were costly, however, and not until competition became keen did transportation rates come down.

Eastern and English capital played a prominent part in this transportational revolution.[27] While the state debts of the country totaled only 13 million dollars before 1820, twenty years later, due primarily to internal improvements, the amount had increased to 200 million dollars. In 1830, there were only 23 miles of railroads; in 1840, over 2,800 miles; in 1850, over 9,000 miles; and by 1860, the number had increased to 30,626 miles. The whole responsibility for this internal improvement construction had been assumed by state or individual enterprise; not until 1850 with the grant of land to the Illinois Central Railroad did the federal government again enter the picture.

Generally speaking, each internal improvement meant a drop in transportational costs. The construction of the Erie Canal caused freight rates from Buffalo to New York to drop from $100 to $15 a ton, and the time was cut from twenty-eight days to eight. The introduction of steam on the Ohio and Mississippi and on the Great Lakes, brought a further drop, and railroad competition still another. The shortening of the time required and the lowering of rates were matters of tremendous importance in the migration of peoples from the East and from Europe. Many of the immigrants called attention to these important items in their letters and travel accounts, for without cheaper rates it is doubtful whether very many could have afforded to settle in the American West. About 1850, the economist Henry C. Carey wrote: "Twelve years ago the fare of a passenger from Chicago, Illinois (by lake and rail to New

27 L. H. Jenks, *The Migration of British Capital to 1875* (New York, 1927), *passim*.

York City), 1,500 miles, was $74.50. It is now but $17. . . . Twelve years since, the cost of transporting a bushel of wheat from Chicago to New York was so great as effectually to keep the grain of that country out of the market. Now a bushel of wheat is transported the whole distance, 1,500 miles for 27 cents. A barrel of flour can be transported from Chicago to New York for 80 cents."[28]

While the river traffic of the West reached its golden age in the 'fifties, yet it must be admitted that the railroad played a vital part, in fact, it set the pace for western development during the rest of the frontier era. With the coming of the railroad frontier, America came into contact for the first time with the forces of the industrial revolution. It was in the 'fifties that the railroad builders, having been successful in England and in the American East, turned their attention to the American West. By this time it could truly be said that the railroad was becoming one of the most important pioneering agencies. As an eminent geographer has put it: "It is the newer parts of the earth that attract the railway builders. For it is there that the railway is the forerunner of development, the pre-pioneer, the base line of agriculture."[29]

It is not necessary here to develop in detail the story of the construction of the railway network in the Mississippi Valley, particularly in the old Northwest, before the Civil War.[30] The most significant fact is the re-entrance of the federal government in 1850 into the field of transportation with the land grant to the State of Illinois for encouragement of railroads.[31] In the seven years after 1850 almost 21 million acres of land were granted by the federal government to subsidize the building of railroads in the Mississippi Valley.[32] In the two years, 1856 and 1857, Congress made grants to forty-five western railroads, almost 9 million acres of which had been approved by the General Land Office by

[28] Quoted in Ernest Bogart, *Economic History of the American People* (New York, 1931), p. 344. By permission of Longmans, Green and Co.

[29] Isaiah Bowman, *The Pioneer Fringe* (New York, 1931), p. 74. By permission of the American Geographical Society.

[30] See Frederic L. Paxson, *History of the American Frontier*, Chap. XLIV, "The Railroad Age"; "The Railroads of the 'Old Northwest' before the Civil War," *The Transactions of the Wisconsin Academy of Science, Arts, and Letters,* Vol. XVII; Robert S. Cotterill, "Southern Railroads and Western Trade, 1840-1850," *The Mississippi Valley Historical Review,* Vol. III (1917); Dan Clark, *The West in American History* (New York, 1937), Chap. XX, "Transportation—From Trail to Rail."

[31] Paul W. Gates, *The Illinois Central Railroad and its Colonization Work* (Cambridge, 1934); *Statutes at Large,* Vol. IX, pp. 466-7.

[32] *De Bow's Commercial Review,* 3rd Ser., Vol. II (1857), p. 518.

1860.[33] Between 1854 and 1857, the Illinois Central Railroad alone sold almost half of its grant—over a million acres—for over 15 million dollars.[34] The sale of the government's alternate sections increased almost in like proportion. During the years 1854 to 1861, the average price received by the Illinois Central Railroad was $13 an acre, which contrasts sharply with the 50 cents per acre to $1.25 per acre received prior to the construction of the railroad.[35] Next to Illinois, probably Missouri with its land subsidy to the Hannibal and St. Joseph Railroad added most to its population in the 'fifties.[36] Certainly the contribution of the railway as a pioneering agency was of incalculable value in promoting settlement in the 'fifties and after.

Cheap and rich loam and the economic opportunity which it afforded in the 'fifties was not the only attractive feature of the Mississippi Valley. One close observer stated that a most powerful incentive "impelling the Anglo-American to bury himself in the wilderness" was freedom in the West, the freedom from deceit and disturbance in the world, the exemption "from the vexing duties and impositions even of the best government," for on the frontier settlers were "neither assailed by the madness of ambition, nor tortured by the poison of party spirit."[37] Another called attention to the good laws—"The aegis of protection and security."[38] The British and Irish emigrant found there the language, laws, usages and manners to which he was accustomed in his homeland.[39] There was no country where the people paid so small an amount in taxes, where the federal government liberally provided by means of grants of land for common school systems and state universities. Add to these advantages those of civil and political liberty, and the fact that the law had no concern with religion.[40] Political and religious freedom and the inducements emanating from a democratic organization of society were undoubtedly strong factors in attracting emigrants, especially from Germany. A Belgian investigator in 1846,

[33] *Report of the Land Commissioner*, 1860, 36 Cong. 2 Sess., S. Ex. Doc. No. 1, p. 67.
[34] Paul W. Gates, "Land Policy of the Illinois Central Railroad," *Journal of Economic and Business History*, Vol. III (1930-31), p. 561.
[35] *ibid.*, p. 564.
[36] Paul W. Gates, "The Railroads of Missouri, 1850-1870," *Missouri Historical Review*, Vol. XXVI (1931-32), pp. 126-42.
[37] Frances Wright, *Society and Manners in America* (London, 1822), p. 367.
[38] *Western Monthly Review*, Vol. III (1830), p. 362.
[39] George Tucker, "Emigration," *Hunt's Merchants' Magazine*, Vol. VIII (1843), p. 158.
[40] Wm. Cobbett, *The Emigrant's Guide* (London, 1829), p. 39.

however, deprecated democratic organization in America as a cause of emigration, insisting that "Land which is cheap of an almost unlimited extent, fertile enough to make capital unnecessary for its exploitation, is a powerful attraction for the agricultural populations of Europe. During the nineteenth century this attraction has been more powerful than any institution made by men."[41]

[41] Quoted in Kirkland, *A History of American Economic Life*, p. 151.

CHAPTER X

INDUSTRIAL-AGRARIAN ALLIANCE

PUBLIC land legislation was one of the most significant factors in the rapid economic development of the United States in the period, 1841 to 1854. Federal largess in the encouragement of this development seemed to know no bounds. Most of this land legislation was made possible by two factors: the ever-increasing political strength of the Mississippi Valley West, and a reversal of the traditional political position of the North Atlantic States which began to vision in the West great opportunities for the investment of capital and vast markets for manufactured goods—the very opportunities which Henry Clay had pointed out two decades before in his so-called American System.

The first in this series of laws which attracted considerable support from the East was the Mineral Lands Act of 1846. Perhaps it was too much to expect that America should continue to be blessed with the policy of prior exploration of mineral resources, which obtained during the 'thirties and early 'forties. The publicity attendant upon the geological reports attracted considerable capital to these western resources. While the mining industry in the lead region of Wisconsin and the copper region of Lake Superior was becoming established Congress might have evolved an intelligent mineral land policy. But many of the geologists, receiving little encouragement from the federal government, were quick to desert the government service for positions with the nascent mining companies. A combination of frontier interests anxious for development, and eastern capitalists hungry for profits, forced Congress in 1846 to abandon the leasing system with respect to mineral lands. The age of exploitation of natural resources other than farm land had arrived.

Since the enactment of the Land Ordinance of 1785, it had been the policy of the federal government to reserve all mineral lands from sale. The Act of March 3, 1807, inaugurated a leasing system providing a 10 per cent royalty on lead-ore lands, though this policy was not actually put into effect until 1822. No doubt this decision to lease the mineral lands originated in experiences during the undeclared war of 1798 against France, for at that time it became apparent that the country was deficient in lead materials so essential to carrying on a war. Desultory and unsystematic management characterized the period between 1822 and 1846. While every major land act specifically exempted mineral lands from entry, nevertheless, without specific knowledge of the location and extent of the resources, many acres of valuable mineral land were appropriated as "agricultural land." Trespassing and plundering were frequent. As early as 1842, there were 44,117 fraudulent entries on the mineral lands of southwestern Wisconsin.[1] The frontier army found itself unable to cope with the situation.

In 1846, the Land Commissioner brought the problem to the attention of Congress. He pointed out that the leasing system had never paid for its operation, and advised that mineral lands be thrown open to entry at the public sale, at private sale, and by preemption. It was better to realize something on these lands than to have them appropriated illegally by settlers, or to have them plundered by trespassers and thus rendered unfit for sale. Undoubtedly the pressure of the western protest against continuing the leasing system also influenced the government to recommend the change. The State of Michigan in 1846 took a firm stand against the perpetuation of a system of "patroonery" on her territory, and insisted that all mineral lands be sold and rendered taxable by her.[2]

In fact, the only objection raised to the proposed abrogation of the leasing system was the fact, or the presumption of the fact, that certain individuals had already obtained extensive tracts in the mineral region, and that these private interests would monopolize the resources if they were offered for sale. Nevertheless, Congress passed an act abolishing the leasing system and instituting a general sales policy.[3] This Act of July 11, 1846, the first of a series, applied only to the lead lands in Illinois, Arkansas, and in the territories of Wisconsin and Iowa. Preemption would be permitted after the auction but at double the minimum. To the general public the minimum price was to be $5 per acre. The purchaser might take as much land as he chose but not less than forty acres, the smallest legal subdivision. Those already in possession of leases might buy their holdings at $2.50 per acre, provided the claimants took the whole tract covered by their respective permits. The next concession

---

[1] Joseph Schafer, *The Wisconsin Lead Region* (Madison, 1932), pp. 114-20.
[2] Resolution of the Michigan House of Representatives printed in the *New York Weekly Tribune*, February 6, 1847.
[3] *Statutes at Large*, Vol. IX, p. 37.

to the mining interests immediately followed. The Act of March 1, 1847, set up the Lake Superior district and provided for the sale of lands at $5 per acre.[4] The Act of March 3, 1847, created the Wisconsin district, extending to it the same privileges.[5] In 1850, the attorney general ruled that iron lands were not included, though it was obvious that it would be difficult to make a classification.

This new mineral land policy which envisaged proper surveys and classification was hardly inaugurated when the gold rush to California set in. Attempts to establish a similar policy in the Pacific West, and later in the Rocky Mountain West, were futile. As a matter of law, these lands were a part of the public domain, but in face of the conditions attendant upon the mad rush the government could do little but stand by and wait for developments. Eastern business interests thwarted all attempts on the part of Congress to bring about regulation, for precious metals provided a business stimulant of incalculable value. While the placer miner still reigned supreme, nevertheless, the mining corporation was in the field. The industrial capitalist with his coterie of companies was getting a foothold in Michigan and Wisconsin; the West Coast frontier was not far beyond. It is little wonder that the South, with its vanishing opportunities even in good agricultural land for its plantation system, looked with suspicion upon this new order of things.

Next in line with a liberalized mineral land policy came new settlement laws which together with the great Preemption Act of 1841 were to attract population to the vacant areas of the West. One of these new laws was the Townsites Act of 1844. It must not be supposed that all of the American West was settled by farmers. A town frontier had always commanded attention; in fact, the townsite interest in the 'thirties became a mania and was one of the conditions contributing to the Panic of 1837. In order to regulate and encourage the settlement of western townsites, Congress passed on May 23, 1844 an act giving to towns preemption rights similar to those granted to individual squatters under the Act of 1841.[6] While this act was not important at first, nevertheless, later history records the fact that a number of western towns took advantage of its generous provisions to add many acres of lands to their corporation limits.

[4] *ibid.*, p. 147.   [5] *ibid.*, p. 179.
[6] *ibid.*, Vol. V, p. 657.

Other settlement laws were designed to attract population to the far-distant territories of the United States. While the general homestead movement was progressing slowly and painfully along a thorny path, the principle was being applied with some success in the distant territories of Florida, Oregon, Washington and New Mexico. In order to encourage settlement in East Florida, which was desirable for a number of reasons but especially for the purpose of national defense, Congress by Act of August 4, 1842, provided that any person being the head of a family or a single man over the age of eighteen, who should make a settlement with continued residence thereon, should be entitled to 160 acres of land. The act was to apply to only 200,000 acres of land.

No sooner was this privilege extended to Florida, than agitation began to extend it to Oregon. In the early settlement of Tennessee, it was pointed out, the government of North Carolina extended a bounty of land to all citizens who might choose to migrate to the Cumberland—now western Tennessee—in order that the western settlements would be built up sufficiently to withstand Indian attacks.[7] Senator George Badger of North Carolina used this same argument in 1850 in support of a donation to Oregon Territory.[8] In order to discover the real origins of the Oregon Donation Act it is necessary, however, to go back to 1843. At that time, Senator Lewis F. Linn introduced a donation bill to encourage the settlement of the Oregon Country. Its preamble declared that "the title of the United States to Oregon is certain and will not be abandoned," and it provided for the erection of a line of forts to the mouth of the Columbia. Though the preamble was stricken out, it nevertheless received much support. Horace Greeley declared in the *Tribune* that "This undertaking is too barefaced. If we get off with $1,000,000 a year, even in the absence of trouble with England, we shall be lucky."[9]

It is interesting to note that Senators Clayton of Delaware, Buchanan of Pennsylvania, and Wright and Woodbury of Vermont voted for this bill at this time. Undoubtedly the expansionist motive was prominent in such support, although Greeley was surprised to find any Easterners voting for it.[10] After the Columbia basin was finally obtained the main argument shifted back to the need for settlement to cope with

---

[7] *Congressional Globe*, 31 Cong. 1 Sess., p. 1,843.   [8] *ibid.*, p. 1,841.
[9] *New York Weekly Tribune*, February 9, 1843.   [10] *ibid.*

the Indians.[11] The act was finally passed, on September 27, 1850, granted to persons who were actual settlers prior to December 1, 1850, a donation of land—320 acres to each single man, and 640 acres to each married man. Such persons as should become settlers in Oregon between December 1, 1850, and December 1, 1853, were to be given grants—160 acres if single and 320 acres if married.

Residence and cultivation of the land for four consecutive years was necessary to secure a patent.[12] The requirement of four years continued residence entailed so much hardship that in February 1853, the Act of 1850 was amended to provide that title could pass after two years of residence, and the act was extended to December 1855. The next year all the provisions of the Oregon Act were extended to the Territory of Washington until December 1, 1855.[13] Another measure similar to the Oregon Act extended donation privileges to the Territory of New Mexico.[14] This last act had no expiration date and lasted until 1883. Furthermore, its terms provided for commutation to cash purchase upon the payment of $1.25 an acre.

The 200,000 acres comprising the armed-occupation donation to Florida were taken up by 1844, but, in spite of the number of entries under the Oregon, Washington, and New Mexican donations, this bounty was not as popular as might have been expected. Many administrative difficulties were encountered. Could the federal government have restricted its donations entirely to actual settlers, the donation legislation might have served as the experiment to test the doctrine of homesteading before it was extended to the nation at large.[15]

Attention also was called during the period of the 'forties to the millions of acres of lands in the Mississippi Valley which had been passed up by settlers because of the fear of floods. Hence the Swamp Lands Act of 1850. In the two decades immediately preceding the Civil War a few voices were raised in the interest of flood control on the Mississippi River. The result was the introduction of federal aid for reclamation. No one can doubt the integrity of some of the authorities who proposed this measure; but, on the other hand, certain exploitative and speculative interests were watching every opportunity to subvert any such well

---

[11] *Cong. Globe*, 31 Cong. 1 Sess., p. 1,841.   [12] *Statutes at Large*, Vol. IX, p. 497.
[13] Act of July 17, 1854, *ibid.*, Vol. X, p. 172.   [14] Act of July 22, 1854, *ibid.*, p. 308.
[15] H. H. Bancroft, *History of Oregon* (The Works of Hubert Howe Bancroft, Vol. XXX, San Francisco, 1888), Vol. II, p. 272.

intentioned subsidies to their own profit. The integrity of some state governments, too, was not above reproach.

The Land Commissioner recommended in 1848 that the swamp lands along the Mississippi and in Florida be ceded to the states in which they lay, on condition that the proceeds be applied to reclaiming them, any balance to go to education and internal improvements.[16]

In 1850, one authority summed up the flood-control problem in this way: "When we survey the vast extent of country which pours its waters into the Mississippi, it is rather a matter of wonder and astonishment that any year should escape the destructive disasters of inundation. . . . As the country is opened and trodden and the timber removed, a greater quantity of water will be thrown into the channels of the rivers, and a higher rise may yet be expected than any which has for years occurred."[17] From the funds obtained from the sale of the reclaimed land along the lower Mississippi it was proposed that a canal be built to carry off the excess water. Such reclamation would save losses annually of five or six million dollars worth of cotton and sugar, not to mention the losses in soil erosion and property damage.

One of the greatest problems of American economic development was thus clearly sensed and stated. The federal government responded by Act of March 2, 1849, granting to Louisiana the submerged lands in the state in aid of the problem of flood control and reclamation. In 1850, Congress made the act general in application, ceding to the states in which they lay the swamp and overflowed lands, with the proviso that "the proceeds of said lands shall be applied, exclusively, so far as necessary, to the purpose of reclaiming said lands by means of levees and drains."[18] The original plan was to grant only such lands as were marked on the government plots as "swamp and unfit for cultivation," but later the Land Commissioner was allowed to sell the lands without reference to the plots. This loophole in the law made possible one of the greatest land-grabs in the history of the public domain. Only a small part of the proceeds of the original grants ever went to the purposes for which they were intended. Millions of acres fell into the hands

[16] At the same time it was suggested that in all states where there remained less than one million acres of public lands these be ceded to the states in which they lay. This was actually a reappearance, though in somewhat modified form, of Benton's cession plan of the 'twenties and 'thirties. See "The Public Domain," *The Emancipator*, Vol. XIII (1848), p. 1.

[17] Mark R. Cockrill, "A Plan to Drain the Lower Mississippi Valley," *De Bow's Commercial Review*, Vol. VIII (1850), pp. 282-4.

[18] Act of September 28, 1850, *Statutes at Large*, Vol. IX, p. 519.

of speculators and politicians. State and local governments in almost every case displayed such ineptness, corruption, and general inefficiency, that one wonders at the congressional decision to extend this land-grant policy in any form.

Nor was the soldier forgotten in the bounties doled out by the federal government in this new era of land history. From the time of the American Revolutionary War, land grants had been made to encourage enlistments and to reward soldiers for valor during military service. Except for the Virginia military bounties of the Revolutionary War period, the first act to involve the public domain directly was that of 1812. However, in this act the bounties were not transferable and they had to be located in specific districts in Illinois, Arkansas, and Missouri. In 1837, a contemporary authority commenting on this bounty-land reserve, thought that "The disposition of this fine country for military bounties" had much retarded settlement. "It was a shortsighted and mistaken policy of the government that dictated this measure. Most of the titles have long since departed from the soldiers for whose benefit the donations were made. Many thousand quarter sections have been sold for taxes by the State, have fallen into the hands of monopolists, and are now past redemption."[19] Heedless of past experience, Congress during the Mexican War period plunged recklessly ahead with this type of legislation until over 26,000,000 acres of land, an area greater than the State of Ohio, had been bestowed upon soldiers. And this was just the beginning, for the Civil War period was yet ahead.

In the period, 1846 to 1856, no less than four military bounty bills became law.[20] The Act of 1847 provided that all noncommissioned officers and soldiers who had served in the Mexican War for not less than a year should receive a quarter section to be located on any part of the surveyed domain. In 1850 the bounty was extended to all who had served in the War of 1812 or in any Indian wars since 1790. The Act of 1852 gave warrants to all officers of militia, volunteers, etc., and further provided that all warrants were assignable. By act of Congress in 1855 a bounty of a quarter section was granted to any soldier, *or his heirs,* if he had served at least fourteen days in any war after 1790; an amenda-

19 J. M. Peck, *A New Guide for Emigrants to the West* (Boston, 2nd Ed., 1837), p. 147.

20 February 11, 1847, *Statutes at Large,* Vol. IX, pp. 123-7; September 28, 1850, *ibid.,* Vol. IX, p. 520; March 22, 1852, *ibid.,* Vol. X, p. 314; May 3, 1855, *ibid.,* Vol. X, p. 701.

tory act the following year extended the act to include soldiers of the Revolutionary War. As Professor Treat pertinently said, "Congress had become wonderfully appreciative of military service or else magnificently lavish in its grants of the public domain."[21]

The benevolent mood of the federal government was also extended to aid the state governments of the New West with that ever-burdensome problem of taxation, many of the newer states having complained that federal ownership of lands within their bounds robbed them of their just share of taxes. The first compact securing exemption from taxation was entered into between the State of Ohio and the United States in 1802. At that time it was agreed that the federal government should continue to dispose of the public lands, and that no state tax could be laid upon these lands until five years after purchase. Inasmuch as the credit system necessitated this arrangement, logically, it should have been abrogated in 1820 when the credit system was abolished. But such was not the case. Although this restriction was raised for the states entering the Union after 1820, it continued to apply to the states which entered the Union between 1802 and 1820. Finally, by Act of January 26, 1847, Congress agreed that those states admitted prior to the Land Act of 1820 might impose a tax upon all lands sold by the United States in these states from the day of the sale, provided that no state should impair the compact which declared that all lands belonging to citizens of the United States residing without said states should never be taxed higher than lands belonging to persons residing therein.[22]

However, this Act of 1847 did not ease the more general problem: the new states were still unable to tax the vast areas of public lands within their boundaries. By the estimate of Senator Charles Sumner in 1849, the public land states, because of their inability to tax the lands of the general government, had lost $72,000,000. This argument of the vassalage of the new states was propounded in the 'thirties by advocates of Calhoun's movement for ceding the public lands to the states in which they were located. In the 'forties and 'fifties the new states used it with telling effect to obtain increased land bounties from Congress for internal improvements and public education. By 1854, the Old South, realizing that the benefits to that section from the public lands were

---

[21] Treat, *The National Land System*, p. 258   [22] *Statutes at Large*, Vol. IX, p. 118.

diminishing rapidly, again became interested in cession.[23] But it was too late; extensive land grants were bringing about rapid settlement of vacant lands.

Perhaps an even more significant example of federal largess to the new states is to be found in the increased aid to the promotion of public education. Senator Stephen A. Douglas succeeded in inserting in the Act of August 14, 1848, for the organization of Oregon Territory, a grant of section 36 in addition to section 16 in each township to be used by that township for common schools.[24] Thereafter the grant of these two sections in each township was made in the organization of every new territory. Of the 500,000 acres turned over to the states by the Distribution-Preemption Act of September 4, 1841, for internal improvements, five states, Wisconsin, Alabama, Iowa, Oregon, and later, Nevada, were able to utilize this grant exclusively for the support of common schools. The Swamp Lands Acts of 1849 and 1850, while intended for the drainage and reclamation of lands, were applied in many western states for the purposes of common education. Thus the new era of the 'forties eased the taxation problem for much of the new West.

But the West soon found itself no longer alone in the field of those who sought educational bounties. Beginning in the early 'forties a movement gained way in the North Atlantic States for the establishment of agricultural colleges. The first issue of the *American Agriculturalist* in 1842 carried an account of steps being taken toward the establishment of the first agricultural school and emphasized the needs for similar institutions. Before long the federal government was being asked to aid in the cause. In the 'fifties a number of states petitioned Congress for public land endowments for this purpose. County and state agricultural societies helped to promote the movement. Many of the eastern states, having received little from the federal government in outright grants, saw in this movement a means of securing a portion of the public domain before it was gone.

The movement came to a head in 1857 when Representative Justin S. Morrill of Vermont introduced a bill providing for a grant to establish agricultural and mechanical arts colleges. It immediately met opposi-

[23] J. Perkins, "The Public Lands and the Land System of the United States," *De Bow's Commercial Review*, Vol. XVII (1854), pp. 151-2.
[24] *Statutes at Large*, Vol. IX, p. 330.

tion. The South argued that it was inexpedient and unconstitutional; some of the western states felt that inasmuch as the grant to the states was to be made on a basis of population it was little more than Clay's distribution idea of the 'thirties in new dress. They felt that the grants to the eastern states would have to be made by means of scrip, which would lead to much speculation and to the appropriation and holding off the market of the best remaining lands in the West. But in spite of the opposition, the bill passed the House on April 22, 1858, by the close vote of 105 to 100.[25] It passed the Senate by an equally close vote. President Buchanan, however, vetoed the measure on the ground that: (1) it was unconstitutional, (2) it deprived the government of much-needed revenue, (3) it would tend to make the states dependent upon the federal government, (4) it would set up colleges in competition with existing educational institutions, and (5) it could not compel states to use the funds for the specified purpose if the states chose to do otherwise.[26] There were other land-grant measures during the Buchanan administration, but southern opposition was so strong that none was successful.

But all this aid to the development of the West dwindles into insignificance when compared to the vast patrimony of land granted in aid of building western transportational facilities. In truth, next to the settler who had received unbounded consideration in the Preemption Act of 1841, the western railroad corporation received just as much attention—if not more. Henry Clay, in 1825, while speaking in favor of extending Jefferson's National Road to the westward, declared that this national internal improvement had been of incalculable value to the country: "Settlement had been multiplied—buildings of all kinds erected—villages had sprung up as if by enchantment.... The effect had been a great addition to the value of property, and an important increase of the wealth of these states through which this great public work had been constructed."[27] But notwithstanding Clay's unyielding campaign for federal subsidization by means of his distribution plan, the period from 1815 to 1840 was characterized rather by the efforts of the individual states and corporations. It is true that there was some aid in the form of land-grant subsidization to such projects as the Miami Canal, the Wa-

[25] *Cong. Globe,* 35 Cong. 1 Sess., p. 1,742.   [26] *ibid.,* 35 Cong. 2 Sess., pp. 1,412-13.
[27] "Mr. Clay's Speech," *Niles' Weekly Register,* Vol. XXVII (1825), pp. 357-61.

bash Canal, and the Illinois Canal, but these exceptions did not prove the rule. Even as early as 1825 the West had begun to clamor for alternate sections to aid in the construction of improvements, but through the Jacksonian era the meager fruits were indeed discouraging. Not until the 'forties was there a popular revival of the Jeffersonian principle of federal aid, and not until 1850 was the principle actually put into legislation.

The ultimate success of the federal land-subsidization principle in the passage of the Illinois Land Grant Act of 1850 was primarily due to the increasing interest, on the part of both the North Atlantic States and the South Atlantic States, in the potential resources of the Mississippi Valley. The Memphis Convention of 1845, presided over by John C. Calhoun, the Chicago Convention of 1847, attended by Horace Greeley, and the St. Louis Convention of 1849, inspired by Thomas Hart Benton, illustrated the growing national interest in railroad construction, particularly interest in building up a system which could later be connected with the Atlantic Coast. The plan to donate to Asa Whitney a grant of land sixty miles wide from Lake Superior to the Pacific Coast to aid in constructing a transcontinental railroad provoked much interest and led to wide discussion of federal aid. Even Calhoun at the Memphis Convention flirted with the federal land-grant idea, contending that a *quid pro quo* was only fair where real benefit was obtained. More than that, he proposed that a bounty might be afforded to the railroads by allowing them to secure iron duty free.[28]

There were, however, certain interests that remained staunchly opposed: representatives from the Atlantic Coast who held that land grants to western interests violated the rights of the old states, and Southerners who, failing to follow Calhoun, deemed the whole principle unconstitutional. The laboring factions of the North Atlantic States in the annual Industrial Congress of 1848 took a firm stand against the proposed Whitney grant, declaring it "an attempt to commit a flagrant wrong against the people."[29] In 1848, President Polk vetoed the so-called Wisconsin Improvement Bill which appropriated one-half million dollars for the improvement of numerous rivers and harbors lying within the limits and jurisdiction of several states, on the ground that such subsidization was unconstitutional. Notwithstanding these opposition ele-

---

[28] Calhoun's view is discussed in *De Bow's Commercial Review*, Vol. I (1846), p. 15.
[29] As reported in the *New York Weekly Tribune*, July 1, 1848.

ments, in 1850 sufficient votes were obtained from the Atlantic States particularly from the North Atlantic, to force through the first great land subsidy.

The success of this land-subsidy measure was due to the efforts of Senator Stephen A. Douglas of Illinois.[30] With the Erie Railroad rapidly forcing its way into the Great Lakes region, and with the lower Mississippi Valley interested in the proposed Mobile and Ohio Railroad, Douglas saw the opportunity of gaining the support of these interests for his proposed Illinois Central Railroad. The Massachusetts Western Railroad having just connected with the Erie, Douglas would not only have much support in New York State, but would also gain the support of Daniel Webster, who, incidentally, was personally interested in western land speculation as well as in railroads.[31]

Perhaps some reference to the debates in Congress will aid one to understand better the votes for and against the land-grant subsidy. Senator Douglas, arguing for the proposal on May 3, 1848, declared that lands of central Illinois had been in the market for twenty-two years and had not sold, primarily because they were situated on large prairies distant from markets and devoid of timber. The building of the railroad would enable the government to dispose readily of all the alternate sections at $2.50 per acre.[32] Nathaniel Niles of Vermont objected on the grounds that the bill was unconstitutional. John Crittenden of Kentucky replied that a precedent had been established way back in 1796 when Congress gave Colonel Zane a grant of land to make a footpath in Ohio.

The question was raised: Why should not grants be made also to the old states? Some doubt was expressed as to whether the grant would enhance the value of government lands. Benton of Missouri felt that the land should be brought into cultivation as soon as possible, and stated his sincere belief that railroad land grants constituted the answer.[33] Andrew P. Butler of South Carolina claimed that as the Nile became the god of the Egyptians and worshipped by them, so the Mississippi was now becoming the god of America. Crittenden of Kentucky challenged the idea that government bounties had been tending westward,

[30] The best and most comprehensive account of the Illinois Central Railroad is that of Paul Wallace Gates, *The Illinois Central Railroad and Its Colonization Work*, Harvard Economic Studies, XLII (Cambridge, 1934).
[31] A. M. Sakolski, *The Great American Land Bubble* (New York, 1932), Chap. XIII, has some interesting material dealing with the land-jobbery behind the passage of this bill.
[32] *Cong. Globe, Appendix*, 30 Cong. 1 Sess., p. 534.   [33] *ibid.*, p. 536.

insisting rather that the means of the government had too long been spent upon the Atlantic frontier. Calhoun of South Carolina made a long speech in favor of the bill. And Douglas, in reply to the argument that speculators and capitalists would get hold of the grant, offered assurances that this would not be the case, inasmuch as the grant would remain in the hands of the State of Illinois until the work was completed. With these brief arguments the bill passed the Senate, May 3, 1848. But the resistance of the Atlantic Coast States prevented its passage in the House. Not until 1850, after considerable logrolling, was the bill forced through that chamber. The act was approved September 20, 1850.[34]

The munificence of this land-grant subsidy attracted the attention of certain New York capitalists who proposed to the governor of Illinois that they take over the construction of the road in return for the donated lands. The road was to be built by July 1854, according to the specified standards of the Massachusetts Western Road.[35] On March 22, 1851, this company accepted through its president, Robert Schuyler, the contract from the state. The grant consisted of alternate sections of 640 acres, six miles in width, on each side of this road, a total of 3,840 acres per mile. The final location of the road determined its length at 670 miles, so the aggregate subsidy amounted to 2,572,800 acres. The railroad

[34] A synopsis of its provisions follows:

Section 1.—Granted rights of way through the public lands, 200 feet wide, with privilege of taking materials for construction: earth, stone, timber, etc.

Section 2.—Granted alternate sections of land, twelve sections wide, the whole length of the road and its branches: one branch to Chicago, one to Salina on the Mississippi, and another to Michigan. In case the lands were occupied, an equivalent quantity could be selected elsewhere, however, not over fifteen miles from the road. The road was to be commenced simultaneously at both ends. The lands were to be sold as the work progressed. The grant did not include lands reserved in the Illinois Canal grant.

Section 3.—The alternate sections reserved to the United States government were not to be sold for less than double the minimum price of public lands.

Section 4.—The road was to remain a public highway for the use of the United States government, free from toll or other charges.

Section 5.—If the road should not be completed in ten years, then the State of Illinois was to pay back to the United States government the proceeds of any land sold, and the remaining land should revert back to the United States.

Section 6.—United States' troops were to be transported on the road at prices fixed by Congress.

Section 7.—The same rights and equivalent lands conveyed and granted to Illinois were to be likewise granted to Mississippi and Alabama to prolong the railroad through those states to Mobile on the Gulf (thus meeting the demands of those who favored the building of the Mobile and Ohio Railroad). *Statutes at Large*, Vol. IX, pp. 466-7.

[35] "Debts and Finances of the States of the Union: Illinois," *Hunt's, Merchants Magazine*, Vol. XXIII (1852), pp. 661-9.

was completed by 1856. In comparison, the total grant to the Mobile and Ohio Railroad comprised 1,156,659 acres.

The passage of the Act of 1850 was heralded throughout the country as the advent of a new era. The editor of *Hunt's Merchants' Magazine* pointed out that with the completion of the Michigan and Southern Railroad, New York City would be connected via Chicago and Cairo with Mobile. The editor exclaimed: "New York will then have a direct connection with the extreme South, through the whole extent of that valley, which, within the lives of some now living, will be the center of the commerce and industry of the continent. All these roads have an immense number of lateral connections with all the important localities, and all contribute not only to the revenues of the Erie Road, but to the trade and welfare of the commercial emporium—New York."[36] It is therefore not surprising that most of the votes in the House from New York and Massachusetts went for the Douglas bill. From Illinois came the happy observation that that state would be connected with the dry-goods marts of New York on the one hand, and with the southern agricultural marts on the other.[37] To the editor of *De Bow's Commercial Review* at New Orleans it was observed that the benefits of this act to the Mobile and Ohio Railroad would be "fully proved by enabling the agriculturalists of western Kentucky and Tennessee, and northern Mississippi, and Alabama, to crop their fields and place their products in the Mobile market twelve to twenty days earlier than can be done from the states north of the Ohio."[38] Which of these interests was to benefit most remained to be seen.

The Act of 1850 opened a new era of land disposition and settlement through the agency of the railroad, an era which lasted until 1871 and during which Congress granted away some 129 million acres of land. In 1852, Congress passed a general right-of-way act, granting to any railroad corporation within the next ten years a one hundred foot right of way through the public domain, with the privilege of using timber and of obtaining additional land for stations. This act provided that the railroads must be completed within the next fifteen years. Together with the land-grant subsidy to the Illinois Central, it literally brought a barrage of land-grant subsidy bills into the Senate, though most of

[36] Vol. XXIII (1850), pp. 655-6.
[37] *People's Journal* quoted in *ibid.*, Vol. XXV (1851), pp. 126-7.
[38] "Mobile and Ohio Railroad," Vol. IV (1849), pp. 89-91.

these were killed in the House. However, by Act of June 10, 1852, Missouri was given 1,764,711 acres for aid in the construction of two railroads in that state. And in this act the section requiring the state to reimburse the federal government for lands sold, in case of default, was omitted. By the Act of February 3, 1853, Arkansas and Missouri received by another grant 2,682,171 acres. By the Act of June 29, 1854, Minnesota Territory received a land subsidy only to lose it because of the unconstitutionality of a grant to a territory.[39]

At this point in the mad scramble for land-grant subsidies, President Pierce made known his determined stand against any further grants. Before 1854, over thirty million acres of land had been withdrawn from public sale with a view to applications for railroad land grants pending in Congress. Pierce boldly abrogated all outstanding withdrawal orders, pointing out that after a quarter century of railroad building, only 17,000 miles had actually been built. He called attention to the enormous absorption of capital withdrawn from the ordinary channels of business, the extravagant rates of interest, and the bankruptcies. "Can it be doubted," he concluded, "that the tendency is to run to excess in this matter? Is it wise to augment this excess by encouraging hopes of sudden wealth expected to flow from magnificent schemes dependent upon the action of Congress? Does the spirit which has produced such results need to be stimulated or checked? Is it not the better rule to leave all these works to private enterprise, regulated, and, when expedient, aided, by the cooperation of States? If constructed by private capital, the stimulant and the check go together, and furnish a salutary restraint against speculative schemes and extravagance. But it is manifest that, with the most effective guards, there is danger of going too fast and too far."[40]

For the next two years Pierce's warning was heeded, but with the completion of the Illinois Central in 1856, the western states renewed their drive for federal aid. The result was that in 1856 and 1857 Congress yielded to the extent of granting subsidies to eight western states (Florida, Alabama, Louisiana, Mississippi, Michigan, Wisconsin, Iowa, and Minnesota), an aggregate of 19,678,179 acres, to aid in the construction of forty-five railroads.[41] In spite of the Panic of 1857, millions

---

[39] Repealed by Act of August 4, 1854. Declared unconstitutional in the case of Rice v. Minnesota and Northwestern Railroad.

[40] Annual Message of December 3, 1853, 33 Cong. 1 Sess., S. Doc. No. 1, p. 19.

[41] See *Statutes at Large* for Acts of May 17, June 3, August 11, 1856 and March 3, 1857.

of acres of land were withdrawn from sale to subsidize 4,649 miles of railroads under the acts of 1856 and 1857. So great was the public pressure against these government withdrawals, that the Land Commissioner in 1858 recommended that settlers be allowed on the reserved sections any time before the public sale.[42] Of the tremendous amount of land that was withdrawn—possibly as much as 100 million acres—18,590,000 acres had been restored by 1860.[43] Here the matter of land grants to states for aid in railroad construction rested until the Lincoln administration.

Up to 1854, it should be noted, the opposition to subsidies in aid of construction of railroads in the Mississippi Valley states had stemmed mainly from that democratic force known as the Land Reform movement. Horace Greeley had been bitterly attacking the whole policy. In 1852, Daniel Webster, asked how he reconciled his advocacy of land-grant subsidies with his stand for homesteading, replied that he sincerely believed that the two principles were not at odds, that land grants made the public lands more valuable.[44] To which Greeley retorted:

"We do not agree with Mr. Webster as to the policy of gigantic land grants for railroads or other purposes. We believe they do essentially interfere with the benign policy of granting lands in limited allotments to actual settlers and improvers, without exacting any price therefrom. . . . Settle the lands compactly, and railroads will be constructed through them rapidly and abundantly. Establish the principle that improved land is a free gift of God, to be dispensed as air and water are, to all who need, and *as* they need, and ample capital will be released from land speculators to construct any number of railroads."[45]

There were many who believed as Greeley did. In fact, the homesteading principle could not be reconciled with the railroad subsidy policy, especially when the latter led to the monopolization of land to the disadvantage of the settler. Was it President Pierce's interest in democracy rather than his sympathy with slavery interests that led him to take this stand against railroad subsidies? For if the corporation was to dominate the remaining good lands in the West, then homesteading would be an empty victory for democratic America.

[42] 35 Cong. 1 Sess., *S. Doc.* No. 1, p. 125.
[43] *ibid.,* 35 Cong. 2 Sess., *S. Doc.* No. 1, p. 76.
[44] Daniel Webster to David A. Neale, March 12, 1852, printed in the *New York Tribune,* March 20, 1852.
[45] *ibid.*

While millions of acres of rich lands in the Mississippi Valley were being doled out, the movement for aid in the construction of transcontinental railroads had been taking an interesting course. The idea of linking the Mississippi Valley with the Pacific Coast had appeared as early as 1832. But not until 1845 did Asa Whitney's plan for the construction of a railroad linking the Great Lakes to Oregon, in return for a grant sixty miles wide along this route, gain any considerable attention throughout the country. Strangely enough, certain people in the South Atlantic States became interested in the Whitney plan, among whom was John C. Calhoun. By 1850, after the organization of Oregon Territory and the admission of California into the Union, this plan came up for more serious consideration. Every junction point along the Great Lakes and the Mississippi River visioned itself the eastern terminus of a transcontinental railroad.

The southern interests had fond hopes of making some point on the lower Mississippi the eastern terminus, but prominent southern authorities soon became convinced that northern support for such a project was well-nigh impossible. As *De Bow's Review* put it: "If there were all the merit in the world in favor, the universal strength of the North is against us."[46] Pointing to the Land Reformers, whose cries against land and monopoly were becoming stronger every day, De Bow believed that within five years' time the prolific sources of revenue from the public lands would be cut off and that the lands henceforth would be given away and not sold. Hence as a second choice he favored Whitney's plan for a railroad from Lake Superior to the Pacific. Some population would be drawn from the South, but he thought that most of it would come from the large northern cities. This would be a good thing, for many of the northern city-folks "without homes or interest except for their daily bread . . . would soon become land owners, not *land reformers. . . .* Such people" then could no longer "be used by the demagogue. They would have means to supply all their wants, and could consume largely of southern products, and could not be supplied from any other source. Being agriculturists, and desiring no protective legislation, would not their wants and their interests be more directly connected with the South than with the North and East?"[47] De Bow, it appears, feared the rising industrialism of the North, and urged the

---

[46] "Pacific Railroad," Vol. IX (1850), p. 601.
[47] *ibid.*

South to support land grants to western railroads as a means of building up southern support in the West, and as a means of staving off the protectionists and land reformers of the North.[48] This strategy, however, came too late; already railroads from the North were reaching out to tap the very West whose support the South hoped to gain. Within the next year the South turned from Whitney's route to one heading westward from some point on the lower Mississippi.

While northern proponents were blocked in their plans by the existence of the Indian Country which had been guaranteed to the tribes "as long as the stars should shine and the rivers flow," the South concentrated its efforts on a route westward through Texas. Undoubtedly it was this growing interest that led to the purchase of the Gila Valley from Mexico in 1853, the transaction known as the Gadsden Purchase. At the same time the northern proponents gained an important victory in the despatching of Manypenny to the Indian Country for the precise purpose of abrogating the perpetual treaties with the Indians so as to make way for a transcontinental railroad via a northern route. Already settlers were breaking into the Indian Country, and it was becoming more evident every day that the country immediately west of Iowa and Missouri would be opened up to settlement. By act of Congress in 1853, the Secretary of War, Jefferson Davis, was directed to employ a part of the corps of topographical engineers to explore all possible routes for a railroad to the Pacific Coast. Inasmuch as Davis was a proponent of a southern route it was not likely that the northern route would be found most desirable.

In the midst of this interest in transcontinental railroads appeared the bill for the organization of Nebraska Territory. Concerning the Kansas-Nebraska Act, it is necessary here to say only that the manipulation of the passage of this act by Stephen A. Douglas changed the whole course of the movement for a transcontinental railroad. The repeal of the Act of 1834 establishing the Indian Country, and the creation of the territories of Kansas and Nebraska, made possible the building of a transcontinental railroad from Chicago westward—a route Douglas was personally interested in—but at the same time, the repeal of the Missouri Compromise and the admission of slavery to these territories precluded any immediate realization of this objective. The eyes of the nation were at once shifted from transcontinental railroad proposals and

[48] *ibid.*, p. 614.

other subjects to the bitter slavery issue. The South became more and more determined in its stand against any important land measure, the benefits of which would accrue to the North.

This realinement of the forces on a North-and-South basis was completed in 1854 with the right-about-face of Horace Greeley, late arch foe of land monopoly and speculation, to a stand favoring the Pacific Railroad. The editor of the *Tribune,* now began to point out the national-defense advantages of such a great communication link. It would save large sums which were being paid for carrying troops, stores, munitions, and mails by way of the Isthmus or Cape Horn. The government was spending forty million dollars annually for the purposes of national defense; the Pacific Railroad, he thought, would be worth half as much as all these expenditures. It would bring San Francisco within ten days of New York, and secure to the Atlantic and inland cities the lucrative and rapidly-increasing trade of the Pacific Coast. Oregon, Washington, and California would be filled with a thrifty, intelligent, and industrious population. While he preferred the northern route, because it was shortest and best, nevertheless, he would take the southern route rather than none at all.[49] In 1857 it seemed to him that no one would object to a grant of two or three miles in width on each side of the track to the builders of the railroad, with free use of timber, stone, coal, iron, and other minerals from the public domain, which inducements, he thought, would reduce the construction costs at least 25 per cent.[50] Greeley's altered stand on land-grant subsidies doubtless indicates the ever-increasing support of the industrial East for the transcontinental project. However, the slavery issue deferred the success of this project, until the secession of the southern states made it possible.

[49] *New York Weekly Tribune,* March 8, 1856.   [50] *ibid.,* January 16, 1857.

CHAPTER XI

SLAVOCRACY OPPOSES FREE LAND

By 1850, after thirty years of effort, no change had yet been made in the minimum price for public lands. Senator Thomas Hart Benton of Missouri had devoted much of his political life to the cause of cheaper land for the frontiersman. Concession after concession had been made to the West, most notable of which was the great Preemption Act of 1841, but the minimum price still remained $1.25 per acre, and the vast volume of offered but unsold land continued to mount yearly as the frontier pushed ever more rapidly to the westward. While the long struggle for the adoption of the principle of graduation bore no fruit during Benton's lifetime, within two years after his death it was recorded on the statute books.

The early history of this movement has already been discussed (in Chapter III). In 1845 the Land Commissioner pointed out that the best lands sold at a price not above $1.25 an acre, while the worst absurdly sold for $1.25. In order to stave off the rising clamor for graduation, Congress passed an act in 1847, allowing all new states to tax lands immediately upon the passage of title.[1] Heretofore, from the time of the passage of the enabling act of Ohio in 1802 up to the 1830's, each new state had agreed not to tax public lands until five years after settlement. This act put an end to a practice inaugurated with the credit system in 1800.

The incipient alliance between the capitalistic interests of the East and the agricultural interests of the West demanded further concessions to the West, in the form either of outright cession or of graduation. The rising industrialism of the East preferred graduation as a solution, for such policy would build up the western population and western markets, while outright cession would interfere with profits for land speculation, and perhaps interfere with land grants to corporations.

In 1854, when the last of many drives to put graduation through Congress was inaugurated, the whole movement was challenged by the conservative slavery interests of the South Atlantic States and by the democratic Land Reform groups in the North Atlantic States. The for-

[1] *Statutes at Large*, Vol. IX, p. 118.

mer group revived Calhoun's old cession ideas in an effort to block graduation, but found little response to their plea to preserve states rights by such a plan.[2] Greeley, representative of the Land Reform interests, declared that graduation was absolutely incompatible with the homestead idea.

"The Homestead Bill," he declared, "looks to the allotment of the public lands in small tracts to actual cultivators; the Graduation Bill is calculated to favor the absorption of that same land in large tracts by extensive proprietors. The cheaper the public lands are held, the more of them a capitalist can buy, and the greater will be the attempt to speculate in them. ... The inevitable tendency of graduation is toward land aggregation and a modified feudalism."[3] After the bill passed the House on April 14, Greeley declared that "The natural effect of this bill will be to give us cheap lands for a few years and dear ones ever after. If the avowed object had been to create a land aristocracy, with the great mass of the laboring population for their dependents and vassals, it would hardly be possible to have framed a bill better adapted to this purpose. ... The House has sent this and the Homestead Bill to the Senate, which, we apprehend, will stifle the Homestead Bill and pass this."[4]

Greeley's prophecy about the bill was correct; the Senate killed the homestead measure and approved graduation. However, the Act of August 3, contained in the third section a provision that the party applying for the graduated price must produce affidavit "that he or she enters the same for his or her own use, and for the purpose of actual settlement or cultivation, ... and that, together with said entry, he or she has not acquired from the United States under the provisions of this Act, more than 320 acres of land." All lands that had been in the market for ten years or upwards and remained unsold were to be put on sale at $1 per acre; those in the market fifteen years or upwards, for 75 cents per acre; twenty years, 25 cents per acre; and thirty years or more, 12½ cents per acre. The act did not apply to lands included in railroad or other internal-improvement grants, nor to mineral lands. Preemption was extended to all lands subject to graduation.[5]

[2] John Perkins, "The Public Lands and the Land System of the United States," *De Bow's Commercial Review*, Vol. XVII (1854), p. 145.
[3] *New York Semi-Weekly Tribune*, April 14, 1854.   [4] *ibid.*, April 18, 1854.
[5] *Statutes at Large*, Vol. X, p. 574.

Greeley's fears about the effect of the bill proved justified. In spite of the third section, the act operated to the advantage of the speculator. Persons took the oath prescribed by the law, but with a mental qualification that the land would be required for actual settlement "at some future time."[6] Two years after passage of the act, it was estimated that more than one-half of all the lands sold for cash were sold for less than the minimum price, while considerably more than one-third sold for barely 12½ cents per acre. The lands were being swept off the market at the rate of thirty to forty millions of acres per annum, about twice as fast as the government was able to perfect the surveys (the total surveyed during 1855 was only 15,315,283 acres).[7] Indeed, the administration of the act became so embarrassing that Congress by Act of March 3, 1857, dispensed with proof of settlement and cultivation. The third section of the Act of June 2, 1862, finally repealed the Graduation Act of 1854, but only after millions of acres of good lands—not inferior lands—had been sacrificed at prices far below $1.25 per acre. The administration of the Graduation Act fully justified the fears of the South and the democratic East in regard to this measure. In reality, the act made land almost as cheap as the later Homestead Act of 1862, and, in the respect that title could pass immediately upon sale, it was perhaps even more liberal than the Homestead Act.

Suddenly—perhaps too suddenly—the South realized that the day was fast approaching when it would no longer receive extensive benefits from the public domain. As long as revenue from the sale of public lands was coming into the national exchequer, the South perceived that there would be no great need for raising the tariff. Heretofore, the public domain had served as a deterrent to federal taxation, and hence at the same time, had increased the sphere of authority of the states. But now, certain representative bodies of the South were beginning to realize that the vast areas of land acquired by the Mexican War were not suited to cotton culture nor to the culture of any plantation staple. The plantation area had actually been expanded to its natural limits.[8] Henceforth, westward expansion would mean the extension of the small-farm frontier, which, because of transportational connections east and west,

---

[6] Report of the Land Commissioner, 1854, 33 Cong. 1 Sess., *S. Ex. Doc.* No. 1, p. 81.

[7] *New York Weekly Tribune*, February 23, 1856.

[8] C. W. Ramsdell, "The Natural Limits of Slavery Expansion," *Mississippi Valley Historical Review*, Vol. XVI, pp. 151-72.

was becoming more and more interested in what the North Atlantic States had to offer.

Not only would the development of western farm lands henceforth redound to the advantage of the industrial East, but the development of the vast timber and mining resources, not to mention the profits from investments in western lands and railroad development, would also benefit the East. It is not surprising that the South began to oppose land legislation which aimed at the development of the West. This section began to sense its increasing economic inferiority, and to claim itself the palladium of vested interests.[9] For instance, a southern source in 1851 notes the "tendency in the North to radicalism," offering as proof their support of "Land Reform: a proposal to give away the public domain to the squatters of all nations and colors; 'the giving every man a farm' principle. Some of its advocates contend that the division shall not end with the public lands, but shall ultimately extend to the private; and antirentism is but one form of this claim."[10] Again, in 1855, another southern authority declared the industrial movement of the North tended toward the enslavement of labor, and hence brought on such movements as trade-unionism and Land Reform.

"Every year in the North a larger number is supported by the alms of the states," he asserted. "The criminal statistics show a frightful increase of crime, especially in the offenses against property; the right to gratuitous education by the forced taxes of the property holder is already a part of the public law, and societies are formed to establish a similar right to an equal division of lands. They declare that the earth is the gift of God for the common use—that no one has a right to monopolize it for himself and his posterity—and that every man has a natural claim to an equal share in its enjoyment. The next step is to deny the right to transmit any kind of property by will or by inheritance, and to force a general redivision in every generation, if not an entire community of ownership."[11]

The North with its Fourieristic, Homestead Exemption, and Land Reform movements in vogue, not to mention a hundred and one other crusades, came to be regarded by the South as the breeder of "isms" and

---

[9] Cole, *Irrepressible Conflict*, p. 58.

[10] M. R. H. G., "The Union, Past and Future," *Hunt's Merchants' Magazine*, Vol. XXIV (1851), p. 427.

[11] Senator Garnett of Virginia, "The South and the Union," *De Bow's Commercial Review*, Vol. XVIII (1855), pp. 689-90.

the instigator of levelling influences of the worst type—all of which were aimed at undermining the existing structure of society. The near-union of Free Soil and Land Reform in 1848 led many a southern politician to examine more closely the traditional alliance between South and West. For if the West was henceforth to become a region settled by small farmers and foreigners rather than by planters and native Americans, if it was to become a region of free-labor and free-soil heresies, if it was to become the adjunct to eastern industrialism, then there was no longer a common basis of interest to support a South and West alinement.

The South, desiring a low tariff and hence low prices on food and manufactured goods, became panicky lest it be faced with economic ruin, as a result of the effective operation of the growing alliance between the industrial East and the small-farming West. It tried to argue that the old agrarian alliance between South and West tied together by Old Man River and a brand new network of railroads was becoming more powerful than ever before. But in reality, the South more than any other section, read the handwriting on the wall. For the time being, it aimed at dominance of the Democratic Party by minority control in order to secure the states' rights doctrine. But such control of American politics by a minority section was tenuous, and at best temporary.

The Kansas-Nebraska Act of 1854 enabled the South to solidify its constituent political elements in opposition to legislation that emanated from the North. Charging that the public lands were being squandered, and that federal government was tending toward consolidation, with the public land office serving as one vast patronage machine, the South in 1854 demanded the cession of the public lands to the states in which they were situated.[12] Southerners contended that their states had received in the disbursements of the federal government very little compensation for the very disproportionate share they had contributed to its revenue. Of the seventy-nine million dollars which came from the sale of the lands in the Old Northwest in 1849, the free gift of Virginia for the sake of the Union, not one cent was received by Virginia. The same was true to a lesser degree of the Carolinas and Georgia regarding the sale of lands in the Southwest. Of the land grants to railroads, the new free states had by 1854 received 18.5 acres to every square mile of sur-

---

[12] J. Perkins, "The Public Lands and the Land System of the United States," *ibid.*, Vol. XVII (1854), pp. 141, 146, 151.

face, while the new slave states had received only 9.3 acres per square mile. Of the donations for education, the free states had received 38.9 acres to the square mile; slave states only 27.7 acres.[13] The tendency was all too plain; the South must resist all further liberal disbursements of the public lands, or better yet, force the cession of the lands to the states. The events of the next few years, however, demonstrated that not for long could the South resist the ever-increasing power of the North. In fact an impasse had been reached.

The first cleavage along the lines of a North and South sectionalism came with the passage of the Kansas-Nebraska Act of 1854. The act provided for the organization of the territories of Kansas and Nebraska, leaving it to the people of the territories to decide whether or not they desired slavery. At one stroke it repealed the Missouri Compromise which forever forbade slavery in the region north of 36° 30′, and at the same time it repealed the Indian Intercourse Act of 1834 guaranteeing that region in perpetuity to the Indians. For the first time, the slave states west of the Appalachians joined with the South Atlantic States in the attempt to open up the West to slavery. Without going into a detailed history of this act, it is important to note that all of the important interests in the North, incongruous though they may have been, were immediately arrayed against the slavocracy. Horace Greeley, apostle of the humanitarian and laboring forces of the North, curtly replied, "If slavery is determined upon the conquest of free territory it will inevitably be resisted and paid in kind. . . . Let but the sentiment gain foothold, and seize and appropriate whatever it can wrest from the hands of free labor, and the banner of reclamation will be raised."[14] To arrest the spread of slavery into the territories, a new party arose to take the place of the old Whig Party, and in its organization Greeley played an important part, not only in drawing together the laborer and employer interests of the East, but also in attracting the agricultural elements of the West.[15]

13 *ibid.*, pp. 435-6.   14 *New York Semi-Weekly Tribune*, January 13, 1854.
15 Professor John R. Commons states that in the rise of the Republican Party "the greatest single factor was Horace Greeley and the *New York Tribune*. See "Horace Greeley and the Working Class Origins of the Republican Party," *Political Science Quarterly*, Vol. XXIV (1909), p. 488. At Ripon, Wisconsin, in 1854, Alvan E. Bovay, formerly prominently associated with the Land Reformers of New York City, manipulated the first political organization to protest the Kansas-Nebraska Bill. See *ibid.*, p. 484.

These diverse political and economic forces operating around the year 1854, reacted upon the progress of the homestead bill through Congress. With the Senate refusing to give much attention to the measure, its second passage in the House on March 6, 1854, by vote of 107 to 72 acquires great significance.[16] In 1854 there were seventeen more Democrats in the House than there had been in 1852, but obviously the vote was not along party lines. Of the additional votes against the bill half came from the slaveholding states west of the Appalachians. Perhaps the true color of the Free-Soilers was indicated by the fact that of the four in the House, two voted for the bill, two against. In 1852, twenty-three members from the slaveholding states failed to vote; in 1854, only fifteen failed to vote. It is apparent from this analysis that some force other than agrarianism had come to play an important rôle.

A study of the Congressional debates of 1854, in fact, reveals that the slavery issue had gained the ascendency over agrarianism and over protection (tariff) and had become the most important of the new conditioning arguments against homesteading. The repeal of the Compromise of 1850 and the rise of the Kansas-Nebraska question were doubtless important factors. As in the case of preemption and graduation, the South now took over the argument, traditionally employed by the old states, that the homestead principle was unconstitutional. Dowdell of Alabama asked: "What clause in the Constitution authorized Congress to give away lands?"[17] Alexander Stephens of Georgia and James M. Mason of Virginia asked the same question.[18] Taking the position formerly held by Henry Clay, they insisted that the proceeds should be distributed for the common use and benefit of all the states. But friends of the bill reminded these opponents that Article IV, Section 3 of the Constitution gave Congress the power "to dispose of and make all needful rules and regulations respecting territory and other property of the United States." The Constitution, they argued, had superseded all the cession deeds of the original states or any agreements pertaining to them. The South also advanced the argument that the homesteading bill was unconstitutional because it was class legislation. For if Congress gives away land to the landless, it might give money to the moneyless, money to the mechanic, to the merchant, to the professional man.[19] Said James A. Pearce of Maryland, "Not one man in a hundred in the

[16] *Congressional Globe*, 33 Cong. 1 Sess., p. 549.   [17] *ibid.*, 33 Cong. 1 Sess., p. 527.
[18] *ibid., Appendix*, p. 524.   [19] *Cong. Globe*, 33 Cong. 1 Sess., pp. 945, 523, 1,814.

old states can avail himself profitably of the [homestead] opportunity."[20] Horace Greeley feared the homestead bill would never get to a third reading. Besides the fact that its chances had been blasted by the "reckless interposition of the Nebraska firebrand," there was also a growing group of men in Congress who expected to be made rich by the railroads, and it was not expected that those who hoped to use the public lands to endow these railroads would vote for homesteading.[21]

By 1854, the South, like the old states formerly, were opposing homesteading on the ground that it would stimulate emigration westward.[22] The old era in which it was easier to purchase new lands than fertilize old lands had passed; taking up new land was now looked upon as an evil.[23] Free land would destroy land values. Southern investments in land must be kept stable. Furthermore, it was argued, free land would be unfair to the eastern farmer, because increased production in the West would mean decreasing food prices.[24] It was further asserted that a 160-acre tract of land would not be sufficient for a plantation.[25]

An even more serious objection from the South was that free land would increase foreign immigration. Thus far, the South had received few of the laborers from abroad. It was now argued that the homestead bill would unlock the poorhouses of Europe and pour upon the United States a population unskilled and untutored in American institutions.[26] There was an attempt on the part of some southern representatives to limit the homesteaders to "native-born citizens."[27] William C. Dawson of Georgia averred in the Senate that the old permanent citizens of the original states had built up this country, and he would do all in his power to prevent placing foreigners on an equal footing.[28] Senator Stephen Adams of Mississippi asserted that opening up the public domain to foreigners would increase crime in the country, and gave statistics from the census of 1850 to show the increase in crime perpetrated

20 ibid., p. 1,772; ibid., Appendix, pp. 1,701-2.

21 New York Semi-Weekly Tribune, February 27, 1854.

22 Cong. Globe, 33 Cong. 1 Sess., p. 506; Letcher of Virginia, p. 526; Millson of Virginia, p. 1,669; Dawson of Georgia, p. 1,772.

23 Phillips of Alabama, ibid., p. 533.

24 Phillips of Alabama, ibid.; Senator Clay of Alabama, p. 1,705; Senator Thompson of Kentucky, p. 946.

25 Millson of Virginia, ibid., p. 505; Benjamin of Louisiana, Appendix, p. 1,073.

26 Dowdell of Alabama, Cong. Globe, 33 Cong. 1 Sess., p. 527.

27 Etheridge of Tennessee, ibid., pp. 534-5.

28 ibid., p. 265.

by foreigners.[29] Obviously, there was considerable economic motivation behind this Know-Nothingism.

The South was also worried about free Negroes: were they to be given privileges under the homestead bill? Senator Archibald Dixon of Kentucky wanted all homestead bills to read "any free white person."[30] Senator John B. Thompson of Kentucky challenged the fair play of northern Senators. "We obtained the land," he said, "by browbeating the Mexicans, by flogging the Indians, and then when you come to make a distribution of the spoils is one-half of the nation to turn round and say to the other half, you smell of the nigger and you shall not have any land; we will give it to the foreigner and you shall not take a particle?"[31] Robert W. Johnson of Alabama declared the homestead bill was "too strongly tinctured with abolitionism." There was objection to the provision of the bill that no state could tax the homestead until patent was issued, for this extension of federal jurisdiction worked to the injury of states' rights.[32] Last but not least, notwithstanding the fact that many Southerners had voted for railroad land grants and other legislation tinged with speculative character, the South feared speculation. In the words of Representative William Dent of Georgia, a rich millionaire could pick out of the gutters men who could be induced to take up land on the share-basis.[33] To this challenge, the friends of the bill replied that "it would be no worse than under the existing law."[34]

An analysis of these debates reveals that the industrial-capitalist interests of the East were becoming less fearful of loss of a labor supply, and more interested in building up western markets, also that the South was less interested in the West and more fearful lest some new legislation injure its "peculiar institution." If homesteading was to succeed, then it must defeat two powerful forces: first, the growing resistance of the southern planters who were convinced that homesteading would no longer benefit slavery; second, the increasing opposition of the speculative interests in the industrial East, who feared that free land would interfere with their profits from the western domain. It was ob-

[29] ibid., pp. 1,740-2.
[30] ibid., pp. 1,740-2; Clay of Alabama, Bayard of Delaware, Geyer of Missouri; and in the House, Brown of Mississippi—all agreed on this free-Negro issue.
[31] ibid., p. 947.
[32] Senator Brown of Mississippi, ibid., p. 1,812; Representative Phillips of Alabama, p. 541; Representative Letcher of Virginia, p. 544; Representative Keith of South Carolina, p. 1,812.
[33] ibid., p. 505.
[34] ibid.

vious that if votes were to be gained they must be gained in the industrial East. The Panic of 1857 effectually silenced speculator interest;
the slavery forces remained the one lone obstacle in the path.

The homestead bill received very little attention in the period from
1855 to 1858. This was primarily due to the fact that the Democratic
Party was coming more and more under the control of the slavocracy,
while the Republican Party of the North, experiencing all the trials and
vicissitudes of a new party organization, was reluctant to take up any
issue other than the one on which it was founded. With the apparent
loss of Kansas in 1857-58, the slavery interests nervously cast around for
other solutions to their problem. The reopening of African slave-trade
and the purchase of Cuba were two solutions which were pressed in
Congress. The advent of the Republican Party, however, nipped these
attempts in the bud. But as the Democratic Party became more and
more identified with the slavery interests, it was obvious that success for
the homestead bill could come only by the efforts of the new Republican
Party.

The outlook was none too hopeful. In 1854, President Pierce had
taken the stand against all departures from existing land policy. President Buchanan was even more set against any changes; it was well
known that he would veto any land measures which displeased the
South, whether they provided subsidies for railroads, for agricultural
colleges, or for homesteaders. In fact, there seemed to be no longer any
pressing need for a homestead measure. The Graduation Act of 1854
had thrown millions of acres of good land on the market at the minimum price of 12½ cents per acre, which, considering the fees, was
about as low as any homestead measure could provide. Too, the Panic
of 1857 had caused a precipitous decline in migration to the westward,
and it was doubtful whether very many of the eastern unemployed had
sufficient money to get to the West.

Nevertheless, in spite of these discouraging conditions, the homestead
bill was finally paraded forth in 1859 with a new escort—the Republican Party. Horace Greeley hailed the drive as the dawn of a new era.
The action on free land, he charged, had been postponed "by the votes
of those who supported the Lecompton and English bills."[35] But "besides this 'peculiar interest,'" he observed, "there is the great railroad

[35] *New York Semi-Weekly Tribune*, May 18, 1858.

land-grant interest, which supposes it would be sadly damaged. . . .
The bounty land warrant interest cannot be easily reconciled. . . . But,
gentlemen speculators! you have had a long day and a merry one! . . .
Your sun has shone and you have made your hay; now stand back and
give the settlers a chance."[36]

The bill was introduced in the House by Galusha Grow of Pennsylvania, on January 4, 1859, and almost immediately Alexander Stephens
of Georgia tried to table it.[37] However, on February 1, the House passed
the measure without debate by a vote of 120 to 76.[38] In this division,
seven negative votes came from the free states, and only three affirmative
votes came from slave states. The bill was introduced in the Senate on
February 1, and was immediately pounced upon by a number of southern members, who finally succeeded in getting it tabled, after Vice-
President Breckinridge cast the deciding vote in the affirmative, making it 29 to 28.[39] The bill was thus sidetracked for that session.

In the thirty-sixth Congress, on February 15, 1860, Galusha Grow
again introduced the bill. Attempts were made by Southerners to table
it, but the measure was forced through under almost a gag rule, thus
avoiding sectional debates. The bill passed the House on March 2, 1860,
by a vote of 115 to 65.[40] Only one negative vote came from a free state—
that of William Montgomery of Pennsylvania—and only one affirmative vote was cast by a member from a slave state. In 1859 nineteen members had failed to vote; in 1860 twenty-seven failed to vote. The
sectionalism division on the homestead measure was thus practically
complete.

Meanwhile, the Senate had been considering its own bill, a measure
introduced by Johnson of Tennessee, which came up for heated discussion on March 19, 1860. This Senate bill was less objectionable than
the House bill. For one thing, the Senate bill did not extend homesteading privileges to aliens nor to foreigners who might come in the future.[41]
A storm broke loose when Senator Benjamin Wade of Ohio attempted
to substitute the Republican House bill for Johnson's Senate bill. To
prevent this move, the southern Democrats tried every sort of legislative
tactic, including an attempt to substitute the idea of ceding the lands to
the states in which they were situated. The Southerners charged that the

---

[36] *ibid.*, February 9, 1859.
[38] *ibid.*, p. 1,725.
[40] *ibid.*, 36 Cong. 1 Sess., p. 1,114.
[37] *Cong. Globe*, 35 Cong. 2 Sess., p. 181.
[39] *ibid.*, pp. 1,074-6.
[41] *ibid.*, p. 1,296.

North was urging the homestead bill as an abolitionist measure, and some Northerners prided themselves that that was the case. It was also charged that the Northerners were pushing the measure to draw votes, especially from the German and Irish elements, in the ensuing Presidential campaign. It is also true that the measure put many northern and western Democrats on the spot.[42] Rather than have the House bill come to a vote, Johnson drew up a substitute bill. Wade of Ohio, supported by his colleague, Pugh, and Douglas of Illinois then tried to have a definite date set for the vote on the measure.[43] This strategy was blocked when it was decided to refer all bills and all amendments back to the Committee on Public Lands, with instructions to report a new bill.

The new Senate bill was reported by Johnson of Tennessee. Its authors had exerted every effort to have the bill satisfactory to all in the Senate and the House, and to the Executive of the United States.[44] Senator Johnson of Arkansas, on the Committee on Public Lands, pointed out the difference between the new Senate bill and the House bill as follows: first, the House bill gave the benefits to heads of families and to those over twenty-one years of age; the new Senate bill gave benefits only to heads of families; secondly, the House bill required no payment for the land while the Senate bill required 25 cents per acre; thirdly, the House bill required five years of consecutive settlement, and then allowed two years more before a patent need be taken out; the Senate bill required residence and cultivation for five years and forfeiture of right if the settler could not pay up at the end of that period; fourthly, the House bill might apply to any land subject to preemption; the Senate bill was confined to land subject to sale at private entry; fifthly, the House bill allowed an alien two years after the expiration of the five-year settlement period to complete his naturalization; the Senate bill required him to take out his first papers at the beginning of the five year period, and complete those papers in the five year period; lastly, in the Senate bill, lands not sold for thirty-five years, and hence held at 12½ cents per acre according to the Graduation Act of 1854, were to be ceded to the states in which they were situated.[45] Gwin of California wanted to amend the bill to allow homesteading on mineral lands.[46]

[42] Stephenson, *Political History of the Public Lands*, pp. 202-3.
[43] *Cong. Globe*, 36 Cong. 1 Sess., pp. 1,660-1.   [44] *ibid.*, pp. 1,748-50.
[45] *ibid.*, pp. 1,750-3.   [46] *ibid.*, pp. 1,754, 1,794, 1,795.

Again, southern Senators did everything possible to prevent the bill from coming to a vote before the meeting of the Democratic convention, and finally succeeded in getting it postponed until May 2. When they came back from their Charleston convention it was evident that a number of western and northern Democrats would allow the bill to come to a vote. The Republican convention was to be held on May 16, and the Democrats could not afford to allow the Republicans to say that the southern Democrats defeated the bill. But just when it seemed that the Southerners might allow the bill to come to a vote, Senator Wade moved that the House bill be substituted.[47] This motion failed by vote of 25 to 30. Finally, on May 11, the compromise bill came to a vote, and passed 44 to 8.[48] The House refused to agree to the Senate bill; on May 30 the House finally asked for a conference committee. But this conference committee failed; a second conference committee also failed. In fact, not until a third conference committee reported a compromise bill did the measure pass both houses. The vote was 36 to 2 in the Senate, and 115 to 51 in the House.[49] As Professor George Stephenson sums up the episode: "Yielding to political necessity both houses concurred by overwhelming majorities."[50]

On June 22, 1860, President Buchanan vetoed this homestead bill. His main objections were these: first, the bill gave the privilege of homesteading to every foreigner who had declared his intention of becoming a citizen, but who was not necessarily the head of a family; second, it was unconstitutional to give lands either to individuals or to states; and third, the price of 25 cents per acre was too low.[51] These objections were in fact the same that had been raised by southern Democrats in Congress. Senator Andrew Johnson of Tennessee charged that the President had not lived up to his word, for Buchanan in his inaugural address had said:

"No nation in the tide of time has ever been blessed with so rich and noble an inheritance as we enjoy in the public lands. In administering this important trust . . . it is our cardinal policy to reserve these lands . . . for actual settlers, and this at moderate prices."[52]

[47] ibid., p. 2,042.
[48] ibid., p. 2,043.
[49] June 19, ibid., pp. 3,179, 3,159.
[50] Stephenson, Political History of the Public Lands, p. 121.
[51] Richardson, Messages and Papers of the Presidents, Vol. VII, pp. 3,130-45.
[52] ibid., p. 2,965.

Horace Greeley, with some asperity, interpreted Buchanan's veto as "one of the natural consequences of elevating to the Presidency a man who from past associations has no sympathy with the poor, and who regards only the interests of speculators. Does any one suppose that Abraham Lincoln would ever veto such a bill?"[53]

53 *New York Weekly Tribune,* June 30, 1860.

CHAPTER XII

BOOM TIMES AND PANIC

THE settlement wave which had spent its fury in the speculation of the 'thirties soon reappeared and spread over the remainder of the better lands of America. To do graphic justice to this magnificent march of humanity into "time's noblest Empire" would require the skill and industry of half a dozen Bentons. "No logical induction, no mathematical demonstration," declared one enthusiastic booster, "can be clearer to our mind, than that here will come together the greatest aggregations of men in cities—outrivalling in splendor as in magnitude, all which past ages have produced."[1] Even the Land Commissioner in his annual report of 1851 stopped short in his official language to acclaim in poetic phrases the greatness of this region. "Imagination can scarcely keep pace," he averred, "with the increase of the western country. The great and fertile valley of the Mississippi which a few years since was the outpost of civilization and the hunting-ground of the savage, has now become the geographical and commercial center of our ocean-bound republic. . . . Villages, towns, populous cities have sprung up as by magic."[2]

In 1850 an authority on population saw "something solemn and almost awful in the incessant advance of the great stream of civilization, which, in America, is continually rolling down from the summit of the Allegheny mountains, and overspreading the boundless forests of the far West. Nothing similar was witnessed in the world before. Vast as were the savage multitudes, which ambition or lust of plunder, under Genghis Khan or Timour, brought down from the plains of Tartary to overwhelm the opulent regions of the earth, they are nothing compared to the ceaseless flood of human beings which is now, in its turn, sent forth from the abodes of civilized man into the desert parts of the world."[3]

"Westward! Westward! is the cry," echoed another enthusiast of 1856. "The cities have come in a day by the Mississippi to vie with

[1] J. W. Scott, "The Great West," *De Bow's Commercial Review*, Vol. XV (1853), pp. 52-3.
[2] Report of the Land Commissioner, 1851, 32 Cong. 1 Sess., *S. Ex. Doc.* No. 1, p. 3.
[3] From Alison's book on *Population*, quoted in *De Bow's Commercial Review*, Vol. IX (1850), pp. 212-13.

Boston and dispute for greatness with New York—and their streets have not yet been paved before on the shores of California passes through the 'golden gate' a commerce that promises to shortly outdo all that London ever saw. Who knows, or can think what shall be there, when the Pacific is an American pond, and the East, or rather the West there, pays no homage."[4] Daniel Webster briefly but pointedly paid his tribute: "The Mississippi Valley will soon be America."[5]

As the wave rolled forward with resistless power, scattering the population over the prairies, thickening it along the rivers, displacing all that was savage, its advance was so rapid and overwhelming that no one for the moment was able to ascertain its bounds. In 1843 the *Tribune* remarked that "Nowadays the West begins at Chicago; soon its Eastern boundary will be the Mississippi or the Rocky Mountains. We have not yet found time to reach it!"[6] Two years later a Cincinnati paper asked: "The West! Where is it? In Ohio, says the Yankee. In Iowa, says the Buckeye. In Oregon, cries he of Iowa. Ohio in the West? Why, we are in the very center of civilization. We will allow New England, after a while, to hang on the hem of our garment."[7] By 1854 writers were beginning to call Ohio an eastern state: "The tide of empire . . . [is] leaving even Ohio behind, and its rapid footsteps making of it a very far down-East state."[8] The wilderness of yesterday, the "stoic of the woods" with his tomahawk, the stalwart pioneer beside his log cabin, the tall forest, and the prowling beast were but memories; stately mansions, cultivated fields, locomotives, the paddle wheels of steamers laden with produce, the fashions of Paris, the civilization and the intellectualism of Europe were the order of the day. By the 1850's it could truly be said that the Mississippi Valley had passed the frontier stage.

The extravagant calculations of wealth and greatness universally applied to the Mississippi Valley as a whole were typical of fanciful estimates of land everywhere, though less so in the Southwest than in the Northwest. The State of Mississippi, for example, was doing everything to recover the prestige lost by bankruptcy and repudiation, assuring the world that she was "the Holland of the central regions of North

---

4 "The Great West," *Friend's Review*, Vol. LX, pp. 573-4.
5 *De Bow's Commercial Review*, Vol. XI (1851), p. 468.
6 *New York Weekly Tribune*, October 26, 1843.
7 "The West," *Cincinnati Weekly Herald*, July 16, 1845.
8 "The Progress of the Republic," *De Bow's Commercial Review*, Vol. XVII (1854), p. 117.

America," and carefully explaining that the remaining public lands within the state boundaries were worth "more than five times the principal, and more than one hundred times the interest of the debt."[9]

Florida was pointing with pride to the development of her lumbering industry, and was anxiously awaiting the day when the government would cede the Everglades for purposes of reclamation.[10] In 1857 Florida announced that the government had nearly completed the removal of the "savage Seminoles," and asked: "Why should not emigrants from Georgia and the Carolinas sometimes turn their steps towards this beautiful and fertile 'Land of Flowers' instead of rushing off in crowds to the bottom lands of the far West?"[11] Louisiana, too, was undertaking to solve the age-old problem of clearing up the foreign titles, a problem inherited from the Spanish and French régimes.[12] Arkansas had plenty of tax-delinquent lands for sale, and invited "emigrants to come and take lands which have been forfeited for taxes," for which no payment would be required.[13] Meanwhile, the Graduation Act of 1854 opened up areas of "the very best lands for a vineyard in the United States"—land worth "from $5 to $10 as soon as entered and secured."[14] The Southwest was thus becoming less interested in the settlement of new lands, since most of the best lands had been taken up before 1837, and it was now a process of consolidating the holdings into cotton or sugar plantations.

The flow of the population in the 'forties thus shifted to the Northwest and to the Pacific Coast. In 1845, the returns showed that "Illinois, Iowa, and Wisconsin," were "by far the greatest favorites with the immigrants."[15] In Wisconsin, particularly, settlement had been rapid. As the fever for speculation subsided after the Panic of 1837, many of the speculative holdings were absorbed by actual settlers.[16] Then too, considerable quantities of state lands were being sold. In 1845 it was declared "that the breadth of the land brought annually under actual cultivation" was now "greater than ever before."[17]

[9] "Resources of Mississippi," *ibid.*, Vol. IX (1850), pp. 559-60.
[10] *ibid.*, Vol. XIV (1853), p. 67; and *ibid.*, Vol. VII (1849), pp. 297-304.
[11] "Fig and Grapes," *Southern Cultivator and Dixie Farmer*, Vol. XVII, p. 152.
[12] *De Bow's Commercial Review*, Vol. X, p. 535; *ibid.*, Vol. XVII, p. 157.
[13] From *Nashua Telegraph* quoted in *New York Weekly Tribune*, October 16, 1847.
[14] "Native Vineyards and Cheap Lands in Arkansas," *Southern Cultivator and Dixie Farmer*, Vol. XVII, p. 316.
[15] "Commercial Chronicle and Review," *Hunt's Merchants' Magazine*, Vol. XIII (1845), p. 472.
[16] *ibid.*, Vol. XII (1845), p. 174.   [17] *ibid.*, Vol. XIII (1845), p. 472.

Three classes were leading the migration into the Northwest: the wheat farmers of New York who could no longer compete with western production, a few wage-earners who had tasted the bitter dregs of the depression, and foreigners who were trying to escape from the Old World's ills. The population of the wheat counties of New York in 1845 showed a decrease below the 1840 level.[18] There were many other factors which gave impetus to the great boom period in the Northwest, notably the repeal of the British Corn Laws, the building of railroads, the attraction of the new mineral lands of the Lake Superior region and of the forest lands of Michigan, Wisconsin, and Minnesota.[19] In 1857, it was predicted by a respectable source that in fifty years Chicago would be larger than New York.[20] Indeed, so rapid was the growth in the upper Mississippi Valley and Great Lakes region that the Biblical prophecy that "a nation should be born in a day" was never more nearly realized.[21]

The frontier after the Panic of 1837 progressed rapidly into Illinois but not as rapidly as might be expected, primarily because of the specter of speculation and the unattractive character of the plains. After 1850, however, with the construction of the Illinois Central Railroad, the plains area was boomed and much of this state was settled despite the speculation that accompanied the settlement process.[22] Then too, the settler's predilection in favor of land that had demonstrated its richness by growing trees was gradually being replaced by appreciation of the advantages of prairie land.[23] In fact, it was averred: "Timber is a great nuisance upon fresh land, beyond what is wanted for posts, rails, and buildings." After the building of the Illinois Central Railroad, timber rafted down the Mississippi could be shipped by rail "far cheaper" than farmers could cut it themselves.[24]

Michigan, like Mississippi, reaped the whirlwind that had been sown in the speculations of 1835-36. This state was at last by 1848 getting its house in order. Its lands, once held by speculators, were being absorbed, and hence cleared and made productive; its public demeanor was

[18] *ibid.*, p. 473.   [19] *supra*, Chap. IX.

[20] J. W. Scott, "Westward Movement of the Center of Population and Industrial Power of North America," *Hunt's Merchants' Magazine*, Vol. XXXVI (1857), p. 202.

[21] "Growth of the North-Western States," *Stryker's American Register*, Vol. VI (1851), p. 305.

[22] See Paul Wallace Gates, "Disposal of the Public Domain in Illinois, 1848-1856," *Journal of Economic and Business History*, Vol. III (1930-31).

[23] Walter Prescott Webb, *The Great Plains* (New York, 1931), *passim*.

[24] "Debts and Finances of the States of the Union: Illinois," *Hunt's Merchants' Magazine*, Vol. XXIII (1852), p. 669.

taking on the countenance of law and order, and its legislation was being enacted in a more cautious manner. Consequently, population was again moving toward Michigan. To cite an example, in Allegan and Ottowa counties, a colony of 2,500 Holland Dutch, with their mechanics and professional men, was expected to increase soon to 10,000.[25] The Michigan Central Railroad was pushing westward across the state; soon the state would be able to throw off the odium of repudiation charges; the burden of indebtedness was expected to "press in future years with a feather's weight."[26] When Horace Greeley visited Detroit in 1847 he noted that the population of the peninsula had increased 50 per cent since his trip there ten years earlier.[27]

Wisconsin, more than any other state of the Northwest, exhibited the spirit of the new boom period. As a Milwaukee newspaper put it, this region seemed to be "stealing the march upon the world."[28] In graphic, poetic narrative, editors East and West sang its praises, picturing this particular portion of the country as the paradise of all earth. "Here where no kingly fist can trammel the soul," declared one enthusiast, "where no omnipresent police can bear fireside converse and secret thoughts to the quick ear of tyranny—where brighter than European skies, are arched above the heads of freer than European men—where a soil, instilled with freedom, clothed in verdure, and decked with flower-gems, has never felt the tread of tyrant or slave—where *esta perpetua* has been inscribed upon a glorious charter of human rights— here are being laid the foundations of a home, where the Celt, the Teutonic, and Scandinavian shall fraternize, and the shamrock and thistle, the lily and the pine, shall mingle their leaves and flowers to symbolize the unity of races and the brotherhood of man."[29] Over and above these virtues was the blessing of health. Wisconsin's "prairies and her openings," this writer pointed out, "yield no noxious vapors, and her mines breathe no deadly pestilence. Here are none of these prevailing diseases incident to the South, the East and other parts of the West."[30]

The lands were already cleared; however, sufficient timber remained for needful purposes—and this combination made Wisconsin lands

[25] J. R. Williams, "Internal Commerce of the West," *ibid.*, Vol. XIV (1848), pp. 19-23.
[26] *ibid.*, p. 23.   [27] *New York Weekly Tribune*, June 12, 1847.
[28] *La Crosse Independent Republican*, June 11, 1856.
[29] Josiah Bond, "Wisconsin, Its Resources, Condition, and Prospects," *Hunt's Merchants' Magazine*, Vol. XXVIII (1853), pp. 445-9.
[30] Bond, "Wisconsin and Its Resources," *ibid.*, Vol. X (1844), p. 556.

better than those of Illinois.[31] The enlargement of the Welland Canal, aided by the Ericson propeller on the Great Lakes, and the extension of the railroads northwest of Chicago, facilitated migration from Europe and the East to its resourceful lands and town sites. Wisconsin's resources in lead, copper, iron, lumber, wool, and wheat would be opened to the world.[32] The development of these mineral and timber resources would create a home market for farm produce, an advantage not possessed by many newer regions of the country. The state also boasted a state agricultural society, an immigration agency, annual fairs, a democratic state constitution, and many other attractive institutions.[33]

Wisconsin was fortunate in having its settlement era correspond with the most democratic period in the history of public land legislation. This period perhaps offered more to the average settler than the later homestead era in which the advantages of liberal land policy were for the most part offset by largess to railroad corporations. Preemption advantages which extended to mineral and forest lands were never more bounteous, and opportunities in rich agricultural lands were probably even greater. The auction had become less operative under the preemption system; in fact, most surveyed lands went at the minimum of $1.25 per acre. If the credit granted under the preemption system was not sufficient, the settler could always resort to the banks. In addition to federal lands, there were also common school and university lands, granted to the state, which were offered at one-tenth of the purchase-money down, and the rest on long credit at 7 per cent per annum.[34]

Weighing all these benefits, one would conclude that the "amount of capital required to purchase a farm" was "about one-tenth as great as in New York." "For ten years to come," this writer on Wisconsin pointed out, "stock of all kinds, can be raised for about one-fourth the cost of raising in New York, and grain for about one-half. The transportation will never exceed 20 per cent, rarely 15, and on wool and similar articles will not exceed 3 to 5 per cent. Should the Pacific railroad become a reality—we will not enter upon the subject—there would

[31] ibid.
[32] J. G. Lathrop, "Wisconsin and the Growth of the Northwest," *De Bow's Commercial Review*, Vol. XIV (1853), pp. 235-6.
[33] ibid.
[34] ibid. In 1853, about one and one-half million acres of school lands were on sale at the state offices in Madison. Balance was payable in ten years, but those lands belonging to the school fund proper were payable in thirty years at 7 per cent per annum.

be such an inversion of present positions, as is unparalleled in the history of commerce."

With the Swamp Land Act of 1850 and the Graduation Act of 1854, the largess of the government became even more extended. Indeed, it was a notable mark of achievement when in 1858, at the end of the boom period, it could be concluded that the "direct sales of lands" had been "mostly to actual settlers. . . . The quantity of land" which had thus "come under the plough had reached, in round numbers, 13,000,-000 acres in farms, taxed in 1857, showing that a considerable proportion of all the lands disposed of" had come under cultivation.[35]

This settlement boom also extended into Iowa and Minnesota, but to a lesser extent. In 1842, Solon Robinson, one of the keenest observers of the agricultural growth of the West, addressing a fair at La Porte, Iowa, could not avoid drawing the comparison "between the encampment of Indians upon the same ground ten years ago, who never broke the soil in search of sustenance, and six thousand happy, healthy, smiling, intelligent cultivators of the earth then gathered together to enjoy the 'farmers' holiday!'" Burlington, just twelve years old in 1845, already boasted of 3,000 inhabitants, 1,000 of this number having settled there within the last two years.[36]

Iowa could point to towns clamoring for charters,[37] to the rich mines around Dubuque, to the rapid spread of the farm-frontier to the westward.[38] Germans began to arrive in large numbers in 1842, and this state was to profit from the settlement of this vigorous teutonic stock.[39] "Scarcely a boat arrives from the Ohio River," a St. Louis writer observed in 1847, "without landing at our wharf a large number of families who are emigrating to the fertile regions of Iowa and Wisconsin. . . . They are, we learn, principally from the enterprising states of New York and Pennsylvania."[40] From the sources of the Des Moines River came the report the next year of the United States Geological Survey conducted by Mr. A. Randall who spoke "in the highest terms of the Prairie de Chien country" which he had traversed. It seemed to him "unexcelled for beauty, agricultural capacity, and mineral re-

---

[35] ibid., Vol. XXXIX (1858) pp. 64-5.
[36] New York Weekly Tribune, August 27, 1845, quoting from the Burlington Hawk-Eye.
[37] Solon Robinson's letter to the editor of American Agriculturalist, Vol. I (1842), p. 312.
[38] John Plumb, Jr., "Iowa Territory," Family Magazine (1840), pp. 153-8.
[39] New York Weekly Tribune, June 25, 1842.
[40] From St. Louis Era, quoted in "Filling up at the West," Emancipator, Vol. XII (1847), p. 4.

sources."[41] Between September 1 and December 1, 1853, the emigration into the state was computed at 50,000.[42]

In 1848, only the rude cabins of a few half breeds marked the site of St. Paul, but by 1857 this great northwestern emporium could boast of "tall spires and elegant buildings . . . commodious warehouses, busy levees . . . fleets of barges and steamboats."[43] The vast lumber districts, the copper and iron on Lake Superior, and the fertile lands in the south, caused Minnesota to pride itself on its future prospects.[44]

The settlement boom carried the population beyond the Missouri, into Kansas, breaking up the Indian Country dedicated by the Act of 1834. In 1852, it was already being asserted in that region that the people could "no longer live without a government." This pronouncement brought up once more the question which had supposedly been "settled forever by the 'compromise.' "[45] For many years this particular region had been designated as the "Great American Desert," but by 1858, that illusion was pretty well dispelled. No longer did one hear of arid wastes stretching into the distance, and presenting impassable barriers to the march of civilization. Instead, green and fertile prairies were being settled with astonishing rapidity; towns and cities were springing up as if by enchantment. Along with the natural growth of this region the artificial stimulus given its growth by the slavery controversy must be taken into consideration.

The movement beyond the Rockies into the Mormon state of Deseret, later Utah, had, in its early stages, primarily a religious appeal. This state, however, had little direct connection with the history of the public lands. A person in the Mormon state might select any unoccupied lot, but no value was attached to land, and one could sell only the improvements.[46]

As for Oregon, part of the story of movement into that state has already been discussed. In 1842, an eastern sea captain visited Portland, where there was not a building to be seen, but in 1850 it was a booming town. For one-half of a tract obtained under the Donation Act, this

---

[41] From *The Prairie de Chien,* quoted in *Hunt's Merchants' Magazine,* Vol. XIX (1848), p. 562.

[42] "Emigration," *Saturday Evening Post,* Vol. XXXIII (1853), p. 3.

[43] "Minnesota: The Growth and Progress of the Northwest," *Hunt's Merchants' Magazine,* Vol. XXXVII (1857), p. 51.

[44] "Minnesota Territory," *Friend's Review,* Vol. IX, pp. 221-2.

[45] Item under heading "General News" in *The Independent,* Vol. IV (1852), p. 175.

[46] "State of Deseret," *Friend's Review,* Vol. III (1850), p. 140.

captain received in 1850 an offer of $30,000. He refused, preferring to break the tract up into small lots and sell them for $500 each.[47]

Thus in spite of the incalculable number of obstacles in the way, the emigrants plodded steadily westward along the Oregon Trail, and every day added to the numbers who were settling the Pacific Northwest. Had it not been for the Mexican War and the discovery of gold in California, Oregon's growth would have been even greater in this period. California was already being looked to as another Arcadia when the gold rush threw into the background the attractions of her rich topsoil.

In the 1840's many thought that the Panic of 1837 had taught its lesson, and that speculation was a thing of the past. Many Congressmen sincerely believed that in passing the Preemption Act of 1841 they had given a permanent blow to speculation, that the speculator would never again have the advantage over the settler in the land market, and that henceforth vacant lands would be reserved for actual settlers. With the return of better times after 1846, however, and the rise in values, especially in land, many an investor's eyes again turned to the American West, where the tide of immigration was flowing as never before in the history of America. The lure of the unearned increment proved too great a temptation; many individuals who had been victims in the inflation of the 'thirties, many who had not, became victims in the 'fifties. Opportunities for fabulous profits from mineral lands, forest lands, rich topsoil along the routes of railroads, or especially advantageous locations were again proclaimed, not only in every commercial city of this country but even across the Atlantic. Indeed, it would have been a miracle had no speculation accompanied the great agricultural boom of the 1850's.

At first, the appreciation of improved property was almost exclusively confined to regions affected by unusual enterprise. Even in 1852, the rise in values was not at all analogous to the speculation of 1835-36, for "cities laid out under water, and commercial depots staked off upon wild prairie lands," were not proving "inviting investments."[48] While it was admitted that occasionally there was a speculative scheme almost as chimerical, and here and there a railroad project with a foundation

[47] "The Rise of Land in Oregon," *ibid.*, p. 765.
[48] "Commercial Chronicle and Review," *Hunt's Merchants' Magazine*, Vol. XXVII (1852), p. 466.

almost as vague, yet on the whole, according to an economist of 1852, the majority of business men were "clear from any hallucination upon these subjects, and rash speculations" were not in fashion.[49]

In the very next year the same person noted that new banks continued "to multiply, and the western states" were "creating, under new free banking laws, a host of small institutions," which increased "so fast" that it was difficult even to keep a list of them.[50] This rapid increase in the number of banks in the western country, and "more especially of banks intended merely to furnish a depreciated circulation," continued to be attended with an unusual amount of fraud and corruption.[51] With plenty of bank credits, with railroads running in every direction, with a great influx of settlers, and with legislation providing for extremely low prices on public lands, the stage was being set for another grand orgy of speculation. Well might the public-spirited citizen pray "to God that the hollow-hearted speculator and political empiric could be induced to leave to wisdom and patriotism the disposition of the public domain!"[52]

At the head of the new speculative parade, was "a class of men known as railroad directors, and internal improvement managers, who, especially," claimed the "fostering care of the government."[53] Since capitalists in the East, and even in England, subscribed millions to build the railroads, this stream of capital did much to enrich the entire West.[54] By 1854, even the humblest proprietor was not hesitant about investing in western railroads, and was reaping a return in the enhanced value of his land. So certain was there to be an increased value in real estate along the lines of these railroads, that whole communities and even states, had levied general taxes to complete the construction of the railroads or even to bring more into existence.[55] The dumping of land onto the market by means of extensive grants for internal improvements, the graduation of prices under the Act of 1854, the throwing open of the mineral lands, the lack of restrictions on the sale of forest lands, the endless amount of scrip issuing from military bounty and swamp lands legislation— all these legislative factors contributed to the boom in land sales.

[49] ibid.   [50] ibid., Vol. XXVIII (1853), p. 344.
[51] ibid.   [52] "Public Lands," Western Democratic Review, Vol. I (1854), pp. 415-23.
[53] ibid.
[54] "Commercial Chronicle and Review," Hunt's Merchants' Magazine, Vol. XXXVI (1857), pp. 578-9.
[55] J. Perkins, "Public Lands and Land System of the United States," De Bow's Commercial Review, Vol. XVII (1854), pp. 153-4.

The California gold rush also did much to prepare the stage. Not only did the pouring of gold into the market bring the country out of the doldrums of the 'forties, but it also conditioned the public mind to a new set of inflated values. As for the land speculation that took place in California as a result of the gold boom, suffice it to say that miners and settlers rushed into the California area and appropriated mining sites, town sites, and agricultural holdings without any respect for the government's title or the Mexican title. Never before had there been such a total disregard for law and order; squatter law reigned supreme. To be sure there had been in former years instances of rushes into Indian reservations, and even more recently, onto the mineral lands of the Lake Superior region, but these were nothing compared with the malappropriations in California. As values rose everywhere, speculation became more and more prevalent.

The California frontier set the pace, but this pace was soon quickened by the spread of the speculative spirit into the realm of railroad lands of the Middle West. As the miner was the pioneer to the Pacific Coast during the 'fifties, so the railroad now became the pioneer for the blazing of new trails in the Middle West. In that section, the speculation was becoming very apparent by 1854, to judge from local newspapers. From a spot as far removed from the focus of speculation as Cleveland, Ohio, came the observation that "thousands" were "rushing or looking to our great cities for the means of building railroads and making other improvements." These people "could make them on their own resources if they had not both hands and arms full of unfenced, unused lands, which they are holding up for five to ten times the price they paid for them, and so preventing the settlement of the country. If every man in Illinois were compelled by law to sell within a year all the land he owns beyond half a section, they would all be richer at the year's end than they are now, while tens of thousands of valuable immigrants . . . would be drawn in to help to do whatever is needful. Every acre of wild lands held on speculation is a . . . drawback not only upon railroads but upon schools, roads, churches, mills, manufactories, etc."[56]

Many groups participated in the speculative boom. When a farmer in Illinois could borrow money to put in a crop of corn, and could clear enough on the crop to pay 20 per cent per annum for the money and still "make a good thing of it," it is apparent why even farmers dared

[56] *Tribune* Correspondent, Cleveland, Ohio, in *New York Daily Tribune*, January 6, 1854.

to enter the speculative ring along with professional speculators.[57] There was a numerous class of small farmers who purchased more land than they would reasonably hope to utilize for many years. Next came the small business men, bankers, editors, judges, lawyers, politicians and government officials. In this class was Stephen A. Douglas, who purchased, around Chicago and Lake Calumet, holdings which netted him enormous profits. More important, however, were the professional speculators. And lastly, there were the eastern capitalists.

Among the more prominent professional speculators were Jonathan Sturgis and Andrew J. Galloway. Sturgis began his purchases in 1836 or 1837 by buying up Revolutionary bounty land warrants of the state of Virginia. With this scrip he located lands at the minimum price per acre. In the early 'fifties he purchased 40,000 acres in the Danville district, through which the Illinois Central was later to run. His holdings ultimately totaled over 100,000 acres. During the rise of the 'fifties he began gradually to unload them on terms of credit. Galloway, on the other hand, was the promoter of the Western Land Agency of Chicago, Illinois, an organization which had field-officers scattered over all the upper Mississippi Valley. Altogether, this company accumulated over 150,000 acres along the Illinois Central Railroad. Of the 14,000,000 acres of land remaining unsold in Illinois, over 12,000,000 acres were sold between 1849 and 1856, and of this amount it is estimated that 6,000,000 went to speculators.[58]

As to the value of this speculation in Illinois during this period, one authority concluded that "the speculators' influence . . . was not always a favorable one. The truth of his advertising literature was often questionable and frequently led to much suffering for the gullible. By holding the best land for higher prices, he forced pioneer settlers with no capital to move farther west in their search for lands after the government holdings had been sold, and thereby retarded the development of the State."[59]

Horace Greeley, visiting Chicago in 1847, commented on the tremendous amount of land being held for rise in prices, and conjectured

[57] "Commercial Chronicle and Review," Hunt's Merchants' Magazine, Vol. XXXVI (1857), pp. 578-9.
[58] Paul Wallace Gates, "The Disposal of the Public Domain in Illinois, 1848-1856," Journal of Economic and Business History, Vol. III (1930-31), p. 228.
[59] ibid., p. 239.

that by 1900 Chicago would surpass New York in size.[60] Truly no city
ever grew so fast as Chicago in the 'fifties. But it was a town "filled with
land sharks" and "downright thieves and blackguards." As one elderly
observer remarked: "Chicago is a humbug! The Great West is a humbug! I am older than you, and I've known bubbles to burst before. Chicago is a bubble, sir! You may depend on't. I remember the crash of '37,
and I tell you that such a state of affairs as exists today in Chicago, presaged that storm. Inflation! Inflation!"[61] Indeed, the piper was soon to
be paid.

Wisconsin's speculations were just as extreme. In the frontier town of
La Crosse, one of the original proprietors of the village bought a lot
in 1851 for $75, and sold it in 1854 for $1,400 cash; nearby agricultural
land, which in 1851 was to be had for $1.25 per acre, was in 1854 "selling
at from $200 down to $20 per acre."[62] As for the farming land in this
state, it was confidently asserted in 1853 that, "All uncertainty is at an
end, and, with ordinary judgment, it is perfectly easy to make purchases which will pay from 12 to 50 per cent per annum on the capital
invested by simple rise in value, if no improvements are made." Many
really believed that this buoyancy in real estates values, "unlike the in-
flations of land manias and speculator's bubbles," would end in general
prosperity instead of in an absorbing "crisis" and an inclusive "smash."[63]

The pressure of currency contraction in 1854 brought no very great
reaction in the frontier areas of the West, and by the end of 1856 the
speculative mania was reaching dangerous heights. In 1857 Horace
Greeley made several observations about a trip into Iowa where speculation was general. "The more I see of land speculation," he wrote, "the
less I like it. Here men are eagerly grasping all the land they can possibly purchase, paying exorbitant usury, putting off needy creditors,
living crowded in wretched huts, in order that they may clutch more
land. . . .

"Everybody complains that speculators, doctors, lawyers, merchants,
etc., are coming in, with too few farmers and mechanics, and everybody

[60] *New York Weekly Tribune*, July 31, 1847. This same opinion was held by J. W. Scott
of New York; see his article, "Westward Movement of the Center of Population and Industrial
Power of North America," *Hunt's Merchants' Magazine*, Vol. XXXVI (1857), p. 202.
[61] The Rev. Dr. Humphrey writing to the *New York Evangelist*, reprinted in *ibid.*, Vol.
XXXVII (1857), pp. 444-5.
[62] *La Crosse Independent Republican*, September 6, 1854.
[63] "Wisconsin: Its Resources, Condition, and Prospects," *Hunt's Merchants' Magazine*, Vol.
XXVIII (1853), pp. 445-9.

is aggravating the distemper thus complained of. Whosoever buys a lot of land that he does not personally need, in the expectation that some one else will soon buy it of him at an advance, is doing what tends to unsettle the public mind, inflame the spirit of speculation and discourage patient industry."[64] A few weeks later from Goshen, Indiana, he wrote: "The men who are building up the villages of last year's origin on the incipient railroads of Iowa, were last year doing the like in Illinois, and three years since in Ohio. He who is doing well in the newest settlement is looking sharply around for a chance to do better in Nebraska or along the lines of railroads leading thither which are soon to be constructed."[65]

But if speculation was rife in Illinois, Wisconsin, and Iowa it was no less so in Minnesota.[66] "Fortunes seemed to be dropping from the skies, and those who would not reach and gather them were but stupids and sluggards," remarked a commentator of the period.[67] Everybody was in debt. Money in the form of Indiana wildcat bills was used, but was becoming scarcer every day. Hotels bulged to overflowing, speculators thronged the streets and merchants could hardly keep their stocks filled up. Both townsite and agricultural-land speculation were sailing into dizzy heights. The boom hit its highest point in the spring and summer of 1857.[68]

The boom in Kansas coincided with the rush of the free-soil and slavery interests to that region. This added stimulus sent land values soaring. The *Leavenworth Journal* reported that a squatter seven miles from that city who originally paid $1.80 per acre for 160 acres of land sold it in 1855 clearing $1,800. The account concluded with the comment that "This can be done in almost any place within a compass of 200 miles of this city."[69] In the same newspaper it was claimed that squatters who had paid $2 per acre for lands near the city were now getting $25 to $50. As for townsite speculation, a New York *Tribune* correspondent wrote from Tecumseh: "The number of towns laid out in this territory is something extraordinary. Every man who owns a quarter section, well located, lays it out at once into a town, so that they dot the maps like the block agencies of a checkerboard. Of course but one in

---

[64] *New York Semi-Weekly Tribune*, February 24, 1857.   [65] *ibid.*, March 3, 1857.
[66] William Walter Folwell, *A History of Minnesota* (4 vols., St. Paul, 1921), Vol. I, p. 362. By permission of the Minnesota Historical Society.
[67] *ibid.*   [68] *ibid.*, pp. 362-3.
[69] Issue of Dec. 11, 1856.

three or four can succeed—the rest must revert into farms."[70] The *Kansas City Enterprise* reported that there were at least one hundred towns in Kansas, but at the most the territory had only a population of 30,000. The editor concluded: "Ninety-nine of these are humbugs—and every land shark in the west is trying to delude the emigrant into the belief that his is the exception. In some towns in the territory, ground is selling at $250 per foot, when there is not corn enough raised within a circuit of 100 miles to feed the dupes that are buying at that price."[71]

Throughout the territory everything was booming—claims were properly advertised in local newspapers, lawyers were doing a great business, especially those connected with the preemption and bounty land practice, money was readily loaned, investments were made for capitalists with 20 per cent return guaranteed, land agencies were setting up everywhere, and emigration companies mostly connected with railroad and steamship companies were established at important points. Such was the picture in Kansas territory in 1857.

In the three years between 1854 and 1857, a stream of capital poured into the Northwest from the East and from England for the building of railroads and for the purchase of lands. Where waves of settlement had advanced far beyond markets, the railroad had come to the rescue. Railroads, found useful and profitable, were so far extended that instead of the means, they became the end. They were no longer constructed to facilitate the cultivation of the soil, but were also used as agencies of local speculation.[72]

Behind this northwestern boom, however, there was another important and impelling force, namely, the tremendous rise in the prices of wheat and corn—due to the failure of crops in Europe. This had brought about a corresponding rise in price of farm lands, and a quickened movement to the vacant lands of the West. As one authority remarked: "Our young men have gone out to the Mississippi, leaving their farms in the older states, because grain was wanted for export at a price which paid better as a whole than the cultivation of ordinary farm produce for a local market nearer home." The same commentator observed that when the reaction sets in, and wheat brings only $1 per bushel on the Chicago market, then "farming land in Connecticut is

[70] *New York Daily Tribune*, May 20, 1857.
[71] Reported in the *La Crosse Independent Republican*, April 15, 1857.
[72] *Hunt's Merchants' Magazine*, Vol. XXXVII (1857), p. 70.

cheaper at $30 per acre than the prairie lands in Iowa at their nominal rate."[73]

In 1857, as in 1837, that keen observer, Horace Greeley, warned the country of the impending panic. In answer to the charge that he was a calamity howler, he asked his readers to "consider the present rage of speculation, especially in western lands, the number of railroads in progress or under contract, the high prices of most staples of food, the infinitude of building operations in city and country, and judge" whether his "word of warning was premature or unnecessary."[74] From the financial editor of *Hunt's Merchants' Magazine* came the retort: "Nothing so surely tends to precipitate a financial crisis and a commercial revulsion, as a weakening of the public confidence in the stability of prosperity. . . . We see no reason why the man of sense may not take a more hopeful view of the future than is just now in general fashion. We do not think the millennium has dawned, or that sunshine will be perpetual; it is well for prudent men to retrench and be cautious amid general recklessness and folly."[75] But the editor did admit, however, that too fast a pace had been set in selling western lands, that too many railroads were being run through these new areas, and that all this expansion was being done upon a "system of reckless expenditure and baseless credit."[76]

Ominous conditions everywhere were pointing to a crash. Money was becoming "scarce and dear"; even in the spring of 1857 it was becoming increasingly difficult to make collections in the West.[77] By August the situation had reached a critical stage, aggravated by the failure of grain crops in the West. On the twenty-fourth day of that month the Ohio Life Insurance and Trust Company of New York failed, and before sundown there were failures in almost every town in the country. As the eastern credit houses called in their loans, the West became literally emptied of money.[78] The speculators left the towns and countryside like rats from a burning ship. St. Paul alone lost almost half its population.[79]

It should be noted, of course, that speculation in railroads and lands were not the only causes of the Panic of 1857. As Professor Arthur H. Cole points out, the volume of trade for the country as a whole had

---

[73] "Commercial Chronicle and Review," *ibid.*, Vol. XXXV (1857), pp. 326-7.
[74] *New York Semi-Weekly Tribune*, March 24, 1857.
[75] "Commercial Chronicle and Review," *Hunt's Merchants' Magazine*, Vol. XXXVI (1857), pp. 457-8.
[76] *ibid.*   [77] *ibid.*, pp. 578-9; Vol. XXXVII (1857), p. 70.
[78] Folwell, *History of Minnesota*, Vol. I, p. 364.   [79] *ibid.*

reached a peak in the early autumn of 1856, after which there followed a broken decline. This swing in the volume of trade was least pronounced in New England and most striking in the West.[80]

Fond hopes that all would be over by the opening of the new year were doomed to bitter disappointment. As the year 1858 neared its end, Greeley wrote from Racine, Wisconsin: "The West is very poor. I think a larger proportion of the people of Michigan, Indiana, Illinois, Wisconsin and Iowa are under the harrow now than at any former period."[81] Poor grain crops and low grain prices, a bumper cotton crop, but falling cotton prices, iron manufacturers everywhere depressed, only a few railroads paying dividends, all stocks at the level of panic prices, ships lying idle in every harbor in the world, immigration at a standstill, wages and rents everywhere declining, and the West especially staggering under a burden of debt which pressed heavier and heavier—such was the economic picture of 1858.[82]

From the General Land Office came the lamentation that less money in proportion to the amount of land offered had been received that year from sales than at any previous period.[83] Real estate values had fallen to such an extent that a property previously valued at $1,500 now proved insufficient to satisfy a claim of $300. In fact, land which in 1856 sold for $50 an acre was in 1858 hard to sell at $20.[84] Greeley again observing the West in 1860, declared, "Some of the railroads [are] worth today just what their rails would sell for as old iron. . . . Worst of all is the moral bankruptcy thus created or developed. City and county loans are repudiated. The creditors are few or distant, the debtors are many, compact and powerful. . . . Wisconsin [at this stage seriously considering the repudiation of her debt as Mississippi had done in the 'forties] hides her burning blushes on the bosom of Mississippi!"[85]

When President Buchanan, in 1858, ordered some land sales in Kansas Territory, the settlers, unable to meet their preemption payments, organized into claim associations and armed themselves to prevent the sale.[86] "Indeed, it is to acknowledge ignorance of the petty despot who

[80] Arthur H. Cole, "Statistical Background of the Crisis of 1857," *Review of Economic Statistics*, Vol. XII (1930), pp. 170-80.

[81] *New York Tribune*, December 25, 1858, quoted in James Ford Rhodes, *A History of the United States Since the Compromise of 1850*, Vol. II, p. 513.

[82] *New York Semi-Weekly Tribune*, January 4, 1859.

[83] 36 Cong. 1 Sess., S. Ex. Doc. No. 1, p. 92.

[84] "Recovery of the West," *Harper's Weekly*, Vol. III (April 9, 1859), p. 226.

[85] *New York Daily Tribune*, March 2, 1860.

[86] Atchison (Kansas Territory) *Freedom's Champion*, April 3, 1858.

rules in Washington," declared an Atchison newspaper, "to suppose that he would be guilty of such an act as doing justice to the people of Kansas by postponing the land sales."[87] Charges were made that marauders from Missouri and Arkansas were pressing these sales.[88] Not only did many of the people of Kansas lose their lands for failure to complete payment, but between the drought and the grasshopper, thousands had to appeal to the country for relief to keep from starving.[89] The suffering in the West brought on by the Panic of 1857 was only alleviated about the time that war broke out between the states.

[87] *ibid.*, May 22, 1858.
[88] "The Kansas Broils," *The Independent*, Vol. XII (1860), p. 4.   [89] *ibid.*, pp. 3-4.

Part III

The Corporation Triumphs

CHAPTER XIII

THE REPUBLICAN VICTORY

IN 1856, the platform of the Republican Party reflected in a general way, but failed to express clearly and concisely, the new industrial-agrarian philosophy upon which it was founded. The party underwent tremendous growth during Buchanan's administration, and looked forward hopefully toward its chances in 1860. It may have been the pressure of the slavery issue which compelled it to seek a compromise candidate from the West. But the manner in which the platform was drawn up at the Chicago convention would seem to indicate that the upper Mississippi Valley was the key to the election.[1] Horace Greeley, serving as a delegate from Oregon, arrived in Chicago several days before the convention opened.[2] In January, after viewing political possibilities in the Northwest, he had written from Davenport that no Democrat other than Douglas or Johnson—Johnson was an active proponent of the homestead principle—could hope for success against the new Republicanism.[3] As a member of the platform committee Greeley probably wrote the homestead plank.[4]

From an analysis of the platform it is hardly an overstatement to say that the new planks were not so much the result of a deep feeling against slavery as of growing needs in the industrial East and the agrarian West.[5] The first eleven planks dealt with the party's antislavery stand—an elaboration of the platform of 1856. But the next five reflected more definitely the interests of the industrial-agrarian alliance upon which the party arose. Inasmuch as this program was to bring about such a fundamental change in the land policy of the Republic, a summary of these planks will be useful:

[1] William E. Dodd, "The Fight for the Northwest, 1860," *American Historical Review,* Vol. XVI (1911), pp. 774-88.

[2] James Parton, *The Life of Horace Greeley* (Boston, 1889), p. 445.

[3] *Dubuque Herald,* September 26, 1860, quoted in Stephenson, *The Political History of the Public Lands, from 1840 to 1862,* p. 234.

[4] It is known that Greeley spent much time in an effort to bring the doubtful states in line with the principles of the platform. See Emerson D. Fite, *The Presidential Campaign of 1860* (New York, 1911), p. 126.

[5] Fite, *ibid.,* emphasizes the industrial needs, Chap. XIII.

12. That . . . sound policy requires such an adjustment of . . . [duties upon] imports as to encourage the development of the industrial interests of the whole country; and we commend the policy of national exchanges, which secures to the working men liberal wages, to agriculture remunerating prices, to mechanics and manufacturers an adequate reward for their skill, labor, and enterprise, and to the nation commercial prosperity and independence.

13. That we protest against any sale or alienation to others of the public lands held by actual settlers, and against any view of the homestead policy which regards the settlers as paupers or supplicants for public bounty; and we demand the passage by Congress of the complete and satisfactory homestead measure which has already passed the house.

14. That the Republican Party is opposed to any change in our naturalization laws or any state legislation by which the rights of citizenship hitherto accorded to emigrants from foreign lands shall be abridged or impaired.

15. That appropriations by Congress for river and harbor improvements of a national character . . . are . . . justified.

16. That a railroad to the Pacific Ocean is imperatively demanded by the interests of the whole country; that the federal government ought to render immediate and efficient aid in its construction.[6]

The South, laden with debts and dependent upon cotton, desiring low prices on food and manufactured goods and hence no tariffs, seemed to face economic destruction if the Republican Party was triumphant in 1860. To secure the votes in the Northwest, the key to the election, the Republicans nominated Abraham Lincoln of Illinois. The agrarian planks of the platform, especially the homestead plank, secured Republican victory in Illinois and perhaps in the rest of the Northwest.[7] The support of the Republican Party by the German and Scandinavian elements of this section was an important factor.[8]

The agrarian West saw the Republican victory from its own distinct point of view. Lincoln held to an economic philosophy which would not have been appreciated at a later date by industrial capitalists.[9] Honest Abe, rail-splitting frontiersman, was true to the spirit of the West; he was interested above all in the maintenance of popular institutions.

[6] Commager, *Documents of American History*, Doc. 192. By permission of F. S. Crofts and Co.
[7] Dodd, *loc. cit.*, p. 787.   [8] Fite, *loc. cit.*, pp. 250, 262.
[9] Richardson, *Messages and Papers of the Presidents*, Vol. VI, p. 57.

He was dismayed at the view that capital was not only equal, but actually superior to labor in the functioning of government. "Capital," he declared in his first annual message, "is only the fruit of labor, and could never have existed if labor had not first existed. Labor is the superior of capital and deserves much higher consideration." His plea was voiced by the great mass of liberal-minded men in both the North and the South. A western viewpoint brought to his mind a picture of "Men with their families—wives, sons, and daughters—[who] work for themselves on their farms, in their houses, and in their shops, taking the whole product to themselves . . . asking no favors of capital on the one hand nor of hired laborers or slaves on the other. . . . The prudent, penniless beginner in the world labors for wages awhile, saves a surplus with which to buy tools or land for himself . . . and at length hires another new beginner to help him. This is the just and generous and prosperous system which opens the way to all. . . . No men living are more worthy to be trusted than those who toil up from poverty. . . . Let them beware of surrendering a political power which they already possess, and which if surrendered will surely be used to close the door of advancement . . . and to fix new disabilities and burdens upon them till all of liberty shall be lost."[10]

Lincoln, like most representatives of the West, viewed the economic situation of his time in the light of the vast areas of unoccupied, fertile lands; he pointed with pride to the fact that after seventy years the national census of 1860 indicated a population eight times that of the Republic in the beginning. He predicted for the near future a population of two hundred and fifty millions. "The struggle of today," he declared, "is not altogether for today; it is for the vast future also." But it was quite impossible to realize, at this time when there was a seeming abundance of good land and a dearth of population, what the economic significance of that struggle for a "vast future" might be in a later day when the country still possessed but half of two hundred and fifty millions. It did not take long for the Republican Party to cover this philosophy with a polished mahogany of silence. Originally the party of Jefferson and of democratic principles, it underwent a profound change. The South in seeking and forcing the issue of Civil War, hastened that change. If the cheap land of the American West constituted the key to opportunity for the common man of America, then the Civil War

[10] *ibid.*, pp. 57-8.

period witnessed the high point of that opportunity. After that conflict was over it was clear that the frontier was passing.

A month before his inauguration, Lincoln declared, "In regard to the homestead bill, . . . I am in favor of settling the wild lands into small parcels so that every poor man may have a home."[11] But only after the southern states had seceded was there a majority in both houses favorable to the Republican program. Even then, the trying problems accompanying the outbreak of the war prevented any immediate fulfillment of the program. Not until early in 1862 was there any concerted effort to deal with problems other than those of the war. Almost coincident with the drive of the emancipationists there arose a demand to carry out in full the platform which, Greeley reminded Congress, was still up-to-date.[12] In spite of the war-prosperity and drain of man power into the army, there was still a surplus population in eastern cities. Greeley urged people to go West. "Young men! Poor men! Widows! Resolve to have a home of your own! If you are able to buy and pay for one in the East, very well; if not, make one in the broad and fertile West!"[13]

Finally on February 28, the homestead bill, which was an almost exact replica of Grow's House bill of 1859, passed the House. On May 6, it passed the Senate by vote of 33 to 7. Knowing that its progress henceforth would not be impeded, Greeley, in the columns of his *Tribune* congratulated the "country on the consummation of one of the most beneficent and vital reforms ever attempted in any age or clime—a reform calculated to diminish sensibly the number of paupers and idlers and increase the proportion of working, independent, self-subsisting farmers in the land evermore. Its blessings will be felt more and more . . . widely for the next twenty years. . . . The clouds that have darkened our national prospects are breaking away, and the sunshine of peace, prosperity and progress, will ere long irradiate the land. Let us rejoice in and gather strength from the prospect."[14]

On May 20, 1862, President Lincoln signed this act, thus extending to the same classes of persons included in the Preemption Act of 1841, the right to a homestead, not exceeding 160 acres, on the surveyed pub-

---

[11] February 1, 1861, Nicolay and Hay, *Compiled Works of Abraham Lincoln*, Vol. I, p. 637.
[12] *New York Daily Tribune*, March 21, 1862. [13] *ibid.*, June 6, 1862.
[14] *New York Semi-Weekly Tribune*, May 9, 1862.

lic domain.[15] Title to the homestead could be acquired by continuous residence, improvement of five years, and the payment of a fee of $34 on the Pacific Coast and $26 in the other states. After six months' actual residence and suitable improvement, the claimant might commute his homestead entry into full title simply by the payment of $1.25 per acre. Any improvement to the extent of an acre or more entitled the claimant to commutation.[16] No lands acquired under the act could in the future become liable to the satisfaction of any debt or debts contracted prior to the issuing of the patent. An affidavit was required of the applicant swearing that he or she was the head of a family or twenty-one years of age, had not borne arms against the United States or given comfort or aid to its enemies, and that such application was "for his or her exclusive use and benefit," and that said entry was "for the purpose of actual settlement and cultivation, and not, either directly or indirectly, for the use or benefit of any other person or persons whomsoever."

Within a fortnight the rest of the Republican program was also on the statute books. The secession of the southern states made possible the selection of a northern route for the Pacific Railroad. By Act of July 1, 1862, Congress incorporated the Union Pacific Railroad Company and authorized it to construct, maintain and enjoy said railroad and telegraph lines. To aid in this construction the act granted a right-of-way of two hundred feet on each side, grounds for stations, buildings, etc., and every alternate section of land, designated by odd sections, per mile on each side and within the limits of ten miles on each side.[17] Mineral lands were exempted from the operation of the grant, but timber land was specifically allowed in the selection. Similar grants were extended to the Leavenworth, Pawnee, and Western Railroad of Kansas and to the Central Pacific of California. Bonds to the extent of $16,000 to every mile for each section of every forty miles (treble this amount through the mountains) were to be issued by the Treasury Department, on the understanding that they would be repaid in thirty years, and that until that time they would constitute first mortgage on the whole line of the railroad. The Act of 1862 was amended in 1864 to provide for doubling the grant of 1862, and changing the mortgage from a first to a second on the railroad property.[18] The munificence of the federal government

[15] *Statutes at Large,* Vol. XII, pp. 392ff.
[16] *Land Commissioners' Letters,* Preemption Division G, Vol. LIX (1865), p. 19.
[17] *Statutes at Large,* Vol. XII, pp. 489ff.   [18] *ibid.,* Vol. XIII, p. 356.

is clear when it is understood that in these two acts, some 40,000,000 acres of land were granted, and over $60,000,000 were lent.

On July 2, 1864, President Lincoln signed the Morrill Act, which granted to each state not in rebellion an amount of land equal to 30,000 acres for each senator and representative in Congress, according to the apportionment of 1860, for the purpose of endowing at least one college in each state "where the leading subject . . . without excluding other scientific and classical studies, and including military tactics," should be "to teach such branches of learning as are related to agriculture and mechanic arts . . . in order to promote the liberal and practical education of the industrial classes in the several pursuits and professions in life."[19] In those states in which there were no public lands, scrip was to be issued at the rate of $1.25 per acre. No mineral lands were to be selected. This act gave a tremendous impetus to the establishment of state universities. Altogether, under this act, some 13,000,000 acres were given to the states.

There was considerable western opposition to this measure, for obviously the eastern states would benefit more than the western ones. An open letter to the New York *Tribune,* protested, above the signature "Free West," that the scheme was "in plain words, a nefarious outrage on the West. If the rich New England States, New York, and Pennsylvania, and others" were "suffering for the want of agricultural colleges let them build them immediately and pay for them themselves; for Kansas, Nebraska, Minnesota, Iowa and Wisconsin will hardly rest patiently and be fleeced of their only source of wealth and power. . . . The passage of the Homestead Bill was a grand thing for the new states; but what good will it do them if the eastern states . . . loot the West of the broad domain thus granted to actual settlers?" To this western attack Greeley replied that it was "mean" for the West to quibble over a few million acres of land granted to the old states, when Congress had passed so munificent a measure as the Homestead Act, the benefits of which would all redound to the West.[20] This does not sound like the Greeleyism of the 'forties and 'fifties!

In the *Montreal Herald* appeared one of the greatest eulogies on the American Homestead Act. This editorial condemned Canadian policy

[19] *ibid.,* Vol. XII, p. 503.   [20] *New York Daily Tribune,* May 27, 1862.

as one which discussed and hesitated about securing a population while the American Congress, on the other hand, "adopted the most comprehensive policy for the encouragement of immigration which has perhaps ever been devised. . . . Partial offers of such gifts have often been made before, but we doubt whether any endowment on so magnificent a scale has ever been conferred on the moneyless sons of labor, not of one country, but of the civilized world. . . . The Homestead law" this editor declared "is the complement of the prohibition of slavery in the Territories, or rather perhaps, one is the complement of the other. . . . The most effective way to shut out slavery is to people the new lands, where it might otherwise seek to extend itself, with men whose position places them in natural antagonism to the plantation system. . . . The civil transactions of the last few months at Washington will make their impression upon ages to come, when the battles on the Potomac and Tennessee will be regarded as mere incidents in history."[21]

The Homestead Act has been heralded as the greatest democratic measure of all history. It marked the climax of the democratic crusade begun in the 'twenties and 'thirties by the West, reinforced in the 'forties by the Land Reformers and labor interests and in the 'fifties by the rising industrial prophets of the East. In truth, the Homestead Act was but the proclamation of a promise that was yet to be fulfilled. The enactment of law is one thing; the operation of that law is another. In the face of the fact that the government had already begun the practice of lavishly bestowing great tracts of land upon states and corporations, many thoughtful observers were beginning to wonder whether the settler would be able to realize upon the Act of 1862. If good, cheap and easily accessible land became scarce, could the settler possibly continue to be the pioneer, the outstanding force, of American democracy? Could it be that the frontier of America—the frontier of opportunity in cheap land—was passing? Unless the government carefully guarded the rest of the domain, the Homestead Act of 1862, it was clear, might have to be regarded not as the loadstone of a new democratic age, but as the capstone of a vanished era.

During the Civil War period all of the benefits accruing from the bestowal of public land bounties in any form were denied to the states

---

[21] Quoted in *ibid.*, May 26, 1862.

in rebellion against the United States. Thus the South received no grants of land for railroad construction, or for the endowing of agricultural colleges, nor any of the benefits accruing from the Homestead Act. But this is only half the story. The most bitter attack upon the southern economic system, aside from the emancipation of the slaves, was the attempt to confiscate the great landed estates and vast tracts of land granted by the federal government to the southern states for railroads and public works. Many northern Congressmen thought no more suitable form of punishment could be devised. Moreover, this plan would kill two birds with one stone, since confiscated lands returned to the public domain could be carved into homesteads and distributed to the faithful soldiers and the loyal landless poor. The dream of the freedman for "forty acres and a mule" might be fulfilled. To many staunch Republicans this seemed an ideal way of peopling the South with loyal party members who would secure the life of that party for years to come.

This movement to confiscate southern lands for homestead purposes was initiated, it appears, by the Secretary of the Interior in his report to Congress on November 29, 1862.[22] A large proportion of the public lands of Texas, said the Secretary, remain unsold, and were "the proper subject of confiscation." Since these lands belonged to the people of Texas, and could not be construed as coming under the acts of Congress for the suppression of the rebellion, he recommended passage of a special act declaring these lands forfeited to the United States and placing them under the operation of the homestead laws. Consequently, numerous bills aimed at confiscation were introduced into Congress, though it was not until 1864 that one received serious attention.

This particular bill, introduced by Representative George W. Julian of Indiana, chairman of the House Committee on Public Lands, provided for the forfeiting of all lands in insurgent districts, such lands to be distributed to soldiers in 80-acre tracts while other loyal persons, without regard for race or color, could procure half that amount.[23] Julian asserted that if homesteading had been adopted in 1832, as suggested by President Jackson, the slavery institution would have died a natural death. This measure, he contended, was necessary inasmuch as the Homestead Law of 1862 was already being threatened by lavish

[22] 37 Cong. 3 Sess., *S. Ex. Doc.*, Vol. I, p. 4.
[23] *Congressional Globe*, 38 Cong. 1 Sess., p. 874.

grants of land to railroads, agricultural colleges, female normal schools, and soldier educational purposes. The war, he said, had been termed a "slaveholders' rebellion," but it was likewise a "landholders' rebellion." The chief owners of slaves had been the principal owners of land; in fact, about five-sixths of the southern lands were owned by slaveholders who constituted only one-fifth of the population. The bill would thus break up land monopoly in the South.

He condemned the honest refusal of President Lincoln to permit the confiscation of the fee simple of the rebel states as the "saddest and grandest mistake of his life." It was a choice, he declared, between two courses: the lands must either be placed in the jurisdiction of the government in trust for the people, or it would fall into the hands of speculators. Julian showed that under the Swamp Lands Acts of 1849 and 1850, some thirty million acres of the best lands in America were granted to the states of Alabama, Florida, Louisiana, Mississippi and Arkansas. Most of these lands, he declared, had been bought up at from 10 to 80 cents an acre by men who had become the most conspicuous rebels. In fact, his bill would provide for the confiscation of the swollen estates of such men as Robert Toombs of Georgia, Jacob Thompson, a former member of Buchanan's cabinet, Jefferson Davis, John Sliddell and Howell Cobb.[24]

Mr. Fernando Wood of New York condemned this policy.[25] He deplored pursuance of the watchword, "booty and beauty," in public lands policy. This measure, he declared, would arouse the darkest passions in order to accomplish a personal, selfish, avaricious, and partisan object. The Negro, in Mr. Wood's opinion, did not need to be rescued from his southern master, but from "the partisan designs and mistaken philanthropy of the North." He charged Julian with trying to put across a bill under the patriotic appeal for the soldier, when his real appeal was for the Negro.

The confiscation bill passed the House, May 12, 1864, by the close vote of 75 to 64.[26] Before the Senate took up the bill, however, confiscation was stopped short by President Lincoln's attorney general, who ordered that all property which had been seized by federal authorities should be restored to its rightful owners.[27] That confiscation had been a serious factor in prolonging the war and was dreaded in the South can be

[24] *ibid.*, p. 2,249.
[25] *ibid.*, pp. 2,233-4.
[26] *ibid.*, p. 2,253.
[27] Edward McPherson, *History of the Rebellion.* p. 148.

gathered from the fact that the Confederate Congress in 1865 made its last appeal to the people of the South on this subject. "Our absolute surrender and submission to the will of the conqueror," the appeal warned, "are the only conditions vouchsafed by our arrogant foe. . . . Not only would property and estates of the vanquished 'rebels' be confiscated, but they would be divided and distributed among our African bondsmen. . . . Failure will compel us to drink the cup of humiliation even to the bitter dregs of having our history written by New England historians."[28]

At the end of the war, a new phase of congressional reconstruction arose with the problem of how to dispose of the remaining public lands in the South. A bill introduced by Mr. John H. Rice of Maine on January 8, 1866, provided that the lands in the southern public-land states were to be disposed of solely through homesteading.[29] The grants were to be 80 acres in extent, only half the amount allowed under the Homestead Act of 1862. Furthermore, no discrimination was to be made as to race or color, and instead of the customary fee of ten dollars charged by the registers at the time of filing, a reduction to half that amount was made.

The Land Commissioner explained in a detailed statistical report to Congress the reason for the departures from the regular homestead policy.[30] In the southern public-land states of Alabama, Mississippi, Louisiana, Arkansas, and Florida there remained a very limited amount of land, a little over forty-six million acres, for distribution among the homeless population. Over fifty-two million acres of agricultural lands were being held vacant by these states, by corporations, and by individuals not engaged in agricultural pursuits. This meant then that one-tenth of the arable land was being held in an unimproved state, though more than two-thirds of the population in this strictly agricultural region were landless. Unless restricted to homestead entries, the rest of the land would also fall into the hands of speculators who would take it up, with governmental scrip and warrants, for 60 or 70 cents an acre.

This measure was necessary, explained Julian of Indiana, to supply homesteads to the poor whites and to the Negroes,[31] and he insisted that

28 Rhodes, *History of the United States,* Vol. V, p. 81, citing *Appleton's Annual Encyclopedia,* 1865, p. 195.
29 *Cong. Globe,* 39 Cong. 1 Sess., p. 135.
30 On February 5, 1866, *ibid.,* p. 715.   31 *ibid.,* p. 716.

it was entirely consistent with and supplementary to the Freedmen's Bureau Act which had just passed Congress.[32] Rice of Maine predicted a rosy future for the South as a result of the passage of the bill.[33] He believed that although the measure was not exactly class legislation, nevertheless, more blacks than whites would be able to avail themselves of its privileges since many of the latter would be excluded from its benefits for having aided the rebel cause.

The bill passed the House, 112 to 24.[34] The Senate Committee on Public Lands added an amendment providing that all who would take an oath of future allegiance to the United States, even though they had borne arms against the Union, could avail themselves of the act. But the Senate changed this amendment to deny the benefits of the act to those who had borne arms, until January 1, 1867. After some readjustments in conference, the bill was agreed to by both houses, and signed by the President on June 21, 1866.[35] In its final form it simply extended the Act of 1862 to the public-land states late in rebellion. Ten years later when most of the public lands had been disposed of, it was repealed.[36]

In 1867, the subject of confiscation was again brought forward, but in a form somewhat different from that of 1864. Representative Julian of Indiana introduced a measure providing for the forfeiture of all public lands that had been given by the federal government to the states of Alabama, Mississippi, Louisiana, and Florida in aid of railroad construction.[37] This Congressman insisted that such forfeiture was necessary, inasmuch as two-thirds of the land opened up under the Act of 1866 was unfit for cultivation.[38] The measure passed the House by vote of 87 to 58 on February 5, 1868, but before it came up in the Senate that body was absorbed in the all-important business of impeaching President Johnson. Confiscation was not again seriously discussed in Congress. Viewed in historical perspective, confiscation was only the beginning of the demand for railroad land-grant forfeiture. Because they had failed to complete construction in the specified time, the southern railroads were already on the defensive. The attack on these railroads, however, was but a part of the general attack on all railroads and as such will be discussed in due course.

[32] Rhodes, *History of the United States*, Vol. V, pp. 598-601.
[33] *Cong. Globe*, 39 Cong. 1 Sess., p. 717.
[35] *Statutes at Large*, Vol. XIV, p. 66.
[37] *Cong. Globe*, 40 Cong. 2 Sess., p. 95.
[34] *ibid.*, p. 748.
[36] *ibid.*, p. 73.
[38] *ibid.*, p. 310.

After the Civil War there was much apprehension lest the homestead law be undermined by wholesale issuing of bounties and land subsidies of various hues and colors. The experience with Mexican War land-bounty legislation was not reassuring. Two groups championed such legislation: soldiers and land speculators. It requires little imagination to picture "a friend of the common people and the gallant defenders of the flag" making a plea for the bounty law, while a horde of speculators wait outside the doors of Congress to reward them with warrants. This had happened in the past.[39]

A homestead bill which had passed the Senate with little discussion on January 14, 1864, precipitated in the House the first important clash between military land-bounty and homestead interests. This bill provided that the soldier who had served a minimum of two years should be able to secure a homestead with only one year's residence. William Holman of Indiana, favoring an outright bounty, asked why there should be any opposition at all. "Congress is all the time," he said, "granting vast bodies of land to railroad corporations, great and overgrown monopolies, and these go to the benefit of speculators, and generally to nobody else."[40] Julian of Indiana wanted the one-year residence clause retained to keep it primarily a homestead measure. It passed in this form, and was signed by President Lincoln, March 21, 1864.[41]

On December 20, that year, a resolution was introduced in the House of Representatives inquiring into the expediency of setting apart a portion of the public lands for the benefit of such soldiers as were disabled during the war, but it failed to come to vote.[42]

The return of peace brought increased pressure upon Congress to discriminate in favor of the soldier in formulating public lands legislation. Every party platform promised him some sort of reward.[43] Nothing substantial, however, was done until the Act of July 15, 1870, was passed.[44] Under its terms, a man who had served a minimum of ninety days in the military or naval forces of the United States was enabled to enter 160 acres of double premium reserved public lands along the railroads—the most-prized land in America—or anywhere in the public domain.

[39] See speeches in Congress. *Cong. Globe*, 41 Cong. 3 Sess., p. 728; 42 Cong. 3 Sess., p. 131; Hibbard, *History of the Public Land Policies*, pp. 126-9.
[40] *Cong. Globe*, 38 Cong. 1 Sess., pp. 1,189-90.
[41] *Statutes at Large*, Vol. XIII, p. 35.   [42] *Cong. Globe*, 38 Cong. 2 Sess., p. 79
[43] Stanwood, *A History of the Presidential Elections*, pp. 301, 302, 320, 324.
[44] *Statutes at Large*, Vol. XVI, p. 320.

Even with the Acts of 1864 and 1870, the friends of liberal land grants to soldiers were not yet satisfied. As might have been expected, the soldier-homestead idea finally devolved into an out and out land-bounty proposal. Mr. William Stoughton of Michigan introduced a bill in 1871 in the House which proposed some radical departures from the homestead law. For instance, the soldier would not be required to begin settlement and improvement immediately after selecting his land, but could wait twelve months if he so desired. Besides, his rights in the bounty were to be assignable.[45]

The chairman of the Committee on Public Lands, Julian, opposed this bill, declaring: "The government is false in its trust, and makes itself an enemy of the people, when it sanctions or permits the monopoly of great bodies of the public domain, which its own landless citizens need for homesteads and are anxious to make tributary to the public domain." He asserted that 90 per cent of the seventy-three million acres of land thus far appropriated under military bounty laws had passed into the hands of speculators. According to the Secretary of War, it was necessary to provide for over two million men, not counting the heirs of those who had died, and this would require over three hundred and sixty million acres of land, or an area eleven times as great as that of the State of Ohio.[46] Since the lands could be had for the asking, it was assumed that nearly all would avail themselves of the privilege. Julian prophesied that should only half do so, it would require every acre that the government could survey for the next twenty-nine years. The result would be a nullification of the Homestead Act and the cessation of the sale of the public lands. If the soldier really needed land, did not the terms of the Homestead Act provide for his need?[47] He concluded by saying: "No legislation that I know of connected with the public domain has been so mischievous, not to say disastrous to the country, . . . [as] this whole system of military land warrants of which the act of 1850 is perhaps the worst."[48]

Another member of the House, Charles Van Wyck of New York, was of the opinion that few soldiers would settle the lands themselves, but would receive a "mere pittance" from the brokers for their war-

[45] *Cong. Globe,* 41 Cong. 3 Sess., p. 583.
[46] For an excellent discussion opposing this legislation see, "Bounty Land and Military Service," *The Republic,* Vol. I (1873), pp. 31-3.
[47] *Cong. Globe,* 41 Cong. 3 Sess., pp. 728-33.
[48] *ibid.,* pp. 756-7.

rants.[49] But friends of the measure argued that the soldier who had withstood the attack of the rebel foe, would be able to "protect his own interests against the body of sharpers and plunderers" who were "swarming every avenue of the government." John B. Hawley of Illinois averred that the soldiers really did not want land bounties, that their principal journal, the *Grand Army Journal,* had declared in favor of cash bounties.[50] Besides, this representative observed, there was a constant struggle in the country between capital and labor, and the result was that the "rich became richer and the poor poorer." It is the duty of the government, said Hawley, to keep open the avenue whereby a man of limited means can procure a tract of good land and thus achieve independence.[51]

In spite of this opposition, however, the bill passed the House by the large majority of 186 to 2.[52] But the Senate refused to consider the measure. In 1872 it again passed the House, this time by vote of 118 to 54.[53] Again the Senate refused to consider the land-bounty bill. To meet the rising demand, however, the Senate that same year did consider a bill which retained the principles of the homestead law, eliminated the "assignable rights" clause, allowed a soldier six months instead of a year to begin his residence on his tract, and permitted the soldier's term of service to be deducted up to four years from the residence requirement.[54] In this form the measure passed both Senate and House, and was signed on April 4, 1872.[55] Thus the Homestead Act was saved from its gravest peril—a universal military land-bounty. The victory, however, was not clear cut, for under the legislation passed great abuses which would endanger the settlers' rights could still arise.

49 *ibid.,* p. 758.
51 *Cong. Globe,* 41 Cong. 3 Sess., pp. 854-5.
53 *ibid.,* 42 Cong. 3 Sess., p. 167.
55 *Statutes at Large,* Vol. XVIII, pp. 49-50.
50 Issue of December 31, 1870.
52 *ibid.,* p. 861.
54 *ibid.,* 42 Cong. 2 Sess., p. 1,884.

CHAPTER XIV

THE DOMAIN THROWN WIDE-OPEN

THE homesteading movement had received great impetus from the fact that free land would promote the settlement of the plains.[1] Before 1862, the region of the High Plains had been looked upon as the Great American Desert; in fact, in the latter 'fifties camels were unsuccessfully introduced into the region in an attempt to solve the transportation problem. Nevertheless, it was hoped that, with the coming of the railroad the problem of penetration and settlement could be solved, and that the region would no longer serve as a barrier between the Mississippi Valley and the Pacific West. But, just about the time the railroads reached the Plains, the cattle range industry began to push up from Texas to meet the railroads. Instead of bringing about the immediate settlement of the High Plains, the railroad served to inaugurate a conflict between the "nester" who desired to settle the country and plow it up into farms, and the cattle man who preferred that the country remain unsettled and that an open and free range be maintained throughout the whole region between Texas and Canada. The nester and the cowboy, however, were not the only participants in this struggle for the High Plains, for the Indian too had a great deal at stake, inasmuch as a large portion of the region had been given over permanently to the red men.

Whether much of the High Plains country would have been settled as soon as it was without the Homestead Act, or whether railroad and speculative interests would have brought about such settlement regardless of what the government did is an interesting problem. In any case one must not underrate the determination of the Republican Party to settle the vacant lands in the West. This determination meant nothing less than an agreement to develop and exploit the remaining resources of the public domain. The industrial-agricultural alliance would hold together as long as that main objective was pursued, notwithstanding the fact that some division was to arise between the East and the West as to what agency—the settler or the corporation—should bring about

[1] The best account of this subject is to be found in Walter P. Webb, *The Great Plains* (New York, 1931), Chap. IX.

the settlement. In pursuit of the objective to settle the arid country, no question arose as to whether the region was more or less adaptable to some industry other than farming. The government thus far had not classified any of its lands, not even forest or mineral lands. It had under consideration various plans for settling the country with free institutions as fast as possible in order to build up an economic barrier against the southern economic system. The public lands were thus thrown wide open to settlement, exploitation, or speculation. In the mad scramble that ensued much legislation was passed that would not have been passed had a more careful survey and classification of the lands been made.

The wisdom of two pieces of legislation, the Timber Culture Act of 1873 and the Desert Land Act of 1877, is open to question. The first of these acts aimed at speeding up the process of settling the arid region of the High Plains. Some of the country was good farming land, but even so it constituted the most uninviting of all frontier regions. Here was pioneering at its worst—the difficulties involved in selecting land, building a home, finding fuel, drilling for water, fighting fierce winds, prairie fires, and grasshoppers were all but insurmountable. Brought into this region by high-pressure advertising of the government and of the railroads, the frontiersmen began the grinding process of harnessing nature—nature in its rawest form.

If the Homestead Act of 1862 was not sufficient encouragement, the government stood ready to furnish aid. In the early 'seventies the Commissioner of the General Land Office recommended that Congress enact legislation to encourage the planting of trees on the prairie lands. In 1872 he suggested inserting such a provision as an amendment of the Homestead Law.[2] Finally on March 3, 1873, Congress passed "an act to encourage the growth of timber on the western prairies"—commonly known as the Timber Culture Act.[3] Under this law any person who would protect and keep in healthy growing condition for ten years, forty acres of timber, the trees to be planted not more than twelve feet apart, would receive title to the quarter section of which the forty acres was a part. Under this act also, homesteaders who had been on their lands for three years and had had one acre of trees under cultivation for the last two years of that time should be given patents. An amendatory

[2] Report of the Land Commissioner, 1872, p. 69.
[3] *Statutes at Large*, Vol. XVII, p. 605.

act of June 14, 1878, reduced the required acreage in trees from forty to ten, and prescribed as the number of trees per acre, 2,700 at the time of planting and 675 when the patent should be granted. Congress evidently believed that if the region could be supplied with timber a desirable class of citizens would settle it.[4]

Convinced that there was a growing conflict between the settlers and the cattle men in the High Plains region, the Land Commissioner recommended that the lands of this area be offered at the earliest moment for cash purchase, and that "thereafter the remaining unsold land be subject to private entry at $1.25 per acre."[5] The past policy of settling this region under the preemption and homestead laws had tended to restrict its development. President Grant in his annual message to Congress in December 1875, recommended the appointment of a commission to visit the West and make suggestions concerning the disposition of the government land.

In response to the recommendations of the President, the Secretary of the Interior, and the Commissioner of the General Land Office, and to the pressure of numerous other influences, Congress enacted the Desert Land Act of March 3, 1877,[6] to apply especially to the states and territories of California, Oregon, Nevada, Washington, Idaho, Montana, Utah, Wyoming, Arizona, New Mexico, and Dakota. It provided as follows:

1. A settler might purchase one section (640 acres) of land if he would irrigate it within three years after filing.

2. He must pay 25 cents per acre at the district land office at the time of filing his application.

3. On proof of final compliance with the law and the payment of one dollar for each additional acre, which could be done any time within three years after filing, the settler would be given title to the tract.

4. Only one entry could be made per person.

5. No assignments of rights would be allowed.

6. The applicant must be a citizen, or have declared his intention of becoming one.

President Hayes apparently had doubts of the advisability of the new law. In his annual message of December 3, 1877, he declared: "These

[4] George W. Kingsbury, *History of Dakota Territory* (2 vols., Chicago, 1915), Vol. I, pp. 77-8.
[5] Report of the Land Commissioner, 1875, pp. 7-9.
[6] *Statutes at Large,* Vol. XIX, p. 377.

lands [west of the hundredth meridian] are practically unsaleable under existing laws, and the suggestion is worthy of consideration that a system of leasehold tenure would make them a source of profit to the United States, while at the same time legalizing the business of cattle raising which is at present carried upon them."[7] In light of the conditions today in the High Plains region, President Hayes' suggestion was an enlightened one, but one which unfortunately, was not heeded.

The gold rushes to the Pacific Coast and Rocky Mountain regions, it will be recalled, prevented the federal government from establishing any policy at all regarding the mineral lands in those regions. But the miners themselves soon organized into associations and began the regulation of their claims, drawing up laws and passing upon cases involving contested claims. "Possessory rights" were so well recognized that their legality went unquestioned; claims were sold not only in the land districts but in the East as well. In time, the territorial or state legislatures and courts accepted the local regulations, passing statutes to sustain their legality. By 1866, there were in the West five hundred organized local districts as well as another five hundred small communities, all operating under local rules and regulations.[8] Chief Justice Chase, in the case of Sparrow vs. Strong which was tried before the Supreme Court in December 1865, commented on this unique situation. "A special kind of law," he declared, "a sort of common law of the miners, the offspring of a nation's irrepressible march . . . has sprung up on the Pacific Coast, and presents in the value of a 'Mining Right' a novel and peculiar question for this court."

The mining West resented all attempts on the part of government, state or federal, to enact any regulatory legislation other than what had already evolved. Regarding the proposal that the federal government tax the quartz ledges in Idaho Territory, a local observer put his finger on the problem, when he observed that "the snug little sum of about two millions of dollars" would have to be "handed in annually from these districts alone; that is, provided it can be collected."[9] While the industry was still mainly confined to placer mining, nevertheless, the

[7] Richardson, *Messages and Papers of the Presidents*, Vol. VII, p. 476.

[8] C. H. Shinn, "Land Laws of the Mining Districts," *Johns Hopkins University Studies*, 2nd Series (1884), pp. 9-11. For a thorough study of a particular region, consult Thomas M. Marshall, "The Miners Laws of Colorado," *American Historical Review*, Vol. XXV, pp. 426-40.

[9] Letters from Owyhee quoted in John Mullan, *Miners' and Travelers' Guide* (New York, 1865), p. 124.

quartz-ledge business was already developing. By 1864, several companies with considerable capital had been formed in New York and London.[10] The governor of Idaho in the same year, called the attention of the territorial legislature "to the [need for] better protection of that hardy class of our population to whom danger is not a sentiment . . . who, amid trackless wastes . . . pursue their enterprises with no capital but their rough lands, with no defender but their revolvers; who, without the knowledge of books, have given the world its choicest geological, geographical, and agricultural information, in tracing ledges, traversing rivers, and exploring valleys, which, but for them, would still have remained an unknown land beyond the Rocky Mountains. . . . Under no circumstances should they lose all the benefits resulting from their regional discoveries, legislation should take the place of litigation and proper amendments be made which would secure to them all their hard-earned rights and privileges."[11]

The territorial law in Montana Territory, which was similar to that in other territories, required $100 worth of work done on the claim within six months after it was recorded.[12] The purpose of this regulation was undoubtedly to prevent individuals from staking out and holding large areas without developing them. The older mining regions were already honeycombed with organized companies. In 1864, the "Comstock Lode" of Nevada was owned by one hundred different companies, whose claims ranged from twenty-five to two thousand feet, and were highly valued.[13] The liberal laws in force in Colorado gave to the fortunate discoverer of a quartz vein two hundred feet of the same and to all others who applied, one hundred feet not already claimed. These claims were recorded in the clerk's office of that mining district, and by such process all rights were secured and respected.[14]

While various bills providing for sale, leasing, and taxing of mineral lands were up before Congress during the Civil War period, there was as yet no strong desire to prevent the destruction of freedom and individualism by large corporations. Consequently, Congress approved with but little discussion on July 26, 1866, a law which made the mineral lands of the public domain, both surveyed and unsurveyed, "free and

---

[10] *The Washoe Star*, November 12, 1864, in *ibid.*, p. 126.

[11] Governor Lyon's message in *ibid.*, p. 131.

[12] Edward G. Hall, *Emigrants', Settlers', and Travelers' Guide and Hand Book* (New York, 1864), p. 57.

[13] *ibid.*, p. 64.   [14] *ibid.*, p. 37.

open to exploration and occupation by all citizens of the United States, and those declaring their intention to become citizens, subject to" regulations prescribed by law, and "subject also to the local customs or rules of miners in the several mining districts, so far as the same" were not "in conflict with the laws of the United States."[15]

This laissez-faire policy contrasted sharply with advice of the Secretary of the Interior that the mineral land should be sold and thus be placed under the guardianship of private owners, for only in that manner could "the great forests of timber, the growth of centuries, and of vast value to the nation be effectually preserved from waste."[16]

The noted geologist, Rossiter Raymond, in his volume, *Mineral Resources of the States and Territories of the Rocky Mountains,* published in 1869, recommended the extension of the public surveys over the public domain of this region and "the reduction of its vast area to order and law." This would dispel "the mischievous feeling that mining is half grab and half gamble."[17] Consequently, Congress passed an act providing for the survey and sale of placer mining lands at $2.50 per acre.[18] And by a still later act mineral lands were constituted a distinctive class subject to special conditions of sale and special schedule of prices. Lode claims were to sell for $5 an acre.[19] The next year iron lands became exempt from the operation of this act and were put on the same basis as nonmineral lands, that is, sale at auction for not less than $1.25 an acre.[20] A special act approved on March 3, 1873, provided for disposal of coal lands by ordinary private entry or by preference right based on priority of possession and improvement. Under this latter act, tracts were limited to 160 acres for individuals and 320 acres for associations; the sale price was $10 per acre if more than fifteen miles from a completed railroad, and $20 if within that distance.

The thirteenth plank of the Republican platform of 1860, it will be recalled, consisted of a "protest against any sale or alienation to others

---

[15] *Statutes at Large,* Vol. XIV, p. 86.

[16] Report of the Secretary of the Interior, 1865, 39 Cong. 1 Sess., *H. Ex. Doc.* Vol. I, Introduction, p. 3. For debates on George W. Julian's bill providing for cash sale according to actual value and protection against speculators, see *Congressional Globe,* 38 Cong. 2 Sess., pp. 684-7.

[17] Quoted in Rickard, *History of American Mining,* p. 108. By permission of the McGraw-Hill Book Co.

[18] July 9, 1870, *Statutes at Large,* Vol. XVI, p. 217.

[19] May 10, 1872, *ibid.,* Vol. XVII, p. 91. For regulation and explanation of lode and placer legislation consult Donaldson, *The Public Domain,* pp. 986-1,007.

[20] February 1873, *Statutes at Large,* Vol. XVII, p. 465.

of the Public Lands held by actual settlers." In the light of the historical background of this plank, there can be little doubt that the Republican Party solemnly pledged itself, at the close of a decade of excessive land speculation—during which Congress had granted exactly 27,876,772 acres of land to western railroad corporations—to reserve the remaining public lands for the common man of America.[21] Contrasting even more sharply with this pronouncement of 1860 is the fact that during President Lincoln's administration 74,395,801 acres of land were granted either directly or indirectly to western railroads. In President Johnson's administration grants included 34,001,297 acres, and in President Grant's administration, 19,231,121 acres. These grants had all taken place before many actual settlers had the opportunity of selecting homesteads under the Act of 1862.

The land granted to western railroads in the 'fifties, together with the grants of the 'sixties and 'seventies, totalled around 180,000,000 acres, an area larger than the whole of the Old Northwest. Thomas Donaldson, an authority on this subject, estimated in 1884 that if the lands embraced in the grants up to June 30, 1880, were all available, and that if the corporations, state and national, built their roads and complied with the laws, it would take 215,000,000 acres of land to satisfy the requirements. The estimate of the General Land Office, in 1878, was 187,000,000 acres. Donaldson believed, however, that justifiable forfeitures would reduce this amount to 154,000,000 acres.[22] Nevertheless, the Land Commissioner reported in 1923 that the whole amount of land granted to states and corporations for railroad purposes from 1850 to 1923 (less the forfeitures) amounted to only 91,239,389 acres directly to corporations and 37,789,169 directly to states, an aggregate of but 129,028,559 acres.[23] A synopsis of these grants as tabulated by Professor Hibbard from this report of 1923 is as follows:

GRANTS TO STATES AND CORPORATIONS FOR RAILROAD PURPOSES—1850 TO
JUNE 30, 1923

State Grants

Illinois	2,595,133.00 acres
Mississippi	1,075,345.12
Alabama	2,746,560.81

[21] *ibid.*, p. 270.　　　　　　　　　　　　　　　　　　　　　　[22] *ibid.*, p. 268.
[23] Report of the Land Commissioner, 1923, pp. 37-8.

Florida	2,217,619.39
Louisiana	372,092.34
Arkansas	2,562,161.89
Missouri	1,837,968.17
Iowa	4,929,849.44
Michigan	3,133,231.58
Wisconsin	3,649,869.15
Minnesota	8,035,577.61
Kansas	4,633,760.73

Total .... 37,789,169.23 acres

Corporation Grants

Union Pacific	11,935,121.46 acres
Central Pacific	6,891,404.94
Central Pacific (successor by consolidation with Western Pacific)	458,786.66
Central Branch Union Pacific	223,080.50
Union Pacific (Kansas Division)	6,175,660.63
Union Pacific (successor to Denver Pacific Ry. Co.)	821,164.15
Burlington & Missouri River in Nebraska	2,374,090.77
Sioux City & Pacific (now Missouri Valley Land Co.)	42,610.95
Northern Pacific	38,916,338.61
Oregon Branch of Central Pacific (California & Oregon)	3,172,610.48
Oregon & California	2,777,591.96
Atlanta & Pacific (now Santa Fé Pacific)	9,878,352.14
Southern Pacific (main line)	4,323,794.01
Southern Pacific (branch line)	2,118,220.48
Oregon Central	128,618.13
New Orleans Pacific	1,001,943.40

Total 91,239,389.27

37,789,169.23

Grand Total .... 129,028,558.50 acres

LAND GRANTS
TO
STATES AND CORPORATIONS FOR
RAILROAD CONSTRUCTION

Reprinted From
The Bureau of Corporation
Report—1913.—The Lumber
Industry, Pt. I, p. 222.

In addition to the grants of land, it must also be remembered that in the case of the transcontinental railroads and its branch lines, Congress granted extensive loans in money. On June 30, 1883, the following amounts of money were due to the government from the railroads mentioned below:

Union Pacific	$ 51,091,655
Central Pacific	45,322,671
Sioux City and Pacific	2,971,262
Central Branch, Union Pacific	2,990,724
	$102,376,312

To these land and money loan subsidies must be added the extensive grants of land made by many states, as well as the money subsidies contributed by states and local governments, together with heavy investments by individual farmers in the stocks and bonds of these railroad corporations.

The rôle of the settler and the railroad corporation, however, tell but part of the story. This particular period of American history was also a significant one for the Indian. Though obscured to a large degree by the Civil War and the attendant problems of Reconstruction, a vast conflict had been taking place during these years for the possession of the lands beyond the Missouri River, and in this struggle the Indians played an important if unsuccessful rôle. From the Sioux uprisings of 1862 in Minnesota to the surrender of Joseph and his Nez Percés to General Miles late in 1877, band after band of plains and mountain Indians made their final stand for the control of the last lands on which they might live in their accustomed manner.

With the opening of Kansas and Nebraska to settlement under the Act of 1854, the Indian problem, which had been comparatively quiescent for more than twenty years, again flared up. The people of the United States had been generally content to look upon the trans-Missouri lands as strictly Indian territory; there had been invasions of this territory, such as the emigrations toward California and Oregon, but being of transient nature and along established paths, they had occasioned only sporadic disturbances. The settlement of the Pacific rim had created only scattered difficulties with the native inhabitants. And so there remained in the early 'fifties, a vast expanse of territory bounded, roughly, on the east by the Missouri River and the States of Missouri and Arkansas, and on the west by the fringe of Pacific settlements, into which the government had transferred, by either forced or voluntary removal, the majority of the Indians of the United States. Here the white man was quite content to let them stay, at least for the time being. The *Report of the Senate Committee for Indian Affairs* had placidly stated in 1836 that "with this uninhabitable region on the west of the Indian territory," the Indian tribes could not be surrounded by white population. It concluded: "They are on the outside of us, and in a place which will forever remain on the outside."[24] As late as 1864 this attitude had so little changed that General Pope could say: "The great region now roamed over by the Indians offers no inducements to settlement and cultivation. . . . There is no longer the necessity of interfering with the wild Indians of the great plains further than to secure immunity of travel for white emigrants."[25]

But even in 1854 the land of desert and mountain, the solid and consolidated Indian country, was being quietly and insidiously invaded, for the Mormons were even then demonstrating that the desert might be cultivated. The spread of population over eastern Kansas and Nebraska in the late 'fifties further contracted the boundaries of the Indian country, and the gold stampede to Colorado and the Rocky Mountain area brought home to the Indians, if it did not to the whites, that the penetration was final, for where one white man came, others would follow.

In this process of penetration the Indians were driven—sometimes with a show of fairness, quite often unfairly and dishonorably, step by step, mile by mile, from lands they had been led to believe would be theirs forever. Advancing civilization gradually pushed into the region after the early 'sixties and succeeded in taking it over almost entirely some fifteen years later. The white man's relations with the Indians in this period do not form a pleasant picture, for there is much of sordidness, meanness, and inefficiency and even cruelty, relieved only occasionally by outcropping of idealism on the part of those in control of Indian affairs and by a few bits of heroism growing out of the actual

---

[24] Quoted by W. C. MacLeod, *The American Indian Frontier* (New York, 1928), p. 466. By permission of Alfred A. Knopf, Inc.

[25] Report of the Secretary of the Interior, 1864, p. 572.

struggles. The anomaly of a treaty-making power exercising sovereignty within the borders of territory subject to the jurisdiction of another sovereign power became most ridiculously apparent after 1860. The land purchase system can only be explained in terms of the wish of the early settlers to have a "just and equitable . . . title to the land."

Though this practice began at so early a date, the actual relation of the Indians to the government of the United States was never defined until 1871, when Congress went on record as opposed to any further Indian treaties. Then the term treaty simply gave way to a substitute term, agreement, for 1871 was no time to inaugurate a radical change in the entire system of Indian land dealings, especially with the bellicose Sioux. Meantime, the question of actual Indian rights in the soil had already engaged the attention of the Supreme Court. In 1823, John Marshall had handed down the following opinion: "It has never been contended that the Indian title amounted to nothing. Their right of possession has never been questioned. The claim of the government extends to the complete ultimate title charged with this right of possession, and to the exclusive power of acquiring that right." A later decision was more explicit. The Court held that though the Indians had no fee in the lands they occupied, yet they have a qualified right of occupancy which could only be extinguished by treaty and upon fair compensation, until which time they were entitled to be protected in their possession. Except for the Indians on the lands ceded by Mexico, these statements formed the basis of the policy of the United States toward Indian lands. Yet awkward relations, the ramifications of which even a Supreme Court could not define, continued to exist between the two races.

Of more obvious significance than the Indian land theory were its results in practice. The Indians, deprived of their lands, had to have other lands upon which to live, unless they took upon themselves the habits of civilization. The system of Indian land purchase had assumed that there would always be a frontier beyond which the Indians might establish themselves. With limitless lands to the west, and others being added, there seemed every basis for such an assumption. Thus the process which went on from the Revolution to the 1850's was described by the Commissioner of Indian Affairs in 1876 in a survey of the whole frontier movement, "A zigzag, ever-varying line, more or less definitely marked, extending from Canada to the Gulf of Mexico, and always slowly moving west, has been known as the 'frontier' or 'border.' Along this border," he continued, "has been an almost incessant struggle, the Indians to retain and the whites to get possession; the war being broken by periods of occasional and temporary peace, which usually followed treaties whereby the Indians agreed to surrender large tracts of their lands. This peace would continue until the land surrendered had been occupied by the whites, when the pressure of emigration would again break over the border, and the Indian by force or treaty, be compelled to surrender another portion of his cherished hunting grounds."[26]

Occasionally the tide of advancing civilization swept around certain Indian groups, leaving them on reservations as on islands. Here they adopted the methods of the whites, and learned the process of agriculture, aided by government annuities growing out of the purchase of their lands. There were, for example, in the 1870's, several thousand Indians living in the State of New York, who were under the direct supervision of the federal government. For the most part these tribes were removed, either because they were unwilling to fit themselves into the white man's mold, or because, as in the case of the powerful southern tribes, their presence was obnoxious to the settlers. Many of the Indian tribes of the plains in the 1860's had made two, three, or more removals. The Winnebagos, for example, had been moved five times from their original home by 1863.

When the frontier crossed the Missouri River frontier, the nation entered upon the final and perhaps the most acute phase of the Indian land problem. It is true that much land remained into which the Indian might have been slowly crowded as heretofore. Had the conditions and nature of settlement in the High Plains been similar to those further east, the removal process might have worked for a considerable time, but when it passed the Missouri, the frontier no longer moved (except for a brief time in Kansas) in a "zigzag, ever-varying line, more or less definitely marked." The trans-Missouri movement was a quick penetration rather than a steady advance. In an amazingly short time the Indians of the plains were surrounded by a civilization from which they could not escape, for they could no longer withdraw westward.

Though General Pope in 1864 looked upon the Indian country as an uninhabitable desert, special commissioners to the Sioux in 1866, reported that it was "hard to find, in the vast unsettled regions of which

26 ibid., 1876, p. 384.

we write, any place where the encroaching scattered miners and white adventurers seem willing to allow the Indians to live unmolested."[27] From this time on agents and commissioners, in reviewing the Indian problem almost invariably came to the conclusion that further removals were impossible. In fact, it may be said that after 1870 no removals of any significance took place except to the Indian Territory, and that even after 1862 removals had no marked westerly tendency but were in the nature of consolidations upon reservations, about which the streams of travel and settlement might pass.

In short, the period from 1862 to 1877, witnessed the breakup, rather than the contraction of the Indian country, and with that new situation in Indian land matters came new and vexatious problems.

By 1862, as many of the Indian tribes as had entered into treaty negotiations with the government were removed to certain tracts of land to which they were given absolute and sole right of occupancy. These reservations usually consisted of portions of former domains, and for the part surrendered by treaty the Indians were to receive compensation. Frequently—and this was the ideal for which the government strove— the Indians agreed to devote themselves to farming on their reserves, and were promised schools and other appurtenances of civilization. Often, if the lands remaining to the Indians were extensive enough, they were allowed to continue the nomadic life of the chase, the agricultural pursuits being deferred until the game should disappear. In any event, the Indians were paid for their lands in the form of annuities, that is, the purchase money was given to them in yearly installments, usually in the form of goods—foods, clothing, and implements for farming or hunting. This dispensation was made through an agent who had a fixed residence on the reservation. He acted as cashier, policeman, physician perhaps, and agricultural instructor. The objective in the minds of the government administrators was that the Indians should, when they had learned how to farm, receive their lands as individuals and become responsible citizens.

This ambitious scheme for the transmutation of savages into citizens in the space of a generation contained several weaknesses.[28] In the first place, the process of treating with the Indians for lands, the pomp and

---

[27] ibid., 1866, p. 172.

[28] Actual granting of lands in severalty took place in some instances in this period, but did not become a general practice until 1887. In some cases Indians were allowed the privileges of homesteading by a law of 1867.

ceremony that attended the signing of documents between two "nations," tended to exaggerate the Indian's idea of his importance in the scheme of government. The Secretary of the Interior, speaking of this situation in 1862, remarked: "The admission of their right to the lands and of the necessity of their consent has given them a feeling of independence, and fostered a desire for vengeance for every supposed violation of their rights."[29] And to make matters worse, these rights were frequently violated. Congress often delayed to appropriate the money for the annuities; vast amounts of money intended for Indian goods were woefully misappropriated; goods received were often of the most inferior sort. Sometimes years elapsed between the signing of a treaty with an Indian tribe and the payment of the stipulated annuities. Meanwhile, the ceded lands filled up with settlers.

Such was the case with the Nez Percé Indians of Idaho, for example. In 1868 the government had not yet carried out the treaty stipulations of 1863 with this tribe.[30] Without the knowledge of the Sioux, an agreement under the treaty of 1851 to furnish certain annuities to them for fifty years was cut to fifteen years, and part of their promised reserve was amended out of existence by the Senate.[31] T. J. Galbraith, agent in charge of the Minnesota Sioux who were responsible for the massacre of 1862, attributed that outbreak largely to the failure of the government to live up to the treaty promises of 1851. Whatever may have been the nature of the Indian's claim under the treaty-annuity system in the minds of the whites, the red man considered it just as valid as the white man's claim.

A third weakness of the reservation system was its tendency to encourage idleness among the Indians. With the passing of the buffalo (the vast herds that thundered across the plains in 1862 had become separated into bands by 1868, and by 1876 were confined to eastern Montana and northern Wyoming), those Indians who had lived by the chase came to depend almost wholly upon the government's aid. They were fed by the proceeds from the lands they were constantly relinquishing. Thus there was no positive need to push them from their outmoded nomadic life to the inevitable one of agriculture. For years the Indians of western Dakota, Nebraska, and Kansas lived lives of leisure,

29 Report of the Secretary of the Interior, 1862, p. 11.
30 *ibid.*, 1868, p. 657.
31 Frederic L. Paxson, *History of the American Frontier* (New York, 1924), p. 486.

hunting only as a pastime, and depending for subsistence on the agency rations for which they were not required to turn a hand.

Even those Indians who evinced a willingness to turn to the agricultural state were unable to develop any sense of providence. If crops were abundant one year, they thought nothing of a possible drought another season, for they knew they would always be fed. The *Nation* in its issue of July 13, 1876, characterized this system "of making distribution of food and clothing in return for the surrender of lands" which the Indians "never really owned, in any sense in which the word is used in civilized jurisprudence," as a "system of legalized pauperism, containing all the evils of pauperism in its worst form." It was "shocking." There was "nothing in our religion, or manners, or laws, or tradition, or polity to give it any countenance or support."[32]

The fourth and final objection to the reservation system strikes at the heart of the Indian problem. It was simply that reservations were an obstacle to progress—the kind of progress, at least, that the West was coveting. The agent of the Osage River Indians in Kansas voiced popular opinion when he said: "The Indian lands are the best in the state, and justice would demand, as well as every consideration of policy and humanity, that these fertile lands should be thrown open to settlement, and the abode of civilized and industrious men."[33] Another agent remarked that the Indian reservations were a disadvantage to all new regions; public interest demanded that the reservation should be opened to the settlement of the whites as soon as practicable.

E. M. McCook, governor of Colorado Territory in 1870, speaking of the large Ute reservation in western Colorado, vehemently declared his belief "that God gave to us the earth, and the fulness thereof, in order that we might utilize and enjoy his gifts. I do not believe in donating to these indolent savages the best portion of my territory, and I do not believe in placing the Indians on an equality with the white man as landholders."[34] A special commissioner to the Sioux in 1874 believed that the article of the treaty of 1868 which gave to the Sioux certain territory in northeastern Wyoming should be abrogated, even without the consent of the Indians, because the territory under the control of the Indians embraced the most productive part of Wyoming Territory, and

---

[32] *The Nation*, July 13, 1876.
[33] Report of the Secretary of the Interior, 1864, p. 536.　　　　[34] *ibid.*, 1870, p. 627.

because it was a great wrong to the citizens of this territory that its domain should not be settled by an enterprising white population.[35]

These extracts suggest the attitude of the entire West toward the Indian lands. Reservations were a good thing only as long as they did not contain land desired by the whites. This attitude placed the administrators of Indian affairs in a serious dilemma. If the Indians were removed to a locality not coveted for white settlement, it was patent that it would be a land in which Indians could not be expected to make a living, and they would therefore become wards of the government in a most complete sense; while if they remained in the desirable sections of the country, the reservations were likely to become surrounded by white settlers, who looked upon the Indian lands with cupidity. To the whites, Indians seemed to be intruders and the friction that naturally grew up between the races resulted in annoyances and outbreaks that were hard for the Indians to bear.

The Indians themselves were quick to recognize the difficulty of their position. The impression seemed to prevail generally among them that it was the Indian's fate to depart, and the white man's destiny to displace him. He took little interest in the development of property which he might soon be forced to relinquish. The Nez Percé Indian agent, J. B. Monteith, maintained that "Forced removal from lands that have been secured them by treaty, and with which their longest and tenderest recollections have been associated, is fatal to all efforts to improve and elevate the Indians. They must be made to feel that the tenure by which they hold their lands is as sacred as that of the white people."[36] The Commissioner of Indian Affairs reiterated this view.

The Indian's attitude found a more satirical expression in a report of the Utah superintendent for 1865: The argument used by the hostile Indians with the peaceful ones is, he wrote "that the Indians now in arms are contending for their homes. . . . That our representation of a desire to concentrate and civilize them, to open farms, and build houses, is only to get them together that they may be slaughtered . . . and the country left to the sole occupancy of the whites. . . . Witnessing the constant stream of emigration and hearing . . . the threats of extermination to their race made against all Indians . . . it is not strange that they are excited and uncertain."[37]

35 *ibid.*, 1874, p. 400.   36 *ibid.*, 1871, p. 954.
37 *ibid.*, 1865, p. 314.

The Secretary of the Interior summed up the general policy of the government regarding Indian removals as follows: "The rapid progress upon the continent will not permit the lands which are required for civilization to be surrendered to savage tribes for hunting grounds [or for farming either]. The government has always demanded the removal of the Indians when their lands were required for agricultural purposes by advancing settlements. Although the consent of the Indians has been obtained in the form of treaties, it is well known that they have yielded to a necessity which they could not resist."[38]

The period of 1862 to 1877 was one in which this yielding to necessity constantly recurred. Tribes were consolidated upon reservations, which were soon cut down because the white man needed the land. The final step was the transferring of the Indians to the Indian Territory to the south. Whereas, in the early 'sixties, no one thought of limiting the extent of Indian reservations in the Plains and Rocky Mountain region, except as concerned mineral lands, yet by 1871 the Secretary of the Interior had come to the conclusion that the solution of the Indian problem was simply to remove all Indians to the Indian Territory, and throw open their lands to white settlement. He called attention to the fact, apparently with some amazement, that in that year every Indian had an average of 588 acres of land.[39] Ten years earlier no one would have cared about Indian acreage, so long as it did not conflict with mining camps or overland trails. But the "Great American Desert" had become populated.

These removals to the Indian Territory, though frequent, were not always easy to effect. Tribes were hesitant about going to a strange land. The Arickarees of Dakota, for example, preferred to "work harder and have less" in order that they might remain in the lands of their ancestors, though their representatives had brought back glowing reports of the new country. More or less voluntary removals on the part of the Kansas Indians, who were familiar with the territory to the south, had placed most of them in that territory by 1877. Certain forced removals had been made, as in the case of the Modocs of Oregon after the outbreak in 1873. But for the most part, the process during the period under consideration was that of the cutting down and the solidifying of Indian domains. In 1871, the Umatilla reservation Indians in Oregon were asked to part with their land, which they refused to

[38] *ibid.*, 1862, p. 11.

[39] *ibid.*, 1871, pp. 6, 7.

do. In 1872, the Shoshone and Bannock tribes of Wyoming ceded a valuable portion of their remaining lands. In March 1873, the Crows of Montana gave up a portion of their reservation, including much valuable mineral land, and the right of way for the Northern Pacific Railway. In September 1873, four million acres of the Confederated Ute reservation in western Colorado were ceded, much of which territory was valuable farming land. Again in 1876, the Sioux gave up claims to the Black Hills. Though these and other cessions were obtained by fair bargaining, and without actual show of force, they were not acceded to because of desire for gain on the part of the Indians, but because the Indians realized the inevitability of white occupation. It is safe to say that the Indians would have preferred to keep their lands.

But though the government's accepted policy was to extinguish Indian title before settlement took place, it was often unable to prevent encroachment, and if settlement so far preceded negotiations that the whites outnumbered the natives, the Indians were powerless to resist, and treaties were taken for granted. Powell and Ingalls, special commissioners to the Indians of the great intermountain basin (Nevada, Utah, southern Idaho, etc.) who reported in 1873, struck this suggestive note: "All the Indians who have been visited by the Commission fully appreciate the hopelessness of contending against the government of the United States, and the tide of civilization. . . . The time has passed when it was necessary to buy peace."[40] None of the Indians had been treated with for their lands, but the commissioners concluded: "It remains only to decide what shall be done with them for the relief of the white people."[41]

The basic causes of Indian disturbances in the period of 1862 to 1877 doubtless lay on the encroachment of whites upon Indian lands. Where this encroachment was made upon a passive group of Indians, the result was simply an injustice done; often the Indians encroached upon were jealous of their rights to the point of defending them, and the result was both injustice and war. The latter type of encroachment was more spectacular; the former, though more insidious, was no less inevitable and effective.

It is also true that the direct causes of Indian trouble were often incidental happenings. The jostling of whites and Indians together in a new and lawless country proved a pregnant source of conflict. The fail

---

[40] *ibid.*, 1873, p. 431.   [41] *ibid*

ure of the government adequately to protect peaceful Indians from their hostile neighbors was another. The Modoc War of 1873 resulted from the juxtaposition of two unfriendly tribes upon one reservation. Retaliation of whites—both civilians and soldiers—upon whole bands of Indians for the misconduct of a few members was one fruitful source of trouble, as was failure on the part of the government to live up to its part of treaty stipulations. Natural hatred of the whites for the so-called inferior race was as much responsible for the continual wars in Arizona and New Mexico, as cases of actual encroachments. But whatever the causes, the testimony of some of the highest military officers of the United States is on record to the effect that, in our Indian Wars, almost without exception, the first aggression was made by the white man.[42]

[42] *ibid.*, 1869, p. 489.

CHAPTER XV

EXPLOITATION UNDER THE SETTLEMENT LAWS

BY 1862 the government had made such great progress in disposing of the public domain that only about one billion acres still remained the property of the United States. Perhaps two-thirds of this remaining domain, however, was not arable land, and could not be parcelled out so easily. The Secretary of the Interior estimated that since the founding of the Republic the average annual income from the sale of land had been about $2,750,000.[1] And moreover, about one-fourth of all the legislation enacted by Congress during this time had related to public lands and to land settlement.

As soon as the Civil War was over, the government launched an impressive program to lure settlers to the remaining vacant lands of the West. In addition to the attractive reports of the Land Office, the Immigration Bureau, the Geological Survey, and the explorations of the Army Corps, there were also the advertisements of railroads and of the state immigration bureaus, not to mention the promotional efforts of many private land companies which were conducting their business in the American and British markets. To these factors should also be added the favorable publicity given to the accounts of travellers who swarmed the West, and to the reports of sportsmen who roamed the High Plains killing off the buffalo. Extraordinary attention was beginning to be given the West in local and eastern newspapers and periodicals, in fact, advertisement of western opportunities appeared everywhere.

From the beginning of the post-Civil War period, the benefits of the homestead law were much overrated. Judging from the tenor of the federal utterances, it appeared that the government no longer regarded the public domain as a source of revenue; in fact, since the passage of the Preemption Act in 1841, the government had often declared that the revenue principle was no longer a consideration. President Grant in his second annual message declared: "The rapid settlement and successful cultivation of them [the public lands] are now justly con-

[1] Report of the Secretary of the Interior, 1864, p. 3.

sidered of more importance to our well-being than is the fund which the sale of them would produce."[2] In 1873, however, he urged caution in securing "access to the balance by the hardy settler who may wish to avail himself" of such lands.[3] By that date Congress had already granted away vast areas of land to corporations, and certain subordinate officials who found it difficult to enforce the law were departing from the principle of reserving the public lands for the settlers.

Perhaps the immediate success of the Homestead Act was misleading. Over one million acres of land were taken out under this act between May 1862, when it went into effect, and June 30, 1863, a period coinciding with the most discouraging year of the Civil War for the Union forces.[4] Nothing was more illustrative of the energy of the American people than the fact that during the war period, settlement continued onto the domain in the West. By improved methods of farming, the land was able to feed not only the million and a half men under arms, but also the multitude of citizens engaged in other pursuits of industry. The amount of land taken out under the Act of 1862 constantly increased until, by 1867, over two and a half million acres had been entered under both homesteading and preemption legislation—about twenty thousand farms added to the freeholds of the Republic.[5] It was noted, however, that 30 to 40 per cent of the farms taken out under the Homestead Act were commuted after six months to preemption or cash payment.[6] By 1869, the Land Commissioner was praising the preemption principle very highly, and declaring that it offered advantages over the Homestead Act.[7] But such extravagant statements regarding the operation of the settlement laws had to be qualified as it became more and more apparent that neither homesteading nor preemption could operate effectively in a wide open public domain. It quickly became evident that neither law could work effectively as long as there were extensive grants to railroads and speculative interests.

By an act of June 2, 1862, preemption was extended to unsurveyed lands on the public domain, while the Homestead Law continued to apply only to surveyed lands. Since there was nothing in the Homestead Act interdicting claimants who were owners of preempted land from entering under the homestead measure, the law was recognized as

---

[2] Richardson, *Messages and Papers of the Presidents*, Vol. VII, p. 110.
[3] *ibid.*, p. 152.   [4] Report of the Land Commissioner, 1863, p. 3.
[5] *ibid.*, 1868, p. 97.   [6] Report of the Secretary of the Interior, 1865, p. 2.
[7] Report of the Land Commissioner, 1869, p. 21.

extending benefits to preemptors also.[8] Thus a person might acquire 160 acres under preemption and another 160 acres under homesteading. One may question whether Congress ever intended any person to have as much as 320 acres of select land. Yet, such was the interpretation of the law. Another ominous situation arose after 1862, when the Land Office was forced to reject many claims because preemption claimants had made only slight improvements on the land claimed.[9] This laxity in complying with the law was due, perhaps in part, to the fact that those who desired to buy land did not intend to live on it, but were holding it for speculative purposes. Also, many persons openly violated the law by making second filings under the Preemption Act, although this was prohibited by section 4 of the amendatory act of March 3, 1843.[10] Similar difficulties were encountered in the administration of the homestead law. Claims were frequently rejected because claimants did not take the oath of allegiance to the United States.[11] Many entries were cancelled because they conflicted with other preemption or homestead entries.[12]

The right of preemption it should be noted attached from the date of actual settlement; that of homestead, from the date of the claimant's entry at the local land office.[13] Since unsurveyed land was open to the first person who filed under the preemption law, it was much safer for a person on unsurveyed land to borrow the money and preempt than to wait for the survey and then file under the homestead law.[14] Many homesteaders lost their claims to preemptors under the operation of these laws.[15] Consequently, there arose much agitation among western Congressmen for the extension of homesteading to unsurveyed lands. In 1871, a bill providing for this concession was referred to the House Committee on Public Lands, but no report was made on it.[16]

[8] *ibid.*, 1863, p. 5.
[9] *Land Commissioner's Letters*, Preemption Division G, Vol. LXXXII (1870), p. 315; Vol. CXLV (1880), pp. 110-11.
[10] *ibid.*, Vol. LXXXII (1870), p. 122; Vol. CXLV (1883), p. 343.
[11] *ibid.*, Vol. LIX (1865), pp. 23, 30, 37, 168, etc.
[12] *Registers' and Receivers' Letters*, Homestead Division G, Vol. CXLV (1884), p. 361; Vol. CXCVI (1885), pp. 25, 49, etc.
[13] Report of the Secretary of the Interior, 1866, p. 2.
[14] Report of the Land Commissioner, 1866, p. 379.
[15] *Land Commissioners' Letters*, Preemption Division G, Vol. CXII (1874), pp. 109, 185 199, etc.
[16] *Congressional Globe*, 41 Cong. 3 Sess., p. 525.

For preemption on unsurveyed and surveyed lands, certain require-ments were specified by law. The settler with the option of securing his title either by homesteading or by preemption often delayed his choice until he was forced into one or the other. This delay led to many administrative difficulties. The Land Commissioner therefore recom-mended that the settler upon any land subject to private sale should be required to reside continuously the whole twelve months upon his tract, and that the settlers upon surveyed, unoffered lands should be required to "prove up" within one year from the date of settlement.[17] It was also recommended that no preemption should be recognized in which set-tlement was not continuous.[18] Had these recommendations been carried out, much corruption in the operation of the settlement laws would have been prevented.

Another major difficulty was encountered in the fact that the pre-emption laws varied greatly from territory to territory, and this lack of uniformity not only caused inefficient administration, but also encour-aged corruption throughout the whole land system.[19] In 1870 this matter was brought to the attention of Congress. The Land Commis-sioner strongly urged the codification of all preemption legislation.[20] A bill drawn up for this purpose was introduced so late that Congress gave it no consideration, although a relatively insignificant law, ap-proved on July 17, 1870, did correct a few of the difficulties.[21]

This one piece of corrective legislation was only a bare beginning of what was actually needed in the way of reform. Revision of the pre-emption laws would not only have been a very exacting job, but it also would have meant the abrogation of certain privileges enjoyed by some of the territories. As an alternative to this task of revising the preemption laws, many thought it would be preferable to abolish the whole system by repealing the Act of 1841 and its amendatory legis-lation.

[17] Report of the Land Commissioner, 1866, p. 370.   [18] *ibid.*, 1863, p. 4.
[19] Report of the Secretary of the Interior, 1866, p. 2.
[20] *Cong. Globe,* 41 Cong. 3 Sess., p. 26.
[21] Report of the Land Commissioner, 1870, p. 179. This act provided that payment be made for preemption claims upon unoffered lands within eighteen months after the expiration of the prescribed date of filing, which date had already been fixed by law, viz., within three months after the settlement upon surveyed unoffered lands and within three months from the filing of the plat of survey in the district land-office where settlement was made before survey. Hence-forth the claimant had to show a continued residence of not less than six months prior to and including the date of application to enter. *Land Commissioners' Letters,* Preemption Bureau, Vol. CXLVIII (1890), p. 460.

To turn again to the homestead law, there is considerable incongruity between the preliminary or original entries, and the number of final entries.[22] These discrepancies become more striking when original and final entries are compared over a period of years. For instance, in the twenty-year period from 1862 to 1882 there were 552,112 original entries, while the final entries totaled only 194,488.[23] A more comprehensive view is furnished by the following tabulation by states for the same period of twenty years.

| | ORIGINAL ENTRIES | | FINAL ENTRIES | |
States	No. Entries	Acres	No. Entries	Acres
Alabama	28,995	2,875,547.12	5,227	542,147.69
Arkansas	44,940	4,095,743.94	11,562	1,142,623.01
California	24,750	3,218,745.16	10,012	1,235,213.09
Dakota	52,733	8,142,999.85	7,806	1,142,263.71
Florida	16,390	1,743,331.41	3,305	353,702.91
Kansas	86,936	11,746,949.80	34,055	4,660,734.83
Minnesota	70,616	8,473,058.89	31,610	3,672,710.61
Mississippi	12,489	1,175,037.45	2,094	203,410.86
Nebraska	64,328	8,183,076.25	29,140	3,566,477.29
Oregon	11,710	1,544,526.43	4,017	551,284.02
Washington	12,668	1,675,162.92	3,360	436,246.96[24]

The reports of the Commissioner of the General Land Office, as far as examined, do not account for this discrepancy. In the southern states there is evidence that in some cases Negroes who had made preliminary entries for homestead tracts were perhaps intimidated by their white neighbors and compelled to withdraw from the lands. Another explanation which seems more plausible and applies to all sections of the country, is that wealthy individuals or corporations employed "dummies" to represent them in filing their claims on timber or mineral tracts, which were, however, described as agricultural lands, and after denuding the tracts of their wealth, these proxy claimants did not conclude the transaction by making final entry.

The Preemption Act of 1841 provided that all assignments and transfers of the preemption right prior to the issuance of the patent

22 Donaldson, *The Public Domain*, p. 359.   23 *ibid.*, p. 1,016
24 *ibid.*

were to be null and void. The homestead laws required proof that the party had not alienated the land, and that no land should be liable to the satisfaction of any debt contracted prior to the issue of the patent. Had the principles of these laws been followed there would have been little opportunity for the numerous abuses prevalent in the 'seventies and 'eighties. In fact, it was one of the anomalies in the operation of the preemption and homestead laws that claimants always sought to excuse deficient residence and meager improvements on the plea of poverty.

It is true that abuses of the public land laws were to a great extent due to inefficient administration, to the conduct of weak and corrupt officials, and to erratic and fanciful decisions; but it is also true that the laws were defective and did not provide adequate safeguards. Many of the local land districts contained over 20,000 square miles. The land officials could not possibly visit all of this vast stretch of territory. All they could do was to consult maps showing the location of the lands and to keep track of the subdivisions which were entered. In fact, the system of making final proof was so loose that it is little wonder that the local land officials failed to check existing fraud.[25] There was, for instance, no way to determine whether a description of a house "twelve by fourteen" referred to inches or to feet; whether "shingle-roof" meant more than two shingles on each side; and whether a house six by eight feet built of rough boards was a "comfortable residence" in latitude forty-six degrees north![26] Moreover, it could hardly be expected that registers and receivers who depended on fees for their salaries would be overzealous in their scrutiny of filings. This example of laxity set by government officials was hardly conducive to honesty on the part of settlers.

Some of the enactments, however, were more clear-cut and exact in phraseology. The Congressional Act of March 2, 1831, as construed by the Supreme Court, made depredations on timber lands in the national domain a criminal offense punishable by fine and imprisonment. In 1855, the enforcement of this statute was placed in the hands of the General Land Office, thus imposing upon the registers and receivers of the local land offices, without additional compensation, the burdensome task of acting as timber agents. These officials were authorized to sell public lands on which timber had been illegally cut at public auction

<hr />

[25] *Registers' and Receivers' Letters*, Homestead Division G, Vol. CXXXV (1876), p. 371.
[26] See illustrations on the next two pages.

A HABITABLE DWELLING

A HOUSE "TWELVE BY FOURTEEN"

Preemption Frauds.

A BONA FIDE RESIDENCE

Preemption Frauds.
From Albert D. Richardson, *Beyond the Mississippi,* 1867.

and to deposit the proceeds in the Treasury of the United States. But in spite of these protective measures designed to save the forests from the invasions of the lawless, depredations increased at such a rate that by the late 'seventies the situation was indeed alarming. Congress during this time made appropriations for the employment of special agents to aid in the enforcement, but they were too small to be effective.

Some of the greatest difficulties in protecting the public forests arose from the fact that there was no single congressional enactment providing a definite method for the disposal of fine timber lands, notably pine lands. The "field notes" of ordinary surveys did not disclose with any degree of accuracy which were pine lands and which were not. Without doubt, purchasers at the auctions formed combinations whereby prices were kept down to merely nominal figures. And lastly, only the best timber, like the pine lands in Wisconsin and Minnesota and the fir lands of the Pacific slope, was in demand; few buyers were interested in the less valuable timber lands.[27]

Another source of trouble was the fact that faulty operation of the preemption and homesteading laws, led to wholesale appropriation of timber lands. This ominous condition was already obvious when the Homestead Act was passed, for the operation of the Preemption Act of 1841 had led to much destruction of forests in the Gulf States, the upper Mississippi River Valley and Great Lakes areas. The rising price of

[27] Report of the Land Commissioner, 1875, p. 10.

lumber brought ever increasing depredations on valuable timber lands all through the West. To obtain access to these lands the spoliators resorted either to outright theft or to loopholes in the general settlement laws. Against such tactics the land officials were all but helpless. Experience had long ago taught the government that when frontier interests conflicted with the law, the law was virtually a dead letter. This was the impasse which confronted the government during the middle 'seventies.

The Act of 1855 was apparently based on the theory that it was better to compromise with the depredators. Wherever trespassers were caught they were forced to pay so much per thousand feet of lumber cut, as well as the costs of the seizure. This was called *stumpage*. In 1864, the Land Commissioner for Nevada Territory, stated that the stumpage value should be not less than one-sixth of the value per thousand feet of the manufactured lumber at the mill.[28] In Minnesota two years later, an increase in the stumpage to four dollars per thousand feet was recommended, for fear the rising price in lumber would cause extensive depredations.[29] The total amount paid into the treasury for depredations on the timber lands from January 1, 1856, to January 1, 1877, was $199,898.[30]

When it became known that the valuable pineries around Denver were being culled out by portable sawmills, the surveyor-general of Colorado Territory advised bringing the land into the market at once in order to realize something on it before it was ruined.[31] The surveyor-general of Washington Territory recommended in the same year that ten million acres of forest lands in his territory be sold before it should become worthless by plundering.[32] The surveyor-general for Florida in 1869 estimated that 50 per cent of the timber sawed within his jurisdiction was stolen off government lands under the cover of preemption claims.[33] In 1879 the Land Commissioner received from Wisconsin many letters protesting that public timber trespassers were becoming so numerous that honest lumbermen could not compete with them.[34]

---

[28] *ibid.*, 1877, p. 19.
[29] Report of Surveyor-General for Minnesota Territory, 1866, p. 441.
[30] Report of the Land Commissioner, 1877, p. 20.
[31] Report of Surveyor-General for Colorado and Utah, 1866, p. 463.
[32] Report of Surveyor-General for Washington Territory, 1866, p. 500.
[33] Report of the Surveyor-General for Florida, 1869, p. 265.
[34] Report of the Land Commissioner, 1879, p. 560.

These few examples are sufficient to show that in the 'seventies the general settlement laws were not operating in the interests of the settler. The homestead law had never been intended to apply to the forest lands of the country. Like the preemption law, it was intended solely as a boon to the settlement of the remaining arable lands. Nevertheless, there was nothing to prevent anyone from securing a settlement-right on timber land, cutting and selling the timber, and then moving on to some other area to repeat the practice. Yet, to cut timber from the land was illegal unless the settler had full title to the land; preemptors and homesteaders might use only timber growing on the land and that for the legitimate purpose of building, fencing, repairs, and firewood.[35] From time to time the Land Commissioner took action on individual cases of depredation, but to identify and prosecute the depredators was very difficult.[36] In general, the western public upheld the government in these prosecutions, for much of the illegal activity was chargeable to the speculator. At times, however, a keen sympathy was expressed for those who supplied the towns with timber and capital.[37]

By the 'eighties, the number of timber depredations had become appalling. In fact, most of the preemption and homestead entries on timber lands had been made fraudulently in the interests of mill men and lumber companies by their employees. A special agent despatched to the Duluth district in 1885 reported that up until 1884 there had been 4,300 final entries in that land district, but that only one hundred settlers living on these entries were actually engaged in farming. It was estimated that less than one-thirtieth of the claims were being taken for actual settlement. According to the county records of this district, the favorite method of obtaining title to the valuable pine and mineral lands of the Duluth district was to hire men to operate under the general settlement laws.[38] Another special agent despatched to Aberdeen, Dakota Territory, reported that fully 75 per cent of the entries made under the preemption laws were for speculative purposes and not for homes or for cultivation. The claimants after proving up often mortgaged their holdings for as large a loan as they could procure, and immediately moved to town or back East to sell the claims.[39]

---

[35] ibid., 1864, p. 37.
[36] Land Commissioners' Letters, Preemption Division G, Vol. LIX (1869), p. 15.
[37] Spring City (Idaho Territory) Owyhee Avalanche, March 7, and May 9, 1874.
[38] ibid., 1885, p. 205.   [39] ibid., p. 206.

The special agent despatched to Colorado Territory reported that four-fifths of the fraudulent entries in Colorado were made under the preemption laws.[40] The letter files of the Land Commissioner are filled with cases in which preemption claims conflicted with timber entries.[41]

In 1887, the investigations of special agents resulted in the holding of more than 2,300 entries covering about 370,000 acres of land for cancellation, while over 1,150 entries covering 180,000 acres were actually cancelled because of fraud.[42] In Colorado, Kansas, and Nebraska during the three years beginning 1885 only about a third of the 73,908 preemption filings and 25,558 preemption claims were perfected by actual entry.[43] In 1887, a special agent reported that out of 1,011 cases of depredations involving $6,146,000, only the amount of $128,642 was actually recovered.[44] In 1891 at least 1,115 cases of depredations involving $2,347,374 were referred to special agents for investigation, but only $53,863 was actually recovered.[45]

The Land Commissioner repeated many times in his annual reports that homestead and preemption laws should not apply to timber lands, particularly to the more valuable pine and fir lands. Frequently the soil of such lands was almost useless for agricultural purposes. In the mountain regions where mining was carried on, vast areas of timber in the vicinity of the mining camps were wantonly destroyed. The Commissioner was justly angered by these destructive inroads on the national timber lands. "In all the pine region of Lake Superior and the Upper Mississippi," he pointed out, "where vast areas have been settled under the pretense of agriculture under the homestead and preemption laws, scarcely a vestige of agriculture appears. The same is true on the Pacific Coast and in the mountain regions of Colorado, Utah, Montana, and Idaho."[46] And, he concluded, "A national calamity is being rapidly and surely brought upon the country by the useless destruction of the forests. Much of this destruction arises from the abuses of the beneficent laws for giving lands to the landless."[47]

The general preemption and homestead laws were not the only laws used to advantage in exploiting the timber lands. Soldiers' additional

[40] ibid., p. 209.
[41] Registers' and Receivers' Letters, Homestead Division G, Vol. CXXXV (1876), p. 365; Land Commissioners' Letters, Preemption Bureau, Vol. CXLV (1883), p. 259.
[42] Report of the Land Commissioner, 1887, p. 133.   [43] ibid., pp. 138-43.
[44] ibid., p. 165.   [45] Report of the Secretary of the Interior, 1891, p. 24.
[46] Report of the Land Commissioner, 1876, p. 8.   [47] ibid., p. 7.

homestead rights, purchased for as low as 40 cents per acre were also utilized to secure double minimum lands heavily forested with valuable pine. On the Mille Lac Indian Reservation, 286 soldiers' homesteads were located on lands worth from $10 to $30 per acre for their timber alone. Looking at the situation as a whole, it is clear that exploitation of the timber resources of the nation was proceeding at such a rate—under laws intended to promote settlement—that unless the government reformed its policy, and reformed it soon, the best timber resources would be gone. Even more serious was the fact that timber rights were being concentrated into large holdings, a tendency distinctly contrary to the democratic principles of American land tenure, and bound to produce dangerous repercussions.

The Timber Culture Act, it will be recalled, had been designed to promote the growth of timber on the vast prairies of the Dakotas and in other public-land regions lacking in timber resources. It provided for the grant of 160 acres of land to persons who would promote the growth of ten acres of timber for a period of eight years. A large number of entries were made under this law, but few were ever completed. In fact, adherence to the letter of the law worked a great hardship upon the settler. Many homesteaders took advantage of the act to get land adjoining their property. The measure was practicable, perhaps desirable, in regions where it was possible to promote the planting and growth of trees, but when applied to the arid regions of the West, it was not only impracticable, but by encouraging the planting of trees where trees could not grow, it actually worked great injustice on honest settlers who had confidence in law and order.[48] In fact, the government was severely criticized by the *Nation* in 1883 for its attempt to forest the western plains.[49]

For the unscrupulous, the Timber Culture Act became another means of illegally acquiring land. By 1880 this law was widely regarded as a failure. In the words of the Land Commissioner in 1883: "Continued experience has demonstrated that these abuses are inherent in the law, and beyond the reach of administrative methods for their correction. Settlement on the land is not required. Even residence within the state

---

[48] Charles S. Sargent, "The Protection of the Forests," *North American Review*, Vol. CXXXV (October 1882), pp. 400-1.

[49] Issue of September 1883, Vol. XXXVII, p. 220.

or territory in which the land is situated is not a condition to an entry. A mere record of entry holds the land for one year without the performance of any act of cultivation. The meager act of breaking five acres, which can be done at the close of the year as well as at the beginning, holds the land for the second year. Comparatively trivial acts hold it for a third year. During these periods relinquishments of the entries are sold to homesteaders or other settlers at such price as the land may require."

"My information," he continued, "leads me to the conclusion that a majority of entries under the Timber Culture Act are made for speculative purposes, and not for the cultivation of the timber. Compliance with the law in these cases is a mere pretense and does not result in the production of timber. . . . My information is that no trees are to be seen over vast regions of country where timber-culture entries have been most numerous. . . . I am convinced that the public interests will be served by a total repeal of the law, and I recommend such a repeal."[50]

Just as tomb robbery was a highly skilled and lucrative trade which kept many Egyptian families in comfort if not in affluence for a good many centuries, so the sale of relinquishments of timber-culture entries became a regular occupation for numerous land agents. Time and time again fictitious entries were made in order to hold land out of the market; tracts frequently passed through the hands of five or six speculators before coming into the possession of actual settlers.[51] The Timber Culture Act was also used to acquire great tracts of land for range purposes. "Within the great stock ranges of Nebraska, Kansas, Colorado, and elsewhere," the Land Commissioner reported in 1885, "one-quarter of nearly every section is covered by a timber-culture entry made for the use of the cattle owners, usually by their herdsmen who make false land-office affidavits as a part of the conditions of their employment."[52]

A company in Dakota had twenty-six quarter-section entries, "judiciously located along streams," made in its interest.[53] An inspector, in 1885, reported that he had seen no instances of success except in the eastern portion of Nebraska and southeastern Dakota, and he doubted "if the trees standing on any timber-culture entry west of the hundredth

50 Report of the Land Commissioner, 1883, pp. 7-8.
51 Hibbard, *History of the Public Land Policies*, p. 418.
52 Report of the Land Commissioner, 1885, p. 72.
53 Hibbard, *History of the Public Land Policies*, p. 419.

meridian would retard a zephyr."[54] A special agent to Dakota Territory declared that 90 per cent of the entries under the Timber Culture Act were made purely for speculation.[55] Another special agent sent to investigate the land system in California reported that only 5 per cent of the entries made under this act and under the Desert Land Act were made in good faith.[56] Still another agent investigating entries in Washington Territory reported that the most extensive fraudulent entries had been made, and that three-fourths of the entries were promoted by persons of wealth.[57]

When the Desert Land Act was passed it was obvious that there had been no agreement between Congress and the Department of the Interior as to the kind of legislative policy desirable for the arid country. The Desert Land Act certainly did not solve the problem. The Land Commissioner himself thought this act was so loosely drawn up that a strict application of its provisions would defeat its main purpose, which was to get water on the land. The act required the irrigation of the entire area of a tract of 160 acres and this was frequently impracticable.[58] "If lands which require no irrigation are given away to any persons who will settle upon them and improve them," the commissioner wondered why the government should "not give away the desert lands upon the same conditions?"[59]

The Secretary of the Interior joined with the Land Commissioner in pointing out the flaws in the law. He was especially insistent upon an amendment requiring competent testimony to the fact that the land entered was of desert character. He also asked that the law specifically forbid sales or encumbrances before the final proof and payment had been consummated.[60] The advice of President Hayes in 1877 to the effect that a system of lease-hold tenure should apply to the desert lands west of the hundredth meridian went entirely unheeded. Even the advice of the most competent authority of that day, Major John Wesley Powell, to the effect that desert holdings should be not less than 2,560

[54] Report of the Land Commissioner, 1885, p. 205.　　[55] *ibid.*, p. 206.
[56] *ibid.*, p. 211.　　[57] *ibid.*, p. 213.
[58] The foremost authority on this subject is John T. Ganoe, "The Beginnings of Irrigation in the United States," *Mississippi Valley Historical Review*, Vol. XXV (June 1938), pp. 59-79.
[59] Report of the Land Commissioner, 1877, p. 33.
[60] Report of the Secretary of the Interior, 1877, p. xxii.

acres in extent, received scant attention in Congress.[61] But Congress, notwithstanding this advice, ventured forth on the plan of homesteading the desert country, and there was little for the executive department to do but attempt to carry out the law.

In 1880 the Land Commissioner termed the act a failure. In many cases of entry the nearest water supply was so inaccessible or so far distant that a great amount of labor and expense was necessary to bring it to the land. And it frequently required at least three years to construct the ditches.[62] In other words, the honest settler could not possibly take advantage of the law, and yet, up to 1893, almost a million acres had been appropriated under this act.

Certainly the genuine settler was not the one who benefited from the act. Many of the entries were not "desert" within the meaning of the law. In 1883, Thomas Donaldson declared in his monumental report on the public domain that tracts taken up under this act were "no more desert than the valley of the Ohio River."[63] Valuable timber lands were actually being embraced in desert land entries, and vast ranges were fenced off by wealthy stock raisers, leaving the actual settler without a range for the family cow.[64]

Donaldson concluded that, "The desert-land act has become an aid to land-grabbing. It should be repealed or a larger area given under it. It is useless for actual settlement, for poor men cannot irrigate it by means of expensive ditches and men of means could not afford to construct ditches for so small an area."[65]

As a means of encouraging irrigation and settlement of the desert country, the Desert Land Law was a failure; but as a way of encouraging trespassing and bringing into existence the cow country, it was most successful.[66] By 1885, the cattle interests were deliberately chasing settlers off their lands, enclosing vast areas and defending these enclosures with armed riders.[67] Such enclosures were being made even in the Indian Territory. Settlers avoided these localities as they would the

---

[61] Report on the Lands of the Arid Region of the United States, 47 Cong. 2 Sess., H. Mis. Doc. No. 45, Pt. IV; also consult The Nation, Vol. XXVI (May 2, 1878), pp. 288-9.

[62] Report of the Land Commissioner, 1880, p. 492.

[63] Donaldson, The Public Domain, p. 1,165.

[64] Donaldson, "The Public Lands of the United States," North American Review, Vol. CXXXIII (1883), p. 207.

[65] Donaldson, The Public Domain, p. 54.

[66] For a comprehensive treatment see: Ernest S. Osgood, The Day of the Cattleman (Minneapolis, 1929).

[67] Report of the Land Commissioner, 1885, p. 225.

plague.[68] Much of this ranch land was taken up by fraudulent means under the provisions of various land laws. A "cattle king" employed a number of men as herders called "cowboys." The herds of cattle were located on a good grassy plat of ground, probably along a stream, and each cowboy was expected and required to make a desert-land entry, a timber-culture entry, and possibly entries under homesteading and preemption. Technically speaking, it was possible under these laws for one person to take out as much as 1,280 acres. A pretense of growing trees or of cultivating the soil could be made while the cattle grazed and fattened on the grassy spots.[69] In Nebraska, claims were taken out under the preemption and homestead laws, proofs were made, and shortly afterwards the land officials heard reports of deeds being executed to cattle companies.[70] The register at Miles City, Montana, reported in 1885 that all lands along the streams flowing into the Yellowstone River had been taken up by cattle ranches.[71]

Not only did these cattle interests use the land, but much of the land they used was ruined by overgrazing. This was even more true of the sheep grazers of Utah. The pasture lands of poor settlers were trampled and bared by flocks, many of whose owners lived in California and the eastern states. Of course, the sheepmen argued that it was "government land" and they had "as much right to its use as anyone."[72] Some idea of the vastness of these ranges may be obtained from the fact that the Musselshell Range of Utah comprised 170 townships or about 3,916,800 acres of government land.[73] The Aztec Cattle Company of Texas was sending outlaws into Arizona and was forcing actual settlers off the land at the point of a gun.[74] Obviously the High Plains region would either have to be given over entirely to the range industry or else the government would have to protect the settler. If the first alternative was determined upon, then the law would have to be made to conform to actual conditions.

While valuable timber and grazing lands were passing into private hands at ridiculously low prices or under the cover of preemption and homestead filings, the same course was being pursued to build up hold-

[68] ibid., p. 205.
[70] ibid., p. 208.
[72] 50 Cong. 1 Sess., H. Ex. Doc. No. 232, p. 3.
[74] ibid., p. 16.

[69] ibid., p. 203.
[71] ibid., p. 280.
[73] ibid., p. 5.

ings of iron lands, particularly in the region of Minnesota.[75] It will be recalled that in the 'fifties and 'sixties many of the valuable copper deposits of the Lake Superior area were acquired under the faulty operation of the preemption law. The Secretary of the Interior had held in 1850 that iron lands were not included in the mineral lands legislation of 1846 and 1847. Nevertheless, interested persons continued to file under the agricultural Preemption Act of 1841, swearing falsely that their tracts did not contain any mineral deposits. Most of the land surveys were not sufficiently detailed to indicate to officials the exact character of the lands; while some areas were reserved from settlement or sale, others were left wide open. Furthermore, under the guise of purchase of timber lands there passed the title to many valuable iron deposits. In the Duluth and St. Cloud districts, which was a timbered and swampy region poorly adapted to agriculture, a special agent found in 1884 that 2,361 homestead entries had been made, including 887 soldiers' additional homesteads. Out of this number 1,000 had been commuted to cash after a declared residence of six months. From this investigation it was evident that less than one-thirtieth of the claims taken up in this region were for actual settlement.[76]

The general settlement laws, however, were not the only means by which unscrupulous individuals and companies acquired holdings in the iron region. Of all the mineral land legislation enacted between 1846 and 1872, not one act dealt with iron lands. In fact, not until February 1873, did Congress provide a legal method for acquiring such lands. At that time it was specified that they should be disposed of on the same terms as nonmineral lands, that is, at auction according to the terms of the Act of 1820, for not less than $1.25 per acre.[77] After a few years it was evident that iron lands were being sold at an average barely above the minimum. Vast holdings were also acquired by buying lands from the state and from railroad corporations, for in spite of the federal government's intention to exclude mineral lands from the various land grants, many timbered areas containing rich iron deposits passed, for instance, to the Northern Pacific Railroad. In addition, numerous entries were made under the Timber and Stone Act of June 3, 1878, and by Indian lands scrip.

[75] The foremost authority on this subject is Fremond P. Wirth, *The Discovery and Exploitation of the Minnesota Iron Lands* (Cedar Rapids, 1937).

[76] Report of the Land Commissioner, 1885, pp. 53-4.

[77] *Statutes at Large,* Vol. XVII, p. 465.

While a great number of the entries embracing iron deposits were undoubtedly fraudulent in character there was little opportunity for the government to recover them once patents had been granted. The same was true of timber lands, inasmuch as it was often difficult to separate these from mineral lands. The General Revision Act of 1891 provided that patent should issue within two years of final report.[78] The Bureau of Corporations, pointed out in its monumental report on the lumber industry, published in 1913, that the "criminal prosecution of timber frauds [under the Timber and Stone Act of June 3, 1878] . . . and of other public frauds as well," was "greatly hindered and in many cases prevented by the statute of limitations . . . which provides that a prosecution for criminal offenses against the United States is barred after a lapse of three years. As to recovery of the lands themselves, fraudulent entries" might be "canceled by the Interior Department at any time prior to patent." But after patent was "issued, any suit by the United States to annul or cancel it and recover the lands must be brought within six years of the date of patent."[79]

Professor Wirth's research on the exploitation of the iron lands in Minnesota reveals the methods by which large holdings were built up in the rich Mesabi range and other areas.[80] For instance, the Minnesota Iron Company, after maneuvering the public surveys to suit its own purposes, acquired a total of 8,772 acres by means of homestead and preemption entries and Sioux Half-Breed scrip.[81] And at Duluth, in 1882, O. T. Higgins, Frank W. Higgins, afterward governor of New York, and the Higgins Land Company obtained at a public sale 11,000 acres at $14,000. Much of this land was valued in 1922 at $50,000 an acre. In 1883, five 40-acre tracts were purchased at $1.25 an acre by Ezra Rust and George L. Burrows in the rich region near Hibbing.[82] In 1882, Morton B. Hull and William Boling purchased 7,500 acres for $22,500.[83] The holdings carved out of lands owned by timber interests and by the railroads were just as impressive, in spite of the fact that after 1887 the State of Minnesota was opposed to the acquisition of large holdings by corporations. Obviously the best iron

[78] ibid., Vol. XXII, p. 1,099.
[79] United States Bureau of Corporations, The Lumber Industry (Washington, D.C., 1913), Part I, p. 263; Wirth, Discovery and Exploitation of the Minnesota Iron Lands, pp. 129-30.
[80] ibid., Chaps. V and VI.   [81] ibid., pp. 138-9.
[82] ibid., p. 159.   [83] ibid., p. 160.

lands passed into private hands before the country was aroused to the danger.

Thomas Donaldson writing on the relationship of mine owners to the government in 1884, observed that "The difficulties of obtaining patent under existing laws are so great . . . that many mine owners prefer to rely upon their possessory title rather than purchase the fee from the government."[84] In the period, 1866 to 1880, there were known to be more than 200,000 mining locations, yet the number of lode or vein claims to which titles were obtained, by compliance with the mining laws, was but 3,978. The government received for these claims, containing 38,435 acres at $5 per acre, a total of $197,778. The number of placer mining claims patented during this same period was 1,303, embracing 110,186 acres at $2.50 per acre, for which the government received $288,767.[85] Of an estimated 5,528,970 acres of public coal lands in the United States, only 10,750 acres had been sold. The only startling defect in the operation of lode and placer mining legislation was the fact that valuable timber lands were entered under the placer laws which allowed areas as large as 160 acres at $1.25 an acre.[86] Wherever there was reason to suspect that the placer mining act was being misused, investigations were made, although it does not appear that this procedure put an end to the abuses.

[84] Donaldson, *The Public Domain*, p. 325.
[85] *ibid.*, p. 324.
[86] *ibid.*, pp. 1,220-1.

CHAPTER XVI

SETTLERS vs. RAILROADS

ALTHOUGH the subject of the disposition of railroad land grants belongs properly to a history of American land settlement, a few facts will illustrate the progress made by the railroads in the dispositions of their landholdings.[1] Not all the railroads pursued the seemingly intended policy of making their lands available at reasonable prices to actual settlers. Since many of the lands were exempt from taxation, the railroads often held them off the market in order to secure higher prices. Some railroads sold their holdings to land companies which were more interested in making money out of the lands than in developing the region through which the railroads passed.

Although the general effectiveness of the railroad as an agency of settlement is still a moot point, one fact is evident, that the railroads in the sale of their lands were more anxious to make money than to secure settlers. It is not difficult to understand, therefore, why the average settler did not benefit extensively from railroad land grant subsidies. In the first place, areas of land many times the size of the grants were withdrawn from the markets, and remained withdrawn until the railroads had finished selecting their lands. Out of the 180,000,000 acres of land granted up to 1880, only 34,000,000 had been definitely located.[2] Thus the settler had to take his homestead many miles distant from the railroad.

Moreover, the price of railroad lands was prohibitive, and the alternate sections of government land had first to be offered at auction where they generally went for more than the minimum of $2.50 per acre. Fifteen million acres of railroad-subsidy land had been disposed

[1] The settlement due to the promotion of the Illinois Central Railroad Company has already been discussed. While Professor Hedges has surveyed the history of the colonization done by the Northern Pacific Railroad, and Miss Edna M. Parker has brought forth much revealing information in her researches on the Southern Pacific Railroad, the subject of railroad land settlement still offers a fertile field for investigation. Consult Paul W. Gates, *The Illinois Central Railroad and Its Colonization Work* (Cambridge, 1934); J. B. Hedges, "Promotion of Immigration to the Pacific Northwest by the Railroads," *Mississippi Valley Historical Review*, Vol. XV (1928), pp. 183-203; Edna M. Parker, "The Southern Pacific Railroad and the Settlement in Southern California," *Pacific Historical Review*, Vol. VI (June 1937), pp. 103-19.

[2] Donaldson, *The Public Domain*, p. 783.

of before 1880 for seventy-two million dollars, or an average of almost $5 an acre. This average ranged from $2.26 on the Oregon and California Railroad to $12.12 on the Chicago, Burlington and Quincy.[3] Few settlers had the money for transportation costs as far as the West Coast; and good lands in the Mississippi Valley were becoming too costly for the settler without means. The homesteader was thus pushed onto the less desirable lands, some of which should never have been taken up for farming purposes at all. And many settlers, discouraged with the prospect of getting a good farm by honest means, became the tools of the crafty corporation which had designs upon timber, mineral or grazing lands. Most of the actual settlers, however, did not submit quietly to the appropriation of the remaining good lands by corporations. They were not slow to recall the declared intention of the government to reserve these lands for actual settlers, as indicated by the Republican platform of 1860 and the Homestead Act of 1862.

Early in the history of railroad land grants, the Department of the Interior had adopted the policy of withdrawing from sale all the lands within the indemnity limits, as soon as a map of the line was filed. In practice, these lands were held until the railroads found it convenient to make their selection.[4] There seems to have been no express authority for the policy, which too often favored the railway over the preemptor or homesteader and thus gave rise to much criticism. In fact, the complaints by the settlers about the administration of lands within the limits of the railway grants greatly encouraged the growth of sentiment in favor of general forfeiture of all the railroad grants.

The terms of the grants to the railroads specifically excepted those lands that were covered by a valid homestead or preemption claim. Yet a great number of people who had penetrated into the West in advance of the railroads found their position very insecure after the era of railway land grants began. This was especially true where the land had not been surveyed or when the settlers had not yet taken the proper legal steps to secure valid claim to the lands they occupied. The railroads very often contested the validity of the settlers' claims. Inconsistent and changing rules of the Interior Department often rendered a claim invalid, although the settlers had adhered to the rules and

[3] ibid.
[4] Lewis H. Haney, *A Congressional History of Railways, 1850-1887* (University of Wisconsin Bulletin No. 342, Madison, 1910), p. 29.

regulations previously in force. At times the purchaser of a tract of land from the original settler would find that because of some technicality the settler could not convey a valid title.

In 1874, an Oregon correspondent for the *New York Sun* questioned the justice of a system which permitted "the local offices to receive applications for homestead and preemption rights and to encourage settlements and improvements on the public domain, only to" receive "instructions from the General Land Office in Washington to drive the settlers away and turn their improved property over to some railroad corporation." The main trouble, insisted the correspondent, was that the Interior Department was conducted almost entirely in the interests of land grabbers and monopolists, that it paid little or no attention to laws or customs.[5]

Regarding the justice of this charge there was great difference of opinion. In spite of legislation upon the subject of preemptors' and homesteaders' rights within the limits of railway land grants many cases occurred which were not covered by the laws. Wide powers, even bordering upon the judicial, were therefore given to the Commissioner of the Public Land Office. He was authorized by Congress to "decide upon principles of equity and justice as recognized in courts of equity, and in accordance with regulations to be settled by the Secretary of the Interior, Attorney General, and the Commissioner conjointly, all cases of suspended entries of public lands and of suspended preemption land claims, and to adjudge in what cases patents shall issue upon the same."[6] In 1861, and again in 1862, the Secretary of the Interior ruled that "If the settler has filed his claim and made the required payment, no party who was a stranger to any interest in the land at the date of entry should be allowed to initiate any proceeding against the entry for the purpose of questioning the good faith of the preemptor, in order to secure the cancellation of his entry on charges of irregularity in the proceedings."[7] This lenient attitude does not harmonize with the views of the *New York Sun* correspondent quoted above.

In the late 'sixties, however, a contrary practice grew up. Investigations were ordered in cases where strangers brought charges of fraud in land claims, and in some cases forfeiture was declared after such investigations. But in 1871, the Land Commissioner recommended

---

[5] *Oregon City Enterprise,* February 27, 1874, quoting the *New York Sun.*
[6] *Revised Statutes,* Sec. 2,450.   [7] Report of the Land Commissioner, 1872, p. 60.

return to the earlier practice.[8] In spite of the fact that this policy invited fraud and irregular proceedings in the administration of the preemption law, he apparently felt that the stricter practice worked hardships upon many persons whose failure to abide by all the technical requirements of the law was due simply to carelessness or to some cause for which they were not responsible. Unfortunately for the settlers, the local land office was occasionally inclined to apply the strict letter of the law, and to cancel the claims of those who had not conformed to all the legal technicalities. If any of the lands thus vacated happened to be numbered odd sections within the limits of their grant, the railroad company claimed the lands and received the benefit of all improvements made thereon by the dispossessed settlers. There is of course no positive proof of collusion between the local land office and the railway company, but the inference that it sometimes existed seems plausible.

Probably a majority of the contested cases related to lands upon which a preemptor or homesteader lived at the time the rights of the railroad attached to the land grant, and which he later abandoned. And not many of these cases turned out favorably for the settler. Before 1871 it was the practice, where land within the odd numbered sections of railroad grants was abandoned by settlers, to hold that the reversion inured to the railroad. Even though the settler had acquired a valid claim before the time of the withdrawal of the lands within the grant, if he abandoned his plot at any period of his right the land passed to the holder of the grant.[9]

In 1871 there was a striking change of practice with regard to abandoned claims. A certain individual named Boyd made application to preempt a tract of land within an odd numbered section inside the limits of the grant to the Burlington and Missouri River Railroad Company in Nebraska. At the date of definite location of the line of the road, this tract had been covered by a homestead entry, but this entry had subsequently been cancelled. It was held in this case that by the terms of the grant all lands to which a homestead right had attached at the date of definite location, whether or not such claim was afterward declared invalid, were exempted from the operation of the grant, and that upon the abandonment or cancellation of such right the lands reverted to the public domain, subject again to the operation of the homestead or preemption laws.[10] This principle was also applied to preemption claims existing on lands at the date of the definite location of the road. Under these rulings the right of the railroad to such lands was no longer recognized.

In July 1872, a new division similar to the divisions for preemption and homesteading, was set up in the Public Land Office for the purpose of handling questions growing out of the adjustment of railroad grants. For under the ruling in the Boyd decision, the class of cases involving conflicts between the claims of settlers and those of the railroads had greatly increased. The examination of such cases involved the determination of the time when the railway grant attached and the exact status of the land in question at that time. If the party originating the claim still held the right to consummate title at that time, the railroad could acquire no rights to the land, even if the claim was later abandoned or cancelled. The right of another person to file a preemption or homestead claim upon the land was fully conceded. If, however, the abandonment or cancellation of the claim took place prior to the time that the rights of the railway company attached to the grant, the lands were awarded to the company.

In the years immediately following, it must be admitted, local land officials did not cooperate heartily in carrying out this decision. In 1873 the Land Commissioner reported that more than 1,100 cases of such conflicts had been entered upon the dockets of the land office, but only about half had been decided. He strongly urged an increase in the office force.[11] By 1876, the number of cases docketed had grown to 2,400, of which 2,158 had been acted upon, and were either settled or remanded.

The question of the validity of the settlers' claims to their lands was often complicated by the fact that a Land Commissioner or Secretary of the Interior occasionally reversed decisions and rulings made by his predecessors. In 1873, for example, the Land Commissioner decided some cases in the settlers' favor under a ruling made by the Secretary of the Interior to the effect that a homestead or preemption entry was valid which was made after the definite location of the road, but before the date of withdrawal of the lands by the local land office. The Secretary of the Interior, reversed the verdict of the Land Commissioner in these particular cases. The Commissioner protested that he had used

[10] *ibid.*, 1872, p. 64.   [11] *ibid.*, 1874, pp. 13-14.

as precedent for his action, the decisions made by the Secretary himself eight months earlier in some similar cases. The Secretary replied that those decisions were made by an acting Secretary who had misunderstood all the facts in the case.[12] The Secretary then went on to say that the decision of the Department now was that the right of the railroad attached at the time of the definite location of the road and not, as formerly held, at the time of withdrawal of the lands by the land office.[13] In an even earlier ruling, contained in an official letter dated January 20, 1870, the Commissioner of the Land Office had declared it the policy of "the Department that where a survey is made in accordance with a resolution of a board of directors of a company authorizing the same, the dates of such survey are to be taken as the definite location of the road."[14] It was possible for a board of directors sitting in a distant city to locate the general limits from which their lands would be taken, and definitely to select and secure title to their lands the moment the survey was completed. In case of any great delay of the proper authorities to give notice to the local land office that these lands should be withdrawn, it often happened that in good faith a settler was allowed to file a preemptors' or homesteaders' claim to land which had been selected by the railroad company. After he had lived upon it for some time, improving and cultivating it, he would be informed that his title was invalid and that the land belonged to the railroad. Not having the shadow of a claim to title he could not bring suit in a regular court in order that the decision of the Secretary of the Interior might be tested by regular judicial authority.[15] Of course, the railroad which benefited from the situation did not care to have the matter taken to the courts.

During 1874, memorials and petitions poured into Congress from dispossessed settlers or from the legislatures of the states and territories in which they resided, asking for legislation to protect their rights.[16] The memorial from the territorial legislature of Washington was especially emphatic in its demands.[17] It accused the government of breach

---

12 The writer was unable to find in the Land Commission Reports any record of the decisions referred to or any clue to the identity of the "Acting Secretary."

13 These facts were set forth in the course of the debate of the Relief Bill of 1876. *Congressional Record,* 44 Cong. 1 Sess., pp. 605-7.

14 *ibid.*   15 Haney, *Congressional History of Railways,* p. 32.

16 See *H. Misc. Doc.* No. 132, 43 Cong. 1 Sess., for a resolution from the legislature of Kansas, and *Doc.* No. 185 for one from Minnesota.

17 *ibid., Doc.* No. 218.

of contract, and held it responsible for damages sustained by those who were dispossessed because they had happened to file their claims between the dates of location of the land and the actual withdrawal of the land by the local land office. In this particular case the lands had not been withdrawn until sixty-five days after the date of the definite location of the land by the railway, and the settlers were not informed that their titles were invalid until after they had lived on their lands for nearly three years. The resolution was exceedingly critical of the Secretary of the Interior: "Do not the honorable Secretary's words and acts clearly convict him of inconsistency, incompetency, and negligence, if nothing more reprehensible?" it asked. "When would he have learned that the sale of these lands to private individuals was illegal or illegally made, if a railroad company had not called his attention to the subject? Why did he not withdraw [these lands] and prevent the sale . . . to innocent purchasers, and thereby protect their rights, or did he infer that they had none?"[18]

In response to these demands Congress passed a number of laws quieting the titles of specific groups of settlers, and in 1875 provided a method by which such conflicts could easily be settled. Where lands were found in the possession of actual settlers whose entries had been allowed subsequently to the time at which, by the ruling of the land office, the right of the railway attached, the railways might relinquish such lands and take others in lieu thereof. The entries of the filings of settlers might be perfected with complete title as though no grant had been made.[19]

However, this optional method of settling contested cases was not broad enough in its scope to benefit very many settlers. Agitation for further remedial legislation continued, and on April 21, 1876, Congress passed an act to confirm preemption and homestead entries of public lands within the limits of railroad grants in cases where such entries had been made under the regulations of the land acts of the United States in force at that time.[20] It specifically confirmed, those entries made in good faith by actual settlers prior to the time when notice of the withdrawal of the lands embraced within the land grant was received at the local land office, and provided that when such settlers had complied with all the terms of the homestead and preemption laws

[18] ibid. [19] Report of the Land Commissioner, 1876, pp. 115-16.
[20] Statutes at Large, Vol. XIX, pp. 35-6.

they should receive patents for their lands. This feature of the law was intended to remedy the conditions created by the decision of the Secretary of the Interior in 1873. Section 2 of the law provided that when, at the time of the withdrawal of the lands within a railway grant, valid preemption or homestead claims existed upon any lands which afterward were abandoned, and were re-entered by preemption or homestead claimants, such entries should be deemed valid and patents should be issued.

The debate on the bill was sharp. Its opponents attempted to postpone its passage, arguing that this was not a matter for legislation, but rather for action by the judiciary. They proposed instead a law enabling the dispossessed settler to file a suit in court. They were very fearful lest the vested property rights of the railroads should be affected, and pointed out that the railroads had issued bonds on their land grants as security, and that their rights to lands thus mortgaged should not be jeopardized. The defenders of the bill argued that provision had been made in a previous law by which the railroad company could receive other lands in lieu of those settled upon. The pertinent arguments in favor of the measure won out,[21] and the bill passed both houses of Congress by large majorities. In the Senate the vote stood 44 to 9.[22]

The framers of this law probably believed that they were providing relief for all those who had made settlements in good faith and had been adversely affected by the decisions of the administrative officials. For a while the law appeared to be adequate for this purpose, owing in large part to the liberal construction given it by Carl Schurz, who was Secretary of the Interior at that time. Schurz even instructed land officers to use the Act of 1876 to secure the rights of settlers who had made settlement on lands after the right of the railroad had attached, but before surveys were made which rendered it possible to distinguish odd from even numbered sections.[23]

In spite of the good intentions of the framers of the Act of 1876, however, a particular class of settlers found themselves excluded from its benefits. Certain decisions made by the Land Commissioners and by the Supreme Court endangered the title of any person who had filed a claim upon land which had previously been abandoned, unless he could present actual proof that the same person held a valid claim to

[21] *Congressional Record,* 44 Cong. 1 Sess., p. 606.
[22] *ibid.,* p. 692.　　　　[23] Report of the Land Commissioner, 1879, pp. 62-3

the land both at the time of the definite location of the railroad grant and at the time of the withdrawal of the lands by the local land office.

During the time that the Boyd decision was in force, it was held that land covered by a valid homestead or preemption claim at the time of *location* of the grant was to be excepted from the grant, even if it was abandoned before the date of withdrawal of the land. But according to the second section of the Act of 1876 requiring that a valid claim should exist at the time of the *withdrawal* of the land the railroad could claim such land. And according to the decision in Weber vs. Western Pacific Railroad Company, to have a valid preemption claim under the second section of the Act of 1876, the prior claimant must have possessed the requisite qualifications and must have met the essential requirements of the laws under which he claimed the land. He must have filed his claim before the location of the railroad lands in order for it to be valid at the date of withdrawal. If this was not the case, any subsequent settler upon the land might have his title contested by the railroad.

This ruling by the Land Commissioner was upheld by the Supreme Court in the case of Turner vs. Atchison, Topeka and Santa Fé Railroad Company. It was held that a preemption or homestead claim which was initiated within the limits of a railway grant after the time the grant took effect, even though prior to the time when the notice of the withdrawal for the company was received at the district office, was not a valid preemption or homestead claim within the meaning of the second section of the Act of 1876, and hence subsequent entries based upon such preemption or homestead claims were not confirmed by that statute.[24] In these contested cases the settler was at a tremendous disadvantage, especially since the Commissioner of the Land Office ruled that the burden of proof was upon the one alleging the existence of a bona fide claim.[25]

In the territory acquired from Mexico in 1848, a great deal of the land was claimed by private individuals under grants from the Mexican government. The treaty with Mexico stipulated that such titles should be recognized, but the claimants had to go through certain legal technicalities in order to have their claims properly recorded on the books of the land office. If they failed to do this within the time specified the land inured to the public domain of the United States. Sometimes as a result of the adjustment of the boundaries of these

[24] *ibid.*, 1880, p. 456.   [25] *ibid.*, pp. 96-7.

grants a portion of the land became government property. While these cases were pending it was the common practice for settlers to occupy these lands, in the anticipation that they would in time become subject to preemption or homestead entry. When such lands happened to fall within the limits of railroad grants, the question arose as to whether they inured to the government or to the railroad. In 1870, there came before the Secretary of the Interior a case involving the status of certain land which had been included in an alleged Mexican grant and which was within the twenty-mile limits of the Western Pacific Railroad. The Mexican grant had been rejected subsequent to the date of the act granting the land to the railroad. The railroad claimed the land, and contested the right of the settlers thereon to file homestead or preemption claims. The Secretary sustained the decision of the Land Commissioner that the right of the road did not attach to such lands upon the rejection of the alleged private claim, but that these lands were reserved from the railroad grant by the terms of the Acts of 1862 and 1864. Therefore they became public domain, liable to homestead and preemption entry.[26]

This ruling was later reversed, as far as California was concerned, by the Secretary of the Interior.[27] Certain lands which were included in the private land, "Los Medanos," were also within the limits of the grant to the Western Pacific Railroad Company. The lands within these limits were withdrawn from sale on January 30, 1865. The line of the road was definitely located in April 1868. Several persons settled upon a portion of the lands in the "Los Medanos" grant, but except in one case after the date of the final location of the road. In 1869, these lands were excluded from the Mexican land grant, and the railroad claimed them. Close examination of the statutes by the attorney for the railroad disclosed a loophole by which the settlers were defeated. A law passed in 1853 withheld lands in California claimed under foreign grant from preemption rights. The Secretary of the Interior agreed to the argument that under this statute the settlers had no valid preemption claim at the time the rights of the railroad attached or at the time the land passed back to the government in 1869. That part of the Boyd decision of 1871 that had excepted from the inclusion in the railroad grant all lands covered by a preemption or homestead entry, *whether such claim*

---

[26] *ibid.*, 1871, p. 179.　　　　　　　　　　　　[27] *ibid.*, 1876, pp. 103-4.

was afterward found valid and subsisting or not, was thus modified in 1873 so that the claim had to be proved *valid.*

The terms of the grant, it is true, excepted the odd-numbered sections of the public land, "sold, reserved, or otherwise disposed of," as well as lands to which a preemption or homestead entry attached at the time the line of road was definitely fixed. The Secretary's refusal to consider lands within fraudulent Mexican claims as "reserved or otherwise disposed of," therefore removed the last obstacle to the claim of the railroad to these lands. In support of his action the Secretary declared that it was the intention of Congress in making the grant, to be generous, and that he did not think the railroad should be deprived of the lands on account of finely spun considerations.

In October 1875, this question was finally settled by the Supreme Court. The Newhall vs. Sawyer case held that such lands were "reserved," and that in consequence they did not pass to the railroad companies under the grants made during such reservation.[28] This decision rectified the injustice done to many settlers in California by the Secretary's decision, and as soon as the patents that had been issued to the railroad companies had been cancelled, these settlers were able to take steps to secure title to their lands.

There were still other situations that gave rise to contests between the railroad company and the settler. In some instances lands supposed to be no longer needed for the purposes of adjusting a railroad grant were restored to the public domain, then later regranted to the railroad. In the interval of the supposed restoration of the land to the public domain, settlers entered in good faith supposing they could get title, but later found their claims contested by the railroad.[29]

The grants made to the Pacific railways contained a provision that if the company had not sold or disposed of all of the land within three years after the completion of the railroad, the remaining lands were to be thrown open to preemption at $1.25 an acre, the money to be collected by the land office, and then turned over to the railroad company. In the case of the Kansas Pacific Railroad Company vs. Dudymott,[30] the railway claimed that the issuing of bonds with the granted lands as security "disposed of," the lands within the terms of the grant and that therefore the land was not open to preemption. The Secretary

[28] *ibid.,* 1877, p. 50. [29] 44 Cong. 1 Sess., *H. Misc. Doc.* No. 109.
[30] Report of the Land Commissioner, 1879, pp. 73-83.

of the Interior pointed out that issuing bonds on the land as security
was the same as mortgaging the land. A party mortgaging land does
not convey the title to anyone else. The Secretary therefore ruled that
so long as the railroad company held the title to the lands it had not
disposed of them, and by the terms of the grant settlers were entitled
to preempt unsold and undisposed lands within the limits of these
railway grants. This was an important decision because it tended to
prevent the holding of lands by the railroad until the unearned increment made them more valuable.

Often settlers bought up the government sections of land within
railroad grants at $2.50 an acre, only to have the government later
declare the grant forfeited on account of the failure of the company to
fulfill the conditions of the grant. The railroad lands, upon being
returned to the public domain, sold at the minimum price of $1.25 an
acre. In justice to those who had paid $2.50 an acre, an act was passed
permitting such persons, without further payment other than regular
fees, to locate on any unoccupied lands an amount equal to their
original entry, excepting, of course, that in case of double minimum
lands only one half the amount could be taken.[31]

From this brief survey of the complex and difficult problems resulting
from the practice of granting great areas of the public domain to aid
railway construction it is clear that while the policy in general brought
many benefits yet it caused great loss and injustice to western settlers. In
the earlier period, before good lands became valuable and scarce, a
dispossessed settler could easily acquire land elsewhere, and the cancellation of his title entailed little loss except the expense of moving and
the expenditure of time and labor put upon improving the land. After
the middle of the 'seventies, however, when desirable farm lands of
the public domain were becoming scarce, dispossession became a much
more serious hardship.

Those settlers who lost their lands to the railroads were usually
unable to make their wrongs known beyond the confines of their
own neighborhoods. Few newspaper or magazine writers championed
the cause of the defenseless settler, or pointed out the means by which
he was being despoiled of his property. Not until the Grangers aroused
the attention of the country to the methods of the great railway corporations in their dealings with individuals did legislators and high

[31] *ibid.*, 1876, pp. 126-7.

government officials begin to take notice of the plight of the dispossessed settlers. It is true that Congress after 1875 attempted rather tardily to define and protect the rights of the settlers in their land claims. But the effectiveness of this relief legislation, depended in great measure upon the interpretation and administration of the provisions of the laws, and the decisions of certain Land Commissioners and Secretaries appeared to favor the railroads rather than the settlers. Naturally, the railroad companies took full advantage of the situation, in spite of the fact that they often violated all principles of justice and equity in so doing.

CHAPTER XVII

MONOPOLY CHALLENGED

FROM the foregoing pages it is obvious that the forces in the settlement of the public domain were becoming more and more monopolistic and consequently less and less democratic. The actual settler by the 'eighties was not in a favored position; in fact, corporations and speculators were definitely in the ascendancy. This was not only the situation with regard to the agricultural lands of the country, but with regard to other kinds of lands as well. The actual settler, the placer miner, the hand logger, and the individual grazer, were all at a disadvantage in competing with the corporation and moneyed interests on the last American frontier. Most of the land laws were designed to favor the individual, but the administration and actual operation of the laws did not. Legal regulations were evaded, the honest settler was thwarted; in fact, a system of landlord-tenant and land concentration was growing up on American soil, which if not checked would soon approach that of feudal Europe.

To defraud the government of a few acres of valuable land was not considered a very grave crime during the formative period of American history. Such defrauding, however, can hardly be blamed upon the frontiersmen as a class, for among them were also to be found honest and enterprising citizens, in fact, the founders of the nation. Nor could the General Land Office in all fairness be charged with the prevailing fraud and corruption, for there were many of the laws that could not have been enforced. If laws were defective, there was little the Land Office could do except make recommendations that they be changed. If public officials were corrupt, public opinion was the only agency for judging their actions and for bringing about their removal. To hold a particular political party accountable for the prevailing system is admissible, but in the last analysis it was the American people who sustained the Republican Party in power during most of this period.

Undoubtedly some responsibility rests upon the shoulders of those capitalists and speculators who openly disregarded the laws to appropriate for themselves vast areas of land. It is true that they forced the settlers to band together and defy the law in order to protect their hold ings. It is true that they helped to foster vast grants of land to railroads, that they were responsible for the exploitation of forest and mineral lands, and that they promoted the vast cattle and sheep ranges of the West. But these same interests furnished capital necessary for building up the new country. They actually contributed a great deal to settlement by building railroads, by bringing in settlers, and by building up towns. And many of them lost heavily in their investments. If eastern and foreign capital in the new country was an evil, it must be admitted that it was accompanied by much good.

Obviously the ultimate responsibility for the chaotic land system must rest at the door of the American people themselves and their representatives in Congress. Not until the people were really aroused could there be any real and vital reform. Irreparable damage had already been done to the nation's resources. Unless Congress should intervene to check the exploitative tendencies in the appropriation of the public lands the remaining resources could not long continue to be appropriated under democratic processes, nor could political processes be expected to protect the resources once they passed into private hands. Apparently the nation was at a crossroads: it must either decide to allow the exploitative processes to continue on their natural course or, through the agency of the government, it must interfere to protect the weak from the strong.

A logical first step in such intervention, seemed to be the codification of existing land legislation. The next step would be the repeal of legislation which had served its purpose and which in its outworn form was serving the ulterior purposes of the exploiters. Beyond this, the remaining resources needed to be carefully classified, farming and grazing lands separated from those of mineral and forest character. Only after these reforms were accomplished could the nation decide what to do with the remaining resources. The government might then adopt a policy which would carefully distinguish those lands which should go to the farmer and small stockman from those which should be developed only by corporations and capital. At the same time it might preserve the destructible and most valuable resources as a permanent national domain which, under strict and intelligent supervision, might be used in such a way as to secure them to the present as well as to the future. Even to initiate this ambitious program of land reform required an outstanding and unfailing leadership which could cope with the strength of those determined upon a course of exploitation. In the 'seventies and the 'eighties such a movement of land reform was inaugurated, and it was destined to serve as the prelude to the later and more important development in American history known as the conservation movement.

In 1875, in a survey of the arid region between the hundredth meridian and the Pacific Coast, there appeared the startling statement that the country was "rapidly approaching the time when the landless and homeless" could no longer hope to "acquire both lands and homes merely by settling them." In clear, unequivocable terms the author of the survey declared: "We have reached the border all along, from Dakota to Texas, where land for nothing is no cheaper than good land at $30 an acre." He concluded that "The phenomenon of the formation and rapid growth of new, rich, and populous states will no more be seen in our present domain, and we must soon face a condition of facts utterly new in the economy of the country, when, not new, but old states must make room for the increase in population, and thereby receive a fresh impetus. And the old song that 'Uncle Sam is rich enough to give us all a farm' will no longer be true, unless we take farms incapable of cultivation."[1]

Immigrant peoples from Europe who easily reached the public domain of the United States from the farthest capital of the Old World, at a cost of only about $70 a person, were fast filling up the remaining arable domain. The immigration of 1879-80 amounted to 450,000 souls. The quantity of land taken up in the arable region in that same fiscal year was about 7,000,000 acres. Thomas Donaldson, contemporary authority on the public lands problem, predicted that "At the same rate of absorption the arable lands so situated in the United States will be all taken within five years or by June 30, 1885."[2] In 1882, however, immigration reached the all-time high of 800,000 persons! Two years later the Land Commissioner advised that the time had arrived when the wastefulness in the disposal of public lands should cease, and that the portion still remaining should be economized for the use of actual settlers only.[3]

[1] W. B. Hazen, "The Great Middle Region of the United States," *North American Review*, Vol. CXX (1875), p. 22.
[2] Donaldson, *The Public Domain*, p. 22.
[3] Report of the Land Commissioner, 1884, p. 16.

Agricultural America of the 'eighties, when contrasted with that of the 'fifties presented a sordid picture. In the 'fifties there was plenty of good rich land which, considering the productive power of the soil, the nearness to markets, and the cheapness of transportation, sold at phenomenally low prices. By the 'eighties the best portions were already disposed of, and prices on land were rising. Since there were no river or canal systems of great consequence, settlers of the inferior lands in the West were at the mercy of the railroads. A report on the internal commerce of the country for 1880 showed that while the freight charges on three of the leading trunk lines of the East were reduced 60 per cent between 1868 and 1880, the increase in the quantity of freight transported during the same interval was more than 200 per cent.[4] Moreover, the rates in the newer regions of the West were extremely high in contrast with those in the East. It was this condition which had led to the Granger movement of the 'seventies.

The western farmer also faced high rates of interest on money borrowed, and an increasing reluctance on the part of bankers to lend. In fact, higher costs for setting up in the farming business in the West were making it more and more difficult for the common man of America to get a farm and to hold it once he got it. As a result of these conditions, "bonanza farming" began to make its appearance in the West.[5] Farms so operated had abundant means for employing the best machinery for utilizing the latest scientific methods. They could easily compete with the old democratic system of land held in small tracts and cultivated by the owner. Under this newer type of farm, however, the workers never developed the thrift and economy that ownership stimulates. Indeed, the industrialization processes had reached the very hinterland of America; the rugged individualism of the arable frontier was beginning to pass.

The country as a whole did not become seriously concerned about the new condition of things until the census of 1880 published, for the first time in American history, statistics bearing on tenancy, mortgages, and the size of land-holdings. Both contemporary and more recent authorities disagree on interpretation of the figures regarding the relative num-

[4] Edward T. Peters, *Century Magazine*, Vol. XXV (n.s., III) (1883), p. 599.
[5] Alva Benton, "Large Land Holdings in North Dakota," *Journal of Land and Public Utility Economics*, Vol. I (1925), pp. 405-13; Harold E. Briggs, "Early Bonanza Farming in the Red River Valley of the North," *Agricultural History*, Vol. VI (1932), pp. 26ff.

ber of tenant farmers. But all admit that there was a decided increase in tenancy. To a recent authority on the subject the census revealed that 26 per cent of the farmers of that period were tenants.[6] A contemporary observer stated that 1,024,601 farms were rented by tenants. Viewed from a slightly different angle, this same observer said that of the 7,670,-443 persons engaged in agriculture in the United States, 2,964,306 were registered as nominal owners of their holdings, the remainder were either tenants paying rent to landlords, or agricultural laborers.[7] In Iowa there was a 24 per cent tenancy and in Illinois, 31 per cent. Conditions in the South emanating from the Reconstruction era doubtless helped greatly to swell the national average. South Carolina had as many as 50 per cent of its families in the tenant classification; Alabama had 47 per cent. Probably what startled the American public were the implications of this tendency rather than the actual figures; yet contemporary observers insisted that America already had the largest tenant-farming class of any country in the world.[8] In fact, it was estimated that the United States had one-half million more tenants than any other nation.[9]

By 1895, it was claimed that 34 per cent of all farmers were renters. Between 1880 and 1930, the number of farms marked a gain of 57 per cent in the country; but the number of tenants showed a gain of 160 per cent—that is, a gain of 639,977 owners as compared with 1,639,764 tenants. With a half century of perspective, a recent authority declares that "Without a doubt, the growth in the number of farm tenants has been persistent, and much greater than for any other group of farmers in the country."[10] Whatever varying interpretation may be put upon the census figures of 1880, one thing is certain: after that date America could no longer boast that the institution of landlordism had obtained no foothold on her soil.

Not only did the statistics show a marked tendency toward tenancy, but they also revealed an alarming increase in the number of farm mortgages. As one contemporary observer averred: "The inquirer is amazed

---

[6] James G. Maddox and Howard A. Turner, "Farm Tenancy in the United States," *Certain Aspects of Land Problems and Government Land Policies* (Part VII of the *Report on Land Planning* of the National Resources Board), Sect. II, p. 21.

[7] Thomas P. Gill, "Landlordism in America," *North American Review*, Vol. CXLII (1886), pp. 55-6.

[8] *ibid.*, p. 57.

[9] "Alien Landlordism in America," *Public Opinion*, Vol. IX (June 21, 1890), p. 244.

[10] Maddox and Turner, "Farm Tenancy in the United States," *loc. cit.*, p. 21.

at the extent to which farmers, nominally owners of their holdings, really hold their land under mortgage, and at the extent to which farmers, in the westerly states and territories especially are plunged into debt."[11] In Illinois and Michigan, two wealthy agricultural states which kept mortgage records, it was revealed in 1886 that the former state had eight million acres of land encumbered by mortgages, aggregating $124,000,000, while in the latter state, one-half of the farms were mortgaged (three-fourths in the newer sections), for a total of $130,000,000.[12] By 1895, about 500,000 of the 4,750,000 farm families in the United States had mortgages.[13] It is difficult to distinguish, however, between mortgages that represent borrowing to meet living expenses and those that represent profitable business enterprise. In the figures for 1895, it was maintained that only 3 per cent represented borrowing to meet living expenses.[14] The tendency in farm indebtedness, like that in tenancy, carried a solemn warning of grave economic conditions.

But the picture is not complete without viewing a third set of facts concerning land tenure in the country. In 1850, the farms of this country averaged 203 acres each; in 1860, around 199 acres; and in 1870, approximately 153 acres.[15] Yet these figures do not reveal the entire picture. It is significant that while the number of farms of more than 1,000 acres fell, between 1860 and 1870, from 5,364 to 3,720; it rose in the next decade from 3,720 to 28,578, an impressive increase of 660 per cent. The tendency was toward large farms, and more striking still is the fact that the rate of increase was greatest in the West.[16]

An article in the *Contemporary Review* in 1868 called attention to these land-monopolization tendencies, asserting that one man alone owned as much as 23,000 acres of western lands, but it attracted very little attention.[17] By the 'eighties, however, there was hardly a prominent periodical in the country which was not carrying articles on the subject. The public became aware that vast areas of agricultural, grazing, timber, and mineral lands were being appropriated by Americans,

[11] Thomas P. Gill, "Landlordism in America," *loc. cit.,* p. 57.

[12] "The Decline of the Farmer," *Belford's Magazine,* Vol. II (April 1889), p. 644.

[13] *Census Bulletins,* 1895, No. 98.   [14] *ibid.*

[15] "Our Public Lands," *Appleton's Journal,* Vol. XI (March 28, 1874), p. 414.

[16] Edward T. Peters, "Evils of Our Public Land Policy," *Century Magazine,* Vol. XXV (February 1883), p. 601.

[17] See Charles H. Pearson, "The Land Question in the United States," *Contemporary Review,* Vol. IX (1868), p. 353.

and even more ominous, by foreign capitalists.[18] By 1886 it was claimed that 26,647,000 acres were owned by foreign land syndicates.[19]

The Scully estate was a much-publicized example of individual land holding. William Scully, it was said, owned 90,000 acres in Illinois, which paid him an annual rent of $200,000.[20] Though Scully came to America in 1851 he was, nevertheless, looked upon as an alien. As one observer remarked: "It is unquestionably the ambition of the Scullys and landlords of their ilk to reproduce in America, as nearly as is practicable and profitable, the conditions which obtain in Ireland."[21]

Thomas Donaldson, the foremost contemporary authority on the public lands, was not alarmed over the tendency toward monopolization. He felt that the power of taxation exercised by legislatures elected by full manhood suffrage would be able to break up the extensive holdings.[22] But Donaldson did not represent the majority view. Public feeling became so strong that in 1885 the *North American Review* sent a special commissioner, Thomas P. Gill, to investigate personally the startling conditions allegedly existing in the states of Illinois, Iowa, Kansas, Nebraska, and Dakota, where bonanza farming was increasing. In his report[23] which appeared in the January 1886 issue he declared it difficult to say which was the more surprising, the extent to which the system popularly known as landlordism was gaining a foothold on American soil, or the ignorance of the American people about the matter.[24] Henry Strong, a man of considerable means, challenged Gill's observations in the next issue of the *Review*. After twenty-five years of observation and experience he was convinced that the tendency was toward smaller farms and a greater number of freeholders.[25] Another authority, Professor D. B. King, upheld Strong's views.[26] But the argument did not end there.

---

[18] See the foregoing Chapter.

[19] *North American Review*, Vol. CXLVI (1886), p. 153.

[20] "Alien Landlorism in America," *Public Opinion*, Vol. IX (June 21, 1890), pp. 244-5. Addison E. Sheldon reveals the total holdings of Scully as comprising more than 210,000 acres in Nebraska, Kansas, Missouri, and Illinois; see *idem, Land Systems and Land Policies in Nebraska* (Nebraska State Historical Society *Publications*, Vol. XXII, 1936), *Appendix*, p. 321.

[21] "Alien Landlordism in America," *Public Opinion*, Vol. IX (June 21, 1890), pp. 244-5.

[22] "The Public Lands of the United States," *North American Review*, Vol. CXXXIII (1882), p. 206.

[23] Thomas P. Gill, "Landlordism in America," Vol. CLXII, pp. 52-67.

[24] *ibid.*, p. 53.   [25] Henry Strong on Alien Landlordism in *ibid.*, p. 250.

[26] *ibid.*, pp. 254-7.

An article by Henry George, whose writings on such subjects as land monopoly, the unearned increment, and single tax were widely known, appeared in the next issue of the *North American Review*. George tore to pieces the arguments of both Strong and King, and gave considerable support to the conclusions reached by Gill.[27] He contended that with the increase in population there was a general tendency toward smaller-sized holdings. He argued that "As society develops, the stock range is succeeded by the farm; the farm of extensive culture by the farm of intensive culture; the grain field by the market garden; and the market garden, in its turn, is cut up into city lots."[28] But he insisted that while this tendency was going on, the ownership of the land was in reality being concentrated into fewer hands and landlordism was increasing.[29]

Tenant farming, he continued, was the intermediary stage through which independent tillers of the soil had passed in other countries, and were beginning to pass in this country, to the condition of agricultural laborers and chronic paupers. If it was true that the number of farms under mortgage actually equalled the number of renters then, George asserted, the farmers who really owned their land were already in the minority in the United States. "But," he concluded, "it needs no reference to census tables or special facts to prove that under present conditions the small American freeholder is doomed. Here are certain broad facts of common knowledge: Our population is increasing. We have now practically reached the limit of our public domain. In agriculture, as in other branches of industry, the march of invention and the improvement of processes of production and exchange tend steadily to the requirement of more capital. The value of land is rising. . . . It necessarily follows that the ownership of land must tend to concentrate, and an increasing proportion of the people to become tributary to the rest. . . . We are on the verge of an event which is, in some respects, the most important that has occurred since Columbus sighted land—the 'fencing in' of the last available quarter section of the American domain."[30]

In the America of the 'fifties there were, it is true, tenants, renters, mortgagors and landlords, but generally speaking the wage earner, the day laborer, or the farm hand could become a freeholder if he so desired. In that day the West was a land of opportunity, a region in which

[27] "More About Alien Landlordism," *ibid.*, pp. 386-401.   [28] *ibid.*, p. 389.
[29] *ibid.*, p. 392.   [30] *ibid.*, pp. 398-9.

the poor man could find salvation. Horace Greeley had in truth portrayed the spirit of his times with the epigram: "Go West young man and grow up with the country." But now in the 'eighties the reverse was more typical. The tenor of the times may perhaps be portrayed by the comment that "no feeling is . . . more obvious than the desire to quit the farm. Whenever the landed proprietor feels able to do so, he moves to town, and our cities and villages grow at the country's expense. Our agriculturists act as if they were ashamed of their calling."[31]

Indeed, the doors of western opportunity were closing; the new frontier was now the city. The census of 1890 officially recorded the disappearance from the census maps of the continuous frontier line of two to six persons per square mile. In face of these new conditions, the immediate and pressing problem for the country was to rid itself of the outworn federal land system. The movement for land reform constituted the closing chapter of the era of the arable domain, and at the same time the prelude to the last phase of public lands history—the conservation of the remaining natural resources.

An article in the *Nation* late in 1870 clearly depicted the increasing doubts about the wisdom of railroad land subsidies: "It is only within the last few years," the article observed, "that a doubt has risen in the public mind as to whether, after all, the policy of giving away the lands almost indiscriminately to great railroad corporations is wise as we thought it to be ten years ago. In the West, especially, this doubt has almost developed into positive opposition, and not only was the cessation of land grants made a prominent issue in many local platforms of both parties, but many leading men in both Houses of Congress, as well as President Grant, have openly expressed their downright hostility to the present system."[32]

By 1870 the opposition to further land grant subsidies to railroads had become so strong that it predicated an end to all future railroad grants. In that year the House of Representatives passed a resolution to the effect that in its judgment "the policy of granting subsidies in public lands to railroad and other corporations ought to be discontinued; and

---

[31] "Decline of the Farm," *Belford's Magazine,* Vol. II (April 1899), p. 643.

[32] J. B. Hodgskin, "The Truth About Land Grants," Vol. XI (December 1870), p. 417. Perhaps George W. Julian, Representative from Indiana, was the foremost congressional opponent of railroad land grants. Another outstanding critic of the corporation grants was Henry George; see his *Our Land and Land Policy, National and State* (San Francisco, 1871).

that every consideration of public policy and equal justice to the whole people requires that the public lands of the United States should be held for the exclusive purpose of securing homesteads to the actual settlers under the homestead and preemption laws, subject to reasonable appropriation of such lands for the purpose of education."[33]

In spite of this declared intention of the House and the growing opposition in the country at large, the very next session of Congress saw a mad rush to push further railroad grants. At least eighteen bills were tabled and forty-one others were referred to a committee. Indeed, almost 20,000,000 acres of land grants slipped through in this session, most prominent of which was the one to the Texas Pacific Railroad. James A. Garfield from Ohio explained his support of this last land grant bill as follows: "I fully share in the general sentiment of the country, that we ought to put a speedy and effective end to the policy of granting lands to railway corporations, but justice to the South dictates this one."[34] It is a question whether Garfield at this period of history was very kindly inclined toward the South. A more important factor in influencing congressional action may have been the effectiveness of the lobby. There is evidence that over one hundred companies were maintaining from two to ten agents in the corridors of the Capitol for the purpose of lobbying and bribing members of Congress.[35]

Nevertheless, the year 1871 marked the end of land grants to railroads. There was not a party platform in 1872 which did not condemn the whole system and insist that the public domain be held for actual settlers. In 1874, the platform of the Democratic Party demanded "reform to stop waste of public lands. . . . The Republicans have squandered 200,000,000 acres on railroads alone."[36]

The cessation of the practice of granting lands in aid of western railroad construction was followed almost immediately by a clamor for forfeiture of grants in cases where the railroad companies had failed to live up to the conditions of the grant. Before 1874 it had been taken for granted that the lands would automatically revert to the government if the conditions of the grant were not complied with. In that year, however, the Supreme Court, in a decision of fundamental significance,

[33] *Congressional Globe*, 41 Cong. 2 Sess., p. 2,095.

[34] *ibid.*, 41 Cong. 3 Sess., p. 1,468.

[35] J. B. Hodgskin, "The Truth About Land Grants," *loc. cit.*, p. 417.

[36] George D. Ellis, *Platforms of Two Great Political Parties, 1856-1928*, p. 32.

declared that the Department of the Interior had no power to declare a grant forfeited.[37]

It thereupon became necessary for Congress to pass a specific act of forfeiture in each case before the government could gain control of the land and open it once more to homestead or preemption entry. Many of the railroads had not lived up to the stipulation of their grants, and in 1876 there was some sentiment in Congress in favor of a general forfeiture law; however, the majority thought that general forfeiture would be harsh and unjust. Two years later another attempt was made to put through a general forfeiture measure. The Committee on Public Lands reported that 100,000,000 acres of land, almost half the amount given to all the railroads, would be restored if such a bill were passed. The annual report of the Land Commissioner showed clearly that an act of this sort was essential, but the bill failed to pass. So Congress continued to resort to the enactment of specific forfeitures.

In the election of 1880, both major parties evaded the land-grants issue. In fact, the editor of the *Nation* charged that the Republicans pointed with pride "to the construction of 5,100 miles of railroad, between 1860 and 1874, largely with money of unfortunate private individuals who lost a large part of their investment."[38] There was evidence, in fact, that railroad building progressed more rapidly after the federal government ceased subsidization than before.[39]

By 1884, the movement for forfeiture was nearing a new high. This was primarily because of the increasing strength of the Democratic Party. Bills and reports in Congress became numerous. All political parties began to demand forfeiture, although the Republicans confined their stand to those cases in which there had been no attempt in good faith to carry out the conditions of the grant. Slowly but surely public pressure made itself felt. In 1876 Grover Cleveland had characterized railroad land grants as "a check to our national development."[40] Cleveland was elected president in 1884, and an act in Congress in 1885 resulted in the revocation of the Texas Pacific grant as well as the grant to a railroad from Portland to Astoria and McMinville. These forfeitures applied to lands adjacent to uncompleted parts of the road. The next year the lands along the uncompleted parts of the Atlantic and

---

[37] Haney, *Congressional History of Railways*, p. 24.
[38] *The Nation*, Vol. XXX (1880), p. 430.
[39] *North American Review*, Vol. CXLII (January 1886), p. 153.
[40] W. V. Hansel, *Life and Times of Grover Cleveland* (Philadelphia, 1888), p. 242.

Pacific Railroad were restored to the public domain, but in this case the right of way was not forfeited. At about the same time, several grants in Alabama, Mississippi and Louisiana were revoked.

A partial victory was gained in 1887 by the passage of an act which provided for the adjustment of all congressional land grants to railways and for the forfeiting of unearned lands.[41] By this comprehensive law the Secretary of the Interior was authorized and directed to take immediate steps to adjust all land grants in accordance with Supreme Court decisions. All patents erroneously issued were to be cancelled and the title restored to the United States. But since this did not mean general forfeiture, the advocates of reform were not satisfied. In 1888 the Democratic Party platform demanded the restoration of 100,000,000 acres of land to the public domain to be "sacredly held as homesteads for our citizens."[42]

Finally, by Act of September 29, 1890, complete victory was won. All grants which were not being utilized when this act was passed were declared forfeited, and the lands thus confiscated were to be restored to the public domain.[43] The measure did not, however, result in any wholesale restorations to the public domain, because generally speaking, the railroad companies successfully contested such forfeitures in the courts.[44] In fact, the legislative victory of 1890 actually brought about restoration of only one-fiftieth of the amount of land demanded by the Democrats in 1888.

If the prodigious grants of land to railroad corporations forced many actual settlers to take lands unfavorably located, it is likely that it was this same lack of available good lands that led the settler to break in upon the Indian reservations. As already shown, it was this pressure upon Indian lands that led to most of the Indian wars between 1862 and 1877.[45] In the mad scramble for the remaining acres of good arable land the settler knew no bounds. To the frontiersman the Indian had always been considered an obstacle in the path of progress. From the very earliest period of American history the red man had been pushed to the westward. But now the closing chapter had set in; the Indian had no

[41] Haney, *Congressional History of Railways*, p. 28.
[42] Ellis, *Platforms of Two Great Political Parties*, p. 73.
[43] *Statutes at Large*, Vol. XXVI, p. 496.
[44] Hibbard, *History of Public Land Policies*, p. 250.   [45] *supra*, Chap. XIV.

escape. He was completely surrounded by the white man's civilization; buffalo and other game were fast disappearing. Most of the Indian tribes of the West defeated in war after war in the period between 1862 and 1877 were humbled and put completely at the mercy of the American government. Any new policy that might be evolved had to be predicated upon the condition that the Indian must relinquish his land to the insatiable white settler, whose only claim to this land before law and God was that he could make better use of it than the red man. While eastern humanitarianism and sympathy were to play a part in its evolution, it was clear from the outset that the prime motivation for this new Indian policy came from a section of the country whose hatred for the Indian knew no bounds. These facts must be borne in mind in surveying the events which led ultimately to the passage of the Dawes Act of 1887.

A sincere desire for the establishment of a portion of the public domain as a permanent abode for the Indians is evident in the annual messages of President Grant. In 1872, he discussed the advisability of reserving all of the Indian Territory south of Kansas (consisting of the present State of Oklahoma) for the Indians, and removing the tribes from other parts of the country to that section. He visualized the Indian Territory as a fertile region, with fabulous agricultural potentialities, which in a few years, would be teeming with prosperous farms cultivated by the Indian braves. He even mentioned the possibilities of a territorial form of government for the Indians which should "protect the Indians from inroads of whites for a term of years, until they become sufficiently advanced in the arts of civilization to guard their own rights, and from the disposal of the lands held by them for the same period."[46]

Recurring again to this subject the next year he wrote: "The Indian Territory south of Kansas and west of Arkansas is sufficient in area and agricultural resources to support all the Indians east of the Rocky Mountains. In time, no doubt, all of them except a few who may elect to make their homes among the white people, will be collected there. As a preparatory step for this consummation, I am now satisfied that a territorial form of government should be given them, which will secure the treaty rights of the original settlers and protect their homestead from alienation for a period of twenty years."[47]

[46] Richardson, *Messages and Papers of the Presidents*, Vol. VII, p. 200.
[47] *ibid.*, p. 252.

The President's views were shared by the Secretary of the Interior and the Commissioner of the General Land Office. As early as 1870 the Commissioner had asked the Secretary of the Interior whether individual Indians who had voluntarily severed their tribal relations, had the right to make entries upon public lands under the homestead law. In a letter dated February 11, 1870, the Secretary of the Interior, replied that Indians who had voluntarily renounced tribal relations might be entitled to homestead rights if they agreed to "forego all claim to or share in any of its [the tribe's] annuities or benefits, and in good faith to perform the duties of citizens of the United States."[48]

The position of the Indian was indeed peculiar. By the Act of Congress of March 3, 1871, no more treaties were to be made between the federal government and Indian tribes. The Indians were wards of the government and were allowed to occupy lands which they did not own, although the government paid them for some of the lands which they were compelled to give up.[49] In view of these considerations the Commissioner of the General Land Office believed that it was unlawful for Indians to make entries on the public domain. He held that the tribal relationship could be dissolved only by the tribe as a tribe with the consent of the government of the United States. Accordingly, he ordered cancellation of all entries that had been made up to that time by Indians, until such action was authorized by congressional legislation.[50] But a year later the commissioner sent to the district land offices a circular which seemed to indicate a reversal of opinion, at least in regard to preemption rights:

An Indian desiring to enter the public land under this act [preemption] must make application to the register and receiver of the proper district land office; also an affidavit setting forth the fact of his Indian character; that he was born in the United States; that he is the head of a family, or has arrived at the age of twenty-one years; that he has abandoned his tribal relations and adopted the habits and pursuits of civilized life; and this must be corroborated by the affidavits of two or more disinterested witnesses.[51]

While the President and other administrative officials of the government were endeavoring to deal fairly with the Indians, to have them settled on lands which might be their own permanent homes, Americans on the frontiers were intruding on the lands of the Indians, and in

[48] Report of the Land Commissioner, 1874, p. 42.
[49] Donaldson, *The Public Domain*, p. 240.
[50] Report of the Land Commissioner, 1874, p. 43.   [51] *ibid.*, 1875, p. 57

some instances, driving them out. President Grant laid the responsibility for the Indian outbreak of 1876, which led to the annihilation of Custer's army, on "hostilities" growing "out of the avarice of the white man, who has violated our treaty stipulations in his search for gold. The question might be asked why the government has not enforced obedience to the terms of the treaty prohibiting the occupation of the Black Hills region by whites. The answer is simple: the first immigrants to the Black Hills were removed by troops, but rumors of rich discoveries of gold took into that region increased numbers. Gold has actually been found in paying quantity, and an effort to remove the miners would only result in the desertion of the bulk of the troops that might be sent there to remove them. All difficulty in this matter has, however, been removed—subject to the approval by Congress—by a treaty ceding the Black Hills and approaches to settlement by citizens."[52] Again the federal government surrendered to the white intruders.

Like his predecessor, President Hayes consistently pled for justice to the Indians, that they be protected in the possession of the land which the government had set aside for them. In his annual message of 1877 he pointed out how "they have been driven from place to place. The purchase money paid to them in some cases for what they called their own has still left them poor. In many instances when they had settled down upon land assigned to them by compact and begun to support themselves by their own labor, they were rudely jostled off and thrust into the wilderness again. Many, if not most, of our Indian wars have had their origin in broken promises and acts of injustice upon our part, and the advance of the Indians in civilization has been slow because the treatment they received did not permit it to be faster and more general."[53]

Two years later, Hayes, supported by the painstaking labors of his Secretary of the Interior, Carl Schurz, recommended to Congress enactment of a law to enable the federal government to give Indians a title in fee, inalienable for twenty-five years, to the farm lands assigned to them by allotment. He also repeated the recommendation contained in his first message, that Congress by law declare Indians eligible for the benefits of the homestead act.[54] These measures were again urged in his fourth and final annual message, December 6, 1880.

[52] Richardson, *Messages and Papers of the Presidents*, Vol. VII, p. 401.
[53] *ibid.*, p. 475.   [54] *ibid.*, p. 576.

If the labors of Carl Schurz as Secretary of the Interior of the Hayes administration awakened the official mind to the need for a new Indian policy, so the novelist, Helen Hunt Jackson, and the editors of eastern periodicals and newspapers helped to arouse the American public. The appearance in 1881 of Helen Hunt Jackson's *Century of Dishonor* with its severe censure of American Indian policy made Easterners aware of the existence of the Indian as an individual and raised the question whether the Indian as well as the foreigner and the Negro might not well be admitted to a part in the American social order. Public opinion ripened and in due course President Cleveland made recommendations which led to the passage of the Dawes Severalty Act in 1887.

This act provided means by which the communal organization of the Indian tribes of the West could be dissolved, their reservations broken up, and the individual members admitted as American citizens.[55] Homesteads were granted by the Dawes Act to individual members of the tribes, 160 acres to heads of families, 80 acres to single adults and orphans, and 40 acres to each dependent child. The remainder of the reservation land of each tribe was to be held in trust for the tribe with the understanding that if these lands were opened to white settlement the government would bestow upon the tribe an adequate payment. Citizenship was conferred upon all Indians who accepted the benefits of the act, but there was also the qualification that no Indian might dispose of his land for twenty-five years. This latter restriction was not eased until 1906 when the Burke Act empowered the Secretary of the Interior to grant full property rights to deserving Indians without waiting for the expiration of the full period, although citizenship was to be deferred until such ownership was granted.

The operation of the Dawes Act of 1887 confirmed the expectations of its proponents. By 1892 agreements had been negotiated with fourteen Indian tribes, restoring to the public domain 26,000,000 acres most of which was already open to settlement. The greatest of the Indian reservations—that of the once powerful Sioux of the plains—consisting of 9,000,000 acres had already been opened to sale and settlement; the 21,000 Sioux Indians had accepted five other separate and very-much reduced reservations.[56] Nor did the old Indian Country escape the

---

[55] *Statutes at Large,* Vol. XXIV, p. 388.
[56] Report of the Secretary of the Interior, 1892, p. 7.

pressure of the grasping whites; at noon on April 22, 1889, extensive areas formerly owned by the Five Civilized Tribes had been opened up, and a year later the Territory of Oklahoma had come into existence. The Secretary of the Interior pointed with pride to the progress being made: "The reservation system and the continuance of tribal relations," he observed, "have been broken to such a degree that what remains of these obstacles to the Indian's progress is light and easily removed. The reservations have been purchased and converted into settlements after due allotments to the Indians in sufficient quantities to enable them each to have a farm. A constant effort has been made to suppress the influence of the Indian chiefs or head men. As a result there has developed among these people a sense of the importance of the individual, an appreciation of his power to take care of himself and of the necessity that this power should be exercised."[57]

By 1906, through the breaking up of the reservation system, some 75,000,000 acres, or about three-fifths of the whole amount of Indian land released by the Dawes Act of 1887, had been appropriated by whites.

[57] *ibid.*, p. 8.

CHAPTER XVIII

REVISION AT LAST

RAILROAD grants and Indian reservations were not the only problems confronting the government in the movement to reform existing land policies. The preemption and homestead laws, and the modified form of the homestead principle in such legislation as the Desert Land and Timber Culture acts had all become the tools of moneyed interests engaged in appropriating the valuable natural resources. Perhaps the preemption system was open to the most serious charges. As early as 1871, the Land Commissioner, who had had eight years of experience in the Land Office, recommended the immediate repeal of the preemption law.[1] He was supported by the Secretary of the Interior, but Congress took no immediate action. Not until January 5, 1875, was a bill introduced into Congress for this purpose. The advocates of this reform dubbed the Preemption Act the "speculator's law" and distinguished it from the "settler's law."[2] In 1879 a similar bill was introduced, but got no further than the second reading. In fact, Congress seemed intent upon easing all restrictions on settlement.

The Act of May 27, 1878, provided that a preemption claim might be commuted into a homestead.[3] And by another, passed May 14, 1880, any settler on land surveyed or unsurveyed, who intended to claim the same under the Homestead Act, was to be allowed a period of time to file his homestead application and to perfect his original entry similar to that provided for preemption claimants. The act also stipulated that the right of the homesteader should relate back to the date of settlement in the same way as preemption.[4] In other words, this act placed homesteaders on an equal footing in all respects with preemptors, and the special utility of the preemption system for purposes of bona fide settlement thus ceased. Any person who might make a preemption entry might now make a homestead entry. Any land that might be

---

[1] Report of the Secretary of the Interior, 1871, p. 12.
[2] 45 Cong. 2 Sess., S. Misc. Doc. No. 80, pp. 5-6.
[3] Report of the Land Office, 1879, p. 417.
[4] Statutes at Large, Vol. XXI, p. 140; Report of the Land Office, 1880, p. 33.

entered under the preemption law might also be entered under the homestead law with the same privileges and guarantees. An individual might now commute from preemption to homestead, or vice versa.[5] Under the homestead law the settler might purchase his land within the same time, upon the same terms, and by the same proofs, as in preemption cases. There was therefore no practical necessity for the continuance of both the preemption and homestead systems. Had Congress been seriously determined on reform, it should have repealed the preemption laws and commutation features of the Homestead Act, a step which would have done much to guarantee bona fide settlements.

Throughout the administration of President Hayes, Carl Schurz, as Secretary of the Department of the Interior, made a serious effort toward law enforcement. If the general settlement laws could have been enforced it seems fair to conclude that they would have been, under this efficient, honest administration. Schurz should also be given credit for focussing public attention on the need for a general revision of the whole land system. He was intent upon two objectives: first, to give the poor and worthy settler an opportunity to establish himself on the land; and second, to inaugurate a campaign to save the timber resources of the country. The following extract from a letter written by the Secretary on August 29, 1877, is typical of his viewpoint: "With regard to the criminal prosecutions of depredators, I would recommend that they be not confined to those mostly poor persons who actually cut timber on public lands with their own hands, but that they be directed as well and principally against the parties who are found to have organized and directed the stealing of timber on the public lands on a large scale."[6]

Early in his administration Schurz made, through his Land Commissioner, several noteworthy recommendations directed toward preservation of the western forests:

1. That Congress "by proper legislation withdraw all lands chiefly valuable for pine timber from the operation of the homestead and preemption laws" and that such lands be sold for cash at an appraised value.

2. That the Secretary of the Interior be authorized by law to sell at just and fair valuation, to be ascertained as Congress may direct, timber from the

[5] *Land Commissioners' Letters*, Preemption Bureau, Vol. XCLV (1880), p. 393.

[6] Report of the Secretary of the Interior, 1877, p. xvii.

public lands in mining districts where it would be contrary to existing laws to sell the land by legal subdivisions.

3. "That Congress be requested to enact a law providing for the care and custody of such timber lands as are unfit for agriculture and for the gradual sale of the timber thereon and for the perpetuation of the growth of timber on such lands by such needful rules and regulations as may be required to that end."[7]

These recommendations contained the essentials of what was later to become the general forest policy for the United States, and Schurz and his administration should be given credit for their inauguration. The proposals had the full support of President Hayes who brought the matter before the country in his annual message of December 3, 1877. He "earnestly recommend[ed] that the measures suggested by the Secretary of the Interior for the suppression of depredations on the timber lands of the United States for the selling of the timber from the public lands, and for the preservation of the forests be embodied in a law, and that, considering the urgent necessity of enabling people of certain states and territories to purchase timber from the public lands in a legal manner, which at present they cannot do, such a law be passed without unavoidable delay."[8]

Congress, so long adamant toward any change in the land system, suddenly rose to action. On April 30, 1878, an appropriation of $7,500—actually an insignificant amount if one considers the magnitude of the task to be achieved—was made to cover the expenses of clerks detailed to investigate fraudulent land entries, trespasses on the public lands, and cases of official misconduct. This appropriation was followed on June 20 by another of $25,000 to "meet the expenses of suppressing depredations upon timber on the public lands."[9] The next year Congress allocated $40,000 for the despatching of fifteen agents to the western states and territories.[10]

Meanwhile, legislation was being rushed through Congress to provide for a classification and sale of timber lands. On June 3, 1878, the Timber Cutting Act and the Timber and Stone Act were passed.[11] For the first time in the history of the public domain, a person could now legally buy timber. The West was almost unanimously in favor of

---

[7] Report of the Land Commissioner, 1877, p. 25.

[8] Richardson, *Messages and Papers of the Presidents,* Vol. VII, p. 476.

[9] Report of the Land Commissioner, 1878, p. 117.

[10] Report of the Secretary of the Interior, 1879, p. 26.

[11] *Statutes at Large,* Vol. XX, pp. 89-90.

these timber laws. The Timber Cutting Act attempted to prevent depredations on the western and southern forests by allowing bona fide settlers and mining interests to cut timber on the public domain for their own legitimate use without charge. The Timber and Stone Act, extending to the states and territories of California, Oregon, Nevada, and Washington, provided for the sale of surveyed lands, valuable chiefly for timber or stone and unfit for cultivation, in quantities of not more than 160 acres at the minimum price of $2.50 per acre.

The immediate results of these reforms, however, were anything but encouraging. In fact, the effect seemed to be to spur on the fraudulent appropriations of valuable resources. Those interests bent on exploitation apparently reasoned that if the government was determined on reform, then they must usurp as much as they could before the doors were closed upon them. The report of the Land Commissioner of 1880 thus constituted a sad commentary on the reforms attempted by the Schurz administration:

"In Alabama the timber trespassers exceed in number and extent those of any other southern state. . . .

"A vast proportion of homestead entries have been fraudulently made by men of wealth and prominence. Several owners of iron works and lumber mills have furnished money to their employees, many of them ignorant and lawless men, to enter the lands in the vicinity of the furnaces and mills, for the sole purpose of acquiring timber thereon. In one instance nearly ten sections of public land were thus entered by an iron company. From lands so entered mill owners in both this state and Florida have cut individually from five thousand to ten thousand logs every season."[12] Similar conditions prevailed in the State of Mississippi, and in Wisconsin, Minnesota and in the Pacific Coast states and territories.[13] The difficulty lay in the fact that the Schurz administration had initiated a reform program which could not be accomplished over night. The meager sums of money appropriated for law enforcement were not sufficient, and Congress was reluctant to continue even these appropriations. The American public was just waking up to the need for action. It is significant to note, therefore, that with all the outburst of energy in the Schurz administration, the platforms of both major political parties were silent on the land issue in 1880.

[12] Report of the Land Commissioner, 1880, pp. 575-7. [13] ibid., p. 579.

Congress obviously was but slightly roused from its lethargy. But elsewhere other forces were at work bringing the land reform movement into fruition. Several professional and scientific organizations of the country, and certain of the nation's leading editors were beginning to sense the seriousness of the situation. Prominent among the recommendations from professional organizations of the country, was that of the National Academy of Sciences which advocated definite reorganization and consolidation of both land and scientific surveys, in which there existed duplication, inaccuracy, and inefficiency.[14] Major J. W. Powell, in charge of the United States Geographic and Geologic Survey of the region beyond the hundredth meridian, along with other scientists, had already pointed out the antiquated, incongruous, and inappropriate character of the land legislation as it was being applied to this region. He strongly advocated classification of the various types of lands, and a scientific system of surveys and disposal for each of the classes defined.[15] Responding to the increased interest in land reform, Congress, on March 3, 1879, authorized the appointment of a commission to investigate the whole land system. Three days later the United States Geological Survey was established, with a director who was to be in charge not only of the geological survey but also of the classification of the public lands. Clarence King became the first director, but resigned in 1880 in favor of Major Powell.[16]

The Public Land Commission, authorized by Act of March 3, was to consist of the Land Commissioner, the director of the Geological Survey, and other civilians appointed by the President. It was ordered to submit to Congress within one year from the time of its organization a report on the following subjects: first, a codification of the laws relating to the survey and disposition of the public domain; second, a system and standard of classification of public lands as arable, irrigable, timber, mineral, etc., having due regard to the humidity of climate, supply of water for irrigation, and other physical characteristics; third, a system of land-parcelling surveys adapted to the economic uses of the several classes of land; and fourth, such recommendations as the Commission deemed wise regarding the disposal of the remaining public domain.[17]

[14] *The Nation*, Vol. XXVIII (January 9, 1879), pp. 27-9.   [15] *ibid.*, May 2, 1878.
[16] Merrill, *The First Hundred Years of American Geology*, p. 551.
[17] *Congressional Record*, 46 Cong. 1 Sess., pp. 2,339-40.

The first move was the calling of a land conference in Washington, D.C., on May 26, composed of Secretary of the Interior Schurz, the Land Commissioner, and various Congressmen and delegates from the Pacific Coast states and territories, for the purpose of considering the growth, preservation, and destruction of timber on the public lands. This conference agreed that the wholesale destruction of timber that was going on in many places in the name of trade, should be promptly and permanently stopped. Investigations continued throughout the year 1879.

The report submitted by the Public Land Commission was a huge document representing much painstaking and professional labor. Perhaps the greatest single item was the codification of nearly three thousand acts of Congress which had been enacted in the history of the public domain.[18]

The report also made several recommendations, most important of which was the proposal for land classification. The whole land system had grown out of the Ordinance of 1785, which was intended for the Northwest Territory, but the laws now applied to an entirely different region. "There was a kind of homogeneity," the report declared, "in the quality and value of the land of . . . [the Old Northwest Territory]. It was all valuable for agriculture and habitation, but in the western portion of our country it is otherwise. Its most conspicuous characteristic from an economic point of view is its heterogeneity. One region is exclusively valuable for mining, another solely for timber, a third for nothing but pasturage, and a fourth serves no useful purpose whatever. . . . Hence it has come to pass that the homestead and preemption laws are not suited for securing the settlement of more than an insignificant portion of the country."[19]

A proposal for the repeal of all the preemption laws and the Timber and Stone Act of 1878 was also included among the Commission's recommendations.[20] The report proposed the sale of grazing lands on the High Plains at a price beginning at $1.25 an acre in 1881 and decreasing to $1 in 1886, 75 cents in 1890, and ultimately to 12½ cents, but with the important proviso that nothing in the recommendation

---

[18] Report of the Secretary of the Interior, 1880, p. 31.
[19] Report of the Public Lands Commission, 1880, 46 Cong. 2 Sess., *H. Ex. Doc.* No. 46, p. 9.
[20] Donaldson, *The Public Domain,* pp. 359 and 678.

was to "interfere with settlement on said pasturage lands . . . under the homestead, homestead pasturage, or irrigation laws."[21]

The attack upon the public land system by scientific organizations and prominent periodicals in the early 'eighties was perhaps unprecedented in the annals of land history. While the demands for the forfeiture of railroad land grants still loomed large on the horizon, there was a growing interest in the conservation of the nation's remaining natural resources, an objective which could be achieved only by complete revision of the land system. In 1883 the Land Commissioner suspended entries in those localities where fraud was most prevalent, but when he asked for an appropriation of $400,000 for further investigation, Congress not only refused, but brought pressure to bear which forced the Commissioner to sanction the fraudulent entries and to reopen the land offices which he had closed.[22]

The whole land reform movement thus seemed to be losing ground in 1884 when Cleveland was elected President on a platform demanding, among other things, the forfeiture of unearned railroad land grants and the reservation of the remaining lands for actual settlers. In spite of the Democratic victory, a Republican Senate and strong Republican opposition in the House might block any attempt on the part of the Democrats to bring about reform.

The appointment of William Andrew Jackson Sparks as Land Commissioner foreshadowed a storm. Although Sparks undoubtedly lacked administrative experience his sympathy for land reform amounted almost to a passion. He had served four terms in Congress but he had never entered extensively into any of the debates. In fact, he was noted for making unnecessary interruptions during serious debates, such as the occasion of the almost laughable verbal altercation with James B. Weaver, Greenback candidate for President in 1880.[23] In fact, there is

[21] *ibid.*, p. 75. This recommendation corresponded to Powell's recommendations at an earlier date. From this report of the Public Land Commission plus the aid and advice of experts and numerous clerks, Thomas Donaldson compiled in 1883 his history of the Public Domain. (47 Cong. 2 Sess., *H. Misc. Doc.* No. 1, Vol. XIX. There is also the 1884 edition.) In many instances, Donaldson simply took sections from the report of the Land Commission and added his personal opinions between the paragraphs. This history might be looked upon as a scrapbook of land legislation intermingled with some original thought and many inaccuracies. Nevertheless, it has filled a most vital need, and has probably been referred to more than any other public document.

[22] Report of the Secretary of the Interior, 1885, p. 37.

[23] See *Congressional Record*, 46 Cong. 3 Sess., pp. 311ff.

evidence that more tact and a greater sense of humor would have kept Sparks out of a great deal of trouble.

Sparks was scarcely sworn into office when on April 3, 1885, he suspended from final action all entries in regions where a considerable amount of fraud had developed. This action included the whole of Colorado except the Ute Reservation, all of Dakota, Idaho, Utah, Washington, New Mexico, Wyoming, and portions of Kansas, Nebraska, and Minnesota. In fact, it applied to the greater part of the public domain. Sparks claimed that this suspension of entries was a public measure, made in the public interest, in order to check conspiracies against the government. The lists of the suspended entries were immediately placed in the hands of special agents for examination and report.[24]

Not content with this step, the Land Commissioner recommended the abolition of the fee system and the substitution of fixed salaries for the registers and receivers of the local land offices.[25] Furthermore, he urged that all general provisions authorizing cash sales of public lands should be abrogated, and a system established for their disposal to actual settlers only.[26] He strenuously recommended the repeal of the preemption laws, the timber culture acts, the Desert Land Act, and the commutation principle of the Homestead Act. In other words, Sparks proposed to reform the land system with one grand stroke. What Congress had failed to accomplish by legislative action, he would achieve by administrative decree. In his annual report he defended his actions as follows:

"At the outset of my administration," reads his annual report, "I was confronted with overwhelming evidence that the public domain was being made the prey of unscrupulous speculation and the worst forms of land monopoly through systematic frauds carried on and consummated under the public land laws. My predecessor had for three years called the attention of Congress to the extent and magnitude of fraudulent appropriations of public lands, and, as shown by his general and special reports, had found it necessary to suspend the issue of patents in several states and territories, either wholly or in certain classes of entries and special districts of the country. . . . Reports of special agents, registers and receivers, and inspectors of surveyors-general and local land offices, communications from United States Attorneys and

---

[24] Report of the Land Commissioner, 1885, p. 202.
[25] ibid., p. 227.   [26] ibid. p. 233.

other officials, and letters from public men and private citizens throughout the country, were laid before me, all detailing one common story of
widespread, persistent public land robbery committed under guise of
the various forms of public land entry."[27]

Sparks had taken a bold step—too bold, in fact, for the Cleveland
administration to bear. Both complaints and congratulations followed
Sparks' action. For the time being Cleveland upheld his reform program, and took pride in the fact that 2,750,000 acres of land had been
saved for the actual settlers. But western Congressmen raised the cry that
stopping the issuance of patents would cause great suffering among the
frontiersmen. Sparks retaliated by going a step further; he indicated
his intention of holding land-grant railroads to the letter of the law,
instead of permitting their agents and attorneys to control the policy
of the Land Office. This stand against the railroads immediately produced an organized movement in Washington to break down the
program of reform and to restore the era of "fraud, favoritism and
fees," as Sparks called it.[28]

Influence was brought to bear upon the Congressmen by an army of
attorneys and money brokers, many of whom, it should be noted were
personally interested, for they had much to lose in case of a decline in
land sales. A systematic flood of petitions and complaints flowed in
from various parts of the country.[29] At this point Congress took up the
fight against the Land Commissioner. A bill providing for the protection of all entries of public lands was introduced into the Senate. A
report from a Senate committee declared that the Government was
responsible for all the actions of the officers of the executive departments.[30] The Senate with its Republican majority thus brought pressure
to bear upon the Democratic administration.

In November 1887 Sparks was dismissed from office. Finally, on
April 6, 1888, the Secretary of the Interior revoked the entire Sparks
reform program.[31] Just before going out of office Sparks reported that
41,323,971 acres of lands fraudulently entered had been restored to the
public domain. At the end of his administration, President Cleveland
proudly pointed to the fact that over 80,000,000 acres of the public
domain had been rescued from "illegal usurpation, improvident grants,

[27] ibid., p. 201.   [28] ibid., 1886, pp. 45-9; New York Tribune, November 12, 1887.
[29] 49 Cong. 2 Sess., H. Ex. Doc. No. 1, pp. 50-69.
[30] 49 Cong. 1 Sess., Senate Reports, No. 44, pp. 1-3.
[31] Report of the Secretary of the Interior, 1889, p. 20.

and fraudulent entries and claims, to be taken for the homesteads of honest industry."[32]

The Republican Land Commissioners of the following administration continued to condemn Sparks and to laud the restoration of the land system to its former status.[33] But their praise of the land system was not long to endure, for the abortive launching of reform measures by Sparks had brought the problem of land reform squarely before the public. In fact, it was the force of public opinion, given additional impetus by the events of the Cleveland administration, that gradually shaped the agitation for reform into a program which the Republicans themselves had to adopt.

The Democratic administration had hardly been inaugurated and the first guns of Sparks' campaign against fraud sounded, before President Cleveland issued a proclamation decreeing that all fences on the public domain should immediately be taken down. This was followed by legislation on the subject.[34] The proclamation came so suddenly and struck so hard that it undoubtedly contributed to bringing about a decline of the western range industry.[35] Land Commissioner Sparks had to bear the brunt of the western reaction. The *Cheyenne Daily Sun,* for instance, held him up to ridicule: "Thou shalt have no other gods than William Andrew Jackson Sparks, and none shalt thou worship. Thou shalt not raise cattle upon the land, neither sheep or asses nor any living thing, but only corn the same as the State of Illinois."[36]

The matter was instrumental in leading to Sparks' resignation, and no sooner had Sparks resigned and the lands been again opened to settlement than cattle and sheep interests engaged in a mad scramble to procure land under the general settlement laws. Though their industry was considerably damaged by the new land legislation, most of the homesteaders of the 'nineties found it well-nigh impossible to conquer the soil of the High Plains.

After this blow at the cattle and sheep interests on the High Plains, the Government made a feeble attempt to aid the homesteader. In 1888 Congress passed an act providing that irrigable desert land should

[32] David S. Muzzey, *The United States of America* (2 vols., New York, 1924), Vol. II, p. 162.
[33] Report of the Land Commissioner, 1889, p. 9; *ibid.,* 1891, pp. 4-6, *ibid.,* 1892, p. 4.
[34] *Statutes at Large,* Vol. XXIII, p. 321.
[35] Ernest S. Osgood, *Day of the Cattleman,* p. 203.
[36] *Cheyenne Sua* in the *Cheyenne Daily Sun,* February 27, 1887, quoted in *ibid.,* p. 207.

be withdrawn from entry.[37] Lacking a geological survey of the arid country, it was practically impossible for local officials to determine just what lands could be irrigated. A slight change in 1890 reduced the size of the entry under the Desert Land Act from 640 acres to 320 acres.[38] But not until the next year, with the passage of the General Land Revision Act, was the Desert Land Act modified so that only 80 acres need be under irrigation at the end of the three-year period, instead of the whole 640 acres as required in the original act.[39] These changes were only a beginning of what was actually needed for the arid country. While its proponents actually thought the new legislation would bring irrigation and actual settlement to the desert country, the truth of the matter was that the opening of the Roosevelt administration found the cattle and sheep interests once more in a position of ascendancy.

Sparks' attack on the land system was but one part of the Democratic program for reform. This reform movement really began, so far as Congress was concerned, in January 1885. On January 13, a bill was introduced providing for the repeal of the preemption laws.[40] It passed the Senate by vote of 26 to 20 on February 12, but was defeated in the House by vote of 166 to 92 on February 26.[41] Thus when Sparks on April 3, 1885, launched his attack on the land system he not only had a precedent established for him by the preceding Land Commissioner who had suspended entries, but he also had the support of a considerable land-reform movement in Congress. But Sparks was too far in advance of Congress. He wanted more than reform; he wanted to revolutionize the land system. In fact, his boldness had the effect of making the attempts of Congress seem quite moderate.

A bill introduced into the House on April 15, 1886, provided for the repeal of the preemption laws, the timber-culture laws, the Desert Land Act, and for a revision of the Homestead Act.[42] The West stood solidly against the repeal of preemption.[43] This bill passed the House on June 7, 1886, by vote of 184 to 42, and was referred to the Republican Senate.[44] There it was amended and passed on June 24 by vote of 34 to 20.[45] The House refused to concur in the amendments; the conference committee failed to agree, and a second conference likewise. Both houses had

[37] *Statutes at Large*, Vol. XXV, p. 527.
[38] *ibid.*, Vol. XXVI, p. 391.
[39] *ibid.*, p. 1,096.
[40] *Congressional Record*, 48 Cong. 2 Sess., p. 648.
[41] *ibid.*, pp. 1,570, 2,209.
[42] *ibid.*, 49 Cong. 1 Sess., p. 3,515.
[43] *ibid.*, p. 5,379.
[44] *ibid.*, p. 5,380.
[45] *ibid.*, p. 6,082.

approved by fairly large majorities the general principle that the Pre-emption, Timber Culture, and Desert Land acts should be repealed, and the bill was being held up by a quibbling over minor details. The Senate contended that all fraudulent claims should be sanctioned, but the House refused to grant this concession. The Senate also contended a person whose title had been questioned by the Land Office should have the right to appeal from the Department of the Interior to the United States Courts.[46] The disagreement seems to have been solely political. A third conference committee, appointed on February 10, 1887, failed to agree,[47] and a fourth reported disagreement on March 3.[48] Because of the deadlock between the two houses, this badly needed reform failed just short of success.

The Democrats were backed by the owners of the stock ranges, who with preemption out of the way, could more easily extend their own operations.[49] In the first session of the forty-eighth Congress a number of successful cattlemen visited Washington and lobbied for the repeal of preemption. During 1888 several bills were introduced into Congress but both Houses stood by waiting for the results of the Presidential election of that year. This election brought in a Republican administration but with only slight Republican majorities in both houses.

A bill for the repeal of preemption was introduced on January 21, 1889, in the House, but failed to get very far.[50] Throughout that year neither house accomplished anything on the land question, their ener-gies being absorbed in other problems. Finally, on February 19, 1890, a bill providing for the repeal of the preemption, timber culture, and desert land laws was introduced in the House by Payson of Illinois.[51] It passed the House on March 23 and passed the Senate with amendments on September 16 by vote of 41 to 3.[52] There was no longer any debate over preemption; the disagreement occurred over the repeal of the timber culture acts. On March 2, 1891, the House agreed to the report of the conference committee, and on March 3, 1891, the bill received the approval of the President.[53]

The Act of 1891 was very short and concise, in contrast to the acts that it superseded. Section 1 repealed the timber culture acts; section 2 amended the Desert Land Act; section 4 repealed the preemption laws,

46 ibid., 49 Cong. 2 Sess., February 10. 1887.　47 ibid., p. 203.
48 ibid., p. 2,743.　49 ibid., pp. 2,031-2.
50 ibid., 50 Cong. 2 Sess., p. 1,059.　51 ibid., 51 Cong. 1 Sess., p. 1,523.
52 ibid., p. 10,094.　53 ibid., 51 Cong. 2 Sess., pp. 3,685, 3,824.

with the proviso that claims initiated before the passage of the act could be perfected under the old laws; section 5 amended the homestead acts to the effect that no commutation was to take place until fourteen months after entry; section 9 provided that henceforth there would be no more auctions of land; and section 24 allowed the President to set aside areas of timber lands as national parks.[54]

The greatest opportunities that the common man of any nation ever possessed disappeared with the passing of the arable frontier of America. Though the remaining area of the public domain—consisting mostly of arid, forest, and mineral lands—was still extensive, it was doubtful whether a man of small capital could share in its blessings. The Revision Act of 1891 climaxed a long period of agitation for a land system which would curtail some of the advantages of men of wealth. But the question was not at this time whether the remaining resources could be better utilized and developed by agencies of considerable wealth, but whether or not the common man should be given the opportunity to develop them. In a sense, then, the passing of the arable frontier did not definitely mean that there was an end to all opportunity in the American West. There still remained some hope that the homesteader might succeed on the High Plains and that the small stockman could succeed in case the homesteader did not. There were a few nooks and crannies left where the individual miners might operate, and there was some evidence that the day of the hand logger was not yet over. If on this last frontier, the government remained true to its proclaimed purpose, there was reason to expect that should the common man fail to work out his own salvation the government would come to his aid.

The closing chapter of the formative period of American history, however, was not to be only a struggle between the common man and the capitalist. It must be remembered that the nation was already aroused to the need for closing the doors of these vast and valuable remaining resources to all private appropriation and exploitation. The East, especially, was becoming convinced of the wisdom of such a policy. If conservation should become a real force in this drama of conflict, the age-old struggle between the common man and the capitalist might indeed be placed in a peculiar light. What would then be

[54] Report of the Land Commissioner, 1891, pp. 41-3; *Statutes at Large*, Vol. XXVI, pp. 1,095-7.

the attitude of that section of the country which embraced these remaining resources? Was this section to be deprived of the wealth that would come from the development of those resources? Was it not to be allowed to make the most of its inheritance?

Truly, here were forces that were to produce one of the bitterest conflicts in American political history. The entrance of the government as a third party into the picture has perhaps tended to obscure the real struggle between the frontier and the established order of society. The West as a political section was to prove itself a force to be reckoned with; in a real sense, the last stand of the American frontier was to be its greatest stand.

Part IV

The Government Forces Conservation

CHAPTER XIX

RISE OF CONSERVATION

Not until late in the nineteenth century, almost coincident with the passing of the American frontier, did a few thinking men begin to realize that the nation's natural resources were being exploited in such an alarming fashion that the time was near when these vast sources of wealth would be completely under the control of a few individuals who had no regard for their proper utilization and little respect for laws which would attempt to regulate their disposition. The agency most responsible for this exploitation was not the individual farmer who typified the earlier period of American history, but the corporation which with abundant capital at its disposal was able to appropriate large areas of valuable land and often to exact an exorbitant tribute from the people who were attempting to build up the civilization of the country. That these corporations had filled a useful part in building the West scarcely anyone would deny, but the abuses which accompanied the corporate exploitative processes were such that many persons began to wonder if the very foundations of democratic America were not in danger.

Conviction that the federal government had been all too generous in its disposition of favors during the period between 1850 and 1870 produced a reaction in the form of an antimonopoly movement which demanded legislation to restore the public domain, and to provide equal opportunity for the many and special privilege to none. But this movement to curb the corporate appropriation of lands was slow in crystallizing into definite action, and meanwhile exploitation continued, the corporations becoming stronger and more resistless in character. Not until after the railroad magnate, the cattle king, the mining baron and the lumber monarch had established a prestige as great as that enjoyed by any capitalist of the eastern industrial order, did the federal government finally pass the first of a series of laws which was ultimately to be distinguished as the conservation movement.

This movement had its roots far back in the nineteenth century. As has been shown, there was from the very beginning some strong opposition to the reckless giving away of land bounties to capitalistic interests. This opposition dwindled as the industrial revolution seized upon the country, and not until after the Civil War did voices again arise to challenge the exploitative interests. Those who were most intimately associated with the nation's land business were the first to sound the warning. The administrations of Hayes and Cleveland were conspicuous for their sponsoring of reforms in the land system. The report of the Public Land Commission of 1880 constituted one of the finest pieces of investigation in the whole history of the public domain. It focussed public attention on the subject in such a way that the government could no longer ignore the problem. The result was fourfold: first, a realization that fraud and corruption existed under the prevailing system; second, a recognition of the urgent need for reform and codification of the land laws; and third, the conviction that thorough survey and classification of the remaining lands, and new legislation to govern their disposition, were highly imperative. The anti-fencing legislation and the railroad land-grant forfeiture act, together with the attempt to curb abuses in the administration of the public lands were indicative of a changing point of view. The passage in 1891 of the General Revision Act climaxed this first period of land reform.

While public attention centered on railroad land grants and cattle kings, the Land Office was mindful of the fact that certain interests were exploiting the public domain of timber resources which were becoming more and more valuable as the years progressed, both because of the rapid industrialization of the country and because of the growing realization that the last timber frontier of America had been reached. The growing tide of sentiment in favor of conserving the timber resources—the birth of Arbor Day in 1872, the creation of Yellowstone National Park by congressional action in that same year, the memorial presented by the American Association for the Advancement of Science in 1873, the passage of the Timber Culture Act of 1873, the rise of forestry associations, the increasing number of conservation articles in popular periodicals—all were indicative of a changing attitude toward the timber resources of America.[1]

As before the Civil War the lumbering interests had ruthlessly stripped the hills of the Great Lakes region and of Alabama, so now in the 1890's they began to extend their operations to the Rocky Moun

[1] John Ise, *The United States Forest Policy* (New Haven, 1920), Chap. I. For the act creating Yellowstone National Park, see *Statutes at Large*, Vol. XVII, pp. 32-3.

tains and Pacific Coast. Perhaps no single factor was more important in the extension of the lumbering frontier to the Far West than the competition of the transcontinental railroads. The Northern Pacific opened service of its own into the Pacific Northwest in July 1887. The Great Northern was completed in 1893, and almost immediately lower rates were instituted because of the competition. The lumber capital of America at once began to drift from the Great Lakes region to the Pacific Northwest, there to exploit the last magnificent stand of timber in America. Although this process began before the Panic of 1893, the lumbering business in the Pacific Northwest did not reach boom proportions until the discovery of gold in the Klondike in 1898.

At first glance it would seem that the General Revision Act of 1891 did much to curb the exploitation of the public domain. The preemption laws were repealed, public sale and private entry abolished, and amendments improved the Desert Land laws and the commutation features of the homesteading legislation. But the Timber Cutting and Timber and Stone acts were still on the statute books, and these pieces of legislation were being employed in a most ruthless manner in the exploitation of the last frontier. The Act of 1891 showed no comprehensive understanding of the land problem. Congress had made no attempt to provide for classification of lands. In the case of agricultural lands, the government had, in fact, locked the barndoor after the horse was stolen. Regarding timber and mineral lands, the act did little more than to legalize plundering. To quote an outstanding authority, "The laws for the disposal of timber on the public domain were worse in 1891 than they had been in 1878, just as they had been worse in 1878 than ever before. Congress had shown utter incapacity to deal intelligently with the public timber, and all hope for future conservation must center in the provision which would take some of the timber land out of the hands of Congress—the provision enabling the President to set aside forest reserves."[2]

This most farsighted provision of the Act of 1891 was the result of outside influence rather than of inspiration on the part of any member of Congress. Much of the credit is due to the Land Office which for a number of years had been proposing forest reservations as the only way to curb exploitation. The immediate prompting, however, came from the American Forestry Association which in 1889 petitioned Congress

---

[2] Ise, loc. cit., pp. 119-20.

for a congressional investigation of the forest resources of the country and for temporary withdrawal of all forest lands from sale.[3] This memorial was read before the House during the discussion of the original bill to repeal the Timber Culture Act. During this same session the American Association for the Advancement of Science sent a memorial to Congress asking for forest reserves in order to preserve favorable hydrologic conditions. President Harrison sent this latter memorial to Congress with a message urging adequate legislation "to the end that the rapid and needless destruction of our great forest areas may be prevented."[4] But very little debate resulted on the proposal in either branch of Congress.

Section 24 of the land act of 1891, later to be known as the Forest Reserve Act of 1891, was an amendment which was added in the conference committee. When put before the Senate it was adopted on February 28, 1891, without comment, but in the House it became the subject of inquiry. In reply, Lewis Payson of Illinois, chairman of the conference committee explained as follows: "We have made a provision in this bill authorizing the President of the United States whenever in his judgment he deems proper to do so, to make a reservation of the timber lands, principally applying to the watersheds of the West, so that the water supply in that country may be preserved from entry . . until legislation shall be passed by Congress whereby these lands shall be opened."[5]

The Committee had been unanimous in its support of this section. Thomas C. McRae of Arkansas, later to win fame as the sponsor of much conservation legislation, arose and expressed grave fear about granting to the President this "extraordinary and dangerous power." Roswell Flower of New York defended the provision, stressing the necessity of protecting the trees around the sources of the rivers of the West, and mentioning particularly the floods on the Missouri and other rivers.[7] With this meager discussion this very important section was allowed to stand. The whole bill was adopted without record vote on March 2, 1891.

Except in New England, California, and a few other places, the passing of the law caused no comment. Scientific associations and a few

---

[3] *Congressional Record*, 51 Cong. 1 Sess., Part 3, p. 2,537.
[4] 51 Cong. 1 Sess., *S. Ex. Doc.* No. 36.
[5] *Congressional Record*, 51 Cong. 2 Sess., pp. 4, 3,547.   [6] *ibid.*, p. 3,613
[7] *ibid.*, p. 3,616.

editors, such as Robert Underwood Johnson of the *Century Magazine*
were interested, but judging from the newspapers there was almost no
excitement at all over the passage of the land reform measure. It is
true that Congress in 1890 had passed laws creating some important
reservations, such as the Big Tree Reservation, but California seemed
more interested in protecting the watersheds of her important cities
than in sponsoring the cause of the timber interests.[8]

During the fiscal year, 1891-92, President Harrison under authority
granted him in Section 24, created six forest reservations including some
three million acres of valuable timber land, the request for such action
coming principally from forestry associations. Two of these were
within the State of Colorado and it was the Colorado State Forestry
Association that was most responsible for their creation. As yet the West
showed little reaction to the beginnings of conservation. During the
fiscal year, 1892-93, nine more reservations were proclaimed, making a
total of fifteen, but still only a slight opposition came from the West.
Regarding the creation of the Pacific Forest Reservation in the state of
Washington, the *Seattle Telegraph* asserted: "If statements made as to
valuable timber, farming and coal bearing lands which are included
in the reservation at Mt. Rainier are true, the boundaries ought to be
recast. There is abundant room for pleasure ground without depriving
the people of property of immense value in a commercial way."[9]

In 1893 President Cleveland refused to create any more reservations
until Congress provided protective legislation for those already created.
In his annual message of December 4, 1893, he "especially commend[ed]
to the attention of the Congress the statements in the Secretary's report
concerning forestry. The time has come when efficient measures should
be taken for the preservation of our forests from indiscriminate and
remediless destruction."[10] A year later he fully endorsed the "recommendation of the Secretary that adequate protection be provided for our
forest reserves, and that a comprehensive forestry system be inaugurated. Such keepers and superintendents as are necessary to protect the
forests already reserved should be provided. I am of the opinion that
there should be an abandonment of the policy sanctioned by present
laws under which the government, for a very small consideration, is
rapidly losing title to immense tracts of lands covered with timber which

8 *Statutes at Large*, Vol. XXVI, pp. 478, 650.   9 Issue of February 16, 1893.
10 53 Cong. 2 Sess., *Senate Journal*, p. 9.

should be properly reserved as permanent sources of timber supply."[11] No more sincere conservationist statement could have been made by any one, but Congress remained indifferent, perhaps partly on account of the financial stringency brought on by the Panic of 1893.

It is clear that President Cleveland fully understood the problems that the administrative divisions of the government had to cope with. No government could administer a faulty law, and no government could provide for good administration without appropriations from Congress.[12] Needless to say, governmental agencies had a most difficult time in carrying out the provisions of the Act of 1891. On May 5, 1891, the Land Commissioner issued rules and regulations for the use of timber on the public domain.[13] These regulations depended on a system of permits which would mean nothing unless there was some policing force.[14] The Forestry Bureau in 1891 worked out on paper a very satisfactory system of protecting the forests. It provided for the establishment of a new division with a superintendent at the head, the institu-

[11] *ibid.*, 53 Cong. 3 Sess., p. 9.

[12] The following table is a financial statement on the protection of the forest reserves, 1891-1899:

Year ending June 30.	Appropriations	Value of Spoliation.	Total amount collected.	Value of pending Suits.	Agents used.
1891	$240,000	$2,347,473	$116,704	$4,451,305	46
1892	220,000	471,610	107,135	1,401,578	95
1893	120,000	195,692	54,552	839,880	82
1894	85,000	1,019,781	23,521	1,481,897	40
1895	75,000	757,761	47,780	1,493,853	42
1896	90,000	696,521	182,699	1,254,566	35
1897	90,000	635,064	111,539	3,129,213	52
1898	185,000	626,182	144,244	3,224,327	48
1899	185,000	743,030	214,178	1,283,213	

[13] A summary of these regulations follow: 1. Settlers were given the right to cut timber for domestic use. 2. Anyone desiring timber from the public lands was to apply in writing, giving complete description of land and timber, and also to append the signatures of four responsible witnesses. 3. Applications were to show that timber to be cut was not needed for public good, and also that cutting was a necessity. 4. For protection of farmers who needed their water supply safeguarded, the notice was required to be published for three weeks. 5. Sawmill men and lumbermen who caused timber to be cut, directly or indirectly, were to be deemed guilty of trespass upon the public timber, and be liable to prosecution and civil suit. (*Congressional Record*, 53 Cong. 1 Sess., Pt. 3, p. 2,373.)

[14] Compiled from the reports of the Land Commissioner, it was found that the number of permits applied for beginning in 1892 and ending in 1897 were as follows: 425, 87, 71, 50, 86, and 96. Fully 50 per cent of these applications were rejected. Among the restrictions listed in one typical permit (to the Anaconda Copper Mining Company) are the following: no trees under twelve inches diameter could be cut, nor more than 50 per cent of the merchantable timber, all slashings had to be disposed of; no timber cut from reservations or settlers' claims, and the holder of the permit agreed not to obtain lumber unlawfully and further agreed to fight forest fires. Cited in *Congressional Record*, 53 Cong. 1 Sess., Pt. 3, p. 2,430.

tion of a ranger service, members of which were to be selected on basis of their abilities, and the whole service to be watched by a number of independent inspectors.[15] The chief of the Forestry Bureau was already pointing out that while his bureau was endeavoring to educate the people on forestry, it was difficult to preach national forest management when there was no evidence of it in the administration of the public domain.[16] The Forestry Bureau incessantly called attention to the need of legislation to prevent forest fires which, it insisted, could be controlled.[17] But Congress did nothing.

On August 4, 1894, the Land Commissioner wrote to Thomas C. McRae of Arkansas, the only member of the House who seemed at that time vitally interested in the problems of the Land Office, that in his opinion the permit system should be done away with and the government should discontinue all free use of timber on the public lands. He was convinced that all permits thus far had been issued to concerns manufacturing lumber. Without appropriations it was impossible for his office to stop the abuses under the law of 1891.[18]

With these difficulties in mind, McRae, a member of the House Committee on Public Lands, initiated a bill designed to remedy many of the defects in the land laws. This measure when first introduced was definitely a conservation measure, but it was so amended that it ultimately took on a countenance quite favorable to the anticonservation forces. Early in 1893 the Land Commissioner had given his opinion that a general law to revise the Act of 1891 should include: (1) provision for the judicious use of timber; (2) provision for the preservation of the timber when needed for water supply; (3) repeal of all existing inconsistent legislation. He also insisted that the power to administer the forest reserves should be given to the Secretary of the Interior, and that Congress should cooperate by providing sufficient money for this administration.[19]

The bill which McRae introduced aimed to embrace the objectives outlined by the Land Commissioner. It bore the stamp of approval of nearly every federal administrative officer; it was endorsed by the

[15] Report of Chief Forester, *Department of Agriculture Report*, 1891, pp. 224-6.
[16] *ibid.*, 1891, p. 223. [17] *ibid.*, 1892, pp. 303-21.
[18] 53 Cong. 2 Sess., *House Reports*, No. 1400.
[19] 52 Cong. 2 Sess., *H. Misc. Doc.* No. 2,437. The Sundry Appropriations Bill for the fiscal year ending June 1893, had cut the already very negligible funds for forest protection to less than 25 per cent of the preceding year's appropriation.

American Forestry Association, the Forestry Congresses, the Iowa Academy of Science, and editors of many prominent periodicals. It was destined to continue under fire through the 53rd, 54th, and 55th Congresses. It constituted the greatest effort to secure protection for forest reserves up to the time of the passage of the Act of 1897.

The McRae bill was definitely a conservation measure, and one which "latter-day conservationists would generally have approved."[20] That part of the law of 1891 known as the Permit Law, whereby the Rocky Mountain states had allowed timber cutting by a resident for use in his state or territory for agriculture, mining, domestic, or manufacturing purposes, provided the timber was not taken out of the state during the term in which it was cut, was definitely repealed by Section 8 of the new bill.[21] In place of the free use of timber in the reserves, the bill provided for the sale of mature timber to the highest bidder and at not less than the appraised value, the receipts from such sale to be used to protect the forests. Section 5 authorized the Secretary of War to detail troops to protect the forests if it should be deemed necessary. As originally reported, the bill contained the statement that the purpose of forest reservations was for the protection of water supply and preservation of timber.

The entire West, from Kansas and the Dakotas on to the Pacific Coast, arose as one to denounce the bill. Jeremiah Simpson of Kansas charged that its provisions empowering the Secretary of the Interior to sell timber had been inserted merely to permit sale of timber on the reservations to corporations hungering for the possession of the forests, and that was "the whole milk in the cocoanut."[22] To meet this initial attack, McRae offered an amendment providing that "no person, company or corporation shall purchase or hold more than four quarter sections of timber," and giving the Secretary of the Interior the power of rejecting all bids. This amendment touched the western forces in a tender spot, and one representative after another denounced the whole measure in no uncertain language.

John A. Pickler of South Dakota insisted that if reserved timber were allowed to be sold it would not be long before all the forests would be cut.[23] Binger Hermann of Oregon declared that the measure should be entitled, "Bill to Despoil the Forests," and that he strongly suspected it

20 Ise, *The United States Forest Policy*, p. 127. By permission of Yale University Press.
21 53 Cong. 1 Sess., *House Reports*, No. 119.
22 *Congressional Record*, 53 Cong. 1 Sess., Pt. 3, p. 2,374.   23 *ibid.*, p. 2,431.

had been drawn up by those conspiring to denude the mountains.[24] William Doolittle of Washington asserted that if the lumbermen ever got upon the reservations they would not stop until every tree was cut. "You might as well turn a dozen wolves into a corral filled with sheep and expect the wolves to protect the sheep as to expect your timber to be protected if you permit the timbermen to go upon the reservations at all."[25]

"You say to the corporations that are able to purchase this timber," declared Charles Hartman of Montana, " 'you may have whatever timber you desire.' But at the same time you say to the honest settlers, the hardhanded miner, or farmer, or stock raiser, 'You can not have a foot of this timber, unless you purchase it in competition with these corporations; unless you do that you must either steal the timber or freeze to death.' "[26] Henry Coffeen of Wyoming warned the Land Committee of the House to be on its guard, for the entire western group was against the bill.

Thomas C. McRae replied to all these arguments. "As long as free permits are granted," he pointed out, "the favored few will not consent to buy. It is not true that this bill is in the interests of capitalists and monopolists. I hurl back all such charges. Whether intentionally or not, you who oppose this bill are the aides of the monopolists who have had the special privilege of cutting government timber for nothing."[27]

At this point Coffeen offered an amendment to strike out the entire bill and repeal all forest reservations except in the three coast states. He insisted that the whole reservation system impeded the progress of the West.[28] John C. Bell of Colorado, agreeing with Coffeen, asserted that the reservations had tied up every stick of wood in Colorado together with many valuable coal lands. With so much opposition, McRae insisted he was willing to meet any reasonable objection by amendments. When the bill came up again several weeks later there was such bitter debate over whether or not it should be considered that it was postponed, and thus the first session ended.

The bill did not come up again for important consideration until December 1894. The western interests were now well prepared and very determined. Coffeen of Wyoming offered an amendment providing

[24] *ibid.*, p. 2,432.
[25] *ibid.*
[26] *ibid.*
[27] *ibid.*, p. 2,433.
[28] *ibid.*, p. 2,434.

for "continuous supplies of timber to the people."[29] Binger Hermann, representative from Oregon, moved to amend so as to provide that "only dead or mature trees" might be sold. He insisted that McRae's bill allowing up to 50 per cent of timber on the reserves to be sold was no better than the robbing of the public domain which had been going on for years.[30] William W. Bowes of California stated that of the five and a half million acres in the reservations in California, scarcely a half million acres of timber worth reserving could be found. David Wells of Wisconsin asserted that the bill was the work of the timber men who wanted to get on to the timber lands. "In the early days in Wisconsin," this Congressman continued, "men bought 40 acres and took the timber off of a whole section. These men, rich," he concluded, "are now in Congress and in the Secretary of the Interior's office; they are expert, and will steal in spite of the law."[31] At a later date he averred that where a million dollars depredations had been reported, only $23,000 had been collected, and at a cost of $60,000 to the government.[32]

By the time the vote was taken on December 17, 1894, the original McRae bill which was proconservation in character, had been so completely altered by western interests that it was practically anticonservation.[33] The Republican West obtained the support of the Democratic South to force the bill through by vote of 159 to 53, with 137 not voting.[34] The amendments, which were all opposed by the Secretary of the Interior in his annual report, provided for retention of the permit system, prohibited the sale of stumpage except dead and mature trees, and allowed mining in the reserves.

In the Senate, a substitute bill was brought up by Henry Teller of Colorado, a member of the Committee on Public Lands, which "represented fairly well what the western men considered right and proper in dealing with the forest reserves."[35] This measure provided first of all that reserves should be created only in order to provide a continuous supply of timber for the people of the state or territory where the reserve was created. Second, no agricultural or mineral lands were to be included—a provision which would protect grazing and mining

---

[29] *ibid.*, 53 Cong. 3 Sess., Pt. 1, p. 86.   [30] *ibid.*, p. 110.
[31] *ibid.*, pp. 111-2.   [32] *ibid.*, pp. 364-6.
[33] Ise, *The United States Forest Policy*, p. 126.
[34] *Congressional Record*, 53 Cong. 3 Sess., Pt. 1, p. 371.
[35] Ise, *The United States Forest Policy*, p. 127.

interests. Timber was to be allowed for nearly all construction purposes in the state or territory. Finally, any settler who found himself in a proclaimed reserve should either be allowed damages or be permitted to select land elsewhere of equal value to his settlement. The Senate passed this bill without debate or record vote, but no agreement was reached in conference.

At the beginning of the 54th Congress, McRae's bill was again introduced, but it did not come up for discussion until June 10, 1896, when it was passed by the House without debate or record vote.[36] The bill was changed somewhat to conform to the Senate bill but evidently ran into difficulties in the Senate Committee of Agriculture and Forestry, for it was never reported out. Thus ended the history of H.R. 119. It would be a mistake to conclude, however, that McRae's efforts were in vain, for the better features of his bill, though somewhat compromised with western sentiment, were to become a part of a later act.

In September 1895, the editor of *Century Magazine,* Robert Underwood Johnson, an ever alert authority on the subject of conservation, printed an editorial entitled "Hope for Forests," in which he expressed high commendation for two events that had occurred in New York City. Both the New York Chamber of Commerce and the Board of Trade had passed resolutions urging study of forest conditions in the United States. The Board of Trade resolution suggested that a commission of experts be appointed to study the extent of the forests and their condition—their relation to the public welfare, the amount of forest lands that should remain open to the public—and more important, to prepare plans for scientific forest management and to recommend suitable legislation. The editor observed that when businessmen got interested in the forests, something was bound to happen.

On November 11, 1895, Johnson wrote the Secretary of the Interior, Hoke Smith, enclosing his editorial. He assured the Secretary that the *Century Magazine* was an ardent supporter of conservation, and that it would appreciate a few words expressing the viewpoint of the proper governmental department. At about the same time, the executive committee of the American Forestry Association, for many years active in the conservation movement, requested the Secretary of the Interior to call upon the National Academy of Sciences for a detailed report on the

[36] *Congressional Record,* 54 Cong. 1 Sess., pp. 6,410-1.

nation's forest assets. On February 15, 1896, Secretary Smith sent a letter to Walcott Gibbs, the president of the National Academy. "Being convinced of the necessity of a radical change in the existing policy with reference to the disposal of and preservation of the forests upon the public domain," he desired the views of the president of the Academy on a number of subjects, to wit: (1) Is it practical or necessary that we preserve the present timber lands as reserves? (2) Does the influence of forests upon soil and water conditions extend far enough to make reservations necessary? (3) What legislation is necessary to remedy the present evils? Owing to the desperate situation of the existing public forest lands, the opinion and advice of the scientists was requested as soon as it could be submitted. The Secretary concluded: "My predecessors in office for the last twenty years have vainly called attention to the inadequacy and confusion of existing laws relating to the public timber lands and consequent absence of intelligent policy in their administration, which will prevent proper development of the country."

Gibbs replied to him on March 2, 1896. "It is needless to remind you," he wrote, "that the matter you refer to the Academy is important and difficult. No subject upon which the Academy has been asked before by the government for advice compares with this in scope. And it is the opinion of thoughtful men that no other economic problem confronting the government of the United States is equal in importance to that offered by the present condition and future fate of forests of western North America."

President Gibbs presented a list of problems to be considered: (1) Were the forests to be publicly or privately owned? (2) How were the forests to be administered so that the people might use timber and not impair the forests? (3) How could continuous, honest management be secured? (4) What provisions should be added so that a plan extending over a period of years might be carried out? He assured the Secretary that such questions could not be answered in a few days' time, that it was a task that would take considerable time for investigation, but that the Academy would furnish the best talent available, provided the government would furnish legal aid and provide all information which might be asked for from time to time.

The Commission which was appointed for this purpose consisted of Professor Charles S. Sargent, eminent arboriculturist; General Henry

L. Abbott, engineer and hydrographer; Professor William H. Brewer of Yale, botanist and agriculturist; Arthur Hague, prominent geologist, and Gifford Pinchot, the latter recommended by President Gibbs, as a young man with a "very high reputation as an arboriculturist."[37] President Gibbs reminded the Secretary that the Commission would serve without compensation, but that money for their expenses should be provided.

The appropriation for the Commission's expenses was included in the Sundry Civil Bill of 1896, and on July 2 the Commission left Washington for the great forest regions of the West. They were in Yellowstone Park on July 8, in Spokane on about July 19, at Crater Lake on August 26, and reached Washington again about October 1. The Commission's visit did not elicit much attention among the regions visited, if news in local newspapers can be taken as an index. The Secretary of the Interior, now David R. Frances, asked for a prompt statement so that it could be incorporated in his annual report. The Commission thereupon furnished him with a written report and also called upon him in person. The outstanding proposal of the Commission without doubt was its recommendation that the President of the United States create thirteen new forest reserves. In conveying the Commission's recommendations to the President, the Secretary made the comment that they "visited *most or all* of the forest reservations and other public forests of the United States, devoting three months of Land Travel, and [they] carefully studied without compensation the work assigned to them. . . . The Commission . . . has performed this responsible duty with *intelligent fidelity*."[38]

In February 1897, before the commission report was published, the chairman, Professor Sargent, took it upon himself to write to President Gibbs of the Academy, recommending the establishment of the thirteen reserves agreed upon by the commission. This letter, however, was written before the commission was ready to make its final recommendations, and its issuance was opposed by Gifford Pinchot, who believed that any recommendation should be accompanied by a statement of the

[37] Pinchot's appointment to this commission apparently began his career. After being graduated from Yale in forestry in 1889, he had gone directly to Biltmore, N.C., to serve in the capacity of developing Mr. Vanderbilt's estate. According to President D. C. Gilman of Johns Hopkins University, though he was still comparatively a young men, nevertheless, he already had great distinction as a forester.

[38] The foregoing paragraphs were abstracted from the Secretary of the Interior Report, 55 Cong. 1 Sess., *S. Ex. Doc.* No. 21, pp. 1-16.

objects sought, and by plans for the administration of the reserves created. President Cleveland, however, got knowledge of Sargent's letter, and determined to create the reserves immediately.[39] At the instance of Secretary Frances, he decided that the 165th anniversary of the birth of George Washington "could be no more appropriately commemorated than by the promulgation . . . of a proclamation establishing these grand Forest Reservations."[40] Hence, on February 22, 1897, thirteen new forest reserves embracing 21,000,000 acres of timber lands, were proclaimed by President Cleveland, the last notable act of his administration.[41] Three were located in Washington, two each in California, Wyoming, and Montana, one each in Utah and South Dakota, one cutting across the state line between Washington and Idaho, and one across the Idaho-Wyoming line.

These lands were withdrawn from entry or sale, except for persons who already had irrigation rights in the reserves, who had legal entries or filings, or mining claims held according to law, provided these exemptions should cease if the law was not complied with. Warning was expressly given to all persons not to enter or make settlements upon the reserved tracts. The Secretary's report accompanying the proclamation concluded with the statement that it fully recognized the fact that the forest reserves, established and corrected, could not remain unless a plan could be effected under which the boundaries could be modified so as to exclude all lands better suited for agricultural purposes than for the products of forests, and under which their timber could be made available for domestic commercial purposes and valuable minerals could be freely sought for and mined within their boundaries. Secretary Frances, commenting on the proclamation said, "The timber growth in most or many of the older states has been ruthlessly laid waste, and in some sections the settlers are realizing its scarcity, its cost for domestic uses growing greater from year to year. Furthermore these forests are the great reserves of the country. They preserve the snow when protected and furnish a good and opportune supply of water in the streams. This forestry committee which has done such good work will now formulate for submission to Congress, through the Secretary of Interior, a forestry policy to provide for the

39 Ise, *The United States Forest Policy*, p. 129.
40 55 Cong. 1 Sess., *S. Misc. Doc.* No. 21, p. 14.
41 Richardson, *Messages and Papers of the Presidents*, Vol. IX, pp. 773-97.

protection of these wonderful reservations from the depredations of sacrilegious man as well as from the ravages of fire."[42]

Needless to say, this executive order unleashed a storm of protest from the West on the subject of public lands, the like of which had not been witnessed since the mid-nineteenth century, when sectionalism held its greatest sway. Within a week after the proclamation scores of protests had arrived in Washington from every state from Nebraska and the Dakotas westward. Local newspapers furnish the best index of public sentiment. As Professor Dicey has so well observed: "Dry legal rules have a new interest and meaning when connected with the varying current of public opinion."[43]

The Denver Republican carried the following headlines on a front-page editorial: "The New Forestry Reserves Result of Arbitrary Action of President Cleveland—Western People Not Consulted—Reserves Made on the Recommendation of a Commission That Made Only A Cursory Examination of the Territory—A Menace to the Interests of the Western States—Colorado for Some Reason was Overlooked." The editorial complained that no senator or representative was consulted where the largest reservations were made. The action, it was pointed out, would retard the growth and settlement of the states interested and shut off the development of great resources.[44] The next day the same newspaper commented: "One trouble with Mr. Cleveland in regard to all matters concerning the West seems to be that he is imbued with an idea that the people of the West, especially those of the Far West, are ignorant, and, at the same time, hostile to the government. What is needed in connection with forest reservations is that no restraint be placed upon prospecting for valuable minerals within the limits of such a reserve, nor upon acquiring a full title to mineral land discovered."

The more conservative *Rocky Mountain News* approved of forest reserves which would effect irrigation protection, but denounced the manner in which Cleveland had made the reserves.[45] Its editor observed that "If the individual rights are not sacrificed, the preservation of our western timber lands is a very proper act. . . . There may yet be shown

[42] Nearly every newspaper in the West carried the complete proclamation together with excerpts from the report and the statement of Secretary Frances.

[43] A. V. Dicey, *Lectures on the Relations Between Law and Public Opinion in England* (London, 1905), *preface,* p. ix.

[44] Issue of February 24, 1897.   [45] Issue of March 1, 1897.

just cause for a modification of the order. On the other hand, there can be no question of the wisdom of guarding the timber about the headwaters of the great streams. It is not the people in the immediate vicinity of these reservations who are most concerned, but the people living along the streams which head therein, and on whose waters must be placed dependence for irrigation. . . . The maintenance and protection of the forests about the headwaters of these western streams means the existence of agriculture and horticulture for a century to come."[46]

On February 26, a mass meeting of 30,000 people was held at Deadwood, South Dakota, protesting that the Black Hills reservation would "affect disastrously all the mining and dependent industries of this region and largely compel its depopulation."[47] From the *Omaha Bee* came the comment that all of the railroads running out of Omaha to the west and northwest had long anticipated the time when much of the territory included in Cleveland's order should form a most valuable territory for them, contributing to the success of the railroads as the country increased in population and in agriculture and mineral wealth. General Solicitor Manderson of the Burlington and Missouri declared: "The great disadvantage of such an order is that settlement of these tracts is absolutely stopped, development of the country is prevented and exploration for mineral wealth must entirely cease."[48] Dickinson, general manager of the Union Pacific, asserted that the order was a great mistake.[49]

From Wyoming came such headlines as: "Senator Clark Roasts the Executive—Not Enough Timber to Fence—Cannon Says Utah Timber is Not Larger than a Jack Rabbit Bush—Western Senators not Consulted."[50] State Engineer Elwood Mead of Wyoming, later to become prominent in irrigation history, declared that many irrigated farms in the Big Horn reservation which had not been filed upon by reason of the absence of surveys were now excluded from entry. Part of this reservation was believed to be rich in mineral wealth but, he added, the reservation did not include the most densely timbered lands of the region where are located the big tree camps of several contractors.[51] The editor of the *Cheyenne Tribune* wrote: "Every right-minded citizen is

---

[46] *ibid.*
[47] From telegram sent to Washington, quoted in *ibid.*, February 27, 1897.
[48] Quoted in *Cheyenne Tribune*, February 25, 1897.   [49] *ibid.*, February 27, 1897.
[50] *ibid.*, February 24, 1897.   [51] *ibid.*, April 1, 1897.

heartily in favor of preserving the forests of the state, but it is well known that the segregating of the forest areas under present laws into reserves whose boundary lines are impassable barriers to the settler who needs timber for fences and logs for cabins, while at the same time the forest fire is allowed to roam unheeded and unchecked, is a dangerous and ridiculous farce. It is in fact more foolish than the making of forest reserves out of hay meadows or miles of rock almost too barren to produce a spear of grass."[52]

On May 13, Mead wrote to Robert U. Johnson, editor of the *Century Magazine,* protesting the manner in which the reserves had been created. He asserted that the people in general were in favor of reserves, but that if reserves were to be an enduring institution the people should be consulted. On March 25, the Governor of Wyoming, in answer to an editorial which appeared in *Forest and Stream* in the issue of March 20, charged that the Forestry Commission by its ignorance had impaired a very worthy cause. He affirmed that 90 per cent of the people of Wyoming were in favor of reservations, but that until the government could provide for their protection it was utterly foolish to shut up resources. In truth, he said, fire was doing much more damage than the ax. In answer to an editorial in *Harper's Weekly* for March 27, which asserted that "if McKinley or Congress rescinds the order of President Cleveland the act will be in the interests of the timber cutters and against the interests of the country dependent on the water supply nourished by these forests," the Governor of Wyoming wrote a public letter to Senator Francis Warren on April 1 denying that any corporations were affected in Wyoming.

California, with the exception perhaps of the Los Angeles region which was interested in irrigation, was also bitterly opposed to the reserves. The editor of the *San Francisco Chronicle* said that while the denudation of forest land diminished the rainfall in some localities, there was no reason to believe that it would do so along the Pacific Coast where cool winds sweep landward from the Pacific, and mountain ranges compel condensation. He declared that natural reforestation was very rapid in California, especially in the redwood region. Even if floods were the result, the damage, he continued, could be more easily borne than an enhanced price for building material and firewood. In California and Oregon, minerals were thus locked up "for no other

[52] *ibid.,* April 4, 1897.

reason than that the wiseacres of the National Academy of Sciences, who nominated the amiable theorists who reported a scheme of forest reservations for the West, believed that what would be well for one part of the country would be the best for all." He concluded that "to save us from floods—which we would one day impound for irrigation and power in any event—they propose not only to make lumber and firewood high but mineral wealth unavailable."[53]

The most vociferous of all opposition came from the State of Washington where the lumbering industry was just becoming established. The depression just began to lift when Cleveland's proclamation spread consternation throughout the state.

The *Seattle Post-Intelligencer* in an editorial on March 1, exclaimed: "By a simple executive order, apparently without the faintest conception on earth of what he was doing, what the character of the country was or whose interests were being imperiled, the President, in the closing hours of his administration, has withdrawn this land from entry under the land laws under the pretext of making a forest reservation of a barren, stony and snow-clad range of mountains which, however, are stored with vast treasures of mineral wealth. No more serious blow was ever inflicted on the people of this state." On March 7, the front page of this newspaper carried a large cartoon representing the situation. On the editorial page was the assertion that the three reserves proclaimed in the state took practically "all the unappropriated lands within the borders which are of any present value, and leave little except the arid lands open to entry." The editor asked if the time had not come when the federal government could renounce its claim upon the public lands and let the individual states regulate the handling of those lands themselves: "At best, the only title which the federal government ever had to the lands was based upon forced concessions which the new states were compelled to make as the price of their admission into the Union." Another editorial declared that one year of withdrawal of the mineral lands would result in the diversion of a heavy amount of capital into the new mineral regions of British Columbia.

From the lumbering district near Tacoma the editor of the local newspaper declared: "This country should be held sacred for and dedicated to the homeless, to those who are willing and anxious to become settlers and lend a helping hand in building up the nation. Pleasure grounds for the rich, extensive parks for sightseers, are all right so long as the territory embraced is not needed for settlement, but so soon as there is demand for it to be used for homes, pasturage for herds and flocks or any other purpose which will add to the country's wealth and the individual happiness of its citizens, this demand should take presidenc [sic] over every other."[54]

In reply to some of these criticisms the *Springfield* (Massachusetts) *Republican* asked: "Who then are the people in Washington and the other states . . . who are making their clamor roar against the act of the President? They belong, no doubt, to that class of timber thieves, and prospectors and ranchmen who make a business of appropriating public land to their own use without authority or expense." To this the editor of the *Seattle Post-Intelligencer* responded that the Springfield editor had abandoned his usual sane position, and called his attention to the fact that the people in whose interest these reservations were supposed to be made were the very ones who were fighting them and that the statement that the reserves did not contain a bit of merchantable timber was true, but that the West did not desire to burden the East with facts.[55] It was public pressure of this type that led to a great mass

"And What is to Become of Us?"

From *Seattle Post-Intelligencer*, March 7, 1897.

[54] *Orting* (Washington) *Oracle*, March 5, 1897.
[55] *Seattle Post-Intelligencer*, March 17, 1897.

meeting in Seattle, to the drawing up of a protest by the Seattle Chamber of Commerce, and to the memorial of protest adopted by the state legislature.

If the newspapers of the West reflected this feeling about forest reserves, it was only natural to expect that the senators and representatives would hold similar views. Senator Frank Mondell of Wyoming, after denying that the reserves in his state were necessary even for water protection, charged that the large one around the eastern and southern side of Yellowstone National Park was created to protect the monopoly of the Northern Pacific. He also blamed the western reserves on the lumbermen of the East and South, who were trying, he said, to hold prices at a high level by restricting the output.[56] He called Cleveland's action "as outrageous an act of arbitrary power as a czar or sultan ever conceived."[57] Senator Clarence Clark of Wyoming declared it to be "an order without the authority of law." It was, he said, part of that solid wall of opposition to western interests. It drew away millions of acres of land which should have been open to happy homes. In Wyoming there was not enough timbers on the reserves to build a four-rail fence around it. As for public land problems, he asserted that the West should be consulted.[58]

In the Senate on February 28, while the Sundry Civil Bill was being considered, Clark offered an amendment which provided for the restoration of the reserves of the public domain as if the executive order had never been issued.[59] This amendment touched off the fireworks. Senator William B. Allison of Iowa opposed to the course being taken, threatened to declare a point of order. William Stewart of Nevada, Thomas Carter of Montana, John L. Wilson of Washington, and Lee Mantle of Montana spoke briefly against the reservations, and the amendment was agreed to.[60] In the House, however, the amendment met stubborn resistance. John F. Lacey of Iowa offered an amendment permitting use of timber for mining purposes on the reservations and giving the President the authority to abolish any or all reserves.[61] The House agreed to this amendment; but in the Senate the western members agreed only reluctantly, claiming that they could not trust the President to revoke his own orders. Mantle declared: "I want to

---

[56] *Congressional Record*, 54 Cong. 2 Sess., Pt. 3, pp. 2,971-3.
[57] *Denver Republican*, February 24, 1897.   [58] *Cheyenne Tribune*, February 24, 1897.
[59] *Congressional Record*, 54 Cong. 2 Sess., Pt. 3, pp. 2,512-3.   [60] *ibid.*, p. 2,517.
[61] *ibid.*, p. 2,677.

say here and now that if these assurances should fail of realization . . . whenever Congress meets in extra session so far as I am personally concerned . . . I shall do my utmost to prevent any important legislation from being crystallized into law until this gross injustice to the people of these states has been remedied and righted."[62] President Cleveland's answer to Lacey's amendment was a pocket veto of the entire Sundry Civil Bill; thus the West was given to understand that the executive had meant what he said.

With the inauguration of William G. McKinley, and the call for a special session of Congress, western interests renewed their hope for modification of Cleveland's order. While the new government was being organized, Charles D. Wolcott of the *Geological Survey,* realizing that the West might force a revocation of the orders creating the forest reserves, went to Senator Richard Pettigrew of South Dakota and convinced him that the occasion presented a wonderful opportunity to bring forward some permanent legislation for the protection of the forest reserves. Wolcott talked that matter over with Secretary of the Interior Bliss, with the forestry commission of the National Academy of Sciences, and even with President McKinley and his cabinet, then finally, using the McRae bill (H.R. 119) as a prototype, drew up a measure which he gave to Pettigrew to introduce into Congress.[63]

On April 8, Pettigrew came forward with a bill slightly altered from the one Wolcott had given him, which he introduced as an amendment to the Sundry Civil Appropriation bill.[64] Western opposition quieted after Pettigrew called attention to section 2, providing for the setting aside of the executive orders of February 22 until March 1, 1898, at which time the order would again become effective. The bill gave the President the power to modify, revoke, or change in any way the reservations already created. This would give western interests time to get their house in order. But more important, perhaps, were certain concessions. One provision defined the objectives of forest reserve as: to secure "favorable conditions for water flow, and to furnish a continuous supply of timber for the record necessities of citizens of the United States." Another excluded agricultural and mineral lands.

[62] *ibid.,* p. 2,930.   [63] Ise, *The United States Forest Policy,* pp. 131-2.
[64] *Congressional Record,* 55 Cong. 1 Sess., Pt. 1, pp. 899-900.

The Secretary of the Interior was authorized to give free timber and stone to settlers, miners, or residents for firewood, fencing, building, mining, prospecting, and other domestic purposes. The reserves were to be open to mining and prospecting. And any person who found his claim included in a forest reserve might relinquish his claim, and in lieu thereof, select an equal area outside.

As an amendment to the appropriation bill, Pettigrew's measure was clearly out of order. So strong were the western forces, however, that when Senator Arthur Gorman of Maryland raised the point of order, it was voted down by a division of 25 to 23. In support of his amendment, Pettigrew asserted that the Black Hills reservation in his state had tied up 15,000 people, many farms and towns, without a stick of firewood because the lands were mineral and hence unsurveyed.[65] Thomas Carter of Montana explained that it would be ill-advised for the administration to revoke outright the executive order of the previous administration, hence the advisability of Pettigrew's measure. Senators George Shoup of Idaho, Stephen White of California, Francis Warren of Wyoming, and George Turner of Washington spoke against Cleveland's order, but seemed to admit that reservations were all right if properly made.

The speech of John L. Wilson of Washington, however, presented one of the best arguments in defense of the western position. "It would seem that it was impossible for the people west of the Missouri River to develop their own domain and their own country in their own way. . . . The people who first settled in New England came and took thousands of acres of land and developed them as they saw fit, and the people who passed from New England across the Alleghany Mountains and settled in the Mississippi Valley took up their lands at a dollar and a quarter an acre without those restrictions required under the Homestead Act of 1860 [sic]. . . . Our people have had to go forward and develop their country by law, and they have observed the law in so far as it has been possible for any citizens to do so. They do not complain of this. It is right and proper and just. What they do complain of is that their material interests—those very things that affect their prosperity and advancement, nay, their very existence as Commonwealths— shall be disposed of by the stroke of the pen, as though we were mere provinces and not sovereign states of this great Union." He concluded

[65] *ibid.*, p. 901.

with a bitter denunciation of the "eastern friends, who are so extremely solicitous for our happiness and our prosperity, and our growth and our development, who control our incomings and our outgoings with such liberality upon their part." And as a parting shot he exclaimed: "Why should we be everlastingly and eternally harassed and annoyed and bedevilled by these scientific gentlemen from Harvard College?"[66]

Pettigrew's amendment was then voted upon and passed 32 to 14.[67] In the House it encountered immediate opposition, particularly from Lacey of Iowa and McRae of Arkansas. McRae took the floor against the complete revocation of the Cleveland order. He spoke at length of the terrible floods then ravaging the Mississippi River and its tributaries, and claimed that they were due to the denudation of forests at the headwaters of those streams, and should thus be a warning to Congress to preserve the forests.[68] The debate continued for some time, shifting to the need of forest fire legislation, to the relative difficulties of the grazing of sheep in the reserves, and to the question of letting the President or Congress repeal the order. Finally, on May 10, the House voted against concurring in Senator Pettigrew's amendment, whereupon the measure went to conference.[69]

The original amendment had allowed any settler who had "initiated" a claim in a forest reserve, no matter how far he had gone with it, to relinquish it and in lieu thereof, select a like area on unreserved land. The conference committee, fearing that this was an open invitation to fraud and speculation, changed this to conform to Lacey's substitute amendment which, in fact, had been taken from McRae's bill (H.R. 119) of 1896. The new provision gave the "settler or owner" only the same claim, right, or title as he had in the forest reserve.[70] The conference thus corrected one danger, but under the vague word "owner" a greater danger was to appear, for it must be remembered that the railroads had many acres of their grants enclosed in the forest reserves. With this one important exception the Pettigrew amendment remained practically unchanged, and was thus reported back. While this change encountered some western opposition it passed the Senate

[66] ibid., pp. 910-16.   [67] ibid., May 6, 1897, p. 924.
[68] ibid., pp. 966-70; Seattle Daily Times, May 11, 1897.
[69] Congressional Record, 55 Cong. 1 Sess., Pt. 1, p. 1,013.
[70] Ise, The United States Forest Policy, p. 140.

by a vote of 32 to 25, and the House 89 to 6.[71] It was signed by President McKinley on June 4, 1897.[72]

Thus ended the most heated land controversy since the days when the homestead issue had divided the nation. During the last stages of the struggle many of the western states had become reconciled somewhat to the institution of forest reserves, but there still remained a great deal of opposition. On the whole, the measure must be regarded as a compromise: the postponement of the reserves for nine months and the provisions permitting mining and agriculture, together with the allowance of free timber to settlers, were out-and-out concessions to the West. The provision allowing the Secretary of the Interior to sell timber and to provide for the protection of the forests was also a concession made to the West, but one which would mean nothing unless Congress appropriated sufficient funds to provide for effective administration.

[71] *Congressional Record,* 55 Cong. 1 Sess., pp. 1,278, 1,284-5.
[72] *Statutes at Large,* Vol. XXX, pp. 35-6.

CHAPTER XX

ROOSEVELT FORCES THE ISSUE

I F the federal government can be charged with plunging recklessly and aimlessly ahead in the evolution of its forest policy, it can also be criticized for being slow and dilatory in evolving a policy for the arid lands. It seems clear in retrospect, that had there been a clearer definition of policy, with proper classification of public lands as forest, mineral, irrigable, range, etc., and a general program adopted for each, united western opposition of the sort that broke out in 1897 would never have appeared. For over twenty-five years it had been a recognized fact that the land west of the hundredth meridian was semiarid if not arid in character. This great region, as different from the country to the east as day is from night, should never have been settled under the land laws which had governed American settlement of the lands to the east.

An enlightened report containing well-advised recommendations was submitted to Congress in 1879 by Major John Wesley Powell.[1] Bills were framed and introduced for the classification of lands as irrigable, timber, and pasturage. Powell, who was interested in preserving the grasslands as a natural resource, advocated that holdings be of not less than 2,560 acres, that each tract should include some irrigable land for the raising of forage and other necessary farm produce, that boundaries be not determined necessarily by the system of rectangular survey but rather by topographic features and water supply, that residences should be grouped together, and that pasturage farms should not be fenced but held in common. In fact, this foremost authority on the subject of the arid region would have legalized conditions then existing in the West.[2] But Congress still felt that the enlarged homestead of 640 acres at 25 cents an acre, as provided for in the Desert Land Act of 1877, was sufficient and refused to consider further legislation.

[1] Report on the Lands of the Arid Region of the United States, 47 Cong. 2 Sess., *H. Misc. Doc.* No. 45, Pt. IV.

[2] Ralph H. Brown, "Utilization and Conservation of Our Arid and Semi-arid Lands," being Chap. VI in *Our Natural Resources and Their Conservation*, ed. A. E. Perkins and J. R. Whitaker (New York, 1936), pp. 123-5.

Not only were the grazing interests neglected, but in the next few years the government attacked the whole range industry as a vicious monopoly which threatened to appropriate the remaining lands to the exclusion of the homesteader. The government made no attempt to reconcile the range industry with farming. Although the homesteader was victorious in the struggle, it remained to be seen whether or not he could conquer the desert country. The prairie grass was plowed under, and the land on which the buffalo and cowboy had roamed was turned into homesteads. Almost immediately the government joined hands with the railroads in promoting settlement of the desert country. The preemption and homestead laws, distinctly unsuited to conditions in the arid country, ultimately proved an invitation to disaster for thousands of settlers who took up lands where there was little hope of continued prosperity. Hardly had the farmer begun his conquest when it became evident that the water necessary for proper cultivation could be secured only by irrigation, and to that problem farmers at once turned their attention.

Throughout the whole arid West enthusiasm ran high. The cattle interests, in order to save themselves, appropriated what available water rights they could get their hands on. Speculators, including railroad companies, under high-pressure advertising, disposed of holdings at inflated prices. Everywhere the desert was expected to bloom like the rose. The successes of ancient Egypt, of the Spanish in California, of the Mormons at Salt Lake, of the Union Colony at Greeley, Colorado, and more recently, the Anahum Colony in California and similar projects in Arizona, all pointed to what could be done in the arid West. No distinction was made between arid lands east of the Rockies and those west; all, it was felt, could be irrigated with but little trouble.

But in practice the homesteader with meager resources soon found that he could not finance and install an irrigation system.[3] Some were able to divert the smaller streams and irrigate the bordering lands, but for the most part, settlers soon found themselves in the meshes of speculating companies. In many western regions avaricious groups with no intention of buying water rights and settling grabbed the land, intending to hold it until some real settlers should come along who were willing to pay handsome prices. Other thrifty promoters preempted

[3] Hibbard, *History of the Public Land Policies*, p. 426. Private capital was solicited for the building of many projects.

the only sources of water, and levied tribute on all settlers. Such terms as a cash payment of $10 to $20 an acre for a "water right" were usual and, moreover, every contract carried the provision for an annual payment called a "water rent." Resort to the courts was useless, for the existing riparian law handed down through the ages protected only the original appropriator of the water. In place of a monopoly of the desert land by the cattle interests, there thus appeared a water monopoly held by speculating interests, which if allowed to stand might convert millions of settlers into tenants.

Such was the state of affairs when in the late 'eighties there came a series of crop failures due to the lack of sufficient rainfall and to insufficient irrigation. This, together with the nation-wide agricultural depression, put reclamation work in an appalling plight. The Panic of 1893 increased the suffering in the arid West. Irrigation projects folded up over night and individual settlers, faced with starvation, had no other recourse than to wend their way back to the East.

These events compelled the federal government to reconsider the problem of arid America. In 1888, Congress approved an act authorizing an investigation to determine the extent to which the arid region of the United States could be redeemed by irrigation, and to select sites for reservoirs necessary for storage and utilization of water for irrigation. The act further provided for the segregation of such lands as could be irrigated or used for reservoirs.[4] In 1888 and 1889 Congress appropriated $350,000 for these surveys in the West. Major Powell, director of the Geological Survey from 1881 to 1894, was active in bringing the matter before the country, and in 1891 published an extensive report on the subject.[5] At about the same time, Senator William Stewart of Nevada, heading a select committee, also reported on the subject.[6] Many Congressmen felt that the existing legislation needed modification before any further measures were passed. An act passed in 1890, apparently in accord with this view, restricted entries under the Desert Land Act of 1877 to 320 acres.[7] Several months later, the General Land Revision Act of 1891 made further modifications, namely, that improvements amounting to $3 per acre, $1 per year for three years, should be put upon the land toward its reclamation; that there should be enough

[4] *Statutes at Large,* Act of October 2, 1888, Vol. XXV, Sec. 1, p. 526.
[5] *Report of United States Geological Survey,* 1891.
[6] 51 Cong. 1 Sess., *Senate Reports,* 1890, No. 928.
[7] *Statutes at Large,* Vol. XXVI, p. 391.

water for the entire area, that one-eighth should be brought under cultivation; and that groups of persons might form associations to water their separate entries.[8]

But these measures did not satisfy the West, which began immediately to demand the cession of all arid lands to the states in which they were situated. This movement, backed by Congressmen from Idaho, Wyoming, and Nebraska, obtained the endorsement of the Land Commissioner in his report for 1891.[9] Meanwhile, controversies over the problem led to a series of Irrigation Congresses, the first held in Salt Lake City, September 15 to 19, 1891; the second in Los Angeles in 1893. These early congresses urged cession of lands to the states for the purpose of developing irrigation. Partly because of the interest aroused by these scientific reports and discussions, and partly because of the suffering in the arid country, Congress passed in 1894 a compromise bill framed by Senator Joseph Carey, chairman of the Senate Committee on Public Lands.

The Carey Act of 1894 aimed to encourage the investment of private capital, and at the same time to secure protection of settlers against pernicious and ineffectual speculative schemes. Through a plan of repayment it was designed eventually to vest the proprietorship of the irrigation system in the settlers themselves.[10] By this act, the Secretary of the Interior was authorized to donate areas of land not exceeding one million acres to any of the arid states, provided that these states should irrigate, reclaim, and occupy said tracts. Not less than 20 acres of every 160 were to be cultivated by each individual settler. States accepting the donation were required to submit a map showing the mode of contemplated irrigation and the course of the water, and were forbidden to lease such lands. After ten years of irrigation the title was to pass to the state or assignees of the state. Not much was said about whether the state was to do the work of installing irrigation systems or to contract with private parties for it, but the latter plan was followed in most cases.[11]

It was becoming more and more difficult for private companies to float bonds for the financing of irrigation projects. The proponents of the act thus hoped that with this governmental encouragement, financial difficulties might be eased and reclamation would continue at a

[8] *ibid.*   [9] See p. 51 of the Report of the Land Commissioner, 1891.
[10] *Statutes at Large,* Vol. XXVIII, p. 422.
[11] Hibbard, *History of the Public Land Policies,* p. 436.

reasonable pace. The act constituted a belated recognition that reclamation was too big an undertaking for the individual settler, or even for groups of settlers, unless there was some encouragement or guarantee given by the state or some other governmental agency.

Though very enthusiastic about the Carey Act of 1894, the western states were in no financial position to take advantage of it.[12] Most of the states had already undertaken legislation in hope of bringing order out of chaos in the reclamation business. Five years after passage of the Act of 1894, only one western state, Wyoming, the home state of Senator Carey, had actually developed lands obtained under its provisions.

While the western states were still hesitating to take advantage of the Carey Act, the feeling began to grow that the federal government should do more than simply donate land for irrigation purposes. Many western interests began to advocate that the federal government should itself construct irrigation works and so safeguard the settler from exploitation. The heterogeneous medley of riparian laws and customs had led to chaos. It was widely recognized that something must be done to bring forth a code of sectional regulations, perhaps the federal government should step in. The grasping water monopoly had not only embittered the relations between states, but had also produced bad feeling and discord between the United States government and the Republic of Mexico. Colorado was monopolizing the waters of the Arkansas River needed for projects previously constructed in Kansas; New Mexico was developing her resources at the expense of Mexican citizens south of the Rio Grande, drying up canals that had supported Mexican communities for centuries.

Some of the states, it is true, were far ahead of others in meeting the various problems. The Los Angeles Circuit Court had already declared that there could be no such thing as private ownership in the natural stream, a decision which paved the way for the abandonment of the old riparian doctrine of prior appropriations.[13] About the same time, the Idaho legislature passed a law prohibiting canal companies from requiring the purchase of a water right as a prerequisite to furnishing water to owners of land along their works. Texas, with the largest amount of waste land of all the states, in 1897 passed an act which reserved to the

[12] Dorothy Lampen, *Economic and Social Aspects of Federal Reclamation* (Ph.D. Thesis, Johns Hopkins University Press, Baltimore, 1930), p. 23.

[13] William Smythe, "Struggle for Water in the West," *Atlantic Monthly*, Vol. LXXXVI (1900), p. 650.

state all unappropriated water, and provided for the condemnation of rights-of-way for ditches.

The Wright Act of California set an example for state regulation and promotion of the financial business connected with irrigation, by providing that where land owners found it necessary to secure water for individual effort they should be allowed to organize an irrigation district and issue district bonds, the proceeds of which would be used to build dams, reservoirs, and canals. In general, considerable progress was being made in the West. But many people thought that greater progress could be made if the federal government would build the most costly items, namely dams, reservoirs, and ditches. The government would thereby set up a yardstick for the financial management of the irrigation industry, and would also bring order out of chaos by encouraging projects in those states where legislation was inadequate.

In 1896, at the Phoenix Irrigation Congress meeting, George H. Maxwell of California took a strong stand in opposition to cession of arid lands to the states, and declared himself in favor of a national irrigation policy. Three years later Maxwell organized the Irrigation Association for the purpose of spreading propaganda throughout the country in favor of a national reclamation law. The discussions in the daily press and among the various scientific associations enlisted the support of many prominent men for this movement. In 1900, both the Republican and Democratic parties, convinced that the subject was of great public interest, inserted in their platforms planks favoring federal aid for reclamation programs of some sort.

Meanwhile, Congress was becoming more and more interested. Beginning in 1894, appropriations were regularly made for the gauging of streams and measuring of the water supply in the arid regions. A very extensive report on the subject appeared in November 1897, under the authorship of Captain Hiram M. Chittenden.[14] Finally, in 1900 and 1901, Representative Francis G. Newlands of Nevada offered a series of bills which contained the essential features later embodied in the National Reclamation Act.

Interest in the subject was keen both in Congress and in the nation at large when Roosevelt succeeded to the Presidency in September 1901. With characteristic boldness and vigor Theodore Roosevelt soon de-

14 55 Cong. 2 Sess., *H. Ex. Doc.* No. 141.

manded the passage of a measure which would embrace a national reclamation policy. In his annual message to Congress in December 1901, he declared that great storage works were necessary to equalize the flow of streams and to save the flood waters. Their construction, it had been conclusively shown, was an undertaking too vast for private effort; nor could it be accomplished by individual states acting alone. "It is properly a national function," he declared, "at least in some of its features. It is as right for the national government to make the streams and rivers of the arid region useful by engineering works for storage, as to make useful the rivers and harbors of the humid region by engineering works of another kind."[15]

Lands reclaimed by federal irrigation works should, he believed, be reserved for actual settlers, and the cost of construction in the long run should, so far as possible, be repaid by the land reclaimed. Beyond the point of constructing the irrigation works, all other operations should be carried on by the settlers themselves in conformity with state law.[16] Obviously the best sites had already been appropriated, but the government could build on sites which had not been appropriated because they required such a great outlay of capital.[17] The President appealed to the common man of America. "Successful homemaking is but another name for the upbuilding of the nation."[18] And, he continued, "Our aim should be not simply to reclaim the largest area of land and provide homes for the largest number of people, but to create for this new industry the best possible social and industrial conditions, and this requires that we not only understand the existing situation, but avail ourselves of the best experience of the time in the solution of its problems."[19]

With this encouragement from the Chief Executive, the Newlands bill was recast to fit the new objectives and quickly pushed through Congress. Opponents claimed that it would encourage agricultural competition with eastern farmers, that it was unconstitutional, that overproduction in foodstuffs would result, and that benefits to be derived would not warrant expenditures. The defenders of federal reclamation declared that it was constitutional inasmuch as it involved the general welfare, that it would relieve the dangers of overpopulation in the cities, that it provided for the conservation of natural resources, that

[15] *Congressional Record*, 57 Cong. 1 Sess., p. 86.   [16] *ibid.*
[17] Richardson, *Messages and Papers of the Presidents*, Vol. XIV, p. 6,657.
[18] *ibid.*, p. 6,658.   [19] *ibid.*, p. 6,660

the produce grown on the projects would be consumed locally, that federal reclamation was no more paternalistic than river and harbor improvements, and finally that the projects would not cost the government a cent since they were to be self-liquidating through repayment by the settlers.[20] Senator Henry C. Hansborough of North Dakota showed that although 112 million acres of land had been disposed of in the 1890's, the prices on farm products were about the same at the end as at the beginning of the decade. "It is the history of all irrigation sections," he pointed out, "that the output of bread foods from irrigated lands rarely meets the local requirements."[21]

The so-called Newlands Act, approved June 17, 1902, simply assigned the receipts from the land sales in the arid states to the construction of storage reservoirs or permanent irrigation works, the water thus made available to be distributed under the water laws of the states.[22] The act gave the Secretary of the Interior authority to make examinations and surveys, and to locate and construct irrigation works for the storage, diversion and development of the streams and rivers. Construction charges were to be repaid to the government in not more than ten annual installments. The Secretary of the Interior, upon recommendation of the Director of the Geological Survey, was to set up an organization known as the Reclamation Service to handle this new government business.

It is to be noted that the federal government was to provide only one thing—water. The government was in no way obligated to help the individual farmer clear his land or equip his farm. No provision was made for the selection of the right type of farmer for the irrigation projects. No consideration whatsoever was given to the guidance of the farmer regarding preparation of his land for crops, the kind of crops to be grown, suitable crop rotations, marketing, or any of the many agricultural problems which beset the farmer in this new and strange environment. In fact, between 1902 and 1923, the federal government was concerned only with the engineering problems which accompanied the construction of the irrigation works.[23]

---

[20] Perkins and Whitaker, *Our Natural Resources and Their Conservation*, pp. 135-6.

[21] *Congressional Record*, 57 Cong. 1 Sess., p. 1,385.

[22] *Statutes at Large*, Vol. XXXII, p. 388.

[23] Elwood Mead, *Rise of Irrigation in the United States* in *The Bureau of Reclamation, Its Functions and Accomplishments* (a government pamphlet prepared for the Pan-Pacific Conference on Education, Rehabilitation, Reclamation, and Recreation, Honolulu, Hawaii, April 11-16, 1927).

The passage of the Newlands Act was heralded throughout the West. A Washington paper contended that the arid lands reclaimed west of the Mississippi would sustain a hundred million people. "The crowded conditions of the eastern communities will be automatically relieved; a happy and contented, home-loving and home-owning people will occupy the present arid region of the West."[24] The *San Francisco Chronicle* declared: "The fight has been made on the principle, and the outcome is the commitment of the nation to the policy of so conserving the waters of the public domain" as to insure "production of the largest possible acreage and support of the largest possible population."[25] Some fears were expressed that politics might play into the location of the sites,[26] and that tedious postponements and dilatory methods might characterize the national reclamation policy.[27] But generally speaking, the West really looked for many advantages to be gained through federal reclamation, especially from the end of speculative monopolization of water and from encouragement to the movement already begun for revision of the water laws in the western states.

Almost from the beginning of the agitation for forest reserves, one of the stock arguments was that not only would timber be preserved, but also in order to promote flood control and irrigation, sites could be reserved for the construction of dams to generate electric power. Once this authority to set apart forest reserves was established, the next step was for the government to manufacture electrical power and to maintain a water supply for the farms and cities within a reasonable distance from the water-power sites. At first, however, few dreamed that the government might utilize its ownership of water-power sites in the forest reserves, originally useful for irrigation and flood-control, to protect the public against water-power monopolies, and that if the government was successful in the region of the national forests it might extend its activity to the rest of the country.

But what was to prevent the government from obtaining water-power sites in the East under the pretext of preserving watersheds? If the conservation of timber and soil was a legitimate exercise of constitutional authority, might the federal government not construe its jurisdiction to embrace the manufacture and sale of electrical power from dams

[24] *Ellensburg* (Washington) *Dawn*, October 18, 1902.   [25] Issue of June 16, 1902.
[26] *ibid.*
[27] *Ellensburg Dawn*, October 18, 1902.

constructed for such conservation purposes? Thus out of the federal government's power to conserve the national resources might ultimately evolve a field of governmental activity that would come directly into conflict with a similar field of the private business. To determine how far the federal government has progressed along this line today, it is necessary only to point to the construction of the great system of dams of the Tennessee Valley, to the Bonneville and Grand Coulee dams on the Columbia, and to Boulder Dam on the Colorado, not to mention numerous other projects completed or nearly completed.

Several significant events foreshadowed the rise of the water-power issue in conservation history. In 1882, Thomas A. Edison had opened the world's first electric plant on Pearl Street in New York.[28] Eight years later, at Ames, Colorado, the world's first hydroelectric plant was constructed.[29] These were the modest beginnings of the era of electricity.

If progress in the East was marked by lightning development, the West was not far behind. Throughout the western country there was lively interest in possibilities of obtaining power from the streams. As early as 1897, at San Diego, a syndicate had just completed one of the largest reservoirs of the country; at San Bernadino a million dollar corporation was planning to supply a chain of cities including Los Angeles with electricity; at San Francisco many interests were eyeing the "unfailing supply of water at a great altitude which could supply motive power to Fresno, Oakland and San Francisco." The editor of the *San Francisco Chronicle,* referring to these news items, could "imagine few greater material benefits than those which would come of such a change."[30] The fact that ultimately 30 per cent of the water power of the country is included in national forests and that 69 per cent of the total horsepower in the streams of the country is in eleven western states alone, indicates the extent of the possibilities for conflict between the government and western interests in this new field of industrial enterprise.[31]

The setting aside of forest reserves authorized by the Act of 1891 precluded all possibility of water-power development and gave rise to the charge of the western interests that the resources were "locked up." In

[28] Samuel S. Wyer, *Study of Electric Light and Power Service* (Columbus, Ohio, Fuel Transportation Educational Foundation, 1932).

[29] *Congressional Record,* 63 Cong. 2 Sess., p. 13,626.   [30] Issue of February 22, 1897.

[31] Samuel T. Dana, *What the National Forests Mean to the Water User* (U.S. Department of Agriculture, Forest Service, Washington, 1919), p. 35.

1896, however, an act was passed providing for limited development in both the public domain and the forest reservations, under permits to be issued by the Secretary of the Interior.[32] These permits allowed rights-of-way and use of parts of the public lands for purposes of generating, manufacturing, or distributing electric power. Two years later the Act of 1898 allowed permits to be issued for rights-of-way for water, canals, or logging roads across the public lands, and for the development of power as subsidiary to the main purpose of irrigation.[33] These two acts were in conflict with the doctrine of prior appropriation of water rights recognized by Congress in the Act of 1866,[34] and it was frequently argued that the federal government had the right to restrict the use of water power on the public lands.

In order to harmonize these apparently conflicting laws, Congress passed an act, signed on February 15, 1901, reorganizing the permit system.[35] The Secretary of the Interior was required to draw up a set of regulations governing issuance of permits. This Act of 1901 is important, because under it a number of the early power permits were issued; in fact, several projects still operate under this law.[36] The power problem had already reached considerable dimensions, but as yet the power interests of the West were not strong enough to challenge seriously the control of federal government.

No nation in world history had so wasted its natural resources or opened up its natural treasure to unbridled exploitation as had the United States of America. But a halt had been called. The grizzled, hardheaded pioneer of the American West and the ever-grasping corporation stood face to face with the challenge of a new American order which demanded an end to the reckless and wasteful methods of the era of laissez-faire. The task which remained was not only to recover lost ground, and to preserve the fragments that were left, but also to educate the public on the intelligent use of the remaining resources. This was a herculean task. Already the best of forest lands had been acquired, by fair means and foul, and the nation's rights in these resources reduced to a minute per cent. In fact, many authorities thought

[32] *Congressional Record*, 54 Cong. 1 Sess., p. 703; *Statutes at Large*, Vol. XXIX, p. 120.
[33] *Congressional Record*, 54 Cong. 2 Sess., pp. 2,458-9.
[34] *Statutes at Large*, Vol. XIV, p. 253.
[35] 56 Cong. 1 Sess., *House Reports*, No. 1,850, p. 402.
[36] Annual Report of the Forester, 1933.

that it was already too late. But governmental authorities insisted that there was still much good land left, and that immediate steps should be taken for its protection.

The nation's forest lands received more serious attention, perhaps, than the other resources. Such inroads had been made on the great stands of timber that it was not difficult to see the end. The day of the hand logger was practically over. The best timber had disappeared from all streams that were easily accessible. Already the most powerful lumber operators, recognizing the warning signs, were disposed to buy logs from the small loggers and retain their large holdings intact, awaiting the inevitable advance in price that would come with the increasing scarcity of the supply.

American consumption of lumber was greater than ever before. It was estimated in 1905, that to supply the Portland mills alone, 80 acres of timber had to be cut every twenty-four hours.[37] Foreign demand was becoming ever more impressive. In fact, the lumber industry was already a big business, and it was doubtful whether the little independent lumberman could survive. A large amount of capital was necessary to provide for the newer manufacturing processes. Tramroads and wire cables were coming into general use, and this newer machinery brought wasteful methods of cutting the timber in the interior. It remained to be seen whether the government could preserve the remaining timber, and whether the government would do anything about the tendencies toward monopolization in the lumber business.

The administrations of Harrison and Cleveland had blazed the way for a national policy of conserving the natural resources. But it was left for the administration of Theodore Roosevelt to place the new national policy on a businesslike basis, to bring the West and East into a working agreement, and to establish a program looking not to the immediate present but many years into the future. The time was ripe for the consolidation of gains already made, and for a statement of national objectives. The press of the country—the newspapers and periodicals—had been ablaze with the discussion of the subject for over a decade. Scientific associations had not only devoted much of their time to the subject, but in 1896-97, after it appeared that Congress would not respond, the National Academy of Arts and Sciences had persuaded President Cleveland to act. Many states had set up conservation com-

[37] *Portland Oregonian*, June 17, 1905.

missions, and railroad companies were experimenting with timber culture in order to insure a future tie supply. By 1897, twenty land-grant colleges were offering instruction in forestry. And last, but not least, in 1900 both major political parties had gone on record in favor of conservation.

At this time of nation-wide enthusiasm, President Roosevelt launched, along with his reclamation, a national program for conservation. During the seven years after 1901, he kept the subject before the country in the boldest and most relentless fashion. When Congress refused to respond he took his message to the people. Under constant prodding action was obtained. If legislation was not forthcoming it was always possible to resort to executive order.

The forest reserves were intrusted to Gifford Pinchot, a very young man indeed for such an important task. Forestry had been Pinchot's study, hobby, and practice for years. At his alma mater he was called "tree mad." A man of considerable wealth, he had studied in Germany and other countries which had not only saved their forests from annihilation, but also were making them pay annual dividends on high valuation, in the case of Bavaria, 10 per cent of the revenues of the kingdom. Pinchot had later managed several practical forest schemes, and had served as a member of the commission of the National Academy of Arts and Sciences that in 1896 had reported on the need for forest reserves. He had inevitably gravitated in 1898 to the position of Chief Forester of the United States.

During Roosevelt's administration he was the real power behind the conservation movement. It was said that the President consulted him more than any other man in Washington. In fact, Pinchot ruled like an autocrat, but with such tact, logic and sincerity, that even the lumbermen and other business men came to respect him and to recognize the business value of conservation. By the end of Roosevelt's administration, Pinchot had built up the Forestry Service into an organization of 1,500 men in charge of 150 million acres of timber resources valued at one billion dollars.

To Roosevelt and Pinchot, and perhaps in a lesser degree to James Wilson, Secretary of Agriculture, and James R. Garfield, Secretary of the Interior, must go the credit for establishing a comprehensive national conservation policy. Their program broadened into a constructive movement, not only for the guarding of irreplaceable resources, but also for the development of other resources, such as irrigation lands, waterways and water power for the benefit of the people as a whole.[38]

Soon after Roosevelt took office, the federal government very definitely announced its intention of conserving the remaining national resources. Both the legislative and executive departments exercised their powers to set apart extensive areas of valuable timber lands into national parks and forest reserves, designed not only to conserve the watersheds so as to assist in flood control, but also to preserve power-sites from the grasping operations of speculators and monopolies, and to afford facilities for the reclamation of arid lands.

The National Reclamation Act of 1902, which was to make possible the reclamation of much of the arid region of the West, almost instantly divided the western forces which had presented such a united front in 1897. But there still remained strong opposition to the program of national conservation. Timber interests were not reconciled; mining interests had been seriously handicapped; there had been no attempt as yet to provide for the grazing interests. To all these interests the forest reserve policy had seemed simply to lock up the resources and prevent their utilization. It was to be expected that these interests would do their best to block the creation of any more reserves.

So aggressively did Roosevelt and Pinchot enforce the laws for the protection of public interests that they aroused much hostility in Congress and in the West. In the latter half of 1902, Secretary of the Interior, Ethan A. Hitchcock, undertook a thorough investigation of conditions in his department. As a result Land Commissioner Binger Hermann was removed and a number of indictments secured against persons who had conspired to defraud the government of large areas of land. The administration pushed this campaign so relentlessly that by the end of Roosevelt's administration many thousands of acres had been restored to the public domain. Some of those who were indicted were able to continue the fight beyond the Roosevelt administration and ultimately to escape punishment when the government dropped the suits against them. Senator Charles W. Fulton alone of the Oregon delegates to Congress in 1903, was not indicted.[39] Not satisfied with a house cleaning, Roosevelt placed the whole forest administration under the civil service in 1904.

[38] Ise, *The United States Forest Policy*, p. 150.
[39] For an account of these prosecutions see *ibid.*, pp. 185-91.

The West applauded Roosevelt in this wholesale cleanup, only a few voices being raised against him. The *Portland Oregonian* and many other western papers were not only supporting the existing forest reserves but from time to time had advocated more reserves. It was a well known fact in the West, if not in Washington, that Land Commissioner Binger Hermann had allowed much fraud to creep into his administration, and when he tried to cover up his misdeeds by a declaration that the reserves should all be abolished, it was the West that denounced him and upheld the forest reserve policy.[40] Hitchcock was not Roosevelt's ideal for the position of Secretary of the Interior; nevertheless, it was he who was responsible for running down and exposing the extensive land frauds. When in 1905 Hitchcock came under attack, much of the Far West came to his support. The editor of the *Portland Oregonian,* in an editorial entitled "His Good Work Tells," declared: "After three years of tireless investigation the government has secured a vast number of indictments. Under backing of the Senate, [Hitchcock] . . . should be given support publicly. Even though the West dislikes him he should be supported, for he is honest."[41]

The West was not all anticonservation by any means. This section of the country had a justifiable grievance against the government's forest-reserve policy. The government itself had unwittingly promoted one of the greatest land steals in history. The Act of 1897, known as the Forest Lieu Land Act, had provided that "in cases in which a tract covered by an unperfected bona fide claim, or by a patent, is included within the limits of a forest reservation the settler or owner thereof may, if he desires to do so, relinquish the tract to the Government, and may select in lieu thereof a tract of vacant land open to settlement not exceeding in area the tract covered by his claim or patent." Ostensibly for the benefit of the settler, it was used as a vehicle of fraud. No matter how barren or worthless the land relinquished, the government, under this act, stood ready to make good with an equal area of the best land that the scrip holder could find elsewhere.[42]

An unfortunate construction of the law that arose during the administration of Binger Hermann opened the way for all land-grant railroads, speculators, and unscrupulous lumber companies in the country to juggle the government out of its valuable timber land in ex-

---

[40] *Portland Oregonian,* August 22, 1901.   [41] Issue of February 20, 1905.
[42] See Ise, *The United States Forest Policy,* p. 331, for large holdings created under this act.

change for worthless holdings within the forest reserves. Quick to see the advantages unwittingly proffered them, the railroads of the West became aggressive advocates of the forest-reserve policy. Nearly a million acres of the finest timber land including the white pine forests in Idaho passed into the hands of these companies.[43]

The West became fighting mad over the lieu land policy. In 1902 when two more bills providing for forest lieu benefits were pending in Congress, the editor of the *Portland Oregonian* declared: "Both bills are vicious and should be killed. They are both framed in the interest of the scrippers who have been endeavoring to grab the mineral lands of this state through the forest lieu land act. . . . We have had too much land scrip issued already. It has invariably been a source of litigation. . . . Congress can relieve the holders of timber lands on the forest reserves by passing a bill providing for a fair compensation for their property in cash on surrendering of their patents."[44]

In spite of all the indictments that followed in the wake of Hitchcock's investigation the laws under which the crimes had been committed still remained on the statute books, although it had been admitted for years that the laws themselves were inherently faulty. Besides the Forest Lieu Land Act, the Timber and Stone Act also remained to offer opportunity and shelter to those who learned the easy way to swindle the government out of valuable timber lands. With the conservation movement in full swing all interests were hurrying to get in before the door was finally shut. Hence in some parts of the West there arose the demand that all forest lands be immediately put into reserves. If the government locked up all its forest lands, lumber interests, speculators and railroads would be compelled to feed the market from their own extensive holdings instead of working off the government holdings. This would be better policy than selling valuable lands under the Timber and Stone Act at a tenth or fifteenth of their value.

The editor of the *Oregonian* thought "This talk about a chance for the poor man . . . contemptible. There is no more reason why the poor man should either steal the nation's heritage, or be presented with a slice of it for one-tenth of its value than that the rich man or even the bugbear corporation should have similar chances on a large scale. . . . The Timber and Stone Act was passed while the nation was sleeping on its

[43] Lute Pease, "The Way of the Land Transgressor" in the *Pacific Monthly* (Portland, Oregon), Vol. XVIII (1907), pp. 486-92.

[44] Issue of June 26, 1902.

ownership. President Roosevelt has still another chance to prove himself the true guardian that we all believe him to be of the timber lands of the United States. . . . The interests of the nation very far outweigh the possible chances that any individual may have for the continuance of the Timber and Stone Act. Let it be repealed!"[45]

That the conservation movement was in many ways aiding the large corporations there is no doubt. Already these interests were expressing themselves openly in favor of the whole program, and their enthusiasm did not wane until indictments began to touch their holdings. As early as 1903 the timber owners of the Northwest had reached a harmonious understanding with Gifford Pinchot,[46] who gave them to understand that the government's policy of withdrawing timber lands from entry and keeping them off the market would cause privately-owned timber to appreciate in value. There is some significance to the statement made by President Chauncey W. Griggs of the Pacific Coast Lumber Manufacturers' Association to the effect that the lumbermen were "working in harmony with Mr. Pinchot,"[47] and to C. A. Weyerhaeuser's belief that "the forest reserve policy" was "all right. The government is doing the right thing. It should save the timber."[48]

Nearly all the lumber and timber journals of the country fell in line with conservation. Many of the articles and editorials in these journals were as alarmist in character as the government bulletins. According to the *Pacific Trade Journal,* Washington timber would not last more than thirty-four years longer, and could last no longer than fifty years even though carefully husbanded.[49] The editor asserted: "With easier and cheaper ways of getting to large markets, the demand for northwestern lumber will increase enormously, and, at the present rate of destruction, two generations hence there may be little left of the great forest areas in which, fifty years ago, the sound of the woodman's ax had never been heard."[50] This frank admission on the part of the lumber interests puzzled the people of the West; many of them became convinced that Roosevelt's conservation program was not the common man's program which it pretended to be.

[45] Issue of February 7, 1905; consult also editorial in issue of February 1, 1905.
[46] John H. Cox, "Organization of the Lumber Industry in the Pacific Northwest" (Ph.D. Thesis, University of California, 1937), p. 174.
[47] *ibid.*, quoting from the *Columbia Review and Oregon Timbermen* (Portland, Oregon), September 1904, p. 33.
[48] *American Lumberman* (Chicago), June 29, 1907, p. 42. [49] Issue of June 1902.
[50] *ibid.*, as reported in Spokane *Spokesman-Review,* June 25, 1902.

Much opposition to the conservation program still came from the grazing country. It will be remembered that in 1897 the mining interests after putting up a stiff fight gained many concessions; in fact, they secured almost unlimited access to the forest reserves. But not so with the grazing interests. Agricultural lands within the reserves were entirely locked up, and only upon application to the Secretary of the Interior together with careful investigation could such lands be restored to entry. This restrictive system in effect, put the homesteader and grazier at the mercy of the Interior Department. These interests insisted that the Act of 1897 did not specifically exclude them from the reserves, and that if there was good agricultural land within the reserves, it should be opened up to them. So great became the western pressure that by 1900 the Secretary of the Interior had established a permit system. This system had no sooner gone into effect than the sheepmen began to charge that the government was not only regulating their business, but was regulating it in such a fashion as to prejudice their interests in favor of the cattle interests and the homesteader. It is much more probable, however, that this permit system once in full operation, benefited large sheep and cattle interests at the expense of the small herders and farmers.

Meanwhile the Roosevelt administration, insisting that the law be respected, made a series of arrests. In most of these, the cases which were tried in the federal district courts, the Act of 1897 was held unconstitutional on the grounds that it delegated legislative powers to an administrative office.[51] But in spite of these court decisions, the Attorney General insisted on prosecuting the sheepmen for trespassing, until in 1903 he found that by use of the injunction he could prevent graziers from trespassing. It was not until 1911 that the Supreme Court declared the Act of 1897 constitutional on the grounds stated.[52] In the meantime the administration took steps to make trespassing a criminal action, while western interests moved in Congress to open the reserves for pasturage and agricultural purposes specifically and to prevent the President from proclaiming any more reserves.

[51] Ise, *The United States Forest Policy*, p. 170.
[52] Case of United States vs. Grimond, 220 *United States* 506.

CHAPTER XXI

THE WEST DEFIANT

THE two industries most grievously concerned over the forest reserves were the lumbering and grazing interests. The Roosevelt administration, at odds with these interests, began in 1904 to swing into action along several lines. To some extent the renewed activity was due to the report of the Public Lands Commission appointed by the President in 1903, to investigate "the conditions, operations, and effect of the present land laws, and to recommend such changes as are needed to affect the largest practicable disposition of the public lands to actual settlers, and to secure in permanence the fullest and most effective use of the resources of the public lands." Modelled after the Donaldson report of the early 'eighties, the report of 1904-05 recommended a number of changes, among which were the repeal of the Forest Lieu Land Act of 1897, the segregation of agricultural lands in forest reserves and opening them to entry under the homesteading laws, and leasing of grasslands, which would provide some control and prevent overgrazing and ruin of millions of acres.[1]

In 1904 the Kinkaid Homestead Act was passed providing for the experiment of homesteading the desert country in western Nebraska.[2] This act permitted a homestead of 640 acres. Though it required improvements valued at $800 and five years' residence, nevertheless, it opened up to farming the remaining Nebraskan lands. Its operation was so successful that there was a general demand for its extension to the rest of the public land states. The act definitely favored the common man rather than the operations of the powerful grazing interests. But it still remained to be seen whether the region beyond the hundredth meridian was better suited for farming or for grazing. It was not until 1909 that the enlarged homestead system was applied generally to the remaining public domain.[3] That, unfortunately, was before the Kinkaid experiment was given a chance of proving itself.

[1] 58 Cong. 3 Sess., *S. Ex. Doc.* No. 189.
[2] *Statutes at Large*, Vol. XXXIII, p. 547; Addison E. Sheldon, *Land Systems and Land Policies in Nebraska*, pp. 156-64.
[3] See Enlarged Homestead Act below, p. 363.

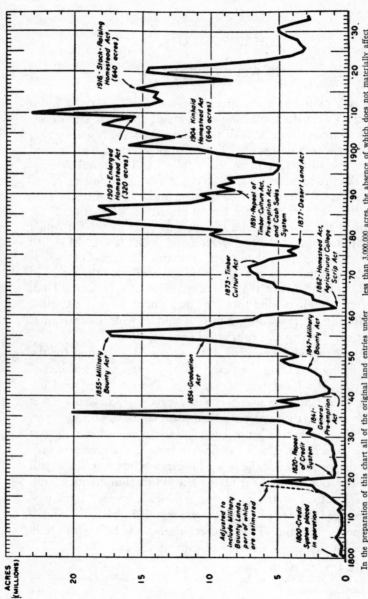

ORIGINAL LAND ENTRIES, 1800-1934

ACRES (MILLIONS)

1800 - Credit System placed in operation

Adjusted to include Military Bounty Lands, part of which are estimated

1820 - Repeal of Credit System

1841 - General Pre-emption Act

1854 - Graduation Act

1855 - Military Bounty Act

1847 - Military Bounty Act

1862 - Homestead Act, Agricultural College Scrip Act

1873 - Timber Culture Act

1877 - Desert Land Act

1891 - Repeal of Timber Culture Act, Pre-emption Act, and Cash Sales System

1904 - Kinkaid Homestead Act (640 acres)

1909 - Enlarged Homestead Act (320 acres)

1916 - Stock-Raising Homestead Act (640 acres)

In the preparation of this chart all of the original land entries under the various laws were compiled, insofar as this was possible. This chart includes the following types of cash entries: Private cash entries, public auction sales, preemption entries, Indian land sales, timber and stone entries under the Act of 1877, mineral-land entries (small), coal-land entries (small), abandoned military reservations, and miscellaneous sales. It also includes entries made with military warrants and various kinds of scrip. Original entries under the Homestead, Timber Culture, and Desert Land Acts are included.

less than 3,000,000 acres, the absence of which does not materially affect the picture here presented.

It should be pointed out that this chart is for original entries. A chart of final entries or one showing the amount of entries going to patent would be substantially different as a large amount of homestead, timber culture, and desert-land entries never were proved up.

The chart does not include lands granted to railroads or States, nor certain small grants to individuals. Nor does it include Indian land sales prior to 1879 nor the sale of Indian allotments at any time. (From

Besides the passage of the Kinkaid Act, several other important changes were made in the land laws. In 1905, the forest reserves were transferred from the Department of the Interior to the Department of Agriculture, on the ground that forestry was a part of the field of agriculture.[4] This latter department immediately entered upon the study of the forest reserve problem, and within the following two years was able to secure legislation which had far-reaching effect. In many ways, the transfer of the national forests to the Department of Agriculture boded ill for the grazing and lumbering interests; for, as might be expected, agricultural administrators were interested in dividing the remaining public domain into as many farms as possible, whether the land was suited for that purpose or not.

In 1905 and 1906, there emanated from Washington, in rapid-fire fashion, a series of laws and regulations which helped to clarify the Rooseveltian program. The first of these regulatory measures repealed the Forest Lieu Act of 1897. This action helped to mollify the Westerners who believed that this law had done more to aid the speculators and corporations than to aid the actual settler. The western position on this measure is supported by the fact that over three million acres of valuable timber land had passed into the hands mostly of large corporations. The Public Land Commission in its report of 1904-05 had urged the repeal of this "vicious piece of legislation." Most western Congressmen favored its repeal, and, it may be noted, a western representative, Mondell of Wyoming, wrote the repeal measure.

The second regulatory measure was an order signed by the Secretary of Agriculture, James Wilson, instituting the system of leasing grazing lands within the forest reserves, such policy to be effective January 1, 1906.[5] Fees at so much per head of stock were to be charged for the privilege of grazing.

Closely following upon these instructions came the executive order from the Interior Department suspending all entries under the Timber and Stone Act, and inaugurating a policy of appraising such lands and selling them at their actual value.[6]

Next in order was a special act passed in 1906 granting the Edison Electric Company of California the right to set up a power plant in the San Bernardino, Sierra, and San Gabriel forest reserves. An annual

[4] *Statutes at Large*, Vol. XXXIII, p. 628.   [5] 59 Cong. 2 Sess., *H. Ex. Doc.* No. 6.
[6] 59 Cong. 2 Sess., *S. Ex. Doc.* No. 141.

rental was to be charged for such purpose. The authority to make a charge rested, it was argued, on the discretionary power conferred by Congress upon the Secretary of the Interior in the Act of 1897. Also, on June 8, 1905, the Secretary of the Interior entered into an agreement with the Secretary of Agriculture whereby the latter was given jurisdiction over applications for rights and privileges within the forest reserves.[7] This agreement placed the authority to issue permits practically in the hands of the Chief Forester, Gifford Pinchot. Furthermore, upon the recommendation of the Reclamation Bureau, Pinchot during the next two years withdrew 2,565 water-power sites upon the pretext that these sites were to be used for ranger stations.[8]

Under the Act of June 11, 1906, known as the Forest Homestead Act, forest-reserve lands which were chiefly valuable for agriculture, and in the opinion of the Secretary of the Interior might be occupied without injury to the forests, were to be open to entry under the homestead laws but on condition that there could be no commutation.[9] It was thought that about 4 per cent of the area of the forest reserves might be opened up to homesteading. From 1906 to 1909, over 1,400,000 acres were taken up under the provisions of this act.

Finally, under an order of June 29, 1906, the President directed the Secretary of the Interior to withdraw from entry all valuable coal lands. Within the next two years over fifty million acres of lands believed to contain coal were withdrawn from entry. For decades valuable coal lands had been passing into private hands under the agricultural land laws. The administration now withdrew such lands until an examination and proper classification could be made. The government could then appraise the coal lands and sell them above the minimum price. As a result, between 1906 and 1909 coal land was sold for $75 to $100 per acre yet without any change in the existing fundamental law. The Secretary of the Interior simply decided that the words "not less than" did not mean "not more than."[10] Thus the withdrawal policy was extended from timber lands to coal lands, and the conservation movement was pointing toward a new objective.

[7] *Decisions of the Department of the Interior and General Land Office*, Vol. XXXIII (Washington, 1905), p. 609.
[8] Report of the Department of Agriculture, 1908 and 1909; also 61 Cong. 2 Sess., *S. Ex. Doc.* No. 610.
[9] *Statutes at Large*, Vol. XXXIV, p. 233.
[10] Report of the Secretary of the Interior, 1909, p. 8.

These reforms in the land laws and regulations did not go unchallenged. In fact, the West was in no mood to agree to a broadening of the conservation program. The grazing states, especially Colorado, Wyoming, and Montana protested vigorously against the new policies. The stockmen of these states were compelled to use the meadows in the forest reserves inasmuch as the lower plains gave out during the hot weather. The sheepmen were especially anxious, for fear that governmental regulation would curtail their operations in favor of the cattle interests. Both these groups looked with suspicion upon a policy which seemed to favor the homesteader.

The report of the Public Lands Commission had declared that any new policy adopted should, above all else, be applied "with special reference to bringing about the largest permanent occupation of the country by actual settlers and homeseekers."[11] Or, as it was phrased in a western agricultural periodical: "Put a family on a quarter section and more cattle can be raised than there can be under the present dispensation. We should put the whole West to its best use and fill it with people."[12] But from Pinedale, Wyoming, came another side of the argument: "Our ranchers have been thoroughly aroused over the determination of the Bureau of Forestry to make the forest reserve self-supporting at the expense of the few ranchers who have faced and endured great privations in order that the Wyoming frontier might be developed and homes made on what was considered desert land. . . . The management of the affairs of the reserves have apparently given good satisfaction but now [these ranchers] . . . are a unit in antagonism. Many things are coming out which might have been otherwise avoided had the department gone over [to] the theory that it is not wise to ride a poor horse to death."[13]

The *Natrina County* (Wyoming) *Tribune* announced the Woolgrowers' Convention to be held at Caspar, under the caption "Woolgrowers' Attention! Pin—chot'll get you Ef you Don't get Together." They warned that everyone in the state of Wyoming "should put his shoulder to the wheel and take a good grip on the spokes and give one good, long, strong pull together. . . . The sheepmen will not be the only ones affected by the leasing of the public range. . . . The leasing of the

[11] Land Commission Report of 1904-05, p. xxi.
[12] *The Denver Field and Farm*, April 14, 1906.
[13] *Centennial* (Wyoming) *Post*, November 4, 1905.

ranges will ruin the small sheepmen. . . . Now is the time to stand still like a donkey with his tail tied down."[14]

The graziers' point of view was stated more clearly in a resolution adopted by stockmen gathered at Laramie:

"We, the stock growers and flockmasters of Albany county," it read, "are now required, whenever called upon to give our time and efforts, without compensation, to assist in putting out forest fires, and we have always, acting in the public interest, safeguarded our forests from destruction.

"We have, struggling with frontier conditions, built up the sheep and cattle interests of this section under many discouragements and have barely been able to win a modest success. . . . The free and unrestricted use of this mountain range has always been enjoyed by us. We have bought our property and built up our ranches on the strength of its continued use without tax or charge. Aided by this public range, under present conditions, we have been hardly able to hold our own, and the imposition of any grazing tax means to us disaster and ruin."[15]

In Congress, most of the attack upon the administration's policy was made in the Senate, with the attack being centered on Secretary of the Interior Hitchcock. Senators from Oregon, Colorado, and Montana were most vociferous in their remarks in favor of the lowly settler, and against a governmental policy that allowed the doling out of millions of acres of rich timber lands to corporations while at the same time it charged for the privilege of grazing on lands which herders had used free of charge for many years. Jonathan P. Dolliver of Iowa, Albert J. Beveridge of Indiana and John C. Spooner of Wisconsin, together with certain Westerners including Francis G. Newlands of Nevada, Reed Smoot of Utah, Fred Dubois of Idaho, Francis Warren of Wyoming, and George Perkins and Frank Flint of California came to the defense of the conservation policy. It was clear that the Reclamation Act of 1902 and the nebulous water-power site legislation were beginning to split the western forces into two opposing camps.

Finally, on February 23, Charles Fulton of Oregon moved an amendment to the appropriation bill, which provided that "Hereafter no forest reserve shall be created, nor shall any addition be made to one heretofore created, within the limits of the States of Oregon, Washington,

[14] Quoted in *ibid.*, January 20, 1906.   [15] *ibid.*, December 16, 1905.

Idaho, Montana, Colorado, or Wyoming except by act of Congress."[16] Some of the western Senators felt that further legislation should later be attempted to reduce those already created. After threat of a filibuster the amendment passed and remained unchanged in the conference committees. The appropriation bill finally passed with the amendment, which included many new provisions, relating to public lands. The amendment might well be called "the Act of 1907."[17] While it did include increased appropriation of one million dollars for the Forest Service, nevertheless, the anticonservationists for the most part had their way. The Forest Reserve Act of 1891 was repealed, which meant that henceforth there could be no more forest reserves in the six most prominent timbered states unless Congress should establish them, and that was not likely. Another important provision allowed 10 per cent of the receipts from the sales of timber and forest revenue to go to the state for schools and roads in counties in which the reserve was situated.

Before President Roosevelt signed this act on March 6, he boldly proclaimed twenty-one new forest reserves in the six northwestern states. This step brought the total number of national forests to 159, covering a total area of over 150 million acres, three times the area at the beginning of Roosevelt's administration. But such arbitrary action on the part of the President stung the West to the quick and provided a bone of contention for many years to come; even as late as 1914 it still brought forth wrath from certain quarters.[18]

Perhaps the most vociferous attacks on the President's action came from the State of Washington. The editor of the *Walla Walla Weekly Statesman,* commenting on the order embracing over four million more acres of Washington timberland, declared that such an action gave to the Weyerhaeuser Timber Company and other large lumber syndicates an undisputed sovereignty over the richest lumber lands of the state. He pointed out that the large corporations already owned most of the lands surrounding the reserves. Under the Forest Reserve Act the government could sell the ripe timber in the reserves to those who wished to buy and who had the price. But the small logger, owning no lands reaching to the reserves, and without means of transportation of any

[16] *Congressional Record,* February 23, 1907, p. 3,720.
[17] *Statutes at Large,* Vol. XXXIV, p. 1,269.
[18] See *Congressional Record,* March 10, 1914, p. 4,633.

kind, would henceforth be barred from bidding for the government timber.[19]

The editor of the *Seattle Post-Intelligencer* asked, "Why not include the state?" He pointed out that Roosevelt was badly misinformed when he spoke of the timber syndicates being opposed to the forest reservation policy. The forest reserve policy, he asserted, was operating to create one of the greatest monopolies in history![20] It was true that the secretary of the Pacific Coast Lumber Manufacturers' Association had called upon the President almost immediately to assure him that the Washington lumbermen thoroughly approved of his recent proclamations.[21] Upon hearing of this call the editor of the *Post-Intelligencer* declared: "It does not follow by any means . . . that all other interests in this state must be sacrificed to insure that the lumbermen of Washington may continue to thrive, prosper, and accumulate fortunes of extraordinary magnitude in proportion to original investment."[22] Two days later the same sheet asserted: "The simple truth is that the President and Mr. Pinchot have a radically erroneous idea of the entire situation. They have an obsession on the subject of land frauds, for which they consider the forest system a panacea."[23] And again, the same editor charged: "The federal government assumes the attitude of the alien landlord, holding perpetually for its own uses millions of acres of land in this state, drawing revenues from them for expenditures elsewhere, and paying no taxes upon its vast holdings."[24]

In an interview, the governor of Washington declared that "Gifford Pinchot, the United States forester, has done more to retard the growth and development of the Northwest than any other man."[25] The editor of the *Seattle Post-Intelligencer* shared the same views. He avowed that "The recent abuses of power have grown to the point that there will be bitter revolt against the entire policy of forest reserves and an appeal to Congress to repeal all of the laws on the subject. The growth of such a great state as Washington can no longer be hampered, and its development hampered, to please a few dilettante experimentalists, however well intentioned and patriotic in purpose they may be. Their idea that the greater part of this state must be kept in a primeval wilderness for the benefit of wealthy lumbermen and city sportsmen does not

[19] Issue of March 9, 1907.   [20] Issue of March 9, 1907.
[21] *ibid.*, March 7, 1907.   [22] *ibid.*, March 8, 1907.
[23] *ibid.*, March 11, 1907.   [24] *ibid.*, March 14, 1907.
[25] As reported in the Boysen (Wyoming) *Copper Mountain Miner*, March 1, 1907.

appeal to the people of Washington, who are inviting immigrants to build up the country."[26]

The opposition to these new reserves was not quite as conspicuous in the Rocky Mountain region as in the Pacific Northwest, although it was significant. The editor of *The Denver Field and Farm* declared that one-fourth of Colorado was now included in forest reserves. He asserted that if Roosevelt continued to create reserves soon there would be little ground left to bury folks on except that of the reserves, and then, he said, the old cowboy song would have to be changed to:

> Bury me not on the range
> Where the taxed cattle are roaming
> And the mangy coyotes yelp and bark
> And the wind in the pines is moaning
>
> On the reserve please bury me not
> For I never would then be free;
> A forest ranger would dig me up
> In order to collect his fee![27]

Public sentiment throughout the West was now so stirred up that western leaders dared to call a convention of protest to meet at Denver, June 19, 1907. Hundreds of delegates arrived, mostly from the grazing states, along with representatives of the administration, including Pinchot, Secretary of the Interior James R. Garfield, and Newell of the Reclamation Service. It was openly charged that the administration encouraged a number of Texas delegates—traditionally opposed to the grazing interests of Colorado, Wyoming, and Montana—to attend the convention. Roosevelt, in characteristic manner, bitterly attacked the convention long before it met, while the Forest Service made use of the mails and newspapers to spread conservationist propaganda into all parts of the West.[28] Just on the eve of the convention the Forest Service released many thousands of acres of agricultural land which had been held in the reserves, apparently hoping by this move to gain the favor of the farming regions.[29] The grazing interests, however, controlled the organization of the convention.

[26] Issue of March 7, 1907.
[27] As reported in the *Centennial* (Wyoming) *Post*, March 30, 1907.
[28] *Cheyenne Daily Leader*, June 7, 1907.   [29] *ibid.*, June 8, 1907

There is some truth in the assertion that the manner in which the convention was organized precluded absolute fairness. Senator Henry M. Teller, chairman of the convention, deliberately chose subjects and speakers in opposition to the administration.[30] Several attempts were made to oust the Roosevelt sympathizers.[31] The administration did not dare interfere, for too many prominent leaders were connected with the opposition movement. Senator Teller of Colorado was perhaps the most distinguished of the western leaders and was senior Senator of all the region west of the Missouri River. Having formerly been Secretary of the Interior, he commanded a fund of knowledge on the land question which few if any could equal. Besides having Pinchot and Garfield present to face the broadside of western fire, Roosevelt sent the convention a tactfully written message in which he declared against the monopolization of resources by a few huge corporations and insisted that the government would continue to favor "a home-building policy, forest reserves and the conservation of both water and timber."[32]

The convention posed as the representative of all western interests, and the resolutions were indeed fairer than was expected. Some critics felt that the homesteader was not fairly represented, yet the resolutions were democratic enough to please even the president himself. Generally speaking, the West was so divided among its varied interests that there could be no unanimity of opinion. A few citations from the western press, however, will be of interest at this point.

In commenting on the convention proceedings, the *Laramie Republican* stated that the views of the majority of the stockmen of the West were not adequately represented. "The big sheepmen," the editor pointed out, "are in favor of the open range without leasing ... [since] in the great majority of cases they have secured control of sufficient land to insure themselves against all possible contingencies." It has been the "practice" to locate all the water in certain sections, thus making it impossible for others to gain a foothold. The homesteader is then given "a cordial invitation to come in and make himself welcome." But since there is "no prospect save that of starvation," he "does not come, and what's more, he never can come and break into holdings of these large owners until there is some kind of legislation that will give

30 *Laramie Republican*, June 22, 1907.
31 *Walla Walla* (Washington) *Weekly Statesman*, June 22, 1907.
32 *Laramie Boomerang*, June 21, 1907.

him control of sufficient land upon which to make a start. One hundred sixty acres of grazing land is extremely inadequate."[33]

The editor of the *Centennial* (Wyoming) *Post* declared that Roosevelt should realize that "he has once more gone too far. The western men of today understand these local conditions as well as Mr. Roosevelt and are equally capable of settling what differences may exist. . . . The President has acted according to his own ideas and in the absence of law."[34]

Congressman Frank Mondell of Wyoming elicited much attention from newspapers in the State of Washington where he attacked the administrative policy of withdrawing coal lands. He warned, "The West is facing probably a serious coal famine next winter because it is impossible to acquire government land for new mines."[35]

"The Far West," asserted the *San Francisco Chronicle* "has formally gone on record . . . and demands that the new states be treated with the same consideration as those commonwealths which have already divided their patrimony among their individual citizens. . . . Just now the popular impression in the East is that the Far West is opposed to the conservation of its forests and that it supports the efforts of the unscrupulous grabbers to steal the public domain." But, the article continued, "the campaign of education inaugurated by the Denver Lands Convention will soon convince it that all that is asked for is even justice for the new states, and that . . . the profits arising from the eleventh hour reform shall not be absorbed by the states that have eaten their cake and now wish to share with those who have scarcely had a chance to nibble theirs."[36]

The resolutions, which were passed practically unanimously by the convention, endorsed the following items: (1) abolition of the leasing system for government grazing lands; (2) administration of forest reserves without interfering with the utilization of the public lands for homes; (3) liberal construction of the irrigation laws; (4) release of timberless land from the forest reserves; (5) removal of restrictions on the settlement of Indian Lands by whites; (6) state control of irrigation; (7) provision for filings on government coal lands; (8) cession of school lands in forest reserves to the state; (9) decrease in size of forest reserves where present area is objectionable to the people; and (10) approval of

---

[33] Issue of June 22, 1907. [34] Issue of June 29, 1907.
[35] As reported in the *Walla Walla* (Washington) *Weekly Statesman*, June 27, 1907.
[36] Issue of June 22, 1907.

the President's attempts to enforce the laws against land fraud per-petrators.[37]

The stand taken by the western interests obviously called for serious attention on the part of the administration. One immediate improve-ment was to be noted in the relations between Washington and the West. In order to arrest the western charges of "bureaucracy" and "red-tape," Secretary of the Interior Garfield, visited regions in the West following the Lands Convention, and determined to inaugurate a policy of local responsibility throughout the whole Interior Department. Henceforth it was expected that every land official, every surveyor general, and every special agent would familiarize himself with the conditions in his district, the needs of the people, the requirements of the homesteader and the farmer, so that when the reports were sent in to Washington, the Interior Department would know that they repre-sented the best interests of the people.[38]

The administration also renewed its efforts to educate the public on long-term policies of conservation and reclamation. The government thereafter made use of every irrigation congress, by sending either the Vice-President or other governmental officials to proclaim the impor-tance of the forest reserves and of the reclamation work. For instance, at the Sacramento Irrigation Congress in 1907, Vice-President Charles W. Fairbanks said: "We now see that some of the older countries in their experience" have found it "necessary to adhere to a national scientific forestry system." This we should do "not only in the interest of our future forests, but in the interest of the important subjects of irrigation and navigation. It is a truism that if the forests are swept away the rainfall quickly flows into the streams and is wasted into the sea, whereas if the trees are properly preserved for the watersheds the rainfall and melting of the snows are stored in nature's reservoirs and are gradually fed into the streams for the benefit of the agriculture and navigation."[39] At the same Congress, Senator G. C. Perkins of California observed that "The strongest ally of irrigation is the forest; without our forests there could be no irrigation."[40]

As he approached the end of his administration, Roosevelt was con-vinced that as yet no really satisfactory national conservation program

[37] Condensed from report of the proceedings in *Laramie Boomerang*, June 24, 1907.
[38] Secretary Garfield's remarks to the *Laramie Boomerang*, June 25, 1907.
[39] As reported in the *San Francisco Chronicle*, September 3, 1907.   [40] *ibid.*

had been established. With so much dissatisfaction in the West, it seemed essential to smooth out the differences, in fact, to establish a program that would pertain to the East as well as the West. So far, the conservation program savored too much of saving the West's resources for the benefit of the East. Why not conserve the East's resources too? This desire on the part of the President led him to appoint several important commissions and to call the great national conservation conference of 1908.

First of all, Roosevelt created the Inland Waterways' Commission to make a thorough study of the river systems of the country, and to suggest means of navigation improvement, power development, irrigation of arid land, flood-control, and soil conservation. Professor Ise, an authority on the forestry policy of the United States, claims that it was while this commission was engaged in inspecting the Mississippi Valley that Pinchot conceived the idea of calling a conference of the governors of all the states to consider the problem of conservation.[41] At any rate, President Roosevelt, approving the suggestion, issued an invitation to the governors of the states and to other public men to meet with him at the White House in May 1908.

For three days, the Governors' Conference discussed all angles of the conservation movement. The object of the meeting was to create a uniform public sentiment looking to the conservation of all natural resources and their ultimate complete utilization in the manner which would yield the most profit with the least waste, so that these resources might be passed down to the future generations unimpaired save by unavoidable wear and tear. Roosevelt hoped that the undefined area of jurisdiction which lies between the state and national government, known as "twilight land," would grow narrower with the lapse of years. Instead, he regretted to say, this area was apparently widening by "judicial decision that in a given case the state cannot act, and then a few years later by other decisions that in practically similar cases the nation cannot act either."

His desire was to be able to hold every·individual or corporation accountable so that his or its acts would be beneficial to the people as a whole. He made it clear that he did not at all object to even very large profits by captains of industry who at their own risk developed the natural resources and made them available to the people, but he

[41] Ise, *The United States Forest Policy*, p. 152.

did object to giving any set of men control in perpetuity of natural resources or opportunities then in public possession, or to the surrender by the public of all power of limitation of profits even during the period of permitted exploitation.[42]

The meeting was significant not only because it brought the conservation question into proper focus, but also because it was the first time in history that the governors of the states had met under one roof. Everywhere it was heralded as an evidence of growing nationalism, but in places in the West it was also regarded as a manifestation of the ascendency of national over state power. A *Seattle Times* editorial, entitled, "The End of Things," called the gathering a "convention of alarmists," but admitted that the meeting of "forty-four sovereign states under one roof" was "more important in its possibilities than any mere problem of coal, wood, iron, and water can possibly be either within this generation or the next."[43]

The Governors' Conference led to the appointment of the National Conservation Commission, with Pinchot as chairman, which made investigations and collected information in cooperation with state commissions and with the Public Land Commission created earlier by Roosevelt.

Not satisfied yet, Roosevelt invited Canada and Mexico to join in the conservation movement, and to attend the first North American Conservation Conference which was to meet in Washington on February 18, 1909. Finally, the President carried the subject to The Hague. Such was the manner in which Roosevelt advertised the urgent necessity for national action in the conservation of the natural resources.

The findings of the National Conservation Commission were made available in December 1908, to a joint Conservation Conference held in Washington. The complete report consisting of three volumes, was finished in January 1909, and forms "the most exhaustive inventory of our natural resources that has ever been made."[44] Inasmuch as various statements and recommendations included in this report were to furnish the basis for legislative action, a brief analysis is in order.

The startling fact was revealed by the National Conservation Commission that most of the public domain had been disposed of, that only

---

[42] See the *Proceedings;* this is what impressed the editor of the *San Francisco Chronicle;* see issue of May 18, 1908.

[43] Issue of May 15, 1908.

[44] Ise, *The United States Forest Policy,* p. 152; 60 Cong. 2 Sess., *S. Ex. Doc.* No. 676.

387 million acres remained open to entry on July 1, 1908. As compared with this figure, 235 million acres remained reserved in national parks and national forests.[45] There appeared to be little need of encouraging settlers to go into this remaining public land, for during the fiscal year ending June 1, 1908, there had been 29,636 entries covering 4,242,710 acres, a greater figure than for any year since 1901 and 1902.[46] It was generally agreed that what was needed was a change in existing legislation to make it accord to changed political, economic and social conditions. The remaining lands should be put to the greatest possible use. In order to accomplish this, a careful classification should be made so that the patentee would know whether he was getting land valuable for agricultural, or timber, and whether the subsurface was mineral or nonmineral. It was realized that the cost for such classification would run high, but it would thwart any attempt to obtain valuable land under laws not legally applicable. Much criticism was already being levelled against the government by homesteaders who were unable to get patents because coal or some other mineral was thought to exist under the surface.[47]

The Commission pointed with pride to the national forests of the United States. It was noted that four-fifths of the forested area had already passed into private hands; nevertheless, the national forests possessed a merchantable timber area of 75 million acres.

There were about 65 million acres of land from which the timber had been removed and which was only suitable for timber culture. It was agreed that reforestation should become a major part of the national program. "Thus far in actual acreage," the Commission reported, "our accomplishment is wholly inadequate. . . . Upon denuded forest lands we have planted only one acre to each 10,000 we have to plant."[48] Stricter fire laws were a necessity. An average of fifty million dollars worth of timber had been destroyed yearly since 1870.[49] But more significant was the fact that exclusive of fire losses, timber was being cut at a rate three and a half times its yearly growth.[50] Under careful management the national forests could yield four times as much, even while considerable waste was eliminated.

[45] Report of the National Conservation Commission, 60 Cong. 2 Sess., Vol. I, p. 75.
[46] ibid., Vol. I, p. 86.
[47] ibid., Vol. III, pp. 408-12.
[48] ibid., Vol. I, p. 63.
[49] ibid., p. 19.
[50] ibid., p. 20.

In addition to the need for reforestation, the report stressed the desirability of additional forest reserves. It recommended that the forest-reserve policy be extended to the East, where it was necessary to preserve timber on the watersheds of the Appalachian and White mountains for the prevention of floods and the preservation of water power. Already, said the report, "delay has entailed enormous preventable damage to forests and farms in these regions, to their developed water powers, and to their vast water powers not yet developed. If delay continues, the damage will be irreparable."[51]

The Commission came to the conclusion that the effects of rainfall in critical regions were not beyond the control of man.[52] The methods of control were incident to agriculture, grazing and forestry. It seemed desirable, therefore, that the government should control grazing land in order to prevent removal of the grass to the extent that great erosion would take place. It was also desirable that agricultural land should be protected in every way possible from excessive wash, and that stream flow should be regulated by proper forestation in regions most vitally concerned. This part of the program obviously should be extended to the eastern as well as to the western states.

Next came the subject of mineral lands. The records of the Geological Survey revealed the startling fact that at the rate consumption was increasing in 1907, practically all minerals with the exception of coal and iron would be exhausted by the end of the twentieth century. In the case of gold, silver, copper, lead and zinc, data were not available. As for gas and oil, these products were becoming more important every day, and inasmuch as use involved complete destruction, it was urged that the government make a thorough inventory of oil-bearing lands. It was estimated that if consumption continued to increase at the then current rate, the supply of petroleum would be exhausted before the middle of the century. The Commission thought it was safe to predict that within the next twenty-five years the known fields of natural gas would be exhausted.[53] It suggested that the life of these valuable resources could be extended by the cooperation of governmental agencies and private enterprise in order to reduce waste, to encourage substitution of common mineral substances for those which

[51] *ibid.*, p. 71.   [52] *ibid.*, Vol. II, p. 709.
[53] *ibid.*, Vol. III, pp. 93-111.

were more rapidly approaching exhaustion, and to increase the efficiency of future mining.

As a first step in this program of conserving mineral resources the federal government was expected not only to classify its remaining lands, but also to bring existing mineral lands legislation into conformity with the recommendations. Under the Coal Lands Act of 1873, only 500,000 acres of public lands had been patented. This small disposition was due to the fact that the area provided for in the act was too small for economical mining. As a result, corporations continued to get title to valuable coal lands under operation of the agricultural land laws. In the case of homesteaders, those who were honest and reported the discovery of coal deposits were immediately deprived of their patent. The law on the one hand seemed to reward the dishonest, and on the other to deprive the honest individual of his just dues. Legitimate business could not be fostered by law which did not lend itself to profitable development. The Commission recommended that the remaining federal coal lands should be leased, reserving the surface for agricultural purposes if suitable.[54]

As for mineral lands other than coal, the Commission reported that up to 1908 only a little over a million acres had been patented, and this land contained not only such precious minerals as gold, but also deposits of sapphires, sheet asphaltum, building stone, oil and gas, which the rules of the Interior Department had put under one and the same law of placer mining. This law, the report declared, had "been a temptation, to which many of the unscrupulous have succumbed, to seek to acquire title to nonmineral lands containing a growth of valuable timber, or to control the course of a stream or a waterfall by means of alleged mineral discoveries and locations, especially under the placer-mining law. This law is exceedingly liberal, the lands being disposed of at $2.50 per acre. . . . In one instance, attempt was made to acquire title to a tract of land five miles long and about fifty feet in width lying upon either side of a stream of water, the obvious purpose being to control the water not to secure the minerals. In a case . . . in California, one individual and his associates had more than 250,000 acres of lands within and about a national forest covered with alleged placer-mining locations, each location being made by eight persons and notice of the location recorded upon the county records. Thereafter, most of

[54] *ibid.*, pp. 417-20.

the claims were conveyed to the instigator of the scheme or to a corporation. . . . Thus fraudulent locations have the effect of depriving both the United States and its citizens of the use and possession of the ground covered thereby, and such claims are only set aside after long and expensive proceedings before the department or in the courts."[55]

With regard to the agricultural land problem, considerable criticism was levelled at the commutation clause of the Homestead Act. The Public Land Commission Report of the early 1880's, it will be recalled, had made this same criticism, but no reform had resulted. Over three million acres out of four million disposed of in 1908 were commuted under the homestead law. No objection would have been raised had these entries been bona fide homesteads, but, said the Commission Report, they became "a part of some large timber holding or parcel of a cattle or sheep ranch."[56] The government received only $400 for a quarter section worth nearly $20,000.

The Commission also recommended the repeal of the Timber and Stone Act of 1878. This act had originally been passed to provide wood lots for homesteaders, but in spite of the required oath that the timber was not to be sold, in actual practice the law had permitted thousands of acres of valuable timber land to be obtained at the minimum price per acre. "In one large operation in Central Oregon," the report stated, "trainloads of women school teachers were shipped out from Minnesota and entered lands under the Timber and Stone Act. A hundred citizens of Oregon made like entries. These lands were then transferred to a timber investor from Minneapolis, Minnesota, transfers going from him by deeds to a corporation. During the past ten years there have been like individual operations in Montana, Idaho, Washington and Colorado."[57] The Commission urged that henceforth the Land Office should appraise all timber entries and sell land at its true value instead of at a minimum of $2.50 per acre.

On December 1, 1908, the Interior Department put this recommendation into effect. Also, in conformity with the report, Congress appropriated $250,000 to be expended by the Land Office for the purpose of recovering those lands that had been fraudulently acquired under the Homesteading and the Timber and Stone acts. As a result, over a million acres were recovered in the year 1909.[58]

55 ibid., Vol. III, pp. 413-16.   56 ibid., p. 390.
57 ibid., p. 389.   58 Report of the Secretary of the Interior, 1909, p. 14.

The Commission called attention to the fact that there were over 30 million acres of arid land which were suitable only for grazing because they could not be irrigated. The free use of the public range, which the law permitted except in the national forests, had resulted in the deterioration of the forage and in some cases absolute ruin of great areas of grasslands because of overstocking and unseasonal use. In many localities "strife, destruction of property, breach of law and even murder" had also followed.[59] The Commission was not very definite in its recommendation on this grazing problem. But it did state, in general terms, that the government should regulate the public range, permitting settlers to enter the land under the homestead laws, allowing fencing for pasturage purposes, preventing overstocking, and insuring the equitable distribution of grazing rights.[60]

Under the subject of agricultural lands the Commission also turned its attention to reclamation and irrigation. It unqualifiedly recommended the repeal of the Desert Land Act or, at the very least, stringent modification of it. Even with the restriction to 320 acres adopted in 1891, the arid land immediately west of the 100th meridian had not been reclaimed. The report of the Public Lands Commission of 1904 and 1905 had stated that the results of the act were disappointing.[61] The small force of inspectors in the Land Office had been unable to check up on the entries. Besides, there was no standard by which to judge irrigable land and determine the water rights or the amount of water necessary to meet the requirements of law. One of the officers of the Land Office remarked: "I may properly say that I have travelled through localities in which more or less extensive areas of lands had been disposed of under the desert land law, and a most critical inspection of these lands failed to reveal the slightest evidence that they had ever received any treatment different from that to which the yet unappropriated public lands in the same localities had been subjected. . . . Acquisition of legal title had been followed by concentration of ownership and subsequent abandonment of all irrigation instrumentalities."[62]

The Commission reviewed the progress in those areas where reclamation was being effected. Under the Carey Act of 1895, up to 1908, more than three million acres had been selected by the states for reclamation,

---

[59] Report of the National Conservation Commission, Vol. I, p. 89.
[60] ibid., Vol. III, p. 358.   [61] See Report in 58 Cong. 3 Sess., S. Ex. Doc. No. 189.
[62] Report of National Conservation Commission, Vol. III, p. 424.

and already 293,000 acres had been approved and patented. As an encouragement to home building, the Commission thought the act was fulfilling its purpose.[63] The National Reclamation Act of 1902 was too new to elicit much attention other than general praise and commendation.

The Roosevelt administration still had time to deal with the problem of agricultural lands in the arid West. The National Conservation Commission had lamented the fact that except for the National Reclamation Act of 1902, there was no suitable legislation for the immense arid area; the Homestead Act of 1862 was considered entirely inadequate. However, the Roosevelt administration had been moving gradually toward a solution. The experiment in western Nebraska under the Kinkaid Homestead Act of 1904 had been fairly successful for the short time it had been in operation. The demand now arose to extend the benefits of this act to the rest of the arid country.

Many of the western regions feared that the government's policy of leasing the arid country to the grazing interests would become permanent, but those most intimately acquainted with the administration knew that it was determined to settle the West with as large a population as possible, and that the farmer was to be favored at the expense of sheep and cattle interests which had monopolized the land for grazing purposes. Hence its determination to plow up the range lands or to encourage the homesteader to set up in the grazing business. But as the editor of the *Laramie Republican* pointed out in 1907, the homesteader and small stockman would never be able to break into the large cattle and sheep holdings of Wyoming and Montana unless the public land laws were changed to give him sufficient land to get a start. One hundred sixty acres was entirely too small an area either for grazing or for farming in the arid country.[64] A commentator in Wyoming clearly stated the problem when he demanded that the government "Quit this Fol-de-Rol of leasing the 'public domain' and give us a 640-acre homestead law which will put the big cattle and sheepman in his respective place and build up the country and state with homes and thereby raise more babies, calves, and lambs, and lessen the taxation on all of us."[65]

Congress, apparently feeling that speculative interests would be attracted, or that irrigation plans would be frustrated, still refused to

[63] *ibid.*, Vol. II, pp. 78-80.   [64] *Laramie Republican*, June 22, 1907.
[65] *Centennial Post*, June 29, 1907.

extend the full benefits of the Kinkaid experiment to the rest of the arid-land states. Instead, a compromise was effected, it being agreed that 320 acres was of suitable size. This Enlarged Homestead Act so-called, specified that one-fourth of the land be cultivated, and that no irrigable, timber, or mineral land should be entered. Conditions being somewhat different in Idaho, the Secretary of the Interior was to permit the settler to live anywhere within twenty miles of his claim, provided that he cultivate one-half of it.[66] Whether the Enlarged Homestead Act would give the homesteader a foothold in the grazing country remained to be seen. And whether the federal government should ever have opened up the grazing country to homesteading was a question that only the future could answer.

[66] Act of February 19, 1909, in *Statutes at Large,* Vol. XXXVI, p. 531.

CHAPTER XXII

TAFT PUSHES ON

I T is a well known fact that Roosevelt chose Taft as his successor because of his desire to see his progressive policies carried forward in the same bold and vigorous fashion that had characterized his own administration. For this reason Pinchot, Roosevelt's *alter ego* in the conservation business, was to be kept on by Taft as Chief Forester. The stage for further action was set. The conservation ideal had been placed before the American public by every known political device; perhaps never before had a body politic been so thoroughly schooled on a subject. The National Conservation Commission had taken an inventory of the nation's natural resources and had set up a program for legislation. In fact, Roosevelt expected Taft to push ahead along all lines, and to yield to no interests whatsoever.

Unfortunately, Taft was to reap the whirlwind which Roosevelt had sown. Roosevelt's arbitrary action in withdrawing valuable forest resources from their natural course of operation without immediately planning for intelligent utilization had produced a so-called anticonservation party located chiefly in the West. Although Roosevelt had blazed the trail, the process of carrying the conservation movement to its ultimate objective—that of embracing all of the nation's remaining natural resources—was not an easy task. Roosevelt had not effectively quieted the opposition; in fact, there had been no conciliation since the President had assumed too much of the attitude that his policy was right and that the West was wrong. As a result, his administration ended with the West in no mood to agree to any extension of the conservation program.

When Taft took over the reins of state in 1909 he immediately came under a withering fire from all western interests. Not temperamentally constituted to follow Roosevelt's methods of arbitrary leadership, and perhaps feeling that discretion was the better part of valor, Taft determined to ask Congress for specific authority to act. Trained and experienced in the field of constitutional law, Taft realized that there was some justice on the side of those who contended that the President had no authority to withdraw resources from their natural course of utilization. He began to question whether or not the Act of 1891 granting the President authority to create national parks had carried with it the power to shut up forests and minerals for the unborn generations of America. In fact, the power to conserve natural resources had never been specifically granted by Congress to the executive department, and it was doubtful whether such a grant would be constitutional.[1] Moreover, it was easier to stretch the authority granted under the Act of 1891 to include forest reserves, than it was to extend this same authority to include mineral lands and water-power sites.

Consequently, at least as far as conservation was concerned, the Taft administration opened with considerable hesitancy on the part of the President. His Secretary of the Interior, Richard Ballinger, was a Westerner, and thus injected a western point of view into administration policy. But the Chief Forester, Pinchot, was determined to carry on the so-called "autocratic" rule that had characterized Roosevelt's administration. From the very beginning Ballinger and Pinchot were at odds, since their points of view were fundamentally different. In 1910, when an investigation was made of fraud in certain entries of Alaskan coal lands, the breach between Ballinger and Pinchot came out into the open. There was little that Taft could do but dismiss Pinchot, though by this action he incurred the everlasting enmity of Roosevelt. There is no need to pursue further the Ballinger-Pinchot episode, except to point out that, so far as the conservation movement was concerned, it indicated that Taft was willing at least to acknowledge that there was a western point of view.

The Inland Waterways Commission had done much to advertise the possibilities of water power in the streams and rivers of the country. In the West, where most of the available water-power sites were enclosed in the forest reserves, this subject had already become a lively one. Vice-President Charles W. Fairbanks, speaking at the Sacramento Irrigation Congress in 1907, said: "We have not fairly begun to appreciate the full value of our streams and rivers. We have not fairly begun to appropriate them to the benefit of our agriculture, industry, and commerce. The waters which come down from the sides of these mountains may be converted into electric power . . . carried hundreds of miles with

[1] "Temporary Withdrawals of Certain Public Lands" in 61 Cong. 2 Sess., *S. Ex. Doc. No. 171*, p. 4,110.

but little loss of the initial energy, and appropriated to lighting and heating cities, operating mines, and driving wheels of industry."[2]

It will be recalled that between 1907 and 1909, Pinchot had withdrawn from entry 2,565 water-power sites, on the pretext that they were to be used for ranger headquarters. Just at the close of Roosevelt's administration, 492 tracts which had been previously withdrawn by the Forest Service were branded as definitely withdrawn from disposal under any of the public land laws except the right-of-way acts. These withdrawals had brought vigorous protests from the western states. Under the Act of 1906, the Secretary of the Interior might grant permits to private interests for the development of these water sites, but it was a foregone conclusion that capital would not be attracted to the development of resources as long as the government held the power of revoking these permits.

When Ballinger came into the Interior Department he questioned the advisability of these power-site withdrawals inasmuch as such action was of doubtful constitutionality and was injurious to western interests. Whatever the real motive behind the withdrawals may have been, Ballinger soon revoked 149 of these sites embracing 28,595 acres.[3] At the same time the Secretary had a bill introduced in Congress which granted the President authority to withdraw water-power sites. In his annual report for 1910, Ballinger defended his action by saying: "In the various public land states and territories containing water-power resources . . . the title to areas greater in extent than that remaining in the Government has long since passed into private ownership and it must be realized that any radical or burdensome restriction imposed by the federal government upon the resource will operate as a servitude on the public lands and discourage their development and use."[4]

He further thought that as the ownership of the water in the stream was held by the states, and as the states had police power to regulate utilities, the transfer of the power sites to them would be a satisfactory method of control.[5] These statements may be compared with those of his predecessor, James R. Garfield, who held that "the proposal for the United States to turn over the lands owned by the United States to the states would be a betrayal of trust because past state legislation does no

[2] Proceedings of the Irrigation Congress reported in the *San Francisco Chronicle*, September 3, 1907.

[3] Report of the Land Office, 1910, p. 111.

[4] Report of the Secretary of the Interior, 1910, p. 19.   [5] *ibid*

justify the belief that the people's interest will be protected. Endless confusion would be probable."[6]

Coincident with the controversy over water-power sites arose the question of whether or not the President had the authority to withdraw mineral lands. In 1909 a Land Classification Board was established to maintain a uniform standard of classification of various kinds of lands. Under the supervision of this board, the Geological Survey every year was to examine the many acres of withdrawn lands and restore the agricultural land to entry.[7] Roosevelt had already withdrawn 68,000,000 acres of coal lands, which constituted practically all the known coal land on the public domain. On September 22, 1909, Secretary Ballinger withdrew 3,000,000 acres of oil and gas lands in Wyoming, California, Utah, and Oregon for the stated purpose of submitting the subject to Congress for legislation.[8] About the same time a great deal of phosphate land was also withdrawn.[9] Thus Taft had broadened the conservation program to include oil lands and water-power sites. With timber, coal, oil and water-power lands withdrawn, the program now was just about all-inclusive so far as the important natural resources were concerned.

Taft now found his policy under fire from all the West, and from many interests in the East as well. He therefore decided to ask Congress to grant him the power to withdraw mineral lands from entry. The result was the Withdrawal Act of 1910.[10] Congress granted the President power to withdraw any public land, such order to remain in force until revoked by him or by act of Congress. The act further stated that no more forest reserves were to be created or additions made thereto within the limits of the States of Oregon, Washington, Idaho, Montana, Colorado, or Wyoming except by act of Congress. An amendment made in 1912 provided that all "withdrawn lands were open to exploration and purchase for metalliferous minerals only."

As a result of the Withdrawal Act, all coal, oil, gas and phosphate lands were withdrawn from entry. In 1911 the Alaskan coal lands were withdrawn. In 1912 two valuable petroleum areas in California, total-

[6] James R. Garfield, "Water-Power from the Standpoint of the National Conservation Commission," *Report of the Colorado Conservation Commission, 1909-1910* (Denver, 1910), p. 158.
[7] Report of the Secretary of the Interior, 1909, Vol. I, p. 15.
[8] John Ise, *The United States Oil Policy* (New Haven, 1926), p. 313.
[9] Report of the Secretary of the Interior, 1909, Vol. I, p. 9.
[10] Act of June 25, 1910, *Statutes at Large,* Vol. XXXVI, p. 847.

ling about 68,000 acres were created Naval Oil Reserves.[11] In the same
year certain lands which indicated deep-seated deposits of copper, iron,
etc., were withdrawn, this action being legalized by an act of Congress.
Thus by the end of Taft's administration, most of the mineral resources
on the public domain were completely locked up, and the West got the
impression that they would never be opened for development since no
plan for their use had yet been adopted.

While the administration was working on its mineral-land conservation policy, legislation was passed on the subject of water-power sites'
withdrawals. Acting on the recommendation of the National Conservation Commission, in July 1909, Representative John W. Weeks of
Massachusetts introduced a bill "to enable any state to cooperate with
any other state or states or with the United States, for the protection of
the watersheds of navigable streams, and to appoint a commission for
the acquisition of lands for the purpose of conserving the navigability of
navigable rivers." The bill provided for an appropriation of $1,000,000
for the current year and $2,000,000 each year until 1916, for the pur-
chase of forest lands in the Appalachian and White Mountains.[12]

During the next two years this bill stirred up more bitter wrangling
in Congress than had any other conservation measure. Its proponents
argued that protection of forests on watersheds would prevent erosion
and floods, and that by insuring a more even water flow navigable rivers
could be made navigable for a greater part of the year. The control of
erosion meant the preservation of the soil in the interests of agriculture;
and the relation of the flow of the rivers meant the development of
water power. It was urged, moreover, that the government in buying up
lands in the southern Appalachians would be preserving the valuable
hardwood timber of that area.[13]

The opponents attacked the bill on the ground that it was unconstitutional, that it was not intended to conserve navigable streams, but was
simply another step to conserve forests, that the effects of forests on
floods was exaggerated, that the bill would involve the government in
a dangerous course requiring the expenditures of millions of dollars,

[11] 68 Cong. 1 Sess., *Senate Reports*, No. 794, p. 3.

[12] 61 Cong. 2 Sess., *House Reports*, No. 1,036; Ise, *The United States Forest Policy*, p. 212.

[13] *Congressional Record*, June 24, 1910, pp. 8,986-92; for a more detailed summary of
arguments, see Ise, *The United States Forest Policy*, pp. 212-14.

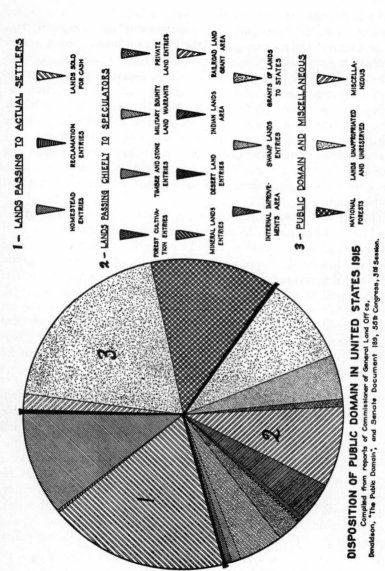

1 – LANDS PASSING TO ACTUAL SETTLERS

HOMESTEAD ENTRIES REClAMATION ENTRIES LANDS SOLD FOR CASH

2 – LANDS PASSING CHIEFLY TO SPECULATORS

FOREST CULTIVATION ENTRIES TIMBER AND STONE ENTRIES MILITARY BOUNTY LAND WARRANTS PRIVATE LAND ENTRIES

MINERAL LANDS ENTRIES DESERT LAND ENTRIES INDIAN LANDS AREA RAILROAD LAND GRANT AREA

INTERNAL IMPROVEMENTS AREA SWAMP LANDS ENTRIES GRANTS OF LANDS TO STATES

3 – PUBLIC DOMAIN AND MISCELLANEOUS

NATIONAL FORESTS LANDS UNAPPROPRIATED AND UNRESERVED MISCELLANEOUS

DISPOSITION OF PUBLIC DOMAIN IN UNITED STATES 1915
Compiled from reports of Commissioner of General Land Office,
Donaldson, "The Public Domain"; and Senate Document 189, 55th Congress, 3rd Session.

From Morison and Commager, *The Growth of the American Republic*. By permission of Oxford University Press.

and that the states should buy their own forests.[14] The bill was backed as Professor Ise has shown, by some of the most influential organizations of the country. The measure passed the House on June 24, 1910, against a very strong opposition, the anticonservation forces mustering 111 votes against 130 for the affirmative. The division on this measure in the House was apparently a clear-cut cleavage between the conservation and anticonservation forces. Yet, the final vote in the Senate on February 15, 1911, 57 to 9 was not clearly drawn; in fact, it is difficult to explain the affirmative vote of the western senators except on the theory that they hoped that the East, by acquiring reserves, would get sick of them and thus help abolish the whole reserve system, or possibly that these senators were not vitally interested since the measure applied to another part of the country.[15]

This act which was approved by the President on March 1, 1911,[16] marked the extension of the conservation movement from the western regional focus to the nation at large. Henceforth, the East as well as the West was to have the responsibility of a national conservation program. The federal government would now be able to establish national forests in the Appalachian Mountains, and such a policy had far-reaching ramifications. In fact, the provisions of this act furnished the authority on which President Franklin Delano Roosevelt some twenty years later based his soil-conservation and water-power programs. In truth, it was a measure of the gravest importance to the future of America, and many interests of the country were not slow to realize its implications.

Meanwhile, Congress had been subjected to a withering fire of protest from farm interests in the West, which charged that much valuable farm land was locked up in the mineral reserves. Congressman Mondell of Wyoming who, at the Denver Land Convention, had protested the Rooseveltian policy of "locking up" the coal lands, introduced into the sixty-second Congress a bill to relieve the situation. He charged that the governmental policy of withdrawing large areas of land from entry, together with the policy of selling coal lands at unreasonably high prices, was paralyzing the western coal industry, creating a coal monopoly, and raising the price to the consumer.[17] He further asserted that the policy

---

14 *Congressional Record*, June 24, 1910, pp. 9,017-25, 9,049-51; February 15, 1911, pp. 2,578, 2,583-94; Ise, *The United States Forest Policy*, pp. 214-17.
15 *ibid.*, pp. 219-20.   16 *Statutes at Large*, Vol. XXXVI, p. 961.
17 *Congressional Record*, 62 Cong. 1 Sess., *Appendix*, p. 55. Mondell's statements appear exaggerated when compared to the thirty-second report of the Geological Survey. Too, if one

of withdrawing agricultural lands from entry until classification could be effected had also injured the agricultural industry of the West, inasmuch as farmers could not get titles to their soil.

Mondell's bill which was passed in 1909, provided that a person who had entered lands classed as agricultural, prior to the discovery of coal, could get patent to his land on condition that he agree to the reservation of the subsurface coal rights by the government.[18] Indemnification for any damages done by the process of mining was to be guaranteed to the farmer, and prior to the disposal of the mining rights, the farmer could mine coal for his own use. By Act of June 22, 1910, any person might enter lands withdrawn or classified as "coal lands," under the agricultural land laws, with the same privileges of compensation and guarantee as in the Act of 1909.[19] This was the beginning of the policy of reserving the title of mineral lands to the government to be held in trust for future generations. It is to be noted that while this legislation quieted those interests which were anxious for the settlement and development of agricultural lands, nevertheless, the coal deposits as well as all other mineral deposits, except metalliferous minerals, were still locked up for purposes of conservation.

The First National Conservation Congress met in Seattle, Washington, from August 25 to 28, 1909. This gathering was practically dominated by lumber representatives, who clamored to endorse the conservation creed. The next year the annual convention of the National Lumber Manufacturers' Association subordinated purely commercial questions to a consideration of the larger problems of lumbering and forestry. Said the editor of the *Spokesman-Review* of Spokane, Washington: "This gathering might have been mistaken for a gathering on conservation. . . . Is Saul among the phophets? Are lumbermen become foresters and conservators? . . . The lumbermen and the foresters are making ready for teamwork. If this powerful association supports forestry much is to be achieved in saving the forests of the United States."[20] If the large lumber interests supported conservation, the smaller interests did not.

studies the figures from 1903 to 1907, it does not seem that Roosevelt's policy of withdrawing lands for the sake of classification really did check unduly the sale of coal lands. (D. Otis Smith, *Major Land Policies of the United States Since 1908*, M.A. Thesis, University of Washington, 1929, p. 59.)

[18] Act of March 3, 1909, *Statutes at Large*, Vol. XXXV, p. 844.   [19] *ibid.*, p. 583.
[20] Issue of June 27, 1910.

Although Roosevelt had proclaimed loudly against the corporations and in favor of the "poor man," the forest reserve policy had actually aided and abetted the consolidation of timber lands into the hands of the few. This fact more than anything else accounts for the western sentiment in favor of conservation but opposed to the manner in which Roosevelt had accomplished it. The West needed settlers, capital and access to the natural resources, otherwise there would be no development. Thus far the government had evolved a plan of selling ripe timber on the forest reserves, but such a sales policy did not favor the small operator. The West claimed that there were still large areas of farm land locked up in the reserves.

As for water-power sites and mineral lands, these resources were to all intents and purposes bottled up, and no plan had been agreed upon for their development, except the permit system which was too restrictive to attract capital. The West thus figured that the government aimed to hold all remaining resources intact for unborn generations and to leave to private interests—mostly corporations who had already appropriated valuable resources—the problem of caring for the present needs of the country. By 1910, the West was more than ever determined to fight. Its leaders were just as much interested in the common man as Roosevelt and Taft had professed to be. The line of action which they now settled upon took the form of a proposal that the conservation program be taken over by the states and administered by them.

Senator William E. Borah of Idaho, in an address before the Senate on June 20, 1910, declared that he did "not accept the modern doctrine that these matters which immediately concern the states in their material and local affairs can be better administered by a bureau from Washington than by the people themselves in their respective states. . . . A state which has her agricultural lands locked up is not on an equality with the state which can devote them to raising foodstuffs for her people. A state which has her mines withdrawn from exploitation must see immigration and all that goes to make a great commonwealth turn from her borders. . . . These power sites are our wealth. . . . They are part of the state's heritage. It is a violation of the Constitution to withhold them from our use. . . . We ask Congress not to adopt a policy, therefore, which will take from us the means by which we must live and thrive, the means by which our citizens are to prosper and our state to grow and take its place with the older states of the Union. We will deal with the monopolist when he comes within our border. We can tax his property, and we can regulate the charges he makes to the people, and, above all, we can disrobe nature of this mantle of idleness with which the theorists and dreamers would clothe her."[21]

It was Thomas Burke's anticonservation stand that led the people of the state of Washington to nominate him to the United States Senate in 1910. In one of his speeches during the campaign, delivered before the State Bankers' Association, Burke declared: "The opinion seems to prevail in the East that the West is opposed to the conservation of natural resources. . . . [Conservation] is in more danger of shipwreck from its overzealous and intolerant advocates than from its avowed opponents. The people of the West believe in forest reservation based upon common sense and scientific principles. They believe in the necessity of protecting our forests against fire and preventable waste, in extending forest reservations over lands better adapted to forest growth than to farming, in preserving the forests on mountain sides and steep hillsides, and in the importance of reforesting deforested areas unsuited to agriculture. . . . But they do not believe in hoarding the wilderness. They do not believe in the sentimental fad that trees are entitled to more consideration than human beings."

Burke continued with a statement that he was utterly opposed to a policy that would make the government a universal landlord over the remaining public lands and the settlers a body of tenants. As for coal and water power, he stated that these factors were essential to the industrial development of the West. It required great capital to develop these resources. He was opposed to a policy of leasing them because such a policy would not attract capital, and besides, a rental for coal lands or royalty for water power would be nothing short of a tax on the people of the state. He suggested that the public land laws be so worded as to provide that in every sale of land containing coal or controlling water power, the right to regulate the price of coal and water power should be reserved to the state. He concluded with the statement: "The people of today have a right to share in the blessings of nature. There is no intention in the West to rob the future, but there is a determined purpose not to let a band of well-meaning sentimentalists rob the present on the plea that it is necessary to hoard Nature's riches for unborn generations."[22]

[21] As reported in the Spokane *Spokesman-Review*, June 21, 1910.
[22] Speech by Thomas Burke in *The Westerner* (Seattle, Washington), August 1910, pp. 10-11.

The editors of many leading western newspapers were opposed to the conservation movement as ultimately defined by Roosevelt and Taft. The editor of the *San Francisco Chronicle* declared: "There is no subject in the whole review of legislation which is evidently and more properly among the rights guaranteed by all the people to all the states than the right to determine the uses of the soil, the waters and the minerals within their boundaries. The general government is a rank usurper in many things which in its arrogance it attempts within the states."[23] On the withdrawal of the Alaskan coal lands, the editor of the same newspaper lamented the government's dictum, declaring that the people of Alaska would have to go without coal until Congress enacted a law permitting development.[24]

After the passage of the Weeks Act, the editor of the *Chronicle* pointed out that the government was planning to buy simply for the sake of reforesting land in the Appalachian and White Mountains which had been denuded by eastern interests. Such a policy meant, he said, that western tax money would go toward buying these eastern forests, that is, "The nation robs the West for the benefit of the East, which seems to be only another application of the good old rule that 'They should take who have the power, and those should keep who can.' "[25] At the same time, this western newspaper suggested the passing of a state law to tax all federal lands in the state, thus forcing a constitutional issue which would doubtlessly go to the Supreme Court for a decision.[26] The editor, however, finally came around to the position of advocating state administration of natural resources.[27] Elsewhere in the West sentiment was much the same. Even some of the most conservative of editors denounced the federal conservation policy notwithstanding the fact that the federal government had heretofore found much support in the West for its reclamation program.

The report of the Secretary of the Interior for 1911 stated that conditions had so radically changed since the Homestead Act was passed in 1862, that alterations should be made which would aid the settler in his conquest of the remaining agricultural domain. Most remaining agricultural land was arid or semiarid.[28] The average homesteader was

23 Issue of March 3, 1911.
24 Issue of June 28, 1911.
25 Issue of February 17, 1911.
26 Issue of February 13, 1911.
27 Editorial "State Conservation" in issue of March 4, 1911.
28 Report of the Secretary of the Interior, 1911, Vol. I, p. 4.

poor; five years was too long a time to wait for his patent—he could not get a mortgage until he obtained it. William E. Borah, in an address before the Senate January 17, 1912, emphasized the pressing importance of the problem. He claimed that 125,000 people left the United States in 1911 to go to Canada, where the Dominion Land Act required only three years residence. In the United States, he charged, there were too many agents watching the homesteader, trying to catch him up on some small technical violations of the law. "If a man does wrong willfully, punish him, of course," said Borah, "but do not compel the homesteader at the end of five years, after his funds have been exhausted, to go up against a pack of lynx-eyed detectives upon the presumption that he is a criminal. . . . The government bets 160 acres against the entry fee of $14 that the settler can't live on the land for five years without starving to death."[29]

Also supporting a change in the homestead law was the report of the House Committee on Public Lands. It showed a significant decrease in the area of land entered during the fiscal year ending June 30, 1911. The report stated that "To reclaim and subdue our remaining public lands requires an expenditure of labor and money far beyond what is generally supposed; it requires determination, courage and energy of a high order, and continuity of purpose which are characteristics and virtues alone of good citizens."[30]

Congress responded by passing the Three Year Homestead Act.[31] It provided that patent was to issue at the end of three years' residence, allowing for a leave of absence of five months in each year. Commutation was to be allowed after fourteen months of actual residence. One-sixteenth of the area was required to be cultivated the second year, and one-eighth of the land the third year. If sickness, climate or other unavoidable cause interfered, the settler was to be allowed an extension of twelve months to begin residence, otherwise it must begin within six months of entry. The grievous problem of commutation, which had plagued the homestead law administration since its beginning, was at last solved. Commutations fell off at once, since it was better for the settler to continue to remain on the land seven months than to pay $200 to commute to cash entry. Commuted homesteads which had amounted to two and one-half million acres in the period from 1910 to

[29] *Congressional Record,* 62 Cong. 2 Sess., pp. 1,010-25.
[30] 62 Cong. 2 Sess., *House Reports,* No. 413.
[31] *Statutes at Large,* Vol. XXXVII, Pt. I, p. 123.

1912, fell off to two-fifths of a million acres in 1915, while in the meantime final homestead entries more than doubled.[32] In 1915, investigation of 950 claims in 95 districts (10 claims in each district) indicated that there was an average of 27 acres cultivated and $790 invested in improvements on each claim proved up.

The new act was a boon to settlers in the untimbered areas, to which it was primarily intended to apply. But its application to timbered regions brought much grief. In such country it was all but physically impossible for a settler to clear twenty acres of timber or brush land in three years. The task was made even more onerous by the fact that the settler who had taken up a homestead under the five-year law must prove up under the provisions of the three-year law. Many settlers in the timbered country at once quit their claims and departed for Canada where the laws were more lenient.[33] Thus, while the law seemed to benefit one section of the West it worked hardship on another.

For several years immediately following the passage of the National Reclamation Act there was great enthusiasm throughout the West. The process of putting magical water on desert land and of making two blades of grass grow where one had grown before was described in superlatives. Everyone was certain that a new day had dawned, and that millions of people would soon fill up the vacant spaces. The advertising connected with the Lewis and Clark Exposition at Portland in 1905 pictured the Pacific Northwest as a region with "glorious climate . . . endless scenery of matchless beauty and grandeur, and soil . . . of inexhaustible fertility."[34] This sort of advertising went for the arid regions, too, for everyone was convinced that it would not now be long until the desert was conquered.[35] In the timbered sections it was claimed that soil that would grow timber would grow anything. There was sufficient water, when it should be controlled by the United States Government, to irrigate millions of acres. Westerners pointed with pride to the possibilities of electrical power development. Power plants were to be erected to generate and transmit electric power hundreds of miles to

[32] Hibbard, *History of Public Land Policies*, p. 396.   [33] *Portland Oregonian*, June 17, 1913.
[34] *ibid.*, August 28, 1904.
[35] "Awakening of the Pacific Northwest," reprint from *Chicago Record-Herald*, August 27, 1904, in *ibid.*, August 28, 1904; "New Agricultural Empire," *ibid.*, July 3, 1904; "Irrigation Here and Elsewhere," *ibid.*, November 23, 1905; "Passing of the Oregon Desert," *ibid.*, March 17, 1905; "Irrigation Outlook," *The Westerner* (Seattle, Washington) November, 1909, pp. 40 *ff.*

points where it could be used for pumping water to irrigation projects and to develop manufacturing plants. Montana, it was claimed, "has the land and she has the water; put these together and the development will astonish the world."[36]

Characteristic of the enthusiasm is the following excerpt from the Seattle *Westerner*: "Mighty indeed is the westward wave of humanity this year. All the country between the Mississippi and the Pacific is a picture of life in which is shown hordes of homeseekers all with eyes open to the possibilities of this promising empire. The magic touch of water thrown upon the erstwhile arid lands, thanks to the government's initiative, is slowly transforming the parched prairie into a Garden of Eden. The call of the West is heard in lands far away. Deserts are being populated; prosperity pulsates throughout the country."[37] Everywhere chambers of commerce, immigration agencies, development bureaus, and other organizations were crying the attractions of their own God-favored localities. California was in the forefront in this campaign of booming. Said the *Portland Oregonian*, "When people tell you in sober earnestness that if the Pilgrim Fathers had landed upon the Pacific Coast instead of the Plymouth Rock the East would today be a desert, you may be sure there is something doing in the way of active development."[38]

With all due credit to the remarkable growth of the Far West, it is only fair to state that the new era was acclaimed too soon, that it was slow in dawning, and that even today there are still many problems to be solved, though perhaps the building of the great dams will help to overcome some of the major obstacles. The western interests did not sufficiently understand the difficult, unyielding, and stubborn character of nature. They did not entirely appreciate the problems of topography. Nor did they realize that little of the timber land was suitable for farming. The government did not move fast enough in its reclaiming of desert land to satisfy the Westerners. Government engineers had under-estimated construction costs; in some cases the actual cost was double the estimate, and the water supply half that expected. Crops could not be raised as soon as was anticipated, and the demand for farm products did not materialize, because "mining camps, lumber mills and similar industries did not grow as fast as agriculture."[39] It was charged that

[36] *ibid.*
[38] *ibid.*
[37] *ibid.*, May 1910, p. 14.
[39] Hibbard, *History of Public Land Policies*, p. 444.

there was a lot of red tape, that the government was too bureaucratic, that government officials were not experienced.

But after all, it must be admitted that the government was not responsible for many of the problems that retarded the reclamation of the arid country. To begin with, the best irrigation sites had been appropriated before the federal government entered the reclamation business, which meant that the government had either to undertake the development of less accessible sites or to follow the even more difficult course of persuading the interests which had appropriated sites to allow the government to develop them. In other words, the government took up the task where private capital refused to make the venture.

At the Irrigation Congress held at Salt Lake City in 1905, Mr. Frederick H. Newell, chief engineer of the Reclamation Service claimed that the cause of delay in the national reclamation program was due to the unwillingness of large land-holding companies to let the government in on terms harmonious with the interests of the homesteaders. In Oregon especially the wagon-road corporations demanded that they be allowed one year to sell their lands on the irrigated area after the completion of the project. "These are thrifty demands," commented the *Oregonian,* "If granted, the wagon-road owners would reap a big harvest of gold through enhancement of the land values by the government work; in fact, they would be speculations on government's expenditure of money in irrigating the land."[40] The editor advised that the government confer upon the Reclamation Service the power of eminent domain "for the condemnation of all the land and all water rights which in any way might burden or limit the usefulness of President Roosevelt's beneficent project for the irrigation of the arid lands."[41] A resolution adopted by the Convention declared that it should not be the purpose of the government to interfere with prior private enterprise nor should private enterprise necessarily interfere to prevent governmental enterprise from reclaiming arid lands.

Very early in the history of reclamation the importance of selecting the right kind of settlers became evident, but states were slow to accept the responsibility. More time was spent in quarrelling over whether one state or another received more of the government's largess.[42] The states

---

[40] Editorial in issue of August 25, 1905. [41] *ibid.*
[42] *ibid.,* November 23, 1905.

were very slow in enacting favorable legislation which would have facilitated federal reclamation.

By 1910 twenty-four projects had been undertaken, but none were yet completed. At this juncture it was found that the Reclamation Fund and accretions would be insufficient to complete the existing projects, let alone to undertake any additional ones. Accordingly, Congress authorized a twenty million dollar land loan to the Reclamation Service, to be repaid out of the Reclamation Fund in twenty equal annual installments beginning in 1920.[43]

By another act of the same date some relief was given to the settler by allowing him a leave of absence, but there was need for a law which would give the entryman five years after water was available to "comply with the requirements of the Homestead Law, irrespective of the time when his entry may have been made."[44] In 1911, a supplement to the Reclamation Act, known as the Warren law, provided a "connecting link between the government works and private systems built in the same vicinity." Many of the private projects which originally depended on the unregulated flow of the streams and consequently were injured by government projects, found consolation in this measure.

The next year, Senator Borah of the Committee on Irrigation and Reclamation came forward with the plea that the settler ought to be able to get a patent on his land before he made final payment on the water right because such a settler could not borrow money on land or sell it until he possessed title.[45] He recommended that a patent be given at the end of five years' cultivation and three years' occupation, reserving to the government a lien on the property. Consequently in that same year an act was passed allowing patent on reclamation entries before the water rights were paid for, provided all other conditions were satisfied and water payments were all met up to the time of issuance of patent.[46]

[43] Act of June 25, 1910, *Statutes at Large,* Vol. XXXVI, p. 835.
[44] *ibid.,* Vol. XXXVI, p. 864; 62 Cong. 2 Sess., *Senate Reports,* No. 540, p. 612.
[45] *ibid.,* No. 688.　　　　　　　　　　[46] *Statutes at Large,* Vol. XXXVII, p. 266.

CHAPTER XXIII

CONCILIATING THE WEST

EARLY in 1913, *Collier's Weekly,* discussing the new administration of President-elect Woodrow Wilson, carried the statement that the new Secretary of the Interior should not be a western man, and inferred that the West was thronging with persons and corporations who were "steadily bent on stealing the public domain." Such an affront could not go unchallenged. The editor of the *Portland Oregonian,* in answer to this jibe voiced what might be considered the typical western viewpoint on the conservation question.

"Here, bluntly and coarsely stated," he asserted, "is the ultraconservationist's view of the settler, the homesteader, the squatter, and the power and colonization concerns that have developed the great West. They have stolen, or are stealing, or desire to steal, something from the United States Government. They are not homebuilders, but felons; not farmers, but rather outlaws; not irrigationists, but thieves; not community developers, but organized land and water-power grabbers.

"The problem of the West is to get the lands settled and cultivated, the water powers appropriated and developed, and the forests logged and made into lumber. Yet the government is directed by the conservationists of the East to withhold its lands, streams and forests from use on the extraordinary ground that the way to make a nation great is to balk and to stigmatize as criminals the men who by their labor and their money reclaim the wastes, populate the wilds and utilize the water powers."[1]

The West, meanwhile, had been anxiously awaiting a statement from Wilson on the conservation question, but no word was forthcoming until January 1913 when the President-elect in his Chicago speech remarked that "A policy of reservation is not a policy of conservation." He explained further that there should be a policy of accessibility of the raw materials of the country to everybody on the same terms. Conservation under the Pinchot administration had meant a reservation or shutting-up of resources in such a manner that the process of monopolization was actually aided and abetted. Slowly the little fellow

---

[1] Editorial "Land and Water Grabbers," *Portland Oregonian,* January 15, 1913.

was being painfully squeezed between the government and the private monopolies. If Wilson's pronouncement meant anything, it meant, first, that the natural resources were to be opened to intelligent use and, second, that these resources henceforth would be administered under a more democratic policy.

The West hailed Wilson's conservation statement as a godsend. Senator Borah of Idaho wrote Wilson a public letter congratulating him on his pronouncement. In clear and concise exposition, Borah showed that the western people were in favor of conservation, but did not favor locking up all the resources from the people. "They believe," he said, "neither in monopoly of individuals nor the monopoly of the government. . . . They so far have been unable to see either the beauty or the benefits of tying up 200 million acres of timber lands and then selling the timber under such terms and conditions that when it reaches the people the price paid is the same as the price paid to the trust from whom we are withholding."

On the subject of reclamation, Borah asserted that the cost was going to be too great for poor men who need homes. "There is no blessing which this government could bestow upon the homeless," he thought, "comparable to that of building at its own expense the great canals necessary to place the water within reach of these lands and [of] then throwing them open to homestead entry. . . . The expense of building ditches should be borne by the government itself. We are putting millions into warships which rot upon the sea. . . . We are putting millions into rivers and harbors and no return to the Treasury is expected. . . . We are putting millions into great canals with no specific return to the Treasury. Why not put these lands, which are the property of the United States Government, in such condition as to make them available for homes? . . . This is real conservation. . . . I am not of your party, but I am of your announced faith in this matter, and shall be anxious to support you."[2]

Nervously the West awaited the appointment of the cabinet. For three months the western press boomed the appointment of western men as Secretary of the Interior and Commissioner of the General Land Office. When Franklin K. Lane of California and Clay Tallman of Nevada were selected for these offices there was cause for great rejoicing throughout the West. As one editor put it: "There is a good

---

[2] Letter of William Borah of Idaho to Woodrow Wilson, President-elect, as it appeared in *ibid.*, January 19, 1913.

occasion for a revolutionary shake-up in the barnacle-encrusted land office, whereby men who know western land by close acquaintance will supplant men who know it only by legal description and special agents' reports. . . . The land laws are to be administered by men from the region where there is public land and who therefore must be familiar from personal observation with the conditions to which they must be applied."[3] Satisfaction was also expressed in the East; even Pinchot approved the appointment of Lane.[4] As events later turned out, however, Lane was to adhere to the western viewpoint, and ultraconservationists were to be disappointed.

Finally, lest the administration forget its promise, there was held at Salt Lake City, June 4 to June 6, a western conservation conference. At this gathering the governors of the eleven western states asserted their determination to protect the rights of states. Resolutions were adopted declaring that the federal government should withdraw from the conservation field as soon as the states became prepared to take over the work of conservation, and that mineral lands which were withheld from entry or classified at prohibitive prices should be open at nominal prices.[5] More specifically, the convention resolved that (1) Each state should have charge of its own conservation work to the exclusion of federal bureaus; (2) The permanent withdrawal or reservation of lands within a state was a policy to condemn; (3) "The best and most economical development of this western territory was accomplished under those methods in vogue when the states of the Middle West were occupied and settled. In our opinion, those methods have never been improved upon, and we advocate a return to these first principles of vested ownership with joint interest and with widely scattered individual responsibility."[6] The conference added further impetus to the western movement for a halt in the alleged federal encroachment upon the states' spheres of authority.

So slow and seemingly ineffective was federal reclamation that open revolt broke out in the Oregon Irrigation Congress of 1913. One authority seemed to strike a popular chord when he advocated joint federal and state development in both the reclamation and power business. Once again the speculators who had bought up land and

    [3] *ibid.*, June 1, 1913.   [4] Ise, *The Oil Policy of the United States*, p. 335.
    [5] Report of Convention in *Portland Oregonian*, June 6, 1913.
    [6] *Congressional Record*, 63 Cong. 1 Sess., p. 2,054, as summarized by Representative Taylor of Colorado.

were holding it from development were scathingly denounced. "Our country is being held back by speculators," said a certain Mr. Walker of Alfalfa, Oregon; "They are acting the 'dog in the manger,' and are preventing many farmers with good intentions from getting water. Adjudication of the water rights would deny them their water titles unless they actually used the water. As the land is worthless without the water, they would be forced to improve their land, sell out or lose their investment."[7]

The Carey Act also came in for some severe criticism in 1913. It was charged that the act had been more successful in tying up lands than in developing them. This act, like the National Reclamation Act, had proved to be an open invitation to the speculator and promoter. Lands had been withdrawn in behalf of individuals, firms, and corporations who possessed no complete engineering data, adequate financial resources, or comprehensive knowledge of the work they were undertaking. Speculators had engaged in projects relying on the sale of water rights to supply funds to complete the irrigation works. Settlers paid in part for their water rights, relying on crops to provide for the additional payments. With water not forthcoming there were no crops, hence no payments to the companies to complete the projects.

It was argued that the Carey Act in recognizing the water company as a middleman was pursuing the wrong policy, for in most cases the middleman had to show a profit as high as 100 per cent in order to attract capital for investment. The editor of the *Portland Oregonian* lamented the irrigation business: "While grave need exists for some enactment that will develop Oregon's arid lands, uncompleted projects begun under inadequate laws and [the] imperfect administration of the past, challenge consideration by the state. The obligation to the unfortunate settlers who have invested therein is not direct, but it plainly exists. Their relief should not be overlooked."[8]

While all the reclamation work in the Far West was not the failure it had been in Oregon, there was, nevertheless, sufficient discontent to demand the attention of the federal government. Hence the West looked forward to the Wilson administration for moderation.

No sooner had Congress convened than the problem of relieving reclamationists from their contractual obligations came up for serious

[7] *Portland Oregonian*, January 10, 1913.　　　　[8] Issue of January 11, 1913.

discussion. Senator Madden of Illinois spoke against any policy that would defer payments without interest, asserting that it was not businesslike and that once the precedent were established it would lead to other demands.[9] On the other hand, it was argued that the settlers could not pay the interest and that there would be a wholesale defalcation. In fact, the government must either extend relief or see the settlers pushed off the projects. Inasmuch as the money for reclamation was not derived from taxation, and inasmuch as the government had been so liberal in the past in spending money for rivers, harbors, good roads, and general improvements, was it not within law and reason to aid the reclamation farmers, many of whom had never received any benefits at all from their lands? Such arguments won over all opposition and a measure passed Congress in 1914 providing for the necessary relief.

Briefly stated, this act allowed the settler twenty years instead of ten to meet the reclamation obligations on his claim. The first annual installment henceforth would not be due until December 1 of the fifth year after the initial payment, and was equal to 5 per cent of the construction charges. The balance was to be paid in fifteen annual installments without interest charge. The bill also provided that after July 1, 1915, all expenses for administering the reclamation law should be met by appropriations from Congress, a provision which took away from the Secretary of the Interior the power of determining the amount to be expended each year.[10] A further step toward pacifying the Westerners was taken in 1916, when the federal government at last agreed that henceforth any public lands within the irrigation districts of states should become subject to state laws.[11] This act not only encouraged the states to take more initiative in developing their own projects, but also invited the states to assume more responsibility in the irrigation industry.

The federal government, however, was not moving fast enough to quiet the growing restlessness throughout the irrigation country. The Reclamation Fund was exhausted and for this reason no more projects could be taken up. Nor was there any hope of replenishing this fund since few projects were paying up and little revenue was coming in from the sale of public lands.[12] Nearly every western state was rent

[9] *Congressional Record*, 63 Cong. 2 Sess., pp. 12,193*ff*.
[10] *Statutes at Large*, Vol. XXXVIII, p. 636.   [11] *ibid.*, Vol. XXXIX, p. 868.
[12] Editorial in *San Francisco Chronicle*, October 17, 1916.

Conservation and Reclamation to 1917.

From Arthur P. Schlesinger, *Political and Social History of the United States, 1829-1925.* By permission of the Macmillan Co.

with bitter fights over water—water for domestic use, water for irrigation, and water for power. In California, San Francisco was absorbed
with the Hetch-Hetchy contest, while Los Angeles was fighting for
the right to use water—and power developed from it—which had been
brought from a long distance.

The editor of the *San Francisco Chronicle,* commenting on the water
struggle, said: "One can hardly go anywhere in this state where there
is not a contest existing or brewing about water. The courts and the
commissions dealing with the subject are overcrowded with water
contests."[13] When, in face of such difficulties, the chief counsel of
the Reclamation Service in an address at El Paso advised federal
physical and financial control of all irrigation, the editor of the *San
Francisco Chronicle* charged that "pork barrelling" and "federal encroachment" by the Reclamation Service had "bungled so awfully" in
what it had undertaken thus far that the government was "suppressing
the report of an investigating body, which was made several months
ago."[14] By the end of 1917 it was asserted that the federal government
alone was responsible for getting the reclamation business into a
"financial hole," and it was up to Congress to tax the nation in order
to pull it out.[15]

The pressure of the democratic forces in Congress in 1916 forced
through legislation dealing with the long-neglected grazing-land problem. Ever since the 1880's a battle had been waged to break up the
holdings of the big cattle interests. Generally speaking, the onslaught
of the Roosevelt administration in favor of the small grazier had been
successful only in certain localities. The system of charging fees for
grazing in the national forests had not changed the conditions of the
alleged grazing monopoly. The Enlarged Homestead Act was not
applicable to most of the grazing area in the mountain states, since
more than 320 acres were necessary for stock farming in that region.
Senator Harvey Ferguson of New Mexico insisted that there were
over 330 million acres not suitable for irrigation, which could be used
only for grazing. Yet, he said, the large stock operators were decidedly
opposed to any further experimenting and were quite content to see a
leasing system extended to all the grazing domain rather than open it

13 Issue of October 23, 1916.   14 Issue of October 26, 1916.
15 *ibid.,* December 22, 1917.

up to homesteading.[16] Senator Robert M. La Follette of Wisconsin expressed a viewpoint held by many of the outside interests when he said, "I'm not one of those who believe that the nomadic stockman, the man who is getting the benefit of public property for nothing and who has had it that way for thirty or forty years, should be continued in that privilege in perpetuity or during the rest of the existence of the United States."[17] Another argument that gained headway was that the grazing country needed more population, that settlement would mean more land for purposes of taxation.

In spite of considerable doubt about the proper solution of the grazing problem, Congress passed the Stock-Raising Homestead Act which was approved December 29, 1916.[18] It provided for grants of 640 acres in "reasonably compact form." It must be land definitely classified as grazing land or as forage crop land and must not contain merchantable timber nor be suitable for irrigation. All coal and mineral deposits were reserved to the government, and in certain cases water holes and bodies of water could be reserved by the Secretary of the Interior. Like the Enlarged Homestead Act of 1912, no commutations were to be allowed. Since no funds were appropriated by Congress for the classification of the grazing lands, no entries were made until 1918. This Act was another democratic thrust aimed at breaking up the grazing-lands monopoly.

In spite of Wilson's declaration against the reservation of resources, the government in 1914 extended the policy of withdrawing coal and mineral lands to include phosphate, nitrate, potash, oil, gas or asphaltic minerals.[19] At one stroke three million acres of phosphate lands in Idaho, Montana and Wyoming were removed from entry. In Congress, Senator Smith of Idaho affirmed his belief that individuals would no longer have any inducement to prospect for minerals if they were not to have any right to what they might discover. Senator Frank Mondell of Wyoming declared that it was monarchical in theory to give only the soil to the settler and reserve everything else to the government.[20] Chester T. Kennan, a Colorado mining engineer, characterized the conservation business as a "reign of terrorism in the western states

[16] *Congressional Record,* 63 Cong. 2 Sess., *Appendix,* pp. 683-5.
[17] *ibid.,* 64 Cong. 1 Sess., p. 1,179; quoted in Hibbard, *History of the Public Land Policies,* p. 400.
[18] *Statutes at Large,* Vol. XXXIX, p. 862.   [19] *ibid.,* Vol. XXXVIII, p. 509.
[20] *Congressional Record,* 63 Cong. 2 Sess., pp. 10,493-4.

through an organized army of forest rangers, mineral examiners, general solicitors, attorneys, press agents and affidavit gleaners."[21]

Just as the western opposition began to reach ominous proportions the administration moved toward the adoption of the leasing system for the mineral lands. This did not immediately suit the West. The laws already provided for the sale of ripe timber on the forest reserves and the leasing of grazing lands in these reserves. The West contended that an extension of the leasing system to mineral lands and water-power sites would result in a complete enslavement of the western states. So far there had been no serious thought of returning a part of the revenues from such a leasing system to the western states, a step which doubtless would have produced a decided change in western sentiment.

Representative Edward T. Taylor of Colorado thought that the leasing system would tend to bring about too great centralization of power in the hands of the federal government, that the western states would be denied the freedom of private property enjoyed by the East. People of the West, he insisted, desired to become "permanent citizens of [the] state, not federal tenants."[22] Secretary of the Interior Lane was in favor of a leasing system in which the western states should share in the royalties, and insisted that this was the only way to safeguard against monopoly.[23] Representative Charles M. Thomson of Illinois maintained that the hydroelectric power companies were the leading opponents of the federal control of land and resources and that the "conflict between the nation and the state was due to some monopoly or corporation ignoring the rights of both state and nation."[24]

Had Congress paid more attention to the proposal of Secretary of the Interior Lane for a leasing system in which the West would share in the royalties, there might have been some settlement of this grievous issue before America entered the World War.[25] But with neither the ultraconservationists nor the rabid anticonservationists willing to yield there could be no compromise. The government could do little except experiment here and there with the leasing system, hoping that the successful operation of this system on Indian Reservations or in Alaska might point the way for a compromise. Looking toward this end, Congress passed an act on October 20, 1914, giving the Secretary of the

21 *ibid.*, pp. 13,574-5.
23 *ibid.*, p. 1,716.
25 *ibid.*, p. 1,716.

22 *ibid.*, p. 15,052.
24 *ibid.*, pp. 14,944-56.

Interior authority to lease certain public coal lands in Alaska.[26] And in 1917 Congress passed a law providing for the renting of potassium lands.[27]

The leasing system remained in the experimental stage until after the World War. As long as the government planned to keep most of the royalties, western opposition to the leasing idea continued unabated. The real opportunity for compromise rested in the hope that the government might evolve a leasing system which would guarantee the western states a substantial part of the royalties accruing from the leasing of the reserved lands.

Meanwhile, western opposition shifted its attention from mineral lands to water-power sites. In this renewed attack upon the governmental policy of reserving water-power sites, the anticonservation movement reached its climax. The whole struggle between the federal government and the West had, in fact, already reached an impasse, which could be broken only by a decision from the Supreme Court. Between 1915 and 1917, certain western interests carefully prepared the ground for this last major offensive. In order to understand this water-power site crisis it will be necessary to go back to 1911 and pick up the threads of the controversy as it stood at that time.

It was the hope of Secretary of the Interior Ballinger in 1910 that the federal government should open up the reserved natural resources as soon as possible to intelligent use. In his annual report of that year he had taken the view that since the ownership of the waters in the streams was held by the states, and since the states had police power to regulate utilities, the transfer of the power sites to the states would be a satisfactory method of control. He felt that power sites on the public domain should be leased, and that legislation should be enacted to protect both the public and the investor.

Several bills with this end in mind having failed, a joint committee was appointed to make a study of the problem and recommend legislation. The findings of this joint committee presaged the major provisions of the Federal Water-Power Act of 1920. The report published in 1911 recommended that right of occupancy for a fixed period of not more than fifty years be guaranteed, that authority be given to the Secretary of Agriculture and the Secretary of the Interior to execute leases for

---

[26] *Statutes at Large,* Vol. XXXVIII, p. 741.   [27] *ibid.,* Vol. XL, p. 297.

water-power development on any public lands under their jurisdiction, that there be a uniformity of leases and a moderate fee charged for use and occupancy of the lands, that there be a revocation of the lease only for breach of conditions or for persistence in charging excessive rates to consumers, that in case of conflict between mineral and water-power development the latter be recognized as the dominant one, that the federal government classify all its water-power sites and open them to development, and that wherever any settler was damaged by water-power development he should be allowed damages therefor.

A bill embodying these provisions was introduced into Congress on March 2, 1911, but failed to pass.[28] In the appropriation act for the Department of Agriculture, however, provision was made for rights of way for a period of not more than fifty years over the public lands and national forests, this easement permitting the construction of electric poles and lines for the transmission of power but not the use of the water.[29]

Thus the matter stood when on March 14, 1912, the Bureau of Corporations published its report on water power. This report revealed that the amount of water power concentrated in the hands of the ten largest power corporations had practically doubled in two years' time. These groups had increased their control of undeveloped power more than twice as fast as they had increased their control of developed power.[30] Carrying the investigations into the Wilson administration, a House Committee revealed in 1914 that twenty-eight private corporations and their subsidiaries owned over 90 per cent of the water power developed on the public lands, and that six of these twenty-eight controlled over 56 per cent of the developed power. The Montana Power Company owned 97 per cent of all developed power in that state. The Utah Securities Corporation had developed 30 per cent of the power in Colorado, 70 per cent in Utah, and 20 per cent in Idaho. Seventeen of these twenty-eight companies controlled about 60 per cent of the water power of the western states; and more significant still, these seventeen companies were affiliated through interlocking directorates, holding companies, and banking connections. After reviewing this situation, the report made the recommendation that it was better for

[28] 62 Cong. 2 Sess., *House Reports*, No. 33,000; 62 Cong. 2 Sess., *S. Ex. Doc.*, No. 274. Hearings before the National Waterways Commission Concerning Water Power, pp. 95, 243.
[29] Act of March 4, 1911, *Statutes at Large*, Vol. XXXVI, p. 1,253.
[30] Bureau of Corporations Report on Water Power, 1912.

Prometheus Bound.
From *Seattle Post-Intelligencer,* September 23, 1915.

the government to postpone the development of the water-power sites on the public domain "rather than to permit them to pass into private ownership to be developed as perpetual monopolies."[31]

So fast was the water power of the United States developed that by 1915, Henry S. Graves, Secretary of Agriculture, asserted that the whole industry was overdeveloped.[32] Thus the bogey of monopoly stilled for the time being the governmental attempt to evolve a policy for the intelligent use of water-power sites on the public domain. Western hopes went glimmering, and about the only recourse was to

[31] 63 Cong. 2 Sess., *House Reports,* No. 842, "Development of Water Power," June 16, 1914.
[32] Report of the Secretary of Agriculture, 1915, p. 175.

resort to a campaign of stirring of public opinion in favor of opening up the resources.

As the governmental policy of locking up the grazing lands had brought forth the protestant convention at Denver in 1907, so in 1915 a convention of representatives from the western states met at Portland to protest the locking up of the water sites as well as the whole conservation program. The pretext for the calling of this convention was the passage of the Ferris Bill in the House. This bill provided for federal control of water power in the western states. It proposed to lease the water-power sites to private or other interests for as long a period as fifty years, reserving to the government the right to take over the improved properties at some future time at the investment values.

Hoping to prevent the passage of this bill in the upper house, the governor of Oregon invited representatives from the thirteen western states to meet at Portland on September 15 to consider the whole problem of conservation but particularly conservation of water-power sites. The convention insisted, by a vote of 28 to 7, that since the water belongs to the state in which it lies or runs that the water power developed from such water should belong to the state in which it is located.[33] The convention was therefore opposed to any measure that would make investments impermanent and unsettled, and that would take from investors the element of reward in enhanced values. A leasing system would deprive the western states of the tax income on improved properties, capital would decline to invest and the industrial progress of the West would be retarded.[34]

Commenting upon the conference, the editor of the *San Francisco Chronicle* observed that "The assumption of paramount sovereignty in respect to water is based upon the theory that the people of the states are incompetent to administer their own property, but that Washington bureaucracy is perfectly competent. . . . The federal government by an assumption of authority which our weak-kneed state government has not the resolution to dispute has absolutely put an end, by prohibitory requirements, to new developments on the public domain. And the states' water continues to run unused to the sea, and the mineral oil is burned to produce power which might be produced by descending

[33] *Seattle Times*, September 24, 1915; *Portland Oregonian*, September 24, 1915; *San Francisco Chronicle*, September 24, 1915.
[34] *Seattle Post-Intelligencer*, September 25, 1915.

water. And the bureaucrats want to tie this up forever."[35] The editor of the *Seattle Times* saw in the conference "a decisive victory for the advocates of states' rights."[36]

The Forest Service, in response to a resolution passed by the Senate in February 1915, made an exhaustive study of the water-power problem and reported in 1916 to the effect that there was "a marked concentration of definite and complete control of a large percentage of developed water power by a few companies . . . that a definite move for concentration of all primary power in central stations was found in all sections of the United States, the rate of which was highest in the South Atlantic states, [but] greatest extent of which was in the western states . . . [and] that there was a considerable overdevelopment in nearly all power centers of the western states, especially in California, Oregon, and Washington, which have installations far in excess of maximum demands."[37]

The water-power sites quarrel was now in its twelfth year of intense fighting and litigation. To those acquainted with the conservation subject, it was obvious that there could be no satisfactory settlement of the issues now that the controversy had reached a point where the East contended that the federal government had the power to control the natural resources and the West insisted that the states possessed that power. The only way out lay in taking the issue to the Supreme Court. Therefore, in 1916 the United States Government sued the Utah Power and Light Company on the grounds that this company had occupied and was using government land in the Bear River Valley without permission. On the other hand, the company claimed that it had vested rights in such land and insisted that the laws of the state and not the federal government obtained over such lands. Furthermore, the company insisted that by local law and custom and by decisions of the state courts it was commonly recognized that these vested rights were acquired when anyone obtained the right to use water. The company asserted that the administrative regulations promulgated by the Forest Service were unconstitutional and that they exceeded the authority necessary for the protection of the national forests.[38]

[35] Issue of September 24, 1915.   [36] Issue of September 21, 1915.
[37] Report of the Secretary of Agriculture, 1916, pp. 175-6.
[38] *Cases Argued before the Supreme Court of the United States,* October Term, 1916 (Rochester, 1917), pp. 242-4.

Justice Van De Vanter delivered the majority opinion of the Supreme Court on March 19, 1917. This decision held that the Congress of the United States alone had the exclusive power as conferred upon it by the Constitution of the United States[39] to determine in what manner and when any lands belonging to the United States might be acquired. Hence, the exercise of the right of eminent domain by the state upon federal government lands within a state was wholly without justification unless Congress approved of it. Finally, the United States Government should receive appropriate compensation inasmuch as the defendants had occupied and used, without sanction and in defiance of law, reserved lands of the United States. This decision not only vindicated the right of jurisdiction of the United States over the public lands, but further substantiated the right exercised by the government to impose a rental charge for the use of the public lands. The decision thus put an end to the states' right movement among the western states. If the West was to continue to oppose conservation it must do so within the pale of constitutionality. The leasing system offered the best compromise between the two extremes of state control and federal reservation, and toward this objective the two contending schools of thought turned their efforts.

The World War prevented the immediate enactment of legislation which would settle the water-power issue and establish the leasing system as a permanent part of the conservation program. By 1920, however, western opposition had not only quieted down but had actually turned into support of the policy, as was indicated in the votes on the two important land measures of that year. This change was due to the fact that the government had revised its leasing plan to provide many benefits to the West—perhaps more benefits to the West than to the nation at large. An act approved on February 25, 1920, provided that most of the public mineral lands should be open to leasing, that each state was to receive 37 1/3 per cent of all royalties accruing within its borders; 50 per cent was to go into the federal Reclamation Fund, and the rest into the miscellaneous fund of the Treasury.[40]

[39] Clause 2, Section 3, Article 4.
[40] *Statutes at Large*, Vol. XLI, p. 438; for a more detailed analysis see Ise, *The United States Oil Policy*, Chap. XXIV.

Even the naval petroleum reserves created in California in 1912 containing some 68,000 acres, and those in Wyoming in 1915 containing about 9,000 acres, were to be opened up, however, with new smaller reservations created for the Navy Department. In many ways, the rush onto the oil lands was much like the rush into Oklahoma in 1887. Airplanes and telegraph were used in the mad stampede to file prospecting permits. Within one year of operation 5,000 applications for permits had been filed.[41]

When an inventory was taken in 1928, it was found that the federal government owned approximately 30,000,000 acres of coal lands, 2,000,000 acres of phosphate lands, 5,000,000 acres of oil land, 7,500,000 acres of potash lands, 169,000 acres of oil-shale land, 12,000 acres of helium land, and 8,500 acres of other mineral lands.[42] The potash act of 1917 was repealed in 1927 and at the same time the General Leasing Act of 1920 was extended to include potassium mineral lands.[43] Sulphur lands were opened to lease April 17, 1926.

By 1928 the total receipts since the passage of the act had amounted to almost $68,000,000, of which the western states received over $22,000,000. Wyoming received the largest share, about $18,000,000. In 1924, a new service known as the Conservation branch was added to the Geological Survey Bureau to serve as guardian of these mineral resources. Thus at last the federal government had evolved a mineral lands conservation program which included an "economic use without waste, and an intelligent distribution . . . as to time."[44]

On February 1, 1918, the Chamber of Commerce of the United States made known the results of a nation-wide referendum which it had conducted on the water-power problem.[45] From this report it was more obvious than ever before that there was a division of opinion in nearly every region of the country on the kind of power legislation desired. On the other hand, it was evident that the whole controversy had unified the desires of the country for some early and effective legislation. Consequently, in the sixty-sixth Congress a special committee was appointed to bring forward a bill. From among many bills,

[41] *ibid.*, p. 353. [42] Report of the Secretary of the Interior, 1928, p. 251.
[43] Report of the Geological Survey, 1927, pp. 62, 64.
[44] Report of the Secretary of the Interior, 1924, p. 32.
[45] Referendum No. 24 of the Chamber of Commerce of the United States on the Report of the Special Committee on Water-Power Development (Washington, February 1, 1918).

H.R. 3184 was finally selected and passed by Congress.[46] President Wilson refused to sign it because the Secretary of the Interior objected to its provision for opening the national parks to all applicants. Senators Jones of Washington and Walsh of Montana came to the rescue, and persuaded the President that the whole bill should not be lost simply because of the defect in one provision. After assurance that corrective legislation would be offered at the earliest possible moment, Wilson signed the bill, June 10, 1920. The amendment providing the correction was duly passed and signed March 3, 1921.

The Federal Power Act of 1920 is long and complicated, covering nine pages of the statute book. Three sections are devoted to the stipulations for setting up the Federal Power Commission, the rest of the act deals with government regulation and control of water power. It is significant to note that most of the recommendations made by the joint committee of 1911 were incorporated in the act. The long fight to unshackle the water power of the public domain at last had been crowned with success. The Power Commission was given the authority to issue licenses for the improvement of navigation and for the development and utilization of power. Sites within the national forests, however, were to come under the administration of the Forest Service. Leases were to run for fifty years, and at their expiration the government had the right either to renew them or to take over the facilities upon two years' notice. Lastly, all public-service licenses were to be regulated by the states, and power rates in interstate commerce were to be reasonable.[47]

The act was neither a victory for the ultraconservationists nor for the rabid anticonservationists; it was a compromise. In a way it was a moral victory for the West, for this section had borne the brunt of the fight and had forced moderation. The West hailed it with great joy. The editor of the *Seattle Post-Intelligencer* declared that: "In the industrial and commercial development of the West it marks the beginning of a new epoch. This part of the country, which has so small a portion of the country's supply of coal and so much potential energy in its streams, shortly will come into its own."[48] The editor of the *Seattle Times* declared: "The enactment of this measure smashes another of the repressive

---

[46] 66 Cong. 1 Sess., *House Reports*, No. 3,184.

[47] *Statutes at Large*, Vol. XLI, p. 1,063; see also discussion of this act in James C. Malin, *The United States After the World War* (New York, 1930).

[48] Issue of June 20, 1920.

policies that were adopted by the government at the height of the conservation excitement. . . . The age of electricity has dawned! This generation of Americans is witnessing the slow passing of steam and the substitution for coal, as an agency for the generation of power, of the harnessed waterfall."[49]

The immediate success of the act was indeed impressive. During the whole twenty-year period before 1920, applications involving only 2,500,000 horsepower had been granted, but in the period from June 10, 1920, to February 10, 1921, eight months' operation, the total applications reached the figure of 13,000,000 horsepower. In spite of the conservative political reaction of the 'twenties, the power figures continued to climb even during the depression period after 1929. But whether the national government could work hand in hand with western private interests in developing the vast water-power resources of the West still remained to be seen.

[49] Issue of June 20, 1920.

CHAPTER XXIV

DEMISE OF THE OLD DOMAIN

THE Wilson administration had settled the most vexatious problems associated with the movement to conserve the nation's resources. In the general evolution of this conservation ideal, there had been, in spite of stubborn western opposition, little real interruption; there had been progress, compromise, and commendable achievement. The changes of administrations from Roosevelt to Taft and from Taft to Wilson had caused no material disturbance. At last the nation's remaining natural resources were carefully placed in trust so that they might be used in the most intelligent manner and developed to their greatest effectiveness but not injured or exploited.

With the major difficulties settled, with all forces pulling together, it was now hoped that regardless of change in parties at the national helm, there would at least be an era of continued progress, if not a golden age in conservation. But fate ruled otherwise. The administration of Warren G. Harding, instead of safeguarding the trust reposed in it, chose instead to open up some of the nation's most valued oil reserves to a process of ruthless exploitation.

It will be recalled that President Taft had created Naval Oil Reserves Nos. 1 and 2 in California in 1912,[1] covering 38,969 and 29,341 acres respectively. Then, in 1915, President Wilson proclaimed Naval Oil Reserve No. 3 near Salt Creek, Wyoming, known as Teapot Dome taking its name from a butte located on the reserve. The Teapot Reserve contained only 9,481 acres, but supposedly was very rich in deposits. These reserves had been specifically designated for the purpose of conserving oil for the navy, and as such constituted an important adjunct of the program for national defense.[2] In spite of serious objections, the Senate bill which became the General Leasing Act of 1920, had been amended in its later stages to provide for the leasing of these naval reserves under special conditions. In June 1920, the

---

[1] See *supra*, pp. 367-8, 395. The best account of the Teapot Dome episode is to be found in Chap. XXV of John Ise, *The United States Oil Policy* (New Haven, 1926); a more personal and colorful account, as well as a more recent appraisal, is found in Chap. XIV of Mark Sullivan *The Twenties* (New York, 1935, Vol. VI of *Our Times; The United States, 1900-1925*).

[2] 68 Cong. 1 Sess., *Senate Reports*, Pt. 3, No. 794.

Wilson administration directed the Secretary of the Navy to take charge of all these reserves, and to use, store, sell or exchange the oil thereof.[3] This move was justified by the more or less plausible explanation that private wells dug on the adjoining lands were draining the naval reserves. This was a considerable trust to place in the care of the Secretary of the Navy, but Josephus Daniels assumed the task and "took scrupulous care to keep the reserves ... what they were intended to be, storehouses for future use."[4] Here the matter rested until the advent of the Harding administration.

By executive order of May 31, 1921, President Harding transferred the administration of these reserves to the Interior Department, where they came under the surveillance of Secretary Albert B. Fall, whose past political and business experience had already stamped him as one of the deadliest enemies of the conservation movement.[5] Fall, exercising his "discretionary power," gave a new intent and meaning to the General Leasing Act when he granted contracts to the Mammoth Oil Company of which Harry F. Sinclair was president, and to the Pan American Company, of which Edward L. Doheny was president. Under the terms of these contracts the private oil companies were permitted to take oil to the point of exhaustion from the petroleum reserves in Wyoming and California respectively, and to use the royalties which, according to the Leasing Act, were to accrue to the government, to pay for the construction of storage tanks on the Atlantic and Pacific coasts.[6]

A letter from a citizen in Wyoming to Senator Kendrick of that state gave rise to the first element of suspicion, and after a personal letter had failed to satisfy Kendrick's curiosity he introduced into the Senate a formal resolution of inquiry. Fall's reply to the Senate resolution did not satisfy Senator Robert M. La Follette, Sr., of Wisconsin, who secured the passage of a resolution which ordered the Public Lands Committee, with Senator Reed Smoot of Utah, author of the General Leasing Act, as chairman, to investigate the situation. The real power of the committee, however, proved to be Senator Thomas J. Walsh, Democrat, of Montana. In the hearings before the committee, Fall refused to admit that the President's action in transferring the

[3] *ibid.*, p. 5.
[4] Sullivan, *The Twenties*, p. 287. By permission of Charles Scribner's Sons.
[5] Ise, *The Oil Policy of the United States*, p. 357.
[6] *Congressional Record*, 67 Cong. 2 Sess., pp. 8,472-80.

naval reserves to the Interior Department was illegal, and insisted that under his "discretionary power" he had the right to lease the reserves to anyone without competitive bidding.[7] Here the committee was blocked. The administration was extremely unfriendly to the investigation, and the American public did not appear to be very much concerned.

Nevertheless, Senator Walsh tried a new lead which later proved the undoing of Fall and his accomplices. The Secretary had suddenly come into possession of much wealth. After a long and complicated investigation, which must have made many a crime detective marvel at Walsh's ability, evidence was uncovered which proved beyond a doubt that Fall had accepted over $100,000 from the beneficiaries of the oil leases. To make a long story short, the committee after taking testimony from a number of witnesses came to the conclusion that fraud and corruption were involved in the oil-lease transactions and recommended that suit be brought in the federal courts against the parties involved, with the intention of cancelling all contracts made. It was the opinion of the committee that the transfer of the administration of the reserves was illegal and that the exchange of royalty certificates for storage tanks was a violation of the spirit if not the letter of the law. Sinclair, refusing to testify before the Committee, was held subject to contempt by the Senate in a vote of 72 to 1. At this point in the story (1924) the scene of action shifted to the courts.

Bills of complaint were filed against the oil companies holding the leases, and trials were held in the federal courts of California and Wyoming, appeals being taken to the circuit courts and finally to the Supreme Court of the United States. President Coolidge, forced by the Senate to discontinue temporarily the Department of Justice because of another corruption scandal, appointed Owen J. Roberts and Atlee W. Pomerene as special counsel to present the government's suits. The Supreme Court decision handed down on December 28, 1927, voided the contracts. The Court held that the "authority to 'store' or 'exchange' does not empower the Secretary of the Navy to use the reserves to regulate or affect the price of oil in the Salt Creek Field, or to induce or aid construction of a pipe line to serve that territory . . . or to use crude oil to pay for storage tanks." Further, it was held that the leases were made without authority and that there was fraudulent collusion

[7] *Record of Hearings*, 67 and 68 Cong., pursuant to Senate Resolutions 101, 147, 282 and 294.

between Fall, Sinclair and Doheny.[8] Thus the oil reserves were restored to the control of the Secretary of the Navy.

Meanwhile, Fall, Sinclair, and the Dohenys, father and son, were charged with conspiracy to defraud the government. Sinclair was found guilty on the Senate contempt charge, sentenced to three months in jail and fined $1,000. On the conspiracy to defraud charge, he was again cited for contempt in 1927, this time for shadowing the jury, and received a second sentence. Finally, after a mistrial and several acquittals, Fall was convicted in 1929 and sentenced to a year in jail and fined $100,000. The jail sentence was served in 1931-1932. Doheny was acquitted. Thus ended one of the most disgraceful episodes in American history: Sinclair had achieved the unique distinction of being the only man ever sentenced for contempt by both the Senate and a court of justice; Fall had "achieved the zenith of ignobility," being "in the whole history of the United States, the first cabinet officer to go to jail."[9]

Fortunately, the success of the Republican public land policy of the 1920's is not to be judged entirely by the Teapot Dome episode. In the fields of reclamation and water power there was thorough investigation and complete reorganization. The reforms inaugurated led to an entirely new era in public land history. This new era was marked by the entrance of the federal government into the reclamation and water-power business as a competitor of private industry, an adventure that was "conducive to much good but perhaps fraught with much evil." This adventure, perhaps, had its inception in the original Reclamation Act of 1902 and in the conservation movement as prosecuted by Theodore Roosevelt; nevertheless, it was the Federal Water-Power Act of the Wilson administration which definitely gave shape to the new idea. If carried to the extreme this policy would result in nothing less than socialization of several important fields of private business.

The immediate origins of this new adventure are found in conditions which faced the Pacific Coast at the close of the World War. This section of America refused to be downed by the depression in agriculture and manufacturing which set in after the Armistice. Westerners clearly remembered Wilson's annual message of December 2, 1918,

[8] *The Federal Reporter,* 2nd Series; Vols. V, X, and XV; *United States Reports,* Vol. CCLXXV.
[9] Sullivan, *The Twenties,* p. 345.

in which he recommended the reclamation of over 300,000,000 acres of land in the West for homes for the soldiers. The General Leasing and Federal Water-Power acts of 1920 gave to investments and development an impetus which was to bring startling growth to some regions of the West Coast. With the transfer of capital from the lumbering industry into new lines of manufacturing, business interests everywhere were once more confident that a new era had set in—an era in which cheap water power would be the key to prosperity. Many people, however, were doubtful whether the private power industry could meet the expanding needs for cheap electrical power. The growing consciousness that there had been too much eastern dominance in the economic development of the Far West was being replaced by a demand for economic independence. For almost a quarter of a century this section had defied the federal government in the conservation movement. That period was definitely past; the Far West now sought the aid of the federal government to complete its growth.

With this new industrial development under way, it was only a matter of time before agricultural interests would also demand legislation to better their lot. This meant, first, financial legislation to relieve the farmers on reclamation projects. Second, it meant opening up many new areas of land for development. It might be argued that these objectives would operate at cross-purposes, that the opening up of new areas of land to irrigation would merely augment the surplus and hence force agricultural prices even lower. But it must be remembered that the Republicans in the 'twenties were preaching the doctrine of plenty; the latter part of the decade was especially marked by credit expansion and development in the manufacturing world and the same theories were applied to agriculture as well. The West was still imbued with the desire for growth. All that was needed, it was thought, was more capital to develop arid lands, minerals, and water power.

In this new line of endeavor the federal government was to be called upon on the one hand to build giant dams for the purpose of generating cheap power for the rising manufacturing industries, and on the other, to reclaim vast areas of arid lands in order to produce the agricultural supplies needed in the new industrial regions.

As has already been noted, the national reclamation fund was exhausted during Wilson's first administration. The inability of the government to complete many projects made it impossible for the settlers to get water, hence it became the duty of the government to extend relief. But this did not solve the problem. The West at this period was apparently more interested in obtaining additional capital for development than it was in getting relief for the irrigation farmer, for such relief at the best could only be regarded as a dole.[10] Hence in 1919 the West demanded direct appropriation of two hundred and fifty million dollars to be used by the reclamation service to complete the projects then under way and to start new ones. It was hoped that this direct appropriation would bring order out of chaos in the reclamation business and that the "awful bungle and prodigious waste of public money" would be brought to an end.[11]

The financial embarrassment in federal reclamation was partially relieved by the General Mineral Leasing Act of 1920, which provided that 50 per cent of the royalties from leasing should go into the reclamation fund. By 1928 the total amount that had accrued to the fund under the operation of this act was nearly thirty-four million dollars, though the grand total in the fund had leaped to $143,000,000.[12] In 1927 the total irrigable area of all the reclamation projects built by the federal government was 1,956,910 acres.[13] Of this amount, 1,378,990 acres were under irrigation. Of course, the actual area irrigated lags behind the irrigable area because the average settler cannot afford to put his whole farm under irrigation the first or second year. In 1928 there were twenty-four federal reclamation projects. Figuring the value of these irrigated lands at an average of $70 per acre, including buildings, machinery and livestock, it thus becomes apparent that approximately $100,000,000 had been added to the farm values of the nation.[14]

To a very great extent the apparent financial success of federal irrigation was due not only to the new capital that was fed into the reclamation fund, but also to the investigation and reorganization of the federal reclamation service that took place between 1923 and 1928. The report of the Secretary of the Interior for 1923 recognized that only one project out of the twenty-eight constructed or in the process of construction had met all the requirements with reference to payments, and that even though extension of time had been allowed on different occasions, a number of them were in a state of insolvency and it was highly

[10] Editorial in *San Francisco Chronicle,* November 24, 1919.
[11] *ibid.*; also *Seattle Daily Times,* September 18, 1920.
[12] Report of the Secretary of the Interior, 1928, Vol. I, pp. 251, 311.
[13] *ibid.,* p. 139.   [14] *ibid.,* p. 28.

questionable whether the government could ever recover the money invested.[15]

As a result of this report, a special committee of advisers, known as the Fact Finders, was appointed to make an exhaustive study of the entire reclamation system—requirements, methods and policies. The Secretary of the Interior, Hubert Work, explained: "This does not mean that the theory of government reclamation is unsound. It means that a new policy must be developed that will safeguard the future from further losses and bring relief to water users."[16] In the more specific instructions he said: "Your committee is requested to survey the whole subject in its entirety; give to the bureau your opinions concerning our operating methods that we may avoid errors, and finally your recommendations which Congress may study and which should ultimately preserve the sanctity of contract, secure to farmers safety for their investments already made, and insure a return of invested funds. I want to improve and extend the service in every way possible, and solicit your suggestions and recommendations." In line with this plan, the Reclamation Service was discontinued and a Bureau established in its place, with David W. Davis, former Governor of Idaho, as commissioner.[17]

This Fact Finders Committee made its report in 1924, listing sixty-six specific recommendations.[18] Among other things it recommended a complete re-classification of irrigated lands. It recognized that there was a great difference in the productivity of holdings and that farms should be classified on this basis and charges fixed accordingly. The committee openly charged that relief measures were not getting at the heart of the problem, inasmuch as continued modification of contracts had led many farmers to think that there was nothing binding about an agreement to pay any stipulated amount. In a special message to Congress, President Coolidge strongly urged that legislation be passed in line with the findings of the advisory committee.

In 1924 and 1925 adjustment and amendatory acts were passed. The Act of December 5, 1924, provided for the determination of the feasibility of a project and its adaptation for actual settlement before construction was authorized; selection of settlers on the basis of industry, experience, character, and capital; classification of the irrigated lands with respect to their ability to support a family and pay water charges;

[15] ibid., 1923, Vol. I; p. 2.   [16] ibid.
[17] ibid., p. 59.   [18] ibid., 1924, p. 6.

the payment of construction charges on the basis of the producing power of the land in annual payments of 5 per cent of the average gross annual return; the taking over of the operation of the projects by a legally organized water users' association or irrigation district; a comprehensive survey to ascertain all pertinent facts where it appeared that on account of lack of fertility of the soil, inadequate water supply, or any other physical cause, settlers were unable to pay construction costs, or whenever it appeared that the cost of any reclamation project had been apportioned or charged upon a smaller area of land than the total area of land under the project."[19] In other words, the new legislation provided for a decentralization of the federal reclamation business by turning over the projects to private irrigators under contracts. A ten-year program entered into by the Reclamation Bureau aimed to complete construction on old projects and to build several new ones. By 1927 arrangements had been made by thirty irrigation "districts and water users' associations on sixteen projects, for the transfer to control of the care and operation of the irrigation works of these projects or division of projects." Already the reforms had resulted in higher percentage of payments being made to the government.

This tightening up of federal regulations resulted in much opposition from the West Coast, especially from Oregon, where Secretary Work refused to extend financial aid unless the state would help get some of the projects into order. Work was rather pessimistic about the whole federal reclamation adventure. In an interview in September 1925, he said: "If the reclamation department had taken time to test a single experiment to its conclusion before starting on a big program, many millions might have been saved. But our enterprising westerners would not have been satisfied. Today we have more than six thousand farms with no farmers on them. The government has invested about $200,000,000 in reclamation projects, of which $27,000,000 probably will never be collected. We have, worst of all, a disposition on the part of some delinquent settlers to repudiate their debts regardless of their ability to pay."[20] It should be remembered, of course, that the agricultural depression in the country at large was embarrassing the administration, and that criticism was everywhere being heaped upon the

[19] *Statutes at Large*, Vol. XLIII, p. 701, as summarized by Elwood Mead, *Bureau of Reclamation, Its Functions and Accomplishments*. See also Report of the Secretary of the Interior, 1927, pp. 20-1.
[20] Quoted in Malin, *The United States After the World War*, p. 253.

Department of the Interior for opening up new acreage to reclamation while the Department of Agriculture was struggling with the surplus problem.

But the arid West had little sympathy with the views of the administration. At the Oregon Irrigation Congress in 1925, the state engineer exclaimed: "Think of $28,000,000 for physical plants and not one red bean for the poor devils endeavoring to eke out an existence against insufferable obstacles. Not a cent to help present settlers out of the doldrums or to encourage new ones to come and try their luck."[21] While the Irrigation Congress admitted that the state should adopt a better settlement and colonization policy, nevertheless, most of the delegates warmly applauded Senator Charles L. McNary who freely criticized Mr. Work and predicted that neither the Secretary "nor any other man nor small group could hold up the West."

Furthermore, McNary charged that the federal government had a moral obligation to develop the West, inasmuch as it was the largest land owner in the western states. The 54 per cent of Oregon's area owned by the government would if taxed—and if the taxes were collected—yield seven millions annually. He insisted on government loans to irrigation farmers to enable them to improve their holdings.[22] There was a general feeling that the federal government having failed in solving the financial problems of the settler and meeting the general problem of colonization, was now trying to pass this burden on to the states, which to many of the delegates was no solution at all.[23] Some insisted that Work resign, and that President Coolidge appoint a man who would be a leader rather than an obstructionist. When, in 1926, Commissioner Mead and Secretary Work ordered the water shut off on an irrigation project at Scottsbluff, Nebraska, because of nonpayment of past charges, the farmers hanged the respective officials in effigy.

This western opposition was somewhat alleviated by the Act of Congress of May 26, 1926, which provided that the Secretary of the Interior be authorized to write off deductions in construction costs where projects had been unproductive.[24] Three years later the Irrigation Districts' Association of California moved to include the irrigation districts of the West in the plan to refund the bonds of eastern and southern levee and drainage districts, issuing in their place non-interest

[21] *Portland Oregonian*, October 7, 1925.   [22] As reported in *ibid.*, October 6, 1925.
[23] *ibid.*, October 7, 1925.   [24] *Statutes at Large*, Vol. XLIV, p. 636.

bearing United States bonds. To California farmers alone the plan would mean an annual saving of five million dollars in interest charges.[25]

While the federal government was attempting to reform the reclamation service, another group of interests in the West was busily engaged in pushing forward the federal power program. The success of the private power interests operating under the Federal Water-Power Act of 1920 has been already pointed out. That was all to the good, but there was an ever-increasing interest in that provision of the Act of 1920 which allowed federal construction of power dams. This idea appeared in the latter part of the Wilson administration, perhaps in 1918, when Arthur P. Davis, head of the Reclamation Service, recommended the building of what later was to become Boulder Dam. By 1921 there was a fairly definite plan for this project, but it was not until the next year that Representative Phil D. Swing introduced a bill in Congress providing for the construction of a high dam near Boulder Canyon.[26]

Almost from the introduction of the bill in Congress, the private power industry of the country became the real force behind the opposition. Its representatives in Congress presented arguments that appealed to various groups and sections. They maintained that the cotton growers of the South would suffer from competition as a result of large cotton production in the Imperial Valley, made possible by irrigation from the dam. The farm interests of the Middle West were warned that the markets would be glutted with farm products. The engineering difficulties were magnified by the argument that silt would fill the dam, salt would render the water unfit for domestic use, and the great size of the structure would make it unsafe.[27] Congressmen from Arizona opposed the bill because, as they claimed, the dam would result in the allocation of water from that state to the use of other commonwealths.

The arguments in favor of the bill were more obvious. Large volumes of water were going to waste which could be used for the irrigation of waste lands, for furnishing water supply for cities, and for developing electric power for the farm and city population and rising industrial concerns. Prominent Californian newspaper editors as well as chambers

[25] *San Francisco Chronicle*, October 11, 1929.
[26] *Congressional Record*, 67 Cong. 2 Sess., p. 13,321.
[27] *Seattle Post-Intelligencer*, December 22, 1928.

of commerce got behind the movement and before long their propaganda was proving an invaluable aid in the promotion of the project.

Finally, on July 18, 1928, the Secretary of the Interior appointed a board of engineers and geologists to investigate the project. Before the year was out, this board pronounced the project practicable. A cost of $165,000,000 was estimated, and a number of changes recommended. The bill passed Congress and was signed by President Coolidge on December 21, 1928.[28] The federal government was to provide the sum of $165,000,000, to be repaid by an amortization from the proceeds of the sale of electric power and of water for irrigation. The passage of the Boulder Dam Act immediately brought into the open a similar project for developing the Columbia River basin.[29]

In marked contrast with all other aspects of public land administration, the Forest Service of the Department of Agriculture showed marked progress in the 'twenties. For the most part the lumber industry and the national government were on comparatively friendly terms. There was no longer any real apprehension on the part of lumber interests that the government was setting up in the lumber business and competing with private industry. In fact, the government was cutting only the ripe timber in the national forests. From 1915 to 1925 the total receipts from the sale of ripe timber in the national forests amounted to $4,108,529.[30] This was a very small amount compared with that harvested from private holdings. Although containing one-fourth of the standing timber of the country, the national forests were furnishing only 2 per cent of the timber cut. The government's purpose was to hold on to its timber until other sources should be more or less depleted, and then undertake to supply the demand by careful cutting, growing, planting, and assisting the states and private owners to recuperate their exhausted holdings. There were already a good many burnt-over and cut-over areas in both the national forests and private holdings where reforestation was necessary if future needs were to be met.[31] Some reforestation had already been attempted. During the year 1922, 7,051 acres of national forest land in eleven states, had been planted in trees. But at that rate of reforestation it would take approximately two hun-

[28] *Statutes at Large,* Vol. XLV, pp. 1,057-66.
[29] *Seattle Post-Intelligencer,* December 22, 1928.
[30] Report of the Department of Agriculture, 1925, p. 6.   [31] *ibid.,* 1927, p. 78.

dred years to reforest the already denuded areas—areas unsuited for anything else.[32]

To study this problem of reforestation, as well as other forestry problems, a select committee of the Senate was appointed in 1923. This committee, after careful inquiry and research, recommended organized forest protection, both private and public, with sufficient cooperation between the two sets of interests, and an equitable adjustment of taxes in order to encourage private interests to carry on commercial reforestation. Besides, efforts should be made to increase nursery stock, because state nurseries were unable to meet the present demand. The growth of wood in the country, the committee felt, should be brought up to a volume equal to the present requirements of American industry.[33] With the country facing a shortage of timber to the extent that more than half of its wood for paper had to come from foreign countries, the time was at hand when further measures should be adopted by the government to aid in a solution of the problem.

In answer to the Committee's recommendations, Congress passed the Clarke-McNary Act, June 7, 1924. This act virtually put the government "into the business of land management and the growing, and marketing of timber on a large scale." It provided for the extension of national forests over lands already publicly owned, allowed for increased purchases of forest lands within watersheds of navigable streams under the Weeks Act of 1911, and encouraged the cooperation between nation and states in forest protection, tree planting, and the acquisition of land needed for reforestation.[34]

In further pursuance of the timber conservation objectives, Congress in 1928, in the McSweeney-McNary Act, provided for the establishment of fourteen experiment stations in the forest regions of the country, with appropriations to the extent of one million dollars annually to maintain these stations.[35]

The Department of Agriculture could indeed point with pride to an excellent forest conservation record. But that was not all. Added to this showing was a very satisfactory administration of the range lands within the national forests. In 1922, there were 1,915,113 cattle, 69,640 horses, 1,888 swine, 6,851,690 sheep and 39,889 goats grazed on national forest land.[36] No longer was there any doubt about the leasing system

[32] ibid., 1923, p. 317.
[33] ibid., 1923, Report of the Forest Service, p. 292.
[34] ibid., 1924, p. 63.
[35] ibid., 1928, p. 102.
[36] ibid., 1923, p. 319.

within the national forests: bloody conflicts among stockmen had disappeared; erosion had been stopped on many areas, hence protecting the watersheds; and in many regions the grass showed a much improved condition. Here was a successful federal experiment which should have pointed the way for a solution to the problem of the vast areas of grass lands of the public domain outside the national forests.

By 1929 the national government still owned more than 340,000,000 acres of land located mostly in the arid and semiarid regions of the West. This figure did not include about 20,000,000 acres of land to which the government held the mineral title, though the surface rights had been disposed of. Of these 340,000,000 acres, there were about 140,000,000 acres of national forests and parks, and about 12,000,000 acres of reserved coal, oil, potash, phosphate and other mineral lands, leaving approximately 190,000,000 acres of land that were unreserved and unappropriated. About 15 per cent of this land was of definite desert character, so there remained approximately 160,000,000 acres of land which was covered by grass or other herbaceous vegetation suitable for grazing.

It will be recalled that the problem of settling these grasslands first appeared in the Civil War period. These broad areas became the battle-ground for the homesteader and for the big stock interests. The government finally decided in favor of the homesteader, but it remained to be seen whether he could actually settle the land. In spite of the fact that the homesteader was given the blessing of the government, by the turn of the century the big stock interests were again threatening control of most of the range lands. At about the same time, the more scientific divisions of the government recommended separation of grass lands from those susceptible of irrigation.

The Interior Department, spurred by Theodore Roosevelt's sympathy with the homesteader, did everything possible to lure population onto the High Plains area at the very time when it was becoming apparent that there was hardly a ghost of a chance that the man of small capital could establish himself there. The Kinkaid Act, applying to Nebraska, the Enlarged Homestead Act of 1909, and the Stock Raising Home-stead Act of 1916, all increased the size of grants, and yet in spite of the impressive number of original entries, the small number of final entries and the great number of abandoned homesteads stood as a grim monument to a mistaken policy.

The World War period, with attendant high prices on agricultural products, provided an unfortunate stimulus to dry farming and to settlement in the semiarid area. In order to encourage production, the government allowed stock-grazing interests to erect fences—in fact, it encouraged the very practices which had been outlawed in the administrations of both Cleveland and Roosevelt. Even more tragic was the fact that the land was not used intelligently; it was exploited. Grazing lands were overgrazed and, in certain regions, actually plowed up in the hope that a crop of wheat might be obtained. With the end of the war came the agricultural depression. The submarginal wheat frontier came to an end. In the 'twenties, the High Plains of America presented a gloomy spectacle: abandoned homesteads everywhere; grazing lands in very poor condition, some beyond rehabilitation; and more significant still, the big stockmen gradually extending their influence as well as their fences over the public domain.

At this point the big grazing interests decided to take a bold step: to urge legislation in Congress that would give them the preference and the perpetual privilege of grazing on the public lands. In 1926 the Stanfield Bill came up in Congress, providing that the public grazing lands should be organized into "grazing districts," requiring the Land Office to hand out *perpetual contracts* to the members of those districts, and keeping out everyone except the contract holders or buyers. The bill, likewise, aimed to throw open the national forests, doing away with the permit system, hence giving over the grazing areas in the forests to the cattle and sheep interests. The contracts as provided for in the bill could be bought and sold, making it possible for the big concerns to buy out the little man.

The bill produced much opposition, even in the West. From one of the western newspapers came this bitter comment: "The Stanfield Grazing Bill raids the public lands quite as effectively as the oil grabbers ever did, and on a larger scale. America wants its public domain left free to the homesteader and the new farmer. It wants its national forests to remain under the field control of the Forest Service, for conservation of timber and water. The bill that turns over all these lands and watersheds, under perpetual contract, to the big stockraisers to use and control and buy and sell as they see fit, is a noxious measure and should be killed."[37] The bill obviously provided no solution of the problem, nor did it gain very much attention in Congress.

At about the same time, the Secretary of the Interior, under fire from various quarters in the country, stated his side of the grazing lands problem: "Under the practice of unrestricted grazing by sufferance, the public lands have been over-grazed to the detriment of the live stock industry and the homesteader, and controversies have arisen among those using the range. . . . The Secretary of the Interior should be authorized by law to designate lands chiefly valuable for their pasturage and to adopt such rules as will insure an equitable use of such areas."

Finally, in 1928, after thirty years or more of discussion, Congress passed an act providing for a trial of the leasing system on that portion of the public domain which was suitable for grazing. An area of 108,804 acres of rough grazing land in the Mizpah-Pumpkin Creek region of southeastern Montana was selected. This region was partly owned by private stockmen. Under the terms of the act these private stockmen entered into an agreement with the government to lease the lands jointly for a period not exceeding ten years.[38] Many observers, however, felt that the problem demanded an immediate solution; the Mizpah-Pumpkin Creek experiment would take too long.

The general reaction to the whole conservation movement which set in with the Republican ascendancy of the 'twenties reached an even greater extreme shortly after Herbert Hoover became President in 1929. With Dr. Ray Lyman Wilbur of California as Secretary of the Interior, a western point of view was again injected into public land policies and administration. Whether this western viewpoint meant an anticonservationist program similar to the Ballinger administration of 1909-10, or a mildly proconservationist program similar to that of Lane in the Wilson administration, remained to be seen.

Secretary Wilbur's program, containing many of President Hoover's ideas, was announced to the country in the summer of 1929 and may be characterized as extremely reactionary.

Speaking at Boise, Idaho, the Secretary of the Interior dramatically presented his plan: "The real conservation problem of the West is

---

[37] *San Francisco Examiner,* March 11, 1926.
[38] Report of the Secretary of the Interior, 1928, p. 53.

the conservation of water. Plant life demands water. . . . From Nebraska west, water and water alone is the key of our future. We need the mountains and the hills and a great protected back country or we cannot have sufficient water for our valleys. . . . There must be a great western strategy for the protection of our watersheds and the plant life on them. . . . *We must replace homestead thinking with watershed thinking, since watersheds are primary to western homes.*"

This move on the part of Secretary Wilbur was followed up by President Hoover who in a speech delivered at Salt Lake City in August, before a conference of western governors, declared that an end should be put to federal landlordism and bureaucracy, and that save for certain mineral rights, the remaining public lands should be ceded to the states in which they lay. "The federal government," he asserted "is incapable of the adequate administration of matters which require so large a measure of local understanding. We must seek every opportunity to retard the expansion of federal bureaucracy and to place our communities in control of their own destinies." He declared further: "Western states have long since passed from their swaddling clothes and are today more competent to manage much of their affairs than is the federal government."

With these introductory statements the President then announced his intention of appointing a commission to study a plan of transferring the unappropriated and unreserved lands—mostly grazing lands —to the western states. He recommended that the commission also study the question of forest reserves, mineral lands, water power, dams and irrigation projects, and scenic parks. Hence the Hoover administration came out openly in a striking defense of the doctrine of states' rights—a stand which was in marked contrast to the centralized, federalistic and bureaucratic tendencies of the more general Hoover political program.[39]

Even in the West public opinion presented a none-too-favorable reaction to the Hoover-Wilbur proposal. Generally speaking, the governors of the western states applauded the move, but the Senators and Representatives were not impressed. Senator Borah of Idaho scoffed at the federal gift of acres "on which a jack rabbit could hardly live," and, pointing to the fact that the federal government had

[39] For a brief analysis of the Hoover-Wilbur plan see: Dr. Ray Lyman Wilbur, "What About Our Public Lands?" *Review of Reviews,* Vol. LXXX (December 1929), pp. 56-7.

already reserved the valuable forest and mineral resources, dubbed the whole cession idea as "skimmed milk." Many Westerners did not believe that states were fit conservation agencies. The prospect of taxing the lands for school purposes hardly outweighed the responsibility of caring for these lands, rehabilitating the grasslands, and building roads and bridges in the ceded areas.[40]

Many people had hopes that the commission would at least compromise with the Forest Service of the Department of Agriculture, which had made some contrary recommendations. This division, with over twenty-five years' experience in the administration of the grazing lands within the national forests, might well have been consulted before the final proposals were drawn up. Instead, for the most part, it was compelled to urge its recommendations on the subject through channels outside the government. Generally speaking, the Forest Service stood squarely opposed to the proposal of ceding the lands to the states, which in turn could sell them at auction to the highest bidder. It was felt that very large units would have to be put up for sale, which would inevitably go to the big stockmen, thus creating a consolidation of holdings, and leaving the homesteaders and small ranchers stranded, perhaps later to be evicted.

Instead of the proposal which the commission was asked to study, Henry B. Graves, head of the Yale University Forestry School and former Chief of the Forest Service, offered the following nine-point program:

1. The adoption of a federal leasing system of control for these public grazing lands similar to that already in operation within the national forests.

2. The leasing of these lands in a manner in which a fair proportion of the proceeds would go to the states within which the lands were located.

3. The addition to the national forests of public grazing lands which could best be administered in conjunction with the national forests (an amount estimated to be about sixteen million acres).

4. The addition to the national forests of areas of the public grazing lands which were covered with forest growth (an amount estimated to be about eight million acres).

[40] "The Public Lands," *Outlook and Independent*, Vol. CLIII (September 11, 1929), p. 54.

5. The establishment of federal grazing reserves on areas where protection of watersheds was deemed essential.

6. The provision for the exchange of owners in order to consolidate the federal and other holdings.

7. In like manner, the provision for grants of land to the states where it was desirable to round out existing holdings or to meet special local problems.

8. The provision for the sale of land to individuals or companies where it was clear that private ownership was the best means to promote the beneficial use of the property, safeguarding the interests of small stockmen, and granting a portion of the proceeds to the states.

9. The transfer of the administration of the public range lands from the Department of the Interior to the Department of Agriculture.

Mr. Graves, whose opinions were supported by Gifford Pinchot, concluded these recommendations with the observation that: "The states in the long run will gain far more from a liberal grant of the annual proceeds from grazing fees and other sources of income than by the effort to handle the lands themselves, especially if the states should undertake to restore them to productiveness and provide the improvements that are necessary."[41]

President Hoover selected James R. Garfield, Secretary of the Interior during the administration of President Theodore Roosevelt, as chairman of the commission. The rest of the members were selected only after consultation with the Secretaries of the Interior and of Agriculture, with the House and Senate Committees on Public Lands and on Agriculture, and with the governors of the public-land states. Six of the members of the commission were from the East and Midwest.[42] Congress provided an appropriation of fifty thousand dollars for the Commission's investigation.

In spite of the fact that the commission was headed by a conservationist of the Roosevelt-Pinchot school, its report published in 1930, gave overwhelming support to the Hoover-Wilbur proposal for ceding the remaining public domain to the states. In several respects it went far beyond the presidential proposal, and it almost completely disregarded the recommendations of the Forest Service, not even mentioning

---

[41] For the Forest Service plan consult the article of Henry B. Graves, "The Public Domain," *The Nation*, Vol. CXXXI (August 6, 1930), pp. 147-9.

[42] For the personnel, consult Ray Lyman Wilbur and William A. Du Puy, *Conservation in the Department of the Interior* (Washington, 1931), p. 168.

the plan advanced by Forester Graves. Furthermore, no explanation was given for the failure of one member of the Commission, Col. William B. Greeley, formerly chief forester, to sign the report. The only conservationist note in the entire document was to be found in the statements providing that certain lands were to be reserved for national defense, reclamation, and for additions to national forests and parks, and that in the process of ceding the lands the states were to be "impressed with a trust for administration and rehabilitation of the public domain." On the other hand, the commission emphasized that "private ownership . . . should be the objective in the final use and disposition of the public domain." Moreover, the report recommended that boards be created for each public-land state to decide what lands should be added to the national forests, and what, if any, should be restored to the public domain.

There were immediate repercussions to the report. Many commentators felt that there would be no conservation of the grazing lands if the states were to receive them. Many of the grazing areas extended over state lines, and conflicting jurisdictions would not make for scientific administration. There was considerable anxiety, also, lest the small stockman and homesteader should be evicted under state programs, for these interests had no voice in the powerful livestock associations nor in the state legislatures. One authority asserted: "The plan, in essence, is one of monopoly and eviction, antisocial, undemocratic." A number of authorities criticized the plan of giving the boards the power to restore lands within the national forests to the public domain. In the light of the fact that the Interior Department as recently as the Harding administration had made strenuous efforts to gain control of the national forests for development, it was not unlikely that these boards might endanger the whole system of national forests.[43]

In fact, the report boded ill for the conservation ideal; it presented too great a chance of return to the old era of politics, corruption, and speculation. One prominent editor concluded his analysis of the report with the terse statement: "When Congress comes to consider the commission's proposals, its duty is clear. It should shelve the report."[44] And that is exactly what Congress did! The Democrats, on gaining control of the House in December 1931, left the Hoover proposal hanging

[43] Ward Shephard, "The Handout Magnificent," *Harper's Monthly*, Vol. CLXIII (October 1931), pp. 594-603.
[44] "Flinging Away an Empire," *The New Republic*, Vol. LXX (February 24, 1932), p. 32.

in mid-air. When the bill embracing the commission's proposals was introduced it was found that not only was the East opposed to it, but also much of the West, including the powerful livestock association interests. Thus ended the dramatic attempt to turn over to the states the remaining public domain.

The opening chants of the Democrats, victorious in the campaign of 1932, indicated that a new deal had come to the conservation movement. Many of the high officials of the new administration—Harold Ickes, Henry Wallace, Henry Morgenthau, Rexford Tugwell, as well as the President himself—were staunch conservationists. While the depression absorbed the immediate attention of President Roosevelt, it was soon apparent that he intended to make a lasting contribution along conservation lines, calling into play not only the natural resources owned by the federal government, but all the nation's natural resources, public and private alike. The expansion of the conservation program from its sectional focus in the West to the nation as a whole—a process which had begun many years before—was now to be carried to completion.

The great task of formulating the new conservation program fell to the Secretary of the Interior, Harold Ickes. Combining the greater objectives of conservation with the more immediate and pressing needs for depression-relief, Ickes developed a program which was revolutionary in many respects. The classification of the nation's resources into crop lands, range lands, forest lands, and mineral lands, which had already been begun, was to be pushed with renewed vigor until the inventory was complete. The Secretary was already convinced that about twenty-five million acres of submarginal lands, mostly privately owned, should be retired through governmental cooperation. The vast irrigation projects about to be approved, together with those already under construction, would make it possible to retire these submarginal lands without interfering with the agricultural production of the rest of the country. One acre of irrigated land was to be provided for every five acres of submarginal land retired. These submarginal lands, together with vast areas of lands which had reverted to the states because of tax delinquency, were to become a part of the public domain. Some were to be added to national forests, others would come under thorough programs of rehabilitation.

Such a plan would be sound conservation policy and also good social policy. Many poor farmers could be relocated on good land, and many of the nation's youth, who would otherwise be unemployed, could be used to care for the nation's valuable forests and aid in reforestation work. The national forest and park program was to be extended to every state in the union, a number of eastern and mid-western states not having thus far shared in this phase of conservation.

Besides this pronouncement in favor of irrigation, resettlement, rehabilitation and more national parks and forests, Mr. Ickes declared himself in favor of extensive water-power development, asserting that nearly every irrigation project was susceptible of development for electrical power purposes. He was opposed to turning over any of this power to private interests; public resources should be held in public trust for public use. In line with this objective, the Secretary defended eastern water development with the argument that it would conserve soil, not to mention the fact that electric power generated by public projects might constitute a yardstick to measure rates charged by private electric utilities.

Lastly, the Secretary dealt with the great unsolved problem of the remaining public domain—some 173,000,000 acres, mostly grazing lands. Scorning the Republican proposal of ceding these lands to the western states, the Secretary boldly declared that these lands should become, like the national forests, a part of the permanent national domain, with grazing use and rehabilitation governed by means of leasing. This plan would insure not only law and order, but also intelligent use and preservation of these grazing resources for years to come.[45]

Even while the Secretary of the Interior was stating the highlights of his program, he could already point to progress toward the fulfillment of its objectives. The Department of Agriculture was busily engaged in studying areas that could be added to the national forests or parks. To meet the social need for relieving the unemployed and also the need for work in the forests, the Civilian Conservation Corps had already been established by Congress. In speaking of the accomplishments of this agency the Secretary proudly boasted: "The young

[45] This summary of the Secretary's proposals was made from a published interview, "The National Domain and the New Deal," between Marquis James and Harold Ickes, *Saturday Evening Post*, Vol. CCVI (December 23, 1933), pp. 10-11.

The Western Domain, 1936.

men of the C.C.C. have in six months accomplished as much that will enhance the happiness of coming generations as has been accomplished by all other agencies dealing with reforestation in the past fifteen years."[46] More than $20,000,000 of C.C.C. funds had been set aside for the purchase of new lands to be added to the national forests.

Congress had also moved far along toward its water-power objective. The Tennessee Valley Authority, created by Act of Congress in May 1933, was busily occupied with a program of constructing dams along

[46] *ibid.*, p. 11.

Irrigation Projects and Federal Dams, 1936.

From Morison and Commager, *The Growth of the American Republic*. By Permission of Oxford University Press.

the Tennessee River in order to control soil erosion, floods, and navigation, as well as to generate electric power. But if the irrigation of the
public lands of the West is to be considered a part of the history of
the public domain, it is apparent that the conservation projects east of
the Rockies, regardless of their significance, also were to become a
part of the history of a new public domain and a new social order.

Perhaps the greatest contribution of the New Deal administration
to the history of the old public domain was the passage of the Taylor
Grazing Act. Among the first orders given by the Secretary of the
Interior was one providing that the fences on the public grazing lands
should come down, with the threat that United States marshals would
be employed if necessary to enforce the decree. Meanwhile, in March
1933, Representative Edward I. Taylor of Colorado had introduced a
bill in Congress whose objects were defined: "To stop injury to the
public grazing lands by preventing overgrazing and soil deterioration;
to provide for their orderly use, improvement and development; to
stabilize the live stock industry upon the public range, and for other
purposes." The bill used the Mizpah River-Pumpkin Creek experiment
of southeastern Montana as a starting point for the proposed program.[47]
After three years of federal regulation this region had been sufficiently
rehabilitated to carry 5,000 head of cattle—2,000 more than before the
experiment was begun. By 1933 numerous requests had already been
made by other western localities for authority to enjoy the same terms as
the Montana project. But rather than deal with the grazing problem
piecemeal, the Secretary favored a general program for the whole
domain.

Consequently, the Taylor Grazing Act, as finally passed in 1934,
provided for the segregation of a maximum of 80,000,000 acres of the
public grasslands to be organized into grazing districts under the control
of the Secretary of the Interior.[48] This act was amended in 1936, increasing the area to be formed into grazing districts to 142,000,000
acres.[49] The Act of 1934 placed in the Interior Department not only
the administration of the grazing districts, the issuance of grazing
permits, etc., but it also granted broad powers to develop water power,
to carry on soil-erosion control, and to provide for the disposition of

[47] *supra*, p. 412.   [48] *Statutes at Large*, Vol. XLVIII, p. 1,269.
[49] *ibid.*, Vol. XLIX, p. 1,976.

land not needed for the grazing districts. Almost immediately the Interior Department entered upon its new task; a Division of Grazing was created, surveys were begun and meetings were held with many western livestock associations.

A compromise measure at its best, the act had its shortcomings. Much criticism was made of the fact that its administration was placed in the Interior Department, when for years—since 1906, in fact—the Department of Agriculture had performed such excellent administration of the grazing areas within the national forests. Also, there was some speculation as to whether the act did not "hand over the public range lands to the tender mercies of 'advisory committees' of the stockmen, who have exploited those lands to their own advantage." At least this was the inference drawn by one authority who emphasized his remarks with the conclusion: "if they really believe the Taylor Grazing Act is a blow at 'special privilege,' then Heaven help democracy. If through the enactment of this bill, this sort of philosophy should be applied to our national forests, turning them over to 'advisory committees' of lumbermen in the name of conservation, we had best begin praying for our children and our children's children."[50]

By March 1935, the entire 165,695,000 acres of remaining domain had been withdrawn by President Roosevelt in preparation for a nation-wide conservation program.[51] These withdrawals, in the words of the President, were made in order to determine "the most useful purpose for which ... [the lands] may be put in furtherance of the land program and conservation and development of national resources." Most of them would be made into grazing districts; others into national forests, parks, and game reserves; and some converted to water-power development. The editor of *Nature Magazine* in commenting on the President's action, said: "It is the hope of all who have the welfare of conservation at heart that this withdrawal means the first definite step in a plan for wise protection and development of the millions of acres which, like red-headed stepchildren of the government, have been allowed to run wild and shift for themselves through many years of tragic neglect."[52]

---

[50] Ed., *Nature Magazine*, Vol. XXXI (January 1938), p. 46.

[51] Two withdrawals were made by President Roosevelt, one by executive order of November 26, 1934, and the other by order of February 5, 1935—both orders based upon the authority provided in the Act of June 25, 1910 (See *supra*, p. 370).

[52] "President Withdraws Public Domain," Vol. XXV (May 1935), p. 263.

In 1936, Mr. Rexford Tugwell, describing the significance of the Act of 1934, declared: "The day [June 28, 1934] on which the President signed the Taylor Act, which virtually closed the public domain to further settlement, laid in its grave a land policy which had long since been dead and which walked abroad only as a troublesome ghost within the living world."[53] In truth, that day—or perhaps February 5, 1935, when the President withdrew all lands from private entry—should be celebrated as the date of the demise of the old public domain; the new domain was one which would not be turned over to private owners— a closed domain to be conserved for the future generations of America. For over forty years historians had been heralding the passing of the frontier; without a doubt the old frontier had now passed.

The history of the public domain from its creation in 1780 to its final official demise in 1935 demarks fairly accurately the formative or frontier era of American history. Within this formative era four periods stand out clearly: the first period, 1780 to 1850, during which time the individual pioneer became the most conspicuous agent in the settlement process; the second period, 1850 to 1862, when the West began to become intensely interested in corporate capital and the corporation almost over night came to challenge the settler's claim to being the foremost agent in occupying and developing the vacant areas to the westward; the third period, 1862 to 1901, a period coinciding with the rise of industrialism in our national history, and a period reflected in the West by the ruthless exploitation by the corporate and capitalistic forces which had gained complete ascendancy over the settler as the pioneering agent; and the last period, 1901 to 1935, which was characterized by the forcing of a program of conservation, ultimately creating the remaining natural resources into a permanent national domain—thereby ending once and for all the open public domain.

Thus ended an era. The land of opportunity—opportunity measured in terms of free land—had officially closed its doors. America had come of age.

---

[53] Rexford G. Tugwell, "Our New National Heritage," *Scribner's Magazine*, Vol. XCIX (March 1936), p. 164.

Bibliography and Index

SELECTIVE BIBLIOGRAPHY OF SECONDARY REFERENCES

Part I

The Settler Breaks the Way, 1776-1850

Introduction—Colonial Precedents:

C. W. Alvord, *The Mississippi Valley in British Politics* (2 vols., Cleveland, 1917); C. M. Andrews, "Land Systems in the American Colonies," *Palgrave's Dictionary of Political Economy*, Vol. II (1923), pp. 556-60; J. C. Ballagh, "The Land System in the South," *Publications of the American Historical Association*, 1897; V. F. Barnes, "Land Tenure in English Colonial Charters of the Seventeenth Century," *Essays in Colonial History Presented to Charles McLean Andrews* (New Haven, 1931), pp. 4-40; P. W. Bidwell and J. I. Falconer, *History of Agriculture in the Northern United States, 1620-1860* (Washington, 1925), pp. 49-66, 70-6; O. P. Chitwood, *A History of Colonial America* (New York, 1931); Melville Egleston, "The Land System of the New England Colonies," *Johns Hopkins University Studies*, 4th Series; A. C. Ford, "Colonial Precedents of Our National Land System as It Existed in 1800," *University of Wisconsin Bulletin No. 352* (Madison, 1910); L. C. Gray, *History of Agriculture in the Southern United States to 1860* (Washington, 1933), Chap. XVII; C. P. Nettels, *Roots of American Civilization* (New York, 1938); H. L. Osgood, *The American Colonies in the Seventeenth Century* (3 vols., New York, 1904-07), Vol. I, Chap. XI; Vol. II, Chap. XI; St. G. L. Sioussat, "The Breakdown of the Royal Management of Lands in the Southern Provinces, 1773-1775," *Agricultural History*, Vol. III (1929), pp. 67-98.

From the Revolution to 1850:

T. B. Abernethy, *Western Lands and the American Revolution* (New York, 1937); H. B. Adams, "Maryland's Influence upon Land Cessions to the United States," *Johns Hopkins University Studies*, 3rd Series, No. 1 (1885); C. W. Alvord, *The Mississippi Valley in British Politics* (2 vols., Cleveland, 1917); J. C. Ballagh, "Southern Economic History: Tariff and Public Lands," American Historical Association, *Annual Report*, 1898, pp. 223-63; B. W. Bond, *The Civilization of the Old Northwest* (New York, 1934); G. S. Callender, *Selections from the Economic History of the United States, 1765-1860* (Boston, 1909), Chaps. XII and XIII; H. J. Carman, *Social and Economic History of the United States* (Vol. I, Boston, 1930); E. Channing, *A History of the United States* (6 vols., New

York, 1905-1926), Vol. III, Chap. XVII; Vol. IV, Chap. XI; and Vol. V, Chaps. II and III; K. W. Colgrove, "The Attitude of Congress toward the Pioneers of the West from 1789 to 1820," *Iowa Journal of History and Politics*, Vol. VIII (1910), pp. 3-129; Vol. IX (1911), pp. 196-302; Milton Conover, *The General Land Office* (Baltimore, 1923); R. S. Cotterill, "The National Land System in the South, 1803-1812," *Mississippi Valley Historical Review*, Vol. XVI (1930), pp. 495-506; Thomas Donaldson, *The Public Domain; Its History* (Washington, 1884); H. U. Faulkner, *American Economic History* (New York, 1935), Chap. IX; Cardinal Goodwin, *The Trans-Mississippi West, 1803-1853* (New York, 1922); B. H. Hibbard, *A History of the Public Land Policies* (New York, 1924); *idem.*, "The Settlement of Public Lands in the United States," *International Review of Agricultural Economics*, Vol. LXI (1916), pp. 97-117; R. T. Hill, *The Public Domain and Democracy* (New York, 1910); J. F. Jameson, *The American Revolution Considered as a Social Movement* (Princeton, 1926); Merrill Jensen, "The Articles of Confederation: A Re-interpretation," *Pacific Historical Review*, Vol. VI (1937); *idem.*, "The Creation of the National Domain, 1781-1784," *Mississippi Valley Historical Review*, Vol. XXVI (1939), pp. 325-43; J. B. McMaster, *History of the People of the United States* (7 vols., New York, 1883-1913), Vol. III, Chap. XVI and Vol. IV, Chap. XXXIII; F. L. Paxson, *History of the American Frontier, 1763-1893* (Boston, 1924); Louis Pelzer, "The Public Domain as a Field for Historical Study," *Iowa Journal of History and Politics*, Vol. XII (1914), pp. 568-78; U. B. Phillips, *American Negro Slavery* (New York, 1918), Chaps. X-XII; R. E. Riegel, *America Moves West* (New York, 1930); R. M. Robbins, "Preemption: A Frontier Triumph," *Mississippi Valley Historical Review*, Vol. XVIII (1931), pp. 331-49; *idem.*, "Horace Greeley: Land Reform and Unemployment, 1837-1862," *Agricultural History*, Vol. VII (1933), pp. 18-41; A. M. Sakolski, *The Great American Land Bubble* (New York, 1927); F. A. Shannon, *Economic History of the People of the United States* (New York, 1934); G. M. Stephenson, *The Political History of the Public Lands from 1840 to 1860* (Boston, 1917); P. J. Treat, *The National Land System, 1785-1820* (New York, 1910); *idem.*, "The Public Lands and the Public Land Policy," *Cyclopedia of American Government* (New York, 1914), Vol. III, pp. 93-7; *idem.*, "Origin of the National Land System under the Confederation," *American Historical Association Annual Report*, Vol. I (1905), pp. 231-39; F. J. Turner, *Rise of the New West* (New York, 1906); *idem., The United States, 1830-1850* (New York, 1935); J. C. Welling, *The Land Politics of the United States* (New York, 1888); R. G. Wellington, *The Political and Sectional Influence of the Public Lands, 1828-1842*

(Cambridge, 1914); *idem.*, "The Tariff and Public Lands from 1828-1833," American Historical Association, *Annual Report,* Vol. I. (1911), pp. 179-85; A. P. Whitaker, *The Spanish-American Frontier* (New York, 1927).

Part II

The West Welcomes the Corporation, 1850-1862

V. E. Chatelain, "The Public Land Officer on the Northwestern Frontier," *Minnesota History,* Vol. XII (1931), pp. 379-89; A. H. Cole, Statistical Background of the Crisis of 1857," *Review of Economic Statistics,* Vol. XII (1930), pp. 170-80; D. A. Clark, *The West in American History* (New York, 1937), Chaps. XVII and XVIII; K. W. Colgrove, "The Attitude of Congress Toward the Pioneers of the West, 1820-1850," *Iowa Journal of History and Politics,* Vol. IX (1911), pp. 196-302; K. Coman, *Economic Beginnings of the Far West* (2 vols., New York, 1925); Thomas Donaldson, *The Public Domain; Its History* (Washington, 1884); P. W. Gates, "The Disposal of the Public Domain in Illinois, 1848-1856," *Journal of Economic and Business History,* Vol. III (1931), pp. 216-30; *idem., The Illinois Central Railroad and Its Colonization Work,* Harvard Economic Studies, Vol. XLII (Cambridge, 1935); *idem.,* "The Railroads of Missouri, 1850-1870," *Missouri Historical Review,* Vol. XXVI (1931-32), pp. 126-42; *idem.,* "Land Policy and Tenancy in the Prairie Counties of Indiana," *Indiana Magazine of History,* Vol. XXXV (1939), pp. 1-26; *idem.,* "Southern Investments in Northern Lands Before the Civil War," *Journal of Southern History,* Vol. V (1939), pp. 155-85; *idem.,* "Large Scale Farming in Illinois, 1850-1870," *Agricultural History,* Vol. VI (1932), pp. 14-25; Cardinal Goodwin, *The Trans-Mississippi West, 1803-1853* (New York, 1922); B. H. Hibbard, *A History of Public Land Policies* (New York, 1924), Chap. VIII; Murray Kane, "Some Considerations of the Safety-Valve Doctrine," *Mississippi Valley Historical Review,* Vol. XXIII (1936), pp. 169-88; H. A. Kellar, (ed.), *Solon Robinson, Pioneer and Agriculturist; Selected Writings, 1825-1845* (2 vols., Indianapolis, 1936); E. C. Kirkland, *A History of American Economic Life* (New York, 1932), Chaps. IV-VII; T. J. Middleton, "Andrew Johnson and the Homestead Law," *Sewannee Review,* Vol. XV (1907), pp. 316-20; F. L. Paxson, *History of the American Frontier, 1763-1893* (Boston, 1924); Louis Pelzer, "Squatter Settlements," *Palimpsest,* Vol. XIV (1933), pp. 77-84; W. J. Peterson, "Population Advance to the Upper Mississippi Valley, 1830-1860," *Iowa Journal of History and Politics,* Vol. XXXII (1934), pp. 312-53; T. A. Rickard, *The Copper Mines of Lake Superior* (New York,

1905); *idem., A History of American Mining* (New York, 1932); Robert Riegel, *America Moves West* (New York, 1930); C. J. Ritchey, "Claim Associations and Pioneer Democracy in Early Minnesota," *Minnesota History,* Vol. IX (1928), pp. 85-95; R. M. Robbins, "Horace Greeley: Land Reform and Unemployment, 1837-1862," *Agricultural History,* Vol. VII (1933), pp. 18-41; E. D. Ross, "Horace Greeley and the West," *Mississippi Valley Historical Review,* Vol. XX (1933), pp. 63-74; A. M. Sakolski, *The Great American Land Bubble* (New York, 1932), Chaps. XII and XIII; J. B. Sanborn, "Political Aspects of Homestead Legislation," *American Historical Review,* Vol. VI (1900), pp. 19-37; Joseph Schafer, *The Social History of American Agriculture* (New York, 1936); *idem., A History of Agriculture in Wisconsin* (Madison, 1932); *idem., The Wisconsin Lead Region* (Madison, 1932); B. F. Shambaugh, "Frontier Land Clubs or Claims Associations," American Historical Association, *Annual Report,* Vol. I (1900), pp. 69-84; F. A. Shannon, *Economic History of the People of the United States* (New York, 1934), Chap. VII; G. M. Stephenson, *Political History of the Public Lands, 1840 to 1862* (Boston, 1917); F. J. Turner, *The Frontier in American History* (New York, 1920), Chaps. IV-VII; W. P. Webb, *The Great Plains* (New York, 1931).

Part III

The Corporation Triumphs, 1862-1901

B. F. Andrews, *The Land Grant of 1862 and the Land Grant Colleges,* U.S. Bureau of Education Bulletin 13 (1918); Stuart Chase, *Rich Land, Poor Land* (New York, 1936); V. E. Chatelain, "The Public Land Officer of the Northwestern Frontier," *Minnesota History,* Vol. XII (1931), pp. 379-89; D. E. Clark, *The West in American History* (New York, 1937), pp. 403-625; Everett Dick, *The Sod-House Frontier, 1854-1890* (New York, 1937); W. J. Donald, "Land Grants for Internal Improvements in the United States," *Journal of Political Economy,* Vol. XIX (1911); Thomas Donaldson, *The Public Domain; Its History* (Washington, 1884); H. H. Dunham, "Some Crucial Years of the General Land Office, 1875-1890," *Agricultural History,* Vol. XI (1937), pp. 227-40; J. T. Ganoe, "The Beginnings of Irrigation in the United States," *Mississippi Valley Historical Review,* Vol. XXV (1938), pp. 59-78; *idem.,* "The Desert Land Act in Operation, 1877-1891," *Agricultural History,* Vol. XI (1937) pp. 142-57; P. W. Gates, "A Fragment of Kansas Land History; the Disposal of the Christian Indian Tract," *Kansas Historical Quarterly,* Vol VI (1937), pp. 227-40; *idem.,* "The Homestead Law in an Incongruous

Land System," *American Historical Review*, Vol. XLI (1936), pp. 652-81; *idem.*, *The Illinois Central Railroad and Its Colonization Work* (Cambridge, 1934); L. C. Gray, "Land Speculation," *Encyclopaedia of Social Sciences*, Vol. IX (New York, 1933), pp. 64-8, 70; *idem.*, "National Land Policies in Retrospect and Prospect," *Journal of Farm Economics*, Vol. XIII (1931), pp. 231-45; A. B. Hart, "The Disposition of Our Public Lands," *Quarterly Journal of Economics*, Vol. I (1887), pp. 169-83, 251-4; J. B. Hedges, "Promotion of Immigration to the Pacific Northwest by Railroads," *Mississippi Valley Historical Review*, Vol. XV (1928), pp. 183-203; B. H. Hibbard, *A History of Public Land Policies* (New York, 1924), Chaps. XVII-XXI; *idem.*, "Homestead," *Encyclopaedia of the Social Sciences*, Vol. VII (1932), pp. 436-41; *idem.*, "Land Grants: The United States," *ibid.*, Vol. IX (1933), pp. 32-6; John Ise, *The United States Forest Policy* (New Haven, 1920); Dorothy Lampen, *Economic and Social Aspects of Federal Reclamation* (Baltimore, 1930); W. C. MacLeod, *The American Indian Frontier* (New York, 1928); T. M. Marshall, "The Miners' Laws of Colorado," *American Historical Review*, Vol. XXV, pp. 426-40; Elwood Mead, *Rise and Future of Irrigation in the United States*, U.S. Department of Agriculture, *Yearbook*, 1899, pp. 591-612; J. B. Milam, "The Opening of the Cherokee Outlet," *Chronicles of Oklahoma*, Vol. IX (1931); Vol. X (1932), pp. 115-37; Ernest Osgood, *The Day of the Cattleman* (Minneapolis, 1929); E. M. Parker, "The Southern Pacific Railroad and Settlement in Southern California," *Pacific Historical Review*, Vol. VI (1937), pp. 103-19; F. L. Paxson, "The Pacific Railroads and the Disappearance of the Frontier in America," American Historical Association, *Annual Report*, 1907, Vol. I, pp. 107-18; *idem.*, *History of the American Frontier, 1763-1893* (Boston, 1924); Louis Pelzer, "A Cattleman's Commonwealth on the Western Range," *Mississippi Valley Historical Review*, Vol. XIII (1926), pp. 30-49; *idem.*, *The Cattleman's Frontier* (Glendale, California, 1936); Gifford Pinchot, "How Conservation Began," *Agricultural History*, Vol. XI (1937), pp. 255-65; J. B. Rae, "Commissioner Sparks and the Railroad Land Grants," *Mississippi Valley Historical Review*, Vol. XXV (1938), pp. 211-30; W. F. Raney, "The Timber Culture Acts," Mississippi Valley Historical Association, *Proceedings*, Vol. X (1919-20), pp. 219-29; T. A. Rickard, *A History of American Mining* (New York, 1932); R. M. Robbins, "The Federal Land System in an Embryo State: Washington Territory, 1853-1890," *Pacific Historical Review*, Vol. IV (1935), pp. 356-75; *idem.*, "The Public Domain in the Era of Exploitation, 1862-1901," *Agricultural History*, Vol. XIII (1939), pp. 97-108; E. D. Ross, "Squandering Our Public Land," *American Scholar*, Vol. II (1933), pp. 77-86; L. B. Schmidt, "The Agricultural Revolution in the Prairies and the Great Plains of the United States," *Agricultural History*, Vol. VIII (1934), pp. 169-95; F. W. Seymour, "Our Indian Land Policy," *Journal of Land and Public Utility Economics*, Vol. II (1926), pp. 93-108; F. A. Shannon, "The Homestead Act and the Labor Surplus," *American Historical Review*, Vol. XLI (1936), pp. 637-51; A. E. Sheldon, *Land Systems and Land Policies in Nebraska* (Lincoln, 1936); C. H. Shinn, "Land Laws of the Mining Districts," *Johns Hopkins University Studies*, 2nd Series (1884); H. A. Smith, "The Early Forestry Movement in the United States," *Agricultural History*, Vol. XII (1938), pp. 326-46; L. O. Stewart, *Public Land Survey; History, Instructions, Methods* (Ames, Iowa, 1935); Arnold Tilden, *The Legislation of the Civil War Period Considered as a Basis of the Agricultural Revolution in the United States* (Los Angeles, 1937); F. J. Turner, *The Frontier in American History* (New York, 1920), Chap. I; W. P. Webb, *The Great Plains* (New York, 1931), Chap. IX; F. P. Wirth, *The Discovery and Exploitation of the Minnesota Iron Lands* (Cedar Rapids, Iowa, 1937).

Part IV

The Government Forces Conservation, 1901-1936

J. H. Anderson, "Jurisdiction over Federal Lands within the States," *North Carolina Law Review*, Vol. VII (1929), pp. 299-306; F. M. Blackmer, "The West, Water and Grazing Laws," *Survey Graphic*, Vol. XXVI (1937), p. 387; F. W. Blackmar, "The Mastery of the Desert," *North American Review*, Vol. CLXXXII (1906), pp. 676-88; R. M. Boening, "History of Irrigation in the State of Washington," *Washington Historical Quarterly*, Vol. IX (1918), pp. 259-76; Vol. X (1919), pp. 21-45; Stuart Chase, *Rich Land, Poor Land* (New York, 1936); Marion Clawson, "The Administration of Federal Range Lands," *Quarterly Journal of Economics*, Vol. LIII (1939), pp. 435-53; A. R. Cordova, "The Taylor Grazing Act," *New Mexican Business Review*, Vol. IV (1935), pp. 193-201; A. P. Davis, "Development of the Colorado River," *Atlantic Monthly*, Vol. CXLIII (1929), pp. 254-63; C. A. Dykstra (ed.), "Colorado River Development and Related Problems," American Academy of Political and Social Science, *Annals*, Vol. CXLVIII (1930), pp. 1-42; J. T. Ganoe, "The Desert Land Act Since 1891," *Agricultural History*, Vol. XI (1937), pp. 266-77; *idem.*, "The Origin of a National Reclamation Policy," *Mississippi Valley Historical Review*, Vol. XVIII (1931), pp. 34-52; P. W. Gates, "American Land Policy and the Taylor Grazing Act," *Land Policy Circular*, October 1935, pp. 15-37; L. C. Gray, "National Land Policies in Retrospect and

Prospect," *Journal of Farm Economics,* Vol. XIII (1931), pp. 231-45; *idem.,* "Our Land Policy Today," *Land Policy Review,* Vol. I (1938), pp. 3-8; B. H. Hibbard, *A History of Public Land Policies* (New York, 1924), Chaps. XXII-XXVIII; John Ise, *The United States Forest Policy* (New Haven, 1920); *idem., The United States Oil Policy* (New Haven, 1926); Dorothy Lampen, *Economic and Social Aspects of Federal Reclamation* (Baltimore, 1930); A. E. Parkins and J. R. Whitaker (eds.), *Our Natural Resources and Their Conservation* (New York, 1936); Gifford Pinchot, "How Conservation Began in the United States," *Agricultural History,* Vol. XI (1937), pp. 255-65; H. A. Smith, "The Early Forestry Movement in the United States," *idem.,* Vol. XII (1938), pp. 326-46; W. J. Trimble, "The Influence of the Passing of the Public Lands," *Atlantic Monthly,* Vol. CXIII (1914), pp. 755-67; F. J. Turner, *The Frontier in American History* (New York, 1920); G. S. Wehrwein, "A Land Policy as a Part of an Agricultural Program," *Journal of Farm Economics,* Vol. VII (1935), pp. 289-304; *idem.,* "The Second Conservation Crusade," *Journal of Land and Public Utility Economics,* Vol. XII (1936), pp. 421-22; C. W. Wright, "The Significance of the Disappearance of Free Land in our Economic Development," *American Economic Review Supplement,* Vol. XVI (1926), pp. 265-71; R. S. Yaʈd, *Our Federal Lands* (New York, 1928).

INDEX

A NOTE ABOUT THE AUTHOR

Roy M. Robbins was born in Richmond, Indiana, in 1904. He received his A.B. degree with highest honors from Earlham College in 1925, and his M.A. and Ph.D. from the University of Wisconsin (1926, 1929). His first teaching was done at the University of Washington (Seattle), and for ten years he was on the staff at Western Reserve University. At Butler University, where Professor Robbins served for sixteen years as head of the Department of History and Political Science and Director of the Division of Graduate Instruction, he received the 1950 Distinguished Faculty Award. From 1954 until 1958 he was Director of the Graduate Division at the University of Omaha, and was appointed Professor of History there in 1958.

As well as contributing articles to scholarly journals, Professor Robbins compiled the Bibliography of American Periodicals in Libraries of Cleveland and Oberlin, Ohio, 1800-1900. From 1954 to 1958 he was a member of the Editorial Board of the *Mississippi Valley Historical Review*.